THE NEW POLITICS OF THE WELFARE STATE

The New Politics of
the Welfare State

Edited by

PAUL PIERSON

OXFORD

UNIVERSITY PRESS

OXFORD
UNIVERSITY PRESS

Great Clarendon Street, Oxford OX2 6DP

Oxford University Press is a department of the University of Oxford.
It furthers the University's objective of excellence in research, scholarship,
and education by publishing worldwide in

Oxford New York

Athens Auckland Bangkok Bogotá Buenos Aires Calcutta
Cape Town Chennai Dar es Salaam Delhi Florence Hong Kong Istanbul
Karachi Kuala Lumpur Madrid Melbourne Mexico City Mumbai
Nairobi Paris São Paulo Shanghai Singapore Taipei Tokyo Toronto Warsaw
with associated companies in Berlin Ibadan

Oxford is a registered trade mark of Oxford University Press
in the UK and in certain other countries

Published in the United States
by Oxford University Press Inc., New York

British Library Cataloguing in Publication Data

Data available

Library of Congress Cataloging in Publication Data
The new politics of the welfare state / edited by Paul Pierson.
p. cm.
Includes bibliographical references and index.
1. Welfare state. 2. Comparative government. I. Pierson, Paul.

JC479.N48 2000   361.6'5—dc21   00-060670

ISBN 0-19-829753-X
ISBN 0-19-829756-4 (Pbk.)

1 3 5 7 9 10 8 6 4 2

Typeset in Times
by Graphicraft Limited, Hong Kong
Printed by T. J. International Padstow, Cornwall

ACKNOWLEDGEMENTS

This volume grows out of two conferences held at the Center for European Studies, Harvard University, in November 1997 and October 1998. The Center remains a wonderful home for this kind of collaborative work, and as usual Charles Maier and Abby Collins were generous in backing this project from the outset. I am grateful to the Center's Program for the Study of Germany and Europe for financial assistance. Lisa Eschenbach provided superb staff support. I have also been fortunate in working with Oxford University Press, and owe thanks to Dominic Byatt and Amanda Watkins for their enthusiasm and efficiency. Many members of the academic community in Cambridge and beyond provided the project's participants with valuable feedback, both during our conferences and afterwards. Acknowledgements for particular help are indicated in various chapters, but I wish to make special note of the extensive and valuable comments I received from Keith Banting and Margaret Weir following the group's first meeting. Miguel Glatzer and Andrew Karch provided important research assistance to me as I was initiating this collaboration. Finally, I would like to thank the other contributors to this volume. Their professionalism, good humour, and energy rendered the administrative tasks associated with editing tolerable and greatly magnified the intellectual and personal rewards.

Cambridge, September 2000   Paul Pierson

CONTENTS

Part III. Adjustment Dynamics Parties, Elections, and Political Institutions

Part IV. Comparing Policy Domains

Conclusion

LIST OF FIGURES

LIST OF TABLES

ABBREVIATIONS

AFDC	Aid to Families with Dependent Children (USA)
ALMP	active labour market policy
BMA	British Medical Association
BVG	German Constitutional Court
CBI	Confederation of British Industry
CDA	Social Committees (Germany)
CDU	Christian Democratic Union (Germany)
CFDT	Confédération Français Démocratique des Travailleurs (France)
CGT	Confédération Générale du Travail (France)
CMEs	coordinated market economies
CPE	comparative political economy
CPI-X	consumer price index minus x
CPP	Canada Pension Plan
CSU	Christian Social Union (Germany)
DB	defined benefit
DC	defined contribution
DHA	District Health Authority (UK)
DOH	Department of Health (UK)
EFO	Edgren, Faxé, and odhner inflation model
EITC	Earned Income Tax Credit (USA)
EMU	Economic and Monetary Union
ERISA	Employee Retirement and Income Security Act (USA)
FDP	Free Democratic Party (Germany)
FDI	foreign direct investment
FO	Force Ouvrière (France)
GRG	1988 Health Care Reform Law (Germany)
GSG	1992 Health Care Structural Reform Law (Germany)
HMO	health maintenance organization (USA)
HQII	high-quality incremental innovation
IRA	individual retirement account (USA)
KV	Kassenärztliche Vereinigungen (Germany)
LMEs	liberal market economies
NA	notional accounts
NAIRU	non-accelerating inflation rate of unemployment
NHS	National Health Service (UK)
NIC	newly industrializing country
NIE	newly industrializing economy
NOGs	1997 Health Care Restructuring Laws (Germany)

NPM   new public management
NZS   New Zealand Superannuation
OSV   Social Insurance Organization Act (Netherlands)
PAYG   pay-as-you-go
PCW   Programme for Competitiveness and Work (Ireland)
PESP   Programme for Economic and Social Progress (Ireland)
PNR   Programme for National Recovery (Ireland)
SERPS State Earnings-Related Pension Scheme (UK)
SPD   Social Democratic Party (Germany)
TECs   Training and Enterprise Councils (UK)
TUC   Trades Union Congress (UK)

LIST OF CONTRIBUTORS

Giuliano Bonoli, Lecturer, Department of Social Work and Social Policy, University of Fribourg.

Susan Giaimo, Assistant Professor, Department of Political Science, Massachusetts Institute of Technology.

Evelyne Huber, Professor of Political Science, University of North Carolina.

Herbert Kitschelt, Professor of Political Science, Duke University.

Philip Manow, Senior Researcher, Max-Planck Institute for the Study of Societies, Cologne.

John Myles, Professor of Sociology, Florida State University.

Paul Pierson, Professor of Government, Harvard University.

Martin Rhodes, Professor of European Public Policy, European University Institute.

Herman Schwartz, Associate Professor of Government and Foreign Affairs, University of Virginia.

John D. Stephens, Professor of Political Science and Sociology, University of North Carolina.

Duane Swank, Associate Professor of Political Science, Marquette University.

Stewart Wood, Fellow and Tutor in Politics, Magdalen College, Oxford University.

Introduction

Investigating the Welfare State at Century's End

Paul Pierson

LONG recognized as a defining feature of the advanced industrial democracies, the welfare state currently commands greater attention than ever. Even at a time of worsening inequality, demands for retrenchment have grown more insistent. In many countries, efforts to introduce significant changes in social policy have provoked sharp conflicts and triggered widespread social unrest. During the past few years, announcements of plans for welfare state cutbacks in France, Germany, and Italy prompted the largest demonstrations in twenty years. In the United States, the Republican attempt to alter core elements of national social policy led to a fierce clash between Congress and President and an unprecedented three-week shutdown of 'non-essential' government services. In France, the Conservative government's efforts to achieve an electoral endorsement of its austerity plans led to a stunning reversal of its overwhelming victory four years earlier. Throughout the world of affluent democracies, the welfare state is at the centre of political discussion and social conflict.

A series of major social, economic, and political shifts leave little doubt that conflict over social policy will continue. Indeed, there is a high probability that it will intensify in many countries. Welfare states face vigorous and mounting criticism in the wake of major global economic change, both because of concerns about competitiveness and because economic shifts have altered domestic balances of political power. In many countries, persistent high unemployment has exacerbated already heavy fiscal burdens. In addition, the financial impact of population ageing will be considerable throughout the OECD. In some countries, demographic pressures on pension and health care systems are so severe that they raise fundamental questions about the sustainability of present arrangements. Finally, for most European countries the formation of Economic and Monetary Union creates new constraints which will intensify demands for retrenchment. Indeed, it was policies announced to meet EMU's strict convergence criteria that prompted protests in France, Italy, and elsewhere.

For all these reasons, we are clearly in a new era of austerity. This era is likely to be long-lived, and it is certain to produce deep social anxieties and painful adjustments. Yet despite the unquestionable centrality of the welfare state to contemporary politics, our understanding of the issues involved remains spotty at best. On the growth of the welfare state there is a huge and sophisticated literature, and well-developed arguments about the sources of variation across programmes, countries, and time (Esping-Andersen 1990; Huber, Ragin, and Stephens 1993). Many disagreements persist, but knowledge has been cumulative; we clearly know far more about the emergence and expansion of welfare states than we did ten or even five years ago. This cannot be said of the dynamics emerging in this new era. Indeed, a systematic programme of research has barely begun. Such a programme is badly needed, both because of the importance of the issues for contemporary social life and because there is good reason to believe that research on the 'golden age' of social policy will provide a rather poor guide to understanding the current period (Pierson 1996).

This is true in part because austerity creates a quite distinct set of political problems, empowers different actors, and dictates new strategies. More fundamentally, the massive scale of the welfare state, which is still a relatively new feature of democratic societies, represents a central yet poorly understood fixture of contemporary politics. In order to comprehend contemporary dynamics, we must integrate into our analyses—in a way that traditional 'theories of the welfare state' did not—the manner in which huge social programmes, and the adaptation of social actors to those pro-grammes, have changed the very contours of contemporary politics. The channelling of from one-fifth to over one-third of GDP through public social policies profoundly influences the distribution of resources, patterns of interests, and prospects for forming or reshaping social coalitions.

This project, which brings together leading researchers from Europe and North America, seeks to increase what we know about the politics of the contemporary welfare state. The focus is on four overlapping themes: (1) the sources and scope of pressures on national welfare states; (2) the role of economic interests, and of systems for representing those interests, in the politics of reform; (3) the implications of electoral politics and the design of political institutions for welfare state adjustment; and (4) the distinctive policy dynamics of particular areas of social provision. The word *overlapping* deserves emphasis. These topics are intimately linked, and both within and across chapters we have attempted to make those linkages explicit. The remainder of this essay focuses on outlining the four themes and introducing the contributions of the chapters to follow.

1. THE SOURCES AND SCOPE OF PRESSURES ON NATIONAL WELFARE STATES

Despite the broad consensus that welfare states everywhere are in trouble, there has been limited progress in untangling the factors that might be generating the difficulty, specifying the processes through which these factors exert pressures on national welfare states, or determining their relative significance (Garrett 1998*b* and A. Martin 1996 are exceptions). In most discussions, 'globalization' is identified as the major threat to central features of national welfare states, and the spectre of globalization provides the organizing frame for the three contributions to Part I of this volume.

Herman Schwartz reviews a series of broad claims about the sources of pressure on the welfare state and argues that globalization's impact is often misconstrued. He carefully distinguishes alternative possible causal connections between changes in the international economy and welfare state distress. In many cases, he finds little evidence for these causal pathways, or evidence that only supports an assessment of modest impact. Yet Schwartz argues that one dimension of globalization has been crucial: a wave of deregulatory pressures emanating from changes in the US political economy, which have led to a dramatic erosion of forms of protected employment in the affected sectors of other countries. Schwartz puts greater weight on globalization than do the Iversen and Pierson chapters that follow—in large part because he employs a considerably broader definition of social protection. At the same time, however, he takes issue with important parts of their alternative characterizations of the nature of recent economic change and its impact on the welfare state.

Central to that alternative characterization is the profound shift in employment structures of the affluent democracies away from manufacturing and towards services. In Iversen's analysis, de-industrialization—caused by the dramatic increases in productivity in the manufacturing sector, not by globalization—is the crucial motor of social change. Iversen directly challenges a variant of the globalization thesis which has been popular among scholars (Garrett 1998*b*; Rodrik 1997): the idea that exposure to the heightened risks of an open economy fuelled the expansion of the welfare state as a form of compensation. Iversen marshals considerable evidence for his view that it is the shrinkage of the manufacturing sector, not economic openness, which fuelled the growth of compensatory social policy. At the same time, he finds little evidence that the various dimensions of globalization constitute a source of real threat to the contemporary welfare state.

Pierson also highlights the role of the shift from manufacturing to services. Rather than focusing on the disruption of employment, however, his concern is the shift in the workforce to activities where productivity improvements are more limited. The result has been slower economic growth, which generates fiscal strain for mature welfare states. For Pierson, this is one of a series of 'post-industrial shifts' that produce severe pressures on the welfare state. Others include the maturation of governmental commitments, the transformation of household structures, and population ageing. These shifts create intense fiscal problems. In addition, social change in a context where programmes are often slow to adapt generates mismatches between the inherited capacities of welfare states and contemporary demands for social provision.

It has become increasingly common to argue that whatever the effects of globalization might be, these are intensely mediated by domestic arrangements, and thus convergence in national social policy structures is not to be expected (Garrett and Lange 1995; Kitschelt et al. 1999*b*). All the authors in this volume share this view. Yet while compatible with this argument, Iversen's and Pierson's critiques are different. They emphasize instead that many of the pressures on the welfare state are wrongly attributed to globalization; they are actually generated primarily within affluent democracies.

Welfare states face pressures to cut back, but how much pressure and from what sources? Understanding the contemporary politics of the welfare state requires answers to these questions, which are too often simply asserted or taken for granted. Explanations of political and policy outcomes become more or less convincing once the scale of particular burdens and constraints are identified. The essays in Part I all seek to show how examining the sources of strain carries implications for identifying who is likely to fight with whom over what. The three authors are not of one mind on this issue. Schwartz, for whom social protection includes regulatory arrangements in sectors such as telecommunications and transportation, is most convinced that some aspects of globalization do play a critical role. Iversen and Pierson (in common with arguments developed in the chapters by Huber and Stephens and Swank) are more doubtful about globalization's impact on the core terrain of the welfare state. All the authors agree that domestic institutions remain crucial in mediating any effects emanating from the international economy. And all the authors agree that whatever the sources of pressure might be, the strains on the mature welfare states of the affluent democracies are very real.

2. ECONOMIC ACTORS, INTEREST INTERMEDIATION, AND WELFARE STATE REFORM

Two claims about the contemporary welfare state are almost certainly true. First, the major economic changes occurring in affluent democracies affect employers' and unions' assessments of major social policies. Second, these same economic actors play a critical role in the politics of welfare state reform. The essays in Part II focus on two topics related to these themes: exploring the linkages between national welfare states and national economies, and examining the processes through which economic actors press their interests on policy makers.

Welfare States and Varieties of Capitalism

A central premiss of this project is that an understanding of the forces reshaping the welfare state requires close attention to the ways in which different national patterns of social policy are embedded in and help to shape distinctive national 'varieties of capitalism'. At the moment we know much less about these issues than we should. Traditionally, neither students of the welfare state nor students of political economy have considered the welfare state an integral part of national economies (for recent exceptions see Iversen and Wren 1998 and Ebbinghaus and Manow 1998). Given the scope of welfare states and their evident impact on—at a minimum—labour markets (Esping-Andersen 1990), this oversight is simply indefensible. Exploring this topic is a central task of the essays in Part II. As emphasized in the chapters by Huber and Stephens, Manow, and Rhodes, welfare states are not just a Polanyian 'protective reaction' against modern capitalism. They are a fundamental part of modern capitalism.

There is growing evidence that social programmes and regulations significantly modify employer and union behaviour. Welfare states alter the costs and benefits associated with particular actions. Most apparent is the impact of the welfare state on a variety of issues related to the management of labour, which is of course a key facet of economic organization. At the level of individual firms, social programmes affect a whole range of factors relevant to choices about hiring and firing and how workers are trained and employed (Soskice 1990). At a minimum, welfare state programmes influence the following: (1) the cost of hiring new workers; (2) the willingness of workers to strike; (3) the strength of 'selective incentives' for workers to organize collectively (Rothstein 1992; Manow 1997*a*); (4) the costs of training workers and the prospects for 'poaching' skilled workers from other firms; (5) the costs of 'shedding' older workers, both in terms of likely worker resistance and the financial expense for firms. In part because they influence the resources available to workers (what Esping-Andersen has termed 'decommodification'), broad social policy arrangements may also influence the attractiveness of alternative bargaining strategies for groups of employers as well as unions. In addition, welfare state structures may have a considerable impact on the availability of investment capital, as has been the case in Japan and, in quite different ways, in Sweden (Estevez-Abe forthcoming; Huber and Stephens 1998). In this volume, Huber and Stephens explore at length the linkages between different types of welfare states and different production regimes. They demonstrate that there are in fact quite different configurations within the universe of affluent democracies, with particular types of welfare states strongly associated with distinct systems of economic organization.

An extremely fruitful way of exploring these linkages and bringing out their political implications is to focus on employers. This approach is adopted in the chapters by Manow and Rhodes, as well as in the contributions of Wood and Giaimo in Part IV. Ironically, the myopia of current scholarship on the welfare state is nowhere more evident than in its very scant treatment of the role of employers in shaping and reshaping social policy (though see C. J. Martin 1995*a*; Mares 1998; Swenson 1997). Most work on social policy has proceeded with the often implicit assumption that employers everywhere and always simply opposed any extension of the welfare state and that employers today would demolish it entirely if they only could. It is true that harsh opposition to expansions of the welfare state has often been concentrated among employers, and that the posture of many employers remains sharply critical. Yet it is clearly too simple to reduce employer participation to an oppositional stance. Employers have often been divided, and as Swenson has emphasized, social policy issues as well as industrial relations ones may reveal evidence of 'cross-class coalitions'.

Even where employers initially opposed particular expansions of the welfare state one cannot simply assume that this stance is etched in stone. For two reasons, the position of employers is likely to become more complex once welfare state initiatives are introduced. First, because employers wield considerable political power, they may have some success over time in 'bending' social policy initiatives into forms that they prefer. Business actors will exploit openings to modify structures, pushing for further expansions of some elements while resisting expansions of others. Second, there is likely to be a process of adaptation among firms. Employers will gradually seek to adjust their own practices in important respects to 'fit' the incentives which social programmes create. Survival rates among the types of firms able to make such adjustments are likely to be higher over time. Thus, capitalists adjust the welfare state, and the welfare state adjusts capitalists. Over time, national welfare states become an important part of the institutional matrix shaping practices at the level of the firm, as well as influencing broader efforts at national economic management.

Such a reinterpretation of the political economy of the welfare state has significant implications. If in fact welfare states are deeply integrated into national variants of capitalism, it is to be expected that employers' attitudes towards welfare state reform will be more complex and ambivalent than is generally assumed. Philip Manow's chapter argues in support of this interpretation. He shows the limits of both a simple model of employer opposition to the welfare state and a more sophisticated variant which locates that opposition in a cross-class alliance of employers and unions vulnerable to international competition ('tradeables'). Thus, stressing the often-strong connections between social policy arrangements and modern economies allows greater precision in identifying the particular aspects of the welfare state which generate the greatest discontent among particular firms or sectors. In turn, this facilitates efforts to specify the kinds of reforms these actors are likely to favour.

In the past ten years, research on the comparative politics of industrial relations has been transformed by a move away from a focus on relationships among unions, social democratic parties, and the state as a result of a growing recognition that employer interests and power were of central importance. One can sense the beginnings of a similar shift in our understandings of contemporary welfare state politics. This is likely to force the reconsideration not only of models of the welfare state but also of prominent models of contemporary political economies. It is hardly plausible that the workings of modern market economies remain hermetically sealed from such massive systems of government intervention.

Employers, Unions, and the Politics of Welfare State Restructuring

The essays in Part I focus primarily on key social and economic transformations while drawing out possible implications for the interests and reform agendas of particular political actors. By exploring the links between welfare states and production regimes, the essays in Part II also seek to clarify the likely interests of particular social actors. At the same time, these essays shift to a more detailed examination of the processes of welfare state restructuring —from identifying potential cleavages to understanding coalition formation and policy change. These issues are the principal focus of the remainder of the volume. In turning to these political processes, the volume's contributors stress the need to recognize two major arenas which shape the dynamics of policy reform. The first is the electoral/partisan arena in which politicians, answerable to voters, make the key decisions. Governments, parliaments, and political parties are central organizational venues. The second arena is that of interest intermediation, in which the political demands of organized social actors are aired and addressed. Of course, these two arenas are linked in many respects. One cannot understand the politics of welfare state adjustment without attending to each, as well as exploring the interconnections between the two.

These two arenas take quite different forms in different countries. In the 'liberal' welfare states (Australia, Canada, Great Britain, New Zealand, and the United States), systems of interest intermediation are fragmented and disorganized, so the electoral/partisan arena is central to the shaping of reform. Elsewhere, key economic interests tend to be more organized and more tightly linked to the machinery of policy making. Here, corporatist or quasi-corporatist policy making complements or even partly supplants the role played by electoral and partisan politics.

The electoral/partisan arena is taken up in Part III. The essays in Part II consider a number of critical issues about the manner in which organized interests, especially those representing the interests of capital and labour, participate in the process of welfare state restructuring. Again, all these

chapters stress that employers as well as unions are deeply implicated in existing social policy arrangements, and that their reform ambitions are generally
oriented towards adjustment rather than dismantling. In his contribution,
Martin Rhodes highlights the participation of employers' organizations as
well as unions in negotiating significant revisions to the post-war social contract. He shows how social pacts have been designed to enhance economic
performance as well as to deal with difficult distributive issues. Furthermore,
Rhodes stresses that social pacts have emerged in contexts where reform
pressures are evident but traditional corporatist institutions were relatively
weak. Thus, far from overwhelming domestic policy makers, the new social
and economic climate may actually invigorate capacities for negotiated
adjustments.

3. POLITICAL INSTITUTIONS, PARTISAN POLITICS, AND POLICY CHANGE

The chapters in Part III focus especially on the electoral/partisan arena.
Under what circumstances can policy makers initiate major reforms, and of
what kind? The starting point for these analyses is the fact that in affluent
democracies the exercise of public authority generally requires electoral
vindication. To say this is not to imply that voters are all-powerful, but it
is to suggest that they are highly relevant actors. Elsewhere, I have argued
that the failure to take voters seriously helps to explain why analysts systematically underestimated the welfare state's resilience over the past two
decades (Pierson 1996). Generally speaking, voters have strong attachments
to the welfare state, and politicians who initiate cutbacks rightly fear electoral
retribution.

   Yet, as outlined elsewhere in the volume, demands to impose austerity are
also intense. How politicians deal with this tension will in part reflect the
structure of the electoral/partisan arena. Key features of that structure may
facilitate or inhibit the formation of viable political coalitions and structure
the terms on which such coalitions can proceed. We argue that two features
require special attention: the character of institutional veto points and the
organization of party systems.

   Various strands of the 'new institutionalism' have underscored the significance of the 'rules of the game'. Here, these rules are broadly construed to
include not only formal political institutions, but regularized (if informal)
patterns of decision making, and rule-like features which may characterize
particular policy arrangements rather than whole political systems (such
as those dictating who has veto power over modifications). The contributors to Part III seek to move beyond broad claims that 'institutions matter'

to more specific propositions about the interaction effects among relevant institutions and to an exploration of how the distinctive features of the contemporary context and policy agenda modify the impact of institutional variables.

The chapters in this section and elsewhere in the volume take up a number of aspects of this issue. In the process, they underscore the complex impact of political institutions on welfare state adjustment. Giuliano Bonoli investigates the impact of concentrated political authority on efforts to carry out politically unpopular welfare state reforms in France, Great Britain, and Switzerland. Here he builds on recent research suggesting that rules affecting the number of veto points in the political system matter a great deal (Immergut 1992; Huber, Ragin, and Stephens 1993). Bonoli shows that centralization indeed increased the possibilities for dramatic reform, but also increased political risks. Furthermore, institutional setting influenced the style and content of reform initiatives as well as their scale. Not surprisingly, unilateral action was common—although not necessarily effective—where power was concentrated. In systems of dispersed authority, negotiated settlements proved to be the norm. Bonoli stresses that these negotiations therefore required quid pro quos. In emphasizing the role of quid pro quos Bonoli also demonstrates the dangers of conflating welfare state change with welfare state retrenchment—a theme also stressed by Rhodes and explored further in the conclusion to this volume.

Duane Swank's quantitative analysis partly confirms Bonoli's conclusion about the impact of concentrated authority on retrenchment initiatives. So does Huber and Stephens' explanation of why the most extensive retrenchment of the welfare state has occurred in Britain and, especially, New Zealand. Yet Swank also notes that if one takes a longer-term perspective, and considers less-direct effects of institutions as well as direct ones, the picture is more complicated. Over the long term, fragmented institutions slowed the growth of the welfare state in the first place. Furthermore, they probably contributed to the development of relatively fragmented, heterogeneous political interests, thus fostering a political environment less favourable to the sustenance of expansive, universal social rights.

In the concluding chapter, I suggest that the analysis of institutional effects is more complicated still. It would be a mistake to simply treat institutions as 'independent variables' which will have similar effects in different settings (e.g. 'an increase of x per cent in the degree of institutional centralization will increase social spending by y per cent'). Instead, we need to pay attention to interaction effects between institutional arrangements and other elements of a particular political configuration. Concentrating political authority in a 'liberal' setting (e.g. New Zealand), where other sources of support for the welfare state are relatively weak, may not have the same consequences as concentrating political authority in a 'Christian democratic' setting (e.g. France). Indeed, the significance of such interaction effects provides a strong justification for analysing distinct regimes of welfare capitalism (following Esping-Andersen), an approach followed in a number of the contributions to this volume. Of course, this is an issue not just for arguments about the role of political institutions, but for all efforts to iden-tify the impact of particular 'variables' across the range of mature welfare states. I therefore take the matter up at some length in the concluding chapter.

Arguments about political institutions clarify one important dimension affecting the capacities of govenments to introduce new social policies. As Herbert Kitschelt argues, a second crucial dimension is the structure of party systems. He makes a convincing case that the investigation of party systems has been a neglected area of research on the politics of the welfare state. Of course, there has been a rich literature on the impact of partisanship on welfare state development, but Kitschelt moves beyond this tradition in two respects. First, he focuses on the contemporary environment and the par-ticular difficulties associated with the politically delicate tasks of managing austerity and restructuring. In particular, he stresses the challenges of a con-text where parties' reputations and capacities to mobilize activists often rest on long-established commitments to social provision.

Kitschelt's second innovation is to treat party systems as strategic fields, where the critical issue is not just the balance of electoral power between left and right but the extent to which governing parties have to worry about exit by key constituencies to other parties.[1] The moves that parties can make depend on the plausible countermoves of competitors. In this framework, the structure of party competition within broadly 'left' or 'right' political groupings can be as consequential as the overall ideo-logical balance in a party system. Kitschelt thus draws attention to the key question of political actors' room for manoeuvre—their capacity to both adopt new positions and embrace new partners in (formal or informal) reform coalitions. As Rhodes stresses, a similar issue arises in the arena of interest intermediation, where the strategies of unions and employers' organizations are shaped not only by those of their interlocutors around the bargaining table, but by organizational competitors who might exploit opportunities stemming from the conclusion of politically painful negoti-ations. In the final chapter, I stress that these arguments highlight a key feature of the new politics of the welfare state. Despite great variation in the terms of debate across countries, a common dynamic is widely shared: the essential question is whether an effective centrist 'restructuring' coalition can emerge between the alternatives of preserving the status quo or radical neoliberal reform.

---

[1] For a different take on related issues, see F. Ross 1998.

4. ANALYSING DISTINCT POLICY SECTORS

'The welfare state' is an umbrella term covering a range of governmental activities that have distinctive characteristics. For instance, the type of government activity (e.g. transfer payment, service provision, regulation of private actors) and the main targets of intervention (e.g. those expected to participate in the labour market vs. those who are not) vary dramatically across sectors. It is widely acknowledged that generalizations about the development of social policy may apply less well to the understanding of particular issue areas. Unfortunately, it has been less common to build an investigation of sectoral variation within the welfare state into systematic research. Understanding the contemporary politics of the welfare state requires examination of the distinctive problems and dynamics which characterize particular sectors.

At the same time, the three 'policy domain' chapters included in Part IV offer opportunities to disaggregate some of the broad claims discussed in the other parts of this project. Focusing on a single policy area over time makes it possible to investigate the processes and outcomes of welfare state reform in greater detail. Authors of each policy essay take up propositions advanced in the other sections of the project which are particularly relevant to their domain and subject them to critical scrutiny. This section thus provides a basis to build on, critique, and add nuance to the more general discussions in Parts I–III.

Part IV includes chapters focusing on three policy domains central to the welfare state: health care, pensions, and labour market policy. Health care and pensions raise crucial issues related to the fiscal pressures on the welfare state. They differ, however, in critical respects. One important divide is the one distinguishing the provision of services from the provision of transfer payments. This difference affects the interaction between public and private sector, the nature of constituencies for each programme, the structuring of coalitions seeking reform, and the possible avenues of policy change.

The lion's share of social expenditure in all of the affluent democracies goes to two areas, health care and pensions. These two sectors generally also provide the core foundations of political support for the welfare state. Not surprisingly, heavy expenditures in these areas have made them major targets for restructuring in most countries. Susan Giaimo's analysis of health care reform in Germany, Great Britain, and the United States shows that there is no single logic of reform—who the key actors are, what they want, and what they can accomplish are all shaped by established arrangements in the health care sector. While employers, for instance, were basically irrelevant in Britain, they were central actors in the other two countries. Yet German employers both wanted and could achieve quite different things than

American employers. All three countries sought cost containment. In the United States, however, the fragmentation of existing arrangements and the weak capacity for negotiated reform left each employer seeking the best deal available in the private marketplace. In turn, this meant that the price of cost containment was a severe worsening of equity problems.

In their chapter on the dynamics of pension reform, Myles and Pierson stress a key feature of public pension systems: the fact that the implications of policy choices only play out over a very long period of time. Almost all pension systems are undergoing major reforms. Yet choices made twenty-five or fifty years ago profoundly shape the nature of the reform options available now. Most countries are severely constrained in their options by the accumulated commitments from decades of experience with social insurance. Only where countries failed to develop large pay-as-you-go pension systems at these earlier junctures has the much-heralded alternative of introducing extensive funded arrangements proven to be a viable option. Myles and Pierson also emphasize the need to legitimate often politically painful revisions to this key element of the post-war social contract. While there has been major change everywhere, in almost all countries this has required broad negotiations, including left-of-centre parties and/or labour unions.

Compared with pensions and health care, labour market policies generate much smaller budgetary demands, but they are widely seen as a critical nexus for relationships between state and market. This issue area thus represents a key policy domain for investigating many of the political economy concerns introduced in Part II. As Stewart Wood shows, the politics of labour market reform in Germany, Sweden, and Great Britain strongly support the more general claims advanced about the connections between welfare state structures and broad organizational features of particular economies. Labour market policies have not converged on a 'liberal', market-oriented model. Barriers to policy reform ('veto points') have been important in slowing change, but more striking is the fact that employers in the more organized market economies have shown limited enthusiasm for liberalization.

In combination, the essays of Part IV develop three important themes which build on the earlier parts of the volume. The first theme is path dependence —the idea that key programmatic arrangements of mature welfare states reflect the operation of self-reinforcing processes over extended periods of time. All of these chapters emphasize the massive implications of previous patterns of policy development in particular countries. These path-dependent processes shift the preferences of key political actors and constrain the range of reform initiatives that are politically plausible in a particular setting. Crucial to an investigation of welfare state restructuring is an appreciation of the ways in which historically constructed and densely interconnected webs of organizations and policies condition what actors want and what they can hope to get.

The second theme is the complexity of identifying actor policy preferences. Largely because of the path-dependent processes described above, actors such as 'employers' find themselves operating in quite different contexts in different countries. Their interests cannot be 'read off' from changes in the international economy. Instead, because of the ways in which firms in different countries have developed over time and because different national welfare state designs are subject to different kinds of pressures (whether internally or externally generated) what employers want is likely to vary substantially across countries; so will their expectations of what they can hope to achieve.

The third theme is the need to transcend simple dichotomous notions of policy change that contrast welfare state dismantling and welfare state resilience, 'more' social provision vs. 'less'. All these chapters emphasize that even in a climate of austerity the agenda for welfare state restructuring generally cannot be reduced to straightforward retrenchment. Instead, revisions involve more complex policy changes, reflecting trade-offs among competing priorities and the need to meet the diverse concerns of various partners in reform coalitions. Appreciating this complexity is critical both for understanding policy outcomes and for grasping the nature of the political processes which facilitate or inhibit reform.

All three of these themes are taken up in the conclusion, which draws heavily on the volume's essays but reflects the editor's views rather than the collective judgements of the contributors. The contemporary politics of the welfare state, I argue, takes shape against a backdrop of both intense pressures for austerity and enduring popularity. The pressures on the welfare state are very real. Changes in the global economy are important, but it is primarily social and economic transformations occurring within affluent democracies that generate fiscal strain. Slower economic growth associated with the transition to a post-industrial economy, the maturation of government policy commitments, and population ageing and changing household structures have all combined to create a context of essentially permanent austerity. At the same time, tax levels strain public tolerance, while payroll contribution rates appear to jeopardize employment. While tax increases have contributed to closing the gap between commitments and resources, it is difficult to imagine that in many European countries changes in revenues alone could be sufficient to maintain fiscal equilibrium. Yet support for the welfare state remains widespread almost everywhere. The core constituencies for social programmes are broad. Furthermore, social actors have made important commitments over extended periods of time to distinct national systems of health care, labour market, and pension policy. These systems are thus deeply embedded in national polities. Finally, most political systems contain major formal or informal veto points which militate against radical change. In most countries, there is little sign that the basic commitments to a mixed economy of welfare face a fundamental political challenge. Nor is there much evidence of convergence towards some neoliberal orthodoxy.

In this context, even strong supporters of the welfare state may come to acknowledge the need for adjustment, and even severe critics may need to face the political realities of continuing popular enthusiasm for social provision. Thus, in most of the affluent democracies, the politics of social policy centres on the renegotiation and restructuring of the terms of the post-war social contract rather than its dismantling. The crucial issue is whether particular national settings facilitate the emergence of such a centrist reform effort, and if so, on what terms.

Clarifying the policy responses of different countries requires the recognition of two complications. First, 'change' cannot be reduced to simply retrenchment. Reform agendas involve complex combinations of efforts to 're-commodify' workers, control costs, and 'recalibrate' welfare states to improve performance in meeting established goals and enhance capacities to meet newly emerging ones. Depending on the structure of dominant political coalitions and on the character of pressures facing particular welfare states, reform agendas will involve quite different combinations of changes along the three dimensions of re-commodification, cost containment, and recalibration.

The second complication is the need to recognize three quite distinct configurations of welfare state politics among the affluent democracies. Gøsta Esping-Andersen's influential typology of liberal, Christian democratic, and social democratic welfare regimes provides a basic framework for distinguishing different dynamics of welfare state reform. Despite many differences among the countries within each grouping, the three 'worlds' do describe distinct social policy configurations, as well as quite different underlying political conditions. These distinct configurations, in interaction with a new socio-economic setting, generate quite different policy challenges and political possibilities.

These three configurations vary systematically in both the intensity and character of adjustment pressures, on the one hand, and the scope of political support for the welfare state, on the other. In the liberal world, reform focuses on cost containment and re-commodification, with the crucial political divide separating those advocating thoroughgoing neoliberal retrenchment and those seeking a more consensual solution that offers compensation to vulnerable groups. In the social democratic world, the focus of reform is on cost containment and recalibrations, which aim at rationalizing programmes to enhance performance in achieving established goals. On the whole, reform has been negotiated, consensual, and incremental. In the Christian democratic world, where pressures to adjust and support for existing programmes clash most intensely, reform has centred on cost containment and recalibration of 'old' programmes to meet new demands. Neoliberal retrenchment is not politically viable. Instead, the focus is on efforts to construct a viable centrist reform coalition. Thus, there is not a single 'new politics' of the welfare state, but different politics in different configurations.

PART I

Sources of Pressure on the Contemporary Welfare State

1

Round up the Usual Suspects!:
Globalization, Domestic Politics, and Welfare State Change

Herman Schwartz

WHO killed the growth of the welfare state? Its seemingly inexorable budgetary, programmatic, and personnel growth in the 1960s and 1970s ground to a halt in the 1980s, accompanied by the mutilation of programmes and rising unemployment. Was it an external intruder—globalization of one sort or another? Was it an inside job—domestic politics and demography? Or, as public choice theory suggests, was death self-inflicted by a combination of producer and client groups? As if this richness of suspects were not problem enough, the identity of the victim is also uncertain. In fact, the central mystery in the relationship between globalization and the welfare state is accurately identifying the victim; it is a mystery of concept formation in which, prosaically, no one is quite sure which dependent variable matters and how it is changing. Spending levels? Policies? Institutions? Wage equality? Employment levels? National autonomy?

Two academic deformations of reality obscure the politics at the heart of this specific mystery. First, the richness of prior research on the formal or overt welfare state—systems of tax funded transfers and state provided or funded social services ameliorating life and economic risks for workers— provides a lamp-post around which enquiries naturally cluster, asking how 'globalization' has affected those programmes, but ignoring areas of darkness away from the lamp. Second, a profound normative bias favouring welfare in most welfare state research obscures the fact that not all welfare is for workers, that the welfare state was never simply an instrumental tool for advancing labour's interests, and that 'welfare'—understood much more broadly as 'social protection'—was about sheltering all income streams,

I thank Aida Hozic and David Waldner, respectively, for many long discussions of the film industry and social sciences in which they raised this alarm. Other useful comments came from Phil Cerny, John Echeverri-Gent, Barry Hindess, Debra Morris, Louis Pauly, Steve Rhoads, and participants in the 'New Politics of the Welfare State' project, where earlier versions were presented. All errors are mine.

not simply wages, from market pressures.[1] Focusing only on formal welfare and workers' interests has led most analysis into a dead end discussion over whether globalization constrains 'national autonomy', as if in the absence of constraint the welfare state would not be politically contested.

In contrast, Polanyi's notion of 'social protection' encompasses a much broader conceptualization of 'welfare' as a shelter for workers and owners from the market. This broader conceptualization permits much more specific attributions of guilt in this case, using the traditional guides of motive, opportunity, and method (or more prosaically, interests, coalitions, and politics). Focusing on social protection shifts attention towards the ways in which the normal operations of the market and deliberate policy choices have eroded certain kinds of property rights, including those nested in the welfare state. Briefly (because the conventions of academic writing demand this now), most social protection after World War II was accomplished by sheltering the service sector (including and especially firms, not workers) from competition; the welfare state was relatively less important. The progressive deregulation and marketization of the service sector has displaced all this covert social protection onto the overt, formal welfare state. It is not the welfare state that has been killed but rather social protection.

The purpose of this essay is to rethink the whole globalization debate and create a more compelling attribution of guilt. So let us conform to the conventions of the mystery rather than academic genre, and survey the allegedly guilty parties before we turn to the victim. We begin with the time-honoured cry: 'Round up the usual suspects!' Was it SAM, ILSA, or RICK?

1. SAM, ILSA, OR RICK?

Most of the suspects in the debate over whether or not globalization did in the welfare state are arguments linking fairly broad pressures to equally uniform changes, and they typically cast conflicts over globalization as fights between capital and labour. But in all of these arguments, the traditional elements of motive, opportunity, and method remain under specified. Are there actors, who are they, and what are their preferences? Which global pressures matter, and—almost as important—from when? What are the intervening mechanisms turning pressures into policy preferences? After I collect all the suspects together into the parlour, you will see that the case against most of them lacks one of the three elements needed for a conviction. Only circumstantial or functional motives are present for most suspects. Causal chains linking the alleged murderer to the corpse are missing. And the variety of weapons is bewildering. In my interrogation I will pay particular attention

[1] One salient exception is Baldwin 1990.

to four issues. First, is the suspected cause in proportion to the alleged effects? Second, can the alleged cause be associated with a plausible set of actors (why do actors act; or how do changes in markets affect actors' interests)? Third, how well does the alleged cause explain the timing of actors' actions (when does it make them act)? Finally, does the alleged cause explain why actors see their proposed (and often realized) policies as plausible solutions to their problems? In this sense, I explicitly take up several challenges posed by Alt and his co-authors to show that while asset specificity is critical in the construction of interests, asset specificity is politically constructed and not an objective fact of economic life (Alt et al. 1996).

Below, I separate the suspects into three groups for interrogation. First, I deal with the obvious external suspects, the 'SAM' arguments about low-wage Southern competition, technological Advances, and Monetary policy constraints. SAM arguments generally correlate global changes to rising inequality, erosion of benefit levels, and heightened unemployment, but they typically lack a causal mechanism. Instead they substitute functional necess-ities for welfare state change or contraction; political actors are driven to retrench the welfare state regardless of preferences.

Then I turn to the domestic 'ILSA' arguments—Inflation control, Low Service sector productivity growth, and Ageing. ILSA arguments usually focus on the political difficulties in changing the welfare state, regardless of any necessity for change, and a strain of ILSA suggests that the welfare state is not really dead. ILSA arguments thus generally have better laid out causal mechanisms with better identified actors. Nonetheless, ILSA arguments also rely heavily on a functionalist link between cause and outcome that recasts the Malthusian tension between agriculture and industry as a tension between services and industry.

Both SAM and ILSA thus turn out to be rather unsatisfactory suspects, largely because they look at the formal welfare state, focusing on spending levels rather than institutional structure, and completely ignoring the shelter-ing of profits that was typical of the Keynesian 'golden era'. They both suffer from a species of functionalism that mistakenly treats an interdependent sequence of events as singular occurrences (i.e. 'Galton's problem'). Finally, they are both weak on method—it's difficult to construct a causal mechanism linking the alleged weapon to the ultimate outcomes.

Consequently, I finally turn to 'RICK'—property Rights, Income streams, and Coalitions, to solve the mystery. RICK arguments link the fear or reality of market and political destruction of actors' property rights (and thus streams of income) to actors' policy preferences for the welfare state understood in its broadest possible form, as social protection, or shelter from market forces. RICK arguments recast the 'external' versus 'internal' dichotomy as a question of market forces to make a tighter case linking motive, opportunity, and method. Constable! Bring in SAM!

2. SAM

The SAM arguments share a common causal effect. Increased trade and financial mobility at the global level correlate with rising income inequality and unemployment (A. Martin 1996). In the first two arguments, this puts fiscal stress on welfare states designed for economic 'fair weather'. In the last, even though some welfare states might be able to handle at least some economic bad weather, financial internationalization constrains monetary policy, preventing expansionist policy in pursuit of lower unemployment. In all three, actors directly translate globally derived fiscal pressures into cutbacks; no motive for institutional changes can be traced in these models.

While the correlation between rising unemployment and fiscal stress is clear, the greatest reductions in formal welfare have occurred largely in the countries with relatively low unemployment rates—the USA, Britain, and New Zealand—not highly unemployed Continental Europe. This suggests the viability of the welfare state rests on political rather than financial foundations, and suggests that SAM arguments lack a causal mechanism for automatically translating economic shocks into cutbacks. Moreover, each of the advanced technology and monetary constraint arguments has a variant that assumes that the welfare state can be expanded despite greater international integration. What do the SAM arguments specifically claim?

Southern Discomfort

The low-wage southern competition argument sees the spectacular rise in foreign direct investment (FDI) flows to the newly industrializing economies (NIEs) after 1970 as a search for relatively cheap and literate workers and links this to declining demand for relatively expensive unskilled labour in the OECD. Adrian Wood argues that southern competition alone accounts for a loss of at least 9 million OECD manufacturing jobs, equivalent to about two-thirds of *Euroland*'s total unemployment in 1998. Similarly, William Cline argues that trade and immigration together account for between 20 and 25 per cent of the observed increase in US wage inequality (Wood 1994: 167; Cline 1996).[2]

Southern competition has two alibis though. First, FDI still disproportionately flows between rich countries relative to either LDC population or purchasing power parity adjusted gross product as a share of total world product (UNCTAD 1993). Second, even if NIE growth displaced OECD

---

[2] I will not discuss rising wage inequality at length, because wage compression was never a core goal of most formal welfare states.

workers, NIE imports created growth in the OECD that in turn could have provided a window for redistribution towards those workers. Net of internal flows, industrializing Asia's share of world merchandise imports doubled to 18 per cent, 1985 to 1995 (OECD 1998*b*: 207). And in the USA, Clinton expanded the tax expenditures for the poor and tried to expand the formal welfare state to encompass health care. In some of the smaller European countries like Denmark, exogenously driven prosperity in the 1990s translated into increased rather than decreased transfers to persons. Southern competition at best explains the weakness of demand at the bottom of the manufacturing labour market. It does not provide a sufficient explanation as to why cutbacks are the natural political response to rising unemployment and inequality or why welfare institutions were restructured.

Advanced Technology

Southern competition's alibi in part rested on the fact that most FDI flows are intra-OECD. Does this throw suspicion on technological advances that facilitated rising intra-OECD competition by lowering transaction costs for management at a distance? Dani Rodrik (1997) provides an argument complementary to the southern competition argument, while abjuring any causal connection between welfare recision and globalization. He argues that increased mobility for goods producing capital has also increased the elasticity of demand for labour across the entire labour market, thus causing stagnant real wages in the USA and more generally the OECD. But Rodrik makes no causal connection between this rising demand elasticity and the crisis of the welfare state. In fact, Rodrik ends by making a partly normative, partly practical argument that globalization implies an even greater need for welfare, lest the unexpected political consequences of globalization undermine the market system as a whole. So while he sees global changes as more consequential than other economists, he obviously thinks these changes do not constrain the provision of welfare. Still, Rodrik provides a point of entry for a broader argument as yet unexplored by economists.

Most FDI does flow to and from rich countries, although the stock of FDI there has fallen from 79.3 per cent of all FDI in 1990 to 68 per cent in 1997 (UNCTAD 1998). One of the less surprising aspects of FDI in manufacturing is that foreign firms generally have higher labour productivity than local firms. (Less surprising, because absent such an advantage, local firms would necessarily out compete foreign investors.) In the six largest OECD economies, on an unweighted basis, the ratio between assets and employment for inwardly investing manufacturing firms at the beginning of the 1990s was 1.6 (versus a nominal economy-wide ratio of 1), suggesting higher capital intensity and lower than average direct employment from FDI (UNCTAD

1993: 5).[3] FDI has carried more efficient production norms from each OECD economy into the others, causing job losses as domestic firms adapt to higher productivity levels or simply exit the market. North–north competition via FDI thus may be responsible for job losses on the same order of magnitude as southern competition, and moreover losses of well paying jobs in steel, autos, and electrical machinery. While wage rates for these kinds of jobs are not affected (as in the southern competition argument), the volume of jobs is reduced. Still, even cast this way we lack specific links between the erosion of manufacturing and service jobs and changes in the welfare state. Most job losses would have occurred in the late 1970s and 1980s, precisely when welfare became politically contested. Why didn't job losers and those afraid of losing jobs demand and get more welfare the way they demanded, and quite often got, more trade protection (see also Iversen, in this volume)? Clearly asset specificity (here job-specific skills) induces a preference for trade policy. But this simply reinforces the tenuous nature of the link between globalization and welfare state changes. This leaves only monetary mechanisms as a suspect in this group.

Money Madness

The financial internationalization argument is similarly straightforward and similarly lacks any direct connection between economic shocks and welfare states' problems. Andrew Martin (1996) summarizes these arguments clearly in order to dismiss them, showing that they all argue that rising financial capital mobility systematically biases macroeconomic policy in favour of deflation. Because countries with floating exchange rates and no capital controls can only make monetary policy operate through the exchange rate, efforts to expand the economy by lowering interest rates only lead to imported inflation and capital flight as the exchange rate falls. Policy makers thus operate under an asymmetrical constraint when faced with unacceptably high unemployment. Whatever their preferences, they can only deflate their economies. Fair weather welfare states thus lack the national autonomy to make any reasonable policy response to rising unemployment.

Geoffrey Garrett rather clearly but perhaps too cavalierly has dismissed this argument, pointing to the absence of significant fiscal and capital tax policy convergence among OECD countries (Garrett 1998*a, b*). Garrett supplements his critique with a positive argument. He argues that social democratic policy makers can deploy powerful supply-side policies, particularly centralized collective bargaining and low relative unit labour costs, to attract capital (see also Boix 1998).

[3] Put differently, because FDI accounts for 20% of manufacturing capital stock, manufacturing employment is roughly 7.5% lower in these OECD countries, an effect similar in magnitude to the losses Wood identifies.

Garrett is clearly correct in dismissing financial integration as a serious challenge to national 'autonomy'. He also correctly criticizes the globalization literature for its obsession with convergence. But he draws the wrong conclusions from the absence of policy convergence, at the policy levels he studies anyway. Logically, the absence of convergence does not demonstrate an absence of effect. Arguments about globalization are ultimately arguments about markets, and markets produce variation. Markets produce winners and losers; different strategies can succeed. Garrett also misconstrues what is at stake because he poses the 'globalization' problem as one of national autonomy in the face of external constraints, rather than asking what autonomy might be used for. He poses the problem this way because he assumes that workers and capital each have internally consistent preferences regarding formal welfare. The left uniformly wants redistribution and the alteration of market outcomes and the right the reinforcement of those outcomes (Garrett 1998*b*: 7). This assumption obliterates any political contestation around welfare inside each camp.

This is a crucial error, because one implication of recent work is that centralized bargaining and large welfare states are an unstable combination because of the way that greater competitive pressures in the international market create conflicts over relative wage levels inside the labour movement (Swenson 1989; Pontusson and Swenson 1996; Iversen 1996). Empirically, the connection between centralized bargaining and capital flows is weak: correlating Garrett's rankings of labour market centralization against FDI inflows and outflows yields coefficients of 0.13 and 0.09, respectively. Garrett does not test whether capital flowed to countries with highly centralized bargaining during the period he studied, 1981–92. This is an odd omission considering that Sweden, which he regards as highly centralized, suffered the second largest outflow of FDI of any OECD country those years, at 2.7 per cent of GDP, only partially offset by well below average inflows running at 0.7 (OECD 1995*e*: 75).[4] So while Garrett correctly dismisses much of the financial mobility argument, he too elides the politics surrounding welfare state change.

Financial and productive capital clearly are more mobile now, but the causal chain linking increased mobility to changes in the welfare state is weak, particularly with respect to the connections between interests, politics, and policy outputs. All three sorts of SAM arguments ultimately depend on two assumptions: that rising unemployment is a sufficient explanation for a weak fiscal basis for the welfare state and that in turn politicians automatically

---

[4] The Netherlands, a traditional capital exporter, had the largest outflow at 2.9% and Britain the third largest at 2.6%. The unweighted OECD average outflow was 1.1% of GDP; the average inflow 0.9%.

TABLE 1.1. *Net change in selected expenditures and fiscal deficits, OECD 18, 1980s–90s (% of GDP, – indicates a fall in spending or deficit)*

Net change in	1980–3	1983–9	1989–93	1993–6	1980–96
Total UE expenditures	0.94	−0.37	1.11	−0.38	1.30
Total social expenditures	1.70	0.20	3.60	−0.70	4.80
Total debt service expenditures	1.40	0.10	0.30	0.10	1.90
Total expenditure	3.60	−3.20	5.20	0.10	5.70
Total taxation (1993–5 only) (Reference: 1970–9 = 4.8 %)	1.10	1.50	0.20	0.20	3.00
Fiscal deficit	2.44	−3.71	4.16	−4.07	−1.18

Source: OECD, *Employment Outlook*, 1997; OECD, *National Accounts Statistics*, various dates.

translate external constraints or rising fiscal stress into welfare state cut-backs (or in Garrett's case, costlessly ameliorate constraints). Certainly rising unemployment raised the relative cost of welfare (tax revenues are down, spending is up); moreover, the Continental welfare states responded to higher unemployment by shifting labour market losers into early retirement and disability programmes, magnifying the fiscal stress. But in most economies the cost of deferred wages—i.e. normal health and pension expenditures—runs at roughly five times the cost of unemployment insurance and early retirement schemes. Absolutely the latter cannot account for the increase in public sector deficits in the last ten years or the twenty years before that. From 1980 to 1996 active and passive unemployment outlays for the eighteen rich OECD countries rose on average by only 1.2 per cent of GDP to 2.97 per cent (OECD 1997*a*). Both unemployment expenditures and fiscal deficits oscillated up and down in response to the business cycle.

But as Table 1.1 shows, factors besides the direct cost of rising unemployment expenses drove the evolution of fiscal deficits. Pro-cyclic unemployment increases surely aggravated deficits, but secular increases in other areas drove the long-term evolution of fiscal stress. Health and old age pensions are the major cause for rising government spending, and thus presumably for fiscal stress. Cumulating deficits and debt service also loom larger than unemployment expenses by the end of the 1980s. As high real interest rates arguably cause both unemployment and high debt service costs, this seems a more appropriate locus for enquiry than unemployment alone.

SAM's second assumption also seems implausible. Much rational choice theorizing about the behaviour of politicians would suggest that in the face of rising demands from their clients they would choose to expand welfare services and transfers, particularly since the interest rate penalty for doing so was not overwhelmingly large. Layna Mosley finds that the financial penalty for running fiscal deficits is a modest 5 basis points (0.05 per cent) on domestic currency debt for every increase in the deficit of 1 per cent of GDP in OECD countries (Mosley 1998: 20–1; Garrett 1998*a*). In the Continental welfare states where unemployment has risen the most and been persistently highest, the fewest cutbacks have occurred. All SAM arguments thus need to connect the kind of external economic pressures they posit to a fleshed out political mechanism. They need to connect interests and preferences to policy outcomes, or in other words, to find not just opportunity but also method and most importantly motives for actors. Perhaps, though, the weak case against the external SAM arguments is irrelevant; maybe it is ILSA who fits the frame better.

3. ILSA

If it is difficult to pin this killing on SAM, the external intruder, perhaps ILSA the maid did it. Most murder after all is domestic. Perhaps Inflation control, Low Service sector productivity growth, and Ageing account for changes in the welfare state. The former argument is most associated with Ton Notermans, the latter two with Paul Pierson.

Inflation Control

Notermans argues that the institutional structures governing post-World War II economies were erected in response to the deflation of the 1930s and consequently were biased towards inflation (Notermans 1999). These institutions naturally could not effectively contain the inflation that emerged in the 1970s, and this inflation forced politicians everywhere to dismantle those institutional structures. Full employment policies, credit market regulation, discretionary monetary policy, and, of course, the welfare state all fell by the wayside. At this point, Notermans's argument becomes symmetrical to and incorporates parts of the SAM financial mobility argument: unemployment rises, no policy response is possible, the welfare state encounters fiscal difficulties. Greater central bank autonomy imposes a domestic constraint on full employment, but capital market and foreign exchange liberalization are external constraints operating in the same way.

Notermans's domestic version of the monetary policy constraint argument at least has the virtues of starting from actors trying to cope with the problems they face, rather than starting from an actorless system imposing constraints, and it also opens up the institutional aspects of the post-war welfare state to scrutiny, unlike Garrett's depoliticized account. But like all the domestic suspects, Notermans's account suffers from a fundamental methodological problem, known as 'Galton's problem', which makes it difficult to sort out logically where constraints on policy really originate. Francis

Galton critiqued Edward Burnett Tylor's explanation for the presence of similar sets of cultural practices in Pacific Island societies (Hamel 1980). Tylor argued that these sets of practices represented functional responses to similar problems in all these societies, and that these practices could reasonably be compared as independent occurrences of the same phenomenon; for statistical purposes, they could be considered independent events. Galton, however, noted that there was a competing, equally plausible logical possibility: that these sets of practices had originated in a single spot and diffused to all the other societies rather than springing up independently. Since the odds of independent multiple emergence are low, Occam's razor favours the external causal argument. Thus, arguments that claim that efforts to change a parallel problem, here inflation-prone institutions, invariably lead for functional reasons to parallel sets of changes to those institutions, cannot eliminate the possibility that these changes originated in one country and diffused to others. Here the likely suspects, aside from those raised in SAM, would be events like the unilateral decision by the US Federal Reserve Bank to raise interest rates in 1979, or, less plausibly, the deliberate propagation of a policy line by elites acting in concert (Gill 1990).

The only suspect immunized against Galton's problem is Ageing, to which we now turn.

The World According to AARP

Clearly people who are living longer, retiring earlier, and demanding more medical care are a growing proportion of all OECD economies' population. It could be argued that ageing has an external component: heightened competition in world markets creates more stress, leading to early retirement. While the Continental welfare states routinely use early retirement to clear labour markets, I do not think I can find a district attorney in the world who would take that one to court. So let us code ageing as a purely domestic suspect for changes in the welfare state.

Paul Pierson (in this volume) has made the strongest case for this.[5] Pension and health spending (much of which goes to old people) amount to two-thirds of government spending in the EU. The secular increase in pension and health spending from 7.1 per cent of OECD GDP to 14.3 per cent in the period 1960 to 1990 is significantly larger than the (cyclic) rise in unemployment expenditures. Moreover, virtually all OECD countries have initiated a debate about or actual policy reforms in old age pensions. These range from tinkering with benefit formulas and eligibility criteria (as in the USA) to wholesale changes like a shift from defined benefit to defined contribution

---

[5] Garrett similarly argues that 'the crisis of the social democratic welfare state is a demographic crisis, not the product of market integration' (Garrett 1998*b*: 21).

plans (as in Sweden) or the creation of mandatory private pensions (as in e.g. Australia). Still, in most countries, these changes are much more consequential fiscally for the future than for now. Only in Britain and in New Zealand has an ongoing fiscal deficit triggered large immediate changes in the indexation formulae and led respectively to slower growth or declining spending in the short run. Worries about an ageing population, Japan perhaps excepted, are worries about the future. So the causality here is backwards: it is hard to see how ageing led to efforts to change the welfare state in the 1980s. The crippling fiscal stresses are over the horizon, and the pension policy reforms made in the 1980s were efforts to head off a crisis that had only limited spillovers into other welfare policy arenas. On the other hand, health care expenditures, including long-term care for the elderly, have been rising, and these are labour-intensive services. Perhaps slow service sector productivity growth has simply priced welfare out of the market?

Violating Baumol's Law

Paul Pierson and others have deployed Baumol's law as a cause for fiscal stress in the welfare state (Pierson, in this volume). Baumol argued that services would become progressively more expensive relative to physical goods because of low productivity growth in services and because wage increases from more productive sectors would inevitably flow on to the service sector. Baumol noted that the labour itself was the object of consumption in much of the service sector, and thus that productivity increased only slowly. Baumol assumed that wage increases in what he called the progressive (manufacturing) sector inevitably flowed over to the constant productivity (service) sector. In turn, labour-intensive welfare state services would become increasingly more expensive, imposing high levels of fiscal stress that ultimately force choices not only between welfare and other goods but also among different categories of welfare spending.

Baumol's law nicely delineates the contours of some of the political struggles that occur in and around the welfare state, allowing us to pinpoint the correct suspect with more certainty. But Baumol's law embodies a relatively static view of the supply side of the market, and takes for granted the political foundations for wage parity. In essence, by assuming that productivity levels in services are more or less fixed, Baumol presents a neo-Malthusian argument in which labour-intensive services rather than the supply of land (and thus agricultural output) is the limiting factor, but in which services simply price themselves out of the market rather than causing mass starvation. However the history of markets is a history of efforts to overcome precisely the kinds of limiting factors and shifts in relative prices Baumol predicts. What distinguishes recent service sector and welfare state reorganization (NB: reorganization, not cutbacks) are attacks on both of Baumol's limiting factors: a pervasive introduction of managerial, organizational, and information technologies that increase productivity; and changes to collective bargaining regimes that delink Baumol's progressive and constant sectors and prevent rapid cross-sectoral transmission of wage gains.

Service sectors like retail and wholesale distribution, transportation, power generation, and telecommunications are important later in this mystery, and there productivity has risen quite rapidly, leading to declining rather than rising prices. (Indeed, declines are often built into regulatory structures as CPI-X pricing formulae.) In Canada, for example, productivity in three of these four sectors rose faster than productivity in the goods-producing sector in 1981–91 (MacLean 1996: 8, 18). But let us put them aside to address directly two core welfare services: health and education.

Health and education are precisely the kinds of services Baumol had in mind in the second part of his article when he predicted the collapse of municipal socialism. In each, labour costs generally amount to 60–85 per cent of operating expenses, and in each we can see both his underlying dynamics at work and efforts to reverse them. Put aside both purely technological productivity gains (e.g. endoscopic surgery requiring fewer personnel and fewer hospitalization days) and technologically driven price increases (e.g. bioengineered pharmaceuticals). Wages in the health sector generally have risen, most strongly for doctors, contributing to a real 450 per cent increase in health care costs from 1967 to 1998 in the USA (Federal Reserve Bank 1999: 8). Why hasn't the normal operation of supply and demand caused entry into the market for provision of medical services and gradually eroded doctors' price premium? Cast as a production problem, why hasn't the market generated close but cheaper substitutes for doctors, or otherwise 'Taylorized' doctors' work practices to strip out (expensive) labour?

Actually it has. In the USA one major thrust of HMO-ization and large group practices has been imposition of strict controls on doctors' use of time. This rationalization of the production process also involves limits on doctors' incomes, with salaries replacing fees and the implicit profit stream in fees being captured by the practice or the HMO. Both organizations have also begun substituting nurses and near-doctors for doctors. So too have universities, where the substitution of expensive tenured faculty with contingent workers has gone even farther.

Clearly, like Marx's prediction of a falling rate of profit, Baumol's law describes a tendency rather than an absolute condition. There is considerable room for rationalization, and precisely because of the operation of Baumol's law considerable pressure to rationalize. While Baumol's law pretends to describe a universal law, perhaps the only universal law in market economies is that when relative prices shift sharply in favour of one kind of input to production, market actors have a powerful incentive to economize or find substitutes. This is precisely what US HMOs (and the employers that favour them) and universities (with much more success) are doing. The differences in outcome are not explained by the irreducible labour content of the service but by the degree to which producers have overcome collective action problems to defend their wages and conditions. This is even clearer if we look outside the USA at professionals in other societies—weakly organized US pharmacists are now essentially wage employees; well organized German pharmacists retain considerable control and enjoy better incomes. So at least part of the service sector's lower productivity is political in origin. It rests on the ability of specific groups of producers to use collective action to defend work norms.

The diffusion of wage gains from Baumol's progressive to constant sectors also rests on political, not market mechanisms. Baumol finessed politics by simply assuming that progressive sector wage increases would translate into rising prices, carrying constant sector wages and prices with them. But Baumol's argument reflects the conditions of the period in which he wrote (1967). In this period wage dispersion fell markedly, cross-sectoral wage links were pervasive, and many markets were characterized by mark-up pricing by firms possessing some degree of oligopolistic power (Goldin and Margo 1992). This led to rising progressive sectoral wages and their transmission to the constant sector. But in perfect product markets, productivity increases lead to declining prices, rather than rising wages. In perfect labour markets, wages would decompress and wage gains would not automatically flow from sector to sector. Quite the opposite: the more labour the progressive sector sheds, the greater the supply and lower the price of labour in the constant sector. While the present period by no means has perfect markets, they more closely approximate that condition than when Baumol wrote.

What then does Baumol's law tell us? Lower service sector productivity clearly is implicated in the cost problems of and fights over the welfare state, particularly in efforts to reorganize production practices and change collective bargaining patterns. Can we indict this simple internal suspect?

No. Oddly enough, Baumol's law provides two incentives to look once more at external suspects. Baumol's law is simply an American inversion of the standard Scandinavian inflation model (the EFO model). In the EFO model, exposed sector (i.e. progressive sector) wages are constrained by world market prices while sheltered sector (constant sector) wages are not. The only way to prevent inflation in the service sector from pricing the exposed sector out of world markets is to assure that sheltered sector wages rise in line with exposed sector wages. Baumol's law thus logically predicts conflicts similar to EFO's: between the traded and non-traded sectors, between progressive and constant sectors. This means that Baumol's law has to be somewhat silent on the question of internal versus external assailants. EFO after all, is a model about global constraints on local choices. Second, the wide dispersion of service sector productivity and remuneration across OECD countries both confirms that Baumol's law has worked its way out in very different ways in different societies, and also creates conditions for extensive arbitrage by firms that can also constrain service sector prices.

Two political considerations temper Baumol's prediction of ineluctably rising absolute or relative services prices. First, as in manufacturing, rising relative wages and prices in services are a function of the structure of production, the wages associated with particular jobs, and collective action by producers. Baumol's law does not work automatically because all of these are inherently political in nature. They are fights over the constitution and defence of property rights and their associated streams of income through collective action. Second, the differential evolution of Baumol's lawlike price pressures provides strong motives for one set of actors to translate the global constraints they experience into local politics. And this suggests that we turn to the suspect who has been sitting quietly in a dark corner so far: RICK—property Rights, Income streams, and Coalitions.

4. RICK

One of the problems pinning the rap on the internal and external suspects above is that if you misidentify the body, it is harder to understand both motive and method, that is to say, the reasons actors transform economic pressures into policy choices and the specific causal mechanism linking pressures, interests, policy preferences, and policy outcomes to a discernable welfare state corpse. Much of the confusion about the relationship between global (and internal) markets and welfare comes from a professional deformation of reality in which academics focus closely on the formal welfare state as an instrument of redistribution only towards workers. Consider the conventional wisdom about politics and about the appropriate dependent variable encapsulated in Garrett's (1998*b*: 7) 'broad' definition of the welfare state:

The most important distributional cleavage in the industrial democracies has long been those who support the market allocation of wealth and risk—the natural constituency of right-wing parties—and those who favor government efforts to alter market outcomes—the left's core base of support. The welfare state—broadly construed to include not only income transfer programs such as unemployment insurance and public pensions but also the provision of social services such as education and health—is the basic policy instrument for redistribution.

Why does the right automatically favour market allocation and the left redistribution? Why is the formal welfare state the only mechanism for redistribution? The astounding thing about the so-called 'golden era', after all, was not widespread recourse to formal welfare by those in the labour market or even the deliberate (if only occasional) use of expansionist monetary policy. The astounding thing about the golden era was stable employment, wages, and investment across all sectors, and predictable access to deferred wages after retirement. States created this stability in reaction to the exposure of virtually all life chances and income streams to the logic and volatility of the market in the long nineteenth century during Polanyi's Great Transformation. They did so not only to benefit workers, and workers alone were not the only actors who benefited from and campaigned for redistribution and stability (Polanyi 1944).

Polanyi's counter-movement after all was about sheltering 'productive organization' from the market. The welfare state is a fiscally visible and expensive modality for providing social protection. But budget financed services and transfers are not the only modality for social protection. After the 1930s states provided social protection—and achieved redistribution—through a wide variety of instruments: trade protection, minimum wages, centralized collective bargaining, product market regulation, zoning, the delegated control over markets to producer groups, and, of course, formal welfare states. The essential feature these all share is that they disconnect or buffer income streams from market outcomes, whether those incomes take the form of wages, employment, or profits. Welfare state analysts call this de-commodification, but golden era de-commodification was not limited to welfare services and transfers. Regulation of the service sector, which created a broad range of property rights for workers and owners (including the state as an owner), de-commodified substantial chunks of capital.

Analysts of the formal welfare state have traditionally preferred to view welfare entitlements as 'social' rights, and there are important reasons for doing so (Klausen 1995). But welfare state related streams of income are also property rights. Welfare state socialization of various life and economic risks created property rights to streams of income from the state, as in the case of defined benefit pensions or disability pensions; by the same token tax-sheltered defined contribution pensions can create a property right if the tax expenditure is linked to the contribution.[6] Similar property rights were constructed outside the formal welfare state after World War II.

These property rights took different forms. The service sector, the source of most post-war employment and employment growth, contained the most expensive and important property rights related to social protection whether expressed as public ownership or regulation of the service sector. These property rights guaranteed stability for wages, employment, and, for regulated

---

[6] Even in the pre-child-tax-credit USA, welfare-related tax expenditures (health, pensions, housing, and the earned income tax credit being the largest) already amounted to almost half as much as formal line item budget spending (Howard 1997: 26).

private owners, steady revenue and profit streams. State regulation dampened or eliminated competition by segmenting markets for services such as telecommunications; road, rail, and air transport; power and water generation and distribution; and retail distribution. These four sectors amount to one-third of most OECD economies and a significant source of producer costs in the manufacturing sector.

Consider how investor-owned power generation utilities in the USA were sheltered from the market. The state offered firms territorial monopolies, access to tax privileged equity capital, and regulated rates of return in order to induce firms to make highly asset-specific investments. In turn firms offered workers stable employment at predictably rising wages linked to the utility's equally predictable expansion of its assets in an environment in which the price of electricity was also predictable. (Workers for state-owned utilities often got the even greater stability of civil service status.)

Because services were sheltered from market pressures, much wider productivity differentials developed internationally across service sectors than in manufacturing, where the GATT permitted increased competition. This can be seen in a simple measure of the relative dispersion of productivity levels in the OECD-19 economies around 1990. If we index US productivity at 100 and rank everyone else accordingly, and then calculate the standard deviation of productivity levels in manufacturing and four critical service sectors, we get 16.1 for manufacturing, 15.8 for telecommunications, 21.1 for retail distribution, 26.8 for electricity generation, and 57.1 for air transport (calculated from Pilat 1996: 107–46). The large dispersion of productivity levels around the mean (i.e. a larger standard deviation) indicates that historically there was much less market pressure to conform with best practice production norms. By 1992, progressive deregulation and privatization in telecommunications unleashed market pressures that essentially eliminated any differences between this service and manufacturing. But in the other three sectors considerable divergences remained.

Because the best data measure productivity after the deregulation wave of the 1980s, we can only surmise the degree of pre-deregulation slack. But in telecommunications, some useful proxies are the 60 per cent reduction in the cost of British and French telephone service after market liberalization or the drop in the share of telecommunications employment in the OECD from 0.81 per cent in 1982 to 0.67 in 1992. Similarly the electricity, gas, and steam sector shed 17.4 per cent of its labour force in the EU-12 post-deregulation, and deregulation of the industrial electricity market in the EU led to a halving of prices for medium-size industrial consumers (Héritier and Schmidt 2000; *Financial Times*, 19 Feb. 1999). Most productivity studies agree that the most significant factors explaining productivity differences in services are government ownership and regulation of labour and product markets (McKinsey 1992; Pilat 1996).

The degree to which regulation created property rights for capital and labour becomes visible in the problem of stranded costs that emerges when states move to deregulate. Stranded costs are the characteristic feature of the regulated service economy and an important clue in our mystery, because they are specific investments, by both capital and labour, that make sense only in a regulated environment. Specificity arises as much from the structure of regulation as from the more objective factors Oliver Williamson (1995) delineates. For example, stranded costs are investments utilities made, using borrowed money, in anticipation of stably rising demand and regulated rates of return on the capital invested. Subsequent deregulation and free market entry 'strands' this investment, saddling existing firms with above average capital costs and lower rates of return than new entrants. Worse, as the income stream this investment generates shrinks, its market value falls. While this term is used specifically for the electricity generation industry and the problem is most acute there, it inheres to most services. Deregulated telephone service in the USA created a long legal battle over whether network owners could charge new entrants the 'historic' (i.e. stranded) cost of creating their networks or only the incremental cost. Analogously, in labour markets, states rewarded civil servants' investment in non-transferable, job-specific skills with guarantees of stable employment. Consequently, states have either bought out civil servants when they privatized state firms or explicitly voided their property rights.

What about the parts of the service sector Baumol fretted about? In more labour-intensive services states' delegation of market control to producer groups solved their collective action problems by allowing them to use selective (dis-) incentives to protect quasi-property rights around specific investments in human capital. As noted above, doctors and lawyers used collective action to restrain entry to their markets, restraining access to training and licensing, and controlling advertising standards, fees, and the definition of jobs allowed to paraprofessionals. Delegated control is typical of but not unique to the professions. Bo Rothstein has shown how Swedish farmers could not control output, and thus prices, collectively until the state delegated taxation power to the Farmers Association, permitting it to impose selective disincentives on overproducers (Rothstein 1991; see also Tilton 1996).

The degree to which the service sector was sheltered, its economic weight, and the salience of stranded costs suggests we need a new autopsy report. The welfare state is not dead. The corpse here is actually social protection delivered through the service sector, and its death has led to intense conflicts around the remaining major source of social protection, the formal welfare state. Fights over retaining or removing social protection—insulation from market outcomes—lie at the heart of welfare state politics in the 1980s and 1990s. Thus, posing the question as 'globalization' versus domestic causes —external intruders versus household suspects—and using the welfare state as the dependent variable misconstrues the motives for the crime. Fights over property rights constructed through state delegation of power to producer groups or state-regulated market segmentation naturally have a substantial domestic component, because deregulation can differentially benefit actors in the same sector even when 'foreign competition' per se is absent. What matters are groups' specific preferences for and political efforts to achieve discrete policy changes around those property rights.

But this discussion has thrown up a new suspect. Perhaps, as the earlier Baumol/EFO discussion suggested, fights over social protection are really fights between traded and non-traded sectors over issues that extend beyond trade protection? Certainly the IPE literature based on Heckscher–Ohlin and Ricardo–Viner models assumes this (Frieden and Rogowski 1996). But the traditional cleavage between traded and non-traded is misleading, as is the emphasis on opportunity costs understood as a loss of potential income for the traded sector. Misleading, not wrong.

The distinction between 'traded' and 'non-traded' is misleading for three reasons. First, all too often it is simply understood as manufacturing versus services. But in many sectors 'internal' competition is the source of market pressures on firms. That is, firms in cognate fields bypass or evade what were always incomplete systems of regulation to capture some of the rents that regulation generated. Thus, non-bank financials invaded banks' territory; para-legals offered cut-rate uncontested divorces; courier and package services eroded postal monopolies; postal monopolies invade each other's markets. All upset delicate balances in which producer groups sought rents for their own aggrandizement while politicians used them to cross-subsidize what were seen as socially desirable services. So an analysis dichotomizing traded and non-traded sectors misses important dynamics leading to deregulation and, of course, attacks on the formal welfare state.

Second, the distinction between traded and non-traded is misleading because few commodities or services are naturally 'non-traded' in the sense that economists meant when they designated services and goods that cannot enter into trade. Economists' classic non-traded service, the haircut, obviously does not cross-borders. But if the structure of regulation permits franchised extensions of multinational (or non-local but domestic) firms to compete with local firms, then parts of the haircut production process are traded. Franchisees' management system, access to liquid capital markets and branding are traded, though the haircut itself cannot cross borders. If significant components of the haircut production process are traded, then few sectors enjoy the natural protection economists talk about. Even domestic mail has become 'traded'; the Dutch Post remails for German customers avoiding high local postage costs (Héritier and Schmidt 2000).

The issue of opportunity costs is also misleading. IPE analysts have invoked opportunity costs in order to provide a micro-foundation for actors' interests and willingness to participate in collective action. Clearly, firms competing in world markets and buying relatively expensive regulated domestic inputs would rather buy cheaper inputs. For them higher domestic costs represent lost profits. And certainly for cognate firms invading regulated firms' territory opportunity costs loom large as the difference between their low (unregulated) cost of production and the high (regulated) price represents additional profit.

But the absolute losses to the firms benefiting from deregulation are not simply losses of income, but rather the destruction of their stranded investments. Deregulation devalues the capital stranded in regulation-specific investments. Consider again the old style barber, making a location and relationally specific investment. This investment was rational when price regulation, zoning, or licensing kept franchisers out of the market. Franchisers/ franchisees' investment by contrast is much less specific because the brand travels in a way that a local barber's does not. The same analysis could be made of the considerably larger stranded investments in electricity generation, water systems, or telecommunications. These sectors have seen considerable cross-national investment ($50 billion in 1998) and contestation for market share subsequent to de-monopolization and/or privatization; they have also seen significant devaluation of investments which were rational to make under a regulated market but cannot generate revenues in a competitive market. As Alt and Gilligan have shown, divergent specificities inside the traded sector (and presumably the non-traded sector as well) mean that the traded sector itself has quite heterogeneous and often unpredictable preferences regarding trade policy (and by extension deregulation and the formal welfare state) (Alt and Gilligan 1994).

The important distinction is not between traded and (the very small number of truly) non-traded sectors, then, but between firms (and employees) that made large specific investments secured as politically generated property rights and firms which either did not, or which had such investments liquidated in prior rounds of deregulation. By looking at the benefits some groups accrue from these property rights, and by looking at the kinds of costs imposed on other groups by a given group's property rights, we can understand fights over welfare and social protection much better. We can construct a much stronger causal chain linking motive and method. As a first cut, suppose we overlay the traditional cleavage between capital and labour with a redefined cleavage between the kinds of firms typically enjoying shelter from market forces and those exposed to markets.

Broadly speaking, by sorting out what are really a large assortment of heterogeneous groups into these four categories we can see that 'welfare state' politics has shifted from primarily being the politics of redistribution among classes which Garrett identifies to being a politics in which groups also try to protect or expand their politically constituted property rights, which is to say partly over the degree to which they are exposed to domestic and international market forces. Sectors/firms already exposed to market pressures deliberately seek to impose market disciplines on sheltered sectors/firms to expose them to competition and so bring down their own cost of production. Sectors/firms still enjoying property rights sheltering their stranded investments try to retain insulation.

Doing this reveals that political conflicts around the welfare state are not solely about aggregate spending levels in the formal welfare state. Fights also centre on institutional changes bringing markets into the formal welfare state and especially into the mechanisms which guaranteed social protection in the service sector. Conflicts are about the specific burdens and benefits that the public sector, the welfare state, and regulation place on specific actors because of their position in the market, and because of different vulnerabilities that different degrees of investment specificity create. Fights over the formal welfare state necessarily involve fights over informal forms of welfare, such as tax expenditures, 'corporate welfare', professional privileges, regulated monopolies, and delegated authority, or in other words, RICK. Below I will briefly sketch out these different group's motives, opportunities, and methods in fights over the property rights created by social protection to show why these fights do not produce policy convergence.

5. MOTIVES, OPPORTUNITIES, AND METHODS

The SAM and ILSA arguments all tend to argue that the welfare state should be changing in roughly the same ways. They all argue that welfare is 'too expensive' and thus that welfare spending should be shrinking. If all welfare states (or all forms of social protection) did change the same way, the case for a functionalist argument would be stronger, although with reasonable doubt remaining as to the internal versus external question. However welfare states are not changing the same way, nor is spending shrinking everywhere (Pierson 1994). Analysts of the public sector discern four emerging models in public administration (Peters 1998). And those building on Gøsta Esping-Andersen's work, like Torben Iversen and Anne Wren, see three major types of response to the emergence of a service economy (or put differently, to the working out of Baumol's law) (Esping-Andersen 1990; Iversen and Wren 1998). Patterned responses suggest an underlying political logic. The public administration studies are content to describe these patterns; Iversen and Wren supply a description based on quantitative analysis, link their argument to Esping-Andersen's rather than advancing a causal mechanism. I intend here to obtain a conviction by tracing out different groups' interests in order to trace out policy preferences and causal mechanisms in the transformation

Policy preference in italics	Firms / producers	Labour
Sheltered	*Limited neoliberalism*	*Responsive state*
Streams of income secured	Traditional (labour-intensive)	Public sector unions in
by property rights created	Service sector	health, education, and
by collective action or	State-owned firms and/or	social services
(producer) regulated markets	regulated monopolies with	Unorganized workers in
	stranded costs	traditional services
	New self-employed and the	Construction unions
	old professions	
	Farmers	
Exposed	*Neoprogressivism*	*Social progressivism*
Streams of income secured	Large export-oriented firms,	Private sector industrial
by (transient) technological	MNCs, franchisers	unions
advantages	Agri-business and food	Public sector unions in
	processing	goods (not service)
	State-owned firms' own	producing firms
	management?	

FIG. 1.1. Cleavages over social protection

of social protection. I will show that RICK orchestrated a conspiracy containing SAM and ILSA. The latter two arguments are not wrong. They are what Hempel called non-rival explanatory sketches lacking fully fleshed out causal mechanisms.

Figure 1.1 lays out the two cleavages identified above, some typical interest groups, and labels for policy syndromes (in italics) in order to trace the connection between motives (interests), policy preferences (methods), and outcomes in fights over social protection. This figure lays out the positions of organized interests and not voters. Like the traditional IPE literature (and Stein Rokkan) I assume votes can be bought; the critical step in the expression of interests as policy lies in the interactions of interest groups and parties seeking the resources they need to win elections. Although the populations in the four cells are fairly heterogeneous in terms of the economic activities they pursue, they are homogeneous in terms of the kinds of property rights and market pressures they confront. As in Helen Milner's analysis of trade preferences, I assume that firms in the same sector but with diverging market positions can express diverging policy preferences (Milner 1988). Conversely firms producing different things can have the same policy stance because they share similar kinds of property rights.

Interests and Policy Preferences: Sheltered Firms and Producers

Sheltered firms and producers enjoy streams of income anchored in property rights whose strength reflects government enforced collective regulation of their markets, guaranteed monopolies, or other politically generated barriers restricting competitive entry or market contestation. These firms or producers made 'regulation' specific investments that were viable given entry barriers, regulated prices, and other devices securing or raising their rate of return. This explains their ferocious defence of the regulations that shelter those immobile investments and their efforts to bolster income streams when those defences fail. These producers and firms pursue an ensemble of policies we can label a 'limited neoliberal' position because it emphasizes the elimination of government and regulation outside of product markets. At the same time it abjures the reform of government or the dismantling of the political supports for their own collective action. Maximally, they want social protection for their capital and no one else.

Sheltered firms' and producers' problem is the intrusion of franchised competitors into previously fragmented and localized markets, and the erosion of barriers to entry that had been supported by collective action. Here I use franchise not only in its common meaning, but also in its older meaning to indicate any firm given licence to operate in a given sector, for example firms bidding for the right to operate a public water system. Franchisers have access to cheaper, more liquid pools of capital because franchisees back them in capital markets; have management strategies using relatively less skilled, cheaper labour, or in utilities, more efficient use of underlying assets; and are branded. Franchisers' investments thus are less asset-specific and risky because they use branding, capital (or information) market access, and management strategies to re-segment markets for undifferentiated goods when political segmentation is removed. Examples of this intrusion include the rise of paraprofessional real estate conveyance firms in the legal market; foreign direct investment (or bidding) in newly opened public utilities; or the replacement of traditional fee for service medical practice by HMOs and investor-owned practices.

Sheltered firms' and producers' relatively greater investment risk (what Frieden and Rogowski misperceive as opportunity costs) explains their ferocious pursuit of reductions in labour costs, personal taxes, and regulations aside from those protecting their product market. Continued regulation and taxation in markets invaded by franchised competitors threatens the very existence of stranded investments, not just the rate of return on those investments. As Tversky's prospect theory tells us, people are generally much more sensitive to losses than to gains (Kahneman and Tversky 1979). Moreover, the gains deregulation creates for producers when they behave as consumers are pretty meaningless if they suffer enormous reductions in their stream of income or have lost their entire investment and are forced out of business.

Sheltered firms and producers also prefer to shift regulatory control out of the state and down to their own organized interest groups. For smaller firms, the fixed costs of regulatory compliance cannot be spread over large and stable revenue flows, so the choice is to contract out for them (at a high cost) or simply evade them (risking legal penalties). Studies of Australian firms have shown that these costs are not trivial, amounting to 4 per cent of turnover and equivalent to 32 per cent of profits in five sampled industries (OECD 1998*b*: 128).[7] Delegation reinforces the ability to use selective (dis-) incentives for collective action in defence of property rights, while minimizing regulatory costs. A partial exception to this pattern is state-owned utilities, where it is the state's capital and not investor capital that is at risk.

Sheltered firms typically prefer the wholesale elimination of publicly socialized health, education, and labour market risks to lower their tax burden. (Except of course where they live off that sector, as in health.) Individuation of risks allows sheltered firms to pass social costs onto larger firms that face organized labour and so must provide a wide range of benefits to buy labour peace. Lower income taxes enable the owners and managers of sheltered firms to purchase 'welfare goods' tailored to their needs, and to maintain a socially defined standard of living in the face of increased competition. In terms of the broader public sector, smaller scale sheltered firms and producers also prefer wholesale privatization of (relatively expensive) public services and deep budget cuts to fund accompanying income tax cuts (since they receive much of their return as what the tax system considers 'income').

The limited neoliberal policy syndrome is most strongly expressed where private ownership in the service sector survived the regulatory impulses of the Great Depression, where financial markets permitted 'deviant' unregulated firms to capitalize themselves more easily, and where individuals can easily purchase insurance against life and economic risks. In short, it is strongest in the Anglo-Saxon welfare states. In this sense Esping-Andersen is quite correct about the importance of programme design in institutionalizing the welfare state's political support. By stamping out private service provision and pricing private service sector employment out of the market, the 'social democratic' welfare state drastically reduced the electoral base for this policy syndrome by lowering the rate of self-employment by 40 per cent relative to the four Anglo-Saxon economies.

Interests and Policy Preferences: Exposed Firms

Exposed firms' income streams depend on their property rights in transient technological advantages for the goods and services they produce. These

---

[7] Similarly, French small business owners (including, naturally, a hair salon) are registering their firms in Britain to avoid taxation on proprietor's income, with savings amounting to 30% of owners' gross pay (*Washington Post*, 16 Apr. 1998, A23).

property rights are not as dependent on collective action or political support. But exposed firms faced quite significant threats of technological leapfrogging, shorter product cycles, and falling prices—deflation—for their products and services as competition intensified in the 1980s and 1990s. All of these factors reduced the potential rate of return on a given investment in R & D or process technology improvements. Looking at price pressures helps explain the timing of political efforts at deregulation and welfare state restructuring. By the late 1990s disinflation had turned from a largely sectoral phenomenon into an economy-wide problem verging on deflation. Simultaneously, these firms felt increased pressure to conform to international rates of return, as financial deregulation broke open illiquid local markets and increased the incentive to diversify into global markets (Germain 1998; Verdier 1998). Downward pressure on prices and profits thus ran headlong into rising expectations about profitability. Disinflation made it harder for exposed firms to accommodate price increases from both sheltered and exposed suppliers. So exposed final producers reacted by transmitting downward price pressures to their parts suppliers. For example, the major US automobile assemblers imitated Japanese norms and began demanding annual 5 per cent price decreases from their global parts networks. Exposed firms want to impose the same sorts of productivity expectations on their public sector and other sheltered suppliers. But this could not be done to public monopolies without first destroying these monopolies' legal standing by introducing competition, and through a pervasive reorganization of the public sector to make government more business-like and responsive to competitive pressures.

Like the original progressive movement in late nineteenth-century America, this 'neoprogressivist' model emphasizes depoliticized and efficient government, and it attacks much 'corporate welfare' (i.e. sheltering) just as the progressives attacked urban machines' patron–client welfare networks. Exposed capital thus is the strongest advocate for the 'new public management' model of public sector reform, involving real wage disciplines, results-oriented management, budgetary transparency, and true costing (Schwartz 1994*a*). New public management does not involve the wholesale programme of deregulation, privatization, and public sector staffing cuts that sheltered firms prefer. Instead it aims at lower costs via higher productivity and via the professionalization and insulation of the state, and at making public sector actors behave more predictably and more like private sector actors who are susceptible to cost reduction pressures. Large exposed firms prefer predictability, because predictability allows them to maximize the return they get from taking targeted risks.

Substantively exposed firms seek increased public sector productivity because they directly and indirectly consume a wide range of public services. Most firms in this sector either face organized labour or value a stable, skilled labour force as a competitive resource. They thus view dismantling the welfare state and desocialization of risks as something that will raise their labour costs rather than reducing them, as a comparison of the incidence of health costs in Canada and the USA shows (C. J. Martin 1995*a*; Giaimo 1998). Exposed firms thus see fiscal discipline as a way to put a hard budget constraint on public producers, a way to attain better credit ratings, and a way to stabilize tax levels, rather than a way to finance tax reductions in individual income tax levels. Fiscal discipline improves the state's credit rating and thus indirectly firms' own rating and borrowing costs. Exposed firms prefer broad-based sales taxes whose regressivity does not affect their upper management, and whose rebate-ability improves their position in export markets. In short, exposed firms prefer to fix the state's service production rather than eliminate it.

Interests and Policy Preferences: Exposed Labour

Exposed labour, like sheltered producers, has a variety of property rights constituted through successful collection action. Most of these rights are secured via the socialization of individual and economic risk, so this group has good reason to prefer a continuation of the welfare state. At the same time, this group faces exactly the same pressures their employers face from falling prices. Falling prices (and heightened competition) puts continual pressure on workers to improve productivity in order to pre-empt any effort by employers to threaten or actually to flee to lower wage regions (as Rodrik and Wood suggest), and to moderate their wage demands to prevent their firms from failing (as Swenson suggests). Exposed sector unions fear that wage pressures emanating from organized sheltered workers will induce their workers to take wage positions detrimental to their long-term employment. But exposed workers also consume public sector services that represent socialized risks, and prefer that to individualized and market-based risk.

Exposed thus labour prefers to reorganize the public sector and welfare state to impose fiscal and wage disciplines on it, but without a recision of public services. Like exposed firms, exposed labour prefers welfare state reorganization to dismantling, but it also prefers continued public owner-ship to privatization and open private–public competition. To the extent that productivity gains are not forthcoming in the public sector, exposed workers have strong incentives to band together with exposed firms to break wage parities with Baumol's constant sector and /or the public sector.

This ensemble can be called 'social progressivism.' As with the neopro-gressivism of exposed firms it emphasizes the more business-like, new public management model, but it diverges by preferring continued socialization of a broad range of risks and a relatively higher level of public spending, ownership, and service provision.

Interests and Policy Preferences: Sheltered Workers

Sheltered workers have a wide range of politically constituted property rights. Generally they enjoy not only the socialization of individual and employment risks that exposed workers enjoy, but they also enjoy significant shelter from market pressures on wage levels and long-term employment. This group fears the de-segmentation of labour markets that previously supported wages and conditions above a 'natural' market level, particularly for the many unskilled workers in this group. De-segmentation occurs when private sector wage disciplines replace public sector norms (through privatization or wholesale changes to collective bargaining regimes) or when licence-based barriers between different labour markets disappear. Consider efforts to remove civil service status from Deutsche Telecom workers, or franchises' substitution of low-wage hair cutters for licensed and experienced cutters, or hospitals' substitution of LPNs for RNs. Sheltered labour thus prefers a stable or growing budget for the public sector, to prop up demand for labour, and a continuation of licence-based barriers inside labour markets. By the same token they oppose anything more than incremental, internally driven reorganization (if any) of the public sector, and any attacks on the continued socialization —i.e. de-commodification—of risks. In effect, they seek to shelter labour markets from world market prices much as sheltered firms seek to shelter their stream of profits from franchisers. The primary method is a public sector with entrenched work norms and rules, and large enough to soak up excess (unskilled?) labour. Aside from direct beneficiaries, who anyway are almost always concerned only about their own specific income stream, this is the largest status quo constituency in the welfare state debate.

In its most positive and forward-looking formulations, this strategy tries to overcome the management problems associated with a bureaucratic welfare state in order to generate continued public support for the public sector (Rothstein 1996). It is a 'high road' strategy for the public sector, emphasizing high-quality services at, of course, high costs, and trying to occupy a market niche different from the low-cost, low-quality US welfare model. The political strategy here tries to retain the support of middle-income voters (or firms) by offering high-quality services, and then using cross-subsidies to also provide high-quality services to poor people. The political strategy here also tries to inculcate a set of values centred on social citizenship; not everything has a 'price'. Consequently, this strategy focuses much more on client service than on NPM style production efficiencies; thus it is a responsive state strategy. Only public sector labour unions possess enough organization to implement this strategy, because most private service industries have fragmented and volatile labour forces. However unionized private sector service workers in regulated product markets are also conscious defenders of their 'local welfare state', i.e. the secure employment conferred on them by sectoral regulation and market segmentation.

6. WHO DID IT?

Initial perceptions about the murder of the welfare state were erroneous. There are more guilty parties than most investigations allege, and the corpse is not the formal welfare state but rather the covert provision of social protection for both capital and labour through service sector regulation. RICK organized the way SAM and ILSA impinged on established forms of social protection. Because RICK shows more precisely how different internal and external pressures matter, indicting RICK overcomes the dispute about internal versus external causes, and shows why a debate about 'autonomy' is misplaced. Our composite suspects SAM and ILSA are neither wholly innocent, nor totally correct. As Hempelian non-rival explanatory sketches, they describe pressures that at least some actors feel. But these sketches impute tropism, automatic reactions, to actors' responses to market pressures. RICK provides a better underlying basis for actors' behaviour, showing why different actors react differently to the same pressures, why actors react at all to those pressures, and why more is at stake for some actors. Looking at the differential erosion of property rights, and the income streams they secure, permits us to generate a more robust causal mechanism that encompasses the causal effects on which the SAM and ILSA sketches are based.

RICK permits us to construct a stylized causal argument that runs like this: in the OECD area, states and collective actors suppressed and contained market pressures on income streams through a regulated service sector and formal welfare state during and after the 1930s. But the incomplete suppression of the market following the Great Depression allowed some firms, mostly in the USA, to generate new competitive strategies that eluded regulatory restraints in the late 1960s. As these actors searched for higher profits in banking, telecommunications and other public utilities, transportation, and retailing they provoked successive waves of deregulation in the USA in the late 1970s and early 1980s. Established, regulated firms either joined the clamour for deregulation (to survive) or exited the market. Competitive markets in the USA generated a range of new production strategies and organizational formats for franchisers and other firms that put new competitive pressures on firms outside the USA.

At the same time deregulation was occurring, the US Federal Reserve Bank shifted to a policy of disinflation, removing mark-up pricing as a plausible strategy for firms in the market. Deregulation in the USA and the Fed's commitment to disinflation set up the dynamics described above, in other countries. On the one hand, regulated firms sought deregulation for their own protection. They could not respond to increasingly plausible customer threats of exit; telecommunication regulation unravelled most quickly because 'call-back' services made exit easy. On the other hand, the Fed's commitment to high real interest rates also made it increasingly important for both exposed firms and the state to push from sheltered sectors into the market. High interest rates made it increasingly expensive for states to simply subsidize state-owned firms given an environment in which operating losses had to be capitalized as public debt. Exposed firms of course faced 'opportunity costs' from continued subsidization of sheltered firms, and so pressed for the elimination of some local forms of social protection and the adaptation of the formal welfare state, just as they had in the USA. Depending on how groups packaged their policy proposal and coalesced with other groups, different flavours of welfare state reorganization and service sector deregulation emerged.

This process did not force states to eliminate the welfare state and did not generate political coalitions with uniformly 'neoliberal' policy preferences (i.e. a preference for a smaller, residual welfare state). Instead most states chose to reformat the welfare state around market forms of regulation. But the survival of most formal welfare state programmes should not obscure the essential disappearance of social protection in the broad service sector as deregulation and privatization thrust millions of workers and thousands of firms into the market. So the broad welfare state was murdered, even though the narrow, formal welfare state survived.

Thinking about the globalization–welfare state question as a problem of markets and social protection thus allows better answers about the timing of change; allows us to locate the sources of change in discrete political decisions in one country (solving Galton's problem); allows us to understand how external and internal changes in markets affect the interests of internal actors; allows us to understand the variety of motives (interests) underlying actors' policy preferences; allows us to understand why actors see certain policy proposals as plausible solutions to their economic problems; and allows us to understand policy proposals spanning different areas as discrete packages.

Here then, are the main points emerging from the interrogation: globalization and the erosion of the welfare state really should be understood as the erosion of politically based property rights and their related streams of income, and as reactions to that erosion. Actors with different kinds of property rights put forward policy prescriptions derived from those different property rights in fights over social protection, the public sector, and the welfare state. A strong case can be made that the causal mechanisms leading to the erosion of social protection find their origin first and foremost in the USA, rather than in markets bubbling up spontaneously everywhere. As in the nineteenth century, the (re-)emergence of markets was planned by market actors and states that stood to benefit from the destruction or reconfiguration of a range of property rights created in the 'golden era' of the Keynesian welfare state. And should we be shocked, *shocked* to find markets going on here? Hardly. As Marx, Weber, and Simmel observed at the turn of the century, once started, markets are extremely difficult to suppress. The wonder is that we enjoyed such a long and beautiful friendship with social protection.

2

The Dynamics of Welfare State Expansion
Trade Openness, De-industrialization, and Partisan Politics

Torben Iversen

RECENTLY, the debate about the future of the welfare state has focused on the effects of globalization. Two opposing views have emerged: a 'pessimistic' one that sees globalization as a serious threat to the continuation of the Keynesian welfare state; and an 'optimistic' one which predicts globalization to be compatible with, and even strengthening, the welfare state. The pessimistic view, prominent in the popular literature and in the press, holds that a large welfare state is incompatible with participation in a fiercely competitive world economy. Optimists, on the other hand, underscore the potential for governments to shape welfare provisions in ways that are compatible with economic efficiency, and they argue that globalization is likely to expose people to greater labour market risks that will raise political demands for public compensation.

For evidence the pessimists can point to the breakdown of the relatively consensus-driven process of welfare expansion during the 1960s and 1970s, and the emergence in the 1980s and 1990s of fierce political battles over welfare state reforms—battles that are at least rhetorically linked to the need for international competitiveness (Rhodes 1996*b*). Yet, overall spending data clearly support the optimists. As illustrated in Figure 2.1, both government consumption of services and social transfers as shares of GDP have risen sharply, and almost without interruption, since the early 1950s. True, the very rapid expansion beginning in the mid-1960s slowed down somewhat in the 1980s, and the fiscal retrenchment associated with the reining in of public deficits in the late 1980s seems to have caused a temporary reduction in public consumption. But there are no signs of any broad-scale retrenchment of the welfare state.

I received many helpful comments on a prior version of this paper from John Freeman, Peter Hall, Herbert Kitschelt, Peter Lange, Paul Pierson, Jonas Pontusson, Dani Rodrik, Michael Shalev, David Soskice, and John Stephens. I am especially grateful to Tom Cusack for his support, data, and advice.

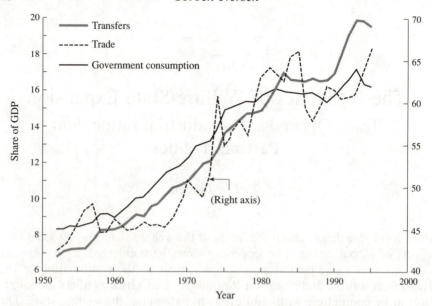

Fig. 2.1. Average public spending and trade across 17 OECD countries, 1952–95

Notes: Government consumption is all spending on public services less military spending; transfers are all government transfers less interest payments and subsidies; trade is exports plus imports divided by the GDP.

Sources: OECD, *National Accounts*, Part II: Detailed Tables (various years).

In fact, the growth in government spending closely tracks the expansion in trade. This tantalizing association, one that also holds for international capital market liberalization, has been argued to reflect a causal relationship. Cameron (1978) and Katzenstein (1985*b*) are important precursors for this line of argument, which has become a major tenet of the contemporary welfare state literature. The argument starts from the premiss that integration into the international economy promises large potential welfare gains especially for small countries, but that such integration exposes economies to the ups and downs of global markets while undermining the capacity of governments to counteract these business cycles. The way governments solve this dilemma, so the argument goes, is by accepting high trade exposure, while simultaneously adopting comprehensive social programmes to compensate people for increased levels of labour market risk (see also Ruggie 1982).

   The original evidence for this thesis was highly suggestive, but inconclusive. Cameron relied on simple cross-sectional correlations across a sample of OECD countries, and Katzenstein focused exclusively on open economies which shared certain basic public policy patterns. Recently, however, more comprehensive evidence has been provided by Garrett (1995, 1998*b*) and by Rodrik (1997, 1998). Both authors make effective use of sophisticated large-N statistical techniques to control for a number of potentially confounding variables. Rodrik accomplishes this by expanding the sample of cases to include developing countries, while Garrett (more in the spirit of Cameron's original article) does so by expanding the number of observations in time. Based on this new evidence, both are confident that trade openness strengthens the welfare state. As Rodrik notes, given the inclusion of so many control variables, the association between trade openness and government spending 'is not a spurious relationship generated by omitted variables' (1998: 1011).

This paper presents a different explanation. Not only are there no compelling theoretical reasons to expect trade openness and welfare spending to be linked, the relationship disappears once we control for a variable that I call de-industrialization. By de-industrialization I have in mind the secular and simultaneous reduction of employment in agriculture and industry beginning in the early 1960s in most countries. This variable turns out to be a very strong predictor of welfare state expansion, and for good reasons. The labour market dislocations associated with de-industrialization are staggering and compare in magnitude to the movement of workers from the countryside to the city during the industrial revolution. In 1960, for example, about 59 per cent of the labour force in the OECD area was employed in the primary sectors; thirty-five years later this figure is down to about 30 per cent. This massive sectoral shift is the outgrowth of deep forces of technological change that have coincided with progressive market saturation—structural-technological conditions that also transformed agriculture.

More specifically I argue that the division between agriculture and industry, on the one hand, and services, on the other, presents a major skill boundary in the economy in the sense that skills travel poorly from the former to the latter. This being the case, the threat of having to move across this boundary is a major risk factor for individual workers because their skills, and hence labour market power, will be downgraded. Employer-provided social benefits do not offer protection against these risks because they are not, as a general rule, transferable. For insurance against these risks, people therefore turn to the state.

The argument is quite compatible with previous work on the early development of the welfare state by Esping-Andersen (1985, 1990), Korpi (1978, 1983), Stephens (1979), and others which underscores the importance of the rise of industry and thus the industrial working class. Indeed it defies credulity—and, as we shall see, also the empirical record—if the decline of agriculture and rise of industry is of major importance for the welfare state, while the massive transformation implied by de-industrialization is irrelevant. Yet, some scholars have taken the link between working-class strength and welfare state development to imply that de-industrialization, and the associated decline of the blue-collar working class, undermine the political support for the welfare state (e.g. Piven 1991). This paper essentially argues the exact opposite: welfare state expansion since the early 1960s has in large measure been driven by de-industrialization and the decline of the blue-collar working class.

But de-industrialization is not the whole story. The speed, and especially the distributional composition, of welfare state expansion vary according to the structure of labour market institutions, and especially the character of electoral and party politics. Where people in the most risky labour market positions are more prone to vote in elections, and where left parties dominate government power, welfare state expansion has entailed a heavy dose of low-priced public services, as well as more egalitarian social transfer programmes and wage policies. Egalitarianism and public sector expansion are causally related to one other, as well as to de-industrialization, because earnings compression undermines the growth of low-productivity, price-sensitive, private service sector jobs (Esping-Andersen 1993, 1994; Iversen and Wren 1998; Glyn 1997). So while de-industrialization has everywhere propelled growth of the welfare state, the distributive aspects of the rising service economy, and the private–public sector mix of employment, vary according to political parameters.

Perhaps the most pressing political question that the de-industrialization thesis highlights is what will happen when the employment structure stabilizes. If the insecurities associated with past de-industrialization spread demands for compensation and for socialization of risks well into the middle classes, once the dust settles, will the process be reversed? Pierson (1994, 1996) has forcefully argued that political 'lock-in effects' may prevent this from happening, and the results in this paper support that argument. The slowdown of the de-industrialization process, however, is likely to undermine support for further expansion and to exacerbate conflicts over the distributive aspects of the welfare state. This is precisely as predicted by the pessimists, but the underlying cause is not globalization.

1. DISCOUNTING TRADE OPENNESS

Figure 2.2 shows the positive cross-national relationship between trade openness and public spending. The figure basically reproduces a similar figure in Rodrik (1998: 1000), and—along with the temporal relationship illustrated in Figure 2.1—conveys the empirical regularity that has given rise to the openness-breeds-spending argument.[1]

---

[1] Switzerland is a rather big outlier and was not included in Rodrik's figure.

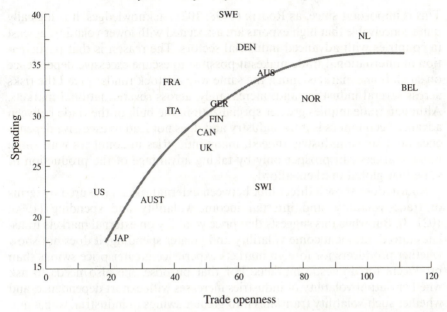

Fig. 2.2. Trade openness and public spending in 16 OECD countries, 1960–93 (%)

Notes: Government spending is civilian government consumption plus social transfers as a percentage of GDP; trade is exports plus imports divided by the GDP.

Sources: OECD, *National Accounts*, Part II: Detailed Tables (1997).

Rodrik explains the relationship between trade and spending by inserting economic risk as an intermediate mechanism:

More open economies have greater exposure to the risks emanating from turbulence in world markets. One can view larger government spending in such economies as performing an insulation function, insofar as the government sector is the 'safe' sector (in terms of employment and purchases from the rest of the economy) relative to other activities, and especially compared to tradables. (1998: 1011)

Garrett fundamentally agrees and elaborates the argument:

[P]erhaps the most important effect of globalization is to increase social dislocations and economic insecurity, as the distribution of incomes and jobs across firms and industries becomes increasingly unstable. The result is that increasing numbers of people have to spend ever more time and money trying to make their future more secure. . . . Given this nexus between globalization and economic insecurity, it is not surprising that government policies that cushion market dislocations by redistributing wealth and risk are at least as popular today as they have ever been. (1998b: 7)

Garrett repeats these claims throughout his book (see e.g. pp. 39, 102, 133), but he makes no effort to demonstrate that labour market volatility is in fact positively related to trade openness (or globalization more generally).

This is important since, as Rodrik (1998: 1021) acknowledges, it is logically quite conceivable that high exports are associated with lower volatility, at least in countries with advanced industrial sectors. The reason is that participation in international trade makes it possible to escape excessive dependence on small home markets, much the same way as stock funds spread the risks across several industries and, increasingly, across several national markets. Although trade implies greater specialization, the bulk of the trade between advanced economies is intra-industry and does not lead to excessive dependence on a single industry. Indeed, many industries in countries with small home markets can prosper only by taking advantage of the production of scale that global markets afford.

Rodrik does show a direct link between external risks, measured by terms of trade volatility, and internal income volatility and spending (1998: 1021–3). But while this suggests that price volatility on external markets translates into domestic income volatility and greater spending, it does not show whether producers for foreign markets experience greater price swings than producers for domestic markets. For that purpose one also needs to ask whether output volatility of industries increases with export dependence, and whether such volatility translates into greater swings in industrial wages and employment. In order to answer this question, I compared the volatility in output, employment, and wages in the manufacturing sectors of sixteen OECD countries with very different levels of export dependence (see Figure 2.3). Output and wages are measured in real terms, and volatility is defined as the standard deviation of annual growth rates between 1970 and 1993. As a baseline for the comparison, the figure also shows volatility in a completely non-traded (but private) service industry: community, social, and personal services (indicated by the three dotted vertical lines).[2]

Contrary to the logic of Garrett's and Rodrik's argument, there is no relationship between the export dependence of manufacturing (measured as the value of exports divided by manufacturing value-added) and any of the volatility measures. The only variable weakly related to export dependence is output volatility, but the association is in the opposite direction of the one implied by the openness argument. Nor is there any evidence that the traded manufacturing sector is more volatile than the average for the completely sheltered service sector. Finally, it is noteworthy that there is no association between the level of volatility and Katzenstein's distinction between small corporatist welfare states and large liberal (or statist) ones.

It can be objected that the presented figures are too aggregated to pick up the volatility experienced in particular industries or even in particular

---

[2] The government sector is less volatile, but it does not make sense to include it in the comparison, since it is supposed to be growing as a consequence of high volatility in exposed sectors.

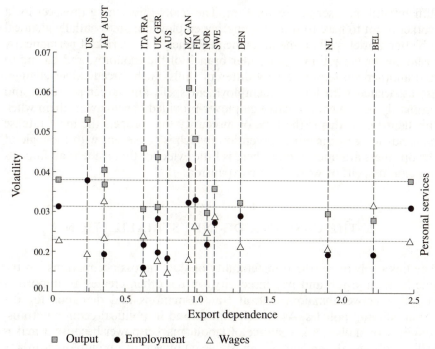

■ Output ● Employment △ Wages

FIG. 2.3. Trade dependence and production volatility across 16 OECD countries

Notes: Export dependence is the total value of manufacturing exports divided by value added; volatility is the standard deviation in the rate of growth in manufacturing output, employment, and wages in the period 1970–93. Output data is not available for Austria; only employment data is available for New Zealand.

Sources: OECD, *The OECD STAN Database* (1994).

firms. However, the pattern does not change if we examine volatility at the more fine-grained 2-digit industry level, and although it is logically possible that volatility varies with trade at even lower levels of aggregation, it is unlikely. The reason is that in order for two countries to have the same volatility at one level of aggregation, but different levels of volatility at a lower level, workers in one country must be systematically less likely to find jobs outside their own specific branch compared to workers in the other country. I know of no theory or evidence that would imply such systematic differences in sector mobility between open and closed economies.

Moreover, the more specific the sectors, the less the effect of volatility on the risks faced by workers. The reason is that when the level of aggregation decreases, the substitutability of workers' skills increases. For example, it is much easier for a metalworker in one car firm to find a job in another car firm than it is for that same worker to find a job in a chemical firm or, more difficult still, in a service sector firm. The really threatening prospect for a worker is not to have to work for another employer in an essentially identical job after a brief spell of unemployment. Rather, it is the risk of permanently losing his or her job in a particular branch of the economy, and having to find another job requiring very different skills. Such forced career changes are associated with longer unemployment spells and larger pay cuts, and ordinarily people cannot carry employer-provided benefits with them when this happens. If this is the type of insecurity that propels the most intense demands for government intervention (which is consistent with the logic of the openness argument), then there is little evidence that trade is an important causal agent of welfare state expansion.

2. THE CASE FOR DE-INDUSTRIALIZATION

The linkage between the transferability of skills across occupations, on the one hand, and job and pay insecurity, on the other, creates an important coupling between major sectoral transformations and demands for de-commodifying policies. As is well understood in political economy, transferability of skills is a key source of labour market power because it makes individuals less dependent on any single employer, or on employers in any particular branch of the economy. Consequently, when jobs are destroyed across firms and industries with low substitutability of skills, it undercuts workers' labour market power and exposes people to greater risks. The largest labour market risks are therefore generated across the interfaces between economic sectors requiring very different forms of skills.

This logic is reinforced when we consider that the mobility of privately provided social benefits, such as health insurance and pensions, tend to be limited by the transferability of skills. The reason is that when skills are firm-specific, employers have an incentive to provide non-transferable company benefits, both as a tool of control over its workforce, and as an incentive for their employees to acquire additional firm-specific skills. Correspondingly, if skills are industry-wide, there is a rationale for employers in that industry to provide benefits that are transferable across firms, but only within the industry. Although the latter depends on the ability of employers to collude in the provision of both skills and benefits, the point is that the transferability of benefits will not exceed the transferability of skills in the absence of state intervention.

The correspondence between the scope of employer-sponsored insurance and the transferability of skills is important in understanding why labour market risks propel demand for state intervention. Since workers who have to transgress the interfaces defined by skill discontinuities simultaneously lose market power and employer-provided benefits, it is only through the mediation of the state that workers can protect themselves against the risks of major shifts in the economic and occupational structure. Such protection comes in the form of state-guaranteed health and old age insurance (which makes it possible to move across sectoral interfaces without losing benefits), early retirement and certain forms of disability insurance (which makes it easier not to have to move across these interfaces), as well as direct employment in relatively secure publicly provided service occupations.

In principle, in order to gauge the extent to which people are exposed to labour market risks of the sort just described we would have to create a 'map' of the labour market in which skill boundaries were marked by thick or thin lines according to the degree of skill transferability across those boundaries. The exposure to risk of any individual could then be calculated as a function of the risk of having to travel across any one of the boundaries times the non-transferability of skills and employer provided benefits. Clearly, the data needed to make such calculations with any degree of confidence are light years away. Just to mention a few difficulties, what measures should we use to gauge skill transferability? How do we assess the comparative scope and transferability of employers benefits? How do we attach probabilities to individual workers' prospect of having to move across any and all of the skill boundaries in the economy?

What makes de-industrialization a useful empirical concept for our purposes are the following:

1. Most skills acquired in manufacturing (and agricultural) occupations travel very poorly to services occupations. Even low-skilled blue-collar workers find it hard to adjust to similarly low-skilled service sector jobs because they lack something that, for want of a better word, is sometimes referred to as 'social skills'. In other words, the distinction between services and the traditional sectors represent a particularly 'thick' skill boundary in the economy.

2. The boundary between manufacturing and services has been subject to a lot of 'traffic' in most countries since the early 1960s. To get a feeling for magnitudes, it is useful to make some comparisons to the employment volatility measure introduced in the previous section. Imagine that instead of using deviations from the mean to measure volatility of employment growth, we used negative deviations from zero (no change). The volatility measure would then jump by a factor of about five, and unlike the original measure, this one would not count 'good news' (employment growth) as a cause for heightened labour market insecurity.

3. To the extent that transferability of private benefits is limited by occupational proximity, forced movement from manufacturing to services is a particularly impenetrable barrier to benefit transfer. Employers in the two

sectors are usually organized in different associations and do not cooperate in the provision of training or benefits. Frequently a switch in employment across the two sectors also requires workers to change their membership in unions and unemployment insurance funds.

De-industrialization, measured as net shifts in employment out of the traditional sectors, is certainly not the only source of labour market risks, and the theoretical argument is much more general. Still, it is difficult to imagine that de-industrialization, as a practical matter, has not been among the most important sources of labour market risks during the past three decades. Not only are the gross figures for de-industrialization large, there is also considerable variance in this variable across time and space.[3] For example, in an early industrializing country like the United States, industrial employment as a percentage of the adult population declined by only 3 percentage points between 1960 and 1995, whereas for a late industrializer like Sweden, the figure is 13 per cent. If we add to these figures the decline of agricultural employment on the ground that it has been driven by a similar process of technological progress coupled with market saturation, these numbers increase to 6 and 22 per cent, respectively.

The difference in these figures translates into very large numbers of people. As a thought experiment, imagine that the USA had gone through the same decline as Sweden in the 1960–95 period. The implied increase in the net number of permanently lost jobs in the primary and secondary sectors of the economy would then have amounted to about 23 million workers! Would such a dramatic rise in the number of dislocated workers have affected popular attitudes towards the state and paved a different path for the development of the American welfare state? There is no way of knowing for certain, of course, but it certainly seems plausible, and we can draw on the comparative evidence for support.

Figure 2.4 shows the association between the average annual figures for de-industrialization—in the sense of the joint employment losses in industry and agriculture—and the comparable figure for the expansion in total government spending. As expected, there is a positive association which is of about the same strength as that between openness and spending (Figure 2.2). There is some clustering around the mean, but this is mainly due to averaging over a 35-year period (as will become apparent later). Most of the countries have gone through periods of both relatively slow and relatively rapid de-industrialization, and the temporal order of these swings varies.

---

[3] There seems to be a misconception that de-industrialization is uniform across countries, and therefore cannot explain cross-national variance in the speed of welfare state expansion. At least this is one of the only reasons I can imagine for why not a single large-N, cross-national study of the welfare state has focused on the effects of de-industrialization.

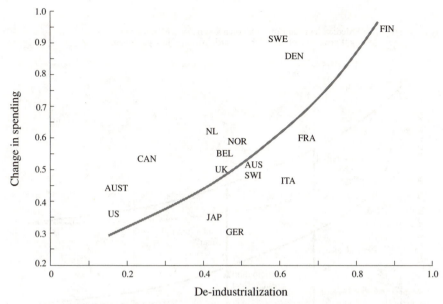

FIG. 2.4. De-industrialization and change in welfare spending for
16 OECD countries, 1960–93

Notes: Government spending is the average annual change in civilian government consumption plus social transfers as a percentage of GDP; de-industrialization is the average annual reduction in employment in industry plus agriculture as a percentage of the working age population.

Sources: OECD, *Labour Force Statistics* (various years); OECD, *National Accounts*, Part II: Detailed Tables (1997).

3. THE LABOUR MARKET RISK STRUCTURE AND PARTISAN POLITICS

In the context of incomplete private markets for risk, the prospect of losing the labour power of one's skills—and hence income, employment, and employer-provided benefits—becomes a powerful motivational force in the formation of policy preferences. In turn, it is the capacity of the state to reduce such uncertainties though transfers and public services that links the labour market risk structure to demands for welfare state expansion. This is why we would expect de-industrialization to be linked to welfare state expansion in democracies. But the welfare state is not merely a source of insurance. It is also a vehicle for partisan politicians to redistribute risks. This can be done by guaranteeing income and employment for those facing high risks—i.e. those with few marketable skills—and imposing a net tax on those

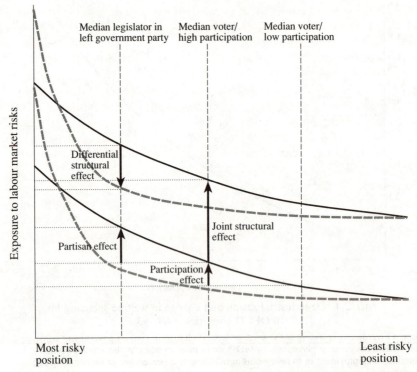

Median legislator in   Median voter/   Median voter/
left government party   high participation   low participation

Exposure to labour market risks

Differential
structural
effect

Joint structural
effect

Partisan effect

Participation
effect

Most risky   Least risky
position   position

FIG. 2.5. The labour market risk structure and the effects of exogenous shocks

in more secure positions. In addition to shifts in the level of risks, it is therefore necessary to take account of factors that affect the distribution of these risks and to determine the political weight accorded to individuals in different locations in the distribution.

Figure 2.5 maps a hypothetical distribution of risks and provides a classification of changes that affects either the distribution or the political salience of particular positions in the distribution. What is labelled *joint structural effects* refer to vertical shifts in the level of the curve, and it is such level-changes that are implied by both the de-industrialization and trade openness arguments. The more people are affected by trade exposure or de-industrialization, so the arguments go, the higher the location of the risk curve. *Differential structural effects* refer to changes in the shape of the risk distribution. For example, it has been argued that technological change in the past three decades has shifted relative labour demand towards high-skilled workers, and away from low-skilled workers (Bound and Johnson 1992; Krueger 1993). A similar effect has been attributed to growing trade with low-wage countries because such trade undercuts the market position of low-skilled workers (Wood 1994; Leamer 1984, 1996). Note, however, that if such changes are truly differential 'i.e. raises risks for some, but lowers them for others' the likely effect will be to reduce the demand for compensation in the centre-right portion of the distribution where the politically pivotal voter is likely to be located. This is in fact the position taken by Rodrik (1997: ch. 4), and it is not obvious how Garrett (1998*b*: 39) can use the Wood–Leamer argument in support of his general openness thesis—i.e. that trade openness spurs demand for compensation.

Just as the shape and location of the risk curve is subject to variation across time and space, so is the 'centre of gravity' of political influence (something Garrett is careful to explain). In particular, as the centre of gravity of political influence shifts from right to left in the distribution, we expect welfare policies to become not only more generous, but also more redistributive. In turn, the literature has focused on three variables that determine this political centre of gravity. Two of these concern electoral politics. What I call *participation effects* occur when vote-abstaining is uneven across the distribution and changes in turnout therefore shift the location of the median voter (Meltzer and Richard 1981). In particular, it is well known that poorly educated and low-income people in tenuous labour market positions are less likely to vote than better educated and higher income people. This leads to the expectation that a higher voter turnout shifts the political centre of gravity to the left (Lijphart 1997), with the expected effect of increasing public spending (Mueller and Murrell 1986) and/or redistribution (Husted and Kenny 1997).[4]

Partisan effects refer to government deviations from median voter preferences. Although it is widely recognized that the median voter exerts a powerful centripetal influence on party platforms in two-party systems (Downs 1957; Cox 1990), as well as on government formation in multi-party systems (Laver and Schofield 1990), there are good reasons to expect that government policies can deviate from the preferences of the median voter. The influence of party activists (Aldrich 1983, 1997; Tsebelis 1990), cross-cutting policy dimensions (Laver and Shepsle 1997; Wren and Iversen 1997), and ideology (Hibbs 1977; Huber, Ragin, and Stephens 1993)—especially in the context of disciplined parties—all point to the possibility for non-centrist party governments. To the extent that this is the case, left governments will pay more heed than right governments to the preferences of those exposed to the greatest labour market risks.

A third factor determining the centre of gravity of influence, not shown in the figure, is the control over policies enjoyed by organized groups. The better organized high risks groups are, the more influence they are likely to

---

[4] For some government services a shift to the preferences of a lower income voter can reduce spending if income elasticity of demand for services is high (Kenny 1978).

exert. The form of organization may also matter because relatively inclusive and centralized labour market organizations diffuse power in the labour
market to groups that would otherwise have little political clout. Centralized
and encompassing labour movements are the most important examples here,
and they have been subject to intensive analysis in the neocorporatist and class
power literatures (e.g. Goldthorpe 1984; Stephens 1979; Korpi 1983, 1989).
We would expect the presence of such organizations to shift the political
centre of gravity to the left.

Summarizing this section, public spending is likely to go up as the general
level of labour market risks rises (the joint structural effect), as participation
increases (the participation effect), and as policy influence shifts to the left
(the partisan effect). On the other hand, a bifurcation of the risk structure—
as the result of shifts in relative demand for different types of labour—is
likely to reduce the generosity of spending. The main contention of this paper
is that de-industrialization, not trade, has been the principal force pushing
the risk-curve—and hence the societal demand for public compensation and
risk-sharing—upwards. By contrast, the primary effect of (left) partisan
politics has been to redistribute risk through particular spending choices.

4. EMPIRICAL EVIDENCE

The evidence presented below covers fifteen OECD countries over a 33-year
period from 1961 to 1993.[5] The data was grouped into 11 three-year periods
primarily to overcome problems of defining a proper lag structure for a model
with a large number of very different types of variables.[6] Hence, the data set
consists of a total of 161 (15 * 11) observations, although fifteen observations
were lost in the regression as a result of lagging some variables.

The 1960–95 period represents the historically most dramatic phase of
growth in welfare spending. Transfer payments more than doubled from
8.5 per cent of GDP in 1960 to over 20 per cent in 1995, and government consumption increased from about 9 per cent of GDP in 1960 to over 16 per cent
in 1995. The cross-national variance in transfers (measured by the coefficient of variation) declined somewhat over time, but it rose for government
consumption. Measured in terms of the difference between the smallest and
biggest 'spenders', divergence increased in both categories of spending. Thus,
the transfers payment gap increased from 10 to 15 per cent of GDP, and

[5] The countries are: Austria, Belgium, Canada, Denmark, Finland, France, Germany
(West), Italy, Japan, Netherlands, Norway, Sweden, Switzerland, United Kingdom, and
United States.
[6] Moreover, for one of the dependent variables, unemployment replacement rates, only bi-
yearly data is available.

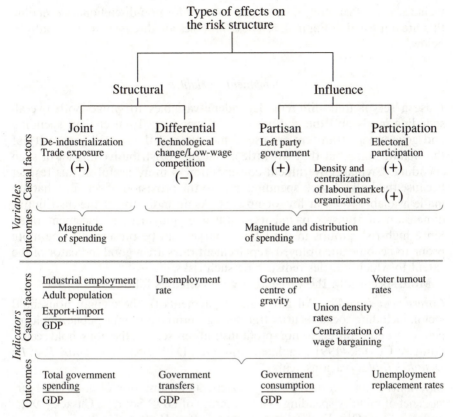

Fig. 2.6. Theoretical variables and their measurement

the government consumption gap from 6 to 15 per cent of GDP. In other words, these data represent not only considerable inter-temporal variance, but also large cross-national differences—a good testing ground for competing explanations of welfare state expansion.

Figure 2.6 summarizes the set of explanatory variables according to their main effect on the labour market risk structure and indicates the way in which each was measured. The direction of the effect on spending of each theoretical variable is also noted with +/− signs which, taken together, constitute the set of hypotheses to be tested. Note in particular that the factors that have been argued to produce joint structural effects—openness and de-industrialization —are predicted to primarily affect total spending, whereas the other factors (whether having differential structural, or influence, effects) are predicted to affect both spending levels and distribution.

The rationale behind the choice of variables, their specific measurement, as well as the data sources are explained below. It should be noted that analysis includes a set of carefully constructed controls for non-discretionary spending that are not listed in Figure 2.6. These variables are discussed under 'controls' below.

Dependent Variables

I use a set of four different dependent variables to gauge both overall spending levels and the composition of spending. Total civilian spending and government transfers are useful measures of the overall generosity of the welfare state, but they say little about the redistributive impact of such spending. Civilian government consumption is more useful in this respect because the bulk of such spending goes to the provision of services that are made available to all at low or no cost. As an indicator of the distributive dimension of transfer payments, I use unemployment replacement rates. Since high-risk groups in the labour market can be presumed to be more prone to become unemployed, replacement rates are a good indicator of the extent to which policies redistribute such risks.[7]

More specifically, the variables are measured as follows:

Government transfers. All government payments to the civilian household sector, including social security transfers, government grants, public employee pensions, and transfers to non-profit institutions serving the household sector. Sources: Cusack (1991), updated from OECD, *National Accounts, Part II: Detailed Tables* (various years).

Government consumption. Total government consumption of goods and services net of military spending as a percentage of GDP. Sources: Cusack (1991), updated from OECD, *National Accounts, Part II: Detailed Tables* (various years), and *The SIPRI Year Book* (Stockholm: SIPRI, various years).

Total spending. The sum of government transfers and government consumption as a percentage of GDP. Sources: as above.

Unemployment replacement rates. The average gross income replacement rate for a 'typical' 40-year worker in various family situations, averaged over three years of unemployment with the first year weighted twice that of the second and third. Source: OECD, *Database on Unemployment Benefit Entitlements and Replacement Rates* (undated).

Independent Theoretical Variables

The measurement of most of the independent variables is straightforward. The main difficulty is to find good indicators for technological change and

---

[7] I focus the analysis of replacement rates on the post oil-shock period, because unemployment compensation was not a contested political issue in the full employment 1960s.

competition from low-wage countries. The latter should be picked up as a differential structural effect from LDC trade (i.e. one that primarily affects distribution), but I also added unemployment rates to the analysis, since these can be seen as reasonable proxies for the effect of changes in relative demand and supply conditions. Since unemployment disproportionately affects those in precarious labour market positions, it should give us a good idea of the extent to which differential structural effects increase or lower spending. Of course, in order to pick up this effect it is necessary to control for the spending effects of unemployment, which is accomplished by the automatic transfer variable described below.

The other theoretical variables are measured as follows:

De-industrialization. 100 minus the sum of manufacturing and agricultural employment as a percentage of the working age population. Since this is often misunderstood, I underscore that the base is the working age population, not the labour force. While government spending may affect the latter, it is highly unlikely to influence the former (it would require changes in the birth rate). Source: OECD, *Labour Force Statistics* (various years).

Trade openness: Total exports and imports of goods and services as percentage of GDP. Source: OECD, *National Accounts, Part II: Detailed Tables* (various years).

Left government centre of gravity. This is an index of the partisan left–right 'centre of gravity' developed by Cusack (1997). It is based on (i) F. G. Castles and Mair's (1984) codings of government parties' placement on a left–right scale, weighted by (ii) their decimal share of cabinet portfolios. The index varies from 0 (extreme right) to 4 (extreme left), although most observations are much closer to the mean. The data was generously made available by Thomas Cusack.

Concentration of union power. This variable is the product of union density and the centralization of union power in wage bargaining. Density is measured as the number of union members relative to the labour force, while centralization is measured by a time-sensitive index of centralization of wage bargaining. Sources: Visser (1989, 1996*c*); Iversen (1998*b*).

Electoral participation. The data is based on voter turnout rates as recorded on an annual basis in Mackie and Rose (1991) and in the *European Journal of Political Research*.

Controls

Two controls deserve particular emphasis. Both are designed to remove non-discretionary elements of government spending, and they are important to get a well-specified model. The first relates transfer payments to changes in unemployment and demographics that generate 'automatic' disbursements of payments according to rules that cannot be readily altered in the short run. Typically, studies control for such effects by including variables for unemployment and the number of people above the pension age. However, Cusack (1997) has developed a more satisfactory measure that takes account of the fact that the generosity of transfers varies across countries. The measure is referred to as *automatic transfers* and defined as follows:

$$Automatic\ transfers = generosity\ (t-1)$$
$$\cdot \Delta\frac{unemployed + population > 65}{population}\ (t).$$

where generosity is the percentage share of transfers in GDP relative to the percentage share of the dependent population in the total population at time $t-1$. In other words, changes in size of the dependent population (the unemployed and the retired) causes an automatic increase in transfers at time t, the size of which depends on the generosity of transfers in the previous period (according to prevailing benefit rules). The source for the unemployment and population figures is OECD, *Labour Force Statistics* (various years).

Another non-discretionary element of spending concerns government consumption. Because productivity increases in public services are generally lower than in the rest of the economy, while especially wage costs tend to follow productivity increases in the rest of the economy, the price level of government services will grow at a faster rate than the general price level (the 'Baumol effect'). At constant provision levels, government consumption will therefore increase as a share of GDP. This non-discretionary effect of relative price changes can be removed by another measure developed by Cusack (1997). It is here called *automatic consumption* and is defined as follows:

$$Automatic\ consumption = \frac{govt.\ consumption}{GDP}\ (t-1)$$
$$\cdot \left(\frac{\Delta govt.\ deflator\ (t)}{govt.\ deflator\ (t-1)}\right) \bigg/ \left(\frac{\Delta GDP\ deflator\ (t)}{GDP\ deflator\ (t-1)}\right)$$

where *govt. deflator* is the price deflator for government services, and *GDP deflator* is the price deflator for the whole GDP. The equation simply says that if prices on government services grow faster than the general price level, government consumption will automatically increase by a proportional amount.

In addition to these variables the analysis included these controls:

Capital markets openness is a measure for capital market liberalization presented in Quinn and Inclan (1997). This control was included to check whether the effect of globalization may run through capital market rather than product market integration.

Per capita income measured in terms of real GDP per capita (in 1985 US dollars at purchasing power equivalents) is intended to capture possible effects of Wagner's 'law'—the notion that demand for welfare services is income elastic (i.e. spending rises with wealth). Source: Penn World Tables.

Unexpected growth is a variable emphasized in Roubini and Sachs (1989). It is defined as real GDP per capita growth at time *t* minus average real per capita growth in the preceding period. The variable is intended to capture the logic that budgeting relies on GDP forecasts based on performance in the recent past. If growth is unexpectedly high, it reduces spending as a proportion of GDP.

Country dummies are included to control for nationally specific effects. For example, Esping-Andersen (1990) has forcefully argued that the institutional blueprints for many of today's welfare states were established in the pre-World War II period, and that these institutional characteristics keep shaping the contemporary development of the welfare state. This dynamic is not captured by any of the other variables and therefore would show up as country specific effects. Likewise Huber, Ragin, and Stephens (1993) have argued that the greater the opportunities for minorities to block new spending bills (i.e. the greater the number of veto points in the political system) the less likely it is that new legislation will be passed or implemented. Since their index of government structures varies across my fifteen cases, but not across time, the effect will be picked up by the country dummies.

5. THE STATISTICAL MODEL

There are numerous ways to model government spending. The most satisfactory from the perspective of being able to disentangle short- and long-term effects is an error correction model, using changes in spending as the dependent variable. This model is also preferable on technical grounds when there is high co-variation between dependent and independent variables across time ('co-integration').[8] Although there are no good tests for co-integration, Figure 2.1 above strongly suggests its presence. The model has the following form:

$$\Delta Spending\ (t) = \beta_1 \cdot Spending\ (t-1) + \beta_2 \cdot De\text{-}industrialization\ (t-1)$$
$$+ \beta_3 \cdot \Delta De\text{-}industrialization\ (t) + \beta_4 \cdot Trade\ openness\ (t-1)$$
$$+ \beta_5 \cdot \Delta Trade\ openness\ (t) + Influence\ var's + Controls + \varepsilon,$$

where *t* refers to time periods, and Δ is the first difference operator.

---

[8] For details, see Beck 1992.

The parameter for the lagged dependent level variable (β_1) indicates whether spending reaches stable equilibrium levels over time, as well as the speed with which this occurs. If an equilibrium does exist, which is the presumption, β_1 must be between 0 and -1. Note also that some independent variables have been entered as both lagged levels—$X(t-1)$—and as first differences—$\Delta X(t)$. Although it is not intuitively obvious, it can be shown that the parameter for a level variable shows the permanent (or long-term) effect of a one-off change in that variable, whereas the parameter for a change variable shows the transitory (or short-term) effect of a one-off change in that variable.

If a variable exhibits only transitory effects, unless it changes continuously, spending will eventually revert back to its original level. Since all the theoretical variables are defined as proportions (either of the GDP or of the working age population) with upper limits, they have no long-term effects on spending unless the parameters for their lagged levels are significant.[9] This does not mean that transitory effects are uninteresting. For example, if the entire effect of de-industrialization were transitory, the implication would be that any expansionary effects would be matched by cutbacks of the same size once the process came to a halt. But the distinction between permanent and transitory effects is a very useful one to keep in mind when interpreting the results.

Finally, it should be noted that the use of differences, rather than levels, as the dependent variable has no substantive implications for the interpretation of the results. The model is mathematically identical to one that uses levels on the left-hand side, and includes a lagged level variable on the right-hand side (to see this, simply add the lagged level of the dependent variable on both sides of the above equation). I use changes as the dependent variable to signal the dynamic nature of both the data and the arguments; it does not preclude an analysis of the causes of differences in levels.[10]

6. FINDINGS

The results of the regression analysis are shown in Table 2.1. Column (1) shows the benchmark model for total spending and includes only the trade openness variable plus the controls. Contrary to the expectation, trade has no statistically significant effect on spending. It is only if we exclude one or both of the automatic spending variables, or replace them with less refined

---

[9] This does not have to be the case. One of the control variables, GDP per capita growth, can in principle continue to grow indefinitely.

[10] Using levels on the LHS, however, has the unfortunate consequence of making the R-squared statistics useless as a measure of explanatory power (because most of the variance will be explained by the LDV).

TABLE 2.1. *The causes of welfare state expansion, 1961–93*

		Total government spending		Government transfers	Government consumption	Replacement rates
		(1)	(2)	(3)	(4)	(5)
Structural variables	Intercept	3.91	−13.12	−3.15	−7.75	−0.31
	Level of dependent variable ($t-1$)	−0.17	−0.25	−0.33	−0.22	−0.71
		(−5.09)***	(−5.74)***	(−6.71)***	(−6.34)***	(−10.93)***
	De-industrialization ($t-1$)		0.25	0.14	0.12	0.01
			(4.05)***	(3.51)***	(3.88)***	(4.00)***
	Change in de-industrialization (t)		0.40	0.27	0.17	0.01
			(4.73)***	(4.18)***	(4.19)***	(3.34)***
	Level of trade openness ($t-1$)	−0.00	−0.01	0.00	−0.01	−0.00
		(−0.01)	(−0.89)	(0.39)	(−1.53)	(−3.59)***
	Change in trade openness (t)	0.00	0.00	0.00	0.01	−0.00
		(0.01)	(0.06)	(0.18)	(0.80)	(−2.54)**
	Unemployment ($t-1$)		−0.12	−0.07	−0.08	0.00
			(−1.74)*	(−1.27)	(−2.66)**	(0.74)
Influence variables	Left government ($t-1$)		0.05	−0.20	0.25	0.03
			(0.24)	(−1.20)	(2.26)**	(3.25)***
	Left government shift (t)		0.20	0.08	0.11	0.02
			(1.09)	(0.59)	(1.18)	(2.84)**
	Voter turnout ($t-1$)		0.05	0.00	0.03	0.00
			(1.60)	(0.09)	(2.32)**	(0.30)
	Change in voter turnout (t)		0.02	−0.00	0.02	−0.00
			(0.50)	(−0.09)	(1.02)	(−0.55)
	Concentration of union power ($t-1$)		0.02	−0.02	0.03	0.00
			(1.05)	(−1.19)	(3.07)***	(0.71)

TABLE 2.1. (cont'd)

	Total government spending		Government transfers	Government consumption	Replacement rates
	(1)	(2)	(3)	(4)	(5)
Capital market liberalization ($t-1$)	0.17	0.06	0.13	-0.03	-0.01
	(1.93)*	(0.60)	(1.71)	(-0.63)	(-2.16)
Per capital income ($t-1$)	-0.00	-0.00	-0.00	-0.00	-0.00
	(-1.41)	(-1.96)*	(-0.68)	(-2.08)**	(-2.33)*
Unexpected growth (t)	-0.56	-0.47	-0.31	-0.17	0.00
	(-9.36)***	(-8.05)***	(-6.82)***	(-5.82)***	(0.27)
Automatic transfers	1.09	0.83	0.65	—	—
	(7.80)***	(5.57)***	(5.47)***		
Automatic consumption	1.24	1.01	—	0.74	—
	(5.78)***	(5.04)***		(7.50)***	
Adj. R Squared (N)	0.69 (150)	0.72 (150)	0.63 (150)	0.67 (150)	0.57 (90)

Control variables

Key: *p < 0.10; **p < 0.05; ***p < 0.01 (based on panel-corrected standard errors).

Note: The results for country dummies are not shown.

ones, that it is possible to get some weak support for the openness hypothesis. What this shows is the importance of having good controls for the automatic spending increases caused by demographic shifts and by changes in the relative prices of government services (see Iversen and Cusack 1998 for a more detailed discussion of this point).[11]

The negative results for trade are unaltered when including the other theoretical variables in the total spending equation (column 2). Although it can always be objected that the trade openness is important for a different set of countries, or for a different period of time, suffice it to say that if trade openness is irrelevant in explaining expansion in welfare spending for fifteen OECD countries over a 33-year period, the scope of the argument is considerably more limited than originally conceived.

De-industrialization and Political Influence Effects

Instead, de-industrialization stands out as the most important factor for explaining overall spending, and its substantive effect is quite remarkable.[12] Thus, a one standard deviation increase in de-industrialization is associated with a permanent increase in spending of 0.9 standard deviations. Another way to convey the implications of these results is to put numbers on our earlier counterfactual thought-experiment of bringing the speed of de-industrialization in the USA up to that of Sweden over the 1960–95 period. The results suggest that this would have increased the equilibrium level of spending in the USA from 25 per cent of GDP (the actual level in 1995) to 40 per cent of GDP which is close to current Swedish levels (which stand at 49 per cent). These are staggering numbers, but perhaps befitting for shocks of the magnitude we are talking about: a net loss of 25 million jobs. If true, this offers a simple explanation for the 'lag' of the US welfare state without any references to the 'exceptional' character of American political culture. At a minimum, these figures show that de-industrialization is an important explanatory variable in accounting for cross-national differences in the size of the welfare state.

Another feature of these results, which has already been acknowledged, deserves emphasis: the effect of de-industrialization persists over time. While we would expect voter participation to have permanent effects on policies (since it permanently alters the preferences that are given political clout) one might have suspected that the effect of de-industrialization would be transitory in nature. But this is not the case. Although the transitory effect, which is large in the first period, quickly dissipates, the total effect of

---

[11] I experimented with log transforming the openness variable, but it has little effect on the results while complicating their interpretation.

[12] The adjusted R-squared also goes up by a substantial 5 percentage points.

de-industrialization remains stable and even creeps up over time (until the point where spending reaches an equilibrium).

It is thus clear that the spending effect of de-industrialization gets 'locked in' by organizational and institutional factors that are exogenous to the present model. This finding supports Pierson's (1994, 1996) thesis that the politics of welfare state retrenchment is not simply the politics of welfare state expansion in reverse. Even though the process of de-industrialization is the causal agent in the expansion of the welfare state, the disappearance of this causal agent will not lead to a full-scale retrenchment—it will 'merely' retard further expansion. However, the character of the political game over welfare policies is likely to change when compromises involving overall expansion are no longer feasible; a point to which I shall return in the final section.

Regarding the control variables in the model, note that income per capita (contrary to Wagner's law) is negative (although only borderline significant).[13] There is no appreciable effects of capital market liberalization, while both the automatic transfer and consumption variables have the predicted (and highly significant) effects. Finally, higher GDP growth, as we would expect, reduces spending by driving up the denominator in the spending variables faster than the numerator.

There are no significant effects on total spending of either the government partisanship variable, voter turnout, or the concentration of union power although they are all in the expected (positive) direction. However, this picture changes in interesting ways once we split spending into its main components: government transfers (column 3) and government consumption (column 4). Concerning transfers, left governments have no effect (or a slightly negative one) on spending, but in the case of government consumption left governments spend significantly more than right ones. Because the total spending results pool effects for both transfers and consumption the net impact is small. Clearly, therefore, left and right governments differ profoundly in their preferences over the form that welfare spending takes. Right governments prefer the use of transfer payments because they do not involve direct state participation in service production, and because transfer payments can be more easily designed to preserve earnings and status differences. Left governments prefer direct public service production, not primarily because it replaces the market, but because equal access to free or low-cost services is highly redistributive. These results are supported by the findings for voter turnout and concentration of union power which both have a significant and permanent upward effect on consumption.

---

[13] This negative finding for Wagner's law is common in the literature, and it is entirely consistent with a labour market risk argument. If income across the economy grows at a faster rate, the potential for future individual income gains is also greater, while the risk of losses are smaller.

Interestingly enough, if trade openness does have any lasting effects on spending, it appears to be a negative one affecting the consumption side (although the effect is not statistically significant). This lends weak support to the argument by trade economists that trade liberalization exposes low-skilled workers to greater competition from low-wage countries (Wood 1994; Leamer 1984, 1996). Since such competition raises the risk curve for those already at the high-risk end of the distribution, while it may well be welfare-improving for all others (similar to the example in Figure 2.5), it reduces the political support for redistributive spending.[14] This logic is also supported by the results for unemployment replacement rates which indicate that both trade and capital market liberalization have significant negative effects. Furthermore, note that the independent effect of unemployment (after control for the automatic spending effects of higher unemployment) is negative and statistically significant. Again, this suggests that differential shifts in the risk structure do indeed have a dampening effect on spending, especially when such spending is redistributive.

Employment Trade-offs and
Political Choices in the Post-industrial Economy

It can be objected to my interpretation of the political variables that left party governments could achieve their distributive goals by altering the distributive effects of transfer payments rather than engaging in direct service provision. Especially in countries where the moderate left has dominated government power, there are no compelling reasons that consumption should be heavily favoured over transfers. After all, the ideological goal of socializing production has been abandoned by virtually all social democratic parties as both unnecessary and potentially damaging for the economy. Yet, social democratic governments have engaged in extensive public provision of social services that could have been supplied through the market. The explanation for this puzzle, I submit, has to do with the interaction between the pursuit of equality, and the logic of service employment expansion.

To see this, first consider the effect of government partisanship on unemployment replacement rates (column 5), which is a good indicator for the redistributive effects of a category of transfers that became politically highly salient following the first oil crisis (before then it was not an issue of partisan contention). Note that in contrast to total transfer payments, left governments are far more likely than right ones to raise replacement rates. Thus, a shift in the government centre of gravity from the moderate right

---

[14] But why this is not the case for transfer payments is an intriguing question. It appears that the trade and unemployment variables are 'stealing' power from each other and alternately accounting for the differential structural effect.

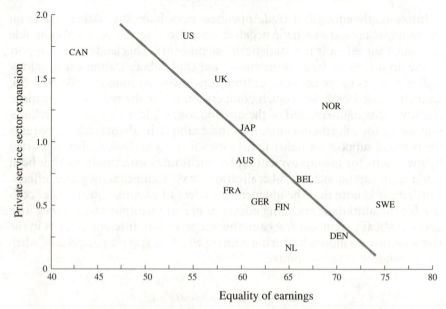

FIG. 2.7. Earnings equality and private service sector expansion, 1970–92

Notes: Equality of earnings is the gross earnings (including all employer contributions for pensions, social security, etc.) of a worker in the bottom decile of the earnings distribution relative to a worker in the middle decile. Private service sector expansion is the average annual increase in employment in all private services as a percentage of the working age population.

Sources: OECD, *OECD Employment Outlook* (1991, 1996); OECD, *International Sectoral Data Base* (1997).

to the moderate left (a change of 2 points on the index) is predicted to raise replacement rates by 14 percentage points.

The effects of left partisanship extend to other aspects of the social wage and to wages proper. The government can—through a variety of social, regulatory, and incomes policies that include, but are not limited to, unemployment compensation policies—influence the overall earnings structure;[15] something that has been recognized in countless studies on the rise of the labour movement and social democracy. What is interesting from our perspective is the way in which such distributive policies condition the expansion of service sector employment (the flip side of de-industrialization), as illustrated in Figure 2.7. The figure shows the relationship between earnings

[15] Policies affecting the earnings structure include minimum wage legislation, mandatory employer social contributions, automatic cost of living adjustments, collective bargaining extension laws, and a host of regulatory measures that affect the strengths of unions and the pressure on employers to compete on the basis of wage costs.

equality—measured as the earnings of a worker in the bottom earnings decile relative to the earnings of the median worker ('d1/d5-ratios') and the average annual increase in private services employment as a percentage of the working age population (the same way we have measured all the other employment variables).[16] The association is strong (Norway is an outlier for obvious reasons) and it holds up over time and after control for a variety of relevant factors (Iversen and Wren 1998). The link between equality and employment is also insensitive to the particular definition of the dependent variable (see Glyn 1997).

The likely explanation for this relationship has to do with slow rates of productivity growth in services—a phenomenon first recognized by Baumol (1967) and informing some subsequent work in economics.[17] Table 2.2 compares OECD's estimates of the total factor productivity growth in different industries and services since 1970 (the earliest date for which this data is available). Note that there is a big productivity gap between industry and services, and that this gap—with the sole exception of construction—holds across all branches and time.[18] The implication is that if wages are compressed across sectors—and d1/d5 ratios are a good measure of such compression— it slows down the expansion of services employment unless demand is highly price-inelastic. For some services—such as producer, educational, and medical services—demand may well be price-inelastic, but for a broad variety of other services—especially wholesale, retail trade, restaurants and hotels, community, social, and personal services—it is probably not.[19]

If the government therefore cares about employment in addition to equality, it is forced to expand the government provision of low-productivity service jobs. This is precisely the pattern documented by Esping-Andersen (1993), and it is consistent with the pattern of partisan effects that we observe in the data. Left governments engage in public policies that advance earnings equality, and they compensate for the adverse employment effects by raising public sector employment. Liberal governments, by contrast, refrain from interfering with the market mechanism and seek to restrict social policies to compensation for labour market risks that affect people across the board. The USA is the archetypical example here with low government consumption at around 12 per cent of GDP, high private service employment at close to 40 per cent of the working age population, and very high (and rising) earnings inequality (Figure 2.8). By contrast, the Scandinavian countries are highly egalitarian and substitute public for private employment

---

[16] The time constraint is dictated by the data which is not available prior to 1970.

[17] See Appelbaum and Schettkat 1994, 1995; De Gregorio, Giovannini, and Wolf 1994; and Rogoff 1996.

[18] For similar results, see Gordon 1987.

[19] I say 'probably' because we really do not have any data on such elasticities, and therefore have to make guesses based on the nature of services.

TABLE 2.2. *Average annual rates of growth in total factor productivity for 14 OECD countries, 1970–94*

	1970–4	1975–8	1979–82	1983–6	1987–90	1991–4	1970–94
AGRICULTURE*	4.6	1.2	3.6	2.5	2.7	n.a.	3.7
INDUSTRY	2.0	1.5	−0.1	1.5	1.4	1.8	1.6
Manufacturing	2.8	1.8	0.1	1.6	1.3	2.7	2.1
Textiles	3.2	0.8	0.3	1.3	0.2	2.2	1.7
Chemicals	3.8	3.7	0.6	0.7	1.4	4.1	2.6
Machinery and equipment	3.6	0.7	0.5	1.7	1.6	3.4	2.6
Electricity, gas, and water	3.0	1.5	−1.3	1.0	0.6	0.5	1.8
Transport, storage, and communication	2.2	1.7	0.3	2.1	3.2	2.0	2.7
Construction	−1.2	0.0	−0.4	0.7	0.3	−0.4	−0.4
SERVICES	0.2	0.2	−0.5	0.4	−0.4	−0.5	−0.2
Private services	0.8	0.2	−0.6	0.7	−0.4	−0.5	0.4
Wholesale, retail, restaurants and hotels	1.8	0.5	−0.9	1.1	0.1	−0.5	0.9
Finance, insurance and real estate	0.4	0.2	−0.4	0.9	−0.4	−0.2	0.0
Community, social and personal services	0.4	0.1	−0.4	0.3	−0.7	−0.6	−0.2
GAP	1.8	1.3	0.4	1.1	1.8	2.3	1.8

* Based on estimated labour productivity; n.a.: data not available.

Source: OECD, *International Sectoral Data Base* (1996).

in services. Thus, government consumption in these countries is between 19 and 24 per cent of GDP, while private service employment is only between 22 and 25 per cent.

A 'conservative' alternative to both the liberal and the social democratic model is to curb labour market inequalities, but refrain from expanding public service production by relying on transfer payments and tax codes which encourage the provision of low-productivity services—caring for old people, child care, preparation of food, etc.—within the family (Esping-Andersen 1994; Huber, Ragin, and Stephens 1993). Belgium, the Netherlands, and Germany are exemplars of this alternative, featuring relatively high levels of earnings equality (Figure 2.8), public consumption at low US levels, but also very low female participation rates of around 60 per cent compared to between 71 and 75 per cent in the USA and Scandinavia.

Summarizing the empirical results, de-industrialization—not trade openness —has been the main engine of welfare state expansion since the early 1960s, and it accounts for the bulk of the inter-temporal and cross-national variance in the rise of transfer payments. But while governments of all stripes have raised spending in response to the labour market dislocations caused by de-industrialization, left governments have shaped transfers in a more egalitarian direction and have compensated for the employment effects of such egalitarianism by engaging in extensive direct government provision of services. Finally, the results suggest that voter turnout is a crucial determinant of the popular demand for, and supply of, welfare spending.

7. OBJECTIONS TO THE ARGUMENT

The empirical results are clearly supportive of the claim that de-industrialization is an important source of welfare state expansion whereas trade or capital market integration is not. But a number of logical and empirical objections can be raised against the findings. In this section I briefly address these objections one at a time.

Trade is the Cause of De-industrialization

It is conceivable that the fierce competition accompanying growing trade, not internally generated changes in technology and demand conditions, is what propels the process of de-industrialization. Especially the growing trade with less developed countries has been argued to cause a range of labour-intensive industries in the north to go out of business (see Wood 1994; Saeger 1997). If that were the case, de-industrialization would become an interesting adjunct to the globalization story, but not an alternative.

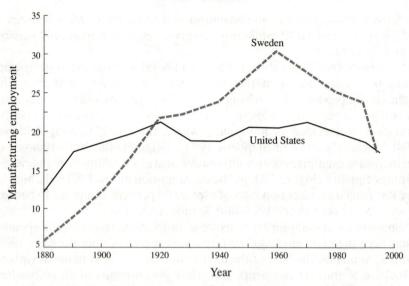

F IG. 2.8. The evolution of manufacturing employment as a percentage of the
working age population in Sweden and the United States, 1880–1995

I am not hostile to this interpretation, but there is no evidence for this view
in the data. Statistically speaking, most of the variance in de-industrialization
is explained by initial levels of industrialization, while openness plays no role.
Using de-industrialization between 1960 and 1993 as the dependent variable,
and the level of industrialization and openness in 1960 as the independent variables, the regression equation is as follows (with standard errors in
parentheses):

De-indus- $= -1.1 + 0.077 *$ Industrialization (1960) $+ 0.005 *$ Openness (1960)
trialization   (0.014)   (0.005)   ($R^2 = 0.71$).

The result for openness is actually weaker if we use openness towards LDC
trade instead of overall trade, and capital market integration is likewise
unrelated to de-industrialization. What the data suggest is that countries
go through sectoral employment cycles where late industrializers generally
industrialize further than other countries in a shorter span of time, and
correspondingly go though the phase of de-industrialization later and more
rapidly. Figure 2.8 illustrates the pattern using manufacturing employment
data for Sweden and the USA since the end of the last century.

A more detailed analysis of the causes of de-industrialization, based on
time series data, shows that the phenomenon is largely explained by a combination of rapid productivity growth in agriculture and manufacturing
combined with a shift in demand away from manufactured goods towards

services (see Iversen and Cusack 1998). There is no evidence that either trade—whether measured as balances or as absolute shares of total or LDC trade—or capital market openness cause de-industrialization. These findings echoes those of a detailed OECD study by Rowthorn and Ramaswamy (1997).

The Results Reflect Reversed Causality

The analysis in Iversen and Cusack (1998) also lends no support to the notion that de-industrialization is the result of, rather than the cause of, welfare state expansion. There is no indication that a rising welfare state, and the associated increase in taxation, has 'crowded out' industrial employment. Despite the economic notion of the distortionary effects of taxation, it appears that workers and unions willingly 'purchase' greater state protection and insurance without trying to pass on the bill in the form of higher real wage demands.

In my experience, most readers are quite willing to accept this result, yet many will maintain that there exists some kind of 'accounting relationship' between the spending and de-industrialization variables. For example, increasing public consumption means employing more people in the public sector, and since public employment is an element in the denominator of the de-industrialization variable, there must be an accounting relationship between spending and de-industrialization. This logic is simply incorrect. The denominator is defined as the total working age population, not as the labour force, and it therefore cannot be affected by spending except through the birth rate. So although it is true that public employment affects an element in the denominator, it is not true that this affects the total size of the denominator. The only logically valid argument about reversed causality is that government spending causes employment in industry and agriculture to decline.

De-industrialization is Absorbed by Natural Attrition

So long as the natural movement of people into retirement 'natural attrition' is sufficiently large, so it may be argued, de-industrialization need not have any effect on the level of labour market risks. Hence, the causal mechanism in the de-industrialization story does not hold. This argument confuses the net effect of a set of variables with the independent effect of these variables. It is true that natural attrition in any market segment will increase the job security of workers by reducing supply relative to demand, just as new entry into a segment will increase job insecurity by raising supply relative to demand. This is why early retirement, as a public policy, is a way to ameliorate such insecurities, and this is why spending on early retirement schemes is causally linked to de-industrialization. This does not alter the thesis that reduction in the labour force due to de-industrialization has an independent, risk-augmenting effect on the labour market. Regardless of the level of natural attrition, we always expect de-industrialization to increase job insecurity.

The Results are Sensitive to the Base Used in the De-industrialization Measure

It will be recalled that de-industrialization is defined as simply 100 minus the employment in the traditional sectors of the economy. The base of 100 could be defended on grounds that it constitutes a natural upper limit (no more than the entire working age population can be engaged in agriculture or industry). But in reality the peak value for traditional sector employment varies across countries, as suggested by Figure 2.9, although we do not necessarily have a 'natural' definition of the relevant reference period in which to identify this peak, nor always the necessary data. The base of 100 is therefore arbitrary, and it may be supposed that this choice affects the results. As it turns out, this choice does not matter because of the inclusion of a full set of country dummies. The only effect of changing the base of the de-industrialization variable is to alter the coefficients on the country dummies. This complicates the interpretation of these coefficients, but since country dummies are already measures of our ignorance, this is really irrelevant. The 'correct' national base for the de-industrialization variable is simply another item in the long list of unknowns that enter into the determination of the country dummy coefficients.

8. CONCLUSION: THE WELFARE STATE AT THE END OF THE INDUSTRIAL SOCIETY

Based on data for fifteen OECD countries over a 35-year period, there is little evidence that trade, or capital mobility for that matter, has played an important role in the expansion of the modern welfare state. Correspondingly, there is no support for the idea, proposed by Katzenstein (1985b), that large countries will become more akin to small corporatist welfare states as they grow increasingly exposed to the vagaries of international markets. On the other hand, there is also little evidence that globalization is a major threat to the welfare state. With a few qualifications that I note below, international variables simply do not appear to be very important in explaining the general dynamics of the modern welfare state.

Instead, what has propelled much of the expansion of the welfare state since the early 1960s is a dynamic process of technological progress

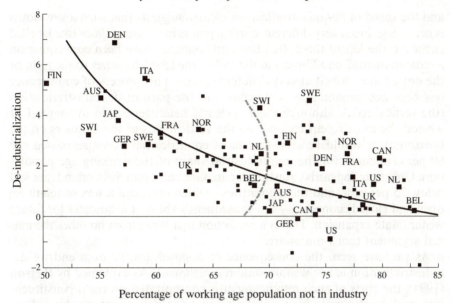

FIG. 2.9. Convergence towards the service economy, 1960–95

Notes: Labelled dots are the first (1960–3) and last (1992–5) observations in the data set. Early observations fall to the left of the dotted line, except in the cases of Canada and the US where both observations are to the right of the line. The un-labelled dots represent the observations of intervening years.

combined with the saturation of markets for agricultural and industrial products. I have referred to this process as de-industrialization because its main feature is the rapid decline in industrial employment, or, if one prefers, the disappearance of the blue-collar working class. The magnitudes of the labour market displacements accompanying de-industrialization compare to those associated with the industrial revolution, and they have shaped popular preferences for government-mediated risk-sharing and social compensation. The speed of the de-industrialization process, however, has varied greatly across countries depending on the timing of industrialization. Moreover, the political-institutional consequences of the process have been mediated by partisan politics. Whereas right governments have expanded income- and status-preserving transfer payments, left governments have altered the social wage in a more egalitarian direction and compensated for the associated job losses in low-productivity private services by expanding government-financed provision of services.

A pressing question remains to be answered: What happens when the de-industrialization process comes to a halt? Figure 2.9, which shows the relationship between the share of the working age population outside industry and the speed of de-industrialization, clearly suggests that such a slowdown is occurring. From very different starting points in the early 1960s (the labelled entries to the left of the dotted line), all countries have been converging on a 'post-industrial' equilibrium in the 1990s (the labelled entries to the right of the dotted line), albeit at very different speeds. This process of convergence has been accompanied by a slowdown in the pace of de-industrialization (the vertical axis), although there is clearly heterogeneity in this regard. If we add the most recent changes on the vertical axis to the numbers on the horizontal, it would be seen that most countries have now surpassed the 80 per cent mark for the non-industrial share of the working age population. Only four 'laggards', Austria, Japan, Germany, and Switzerland, are still below 75 per cent, and these countries—which represent a mix of relatively open and closed economies—are consequently the best candidates for future welfare state expansion. This is a prediction that flows from no other theoretical argument that I am aware.

As we have seen, the consequence of a slowdown, or even end to, de-industrialization is not welfare state retrenchment. As explained by Pierson (1994), the costs of such retrenchment is concentrated on vocal constituencies, and most people have simply become too dependent on the welfare state to want its dismantlement. However, the slowdown is likely to be accompanied by more intense distributive battles between those in secure and those in insecure labour market positions. If people in secure positions know that they are highly unlikely to end up in insecure ones, i.e. face low labour market risks, they have less reason to be solidaristic with those in insecure positions. This effect is reinforced by processes that have resulted in an increasing bifurcation of the labour market risk structure. The shift in demand away from low-skilled and towards high-skilled workers 'whether due to the introduction of more skill-intensive technologies, growing exposure to competition from low-wage countries, or a combination' has been an important factor in this bifurcation. The increase in the number of single-parent families and the division of services into a low-skilled and a knowledge-intensive sector may also have contributed to the division between secure and insecure workers.

The form that these distributive conflicts take varies across countries depending on past policy responses to de-industrialization. In Scandinavia, where the welfare state has taken a distinct public service character, calls have intensified for the privatization of more and more services (Stephens 1996). In addition, solidaristic wage policies have run into difficulties, at least partly because the high-skilled/well-educated segment of the labour force have sought to break out of the centralized bargaining system and take advantage of their improved labour market position (Pontusson and Swenson 1996; Iversen 1996, 1999a). In the United States recent conflicts have centred around the introduction of tougher means-testing as well as a strengthening of the incentives for people on welfare to take jobs in the low-paid service sector (Myles 1996). In still other countries, such as Italy and the Netherlands, where service jobs are scarce in both the private and public sectors, conflicts have intensified between 'insiders' and 'outsiders' (Esping-Andersen 1993). Political demands for the exclusion of foreigners in benefiting from the welfare state seem to have intensified everywhere.

Whatever their particular form, however, one of the most important implications of the de-industrialization argument is that the emergence of the mature 'post-industrial' economy will be associated with an intensification of distributive conflicts. This general conclusion stands in sharp contrast to the post-materialism thesis advanced by Inglehart (1987, 1990) and others, but it helps us to understand why contentious welfare state reforms in many countries rose to the top of the political agenda in the 1980s and 1990s.

3

Post-Industrial Pressures on the Mature Welfare States

Paul Pierson

SIGNS of strain are everywhere. The struggle to balance budgets is unending, even as many governments cope with levels of debt unprecedented in peacetime. Taxes have reached stress-inducing levels, and, especially in Europe, generate growing apprehension about the consequences for economic growth and employment. Critics on all sides argue that 'old' welfare states seem unresponsive to new social demands. The capacities of nation-states to address domestic problems seem to have declined (Cable 1995). Despite their striking resilience over a quarter-century of 'crisis', welfare states are widely held to be under siege.

The oft-employed metaphor of the siege is revealing, for it evokes an image of national fortresses of social protection, struggling to resist assault from external enemies. For many observers, especially in the popular press, the principal source of the welfare state's troubles is the rapidly changing world economy. The basic outlines of this new conventional wisdom are well known. 'Globalization' undermines the capacity of nation-states to control their own affairs and generates acute pressures on the welfare states of advanced industrial societies. Integration of financial markets has greatly curtailed national autonomy in macroeconomic policy, leading to a policy convergence towards low deficits and monetarism. Footloose capital undermines state revenues as corporate taxation declines. It also weakens the bargaining power of the state and organized labour, allowing employers to demand curtailment of public social provision. Perhaps most fundamental in the eyes of many is the rise of competition from newly industrialized countries (NICs). NICs compete in markets which traditionally generated manufacturing employment in advanced industrial societies, but the workers in these new competitors earn much lower wages. Thus to many, pressures associated with global economic

For helpful comments on previous drafts I thank the participants in the New Politics project and, especially, Ann Orloff. I am grateful to Miguel Glatzer for extensive research and useful discussions, to Andrew Karch, Effi Tomaras, and Erin Delaney for additional research assistance, and to the Program for the Study of Germany and Europe for financial support.

change create a new context where the generous social provision characteristic of advanced industrial societies represents an unaffordable luxury.
There is a widespread sentiment that this new global environment threatens
a 'race to the bottom', or at least convergence on the much more modest
level of social provision characteristic of 'liberal' welfare states like the United
States or United Kingdom.

This essay offers a sceptical evaluation of this globalization scenario. Such
scepticism is indeed becoming more common, as many of the core claims
are subjected to more intensive scrutiny (cf. Krugman 1996; A. Martin 1996;
Garrett 1998*b*; Swank 1998*a*; Swank, in this volume; Iversen, in this volume).
In particular, the suggestion that increased trade and the rise of new economic competitors is the principal source of greater wage dispersion, slow
income growth, and higher unemployment in the affluent democracies is now
seen as more suspect.

Why has the globalization thesis been widely accepted in popular discussion
if the direct evidence supporting it is at best weak? The answer is straightforward. What makes the globalization thesis so convincing to many is the
undeniable difficulty that governments now face in funding their social policy
commitments. Austerity has been on the agenda everywhere, and the intensity
of fiscal pressures is clearly growing. Governments appear increasingly unable
to respond to new demands. The correlation in timing between globalization,
on the one hand, and both mounting demands for austerity and strong indica-
tions of lost policy making capacity, on the other, has lent credence to claims
of a causal relationship between globalization and a weakening nation-state.

Rather than directly examining the causal arguments associated with the
globalization thesis, however, this essay takes an alternative tack. It focuses
on trends within the affluent democracies which constitute potential sources
of the strains generally attributed to globalization. The motivation for this
alternative approach has been well summarized by Neil Fligstein:

it is a strong claim to assert that any one structural shift is causing everything we
observe. Given what we know about how most social processes work, they usually
reflect complex causes working together in different ways across time and space. It
should take a lot of evidence to convince us that the globalization story is true.
(Fligstein 1998: 9–10)

I heartily concur. Very broad claims have been made about the connection
between international economic change and the development of national
polities. A great many things are indeed changing in the world, and this sense
of transformation has fuelled such speculation. But many of the important
shifts occurring are related only loosely, or not at all, to the changing international political economy.

In evaluating causal claims, such as the argument that 'increased international economic integration produces intense demands for austerity and

severely weakens the capacities of nation-states to respond to domestic problems', social scientists have recently become more conscious of the need to
make counterfactuals explicit. Arguing that 'A caused B' implies that 'if
A had not occurred, B would not have occurred' (Fearon 1991). It is the
counterfactual of the globalization thesis which I wish to assess. Developing
counterfactuals is difficult. Where we cannot run a controlled experiment,
it is hard to prove what would have happened if A had not occurred. Nonetheless, the available evidence casts doubt on the claim that in the absence
of growing economic integration welfare states would be under dramatically
less pressure, and national policy makers markedly more capable of addressing new public demands.

My central argument is that while welfare states indeed face unprecedented
budgetary stress, it seems likely that this stress is primarily related to a series
of 'post-industrial' changes occurring within advanced industrial democracies
themselves, as the employment profiles of affluent societies have become
increasingly service-based, as their welfare states have matured, as populations
have aged, and as radical changes in household structures have taken place.[1]
To focus on globalization is to mistake the essential nature of the problem.

Perhaps, one might say, it does not matter. Regardless of the sources of
pressure, the strains are very real. Yet it is important to get the causal story
right. In the final section of this essay I argue that a recognition of the diverse
post-industrial transformations carries important implications for our
understandings of the pressure points on contemporary welfare states, the
possible policy alternatives that are likely to dominate political agendas, and
potential cleavage patterns related to proposed reforms. Without claiming
that policy programmes and cleavages can be directly 'read off' an accurate
account of social strains, such an account is surely relevant to developing
plausible political scenarios. More generally, since these diverse trends often
take quite distinct shapes in different welfare regimes, a focus on domestic
transformations provides a much-needed corrective to simplistic arguments
about the likelihood of convergence towards some single model of social provision in the contemporary period.

1. INVESTIGATING THE COUNTERFACTUAL: THE
MULTIPLE TRANSITIONS OF POST-INDUSTRIALISM

In addition to growing global linkages, four profound transitions have
been taking place in the advanced industrial economies: the slowdown in

---

[1] To link these transitions together as 'post-industrial' is slightly awkward, but just as the
term 'globalization' effectively highlights a range of quite distinct international processes, post-
industrialism focuses attention on important domestic socio-economic transformations.

the growth of productivity (and consequently economic growth) associated with a massive shift from manufacturing to service employment; the gradual expansion, maturation, and 'growth to limits' of governmental commitments; the demographic shift to an older population; and the restructuring of households and their relationship to the world of paid employment. Each of these transitions constitutes a powerful and continuing source of pressure on the welfare states of affluent democracies. Globalization is essentially unrelated to the last three of these transitions; its links to the first transformation are at best quite modest.

In short, my counterfactual runs as follows: the slower economic growth and related problems associated with rising service sector employment, the tremendous expansion of governmental commitments, the fiscal demands stemming from population ageing in countries with mature social programmes, and the restructuring of households would, by themselves, have generated much of the current turmoil around the welfare state. Had economic openness remained constant over the past quarter-century, governments would nonetheless face increasing inflexibility and intense fiscal pressure, including tendencies towards deficit spending and demands for programme cutbacks and policy reform. Globalization accompanied these transitions; it has undoubtedly accentuated and modified the pressures on welfare states in important respects. Yet it is these multiple transitions to post-industrialism that have made the real difference.

Slower Productivity Growth, the Rise of the Service Sector, and Welfare State Strain[2]

The first transition, to slower growth of productivity, is now so taken for granted that we forget what a profound impact it has had on the workings of advanced economies. Over time, productivity improvements are the key to sustaining economic growth. It is this slowdown in growth that lies behind much of the current concern about OECD economies. If 3 to 4 per cent economic growth had continued over the past quarter-century, many of our current problems would never have materialized.

It is hard to see how slower productivity growth can plausibly be attributed to increasing international exchange. There is, in fact, a broad consensus among economists that such exchange should be efficiency-enhancing —that it facilitates the allocation of resources to their most productive use and therefore should increase productivity growth rather than retard it. Thus, the sources of slower productivity growth appear to be largely endogenous rather than exogenous to national economies.

[2] This section owes a considerable debt to the work of my colleagues Torben Iversen and Anne Wren.

TABLE 3.1. *Industrial countries: growth of output and employment*

	1960–70	1971–94	1960–94
Output			
Manufacturing	6.3	2.5	3.6
Services	5.3	3.3	3.8
Output per person employed			
Manufacturing	4.6	3.1	3.6
Services	3.0	1.1	1.6
Employment			
Manufacturing	1.7	−0.6	0.0
Services	2.4	2.2	2.2

Source: Rowthorn and Ramaswamy 1997.

While there remains uncertainty concerning the full explanation for declining productivity growth, a central culprit almost certainly has been the massive shift in employment from relatively dynamic manufacturing activities to generally less dynamic service provision. William Baumol long ago pointed out that service industries were generally unable to match the productivity increases typical of manufacturing, and that this would be especially true when services were particularly labour-intensive (e.g. in education, child care, and many aspects of health care) (Baumol 1967). In many services, it is essentially the labour effort itself that we wish to consume. Such activities are resistant to the processes of standardization and replication that are central to efficiency gains in manufacturing. It is extremely difficult in most services to generate the large, continuous increases in productivity typical of manufacturing (Rowthorn and Ramaswamy 1997). Table 3.1 reveals a large and consistent gap in productivity increases between services and manufacturing from 1960 to 1994 in the OECD.[3]

The limited capacity for productivity improvements in services has a number of implications. Relative prices of manufacturing goods are likely to fall. In the United States, for instance, prices of services relative to the price of manufactured goods increased by 22.9 per cent between 1970 and 1990 (Krugman and Lawrence 1994). If, however, demand for services is price-inelastic—remaining high despite rising relative prices—then the relative weight of services in employment will increase.[4] Given stable relative demand for

---

[3] Schwarz (in this volume) rightly notes that there often may be possibilities for productivity improvement or substitution. What is less likely is that such possibilities will allow services to match the productivity growth typical of manufacturing. It is this imbalance, not absolute stagnation, which generates 'Baumol's disease', and it is this persistent imbalance which is clearly signalled by the data in Table 3.1.

[4] In fact the real output share of manufacturing has been relatively constant, probably because the relatively low income elasticity of demand for manufactures has offset the falling relative prices resulting from manufacturing's higher productivity (Rowthorn and Ramaswamy 1997).

FIG. 3.1. Manufacturing and service employment 1960–94
(% civilian employment, OECD average)

Source: OECD, *Historical Statistics, 1960–94* (Paris: OECD).

services and manufactures, large gaps in productivity will mean fewer and fewer workers in manufacturing, and more and more in services. Indeed, as Iversen emphasizes (in this volume), there has been a massive, steady shift in the employment structures of all advanced industrial economies, away from increasingly efficient manufacturing and towards relatively stagnant service provision (see Figure 3.1).

Paul Krugman has stressed that we must recognize a

seemingly paradoxical principle: the kinds of jobs that grow over time are not the things we do well but the things we do badly. The American economy has become supremely efficient at growing food; as a result, we are able to feed ourselves and a good part of the rest of the world while employing only two percent of the work force on the farm. On the other hand, it takes as many people to serve a meal or man a cash register as it always did; that's why so many of the jobs our economy creates are in food service and retail trade. Industries that achieve rapid productivity growth tend to lose jobs, not gain them. (Krugman 1996: 212–13)

Over time, more and more workers are engaged in service provision, where possibilities for productivity improvements are more limited. Inevitably, the consequence will be a slowdown in overall productivity growth, and, all other things being equal, slower economic growth (Appelbaum and Schettkat 1994; Rowthorn and Ramaswamy 1997; see also Iversen and Wren 1998).

It is important to stress that this first 'post-industrial' transition to massive service employment is fundamentally endogenous to domestic economies, based on crucial differences in the possibilities for efficiency improvements in different economic activities (Baumol, Blackman, and Wolff 1989). As Robert Rowthorn and Ramana Ramaswamy put it, 'deindustrialization is simply the natural outcome of the process of successful economic development, and is in general, associated with rising living standards' (Rowthorn and Ramaswamy 1997: 14). That being said, the lower productivity growth associated with expanded activity in services generates acute problems for welfare states. Most directly, slower overall economic growth impedes the growth of wages and salaries, on which the revenues of the welfare state heavily depend— especially but not only in systems heavily dependent on payroll contributions (see Myles and Pierson, in this volume). One can see this clearly in an examination of pension costs. With benefits indexed to prices (at least after retirement), high real wage growth provides an expanding base for financing pension payments. As the growth of real wages slows, however, higher payroll taxes are required to finance higher benefits. In Sweden, for instance, sustained 2 per cent real growth would necessitate payroll tax rates of 23.3 per cent in the year 2025 to meet existing pension commitments. If instead the growth rate were to be 1 per cent, the payroll tax rate would have to rise to 33.1 per cent (Anderson 1998: 13). Thus, low growth has a direct impact on the welfare state's fiscal health. In addition, if slower growth contributes to higher unemployment (e.g. because of labour market rigidities), it further retards revenues while forcing up expenditures.

Nor are the implications of this post-industrial transition limited to simply slower economic growth. Esping-Andersen (1996c), Scharpf (1997b), and Iversen and Wren (1998) have highlighted the contribution of the shift towards service employment to many of the central challenges facing post-industrial political economies in general and welfare states in particular. In Iversen and Wren's elegant formulation, this post-industrial transition confronts governments with a 'trilemma of the service economy', in which the goals of employment growth, wage equality, and budgetary constraint come into increasing conflict. Service sector employment, prone to productivity stagnation and often low-wage, can be generated in only two ways: through the private sector, at the price of increased wage inequality, or through the public sector, where wages may be kept artificially high but at the cost of increased budgetary pressure. Alternatively, countries that manage to hold the line on wage equality and budgetary restraint are likely to see little service sector employment growth and hence rising unemployment.

Strikingly, the three typical responses to this trilemma largely mirror the three regimes (Christian democratic, social democratic, and liberal) identified in Esping-Andersen's *Three Worlds of Welfare Capitalism* (Esping-Andersen 1990). Welfare states in each regime face problems associated with the rise of the service economy, but the nature of the problem depends upon regime type (Esping-Andersen 1996*b*; Iversen and Wren 1998). Social democratic welfare states have increased employment without worsening wage inequality by expanding the public service sector. The budgetary costs of this strategy, however, are increasingly stiff. Public sector social service employment is acutely prone to 'Baumol's disease'. Significant areas of the welfare state involve service provision in 'non-dynamic' sectors. Child care, elder care, education, and other social services are clear examples; health care is a more ambiguous one. Over the long run, such sectors invariably face a secular deterioration in relative prices. Governments have to run faster and faster in order to stand still. If reduction in wages for public employees is not an option, such sectors face the unenviable and continuous prospect of increases in outlays, declining quality of services, or both.[5]

Welfare states in the other regimes face distinct problems, but these are also linked to the changing role of the service sector. For the Christian democratic societies of Continental Europe, public service employment is limited and labour market regulations and high fixed costs (including payroll taxes) impede private service sector employment growth (Scharpf 1997*b*). The dominant problem is lagging employment, with increasingly disturbing implications—not the least of which is the 'death-spiral' scenario of low employment requiring higher payroll contributions, which further lower employment (Esping-Andersen 1996*c*).

In the liberal welfare states, the problems of lost budgetary restraint and unemployment have been largely avoided through policies which encourage the expansion of low-wage private sector service employment. In these countries, the costs include mounting poverty and inequality, large gaps in the support for human capital development, and a host of associated social problems. Again, this scenario places pressures on welfare states—although many of these pressures may simply go unmet.

Here we have a slow-moving but inexorable social process with major ramifications. Less dramatic and exotic than globalization, the shift to services nonetheless represents a profound social transformation. By themselves, the stagnation of service sector productivity and the related decline in overall economic growth after 1973 probably go a long way towards explaining the current predicaments of mature welfare states. Equally important, as the work of Esping-Andersen and Iversen and Wren demonstrates, a focus on this post-industrial transition allows us to zero in on the distinctive predicaments facing different welfare state regimes. I return to this issue in the conclusion.

---

[5] This is of course a problem facing such activities in all countries. It affects public services in all welfare states, but these sectors are not as extensive elsewhere as they are in social democratic countries. Nor is the problem eliminated by transferring such activities to the private sector, as has occurred in liberal welfare states. However, we can expect both the political and economic dynamics to be quite different when Baumol-style cost diseases operate in the private sector. More on this below.

The Expansion of Governmental Commitments and Welfare State Maturation

A second source of pressure is simply the transition to mature welfare states and an expanded set of governmental commitments which has occurred throughout the industrialized world in the post-war period (Flora 1986; Klein and O'Higgins 1988). Welfare states grew at a remarkable pace from 1945 to 1973, far faster than the (very rapid) growth of real GDP. Countries adopted new programmes, 'filling in' their coverage of social risks associated with industrialization. In addition, they expanded eligibility and increased the benefits of existing pensions, disability, and unemployment insurance programmes. Although the pace of expansion slowed down considerably after 1973, most welfare states continued to grow. The wide scope of established governmental commitments is a defining feature of affluent, post-industrial democracies. By themselves, these expanded governmental commitments generate persistent budgetary pressure and a pronounced loss of policy flexibility in the contemporary period.

By far the most important components of this expanding array of governmental commitments are health care provision and pensions. In the EU, these two policy areas accounted for just under two-thirds of total social protection outlays in 1991. Pensions alone accounted for roughly 40 per cent of expenditures on social protection. As will be discussed below, this is partly related to population ageing, but it also fundamentally reflects the expansion and maturation of public pension programmes. Increasingly generous pension systems developed over the past four decades have greatly magnified the fiscal implications of demographic change.

Throughout the OECD, pension benefits are considerably higher than they were forty years ago, not just in real terms but as a percentage of average wages. Almost everywhere, rising outlays in the post-1973 period stem in significant part from more generous benefit provisions, expanded programme coverage, and the gradual maturation of systems in which benefits depend on contributions over a full working life. In the United States, for example, median social security benefits increased from 33 per cent of average male wages in 1950 to 55 per cent by 1980 (Smolensky, Danziger, and Gottschalk 1988: 44). Over the same period, the percentage of elderly Americans receiving social security increased from 16 to 90 per cent (Ball 1988: 28). Substantial benefit increases were enacted in most countries in the 1960s and 1970s. In part at least, governments used promises of pension improvements to purchase labour peace while deferring the costs (Myles 1988). In combination, these trends in benefit levels, programme maturation, and pensioner populations have led to major increases in pensions spending in most OECD countries. Between 1960 and 1990, public expenditures on pensions in the OECD increased from 4.6 to 8.5 per cent of GDP (see

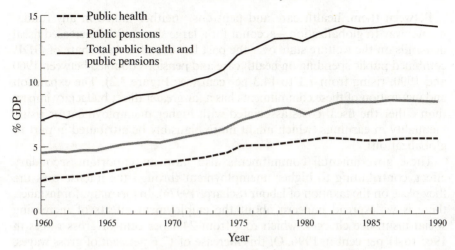

FIG. 3.2 Public spending on pensions and health 1960–90
(% GDP, average for 20 OECD countries)

Countries: Australia, Austria, Belgium (pensions: 1971–), Canada, Denmark, Finland, France, Germany, Greece (pensions: 1962–89), Ireland, Italy, Japan, Netherlands, New Zealand, Norway, Portugal (pensions: 1962– ; public health: 1970–), Spain (pensions: 1967–), Sweden, UK, US. Pensions data contains 1980 break in series.

Sources: OECD, *New Orientations for Social Policy* (1994); OECD, *Reforming Public Pensions* (1988).

Figure 3.2). As will be discussed further below, these commitments contribute to both the sense of fiscal strain and the declining freedom of movement which governments confront today.

Health care represents the other massive social commitment of OECD governments. Again, both the coverage and scope of health care systems expanded dramatically in the post-war period, as governments extended their promises in this critical area of social provision. In the fifteen countries of the European Union, coverage rates of public health care systems increased from an average of 72.2 per cent in 1960 to 97.4 per cent by 1995 (OECD 1998*d*).[6] In addition, the costs of health care have risen inexorably (in part because of the relative price effect in service provision discussed above). As with pensions, this consolidating governmental commitment to health care provision has led to dramatically higher spending. Between 1960 and 1991, average public spending in the OECD on health care increased from 2.5 per cent of GDP to 6.0 per cent of GDP.

[6] With the exception of Germany and the Netherlands, all of these countries now have coverage rates of 99 or 100%.

Between them, health care and pensions—neither linked in any fundamental way to globalization—account for a large share of the increased fiscal
demands on the welfare state over the past few decades. As a share of GDP,
combined public spending on health care and pensions doubled between 1960
and 1990, rising from 7.1 to 14.3 per cent (see Figure 3.2). The expansion
and maturation of these commitments has a far greater direct budgetary impact
than either the fiscal costs associated with higher unemployment or rising
inequality in earnings (which might more plausibly be attributed in part to
globalization).

These governmental commitments also have an important secondary
effect, contributing to higher unemployment through the intense pressure
they place on the taxation of labour (Scharpf 1997*b*). In Germany, for instance,
there is widespread concern about the employment effects of increasing
social insurance charges, which rose from 24.4 per cent of gross wages in
1965 to 41 per cent in 1996. Of this increase of 17.6 per cent of gross wages,
only 4.5 per cent is for unemployment insurance. The remaining 13.1 per
cent is accounted for by rising contribution rates for pensions, health insurance, and the new long-term care insurance programme (Manow 1997*a*:
table 3).

Welfare states matured between 1960 and 1990. For three reasons—none
of which has anything to do with globalization—this maturation process was
bound to lead eventually to a slowdown in programme growth, increased
budgetary stress, and a loss of policy flexibility. First, as social provision
accounted for a growing share of the economy, the opportunity cost associated with further expansions has risen (Klein and O'Higgins 1988). If social
expenditure grows at twice the rate of national income, the cost in foregone
resources is much greater when social spending is 30 per cent of GDP than
it was when that share was 15 per cent of GDP. Second, the pain of taxation has grown over time as rising social expenditures required government
officials to reach further and further down the income distribution in search
of revenues. Mature welfare states require a heavy tax burden on average and
even below-average income households, which necessarily produces growing political tension over expenditure levels. Finally, as maturing welfare states
gradually expanded, the costs of increased generosity (e.g. the impact on
work incentives) were likely to grow, leading to greater controversy. Many
welfare states have failed to adequately address new (or newly recognized)
social risks associated with changing family structure, gender relations, and
the spread of atypical work (see below). In traditional domains such as health
care, pensions, disability, and unemployment, however, welfare states are often
working at the margin—that is, they have grown to limits. As replacement
rates for unemployment insurance or early retirement approached 100 per
cent of wages, the case for stopping expansion, or for rolling back some
instances of overreach, was bound to become stronger.

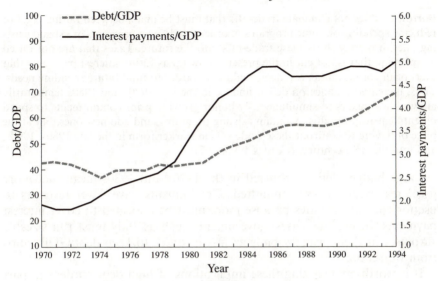

FIG. 3.3. Debt/GDP and interest payments/GDP: G7 countries 1970–94
Source: Tanzi and Fanizza 1996.

All of these correlates of maturing welfare states help to account for a heightened sensitivity to the costs of social provision. There is nothing surprising about any of these tendencies—and certainly no need to invoke globalization to account for them. Rather, they are simple consequences of a core transition of modern affluent societies: the more complete institutionalization of governmental commitments.

A closely related phenomenon is perhaps less 'natural' but nonetheless highly significant: the decline of fiscal slack associated with years of extensive government borrowing. As Figure 3.3 indicates, government debt and associated interest payments have risen considerably over the past two decades (Tanzi and Fanizza 1996). For the industrial countries as a group, spending on interest payments rose from roughly 2 per cent of GDP in 1970 to over 5 per cent of GDP in 1994. This is roughly equal to the increase in spending directly associated with higher unemployment in Europe.[7] Part of this historically unprecedented rise in peacetime debt resulted from miscalculations about the possibilities for reflation in the late 1970s, but it also reflects the mounting fiscal demands outlined above, the willingness of elected officials to defer painful choices, and the relentless logic of compound interest. As Joseph Cordes puts it,

[7] A recent OECD study compared public expenditures on active and passive labour market measures in seven European countries between 1980 and 1993, a period when unemployment in Europe increased from about 6% to around 11%. The average increase in expenditures was around 3% of GDP (OECD 1996g: 24).

Borrowing does not eliminate trade-offs that must be made between raising taxes or reducing spending on some programs in order to add new programs or expand existing ones; it merely shifts these trade-offs into the future. Taxes that are not raised or spending that is not cut in the present show up as future interest payments that exert prior claims on tax revenues, making it harder to fund future spending needs. Thus, increased reliance on deficit finance in the late 1970s and 1980s temporarily allowed lawmakers to simultaneously honor growing prior commitments to spend on entitlement programs, maintain existing programs, and add new ones, but at the price of having to confront these trade-offs in starker form in the late 1980s, 1990s, and into the next century. (Cordes 1996: 107)

Large budget deficits incurred in the 1970s and 1980s mean that more fiscal resources are pre-committed. Governments have fewer revenues to use for current activities because more must be allocated to cover interest payments. In extreme cases, governments such as Italy must run sizeable surpluses in their primary budgets just in order to keep debt/GDP ratios from worsening.

It is worth emphasizing these implications of high debt burdens in part because in Europe the pressures for constraint which they generate will often be attributed to the Maastricht criteria associated with monetary union. EMU is likely to have considerable consequences, exacerbating and channelling pressures for fiscal retrenchment (Pitruzzello 1997). Yet it is essential to realize that the broad constraint on government debt/GDP ratios, and the implications of rising interest payments, would exist in a world without EMU. Nor are the constraints generated by these commitments a product of globalization. Indeed, while the opening of financial markets is often depicted as a crucial curb on the autonomy of national policy makers, financial deregulation has driven down interest rates for many treasuries, arguably facilitating the capacity to borrow.

The vast array of governmental commitments which has accumulated over time is a fundamental feature of post-industrial societies. There is tremendous cross-national variation in the scope and character of these commitments, but they have expanded everywhere. Pensions and health care, perhaps the sectors of the welfare state least connected to processes of globalization, have been at the core of this transformation. This second post-industrial shift and its ripple effects (such as the possible impact on unemployment and the implications of efforts to defer the bill for meeting these commitments) are central to the growing sense of budgetary stress and loss of policy control which characterizes the affluent democracies. As C. Eugene Steuerle and Masahiro Kawai argue, 'most industrial countries are finding that their spending obligations arise more and more from the past . . . If the governments of the industrial world seem to be at bay, these common fiscal problems, more than almost any other factors, have put them there' (Steuerle and Kawai 1996: 1).

Population Ageing

The third critical post-industrial transition is demographic, or more accurately, the evolving interaction between demography and mature social programmes. The populations of the advanced industrial democracies have been ageing, both because birth rates have fallen and because people are living longer. In the OECD, the share of the population over 65 rose from 9.4 per cent in 1960 to 13 per cent in 1990 and is projected to reach 13.9 per cent by the year 2000 (OECD 1988: 12, 22). This represents a very considerable shift—a 50 per cent increase in the elderly's share of the population—with clear implications for public expenditures, since all welfare states are heavily tilted towards the elderly.

And yet this demographic transition is still in an early phase. The increase since 1960 accounts for roughly one-third of the projected total growth in the elderly's share of the population, which is anticipated to eventually reach 23 per cent of the population. The bulk of this demographic transition in most OECD countries will occur between 2010 and 2035 (OECD 1995a). In a more fundamental sense, even a greater proportion of the demographic transition lies ahead. Over the past few decades, the fiscal impact of population ageing has been muted by the very large 'baby boom' cohorts following the current elderly through the life course. Because these large cohorts are in their peak earning years, they provide a solid foundation for financing social benefits for the elderly. The situation will be quite different when the huge baby boom generation moves into retirement and must be supported by a workforce made up of the considerably smaller cohorts which follow. In the OECD, the ratio of the working-aged (15–64) to those over 65 fell by a third between 1960 and 1990 (from 7.5 to 5.0), but it is expected to fall by half between 1990 and 2040 (5.0 to 2.5) (Scherer 1996).

Associated fiscal pressures are beginning to mount. Under policies in effect in 1996, population ageing was projected to produce an additional increase in pensions spending of 3.9 per cent of GDP across the OECD between 2000 and 2030. Particular countries such as Japan (6.3%), Italy (7.7%), and the Netherlands (6.9%) face much larger increases (OECD 1996a: table 12, p. 25). Given the high levels of taxes in many of these countries, and the other sources of fiscal pressure already discussed, these looming increases in pension outlays are attracting considerable attention. Unfunded pension liabilities should be seen as an additional set of commitments, similar to public debt but less visible, which place limits on the flexibility and responsiveness of public officials.

Population ageing is an important factor at work in another area where the welfare state faces strains: the provision of health care. Because the elderly are the biggest consumers of health care, population ageing leads directly to higher health costs. Between 2000 and 2030, population ageing alone is expected to add 1.7 per cent of GDP to health care expenditure in the OECD

(OECD 1996*a*: 25). In combination with pensions, this suggests an average increase in outlays of 5.6 per cent of GDP in the OECD attributable to population ageing alone.

The demographic shift underway is profound, and its effects are felt precisely in the most expensive areas of the welfare state. This is thus a central source of fiscal pressure on national systems of social provision. Like the other two transitions of slower economic growth and the maturation of governmental commitments, the phenomenon of population ageing is slow-moving and undramatic, but it has fundamental consequences over time.

The Transformation of Household Structures

A final transition, equally slow-moving but equally revolutionary, has been the reconfiguration of both household structures and the relationship between households and the world of work. In this case, I group together a number of distinct but interconnected changes: a massive increase in women's labour force participation rates, falling fertility rates, and the fragmentation of households resulting from a sharp rise in single-parent households (due to the increasing prevalence of both divorce and of out-of-wedlock births) and the increasing tendency of single adults and the aged to live on their own. These transformations have led to strains on welfare states designed for a traditional 'male-breadwinner' household structure of intact (or even extended) families, with men acting as wage earners and women providing a variety of non-market services, including child care and elder care within the household.

Social welfare has never been based on a state/market division of labour, but rather on a tripartite division among the state, the market, and private households (Orloff 1993; Sainsbury 1994; O'Connor 1996). Thus, dramatic changes in household structures, and in relationships between the market and the household, have had considerable consequences for welfare states. And because systems of public policy have provided quite varied systems of incentives and supports for particular mixes of state, market, and household activity these changing circumstances have had quite distinctive consequences for different welfare states (Esping-Andersen 1999).

Here I can only briefly highlight four of the most important transformations that are taking place. First, and most critical, the increase in women's labour force participation has been among the most dramatic social shifts of the past generation. In the eleven countries for which the International Labour Office has data for the full time period, labour market activity rates for women aged 15–64 increased from an average of 33.3 per cent in 1960 to an average of 61.9 per cent in 1996 (ILO 1990, 1993, 1997).[8] The degree of

---

[8] The countries are Canada, Denmark, Finland, France, Ireland, Italy, the Netherlands, Norway, Portugal, Spain, and the United States.

change and current levels of participation vary markedly across countries, but the basic trend has been universal.

This remarkable shift has had multiple, often conflicting implications for mature welfare states. Expanding women's labour force participation is central to what Esping Andersen (1999) terms 'defamilialization' and Orloff (1993) would term the heightened capacity of women to form autonomous households. Prospects for increased economic autonomy sometimes reduce the need of women to rely on the state for financial support. At the same time, the movement of women into the paid labour market provides new sources of badly needed tax revenue. Indeed as Huber and Stephens argue in this volume, and as Esping-Andersen has also stressed, reinforcing this trend is probably critical for sustaining the welfare state's long-term fiscal equilibrium. The welfare state's fiscal base looks especially precarious in those countries, typically 'conservative' or 'Continental' welfare states, where women's labour force participation remains relatively low.

At the same time, however, the new possibilities associated with expanded women's labour force participation may also fuel processes of household fragmentation which place new burdens on public social provision. I discuss this issue below. Furthermore, as Orloff has noted, with the movement of women into the labour force 'there are new risks to be insured against —risks, particularly facing women workers, of income interruption due to maternity and participation in caregiving activities' (Orloff 1999: 8). Thus, maternity and parental leave expenses, and the provision of (tax-financed) social security 'credits' for child or elder care, may be added to the pressures on the public purse.

Probably of greater consequence for systems of social provision is the fact that women working outside the home need increased help with social tasks previously carried out within the household, including care for children, the elderly, and the disabled. Strikingly, this is in many cases not an instance of maturing commitments but one of new or expanded initiatives. As Mary Daly puts it, support for caring constitutes 'one of the few growth areas in contemporary welfare states' (Daly 1998: 14; Daly 1997). Whether these previously non-marketized services are provided through public means or through private but marketized means, associated pressures on the welfare state have been increasing. And since the caring services are classic representatives of Baumol's 'non-progressive' sector, the costs of caring provision can be expected to grow over time, even in the absence of demographic shifts.

If such caring services are provided publicly, there will be direct and substantial budgetary consequences. In effect, the state is now paying for many services which used to be provided 'for free' within the context of 'male breadwinner' households or broader kinship networks. The expansion of public sector caring services has been quite uneven across countries

(Gornick, Meyers, and Ross 1998). This is true in part because such a trend is strongly self-reinforcing: the creation of public social services creates both a supply of jobs for women and facilitates the movement of more women into paid employment, which in turn fuels political demand for more public social services (Huber and Stephens 1999). As is well known, the expansion of these programmes has been especially prominent in the countries of Scandinavia (and also in France), which offer comparatively generous supports for child and elder care. In Denmark, for example, households have something close to guaranteed access to public child care and elder care (Ungerson 1997).

Such programmes can be very expensive. By 1995, Denmark, Norway, and Sweden were all spending over 3 per cent of GDP on public and mandatory private expenditures related to services for the elderly and disabled, although the rest of the OECD nations still spent far less (Daly 1998: table A.2). In most countries, however, public funding of caregiving has expanded significantly. Among nineteen OECD countries reviewed by Daly, the United States was the only one in which less than one-quarter of children aged 3–6 were in publicly funded childcare; in 13 of the 19, public coverage exceeded 50 per cent (Daly 1998: table A.1).

In most OECD countries, however, direct public provision of caring services remains limited. Nonetheless, the welfare state feels the indirect effects of the shift towards private, marketized care arrangements (a process which, in line with women's labour force participation rates, has proceeded further in the 'liberal' welfare states than the 'conservative' or 'Christian democratic' ones). If services are provided privately, both the need for care and problems of affordability will become increasingly prominent over time. These pressures will lead to growing demand for subsidies (e.g. in the form of tax expenditures), increased transfer payments (often means-tested) for households with children, or expanded public provision. Thus, even the harsh welfare 'reform' enacted in the United States to move poor mothers into the paid labour market has been accompanied in many states by substantial increases in publicly subsidized child care. In the conservative welfare states, governments seeking to preserve traditional household structures face growing pressures to 'pay' at least something for the household's (i.e. women's) provision of caring services, whether through family allowances, pension credits, or direct payments to those caring at home for the elderly or disabled.

A second major change has been a sharp fall in fertility rates. Cultural change, the availability of birth control, and the expansion of opportunities for women have all led fertility rates to fall sharply across the OECD. Increasing women's labour force participation clearly has played a role here, although it is critical to note that fertility rates are generally now lowest in those countries where women's labour force participation rates are lowest, and where the availability of jobs for women and policies which support the ability of households to combine work and child-rearing are most limited (Esping-Andersen 1999).

As Huber and Stephens stress in their contribution to this volume, the consequences of low fertility for the welfare state are profound (cf. Esping-Andersen 1999). Welfare states that make generous provision for those at the end of the life course are vulnerable to sharp declines in the size of younger populations. Indeed, it is not declining mortality rates that largely explain the trend of population ageing discussed in detail above, since mortality rates have fallen for all ages. Rather, the shift towards an older population structure largely stems from declining fertility.

The third major change in household structure in most of the affluent democracies has been a dramatic increase in the share of single-parent households. Divorce rates have generally risen sharply over the past three decades. In nine OECD countries for which data is available, the divorce rate (per 1,000 married women) rose from an average of 4.1 in 1960 to 10.8 in 1986 (Sorrentino 1990: 44).[9] In the same countries, the prevalence of out of wedlock births increased from 5.4 per cent of all births to 21.4 per cent (Sorrentino 1990: 45). Although the comparative data does not go back so far, the result of these trends has been a sizeable increase in the share of single-parent households among all families with children. In the United States, this share rose from 9.1 per cent in 1960 to 22.9 per cent in 1988. More typical were the German figures, where the share of single-parent households rose from 8 per cent in 1972 to 13.5 per cent in 1988.

The increasing share of single-parent households puts considerable strain on welfare states. Single-parent households, mostly female-headed, are significantly more likely than other families to have low incomes and experience poverty unless the state steps in to fill the gap. Such families often cannot draw on the father's economic resources and must contend with both the limited earning capacities of many women in the labour market and the extraordinary difficulties a single parent faces in combining work and family responsibilities.

A final shift, related to but distinct from the first three, has been the decline in average household size. Households are fracturing. Both young people and the elderly are increasingly prone to be living on their own, and adults are more likely to separate or never form joint households to begin with.[10] While population growth aside from immigration has stopped in many OECD

[9] The countries covered were the United States, Canada, Japan, Denmark, France, Germany, the Netherlands, Sweden, and the United Kingdom. Unless otherwise indicated, all figures in this section refer to that set of countries.

[10] In Japan, fully one-quarter of households in 1960 were made up of married couples living with both their parents and their children; such households constituted 12% of the total by 1985. In Germany, 'stem' families comprising more than two generations made up 11% of the population in 1961, but less than 4% in 1981 (Sorrentino 1990: 45).

countries, the number of households continues to increase significantly. Average household size fell from 3.3 in 1960 to 2.6 by the late 1980s—a drop not fully accounted for by declining fertility rates. Almost everywhere, the fastest growing household type consists of individuals living alone.

The trend towards smaller households has multiple effects, but most important for the welfare state is the difficulty which small households are likely to have in internalizing many aspects of social provision. Large households, including extended families, can share resources and care responsibilities for children, the disabled, and the elderly. Those living in more fragmented family units, and especially those living alone, are more likely to need to turn outside the home for help, often to the state.

It is much more difficult to quantify the consequences of these shifts for the welfare state than the three transitions previously discussed. In pure budgetary terms, the impact is probably more modest because of the significant positive as well as negative fiscal effects of the overall trends. The changes in the role and structure of households has an additional impact, however, which is to generate an understandable and often intense perception of mismatch between the needs of 'new' households and the capabilities of 'old' welfare state structures (Esping-Andersen 1999). Even though this has been the greatest area of new or expanded state initiatives of social protection, such efforts have generally lagged behind the pace of social change.[11] Thus, this post-industrial transition contributes to perceptions of both heightened fiscal strain and diminished public capacity to respond to emergent social needs.

As with the three other transitions discussed, the transformation of the household draws our attention back to domestic processes. In contrast to common variants of the globalization thesis, the current analysis suggests that the affluent, post-industrial democracies have been changing not in one big way, but in many ways. To complete my original counterfactual: the fundamental symptoms of declining governmental capacity and mounting budgetary stress would clearly be with us even in the absence of trends associated with globalization. This is not to suggest that increasing economic integration is unimportant, or to dismiss the linkages between international and domestic developments. Such links, however, are likely to be more modest, complex, and bi-directional than is commonly suggested. At the same time, we need to pay more attention than has recently been the case to profound social transformations that are essentially domestic in character. Societies are becoming more service-based, with a consequential decline in

---

[11] Just as Myles and Pierson (in this volume) argue that the timing of pension system consolidation has a crucial effect on the dynamics of policy reform, so timing matters for efforts to transform gendered aspects of social policy regimes. Current mobilization efforts are likely to be profoundly effected by the fact that such initiatives are occurring against a general backdrop of austerity rather than the expansionary context of the 1950s and 1960s.

productivity growth. Social programmes have grown to maturity. Populations are getting older. Household structures are changing dramatically. These trends, loosely lumped under the label of post-industrialism, explain most of the strain facing the welfare states of affluent societies.

2. IMPLICATIONS FOR THE NEW POLITICS OF THE WELFARE STATE

One could reasonably ask how much any of this matters. To say that the role of globalization in the transformation of welfare states has been over-stated is not to deny that fiscal strains on welfare states are real. Quite the contrary. Welfare states are under intense budgetary pressure, and that pressure is likely to remain and indeed intensify. In this crucial respect the current analysis echoes a central implication of the globalization story. For practical purposes, we have reached a situation of permanent austerity.

Clarifying causality is important, however, for thinking about likely reform agendas and for indicating potential political cleavages. If one's goal is to understand the actions of policy makers, it is important to have a clear sense of the problems they actually confront (though here it is crucial to acknowledge that their perceptions of those problems are critical). Here I wish to briefly sketch out several implications of my argument for an investigation of contemporary welfare state politics.

Distinct Countries, Distinct Problems

Simple versions of the globalization story flatten national differences. If globalization creates a set of overriding imperatives, national characteristics decline in significance. At most, perhaps, these characteristics determine the distance that countries need to travel, and the particular route (more painful or more contentious, say) that they will take.

By contrast, this investigation of trends strongly implies that the growing turbulence around the welfare state retains a distinctly national character. This is clearest with respect to population ageing, where the current and pro-jected pressure on social provision varies quite dramatically across countries (OECD 1995a). This variation depends, critically, on the generosity of pension benefits, fertility rates, and labour force participation rates, especially among women (Esping-Andersen 1996c). Countries vary considerably in the extent to which they have approached a full menu of comprehensive social provi-sion at benefit levels which generate high replacement rates. The Christian democratic welfare state regimes, along with Japan, combine a number of features which will make the pressures associated with population ageing particularly intense. Other countries, such as Ireland and Great Britain, face almost no fiscal strains associated with population ageing. In the United States, pressures on pensions are likely to be modest, but miserable performance in health care cost containment means that fiscal strain in public health care budgets will be acute (Steuerle 1996). Under policies in effect in 1995, pension outlays were projected to peak at over 15 per cent of GDP in Japan, Germany, and Italy (and nearly 15 per cent in France), but to remain well under 10 per cent of GDP in Canada, the United Kingdom, and the United States (OECD 1995a: fig. 13).

The same point applies to the shift to services which typifies post-industrial economies. As Esping-Andersen and Iversen and Wren have explored, while this transition is common to all advanced economies, it places fundamentally different stress points on distinct national models. Social democratic welfare states wrestle with fiscal overload, Christian democratic regimes with mounting unemployment, and liberal ones with worsening wage inequality and high poverty rates. Post-industrial politics, as Iversen and Wren put it, remains 'materialist' politics.

And of course the same can be said for issues related to changing household structures. Although the social trends discussed above are essentially universal in the OECD countries, they have proceeded at different paces and from different starting points. These trends interact with widely divergent systems of public policy. The result is that there remains enormous variation in outcomes across countries (Daly 1998). The character of pressures, political demands, and processes of mobilization are likely to look very different in these distinct contexts.[12]

Thus, this analysis not only points to multiple sources of pressure rather than one overarching process; it also underscores both the extent to which each of these pressures varies cross-nationally and how the specific form in which such pressures appear is shaped by particular patterns of public policy. These variations alone limit the prospects for cross-national convergence, even before one begins to consider how demands for reform are filtered through widely divergent political processes.

The Content of National Reform Agendas

Understanding the sources of strain on national welfare states also allows one to highlight probable programmatic agendas. One's search for solutions is likely to be shaped by understandings of where pressures come from. For instance, both restrictions in trade policy and efforts to increase worker 'flexibility' in export industries look like better candidates for reform if

---

[12] As O'Connor, Orloff, and Shaver (1999) demonstrate in their comparison of liberal cases, there is in fact quite considerable variation within even a single 'family' of gender regimes.

newly industrializing competitors in manufacturing are retarding economic growth than either does if the source is, for instance, slower productivity improvements in services.

The current analysis suggests some of the crucial policy levers for social reformers. In coping with the Iversen/Wren trilemma, instruments to generate service sector employment and improvements in service sector productivity are essential. The appropriate instruments and opportunities may vary considerably depending on the particular 'variety of capitalism' and welfare state regime in place in a particular country (Hall 1998). For instance, Fritz Scharpf (Sharpf 1997*b*) has argued vigorously that some variant of a negative income tax (perhaps engineered through a reform of payroll taxes) could have a big impact on the expansion of service sector employment in the conservative welfare states.

A second major item on most reform agendas will be instruments to manage the budgetary pressures associated with population ageing. Pension systems have become major targets of welfare state reform—understandably, given the budgetary implications of current trends in most countries. Myles and Pierson's chapter considers these responses in detail.

A focus on post-industrial pressures also highlights a critical aspect of agenda formation which alternative perspectives obscure: the tremendous importance of the timing of welfare state reform and the extent to which it is oriented towards long-term issues. The significance of pre-existing commitments in mature welfare states means that contemporary political choices will have long-lasting consequences. Given the difficulty of rolling back social provisions once made, and the powerful impact of compounding on benefit systems which are indexed, a central aspect of reform involves the implementation of policy changes with long lead times.

An illustration from pension systems may clarify this point. The IMF has recently calculated 'contribution gaps' in national pension systems, meaning the rise in average contributions (or cut in benefits) needed over the 1995–2050 period to equalize the government's net asset position in 2050 with its net asset position in 1995. Among the major industrial countries, the average contribution gap is 1.8 per cent of GDP.[13] The IMF spells out the implications of delaying reform:

For the average industrial country, a delay of ten years in addressing pension plan imbalances will permanently increase the contribution rate that will eventually be needed by 0.7 percent of GDP; a 30-year delay would increase the gap to almost 5 percent of GDP. The earlier an adjustment is made, the smaller the adjustment needed. (IMF 1996: 55)

[13] Note that this implies increases in contribution rates of substantially more than 1.8%, since payroll taxes are imposed only on wages, and generally on something considerably less than a country's total wage bill.

The costs of delay are thus very large. In short, both the time-horizons of policy reformers, and their capacity to execute reform in a timely manner become crucial. It is not just a question of how countries implement reform, but when they do so. In this context, the political capacity of systems not only to mobilize support for long-term adjustments but to do so in a relatively speedy fashion should be viewed as a variable of central importance for political scientists.

The Structure of Political Cleavages

Perhaps most important, identifying the major pressures on the welfare state and central programmatic agendas has implications for the analysis of potential cleavages. Once one has a sense of the policy instruments which are likely to be targets for reform, one can seek to identify potential winners and losers from such reforms. As a number of contributors to this volume point out, there is nothing automatic about the process through which such potential cleavages become activated in politics. Nonetheless, they offer helpful clues.

If the welfare state indeed faces permanent austerity, this alone is likely to transform political conflicts over the restructuring of policy. The pressures associated with post-industrialism, intensified in some respects by globalization, also indicate that sustaining existing policy arrangements without adjustment is an increasingly unrealistic option. Continuing low growth coupled with the challenges of creating service sector employment, population ageing, the shifting structure of households, and the overcommitments of existing policies are already generating intense pressures. Tax levels strain public tolerance. Payroll tax burdens and their possible adverse impact on employment and wages create increasingly severe tensions within the traditional support coalitions of the welfare state, particularly in the ranks of private sector unions (Visser and Hemerijck 1997). Barring an extremely unlikely return to an era of high economic growth, fiscal pressures on welfare states are certain to intensify. While tax increases may contribute to closing the gap between commitments and resources, it is difficult to imagine that in many European countries changes in revenues alone could be sufficient to maintain fiscal equilibrium. Thus, even strong supporters of the welfare state increasingly acknowledge that sustaining basic arrangements will require significant reforms.

Welfare state conflict is often portrayed as a clash between those wedded to the status quo and those eager to dismantle basic social protections. In countries where aggressive advocates of neoliberalism have been in power, such as New Zealand and until recently the United Kingdom, this has not been too inaccurate a portrayal. Yet in a climate where social trends make pressures on budgets intense and unrelenting, political cleavages are likely to become more complex. Those seeking restructuring will include many who wish to preserve key elements of the social contract while modernizing it in a manner which contributes to economic performance, does not create unsustainable budgetary burdens, and gives emerging social demands some chance of competing for public attention and resources with well-established ones. In a climate of permanent austerity, restructuring must be distinguished from retrenchment or dismantling, and a simple cleavage between 'pro' and 'anti' welfare state forces is unlikely to emerge. Coalitions among actors with different motivations may be common. For example, poverty advocates may join retrenchment initatives when some of the savings are allocated to expand programmes for the poor (Myles and Pierson 1997). Women's groups may support or acquiesce to austere pension reforms if some of the savings are allocated to address their concerns (Bonoli, in this volume).

The arguments developed here have additional implications for the investigation of cleavages. The dominant political divide suggested by research on globalization has been a split between the tradeable and non-tradeable sectors, often portrayed as essentially a divide between most employers and private sector workers, on the one hand, and public sector workers, on the other (Swenson 1991*b*; Frieden and Rogowski 1996). It is worth noting in passing that one possible implication of the current analysis is that the share of employment in tradeables is actually declining over time, since most services remain non-tradeable. To the extent that such economic cleavages play out in the electoral arena, the declining numbers employed in tradeable sectors may be of significance. My main point here, however, is not to contest this notion of a potential cleavage based on exposure to trade, but to suggest that given the several distinct sources of strain on national systems of social provision, processes of welfare state reform may also activate a number of competing cleavages.

Pension reform, for instance, is high on the agenda almost everywhere. Here, proposed reforms will have major implications for the distribution of benefits and burdens along the lines of income, class, gender, and age. A critical question will be the extent to which adjustments in pension systems fall on those currently in retirement as opposed to current workers. Decisions to tighten links between pension contributions and benefits are likely to disadvantage most women and many blue-collar workers. By contrast, in most cases (countries such as France, which offer especially generous arrangements for public sector workers, are exceptions), these controversial reforms of public pension systems are not likely to produce intense divisions between public and private sector workers. A critical issue, however, will be the manner in which both public and private sector unions choose to balance the conflicting interests of different generations of workers.

Similarly, in the case of health care, pressures for cost containment will generate distinctive divides. Although some countries have massive public sector employment in health care, most do not. Pressures for cost containment in most countries will not fall on public sector workers, but on health care consumers (potentially including cost-shifting to employers where they play a role in health care financing), suppliers (including those in the tradeable sector, such as pharmaceutical firms and equipment manufacturers), and providers (hospitals and medical personnel). The range of potential cleavages in health care reform is likely to be highly diverse, and coalition formation may take quite different paths in different countries.

One needs to be very careful in moving from arguments about cleavages to arguments about coalitions. There is nothing automatic about the process that transforms (theoretically derived) 'winners' and 'losers' from particular reform initiatives into competing flesh-and-blood coalitions. This becomes especially true as the potential lines of cleavages multiply, creating the 'multi-dimensional choice' environments and cycling opportunities that formal theory tells us inhibit the formation of stable, coherent political alignments. Yet who wins and loses from particular patterns of welfare state adjustment (or non-adjustment) is unlikely to be irrelevant to coalition formation. By clarifying what is at stake we can expect to make some progress in identifying the probable stakeholders and their most plausible allies. At a minimum, however, my argument implies a cautionary warning against the scenario of a looming political struggle between public and private sector workers.

Indeed, the broader point of the essay is to caution against the acceptance of a grossly-oversimplified vision of national welfare states under siege from the rising forces of footloose global capital. There is some truth to that account, but far less than is usually suggested. More accurate, if admittedly far less parsimonious, would be an attempt to recognize the implications of multiple, overlapping social transformations occurring within (and interacting with) contexts of quite different national systems of social provision. Developing and evaluating claims about reform dynamics in this more complicated world is an arduous task, but an unavoidable one.

PART II

Adjustment Dynamics:
Economic Actors and Systems of Interest Intermediation

4

Welfare State and Production Regimes in the Era of Retrenchment

Evelyne Huber and John D. Stephens

In recent years, two parallel developments in social science research have advanced our understanding of the institutional configurations of advanced industrial societies, the growing interest in different typologies of welfare states, on the one hand, and the deepening study of varieties of capitalism, on the other. Since the publication of Esping-Andersen's *Three Worlds of Welfare Capitalism* (1990), the dominant approach to the study of welfare states in advanced capitalist democracies has been to study variations in welfare state provisions through the lens of a typology of three or four types of 'welfare state regimes'. In the study of varieties of capitalism, Soskice's (1999) distinction between flexibly coordinated and deregulated market economies focused investigators' attention on the nature of relations among enterprises as well as between enterprises and financial institutions and between them and the government (Albert 1991; Soskice 1999). Thus, it added to the literature on corporatism that had focused mainly on institutionalized interaction between the government, labour, and employers. Of course, the role of organized labour in coordinated market economies retained its importance in the literature on varieties of capitalism, or on what came to be called production regimes (Hollingsworth, Schmitter, and Streeck 1993; Soskice 1999). However, this literature has not really been integrated with the study of welfare states. In their 1992 article Esping-Andersen and Kolberg argued that welfare state regimes are interrelated with different labour market institutions and policies. We expand on this idea here and attempt to link the study of welfare state regimes more systematically to the study of production regimes.[1]

Earlier versions of this chapter were presented at seminars at the Institute for Advanced Study and Princeton University, and at the two conferences at Harvard on which this volume is based. We would like to thank the Institute for Advanced Study for support and a stimulating environment, and the participants in these seminars and conferences for helpful comments, particularly Mauro Guillén, Torben Iversen, Herbert Kitschelt, John Myles, Paul Pierson, Herman Schwartz, Duane Swank, Michael Walzer, and Bruce Western.

[1] Our efforts here run parallel to those of Ebbinghaus and Manow (1998).

We conceptualize production regimes in a parallel manner to welfare state regimes, to denote a configuration of institutions and policies. In the case of production regimes, the relevant institutions are private and public enterprises (industrial and financial), associations of capital interests (business associations and employers' organizations) and of labour, labour market institutions, and governmental agencies involved in economic policy making, as well as the patterns of interaction among all of them; the relevant policies are labour market policy, macroeconomic policy, trade policy, industrial policy, and financial regulation. These institutions constitute national frameworks of incentives and constraints (Soskice 1999) that shape the behaviour of actors and are relatively impervious to short-run political manipulation.

Our analysis proceeds in three steps. First, we provide a conceptualization of welfare state and production regimes and an analysis of their performance up to the 1980s. Second, we analyse pressures on these regimes and resulting welfare state roll-backs since the 1980s. Third, we offer an assessment of possible future paths to adaptation, recovery, and consolidation.

1. WELFARE STATE AND PRODUCTION REGIMES

In his path-breaking work on social policy regimes, Esping-Andersen argues that (1) welfare states vary along multiple dimensions and (2) they cluster around three distinct regimes. While subsequent work on the welfare state has disputed varying aspects of Esping-Andersen's argument,[2] his typology has proved to be a highly useful heuristic explanatory device which we adopt, with a few modifications. First, following F. G. Castles and Mitchell (1993), we distinguish an Antipodean type of 'wage-earner welfare state' (Table 4.1). While these two countries have converged on the liberal welfare states since the beginning of the era of retrenchment which we somewhat arbitrarily date as commencing in 1980, they were quite distinctive at this point in time. Second, we label his conservative/corporativistic group 'Christian democratic'. This labelling is consistent with the 'liberal' and 'social democratic' labels in that it underlines the main political force behind the creation of these welfare states. More important, the label gets away from the misleading implication of Esping-Andersen's work that the 'conservative' welfare states of Continental Europe reinforce inequalities created in the market and thus preserve the stratification system.

---

[2] The main points of criticism concerned the number and type of regimes, the classification of various countries, and the degree to which countries cluster into the three (or four) distinct groups.

We leave it as an open question how clearly countries clustered into four distinct types.[3] We do contend that within a given country, different aspects of the welfare state 'fit' together and 'fit' with different aspects of the production regimes, in particular their labour market components. This 'fit', however, is not a one-to-one correspondence between a whole configuration of welfare state and production regimes. Rather, an essentially similar set of inter-enterprise and employer/labour/government relationships can be the framework within which different specific—but not any—welfare state regimes emerge; conversely, the same welfare state regime is compatible with different—but not any—labour market institutions and policies. The groups themselves vary in their homogeneity, with the Scandinavian social democratic group being the most homogeneous and the Continental Christian democratic being the most heterogeneous, particularly if one includes production regimes into the analysis. Accordingly, we have divided the Christian democratic group into three subgroups.

The data in Table 4.1 outline the basic differences between the policy and institutional configurations in the different types of welfare states.[4] All data are for 1980 or the closest possible year and thus represent a cut in time before significant retrenchment in all but a few cases. The first two columns document, in conjunction with the implicit absent category—years of secular centre and right cabinet—the differences in the political underpinnings of the groups.[5] The Scandinavian countries were distinctive in terms of their years of social democratic governance.[6] Liberal welfare states were characterized by the absence of Christian democratic government and, with the exception of Britain, little or no influence of social democracy in government. The 'wage-earner' welfare states were characterized by strong labour parties, who nonetheless were narrowly defeated in most elections between 1945 and 1980, and by strong unions (see Table 4.2). Thus, the Antipodean labour

---

[3] Japan does not fit into any type and is being treated as a case apart. The economy is a group-coordinated market economy (Soskice 1999) and the welfare state comes closest to a residual model, with very low benefits through the public programmes in pensions and health care. The pillars of the system of social provision are private programmes in the large corporations, from which only a minority of the labour force benefits, and the family (Pempel 1997).

[4] See Appendix to this chapter for data definitions and sources in all tables.

[5] Political differences are not the only factor which distinguishes the groups. Size of the domestic economy, the timing of industrialization, market structure, export product specialization, export orientation, among other factors have shaped the associated labour market and production regimes which in turn have a feedback effect on the welfare state regimes (e.g. see Stephens 1979; Katzenstein 1985b; Hall 1986; Wallerstein 1990). It is beyond this paper to trace these links. We do this in a work in progress (Huber and Stephens, forthcoming).

[6] In the mid-1960s Finland experienced a 'system shift' marked by the coming to power of a social democratic led government including the communists, and by unification of unions and the development of a corporatist social pact with the employers. In the subsequent two and a half decades, Finland caught up with its Nordic neighbours in terms of welfare state generosity (Stephens 1996; Huber and Stephens 1998).

TABLE 4.1. *Welfare state regimes, circa 1980*

	1 Left Cabinet years	2 Christian Democratic Cabinet years	3 Social security expenditure	4 Transfer payments	5 Total taxes	6 Public HEW employment
Social Democratic Welfare States						
Sweden	30	0	31	18	56	20
Norway	28	1	20	14	53	15
Denmark	25	0	26	17	52	18
Finland	14	0	17	9	36	9
Mean	24.3	0.3	23.6	14.5	49.4	15.5
Christian Democratic Welfare States						
Austria	20	15	21	19	46	4
Belgium	14	19	21	21	43	6
Netherlands	8	22	27	26	53	4
Germany	11	16	23	17	45	4
France	3	4	25	19	45	7
Italy	3	30	20	14	33	5
Switzerland	9	10	13	13	33	5
Mean	9.6	16.4	21.6	18.4	42.4	5.0
Liberal Welfare States						
Canada	0	0	13	10	36	7
Ireland	3	0	19	13	39	
UK	16	0	17	12	40	8
USA	0	0	12	11	31	5
Mean	4.7	0.0	15.2	11.5	36.5	6.7
'Wage Earner' Welfare States						
Australia	7	0	11	8	31	7
New Zealand	10	0	16	10	.	
Japan	0	0	10	10	28	3

(1) Left Cabinet: Scored 1 for each year when the left is in government alone, scored as a fraction of the left's seats in parliament of all governing parties' seats for coalition governments from 1946 to 1980 (HRS*).

(2) Christian Democratic Cabinet: Religious parties' government share, coded as for left cabinet (HRS).

(3) Social security benefit expenditure as a percentage of GDP (HRS, ILO†).

(4) Social security transfers as a percentage of GDP (HRS, OECD°).

(5) Total taxes as a percentage of GDP (HRS, OECD).

(6) Public health, education, and welfare employment as a percentage of the working-age population (WEEP•). Canadian figure provided by John Myles on the basis of Statistics Canada data.

* Data from the Huber, Ragin, and Stephens (1997) data set.

° Original data source is OECD.

† Original data source is International Labour Office.

• Data from the Welfare State Exit Entry Project, Science Center—Berlin.

7 Health expenditure % public	8 Health employment % public	9 Pension expenditure % public	10 Spending on non-aged	11 Decommodification index	12 Support for mothers employment
Social Democratic Welfare States					
92	92	86	12.7	39	62
98	88	82	8.5	38	43
85	85	71	11.5	38	64
79	88	69	10.5	29	66
88.5	88.3	77.0	10.8	36.2	58.8
Christian Democratic Welfare States					
69	59	68	4.1	31	
82	31	60	10.2	32	59
76	16	69	12.6	32	34
79	34	70	8.0	28	36
79	63	68	7.5	28	53
84	75	72	3.4	24	36
68	47	71		30	
76.7	46.4	68.3	7.6	29.3	43.6
Liberal Welfare States					
75	78	58	5.7	22	35
92		55	6.8	23	
90	95	67	9.2	23	22
42	23	61	4.5	14	14
74.8	65.3	60.3	6.6	20.6	23.7
'Wage Earner' Welfare States					
62	58	59	2.8	13	22
84		88	3.1	17	
71	19	54	2.4	27	

(7) Public health expenditure as a percentage of total health expenditure (HRS, OECD).

(8) Public health employment as a percentage of total health employment (WEEP). Canadian figure provided by John Myles on the basis of Statistics Canada data.

(9) Public pension spending as a percentage of total pension spending (Esping-Andersen 1990: 85).

(10) Spending on the non-aged as a percentage of GDP (OECD 1996d: 107).

(11) De-commodification index (Esping-Andersen 1990: 52).

(12) Support for mothers' employment (Gornick et al. 1998).

movements relied on 'social protection by other means', that is, through highly regulated labour markets (F. G. Castles 1985). Since the Christian democratic welfare states were the most heterogeneous, we have broken them down into three subgroups. The first 'group' contains the lone country of Austria. It is the only Christian democratic welfare state in which social democracy is more influential than Christian democracy. Its production regime, particularly relations between capital, labour, and the government, and to a lesser extent its labour market policies, were closer to the social democratic model than to the Christian democratic. In the next group, Belgium, Netherlands, and Germany, social democracy was influential but not as influential as Christian democracy. Along with Austria, these countries also were more generous than the other three Christian democratic countries on most of the welfare state indicators in Table 4.1. These countries also shared—to different degrees— production regime characteristics with the Nordic economies which set them off from the other three countries in the Christian democratic group.

As one can see from the table, both the Christian democratic and social democratic welfare states were much more generous than the other groups in terms of their social expenditure (columns 3, 4, 7). Indeed, it would appear that the Christian democratic welfare states actually provided more generous transfer payments than the social democratic welfare states. While it is true that they spent more on transfers and they were 'transfer heavy' as compared to the 'service heavy' social democratic welfare states (Huber, Ragin, and Stephens 1993; Huber and Stephens 2000), the transfer spending figures in Table 4.1 for Christian democratic welfare states were high in part because the target populations (the unemployed and people on early retirement) were large.

Esping-Andersen's de-commodification index (column 11) is a better indicator of the generosity of transfer entitlements than the transfer expenditure figure. It is a composite measure of the characteristics of three income transfer programmes (pensions, sick pay, and unemployment compensation), the components of which are various measures of qualifying conditions and benefit duration and income replacements for two categories of workers, a 'standard production worker' and those qualifying for only minimum benefits (Esping-Andersen 1990: 49, 54). One can see from the index that social democratic welfare state transfer systems were more generous than the Christian democratic ones. Other data from the Social Citizenship Indicators Project at the University of Stockholm and other sources indicate that a principal reason for the difference between the social democratic and Christian democratic welfare states on the index was that income replacement rates among those with minimum qualifying conditions were much better in the Nordic countries (Palme 1990; Kangas 1991; Carroll 1994; OECD 1994c).

It was not, however, in the structure of transfers that the social democratic welfare states and Christian democratic welfare states differed most. As we have shown in an analysis of pooled times series data, the most distinctive feature of the social democratic welfare state was the public funding and delivery of social services (Huber and Stephens 2000). One can see the dramatic differences in this regard from the figures for public health, education, and welfare employment as a percentage of the working age population in column 6 of Table 4.1. In the case of health care, it is clear from a comparison of the figures in columns 7 and 8 that other welfare states pick up the tab for health but are not the primary deliverers of it. Outside of the Nordic countries, only three other countries, the UK, New Zealand, and, from 1978, Italy, had national health services and in two of these (UK and New Zealand), they were products of social democratic governments. The expansion of additional social programmes; child care, elderly care, job training programmes, temporary employment programmes in the public services, after school programmes, to name a few examples; along with improvement of maternal and parental leave programmes were the main areas of welfare state innovation in the Nordic countries in the 1970s and 1980s. The difference in the level of public social services was the reason why taxation levels in social democratic welfare states were significantly higher than in the Christian democratic welfare states, averaging close to 49 per cent of GDP compared to 42 per cent in the latter group (Table 4.1, column 5) despite the fact that transfer payments were actually lower on the average in the social democratic welfare states.

Two distinctive features of the social service intensiveness of the social democratic welfare states are worth underlining. First, they were 'women friendly' and promoted the expansion of women's labour force participation which we examine below. This is reflected in the index in column 12 which measures the extent to which a wide range of social provisions facilitate mothers with young children entering the labour force. Second, they were aimed at the non-aged as can be seen from the OECD figures on spending on the non-aged as percentage of GDP in column 10 of Table 4.1.[7] In both cases, these distinctive features involved investment in human capital and in the mobilization of labour.

Turning now to the relationship between welfare state and production regimes, we take as our point of departure Soskice's (1999) conceptualization and add a more explicit treatment of the role of the state. Soskice emphasizes employer organization and relationships between companies and financial institutions as defining characteristics of production regimes. Employer organization takes three distinctive forms: coordination at the industry or sub-industry level in Germany and in most Northern European economies (industry-coordinated market economies); coordination among groups of companies across industries in Japan and Korea (group-coordinated market economies); or absence of coordination in the deregulated systems of the Anglo-American countries (uncoordinated market economies). He notes that France was an example for a different type of production regime, where the state played the leading role. In coordinated economies, employers are able to organize collectively in training their labour force, sharing technology, providing export marketing services and advice for R & D and for product innovation, setting product standards, and bargaining with employees. The

---

[7] These figures underestimate the differences between the social democratic and Christian democratic welfare states because they include spending on early pensions and disability pensions which were employed as means of labour force reduction in a number of the Christian democratic welfare states at this time.

capacity for collective action on the part of employers shapes stable patterns of economic governance encompassing a country's financial system, its vocational training, and its system of industrial relations.

A central characteristic of the coordinated economies is the generalized acceptance by all major actors of the imperative of successful competition in open world markets. Successful competition in turn requires a high skill level of the labour force and the ability of unions to deliver wage restraint to the extent needed to preserve an internationally competitive position. In the industry-coordinated market economies of Central and Northern Europe, initial labour skills are effectively organized in companies or with strong company and union involvement in public schools. Unions are organized mainly along industrial lines and play an important cooperative role in organizing working conditions within companies and in setting wage levels for the economy as a whole. Banks and industries are closely linked providing industries with preferential sources of long-term credit, or the state plays a major role in bank ownership and performs a similar role in preferential credit provision for industry. In uncoordinated market economies, in contrast to both types of coordinated economy, training for lower level workers is not undertaken by private business and is generally ineffective. Private sector trade unions are viewed as impediments in employer decision making, have little role in coordinating their activities, and are weak. Bank–industry ties are weak and industries must rely on competitive markets to raise capital.

While Soskice's analysis focuses heavily on factors underpinning competitiveness in manufacturing and on organization of capital and labour, these institutional frameworks can be seen as national/economy wide (see Kitschelt et al. 1999) and as further differentiated by the extent of state involvement in capital and labour markets. With this extension, one can distinguish a Nordic pattern in which there was economy-wide bargaining and a large state role in economic management from the Continental pattern in which bargaining was generally carried on at the industry level and the state's role was more muted. In the social democratic welfare states and the Northern tier of Christian democratic welfare states, the combination of strong unions and dependence on competitive exports necessitated a policy of wage restraint and the centralization of unions, employers' organizations, and the bargaining process made such a policy possible, with the temporary exception of the Netherlands. The unions' 'side payment' for wage restraint, at least up to the mid-1970s, was full employment and the development of the generous welfare state described above.

In the case of the Nordic countries and Austria, fiscal and monetary policies were moderately counter-cyclical and backed up by occasional devaluations.[8] The core of the long-term growth/employment policy, however, was a com-

---

[8] Austria and Finland were partial exceptions in that the Austrian currency was pegged informally to the German Mark in the 1960s already, and Finnish fiscal and monetary policies tended to be pro-cyclical.

bination of supply-side and tax policies which themselves largely affected the supply side.[9] Key among the supply-side policies were an active labour market policy (though in Austria only from the 1970s on), regional policies, and support for selected industries. Tax policies heavily favoured reinvestment of profits over distribution and industrial investors over consumers. Interest rates were kept low through credit rationing, state supply of cheap credit, and through public sector surpluses. These policies were predicated on financial controls. In addition, fiscal policy was generally austere: these countries usually ran budget surpluses. The demand side of the growth/employment models in these small countries was only in part internally generated; it was to a large part a result of demand for exports created by the vigorous post-war growth in the core advanced capitalist economies of North America and Europe.

Table 4.2 outlines some of the parameters of the production regimes, particularly labour market institutions, corresponding to the welfare state types. Given that at least some strands of the literature on corporatism consider social democratic government to have been a precondition for corporatism (Western 1991), it is not surprising that countries with social democratic welfare states were highly corporatist as indicated by Lehmbruch's (1984) scale of corporatism (column 4). The countries with Christian democratic welfare states, particularly the four countries of the Northern tier, were also highly corporatistic. However, if one wants to draw a distinction between the formal institutional features of corporatism and the effective participation of labour in the sense of exercising significant influence through these institutions, then one could not classify the Netherlands as equally strongly corporatist as Sweden, Norway, and Austria.

Union organization and coverage were very high in the social democratic countries and only slightly lower in the wage-earner welfare states. While union density was lower in the Christian democratic countries, coverage of union contracts was quite high due to agreements between employers and unions which extend union agreements to non-unionized workers or to government legislation which achieved the same end. Wage setting was also very centralized in the social democratic and wage-earner welfare states and very decentralized in the liberal welfare states with the Christian democratic welfare states falling in between. However, just as in the case of corporatism, one must be careful in ranking countries in terms of bargaining centralization on the basis of formal institutional arrangements only. On the Wallerstein (forthcoming) measure (column 5), both Austria and Germany appear to have had relatively low wage-setting centralization. If one looks at where collective agreements were signed, this is plausible, as in both countries agreements were signed at the industrial level and not at the national level. However,

---

[9] Because of the heterogeneity of the Christian democratic pattern of state intervention and macroeconomic management and the idiosyncrasy of the Antipodean pattern, it is impossible to give a complete accounting of all four production regimes here. See Huber and Stephens, forthcoming, chs. 4 and 5.

TABLE 4.2. *Labor market regimes, circa 1980*

	1 Female labour force participation	2 Union density %	3 Union coverage	4 Corporatism index	5 Centralization of wage setting	6 Wage dispersion†	7 Active labour market policy spending / unemployment†
Social Democratic Welfare States							
Sweden	74	82	83	4	60	2.0	75
Norway	62	59	75	4	57	2.0	26
Denmark	71	70		3	60	2.1	20
Finland	70	73	95	3		2.5	18
Mean	69.3	71.1	84.3	3.5	59.0	2.2	35
Christian Democratic Welfare States							
Austria	49	66	71	4	20	3.5	8
Belgium	47	72	90	3	34	2.4	10
Netherlands	35	38	60	4	47	2.5	10
Germany	51	40	76	3	20	2.7	10
France	54	28	92	*	20	3.3	7
Italy	39	51		2	40	2.6	4
Switzerland	54	35		3		2.7	23
Mean	47.0	47.0	77.8	3.2	30.2	2.8	10

	(1)	(2)	(3)	(4)	(5)	(6)	(7)
Liberal Welfare States							
Canada	57	31	38	1	9	4.0	6
Ireland	36	68		3			9
UK	58	48	47	2	28	2.8	6
USA	60	25	18	1	6	4.8	4
Mean	52.8	43.0	34.3	1.8	14.3	3.9	6
'Wage Earner' Welfare States							
Australia	53	51	80	1	40	2.8	5
New Zealand	45	59	67	1		2.9	20
Japan	54	31	21	*	16	3.0	6

* concertation without labor, † mid-eighties data for Belgium, Netherlands, and New Zealand, 1991 for Switzerland.

(1) Female labour force participation: percentage of women age 15 to 64 in the labour force (HRS, OECD).

(2) Union density: union membership as a percentage of total wage and salary earners (HRS, Visser 1996b).

(3) Union coverage: union contract coverage as a percentage of total wage and salary earners (Traxler 1994).

(4) Corporatism index (Lehmbruch 1984).

(5) Centralization of wage setting (Wallerstein, forthcoming).

(6) Wage dispersion: 90–10 ratio: the wages of a full-time employee at the 90th percentile of the wage distribution as a multiple of one at the 10th percentile (OECD 1996a).

(7) Active labour market spending as percentage of GDP divided by the percentage of the labour force unemployed. Calculated according to Nickell (1997) by David Bradley.

as Soskice (1990*b*) makes clear, one must distinguish between the degree of centralization of bargaining institutions and the degree of coordination of wage setting. In Germany as well as in Austria, there traditionally was a high degree of economy-wide coordination of wage setting, more formal in Austria and more informal—but not less effective—in Germany.

As a result of the differences in union organization, bargaining centralization, wage setting, and union contract coverage, wage dispersion was much greater in the liberal states than in the social democratic states again with the Christian democratic welfare and the wage-earner welfare states falling in between, but in this case closer to the social democratic group. In fact, other than in Austria, wage dispersion in the Northern tier countries was much more similar to that in the Nordic countries.[10]

The social democratic welfare states were very different from the Christian democratic welfare states, including the Northern tier, and the wage-earner welfare states in terms of women's labour force participation and, as a result, in the levels of total labour force participation of the working-age population. The high level of women's labour force participation was both a result and a cause of the Nordic welfare state/labour market pattern (Huber and Stephens 2000). The growth of women's labour force participation beginning in the 1960s stimulated demands by women for the expansion of child care and other social services which, along with social democratic governance, helped fuel the growth of public social service sector employment. These public social service jobs were filled very disproportionately by women, so this in turn stimulated a further expansion of women's labour force participation. The Continental Christian democratic welfare states followed a quite different trajectory. Foreign labour was imported in large numbers, arguably due to a combination of Christian democratic emphasis on the traditional male breadwinner family and weaker union influence on labour recruitment policies. Moreover, in these countries, union contracts cover a large proportion of the labour force, which prevented a rapid expansion of a low-wage service sector, a source of employment for women in liberal welfare states (Esping-Andersen 1990). As a result women's labour force participation was the lowest in the Continental Christian democratic welfare states of the three welfare state types, despite the fact that social policy is more 'working mother friendly' in the Christian democratic than the liberal welfare states (compare column 1 of Table 4.2 with column 12 of Table 4.1).

As a result of these labour market configurations, then, both social democratic and Christian democratic welfare states did not produce the dualist labour markets with a low-wage sector, largely though not entirely in services, a characteristic of the liberal welfare states.[11] This 'fits' with the

---

[10] For a discussion of Austria's outlier status in this regard, see Pontusson 1996.

[11] Italy does have a low-wage sector in the black market and Spain and Portugal have yet larger black and informal sectors.

generous welfare states of these countries and with an overall 'high road' economic strategy, based on high-quality/high-wage manufacturing for export, and thus with the type of production regime these countries have.

As we pointed out above, adding characteristics of the production regime to the analysis challenges the assumption that countries follow clear patterns and form neat clusters. So, for instance, while most of the Christian democratic welfare states of Continental Europe were coordinated market economies, Soskice points out that the Netherlands and Italy only partly fit this designation and France had a state-led production regime. Or, Denmark had different inter-firm relations from and relied much more on small to medium firms for export than do the other Scandinavian countries, yet it developed a social democratic welfare state regime. Rather than abandoning the typology of welfare states and production regimes altogether, though, our solution is to treat the types as ideal types to which countries more or less conform. Moreover, we would contend that within each country, certain—though not all—aspects of its welfare state and production regimes do 'fit' each other. Specifically, wage levels and benefit levels have to fit, and labour market and social policies have to be in accord such as not to create perverse incentives. In addition, the type of production for the world market has to fit with the qualification of the labour force and with wage and benefit levels. Business/labour/government coordination in R & D, training, and wage setting makes it possible to engage in high-quality production and thus to sustain high wages and a high social wage.

The production regimes of the wage-earner welfare states were quite unique. As we mentioned above, this type of welfare state regime delivered social protection primarily through the wage regulation system which provided a male breadwinner wage and a number of social benefits to the wage earner. It was developed early in this century in an explicit compromise in which industry received protection and was enabled by the transfer of resources from a highly productive primary product export sector.

The combined welfare state regimes and production regimes, particularly their labour market aspects, result in very large differences in the distributive outcomes in the three groups of welfare states, as one can see from Table 4.3, which is based on Luxembourg Income Surveys for the nearest possible date to 1980.[12] The differences in income distribution after direct taxes and transfer payments between the social democratic welfare states and the Northern tier of Christian democratic welfare states and the other countries were particularly striking (column 1). These figures do not include the distributive effect of free or subsidized public goods and services which would increase equality in all welfare states (Saunders 1991), but particularly in the social democratic welfare states.

---

[12] The only exception to this rule is the French case. For France, we use the 1984 BF LIS data because LIS considers them to be more reliable.

TABLE 4.3. *Welfare state outcome, circa 1980*

	1 Year of LIS Survey	2 Post tax transfer Gini	3 Redistribution resulting from taxes and tranfers	4 Post tax transfer Gini—Aged	5 % of group in poverty 25–59	6 Aged	 Single mothers
Social Democratic Welfare States							
Sweden	1981	0.20	52	0.16	4.8	0.3	7.7
Norway	1979	0.22	40	0.26	3.7	4.7	12.1
Denmark	1987	0.26	36	0.24	4.8	9.2	4.5
Finland	1987	0.21	38	0.22	3.0	3.0	4.8
Mean		0.22	41.4	0.22	4.1	4.3	7.3
Christian Democratic Welfare States							
Austria	1987	0.23		0.25	2.3	6.0	13.3
Belgium	1985	0.23	46	0.23	4.4	6.0	14.2
Netherlands	1983	0.28	38	0.27	6.7	3.9	6.6
Germany	1981	0.25	38	0.29	4.2	10.0	6.0
France	1984	0.33	34	0.37	15.9	18.9	22.8
Italy	1986	0.31	28	0.30	10.5	8.3	17.5
Switzerland	1982	0.32	21	0.37	6.1	15.2	22.4
Mean		0.28	34.2	0.30	7.1	9.8	14.7
Liberal Welfare States							
Canada	1981	0.29	24	0.31	10.3	9.3	42.0
Ireland	1987	0.33	35	0.32	10.9	4.9	15.4
UK	1979	0.27	33	0.26	5.5	4.8	10.8
USA	1979	0.31	26	0.34	11.9	21.8	42.3
Mean		0.30	29.4	0.31	9.7	10.2	27.6
'Wage Earner' Welfare States							
Australia	1981	0.29	29	0.29	9.3	5.3	44.8

All data in Table 4.3 are from Luxembourg Income Surveys. The calculations were done by David Bradley with household adjustments and other definitions such that the figures are consistent with those in Mitchell (1991), Atkinson, Rainwater, and Smeeding (1995), and those periodically updated at the LIS website (http://lissy.ceps.lu).

(1) Gini index for disposable household income.

(2) Redistribution: percentage reduction in the Gini index for pre-tax and transfer income caused by taxes and transfers (Mitchell 1991).

(3) Gini index for disposable household income among the aged.

(4) Poverty—Age 25–59: percentage of households in which the household head is between 24 and 60 with disposable incomes below 50% of the average disposable household income.

(5) Poverty—Aged: percentage of households in which the household head is over 65 with disposable incomes below 50% of the average disposable household income.

(6) Poverty—Single mothers: percentage of single mothers with disposable incomes below 50% of the average disposable (post-tax and post-transfer) household income.

Columns 4–6 of Table 4.3 document differences in poverty levels in countries with different welfare state regimes. Poverty is defined as less than 50 per cent of median income in the country in question. It is clear that again the social democratic welfare states did very well in combating poverty and the liberal welfare states very poorly. The Northern tier of Christian democratic welfare states were almost as effective as the social democratic welfare states (though again one has to observe that free or subsidized public goods and services are not included in these figures). Cross-national differences in disposable income inequality were in part a product of variations in market income inequality and these in turn are in large part a product of wage dispersion and unemployment levels. From Tables 4.2, 4.3, and 4.4, one can see that part of the reason for egalitarian outcomes in the social democratic welfare states and the Northern tier of Christian democratic welfare states is that, in the early 1980s, these countries had compressed wage differentials or low unemployment or both.

As to the redistribution effected by taxes and transfers, Korpi and Palme's (1998) analysis demonstrates that the systems which combine 'basic security', usually transfers with flat rate benefits, and 'income security', transfers with earnings-related benefits, have the greatest redistributive impact. The Nordic pension systems which combined a flat rate citizenship pension and an earnings-related supplement are good examples of this type, and Korpi and Palme point out that most other programmes and thus the Nordic welfare states as a whole had this structure. In contrast to the social democratic welfare states, entitlements in the Christian democratic welfare states were primarily employment based and earnings related. They generally lacked the basic security tier; the task of meeting the needs of those outside the labour market falls to means-tested benefits. What is very surprising is that the Christian democratic welfare states with their great reliance on employment-based, earnings-related benefits were more egalitarian in their impact than the liberal welfare states with their greater reliance on programmes targeted to the needy. That this is true can be readily seen from Table 4.3. Part of the explanation, Korpi and Palme argue, is that the Christian democratic welfare states were simply much larger: though their benefit structures were less egalitarian, they more than make up for it in greater expenditure. In addition, where benefits are generous, they tend to squeeze out private alternatives as can be seen from column 9 of Table 4.1 (see Kangas and Palme 1993; Stephens 1995). As Kangas and Palme show, these private alternatives are invariably much more inegalitarian than the most inegalitarian of public pension systems (the Finnish).[13]

---

[13] This begs the question of why targeted welfare states (and targeted welfare policies within welfare states) are so ungenerous. The answer generally given in the comparative welfare states literature is that precisely because they are targeted, they have a narrow support base and thus few supporters and many opponents.

As to the policy measures which are most effective in combating poverty, we can give more precise answers, particularly with regard to the two groups most vulnerable to poverty, the aged and single mothers. Palme's (1990) data on minimum pensions for the early 1980s make it abundantly clear that the level of minimum pensions was the main factor which accounts for the international differences in poverty levels among the aged. As for single mothers, the two factors which appear to explain the most variation in poverty rates are family allowances and high levels of labour force participation among young women which in turn is in part a product of policies supporting mothers' employment. For the working-age population, levels of wage dispersion and low levels of unemployment would appear to be the most important factors determining pre-tax/transfer distributive outcomes. For those dependent on transfers, unemployment compensation and social assistance are obviously important measures for poverty reduction. Since child allowances are generally flat rate and in no case vary directly with income, they are also an effective means of combating poverty, not just among single mothers but among all low-income families.[14]

Table 4.4 outlines the performance of the different countries, again grouped by welfare state regimes, in growth and employment. As the table indicates, it is difficult to maintain that the generous social democratic and Christian democratic welfare states have been a clear drag on economic growth or unemployment levels. A more complex argument might be made in which it is claimed that generous social policy and high taxes produce micro-level disincentives which are a drag on growth, but then the associated production regimes provide contrary incentives which more than make up for the disincentives.[15] Both the social democratic and Christian democratic welfare states were built in economies very open to trade and, especially in the social democratic welfare states, they were built around the interest of the export sector workers whose unions were the dominant force within their respective union movements. These workers and unions had and have strong interests in the competitiveness of the export economies of their countries. These countries chose a high road niche in the world economy based on highly skilled and educated labour, cooperative production, and capital-intensive production techniques, which is compatible with both high wages and generous social benefits.

---

[14] See Huber and Stephens, forthcoming, ch. 4, for a detailed discussion of the link between labour market and policy configurations and the variations in poverty rates across the regimes.

[15] For instance, in a 1996 issue of *The Economic Journal*, Agell (1996) claims that micro-level disincentives were a serious problem in Sweden, while Korpi (1996) and Dowrick (1996) argue the aggregate growth figures do not sustain the view that the welfare state is a drag on growth. What we are pointing out in the text is that both could be true. In fact, a recent comprehensive review of the empirical literature on the work disincentives of taxes and social benefits reveals that the studies to date yield very contradictory findings (Atkinson and Mogensen 1993).

TABLE 4.4. *Unemployment and growth*

	Unemployment				Growth			
	1960–73	1974–9	1980–9	1990–4	1960–73	1973–9	1979–89	1990–3
Social Democratic Welfare States								
Sweden	1.9	1.9	2.4	5.2	3.4	1.5	1.8	−1.6
Norway	1.0	1.8	2.7	5.6	3.5	4.4	2.3	2.0
Denmark	1.4	6.0	8.1	10.9	3.6	1.6	1.8	1.0
Finland	2.0	4.6	5.1	12.3	4.5	1.8	3.2	−3.6
Mean	1.6	3.6	4.6	8.5	3.8	2.3	2.3	−0.6
Christian Democratic Welfare States								
Austria	1.7	1.6	3.3	3.9	4.3	3.0	1.9	1.0
Belgium	2.2	5.7	11.3	10.7	4.4	2.1	1.9	1.2
Netherlands	1.3	5.0	9.7	6.2	3.6	1.9	1.1	1.2
Germany	0.8	3.4	6.7	7.8	3.7	2.5	1.7	2.1
France	2.0	4.6	9.1	10.6	4.3	2.3	1.6	0.2
Italy	5.3	6.3	9.3	10.6	4.6	3.2	2.4	0.7
Switzerland	0.0	0.4	0.6	2.7	3.0	−0.1	1.8	−0.8
Mean	1.9	3.9	7.1	7.5	4.0	2.1	1.8	0.8
Liberal Welfare States								
Canada	5.0	7.2	9.3	10.3	3.6	2.9	1.8	−1.0
Ireland	5.2	7.6	14.3	14.9	3.7	3.3	2.7	4.8
UK	1.9	4.2	9.5	8.4	2.6	1.5	2.2	−0.3
USA	5.0	7.0	7.6	6.6	2.6	1.4	1.5	0.8
Mean	4.3	6.5	10.2	10.1	3.1	2.3	2.1	1.1
'Wage Earner' Welfare States								
Australia	2.0	5.1	7.5	9.6	3.2	1.5	1.8	0.3
New Zealand	0.2	0.8	4.4	9.2	2.2	−0.2	1.4	0.6
Japan	1.3	1.8	2.4	2.3	8.3	2.5	3.4	2.2
Grand Mean	2.2	4.2	6.9	8.2	3.8	2.1	2.0	0.6

Unemployment: unemployment as a percentage of the total labour force (OECD, HRS).
Growth: growth of real GDP per capita (OECD 1995*b*: 50).

2. WELFARE STATE RETRENCHMENT AND CHANGES IN PRODUCTION REGIMES SINCE 1980

In our quantitative and comparative case work on welfare states in the era of retrenchment (Huber and Stephens 1998, forthcoming, chs. 6 and 7; Stephens, Huber, and Ray 1999), we find that roll-backs and 'restructurings' in welfare state programmes have been a universal phenomenon in the past two decades. We distinguish 'restructuring' from roll-back as some programmes, most significantly public pension systems, have been significantly restructured in a fashion in which the benefits have not been significantly cut but contributions or taxes have been increased to make the pension systems viable.

Indeed, pension systems have a special dynamic and because they are dealt with at length in Myles and Pierson's contribution to this volume we will simply make a few observations on the antecedent causes of changes in pension system. As Myles and Pierson (in this volume; Myles 1997) point out, the pressures on pensions system were created by a combination of demographic and economic change. As a result of increasing longevity and declining birth rates, the populations of advanced industrial democracies have aged and will continue to do so as the post-World War II generation moves into retirement. The decline in wage growth and increase in the returns on capital in the present era as compared to the Golden Age made the PAYG systems designed in the previous era unviable and made more fully funded systems more attractive alternatives. We would add that, to the extent that financial internationalization has contributed to slower wage growth and higher interest rates as we will argue below, it contributed to the pressures to restructure the pension systems.

As to actual cutbacks—reductions in social benefits and social services— our case studies indicate two different dynamics: ideologically driven cuts, which occurred in only a few cases, and unemployment driven cuts, which were pervasive. It is the timing and severity of the latter type of roll-backs that argues that they were largely unemployment driven. The countries where unemployment rose early (Denmark and the Netherlands) initiated cuts in the mid-1970s, the countries where unemployment rose late (Sweden, Norway, Finland) continued to expand welfare state entitlements until the late 1980s. The countries where unemployment levels remained very high for a long time (e.g. the Netherlands) made deeper cuts than the countries where they remained more moderate (e.g. Norway). This is not to say that all the policy changes were somehow dictated by economic constraints; perceptions and beliefs about the effectiveness of different policies in achieving certain goals did play a role. Thus, the rising hegemony of neoliberal doctrines certainly contributed to the roll-backs.

These roll-backs in most cases did no more than reduce the increase in welfare state expenditures. In fact, if we look at the aggregate data for the different welfare state types, the average annual increase in most indicators of welfare state expenditures in the 1970s was higher than it had been in the Golden Age, and it continued to increase in the 1980s though at a slower pace than in the previous two periods. Essentially, in the 1970s governments countered the deteriorating economic situation with traditional Keynesian counter-cyclical policies, but by the 1980s they had all realized that the rules of the economic game had changed and demanded new approaches. Still, the increase in claimants of benefits kept pushing up expenditures.

Retrenchments generally began with lags in adjustments of benefits to inflation and increased co-payments for welfare state services, particularly health care. The data on public share of total health care expenditures reflect these economizing measures; the average annual increase in the public share was already lower in the 1970s than in the earlier period, and in the 1980s the public share declined. Increases in waiting days for benefits, decreases in the length of time for which the most generous benefits could be claimed, and decreases in replacement rates followed. Eligibility criteria for a variety of programmes were stiffened, particularly for unemployment and disability benefits. In the case of pensions, cuts in benefits promised for the future but not yet enjoyed by retirees were implemented in some countries. Thus, though retirees will enjoy equal or higher benefits in the future than in the present, they will not enjoy the benefits they would have enjoyed under previous legislation.[16] Only rarely were entire programmes abandoned or radically changed, such as the maternity and death grants and the child benefit in Britain or the universal health care system in New Zealand. Nevertheless, the cumulation of all these changes meant in some cases a significant reduction of entitlements, though not a system shift.

Our data show a sharp decline in partisan effects on welfare state expansion/retrenchment, with one important exception, public social service employment. Curtailment of entitlements, or at best defence of existing entitlements, was on the agenda everywhere. As Pierson argues (1996; also see Huber and Stephens 1993, 1998), the politics of retrenchment are different from the politics of welfare state expansion. The right was constrained in its ability to cut by the popularity of most of the large welfare state programmes, and the left was constrained in its ability to raise taxes to keep the programmes on a sound financial basis by the economic slowdown. This is not to say that there have not been significant differences in the rhetoric of political parties with regards to desirable welfare state reforms, but simply that electoral constraints worked against radical departures from established welfare state models. In our data analysis, the only indicator on which we found continued partisan effects was public employment, a result which was driven by the expansion of the public social service sector in Scandinavia that continued throughout the 1980s. As the unemployment crisis hit Scandinavia in the early 1990s, the expansion of public employment ceased.

There were only a few cases of large-scale ideologically driven cuts. The most dramatic were by Thatcher in Britain, the National (conservative) government in New Zealand, and the Reagan administration in the United States. In the case of the Reagan administration the cuts were focused on cash and in kind benefits to the poor, a small but highly vulnerable minority, while Social Security was preserved by a large increase in the contributions.

---

[16] Alber (1998*b*) shows that these reductions, which one might term 'real but not apparent' (to the beneficiary, which is why they could be implemented), were quite significant in the case of German pensions. He also points out that cutbacks were often accompanied by new extensions of social programmes in Germany and Austria, and to some extent even in the Netherlands.

In any case, the United States cannot have been said to have made a 'system shift' if only because it already had the least generous welfare state of any advanced industrial democracy. Only in Great Britain and New Zealand could one speak of an actual system shift from welfare state regimes that used to provide basic income security to welfare state regimes that are essentially residualist, relying heavily on means testing. We argue that the exceptional nature of these two cases can be traced to their political systems which concentrate power (unicameral or very weakly bicameral parliamentary governments in unitary political systems) and make it possible to rule without a majority of popular support (single member districts and plurality elections which allow parties with a minority of votes to enjoy large parliamentary majorities). Thus, in both cases, the conservative governments were able to pass legislation which was deeply unpopular.

Despite these common trends to retrenchment and the rarity of ideologically motivated roll-backs, there were very important differences between welfare states in how they handled the higher unemployment which reflected the type of welfare state regime. These differences become visible if one looks at activity rates. The well-developed Christian democratic welfare states attempted to deal with unemployment by decreasing the labour supply. Older workers were helped into early retirement or provided with disability pensions. For example, labour force participation among male workers in the age group 60–64 fell from around 70 to 22 per cent between 1973 and 1991 in the Netherlands (Hemerijck and Kloosterman 1994). In the well-developed social democratic welfare states, in contrast, active labour market policies were used to keep up employment. Thus, in 1994 at the peak of the Nordic crisis, labour force participation among males aged 55–64, was at 64 per cent in the four Nordic countries compared to 42 per cent in five Christian democratic welfare states for which there is comparable data (OECD 1996*f*: 34).[17]

If we look at total activity rates, including women, the differences become even more pronounced. As noted above, the only large welfare state expansion in the 1980s was the expansion of public social services in Scandinavia. Since most of these jobs were filled by women, female labour force participation continued to expand during this decade. This expansion was facilitated by other social reforms, such as expanded parental leave provisions. As a result, by 1993 an average of 72 per cent of women worked in the Scandinavian countries, as opposed to only 54 per cent in the countries with Christian democratic welfare states. This made for much more favourable ratios of the total working to non-working population in the former compared to the latter (see Table 4.2).

[17] The corresponding figures for liberal welfare states is 64% and for the Antipodes 62%. Among the social democratic welfare states, Finland is the exception as only 43% of men of the 55–64 age group are in the labour force.

Given the crucial role that the rise in unemployment has had in stimulating welfare state retrenchment, we have to seek to understand the reasons for the dramatic increases in unemployment in the 1980s and early 1990s (see Table 4.4). Here we can only summarize the arguments we make elsewhere at length (Huber and Stephens 1998; Stephens 1996; Huber and Stephens, forthcoming, chs. 6 and 7). First, let us dispense with the standard argument that regularly appears in the *Economist* and European reporting in the *New York Times*, that is, with globalization the countries with generous welfare states and high wages were increasingly exposed to trade competition and their generous social provisions made them uncompetitive in ever more open world markets. In fact, the generous welfare states of Northern Europe were developed in very trade open economies in which the performance of the export sector was pivotal for the economic welfare of the country. Moreover, the export sectors of countries such as Sweden and Germany were performing incredibly well in the mid-1990s at precisely the same time when the governments of those countries were cutting social benefits (Huber and Stephens 1998; Pierson, in this volume; Manow and Seils 1999). Thus, it is clear that export competitiveness was not the cause of the retrenchment, at least not as a direct economic constraint. The issue did lend itself to effective rhetoric from the right and business and may have made an indirect contribution to legitimizing cuts (see Swank 1998*b*).

Underlying the growth in unemployment would appear to be a decline in the growth of employment which in turn could be attributed to the decline in economic growth. Per capita growth rates did fall from 3.8 per cent in the period 1960–73 to 2.6 per cent in the 1980s. However, as Glyn (1995*a*: 2) points out, it is not true that employment growth in the OECD was significantly faster in the period 1960–73 than in 1973–93.[18] Of course, many of the jobs produced in the 1980s were part-time jobs. This must be considered if we are concerned with increases in citizens' well-being, but conventional unemployment rates count part-timers as employed so this cannot explain the increase in unemployment. As Glyn observes, the data show conclusively that observers who explain the current problem as one of 'jobless growth' miss the mark completely. While this may be true of manufacturing, if anything the opposite is true of the economy as a whole: given that average annual per capita growth was significantly lower in the post-1973 period (see Table 4.4), these economies were clearly producing more jobs for each per cent of growth than they were in the 1960s.

This counter-intuitive finding is explained by the sectoral changes in the economy correctly pointed to as a main source of lower growth rates in the

---

[18] According to Glyn's figures for all OECD countries, it was actually higher after 1973 (1.2 vs. 1.1% per annum). For the eighteen countries examined here, it was slightly lower in the period after 1973.

contemporary period by Iversen (in this volume) and Pierson (in this volume; also see Maier 1985). As sectoral composition of the economy has shifted from the high productivity growth manufacturing sector to the lower productivity growth service sector, growth has declined. By the same token, each per cent increase in growth results in a larger increase in employment precisely because of the greater labour intensity of services. While we would agree with the contention that the lower growth rates caused by the sectoral shift have had a direct impact on social policy because higher growth rates facilitate the simultaneous expansion of private and public consumption, the sectoral shift has not exerted pressures on the generous welfare states by causing increasing unemployment.

Since the growth of the working age population is actually lower in the period after 1973 than before, it must be that rising participation rates explain the rise in unemployment. Glyn correctly observes that this goes far in helping us to explain the secular trend within countries, but is of more limited use in explaining the differences between countries. From Table 4.5, we can see that in the earlier period the entry of women into the labour force was entirely offset by the exit of men from the labour force. Since this was an era of full employment, it is a good guess that the exit of men was almost entirely voluntary and due to the lengthening education and declining retirement ages. By contrast, in the more recent period, women have entered the labour force at double the rates that men have exited. Moreover, we know that in this period, a significant portion of the exit of men was involuntary as they were forced into early retirement by high unemployment. With regard to the pattern across countries, only within the Christian democratic group do variations in participation rates of men and women give one much leverage in explaining variations in rates of unemployment. In Switzerland and Austria, the small increase in women's labour force participation was counterbalanced by declines among men which helps explain why these two countries faired better in their unemployment rates than the other countries in this group. In the social democratic welfare states, the big increase in women's labour force participation occurred while these countries maintained close to full employment.

The change in the sectoral composition in the labour force is not the only cause of the decline in growth rates after 1973. Unlike sector change, these other changes which have affected growth do not appear to have automatic counterbalancing effects on unemployment. We would argue that, ceteris paribus, higher growth rates would have produced more jobs and less unemployment and that one of the key requirements for higher growth would have been higher investment levels. Many economists argue that capital stock has no impact on unemployment and inflation, and that the problem of job creation is to be solved through the stimulation of more employment on existing capital stock by making labour markets more flexible. However, as Rowthorn (1995) forcefully argues, there are good theoretical reasons and

TABLE 4.5. *Labor force participation by gender*

	Female labour force, % of females 15–64					Male labour force, % of males 15–64				
	1960	1973	1980	1990	1994	1960	1973	1980	1990	1994
Sweden	50	65	77	76	76	99	89	86	86	79
Norway	36	50	66	71	71	92	87	87	85	82
Denmark	44	63	74	78	78	100	90	88	90	87
Finland	66	66	73	70	70	91	80	82	81	78
Mean	48.9	60.9	72.3	73.7	73.7	95.4	86.4	85.7	85.2	81.5
Austria	52	53	50	59	59	92	86	82	80	81
Belgium	36	42	49	54	54	86	83	77	73	73
Netherlands	26	30	40	56	56	98	84	77	80	79
Germany	49	51	52	61	61	94	89	83	80	78
France	47	51	54	59	59	95	85	78	75	75
Italy	40	34	40	43	43	95	85	81	79	75
Switzerland	51	54	54	59	58	100	100	94	95	93
Mean	43.0	44.9	48.5	55.7	55.6	94.3	87.4	81.7	80.4	78.8
Canada	34	49	60	65	65	91	87	85	85	78
Ireland	35	34	38	41	41	99	96	92	90	89
UK	46	54	57	65	65	99	92	88	86	84
USA	43	52	62	69	69	91	86	84	85	85
Mean	39.3	47.3	54.2	60.2	60.2	94.9	90.1	87.1	86.6	84.1
Australia	34	49	53	62	62	97	91	87	86	85
New Zealand	31	41	46	63	63	94	89	85	83	83
Japan	60	52	57	62	62	92	90	89	88	90
Grand Mean	43.3	49.4	55.6	61.8	61.8	94.7	88.2	84.6	83.7	81.8

Female labour force participation: percentage of women age 15 to 64 in the labour force (HRS, OECD).
Male labour force participation: percentage of men age 15 to 64 in the labour force (HRS, OECD).

strong empirical evidence linking the growth of capital stock to growth of employment. He works within a non-accelerating inflation rate of unemployment (NAIRU) framework and assumes no central coordination of wage and price setting. In his model, additional capital stock reduces the inflationary conflict over income distribution and thus allows the NAIRU to stabilize at a lower level. Growth in capital stock causes productivity growth which in turn permits growth in real wages and reduces the saliency of the struggle over the share of labour versus capital income. His model works in the context of non-coordinated bargaining, and it is even more plausible that the labour market partners in a coordinated economy would take advantage of higher growth rates to opt for relative wage restraint in the interest of higher investment and employment levels. Empirical support for these arguments is provided by a regression analysis estimating the effects of growth in capital stock (1960–92) in ten OECD countries on employment, which shows a large, statistically significant effect (Rowthorn 1995: 33–4).

Our own data show a fall of gross fixed capital formation from 24 per cent of GDP in the 1960s to 21 per cent of GDP in the 1980s. Three important immediate causes of this decline in investment are a decline in the rate of profit on productive investment, a decline in net savings (from 14.4 per cent of GDP in 1960–73 to 9.1 per cent in the 1980s and then down to 7.7 per cent in 1990–3), and an increase in real interest rates (from 1.4 per cent to 3.8 per cent to 5.6 per cent in the three periods) (OECD 1995*b*: 77, 108).[19] The deregulation of international and domestic financial markets is partly responsible for this increase in interest rates.[20] As a result of the elimination of controls on capital flows between countries, governments cannot control both the interest rate and exchange rate. If a government decides to pursue a stable exchange rate, it must accept the interest rate which is determined by international financial markets. As a result of decontrol of domestic financial markets (which was in many cases stimulated by international financial deregulation), government's ability to privilege business investors over other borrowers also became more limited.

In fact, the coordinated market economies, most of which relied on some form of capital controls, experienced a significant decline in gross fixed capital formation from the 1960s through the 1980s, whereas the liberal market economies experienced no such decline. Nevertheless, the level of gross fixed capital formation in the CMEs remained above that of the LMEs.[21] In Germany, where capital controls were not a factor, financial internationalization has also had a negative effect on the traditional model of investment financing, insofar as the special long-term relationships between banks and corporations are becoming weaker (Streeck 1997*b*; Manow and Seils 1999).

External financial decontrol also limits a government's ability to employ fiscal stimulation as a tool, as fiscal deficits are considered risky by financial markets and either require a risk premium on interest rates or put downward pressure on foreign exchange reserves. Thus, at least a portion of the increase in unemployment can be linked to globalization in the form of deregulated capital markets. However, it is important to recognize the importance of political decisions and conjunctural developments in explaining the current high levels of unemployment in Europe. Though it almost certainly was

---

[19] Rowthorn (1995) emphasizes the decline in the rate of profit and the real cost of borrowing. The figures for gross fixed capital formation and savings are for all eighteen countries included in the other tables in this chapter. The figures for real interest rates are only for the nine countries for which OECD (1995*b*: 108) presents data for all three periods. For the most recent period, this table has data for seventeen countries. The additional countries raise the average real interest rate across the countries to 6.2%.

[20] Another part of the reason is competition from non-OECD countries for investment funds (Rowthorn 1995).

[21] Our calculations, based on OECD (1995*b*: 73).

not a conscious decision, or at least not seen in these terms, the Christian democratic welfare states, faced with a growing supply of (female) labour rejected the alternatives of creating a low-wage market in private services along American lines or expanding public services (and thus raising taxes) along Nordic lines.[22]

When we talk about conjunctural developments, we do not mean to imply that these developments are necessarily cyclical and transitory; rather, we want to distinguish them from secular changes that are clearly irreversible. With regard to conjunctural elements of the present employment crisis in Europe, then, one can begin with the contribution of the debt build-up of the 1970s to the current high levels of interest rates. With only two exceptions, the countries included in our quantitative analysis increased expenditure faster, in most cases much faster, than revenue in the 1970s and then did the reverse in the 1980s, but not enough to erase the debt, and in many cases the deficits, inherited from the 1970s. This legacy, plus the development of the EMS, the collapse of the Soviet Union, German reunification, the Maastricht accord and the development of the EMU led, in sequence and in combination, to the extremely austere monetary and fiscal policy now prevalent in Europe (Hall 1998; Soskice, in press). With open financial markets and the EMS system of fixed exchange rates, interest rates in European countries were determined by financial markets and, given the pivotal role of Germany in the European economy, this increasingly meant that the Bundesbank set European interest rates imposing its traditional non-accommodating policies on the rest of the region. The collapse of the Soviet Union and with it the Soviet economy sent a negative shock to all countries with exports to the Soviet Union, a shock which was a major blow to the Finnish economy and a minor one to a number of others. The budget deficits caused by German reunification stimulated an exceptionally austere response on the part of the Bundesbank which was then communicated to the rest of Europe.[23] The convergence criteria contained in the Maastricht accord pressed further austerity on all governments, even those not committed to becoming EMU members, such as Sweden, and even on those outside of the EU, such as Norway.

In the cases of Finland, Sweden, and to a lesser extent Norway, government policy mistakes strongly contributed to, indeed, may have created the crisis.[24] All three countries deregulated their financial markets in the 1980s which led to booms in consumer spending and skyrocketing real estate prices and

[22] It should be pointed out here that the US unemployment performance in the 1980s, with 7.5% of the labour force unemployed, was hardly outstanding, and liberal welfare states as a group registered higher levels of unemployment than the Christian democratic welfare states, so it is not surprising that the liberal welfare states were not looked to as a model. The US unemployment performance only began to look attractive once the conjunctural features discussed in the following paragraphs kicked in during the 1990s.

[23] See Czada (1998) for a discussion of the enormous impact of unification on the German production regime and welfare state.

[24] See Huber and Stephens (1998) for a more detailed analysis.

to overheating of the domestic economy and wage inflation. In the bust that followed the boom, property values collapsed which caused bank insolvency and consumer retrenchment, which in turn aggravated the deep recession. The bank bailout cost the Swedish government 5 per cent of GDP and the Finnish government 7 per cent of GDP, greatly adding to the deficit in both countries.

The changes in the international financial system and resultant changes in the setting of monetary and fiscal policy fundamentally changed the wage bargaining process in Scandinavia, resulting in a convergence on the Northern European model.[25] As Iversen (1998b) points out, there are two different ways in which CMEs can produce wage moderation and low unemployment. The first one, associated with Scandinavia and, before 1973, Austria, combined centralized wage bargaining with accommodating monetary and fiscal policy and was associated with more nominal wage inflation than the alternative model. That model is best exemplified by Germany and it combined industry-level coordinated wage bargaining with non-accommodating monetary policy and resulted in little nominal wage inflation. For this system to result in little unemployment, it is necessary for the monetary authorities to send such a strong signal that inflation will not be tolerated that the labour market partners bargain with expectations of very low inflation. As pointed out above, the current monetary arrangements in Europe impose such a regime on all countries. Though this new system requires adjustments on the part of labour market actors, there is no reason to suppose that it cannot produce wage restraint and low unemployment in Scandinavia, as it has in Germany in the past. The apparent learning process in Sweden over the last two bargaining rounds (1995—inflationary; 1998—moderate) supports this view.[26]

[25] Iversen, Pontusson, and Soskice (in press) also argue that Scandinavian bargaining systems converged on the Northern European type but emphasize the movement towards decentralization. This movement is not as dramatic as the one discussed in what follows, as Norway and Finland experienced very little change and the interpretation of the changes in Denmark is disputed (compare Iversen 1996 and Wallerstein and Golden 1997), leaving Sweden as the only country with undisputed major changes.

[26] Iversen's argument would predict that Sweden would be successful because Sweden has moved to a system of coordinated industry-level bargaining. According to his argument, those countries with centralized bargaining should have greater difficulty in adapting to such a regime because unions' wage compression goals conflict with other goals, but he admits that this depends on the weight unions place on wage solidarism. The fact that Finnish unions have never had a wage compression policy indicates that the link between centralization and wage compression is not that strong. Admittedly, the wage bargaining systems in the Nordic area are in flux and thus it is hazardous to say that a new equilibrium has been found. The fact that Germany is likely to be the fulcrum of European wage setting and thus much depends on the response of the German unions to the transition to a European monetary authority, and on the monetary authority's response to European vs. German inflation (Soskice and Iversen 1998) makes any prediction yet more hazardous. See Huber and Stephens, forthcoming, ch. 8, for a further discussion.

A final change in production regimes of the Nordic countries; of the Continental European CMEs whose production regimes included an important role for state ownership and intervention, such as Austria and France; and of both of the Antipodean countries, but particularly New Zealand, has been a strong trend to privatization of state enterprises or marketization of the operation of not only state enterprises but also public administration. A key motive behind these moves in most cases has been fiscal retrenchment, with the sale of state enterprises giving the government a one-shot deficit reduction and the rationalization of public enterprises to put them on a profit-making basis resulting in a much smaller but continuing boost to the budget. The immediate effect of privatization or marketization is increased unemployment as personnel kept on for non-economic reasons are laid off. The longer term effect is less clear. Arguably, the employment effects could be positive as the now profitable enterprises begin to invest and take on new employees.

In contrast to the European and North American cases, the production regimes of the Antipodes did undergo a system shift as a result of changes in the international economic environment. As a result of long-term secular changes in commodity prices, the Australasian production regimes became unviable because they were based on rents transferred from the primary product sector to a protected manufacturing sector. These rents were highly adversely affected by these changes in international markets. In both countries, the wage regulation system, which was the core of the system of social protection, was changed substantially—in New Zealand completely abolished —and this, along with the rise in unemployment, exposed workers to much higher levels of risk of poverty than had earlier been the case. Add to this other marketizing reforms (see F. G. Castles, Gerritsen, and Vowles 1996; Schwartz 1994*a*, 1994*b*, 1998), and it becomes apparent that the production regimes of the Antipodes have converged on the liberal type. However, there are strong differences between the two countries with regard to not only the extent of labour market deregulation but also changes in the social policy regime proper. In Australia, Labor attempted not only to compensate those hit hardest by the ongoing changes with targetted programmes, it also introduced two universalistic policies, medical care and supplementary pensions, which make the Australian social policy regime one of the most generous in the liberal group. By contrast, the conservative government elected in 1990 in New Zealand and unchecked by veto points in the country's unicameral unitary system carried out deeply unpopular reforms which completely deregulated the labour market and substantially cut social benefits.

To conclude this section, let us summarize the main changes in production and welfare state regimes, their interrelationship, and their relationship to globalization. First, the changes in the production regimes are greatest in those countries which relied most on political control of markets, above all the Nordic countries, some of the Continental CMEs, and the Antipodes. The rationalization of the public sector and privatization of state enterprises certainly contributed to the rise in unemployment in the short term, but the long-term and future effects are less clear. Although the developments fit uneasily under the rubric of globalization, it is clear that changes in the international economy fundamentally changed the Antipodean production regimes, moving them into the liberal group. Deregulation of international and domestic financial markets represented a profound change for the CMEs, especially the Nordic countries and Continental CMEs who relied on financial controls. It deprived them of instruments by which they delivered low-interest loan capital to business investors, and of stimulative fiscal and monetary countercylical tools. Financial deregulation along with the debt legacy of the 1970s contributed to higher interest rates and arguably lower growth across the advanced capitalist world in the 1980s. In this environment, only the Nordic welfare states managed to absorb the growing labour force participation caused by the inflow of women into the labour force, and this was accomplished by expanding public sector employment. In the 1990s, the conjunctural features affecting Europe as a whole and the developments specific to the Nordic group are certainly much more important than longer term secular changes, such as globalization, sectoral change in the economy, and the rise in labour force participation, in explaining the additional rise in unemployment and thus welfare state retrenchment.[27]

3. PROSPECTS FOR THE FUTURE

In this final section, we speculate about the future of development of the welfare state, particularly the prospects for the maintenance of the more generous and egalitarian Northern European welfare states, which the popular versions of the globalization thesis see as unviable. Our analysis is largely in agreement with Pierson's views on the impact of globalization (in this volume). While the economic environment of the late 1980s and early 1990s was difficult for these welfare states, relatively little of this can be directly attributed to globalization as commonly understood (also see Swank 1998*b*, in this volume). Increased trade openness did not lead to retrenchment as these countries' economies have always been trade open and the export sectors continue to do quite well. It is true that increased financial openness made at least some contribution to the decline in growth by depriving

---

[27] Only to the extent that the development of monetary arrangements in Europe can be strongly linked to financial internationalization can the present high levels of unemployment be strongly linked to globalization.

governments of tools to encourage investment and to combat economic downturns. Moreover, it has contributed to the rise in real interest rates across OECD countries, although the debt and deficit burden inherited from the 1970s was also an important contributor here. Nevertheless, the most important sources of the employment crisis in Europe in the mid-1990s, and thus of the pressures on the welfare state, have been (1) the failure of the Christian democratic welfare states to absorb the growing female labour force, (2) the failures of the Scandinavian welfare states to manage counter-cylical policy between the mid-1980s and early 1990s, (3) the collapse of the Soviet economy, (4) German reunification, and (5) the evolution of European monetary arrangements which have translated German austerity into European austerity (Soskice, in press). In addition, as many authors have pointed out, changing demographics have contributed to difficulties of pension and health care systems. In our concluding remarks, we deal in turn with the future of the European conjuncture, the changing demographic burden, and national policies for increasing employment and growth. In connection with the latter, we address the OECD Jobs Study solution to the advanced industrial economies' employment problem.

It is perhaps most difficult to say anything about the future evolution of European monetary arrangements, since nobody can say with much certainty what will happen.[28] Suffice it to make a few observations here. As our data show, almost all advanced industrial countries responded to the shocks of the 1970s with a large run up of debt, which appeared to be rational given the negative real interest rates prevailing at the time and the assumption that the industrial world was just facing a cyclical downturn and not a fundamentally changed world. While virtually all governments regardless of political colouring realized in the 1980s that the world had indeed changed and began to increase revenue faster than expenditure, most of them did not do this fast enough to reduce deficits much by the end of the period of expansion, much less to reduce the accumulated debt. Thus, they were in a very bad position to meet the convergence criteria specified in the Maastricht accord.

In the cases of Sweden and Finland, the governments found themselves in a good budgetary situation at the end of the 1980s when the crisis hit, but they quickly began to record high deficits and skyrocketing debt. However, as the 1990s were about to close, the situation looked much rosier for the Nordic social democratic welfare states. By 1998, budget surpluses were recorded by all but Finland, where the deficit was under 2 per cent of GDP; inflation was low; the latest wage round had generally delivered non-inflationary wage increases; and exports were doing well, in some cases booming. Only unemployment was problematic and even it had fallen to

---

[28] See Cameron (1998) for an overview of near-term possibilities.

6 per cent in Sweden and Denmark by early 1999. In any case, given the budgetary situation, it could no longer be said that the countries could not afford their welfare states. In the Northern European Christian democratic welfare states, the Austrian economy continued to perform well and the turnaround in the Netherlands was being heralded as a 'miracle' (Visser and Hemerijck 1998), with unemployment falling to 6 per cent.[29] While the unemployment performance elsewhere in Europe was deeply problematic, almost all countries were moving towards reduced deficits under the pressure of Maastricht.

While the short-term effects of the move to budget surplus across Europe are higher, probably much higher, unemployment, the long-term effect is to push Continental Europe towards the traditional social democratic model of the Golden Age in which the social democratic countries ran budget surpluses across economic cycles which facilitated the supply-side, low-interest rate policy pursued by these countries. Thus, though in the short to medium term, this means more unemployment, the longer term picture is not so bleak.

There is wide agreement that the demographic structure, the combination of higher life expectancy and declining fertility, is and will be a problem for welfare states, particularly those with a transfer and pensioner bias (e.g. see Pierson, in this volume; Esping-Andersen 1997). In the political discussion, this problem is often portrayed as a time bomb that is certain to destroy welfare states as we know them. However, the figures in Table 4.6 suggest that the increase in the aged dependency ratio will not be as dramatic as often claimed, and that there is considerable variation among countries. In Scandinavia, the changes for the worse in this ratio were larger in the past thirty years than they will be in the next thirty; in the Continental European countries, the decline in the ratio of active labour force age population to those 65 and over in the future will be somewhat steeper than it was over the past thirty years, and only in the liberal welfare states and the Antipodes will the decline be much greater.

Moreover, while it is true that the elderly are disproportionate burdens on welfare state services and transfers, the young are dependent (on education, child care, child allowances, etc.) also. If one includes them as part of the dependency ratio, then demographic change will be less burdensome than is conventionally assumed (Table 4.6). One can take this a step further. The relevant figure is not the ratio of dependents to adults but rather to those actually supporting the welfare state through employment and thus a contribution to the tax base. This figure, the ratio of the working population to

---

[29] We put miracle in quotation marks because the dramatic decrease in unemployment in the Netherlands was achieved largely as a result of an increase in part-time work; aggregate hours worked remained among the lowest in Europe.

TABLE 4.6. *Ratios of active to dependent populations*

	Working age population per elderly person			Working age population per dependent person			Ratio of working population to non-working population		
	1960	1990	2020	1960	1990	2020	1960	1980	1989
Social Democratic Welfare States									
Sweden	5.5	3.6	3.0	1.9	1.8	1.6	0.92	1.04	1.11
Norway	5.7	4.0	3.6	1.7	1.8	1.7	0.67	0.88	0.94
Denmark	6.0	4.3	3.3	1.8	2.1	1.8	0.81	0.95	1.06
Finland	8.5	5.0	2.9	1.7	2.1	1.7	0.92	0.97	1.01
Mean	6.4	4.2	3.2	1.8	2.0	1.7	0.83	0.96	1.03
Christian Democratic Welfare States									
Austria	5.4	4.5	3.3	1.9	2.1	2.0	0.87	0.69	0.78
Belgium	5.2	4.5	3.1	1.8	2.0	1.8	0.64	0.61	0.61
Netherlands	6.8	5.4	3.2	1.6	2.2	1.8	0.57	0.56	0.71
Germany	5.8	4.6	3.3	2.1	2.2	2.0	0.89	0.78	0.81
France	5.3	4.7	3.0	1.6	1.9	1.7	0.76	0.68	0.65
Italy	7.0	4.7	2.7	1.9	2.2	1.8	0.74	0.60	0.60
Switzerland	6.2	4.5	3.2	1.8	2.0	1.8	1.00	0.98	1.10
Mean	6.0	4.7	3.1	1.8	2.1	1.8	0.78	0.70	0.75
Liberal Welfare States									
Canada	7.7	5.9	3.1	1.4	2.1	1.8	0.53	0.81	0.92
Ireland	5.2	5.4	4.0	1.4	1.6	1.8	0.59	0.51	0.45
UK	5.5	4.2	3.5	1.9	1.8	1.8	0.86	0.82	0.88
USA	6.5	5.3	3.6	1.5	1.9	1.8	0.61	0.80	0.93
Mean	6.2	5.2	3.6	1.6	1.9	1.8	0.65	0.74	0.80
Antipodes									
Australia	7.2	6.0	3.7	1.6	2.0	1.9	0.66	0.76	0.86
New Zealand	9.0	5.8	4.1	1.4	1.9	1.9	0.58	0.68	0.78
Japan	11.2	5.8		1.8	2.3		0.91	0.90	0.99

Working age population per elderly person: population aged 15–64 years/population over 64 years. (OECD 1994*b*: 100) supplemented by calculations by the authors based on UN (1996) data for countries and years with missing data.

Working age population per dependent person: population aged 15–64 years/(population over 64 years + population under 15 years). (OECD 1994*b*: 100) supplemented by calculations by the authors based on UN (1996) data for countries and years with missing data.

Ratio of working population to non-working population: employed population/unemployed and inactive population (all ages) (HRS, OECD).

the total non-working population (including the aged, youth, the unemployed, and adults not in the workforce) is shown in the last three columns of Table 4.6. In this comparison, the social democratic welfare states do best, followed by the liberal welfare states, then the Antipodean, and finally the Christian democratic welfare states. Underlying these figures are the differing levels of women's labour force participation shown in Table 4.5. The two tables also underline another advantage of social democratic welfare states, not only are their active to non-active ratios very favourable, the demands on the economies to produce more jobs due to the entry of women in the labour force will decline in the future as these countries approach a situation in which the adult female population is fully active in the workforce.

Female labour force participation clearly needs to be increased in the Christian democratic countries in order to increase the tax base of the welfare state. As Esping-Andersen (1997) points out, higher female labour force participation is needed to not only counteract a deterioration of dependency ratios resulting from an ageing population and declining fertility rates, but also to reduce the household risk of falling into poverty resulting from the spread of non-traditional families and less stable labour markets. (All this is quite in addition to value-based arguments having to do with personal autonomy and power relations in the family.) In order to improve dependency ratios, of course, female labour force participation needs to be compatible with child-raising; if it is not, it will be accompanied by lower fertility. This suggests that the Christian democratic welfare states need to be adapted to these requirements and follow the Scandinavian model in the area of welfare state service expansion, particularly in the areas of child and elderly care. Given the demands of the EMU and the fiscal deficits of most Continental countries, this does not appear to be a very likely avenue of reform, since significantly expanding public employment would entail increases in expenditure and taxes. However, small steps in this direction might be taken, and other measures which do not increase the fiscal burden but would facilitate female labour force participation, such as changing the tax code to individual rather than household taxation, might be implemented.

On the other hand, one should keep in mind that the Christian democratic welfare states are performing better than the liberal welfare states at present, despite the unfavourable active to inactive ratio, in keeping people out of poverty, because they are embedded in production regimes with greater contract coverage and thus less inequality in the primary income distribution, and because of the greater generosity of their benefits. Thus, as we point out below, the liberal approach to dealing with the growing burden of an inactive population, deregulation of the production regime, and residualization of the welfare state, with the hope that the market will produce more low-wage jobs, imposes sufficient social costs that it is unlikely that it will be pursued for political reasons. A more realistic goal, and in our view a more desirable one, is to increase the activity ratio within the parameters of the existing production and welfare state regime. As just noted, the obvious strategy to increase activity rates is to increase women's labour force participation by providing legal protection and services that make it easier to combine child-rearing and working life. A second important strategy is the development of an active labour market policy with heavy emphasis on training and retraining.

This prescription, of course, raises the question of where the jobs are supposed to come from that are to be filled by women entering the labour market. The recent success of the Netherlands, Denmark, and Sweden in lowering unemployment from double-digit levels to around 6 per cent suggests that wage restraint, which has been pivotal in both cases, will be a critical part of the model in CMEs. Our analysis in the last section suggests that policies to raise investment levels are a second element of a strategy to create more employment. In what follows, we discuss the policies and prospects in both areas in sequence and then compare our jobs strategy with that of the OECD.

Developments in European monetary arrangements have imposed the equivalent of independent central banks pursuing non-accommodating monetary policy on all of Europe. As the work cited above indicates (Soskice 1990; Iversen 1998*b*; Hall and Franzese, in press; Soskice, in press), the combination of central bank independence and coordinated industry-level bargaining should yield effective wage restraint. According to Iversen (1998*b*) countries with centralized bargaining (now only Norway and Finland) should have more difficulty in restraining wages because centralized bargaining is associated with wage solidarity policies which in turn is associated with wage drift. Here one must be more precise than Iversen and distinguish between what in the Swedish context is referred to as stage 1 (equal pay for equal work) and stage 2 of the wage policy of solidarity (wage compression between skill levels). We would argue that it is the skill differential compressions which are problematic for wage restraint. Moreover, both the theoretical argument of Moene and Wallerstein (1999) and empirical analysis of Hibbs and Locking (1995) indicate that, consistent with Rehn–Meidner arguments, the first stage of the Swedish solidaristic wage policy enhanced productivity growth whereas the second stage retarded it. The association of stage 2 with centralized bargaining is not as tight as that of stage 1, as the Finnish movement has never pursued it.[30] In any case, the latest wage bargaining rounds in both Finland and Sweden yielded moderate wage increases, so it is clear that centralized bargaining can produce wage moderation even in the present European monetary environment.[31]

Our remarks in the previous paragraph indicate that there are reasons to give up wage compression policies and indeed that is what we have argued (Huber and Stephens 1998: 391–2). To the extent that the wage compression policy was actually successful, the inevitable result of abandoning it will

[30] We do not dispute Iversen's (1998*b*) and Pontusson and Swenson's (1996) contention that a central motivation of Swedish employers in ending centralized bargaining was to end wage compression. Interviews we conducted with economists at both the Swedish employers federation and at LO, the trade union confederation, confirm this.

[31] Note we say 'can produce' and not 'will produce' or even 'probably will produce' as the system is very much in flux now as we point out in note 26.

be greater wage dispersion, as has occurred in Sweden since the end of centralized bargaining. Greater wage dispersion would, in turn, appear to result in greater inequality of disposable income, greater gender differences in income, and greater poverty. Therefore, abandoning wage compression would appear to be abandoning central goals of social democracy. The data available indicate that the loss would be minimal. As one can see from Table 4.2, with the exception of Austria, the differences in wage dispersion between Norway, Denmark, and Sweden and the other social democratic and Northern tier Christian democratic welfare states are not large.[32] Moreover, the differences in poverty levels of households whose heads are aged 25–59 and in inequality of disposable household income are yet smaller. The Austrian case is highly instructive as it combines moderate levels of wage dispersion with very equal levels of disposable household income.[33]

We noted above that one proximate cause of lower levels of growth in the post-1973 period was the lower levels of investment and pointed out that the internationalization of capital markets has made it much more difficult for governments to stimulate investment. In countries in which corportatist bargaining arrangements have survived or could be revived, one possible way to encourage investment and secure wage restraint on the part of unions might be to make an explicit bargain exchanging wage moderation for domestic investment commitments of corporations. Given the internationalization of production, the commitment to domestic investment is essential lest wage restraint help finance investments elsewhere. The future obstacles to the achievement of such corporatist bargains resulting from a loss of interest on the part of employers in domestic class compromises are extremely difficult to gauge. On the one hand, company executives will increasingly follow the logic of the global interests of corporations. On the other hand, the advantages offered by the production regimes in coordinated economies, particularly high skill levels of the labour force, social peace, and policy

---

[32] This is not all that surprising if one considers that wage compression was only pursued within the respective trade union confederations, not between them.

[33] Unfortunately, the data available for Sweden do not allow us to construct a very clear picture of the trends through time. The OECD data on 90–10 ratios indicate a very small change in wage dispersion from the 2.0 shown in Table 4.2 for 1981 to 2.1 in 1991. Hibbs and Locking (1995) show a much larger increase in wage dispersion among LO members after the end of centralized bargaining, though wage dispersion in 1990 was still considerably lower than it was when the stage 2 wage compression policy was initiated in the late 1960s. From the LIS data, we can say with some confidence that inequality in disposable household income increased from 0.20 in 1981 to 0.22 in 1987 to 0.23 in 1992, though without decomposing the data, one cannot say what contributed to this outcome. The fact that most of the change had occurred by 1987 indicates that it was probably due to changes in the labour market, including the end of centralized bargaining, and occupational structure, and not to the tax reform, welfare state cuts, and rise in unemployment, all of which came later.

predictability, may well sustain the interest of executives in the stability of these production regimes and their position in them. Moreover, the world financial turmoil and recessions of 1997 and 1998 can be assumed to have strengthened the importance of home bases in the strategies of corporations headquartered in coordinated economies.

A proximate cause of lower investment has been the lower savings rate. As we have argued (Huber and Stephens 1998: 392–4), an extremely promising method of raising the savings rate is to fund or more fully fund social insurance. There has already been a trend in this direction in public pension systems in a few countries, notably Sweden and Canada (Myles and Pierson, in this volume); this could be extended in the case of pensions and applied to other social insurance systems as well.[34] It would also have the advantage that it would make social insurance systems more solvent and thus more resistant to cutbacks in hard economic times.

A third potential path to investment stimulation is the lowering of pay-roll taxes in exchange for domestic investment commitments, which in turn entails reforming the financing and structure of social security schemes. Restructuring of social security schemes with some tightening of eligibility rules and a slight reduction of benefits is unlikely to produce the desired amount of savings, so that it needs to be accompanied by a shift to greater financing from general revenue. As the experience with social security reform in Continental Europe has shown, consent of unions is essential to make significant reforms work without major disruptions. Such consent is greatly facilitated by tripartite corporatist bargaining through which unions can be convinced that reform is indispensable and can be offered some measure of compensation. Whether these are traditional corporatist bargains, or the new 'competitive corporatist' bargains as conceptualized by Rhodes (in this volume) seems to matter less than that the negotiations be inclusive, with wide representation of union and employer organizations.

This model of reducing labour costs through wage restraint and reduction of payroll taxes has been conceived largely to keep or make exports competitive, that is, with reference to the tradeable sector. However, it can also be applied to the non-tradeable sector, to both public and private service sector enterprises. Wage restraint in the public service sector can increase public savings and investments and, along with a reduction in payroll taxes,

---

[34] Evidence from Denmark and Australia indicates that introducing a funded system (in these cases an earnings-related tier) where there was none is likely to produce a fall in private savings that offsets the increased savings which the new funded pension system creates. Arguably, the increased guaranteed income levels in retirement lead people to save less. Our suggestion is to move from currently unfunded systems to partially funded systems or to move from partially funded systems to more fully funded ones. Since benefits are not being increased, there should not be a decline in savings due to anticipated increases in retirement income.

it can be traded off for investment commitments by private service enter-prises. The effectiveness of reducing the state's contributions for public employees to the social security schemes, the equivalent of payroll taxes, is limited in terms of increasing public savings, of course, because of the need to find alternative sources of financing out of general revenue.

If one assumes that technological progress and productivity increases in the manufacturing sector continue and keep the rate of job creation relatively low despite increased investment, one needs to look to the service sector as the major potential creator of jobs. The OECD Jobs Study has argued that low productivity growth in this sector means that these jobs must be low-wage jobs (OECD 1994c). The OECD strategy for creating jobs in this sector is to increase wage dispersion, deregulate labour markets, and cut social benefits, such as unemployment compensation, which raise the reservation wage. Thus, though based on a much more sophisticated analysis, the OECD formula is identical to that of conservative proponents of the globalization thesis. The American case with its large low-wage private service sector and current low levels of unemployment would appear to support the OECD's view. But there are reasons to be sceptical of (1) whether the US model was that successful and, if so, whether it was due to increased wage dispersion, (2) whether movement in this direction by the Christian democratic and social democratic welfare states would have large employment creation effects, (3) if they did, whether it would be worth the social costs of doing so, and (4) whether it is politically feasible for European governments to move in this direction even if it were deemed desirable.

On the first point, R. B. Freeman (1995b) argues that if one adjusts the unemployment rates for the increase in incarceration, which has trebled since 1980, the US performance does not look so outstanding. Western and Beckett (1999) have estimated that an inclusion of the prison population would raise unemployment levels among males by a negligible amount in Europe but by almost 2 per cent in the United States. Freeman also presents extensive data demonstrating that increased wage dispersion in the United States did not contribute to employment growth. Still the OECD argument might be saved by contending that the pre-existing levels of wage dispersion, labour market flexibility, and low welfare state benefits were a precondition for the vigorous growth of the private service sector in the USA.

On the second point, the experiences of the two countries which made the most dramatic moves in the direction suggested by the OECD, the United Kingdom and New Zealand, do not support the view that the American experience is replicable. Both countries have had modest upturns in employ-ment recently but both are still above 6 per cent unemployment and thus are not faring better than the Netherlands, Denmark, or Sweden. And they are paying the social costs paid by the USA for some time now. Despite the decline in unemployment in the USA, poverty increased modestly from

16.4 per cent of households in 1979 to 17.9 per cent in 1994, and inequality increased substantially, with the gini index for disposable income rising from the 0.31 shown in Table 4.3 for 1979 to 0.37 in 1994. The UK clearly moved to the American model in both respects as poverty increased from 5.7 per cent in 1979 to 10.6 per cent in 1995, and inequality increased from the 0.27 shown in Table 4.3 for 1979 to 0.35.[35] For single mothers, the percentage in poverty increased from 11 to 28 per cent. This increase in inequality was the largest recorded in the LIS data and moved the UK to a position second only to the USA as the most inegalitarian country among the eighteen analysed here. Unfortunately, LIS does not have data on New Zealand, but Easton's (1996) figures show very large increases in poverty and inequality in the early 1990s. Thus, New Zealand and the United Kingdom are paying the social costs while performing in terms of unemployment levels no better than countries such as the Netherlands, Denmark, and Sweden that have retained their generous welfare states and have experienced no or small increases in inequality and poverty. Fortunately, it is not likely that any other country in Europe would move as vigorously in the direction charted by the OECD jobs strategy as these two countries have because, as discussed in the previous section, the unique political conditions which allowed such unpopular policies to be implemented in these countries are not replicated elsewhere.[36]

If we reject the American way as codified in the OECD jobs strategy, we need to be able to identify policy options for creating service jobs with adequate wages and social protection. One option is expansion of social services in the public sector, where employees enjoy public sector working conditions. A second option is expansion of public funding of social services provided by the private sector, with working conditions determined by collective bargaining or by stipulations of minimum standards for firms bidding for contracts. Certainly, outside the Scandinavian countries there is much room for expanded social services, particularly in child care, elderly care, and continuing education. The obvious problem with both of these options is the burden on the government budget. However, if preceded by wage moderation as suggested above and accompanied by higher investment and—albeit modest—employment growth in manufacturing, the tax base will be enlarged and new resources will become available. A third option might be to stimulate productivity in the private service sector through support for R & D and skills training, a kind of 'industrial policy' for the service

---

[35] All of the figures are from LIS data and were obtained from the LIS website <http://lissy.ceps.lu/>. The calculations were made by Koen Vleminckx.

[36] We do not want to indicate that we find the OECD recommendations totally without merit. We agree with some of their suggestions for decreasing labour market rigidity and take up several of their suggestions in the following paragraphs.

sector, such as that successfully pursued by Denmark in the 1980s (Benner, Vad, and Schludi 1999). Certainly, in the area of business services this is feasible, as there are highly productive activities and firms there; the challenge is to extend this into the area of personal services.

One frequently suggested prescription for job creation is job flexibilization or job sharing, in the sense of creating more part-time positions and improving social protection associated with part-time work. Certainly from a social equity point of view, two people employed half-time are preferable to one employed full-time and the other one unemployed. The question is to what extent this solution increases aggregate employment, productivity, and the value of goods and services produced. Maybe the easiest positive answer can be given for productivity of labour. In most jobs, people are hard put to keep up maximum performance for eight hours; average productivity during a four-hour stretch is clearly likely to be higher. A second positive impact is the uninterrupted contact with the labour market and thus the continued employability of both workers, which should reduce frictional unemployment and thus increase the total number of hours worked. More hours worked and higher average productivity in turn will increase the total value of the goods and services produced in the society.

If there are indeed policy options to sustain generous welfare states and deal successfully with pressures on coordinated production regimes, what are the political conditions for their pursuit? Are we likely to see a return of partisan effects on social policy? Here we necessarily have to be extremely speculative and make one important assumption—that there not be any further economic shocks emanating in global markets. As long as unemployment crises dictated an agenda of curtailment of welfare state expenditures, the range of political choices was extremely restricted. Social democratic parties were forced to adopt austerity measures, and the constraints of blame avoidance kept centrist and right-wing parties from making very deep cuts. If we are correct that the cuts were mostly driven by unemployment and that at least some of the unemployment was cyclical, in some cases aggravated by policy mistakes, then we would assume these pressures to relent as unemployment recedes from crisis levels, albeit still to levels above those of the Golden Age.[37] Weakened fiscal pressures as a result of more people working and contributing taxes and fewer people claiming benefits then introduce potentially new political dynamics. It will no longer necessarily be the politics of retrenchment. Nor will it be a return to the dynamics of welfare state

---

[37] There is another tall assumption behind this argument, which is that Germany can recover from the shock of unification with the production regime preserved in its essentials. In other words, German unification needs to be seen as a temporary shock rather than as a terminal burden on the German production regime and welfare state, with lasting deep recessionary effects on the rest of Europe.

construction; the welfare states in the social democratic and Christian democratic categories are fully developed, and the lower growth rates will keep resources comparatively scarce. Rather, it is likely to develop into a politics of rejuvenation and adaptation. Still, there will be potentially different approaches to these new challenges preferred by different political actors.

Of course, the strength of the partisan effect will depend very heavily on the distinctiveness of incumbency, both in terms of single-party government versus coalition government and of stability of governments. Where voter alignments and party systems get more fluid, long-term single-party or single-block governments become less likely and policy preferences of incumbents will have a lower probability of being converted into policy. Since the late 1960s there has been a general trend towards greater volatility of electorates and the emergence of new small parties (Wolinetz 1990), but this trend has by no means been uniform across countries. The loss of vote share by established political parties from the 1960s to the 1990s has been higher than 25 per cent in Austria, France, Italy, and New Zealand, but 10 per cent or less in Denmark, the United States, Belgium, the Netherlands, and Germany (Kitschelt, in this volume). In some cases, established parties have been forced into coalitions with rather precarious stability, and the greater need for compromise is most likely to overwhelm partisan preferences and thus a partisan effect on the future development of welfare state regimes in these cases. So, as welfare states are confronted with new challenges under non-crisis conditions, we would hypothesize a resurgence of some partisan differences in policy outcomes.

5

Comparative Institutional Advantages of Welfare State Regimes and New Coalitions in Welfare State Reforms

Philip Manow

THE welfare state, it has been said, was the 'principal institution in the construction of different models of post-war capitalism' (Esping-Andersen 1990: 5). If one accepts this premiss by and large, then one is led to ask how much current welfare reforms are encouraged or constrained by the degree to which social protection has become a central and indispensable part of different national market economies. Since we now know that market economies come in a limited variety (see Hall and Soskice, forthcoming; Crouch and Streeck 1997; Hollingsworth and Boyer 1997; Kitschelt et al. 1999*b*) and since we also know that central factors of variance between different models of capitalism are the degree to which and the form in which the welfare state has become a 'fundamental force in the organization and stratification of modern economies' (Esping-Andersen 1990: 159), we have to question whether this also has had an impact on the way welfare states have adjusted and are still adjusting to the more unfavourable economic conditions that have prevailed since the mid-1970s. Do current welfare reforms and the interest coalitions that are formed during these reform processes mirror the function of the welfare state within national models of production? Are certain types of welfare states more vulnerable than others because they are less or, for that matter, more closely linked to other core institutions of the economy? Have welfare reforms themselves become the main road leading to renewed economic competitiveness in internationalized markets (see Rhodes, in this volume), or does globalization stabilize rather than threaten certain welfare arrangements precisely because the welfare state contributes substantially to the performance profile of national economies?

I gratefully acknowledge comments on earlier versions of this paper by Paul Pierson, Torben Iversen, Isabela Mares, George Ross, and the participants of the 'New Politics of Welfare' Project group. I thank Dona Geyer for language corrections and Annette Vogel for editorial help.

This chapter addresses these questions. In Section 1, I will first offer a critical account of contributions that predict the formation of new political coalitions along the cleavage line between those firms and workers that are forced to adjust to international market pressures and those that enjoy domestic shelter from globalized markets. I will further discuss briefly the relative importance of the electorate in current welfare reforms as compared with the role played by organized interests of capital and labour. Second, I will present a transaction cost argument that seeks to identify one central logic linking production and protection in the Continental welfare states and co-ordinated market economies, respectively (Section 2). The central argument in this section—which is in contrast to the dominant perception in the literature—is that generous welfare state programmes may enhance and not diminish international competitiveness and can be part of the comparative institutional advantage of an economy rather than solely contributing to its comparative cost disadvantage (see for this distinction Hall 1997). Hence, I claim that globalization may not only exert financial pressures on the welfare state but, at the same time, may further increase the importance of economically beneficial side-effects of social policy. Concurrently, a close linkage between production and protection regimes may diminish incentives for firms to exit a costly national welfare regime, that is, to engage in location arbitrage.

This has consequences for political coalition building. I hold that welfare reforms and the reform coalitions tend to reflect both aspects, the direct economic costs and the indirect economic benefits of given welfare regimes. And reforms reflect the relative power positions of both the 'individual programme beneficiaries' exerting influence through the 'numerical democracy channel' and the 'corporate programme beneficiaries' protecting their interests through the 'corporate bargaining channel'—to use Stein Rokkan's terms. The relative importance of either the electoral or the corporate-bargaining agenda may depend primarily on the institutional set-up of the welfare state itself, whether it ascribes an important role to organized capital and labour or whether welfare entitlements are granted by the state to the individual as a universal citizen right without institutions or corporate actors playing a mediating role. I will conclude by briefly discussing the implications of my argument for the present debate on the compensatory role of the welfare state in a globalized economy (Section 3).

1. THE NEW POLITICS OF WELFARE REFORM

It has been argued very convincingly that welfare retrenchment follows a different logic as compared to welfare expansion (Pierson 1994). In particular it is not necessarily true that those who have been strong proponents of welfare state expansion in the past are also natural candidates for its defence in the reform struggles of the present. While it may be true that the 'principal forces that built the welfare state seem now to have lost ground—notably trade unions and social democratic parties, but also Christian Democracy' (Esping-Andersen 1997: 244), this does not mean that the welfare state stands alone without a single ally (Pierson 1994).

The main reason given for the difference of welfare expansion as compared with welfare contraction is that social programmes nurture their own clientele. Jack Walker, referring to the impressive growth of American interest groups, has argued that it is not primarily organized interests that succeed in getting public programmes tailored to their particular needs, but more often it is public programmes that give birth to corresponding interest groups, which then support the programme's maintenance or expansion and protect it from political attacks. In this way, the welfare state seems to generate 'positive policy feedback' as well (Pierson 1996). Apparently, Say's law that each supply generates its own demand has a political counterpart. Not only do administrators, organizations, and welfare professions develop an interest in generous social programmes, but, not very surprisingly, the beneficiaries of these programmes also begin to wonder how they ever could have lived without them. Thus, scholars often conclude that 'the support of electorates for a "fat" rather than "lean" welfare state, buttressed by the defense of the status quo by vested interests, makes anything other than tinkering very difficult' (Rhodes 1996a: 307).

In taking this argument a little further, however, one can reach quite a different conclusion. For one thing, today's welfare state can no longer count automatically on the support of its traditional allies in the workers' movement and in the labour party. Moreover, in many countries, unions (and social democrats) seem to have joined the ranks of those who favour profound welfare reform. While it is certainly true that social programmes create their own clientele and feed their own source of support, the very invulnerability and political 'self-sustainability' of the system may even transform the traditional backers of the welfare state into today's challengers. Clearly, unions and social democratic parties have not simply changed sides and become members of the neoliberal crowd. However, in a number of countries, unions and certain 'modernizing' sections of the social democratic parties have fought for profound welfare reform, including the lowering of generous replacement ratios, the privatization of social services, the introduction of stronger eligibility tests and longer qualifying periods, the reduction of sick pay or pension entitlements, the introduction of stronger incentives to return from welfare to work, etc. In the Netherlands (Visser and Hemerijck 1997), Sweden (Clayton and Pontusson 1998; Stephens 1996), Italy (Baccaro and Locke 1996a), New Zealand (Schwartz 1994b), and Japan (Kume 1997), predominately private sector unions seem to have entered either openly or silently into cross-class coalitions with employers and reform-minded politicians and/ or bureaucrats. The common goal of these—sometimes bizarre[1]—alliances has been the restructuring of the welfare state, including a reversal of the expansive trend in social spending, thorough administrative reform, and the reduction of heavy tax burdens. At the same time, observers note that employers do not always side with those who try to scale back high levels of welfare entitlement and to lower the cost burden imposed by a generous welfare state (cf. Thelen 1999; Mares 1996; S. Wood 1997*b*). Coalition formation in the process of welfare reform apparently does not happen along simple lines.

The prominent involvement of unions in current welfare reform poses considerable difficulties for an approach that ascribes to the labour movement an invariant, almost 'ontological' interest in de-commodification, universal and generous social protection, and full-employment policies. The same is true for the role of business in current reforms of the welfare state that contradicts widely held beliefs that business is invariantly and uniformly in favour of welfare retrenchment and programme cutbacks. In this respect—and not only there—recent analyses of the early periods of welfare state expansion *do* teach a highly informative lesson for the present era of welfare contraction and cutbacks. They show convincingly that business has indeed often played a highly significant supportive role in welfare state growth and that business interests have left a significant imprint on the institutional character of developed welfare states (cf. Mares 1998; Swenson 1997).

The picture becomes even more complicated with respect to the 'positive-feedback thesis', which ascribes to the welfare state the capacity to mobilize sufficient support to protect itself from political attacks (cf. Pierson 1994, 1996). This argument has especially emphasized the role of the ballot as a powerful weapon against attempts at welfare retrenchment. The political calculus of blame-avoidance (Weaver 1986) and the fear of electoral defeat strongly motivate politicians to pursue prudent tactics in social policy reform. However, this argument apparently harbours a 'Westminster-bias' (cf. Visser and Hemerijck 1997). The role of the electoral mechanism in welfare reform is less predominant in most of the Continental welfare states: here, particular spending programmes have very rarely given rise to special interest groups, and social policy is often considered to be a part of a 'corporatist complex', in which the state cannot intervene unilaterally, but is bound to a negotiated consensus with organized labour and capital. Within this political-institutional setting welfare reforms often follow a different logic.

---

[1] Take the Japanese case, in which private sector unions, employers' associations, and reform-minded LDP-members of Parliament rallied against the socialist public sector unions, which fought side by side with the conservative ministerial bureaucracy for the preservation of the status quo.

The current renaissance of central corporatist concertation in a couple of European countries (Pochet and Fajertag 1997; Schmitter and Grote 1997; Rhodes 1998, and in this volume) which is associated with a significant extension of the range of negotiable topics from the traditional issues of income policy (Flanagan, Soskice, and Ulman 1983) to questions including education and training, working hours, taxation, and most prominently, welfare reform, has been interpreted as a strategy by which 'governments . . . are seeking additional legitimacy for welfare reform *that they are increasingly failing to find at elections*' (Rhodes 1998: 13, my emphasis; see also Regini and Regalia 1997; Rhodes, in this volume). While historical-institutionalist accounts of the formative period of the welfare state have examined in particular state structures, the relative autonomy of bureaucratic elites, the importance of partisan politics, etc., today the pervasiveness and political weight of the welfare state well justify the need to explain the fate of current reforms primarily by looking at the structures of the various welfare programmes themselves: Who benefits? How broad is a programme's coverage? How visible would cuts in entitlements be? Included in this perspective, however, has to be the relative importance of corporate actors, in particular organized labour and capital. And here an additional set of questions gains relevance: Which firms and workers benefit from welfare programmes? Does the institutional structure of the welfare state allow for or does it impede cross-class coalition building? To what degree are welfare state programmes tailored to fit the 'national systems of production', etc.?

Although these questions have been already addressed from time to time in the debate on globalization and in the comparative political economy literature, the debate has generally remained on the level of very broad assumptions concerning the interests of the unions and business in welfare reforms and has usually lacked detailed information on the concrete cost-benefit structure of specific social spending programmes. The most common explanation for the new cross-class alliances in welfare reforms is quite straightforward. Labor–capital alliances are caused by a new cleavage between workers and firms in the traded and non-traded sectors. Firms in sheltered sectors of the economy, according to the argument, can better externalize higher costs via price increases (or are dependent rather on the public budget than on the market). Firms in the exposed sectors have to be essentially price takers. If the range of tradeable goods increases via the reduction of both technical (advanced transportation technologies) and legal/economic (trade liberalization) transaction costs (Frieden and Rogowski 1996), firms are increasingly forced to change their strategy from cost externalization via price increases to cost cutting by wage reduction, rationalization, and labour shedding. The same applies for the liberalized sectors of the economy that are no longer financed out of public budgets or enjoy a monopoly granted by the state, but must now survive on their own in fiercely contested and increasingly international markets. If the internationalization of markets, the economic integration of regional trading blocks, and the large-scale privatization of public services in telecommunications, energy, and transportation lead to a growth in the share of the exposed sector in relation to the sheltered sector, the overall pressure on high wages and generous welfare benefits increases too. And this alters unions' and workers' stance towards encompassing and generous social protection: 'with increased openness and intensified international competition, workers and employers in exposed sectors become acutely concerned with containing the upward pressure on domestic costs generated by large public sectors'—and, of course, by generous welfare states (Clayton and Pontusson 1998: 97). 'In this context a new political-economic cleavage between sheltered and exposed sectors opens up' (ibid.).[2] Note that the exposed/sheltered cleavage thesis already acknowledges the importance of the corporate actors of capital and labour in current reforms of the welfare state, in addition to or even in place of the importance of the electoral agenda.

However, the exposed/sheltered sector thesis is based on a problematic assumption about the interests of unions and firms in these reforms. Similar to arguments that have been put forward in the debate on wage bargaining in the open economy (cf. Swenson 1989; Iversen 1996; Lange et al. 1995), the literature on the impact of a new exposed/sheltered divide in welfare state reform perceives workers' and employers' social security contributions primarily or solely as (non-wage) labour costs. Analogous to the argument that 'exposed workers and employers' support wage restraint in the sheltered sector is the subsequent claim by scholars that these same firms and workers are also interested in maintaining non-wage labour costs at a level that would not endanger the international competitiveness of national products. Thus, the literature predicts the emergence of a new line of conflict primarily between the private and the public sector.[3] The argument holds that while private sector unions are likely to have an interest in reducing the unfavourable

---

[2] Clayton and Pontusson do not sufficiently explain why employers in the exposed sector should be interested in defending the high levels of welfare spending enjoyed by their workers while they at the same time try to form a coalition with them that fights for public sector reform. They write: 'Left to their own devices, export-oriented employers would probably have favored across-the-board cuts in the welfare state, but the maintenance of basic social insurance entitlements is a condition for private sector unions to support public sector cutbacks and reforms' (Clayton and Pontusson 1998: 97). This is an implausible argument. While workers in the exposed and sheltered sectors of the economy may have opposing interests, one must make an additional assumption in order to explain why employers in the exposed sector should side with their workers. As will become clear below, these assumptions must depend on arguments referring to the 'comparative institutional advantages' that certain welfare states offer to employers as well.

[3] This division is believed to become further intensified by the different levels of productivity in the sheltered/non-traded and in the exposed/traded sectors: 'Industrial policies and the welfare state must be paid for by taxes to which the traded sector would contribute disproportionately (given its productivity)—further reducing the sector's international competitiveness' (Garrett and Lange 1996: 56).

TABLE 5.1. Selected features of European welfare states

	Austria	Belgium	Denmark	Germany	France	Ireland	Italy	Netherlands	Portugal	Spain	Sweden	UK	OECD
Openness (1990–6)	62.5	82.7	55.7	42.8	39.9	87.0	39.1	76.3	55.6	37.3	54.3	45.9	51.6
Total social expenditure (1990–5)	26.5	28.0	30.6	28.0	28.6	19.9	24.7	29.5	16.6	21.2	35.0	22.1	24.5
Total government outlays (1990–5)	51.7	56.0	61.3	48.9	52.8	41.7	54.8	57.1	44.0	45.8	67.0	44.2	49.6
Public employment (1990–7)	13.9	10.6	22.1	9.9	14.2	9.2	9.1	7.0	11.4	7.4	23.8	11.4	12.8
Corporatism index	17	10	14	12	7	…	5	11	…	…	15	6	…
Collective bargaining coverage rate (1990)	98	90	…	90	92	…	…	71	79	68	83	47	…
Union density (1994)	42	54	76	29	9	…	39	26	32	19	91	34	40

Openness: OECD, *Statistical Compendium* (National Accounts) (1997).

Total social expenditures: Willem Adema, *Social Expenditure Statistics of OECD Member Countries* (Paris: OECD, 1998).

Total government outlays: OECD, *Historical Statistics* (various issues).

Public employment [Government employment/population (15–64)/100]: OECD, *Statistical Compendium* (Economic Outlook) (1998).

Corporatism index: Calmfors and Driffill 1988.

Collective bargaining coverage rate: OECD, *Employment Outlook* (1994), 173; data for France, Germany, and Portugal refer to the years 1985, 1992, and 1991, respectively.

Union density: OECD, *Employment Outlook* (1997), 71.

impact of high taxes, high domestic prices, and high social insurance contributions on production costs, public sector unions not only have no such
interest, they often take the opposite stance. Public sector unions commonly
favour a further expansion of welfare spending and the continuing growth of
the welfare sector, since they recruit a considerable number of their members
from the public (welfare) service sector (cf. Garrett and Way 1999).

This line of argument seems to run, first of all, into an empirical problem:
those countries that, according to the exposed/sheltered cleavage thesis,
should be most likely to give rise to the predicted new cross-class coalitions,
namely those European countries with very open economies, with a generous
level of social spending or a large public sector and a medium-to-high level
of unionization, have not figured prominently among the group of countries
in which 'contracted change' and 'competitive corporatism' (see Rhodes,
in this volume), based upon a joint interest of exposed sector unions and
employers, have been the preferred paths of adjustment. Instead, social pacts
have been prominent exactly in those countries that are less open, that have
neither strong labour movements nor are particularly renowned for a strong
neocorporatist tradition: Italy, Spain, Portugal, Ireland, Finland, just to name
the most important examples (Pochet and Fajertag 1997; Schmitter and Grote
1997). Most of these countries also do not rank particularly high on the
scale of social spending (see Table 5.1).

According to the exposed/sheltered divide thesis, the Southern European countries of Italy, Spain, and Portugal, or the Anglo-Saxon periphery
(Ireland) are 'unsuspected places' (see Rhodes, in this volume; Schmitter
and Grote 1997: 7) for 'tripartitely negotiated' welfare reforms. Rather one
would expect these social pacts to take place on the Continent, in countries with an open economy, generous welfare states, and relatively strong
labour unions. This would be anticipated all the more in the light of the
observation that the Continental corporate welfare states seem to combine
the unattractive features of being both very costly and highly ineffective in
generating employment—a combination that has been often described as
the pathology of welfare without work (Esping-Andersen 1996c; Scharpf
1997b; cf. Iversen and Wren 1998; Huber and Stephens 1998). This should
make them the most natural candidates for profound reform efforts and
also for the emergence of cross-class coalitions since full employment can
still be considered to be the unions' most important policy objective. Given
the 'frozen landscapes' (Esping-Andersen 1996) of the Continental welfare
states and the prominence of reform pacts in Italy, Portugal, Spain, or Ireland,
one doubts whether the simple distinction between sheltered versus exposed
sectors adequately explains the entire variety of interests among the core
political agents. In particular, it might be misleading to analyse interest
positions of exposed and sheltered firms and workers concerning welfare
reforms in strict analogy to their interests with respect to wage setting.

I hold that the problems of the exposed/sheltered hypothesis arise primarily because it presumes that competition is almost always price competition and that welfare state programmes are only a deadweight for business (and nowadays have also become so for exposed-sector unions). That both these presumptions do not necessarily have to hold true is at least implicitly argued by a new body of literature in which it is argued that the 'comparative institutional advantages' (Hall 1997) of modern market economies are often much more important than the relative cost advantages resulting from low levels of taxation, low social spending, or from a lean public sector. The notion of comparative institutional advantages draws attention to the fact that the exclusive focus on the relative level of social spending or on the level of real wages might not be sufficient to assess the relative competitiveness of welfare states and national systems of production.

In order to understand the economic impact of a welfare state regime on firms and modes of production, one has to take a closer look at the programme's benefit structures and their links with other core features of the economy. Precisely such a perspective is provided by the new comparative political economy (CPE) literature. So far, this body of literature has largely ignored the welfare state as an important element in the political economy of advanced market economies.[4] Instead, it has concentrated on industrial relations, financial systems, systems of vocational training, and 'national systems of innovation'. The central thesis of this literature, however, is that these 'extra-economic' features of modern market economies have a crucial impact on the operation of market forces in the advanced industrialized nations and that they can explain much of the observed systematic differences in economic performance between them. The CPE literature holds that these different institutional arrangements represent complementary, coherent, mutual 'fitting' complexes that give rise to distinct patterns of economic performance. The literature on the 'varieties of capitalism' (Soskice 1990*a*, *b*; Hollingsworth et al. 1993; Berger and Dore 1996; Hollingsworth and Boyer 1997; Crouch and Streeck 1997; Kitschelt et al. 1999; Hall and Soskice, forthcoming) especially highlights the distinct ways in which markets are institutionally embedded. All evidence provided by this new literature points to the fact that differences in the 'institutional environment' of modern market economies go a long way in explaining the nationally distinct patterns of economic performance. These patterns have been distinguished mainly by the different degrees to which an economy allows for long-term economic coordination among firms, between lender and borrower of investment capital, and between managers and workers (see Soskice 1990*a*, 1990*b*, 1999).

---

[4] There are however clear signals that this will soon change. See the important contribution by Mares 1998. See also the contributions in Ebbinghaus and Manow, forthcoming.

As I argue here, the welfare state must be perceived as an important part of this institutional complex. The welfare state has contributed significantly to the emergence of distinct profiles of economic performance in the advanced industrialized nations. Thus, understanding the micro-links between production and labour regimes, on the one hand, and social protection regimes, on the other, is a precondition for understanding the interests of the central corporate actors in contemporary welfare reforms. Yet how exactly can we conceive of the welfare state as a 'fundamental force in the organization and stratification of contemporary capitalism'? Which kind of micro-links exist between the realms of protection and production? These are the questions I will now address.

2. THE COMPARATIVE ADVANTAGE OF A TIGHT PROTECTION/PRODUCTION NEXUS

This section claims that the welfare state plays a crucial economic role especially with regard to its impact on the long-term cooperation and co-ordination among the core economic agents within a national system of production.

Successful long-term economic coordination presupposes institutions that enable economic agents to engage and invest in long-term and trusted transactions. The central thesis of this section is that the welfare state can be such a supportive institution. If coordination is made possible because markets are deeply embedded institutionally, investments either in specific skills, in special 'machinery', or in economic transaction chains with a long time-horizon become possible—investments that would either be impossible or very costly in a spot-market context. Subsequently, these investments can translate into a comparative advantage for the firm, the sector, or the economy as a whole (Lazonick 1990, 1991). Economic coordination can enable the creation of special market niches that are not at all or only scarcely contested by competitors. With economic coordination, high fixed costs can co-exist with low unit costs (Lazonick 1992).

This argument can be located within a more general transaction-cost framework. The notion of 'asset specificity' is central in this respect. Stated in very broad terms, the transaction-cost theory of industrial organization holds that 'the more specific the assets in question to their current use, the greater the incentive for their owners to carry out economic activity within one economic entity rather than in spot markets at arm's length. This leads to predictions about the degree to which industries or firms will be characterized by vertical integration and long-term contractual arrangements' (Alt et al. 1996: 700–1). Generalized for entire production systems, this argument maintains that economic agents possess a comparative advantage vis-à-vis their competitors—in certain market segments—if institutions reduce the high degree of vulnerability involved in long-chain transactions and of long-term investments. Successful economic coordination allows economic agents to gain quasi-rents—they can 'cash in' the lower transaction costs that come with their highly asset-specific investments. On their own, employers and workers are usually not capable of creating institutions that would make long-term stable coordination among them possible, because the creation of these institutions is subject to the very same coordination and enforcement problems that these institutions then would be able to alleviate. Normally, external intervention, i.e. predominantly state intervention, into employment relations is critical for establishing long-term economic coordination. Thus, either the state or dense regional or family networks providing the necessary trust to rule out 'opportunism' can create the structures and institutions within which successful and time-stable economic coordination can take place.

Social policy is a central domain for both direct or indirect state intervention into the employment relation. Social policy may translate directly into an economic advantage because a high social wage poses a 'beneficial constraint' (Streeck 1997a) for employers and employees—a beneficial constraint that is said to force economic agents to search for high-skill/high-wage production strategies. But state intervention into employment relations may be also important because it potentially (depending on the form of intervention, see below) allows forms of productive economic coordination and cooperation which would be infeasible otherwise. This coordination then helps firms to pursue strategies with which they can 'bite a chunk out of the market'. As a consequence, they can earn above-average profits because they have a comparative advantage over their less coordinated competitors. Thus, it is the form of state intervention into labour relations and the specific institutions thereby created that may enable economic agents to occupy market segments and competition-sheltered niches. In turn, this may make it possible to pay out wages above the competitive minimum and may create avenues for redistributive policies. Hence, the welfare state may be economically beneficial not only because it provides both 'market security for capitalists as well as social security for workers' (Swenson 1997: 69) by imposing the same social costs on all firms—an argument that applies especially to welfare states in a closed economy—but also because it may allow firms to specialize and to develop comparative advantages over less coordinated competitors. This argument highlights the potentially positive economic externalities of social intervention in an open economy. In essence, the welfare state can provide firms with 'external economies' (Alfred Marshall) by offering an infrastructure for economic cooperation. Note that the transaction-cost argument referring to the 'economic value of social policy' implies a different prediction with regard to the sustainability of generous levels of social protection within an internationalized market as compared to the 'market security' argument put forward by Peter Swenson. Whereas employers' interest in market security provided by uniform standards of social protection should quickly vanish in an international environment in which anything but a least common denominator standard is out of reach, the interest in the beneficial economic side-effects of welfare programmes should remain in place and may even increase within a global market.

But which forms of social intervention into the market have been and still are particularly supportive of long-term economic coordination and can enhance competitiveness? I argue that the welfare regimes which potentially enhance competitiveness are those which have established a strong nexus between production and protection, i.e. which have managed to integrate organized capital and labour into the welfare state and which have linked entitlements to the employment relation.[5] I am referring to the welfare states of Continental Europe that are based upon occupational principles, show only moderate to low levels of redistribution, and honour long-term employment careers. The Japanese model of life-long employment plus encompassing company welfare provides a very similar set of incentives with regard to the acquisition of skills, the pursuit of a secure career, and a low wage differentiation among the workforce. In both social insurance systems, a high degree of programme fragmentation corresponds to a targeting of benefits to clearly delineated groups of workers. These different variants of the occupationally based welfare regime come close to what Titmuss has labelled the 'industrial achievement-performance model of social policy' (Titmuss 1974). This model can support long-term economic coordination in numerous ways. For example, earning-related premiums and benefits justify high replacement ratios and legitimize the maintenance of pay differentials at retirement. If linked to levels of qualification, long-term pay differentials may make it profitable for workers to invest in the acquisition of additional skills. Moreover, skill investments might be protected against

---

[5] It is not possible here to give a full historical account as to why certain welfare states have developed into employment-based systems integrating capital and labour, while others either reveal mainly clientelistic features (the southern model of social policy; see Ferrera 1997) or are almost entirely based on the status of citizenship rather than employment (the liberal, Anglo-Saxon model; see Esping-Andersen 1990). While there are two factors frequently mentioned in the literature: late versus early industrialization and successful vs. unsuccessful liberal–labour coalition building (cf. Luebbert 1991), I hold that a third important variable is regularly overlooked: state tradition, in particular the different traditions of patrimonial absolutism (Southern Europe), bureaucratic absolutism (Continental Europe) and bureaucratic constitutionalism (UK and Scandinavia); see Ertman (1997). Mobilization of societal interests followed different paths in these three settings. To state it very generally: the logic of interest mediation was clientelistic in the first setting, associational in the second, and electoral in the third setting. This argument, however, must be elaborated upon elsewhere.

the danger of rapid deskilling during periods of unemployment by stipulating generous criteria for the 'acceptability' of alternative job offers and by
establishing a long period of eligibility for strictly income-related benefits.
Again, a functional equivalent would be the implicit promise of a no-dismissal
policy.[6] These income-related welfare provisions can support production
regimes that put premiums on long-term strategies to invest in skills, to
follow more long-range career plans, and to particularly emphasize the social
status of a job. Welfare provisions that are closely linked to employment relations can shelter these strategies from market insecurity, stretching the time
horizon of workers beyond the period of a single labour contract.[7]

Furthermore, welfare schemes that were targeted at the upper segment
of the labour market often provided unions with critical organizational support (see the importance of the Ghent system for union organization; cf.
Rothstein 1992). Unions could fill posts and had a say in big-ticket budget
issues. Pension funds have been used to finance workers' housing, which in
turn provided unions with selective incentives to induce workers to join the
union. Alternatively, welfare funds have been used for corporate finance, for
providing firms with low-interest credit and 'patient capital' (see Estevez-Abe,
forthcoming for the Japanese case), thus allowing long-term strategic investments and relieving firms from the pressure of instant profit maximization.
Legal counselling in questions of social insurance often figured as another
important selective incentive offered by unions to their membership. Historically, this strengthened unions as well as organizations (see Manow 1997*a*
for Germany). As a consequence, unions could make labour contracts binding either by intervening politically, or by threatening to strike and by cap-
italizing on their powerful position within collective bargaining. Employers
had to take the unions into account and anticipate their enduring presence.
This in turn forced employers to organize and to pursue more long-term

Replacement rates of public pensions in relation to income level

1992	$20,000	$50,000
UK	50%	26%
US	65%	40%
Japan	54%	54%
Germany	70%	59%

Source: Davis 1995: 43.

  [6] Take the degree of 'linearity' of pension replacement ratios with levels of previous income
as an example. Here coordinated market economies reveal a clearly distinct pattern compared
with liberal market economies.
  [7] In this sense, generous earning-related pensions can be a partial functional equivalent to
seniority wages and lifetime employment.

strategies as well. Binding labour contracts provided both sides, employers and employees, with a long-range perspective. Under these circumstances, certain organizational and individual (skill) investments became profitable that would not have been so in a spot-market context.

Moreover, since the 'industrial achievement-performance' welfare state model already focused on a worker's status, unions no longer had to bargain much over detailed job descriptions. Unions were less resistant to in-house flexibility—thus they could pursue less adversarial bargaining strategies that led to the emergence of trust-based methods of production. The transition from trade unions to either industrial unions or company unions was thus facilitated by occupational-based welfare states. Note that both industrial and company unions organize skilled and unskilled workers and therefore had an interest in a comparatively narrow wage spread. This again motivated policies of up-skilling and supported a high-wage/high-productivity equilibrium. Furthermore, the joint administration of welfare schemes by workers' and employers' associations often meant that the regulations concerning bene-fits, eligibility, coverage, etc., could be tailored especially to the needs of the 'social partners'. The welfare state was increasingly designed to serve their particular needs. This is most evident in the diverse pathways into early retire-ment through which unions and employers, especially in exposed sectors of the economy, could transfer the costs of economic adjustment to the broader risk community of those paying into the social insurance system (Kohli et al. 1991). Generous unemployment and (early) retirement and disability benefits could buffer the adverse effects of cyclical downswings on companies with-out destroying the by and large peaceful and consensual relation between workers and managers on which production was based. This is an import-ant precondition for the type of investment in fixed capital (employers) or in skills (employees) that will not pay off instantaneously but only at a much later date. Therefore, the joint administration of welfare schemes could both partially support and partially substitute the corporatist concertation of business and labour in the central political arena (cf. Manow 1997*a*).

Hence, the vulnerability and 'competitiveness' of contemporary welfare states within an internationalized economy is a question of distribution and of pro-duction (see Rhodes's notion of 'productive' and 'distributive coalitions' in welfare reform; in this volume). The institutional set-up of a given welfare state and its impact on the national system of production is possibly of greater relevance than the 'relative generosity' or, for that matter, the extent to which the welfare state succeeds in the de-commodification of labour. Furthermore, transaction-cost arguments suggest that a close link coupling 'production' and 'protection' in a country might substantially reduce the mobility of firms and might undermine the credibility of business' threats to relocate out of the country. Elaborated welfare state programmes, which firms have learned to 'exploit' (while they continue to complain publicly about their drawbacks) and to which they have adapted their mode of production, may lessen a firm's temptation to relocate even though some production costs could be lowered significantly if the business moved somewhere else. The more the comparative advantage of a production model is based upon a certain institutional environment, the weaker the incentives are for firms to leave this environment. Hence, an encompassing/expensive employment-based welfare state may not be the reason why business relocates abroad, but it may indeed substantially reduce the tendency of business to engage in 'regime shopping' —making the welfare state less of an incentive and more of an impediment to business mobility. In turn, business would lobby more intensively to maintain the welfare state features it values and to reform those features it does not (cf. Alt et al. 1996). We can safely expect that business uses the exit threat in its lobbying efforts thus exploiting the asymmetrical information between firms and policy makers over the firms' true cost-functions.

Take for example the specialization of German firms in flexible quality production (Streeck 1996) or high-quality incremental innovation (HQII) (Carlin and Soskice 1997). This production strategy depends critically on the institutional support provided by the dual system of vocational training, the uniform wages set in industry-wide collective bargaining, and income-based pension and unemployment schemes, to name a few factors (see Soskice et al. 1997). Firms that have specialized in this form of production have made asset-specific investments, which would be lost should the business relocate (see Alt et al. 1996). The same is true for workers whose skill acquirement is based upon expectations of the future—a future that is once again shaped greatly by the way welfare programmes link current employment to later welfare entitlements. Given the strong nexus between welfare state programmes and labour and production regimes, it is no surprise that employers and unions alike oppose reforms that would endanger core features of the German system (see S. Wood 1997*b*, and in this volume; Thelen 1999; Mares 1996; a very similar argument for another prominent coordinated market economy, Japan, is provided by S. Vogel 1998).

Thus, the importance of unions and employers' associations in reforming the Continental welfare state arises from both their institutional role in the administration of these schemes and from the important economic benefits which are at stake for them. In generalizing from the above example we may roughly distinguish some basic patterns of welfare state adjustments in Western European countries. If one follows the transaction-cost argument outlined above, the salience of the 'economic cost' argument over the 'institutional benefit' argument depends upon how closely the welfare state and the economy are linked. Where such linkages do not exist, such as in liberal or residual welfare states and in liberal market economies, welfare reform often does seem to be characterized by a simple distributive conflict. Welfare reforms follow primarily an electoral logic, politicians design their proposals to woo the average voter. Adjustments to market pressure take place in the form of welfare retrenchment, and employment-related welfare schemes tend to be privatized. Yet at the same time, universal provision with basic social services becomes (relatively) more important (e.g. health care or care for the elderly). In Continental welfare states, business and labour play more leading and not necessarily conflicting roles in welfare reforms. With regard to their position much depends on the skill- and capital-intensity of production, the firm size, the relative importance of social transfer payments to the core workforce as compared with spending for social services, and the representation of interests in the administrative structure of the welfare state. In short: much depends on which kind of firms or industries and worker especially profit from existing arrangements. Of course, the organizational strength and interest homogeneity of unions and employers' associations also have a great impact. Often unions protect existing arrangements not because it is in the interest of their core clientele, but because it is in the interest of the organizations themselves to protect union-run schemes or because the union rank and file has developed a vested interest in welfare state administration. Generally, the Continental welfare states experienced little change during the 1990s, since both employers and unions often showed lukewarm support at best for attempts at profound reform. Programmes directly relevant to production and labour regimes, such as early retirement schemes, unemployment insurance, or active labour market policies, were often exempt from retrenchment. In some cases, programmes were even expanded considerably. Efforts to contain costs concentrated instead on health care and related social services.

Unlike either the liberal or the Continental welfare states, the tradition of 'clientelismo' in the southern model of welfare (cf. Ferrera 1996, 1997) has given unions, employers' associations, and reform-minded politicians the opportunity to free the welfare state from slack and to improve the efficiency of the social security systems while cutting costs. The abuse of the welfare state by its clientele actually brought about a tripartite win–win solution, in which 'vices could be turned into virtues' (cf. Levy 1999) while social spending could be contained—or at least a further growth in welfare expenditures could be forestalled. Yet, what is especially important in the context of our argument is that centrally negotiated welfare reforms in the European periphery have to be perceived as attempts to emulate the patterns of economic and social policy coordination between the social partners that are already deeply entrenched in the welfare states of the European core. In this perspective 'contracted change' in Italy, Spain, Portugal, Ireland, Finland, etc. takes place not despite, but because of the lack of the institutional precondition for corporatist concertation and long-term economic coordination.[8]

---

[8] And the revival of corporatist concertation in Belgium and the Netherlands can be understood as a reaction to the degeneration that corporatism experienced in these two countries during the late 1970s and early 1980s (see for the Dutch case, Visser and Hemerijck 1997).

I hold that these patterns of adjustment briefly outlined here can hardly be understood without reference to the different interests of business and unions in welfare reform, given that these central actors are situated so differently in the various types of European welfare regimes. At the same time, this argument suggests that we will rather see internal shifts between different social programmes than an overall pattern of welfare retrenchment as an answer to increased economic pressures. As a general pattern however we will see the resilience of coordination between organized capital and labour within the open economies of Europe and the continuing influence of these corporate actors on the fate and character of future welfare reforms. Moreover, given the extremely poor labour market performance of the Continental welfare states, the presented analysis suggests that we reinterpret our understanding of 'better performing' and 'badly performing socioeconomic institutions' (cf. Garrett and Lange 1996: 52–3). I maintain that it is the political relevance of micro-level competitiveness in addition to or even in place of macro-economic performance, the high stakes involved for unions and business in welfare reform, and the increased importance of the corporate actors of both capital and labour in the contemporary political reform processes that explain the apparent mismatch between factual problem load and actual reforms undertaken in the Continental welfare states.

In the last section, I will briefly highlight some implications of the presented argument for the current debate on welfare state adjustments within increasingly international markets.

3. COMPETITIVE WELFARE STATES IN THE OPEN ECONOMY

In the debate over the fate of the welfare state in the open economy the traditional view holds that the welfare state is a kind of *post hoc* domestic compensation for the social costs of economic integration into world markets. I have tried to show that this interpretation leaves out an important part of the story. That the welfare state is not essentially 'autarchic . . . protective and nationalistic' (Myrdal 1957: 13 and 15) has already been argued very convincingly by Peter Katzenstein, who maintains that domestic intervention and expansive public spending are not only very compatible with a high degree of integration into world markets, but can indeed support such development (Katzenstein 1984, 1985b; see Garrett 1995). From this perspective, social policy is conceived of as a 'functional equivalent' for protectionism, albeit one securing a higher welfare level for the entire society (Ruggie 1982). The welfare state is said to compensate domestic losers out of the revenue accrued by the winners on internationalized markets (cf. Leibfried and Rieger

1998). In this way, broad political support for liberal trade regimes is secured (Rodrik 1997; Garrett 1998*b*). For instance, active labour market policy may ease the adjustment to shifts between industrial sectors or in product markets and thus may 'facilitate rapid and positive adjustment to changes in international market conditions' (Garrett and Lange 1991: 546). A credible political commitment to full employment allows unions to follow a wage-restraint strategy and thus maximize long-term income and job security instead of struggling for immediate wage hikes. This secures the competitiveness of national products on the world market. John Ruggie has called this the 'grand domestic bargain: societies were asked to embrace the change and dislocation attending international liberalization, but the state promised to cushion those effects by means of its newly acquired domestic economic and social policy roles' (Ruggie 1997: 6; for a fundamental critique of this argument see Iversen, in this volume).

But the conservative welfare states of the Continent have often preferred to finance unemployment instead of active labour market policies. And not everywhere was the labour movement sufficiently centralized, not everywhere allowed the political institutions for corporatist concertation of capital and labour, and not everywhere were central banks willing to follow a loose monetary policy in order for the corporatist exchange between unions and (leftist) governments to take place (cf. Scharpf 1987). Hence, 'social democratic corporatism' turned out to be just one way to combine an open economy with a generous welfare state. The 'Keynesian welfare state' (cf. Garrett and Lange 1996; Garrett 1995), with its core features of 'Keynesian demand management, capital controls, industrial policy, and extensive public provision of welfare and other social services' (Garrett and Lange 1996: 61), does not exhaust the source of potential linkages between domestic welfare and a liberal trade regime and should not be treated as the sole reference model against which the probability of neoliberal deregulation of advanced welfare states can be assessed (cf. Iversen 1999*a*). Moreover, the Continental compromise between external openness and internal compensation seems to be at least as stable politically as the social democratic compromise, despite the fact that its employment performance is much poorer.

By looking at the micro-effects of welfare regimes, it becomes obvious that the welfare state can well support high degrees of world market integration without having to maintain the Keynesian macroeconomic equilibrium between wage restraint practised in central corporatist wage-setting systems, full employment policies, and monetary and fiscal policies that support business investments. Although countries that have not followed the traditional, nordic social democratic strategy might have performed less well with respect to employment, high unemployment in the Continental countries was not incompatible with high degrees of trade openness (see Huber and Stephens, in this volume, Table 4.3). The lack of active labour market policies and generous government spending did not affect the high degree of international competitiveness of business in these countries. These obvious limitations to the explanatory power of the compensation hypothesis are underscored by the argument presented here, which emphasizes that 'international liberalization' does not necessarily start a chain reaction that ends up with 'domestic compensation' (Katzenstein 1985: 39). Instead, domestic social intervention often enables firms to become international in the first place. Ironically, it is the Continental welfare state itself that often generates the 'domestic losers' of world market integration if a high, but still internationally competitive social wage generates severe problems for domestic employment in the low-skill/low-productivity (service) labour segments (cf. Scharpf 1997*b*; Iversen and Wren 1998; for Germany, Manow and Seils 1999).

6

The Political Economy of Social Pacts: 'Competitive Corporatism' and European Welfare Reform

Martin Rhodes

ONE of the most significant achievements of the post-war era has been the reconciliation of economic growth with varying degrees of social justice within Western European welfare states. Yet the capacity for achieving this compromise has been thrown into question by a number of major challenges. Pressures for retrenchment including 'globalization', low economic growth, and unsustainable public sector deficits have hit up against counter-pressures for larger social outlays. The latter comprise demographic change (a higher ratio of active citizens to passive welfare recipients), the rising cost of health care, the appearance of new social risks linked to high and persisting rates of unemployment and the changing nature of the labour market, household patterns, and family/gender relationships.

At the same time, the 'disorganizing' impact of socio-economic change (post-Fordism and the transformation of production, the emergence of the service economy, and the breakdown of former welfare-supporting coalitions) has purportedly rendered impotent the capacity of welfare systems to negotiate their way to a new and sustainable equilibrium. Efficiency and equality, growth and redistribution, competitiveness and solidarity are frequently referred to as polar opposites, able only to thrive at each other's expense. In many quarters, this formulation of the problem has become accepted as common wisdom.

Yet one of the most important, but until now neglected, aspects of the 'new politics of welfare' in Western Europe are new nationally negotiated social pacts, designed precisely to bridge these apparent polar opposites. These were referred to in a previous article (Rhodes 1998) as 'competitive corporatism' (an apparent oxymoron) in order to signal their search for elaborate equity-based compromises and trade-offs. These pacts, which have proliferated since the late 1980s, have major implications for welfare states by bridging, and

I am grateful to Jonathan Zeitlin for his very useful comments on an earlier version of this article.

innovating in linkages between social security systems and employment rules and wage bargaining.

Despite important differences between them—due to membership of diverse welfare state models and industrial relations traditions—all social pacts consist of new market-conforming policy mixes. But they are far from being vehicles for neoliberal hegemony or economic nationalism (cf. Streeck 1996). The essential argument of Section 1 of this chapter is that the emergence of social pacts is rather linked to common domestic and external pressures for reform in the European Union. As is argued in some detail, contrary to the expectations of many commentators, these pressures are neither 'disorganizing' European capitalism nor neutralizing the power of the state, although they certainly do present a series of challenges unprecedented in the post-war era. While governments may have lost their power to expand social spending at will, due largely to their inability to sustain growing public deficits, they remain the principal architects of welfare states and employment systems.

Furthermore, rather than fragmenting political-economic structures, the impact of pressures for reform have in many instances modified or even bolstered efforts at coordination via bargaining. For, as discussed in Section 2, which introduces the notion of 'competitive corporatism', underpinning these pacts are varying degrees of associational cohesion and the development to one extent or another of two types of coalition—seeking distributional deals and productivity gains—with complex linkages and overlaps between them. In ideal-typical terms, it can be suggested that 'competitive corporatism' is successfully achieved if underpinned by a close but flexible interlocking of the two. Admittedly, certain countries will be unable to put such pacts in place. The recent experiences of Germany (where coalitions seem to form more readily at the regional (länder) level, Belgium (where successful experiments along Dutch lines have been ruled out by the salience of ethno-linguistic conflict), and France (where concertation has always been prevented by the weaknesses and fragmentation of union and employers' organizations) all attest to problems of innovating in relations between private and public actors in complex political economies.

1. THE POLITICAL ECONOMY OF
NEGOTIATED REFORM

Social Pacts and European Welfare Reform

Despite the forecasts of the bulk of analysis in recent years, corporatism— apparently a now defunct feature of Europe's organized political economies of the 1950s–1970s—has not gone away, either as a mechanism for coordinating wage bargaining or for negotiating wider policy options. Indeed, recent years have witnessed the preservation (in modified form) of corporatism in countries where it has always been strong, as well as its emergence in those where the traditional prerequisites (e.g. strong, centralized, hierarchically ordered interest associations) have been weak.

Apart from Sweden, the traditional corporatist countries of Central and Northern Europe have seen their centralized or coordinated bargaining systems modified or recast rather than abandoned. The Swedish case, in which coordinated bargaining broke down under pressure from employers and the strains of sustaining solidarity wages in a more competitive international environment, turned out to be the exception (Wallerstein and Golden 1997). By contrast, bargaining remains 'centralized' in Finland, Denmark, and Norway, even if the structures of bargaining have become more supple as a result of buffeting by macroeconomic policy turbulence in the 1980s. In Denmark, the 1990s have seen the emergence of five large bargaining cartels, with even greater controls on plant-level bargaining than in the past. Meanwhile, state influence has ensured that the 'free and voluntarist' system of collective negotiation has taken account of new contingencies, especially participation in phases 1 and 2 of EMU (Lind 1997). In Norway, centralized negotiations were re-established in the late 1980s after a period of industry-level bargaining. In 1992, the so-called 'solidarity alternative' (*solidaritetsalternativet*) forged with the trade union confederation, LO, put in place an incomes policy to help strengthen the competitiveness of Norwegian companies and reduce unemployment (Dølvik and Martin 1997). In Finland, a reunification of blue-collar unions in the late 1960s has assisted the government's strategy in the 1990s of combining fiscal consolidation with a centralized wage bargaining (Kiander 1997). Institutional adaptation and preservation of social consensus has helped the Nordic welfare states weather the recessions of the 1980s and 1990s while also accommodating pressures for changes in social programmes and labour market regulation. As the authors of a recent survey conclude, despite some 'shaky ground' there is no evidence of retrenchment and dismantling and 'all of the traditional hallmarks of the Nordic model appeared to be very much alive' (Heikkilä et al. 1999: 271). Meanwhile Austria—with especially high levels of openness and tertiarization (purportedly the two major threats to social partnership and negotiated reform)—has also remained highly corporatist, although with considerable flexibility in its wage bargaining structures (Traxler 1997*b*; Wallerstein, Golden, and Lange 1997).

Then there are the countries—all to be discussed in detail below—where new social pacts have grown on apparently arid ground In some, a moribund corporatist tradition has been revitalized. Among these the Netherlands takes pride of place. After an interlude of industrial relations strife, the mid-1980s saw a revival of Dutch corporatist policy making—again with flexible, decentralized bargains within a coordinated structure. This has produced something of a model—to be discussed in greater detail below—for advocates of a 'third way' between neoliberal deregulation and the traditional solidaristic European model (Visser and Hemerijck 1997). In Ireland, a country which frequently tried but failed to put in place a workable incomes policy in the 1970s (Hardiman 1988) has now developed a rather comprehensive social pact. Negotiated in successive phases—in 1987, 1990, 1993 and most recently in 1997—this pact has addressed tax, education, health, and social welfare issues in addition to incomes.

The real surprises are Italy, Portugal, and Spain. In these countries, the institutional preconditions for national pacts are particularly weak, and the potential for conflict—over both labour market and social policy reform—especially high given the intensity of pressures for change and the strength of veto groups (Ferrera 1996; Rhodes 1997a). In Italy, negotiations in the early 1990s on reforming automatic wage-indexation were extended to the rationalization of bargaining structures, the reform of workplace union representation, improvements to the training system, the legalization of temporary work agencies, employment regulation reform, and the May 1995 agreement on pension reform. In Portugal, five tripartite pacts since 1987 have focused on incomes and social and labour market measures. The 1996 agreement also covers social security issues, including a minimum wage, a reduction of income tax for low-income groups, and a more favourable tax treatment of a range of benefits, including health and education and pensions. In Spain, a long period blockage in welfare and labour market reform has given way to a new national bargain—the Toledo Pact—allowing progress on pensions reform and innovations in loosening up a highly rigid labour market (Rhodes 1998). In all cases, a process of new coalition building has been embarked upon, with greater success in some than in others. In those countries with weak prerequisites for national bargains, functional equivalents have been put in place, either by institution building (making representational change part of the bargain) or via complex package deals (extending the bargain from incomes policy to social security and tax reform).

Why is this happening? A good place to start is the globalization debate —a logical embarkation point given that trade competition, global financial markets, and the power of transnational capital has supposedly made such corporatist pacts impossible.

'Disorganized' Capitalism? Globalization and Socio-economic Change

Globalization

Many engaged in the debate about the welfare state's future have tended to downplay or at least relativize the impact of globalization and its interaction with other, domestic, challenges (e.g. Pierson 1997d; Fligstein 1998).

The following argument takes the globalization arguments more seriously, while also maintaining that globalization works within domestic national contexts. Indeed, it is the relationship between external pressures (both in the international and integrating European economies) that is rendering the search for new negotiated solutions essential in much of Continental Europe. Given the prevalence of 'strong globalization' assumptions it is worth stating from the outset that national economies have neither been wholly absorbed into a new global order nor their governments totally incapacitated. Non-tradeables remain important in most European economies and national comparative advantage and specialization remain critical for international competition (see Perraton et al. 1997). Good arguments for the compatibility of large welfare states with internationalization are regularly rehearsed. Welfare states emerged in line with the growing openness of economies and facilitated the consequent process of socio-economic adjustment (e.g. Rieger and Leibfried 1998). Government consumption appears to play an important insulating role in economies subject to external shocks (Rodrik 1996).

Moreover, rather than globalization being the main culprit welfare states have, as Pierson (1997*d*) argues, generated many of their own problems. By helping improve living standards and lifespans they have created new needs that social services were not originally designed to meet. Rising health care costs and pensions provisions have contributed massively to welfare budgets and fiscal strains. Other problems—e.g. the decline in demand for low or unskilled manufacturing workers—stem from the increasingly post-industrial nature of advanced societies (Rowthorn and Ramaswamy 1997). Post-industrial change has created a 'service sector trilemma' (Iversen and Wren 1998) in which the goals of employment growth, wage equality, and budgetary constraint come increasingly into conflict (see also Esping-Andersen 1996*a* and Scharpf 1997*a*; 1999). Creating private service sector employment may entail lower wage and non-wage costs, risking greater inequality, while generating such employment in the public sector has hit up against budget limits in many countries. The interaction between these developments and globalization are far from straightforward. To cite Pierson (1997*d*), while 'it is important to recognize the linkages between international and domestic developments . . . such links are likely to be more modest, complex and bi-directional than is commonly suggested.'

But these links do exist and should be taken seriously. Consider the issue of trade competition. The thesis that trade with the South will lead to declining demand for unskilled labour and either lower wages or higher unemployment in the North (as strongly argued, for example, by A. Wood 1994, 1995) has been contested. Thus better qualifications command a return to human capital and protect many workers in the North (R. B. Freeman 1995*a*). Specialization in different goods reduces downward wage pressures in developed nations (Thygesen, Kosai, and Lawrence 1996). Others (e.g. Slaughter and Swagel 1997) argue that technological change is the principal culprit in the shift from lower to higher skilled labour demand. It is unlikely, though, that trade has nothing to do with this. Snower (1997) links trade competition with skill-biased technological change and 'the organizational revolution' in firms (flatter hierarchies, flexible specialization, the adoption of 'lean' and 'just-in-time' methods), which adds a further dimension to the service sector trilemma. By making jobs less secure, argues Snower, these developments create greater reliance on unemployment insurance, public support for education and training, and a wide variety of welfare services. This may create a 'quicksand effect' as welfare structures designed for a different era get weighed down, generating negative effects, destroying incentives, and making redistributive policies inefficient. Such developments can be generated not just by international, but by more competitive intra-European trade, circumventing the argument that trade with the rest of the world (around 14 per cent) is too small to explain European employment problems (cf. Fligstein 1998).

What about the globalization of finance? Although its effect is often exaggerated, the interaction of a number of developments should be acknowledged. First, there is the Mundell–Fleming theorem or the 'unholy trinity' which states that exchange rate stability, capital mobility, and domestic monetary independence cannot be achieved simultaneously (Andrews 1994; see also Webb 1991; Frieden 1991; Goodman and Pauly 1993). In an environment of international austerity, it becomes increasingly costly for individual states to pursue an expansionary monetary policy as part of an effort to stimulate growth and employment. Second, the emergence in the 1970s of a new world market for capital has resulted in an explosion of global short-term flows, making capital restrictions more difficult to maintain. In the absence of relative capital immobility, domestic policy priorities—e.g. full employment—must be subordinated to defending the balance of payments, a priority to which both fiscal and monetary policies are redirected (Moses 1995). Third, increased financial integration has increased the social and political power of capital—in particular capitalists with mobile or diversified assets. The power of multinationals to 'arbitrage' diverse national structures and force deep, structural convergence across diverse societies has been described as 'chimerical' (Pauly and Reich 1997: 24 ff.). And the evidence shows that the bulk of FDI continues to go to relatively high-wage and high-tax countries (Weiss 1997: 10). Nevertheless, the relocation threat can exert a powerful influence on domestic policy and institutional arrangements, as shown, for example, in Germany where large firms have used it to weaken the power of unions and force concession bargaining (F. Mueller 1996).

Then there is tax competition. Swank (1998*a*) has argued against the claim that international capital mobility has generated a shift away from capital taxation. Governments continue to rely on corporate taxes for a significant, and in some cases, a growing share of revenue. Changes in the structure and rates of taxation have coincided with attempts to make the overall changes revenue neutral or protect the revenue needs of the state. Rate cuts have been offset by broadening the tax base and eliminating investment-related allowances, credits, and exemptions. Nevertheless, Clayton and Pontusson (1998) argue that even if corporate tax reforms have not shifted the tax burden onto labour, by limiting the use of the tax code as a means of boosting invest-ment and employment, life is made a lot harder for social democratic gov-ernments. As Ganghof and Genschel (1999) point out, while revenues from capital income taxation may not have fallen since the 1980s, on average, they have also not increased. This has contributed to the fact that the average total tax ratio of the eighteen most advanced (and largest) OECD countries has stagnated since the mid-1980s and has failed to keep up with increas-ing public expenditures. Tax competition may not be the main cause of the financing problems of the welfare state, but it has constrained policy responses by making some forms of revenue-raising more costly at a time when pressures for increased spending abound.

What are the policy implications for European welfare states? Interpre-tations differ. While Garrett (1995, 1998*b*) concludes that the 'propensity to deficit-spend' has not been constrained by increasing trade and capital mobility, he also points out that the integration of financial markets has put a premium on left-wing policies in terms of higher interest rates. Keohane and Milner (1996) suggest that financial market integration or capital mobil-ity have potentially a much more detrimental effect on the policy making autonomy of Left-Labour governments than trade integration. Swank, on the other hand, argues that more important are the pressures placed on taxation by trade competition and low rates of growth (1998*a*: 678–9). Whatever the particular interpretation, at a time when EMU has forced a reduction in deficits and debts, and rendered competitive devaluation impossible for its member countries, even a 'globalization sceptic' has to accept the con-straining nature of these developments.

But the way out of this conundrum does not necessarily involve neoliberal deregulation. Thus many countries are engaged in policy innovations to reduce the 'quicksand' effect of social policy provisions by tackling the costs of transfer-heavy welfare states and redesigning benefit formulas so as to make them both financially sustainable and more employment friendly. They are also reconfiguring a range of fiscal policies and their relationship with social security expenditure. Moreover none of the above are necessarily inimical to negotiated paths of adjustment. Nor is responding to the accentuated power of the markets. As Glyn (1995*b*) has argued, globalization has often been made the scapegoat for the failure of certain countries to control their domes-tic sources of social conflict and spending. The real task is to build or rebuild domestic coalitions and arrangements containing trade-offs that make such policies 'credible'. The same can be said of multinationals, often assumed to be instrumental in diminishing state autonomy. Domestic bargaining arenas in all parts of the world impose huge social, political, and financial constraints on multinationals (Ruigrok and Tulder 1995) and the 'rootlessness' of such firms has been much exaggerated. They too can be linked into new national bargains sustaining high-wage, high-productivity solutions.

Socio-economic Change

Such bargains are supposedly made harder by broader processes of socio-economic change, some of which are also linked to globalization. Crepaz (1992) maintained that corporatist policies had retained their capacity to achieve their desired macroeconomic goals in the 1980s but he was a lone voice. Most concurred that organizational fragmentation and decentralization, spurred on by flexible specialization and the 'disorganizing' effects of globalization, had brought the corporatist era to a close. Grahl and Teague (1997: 418) argued that 'as a strategic programme for the resolution of employment issues, neo-corporatism is moribund—defeated on the ground by the actual evolution of employment relations before reluctant abandonment by its academic proponents'. Lash and Urry (1987) developed a persuasive thesis that the transition to post-Fordism meant a widespread process of flexible decentralization, undermining traditional hierarchies and associations. Others, such as Hirst and Zeitlin (1991) were more cautious, suggesting that while not necessarily undercutting corporatist concertation, flexible specialization did require increased scope for the adjustment of employment arrangements at the firm or local levels. Invoking changes in the macroeconomic environment, Streeck and Schmitter (1991) powerfully argued that a combination of the business cycle effect and European integration would unravel the logic of corporatist exchange. Loose labour markets meant less need for centralized bargaining institutions for stabilizing wages and prices while an integrated European economy with constrained macroeconomic policies would reduce the scope for state package deals or side payments to unions and employers. Gobeyn (1993: 20) neatly summarized a common view: 'contemporary economic realities—slow growth, deindustrialization, the continuing installations on shop floors of labor-saving technologies—make corporatism largely unnecessary. Market forces alone can presently achieve labor discipline and wage demand moderation.'

In reality, the effects of contemporary socio-economic change are much less straightforward. Contradictory tendencies are at work. Decentralization in centralized industrial relations systems has occurred. The new international division of labour within large transnational firms and the presence of the latter national bargaining arenas have made collective bargaining more complex. So too have divided interests between traded and non-traded capital and labour. A shift to more sectorally based forms of bargaining has followed employer and worker demands for greater wage differentiation. Meanwhile, employers in all systems are searching for greater company- and plant-level flexibility in three areas: internal (or functional) flexibility in the workplace; external (or numerical) flexibility vis-à-vis the wider labour market; and greater pay flexibility at local levels. At the same time, the creation of the single market and the achievement of EMU have placed new pressures on wage-cost competition.

But labour market rules and the wider systems of social security to which they are often linked are not dysfunctional for growth as such. Nor is it the case that labour market institutions are in the grip of such deep uncertainty that the importation of the UK's neoliberal deregulation policies to the rest of Europe is on the cards (cf. Grahl and Teague 1997; Teague and Grahl 1998). Given the service sector 'trilemma' there may have to be some selective deregulation of the labour market to enhance flexible (i.e. part-time or temporary) employment. There are also varying degrees of insider/outsider dualism in the labour markets of many countries, created by over-protective regulations for those in full-time, standard employment (see Siebert 1997). But as Hall (1998) argues, there is no reason to expect that this will push Europe's organized, cooperative economies down the slippery slope to Anglo-Saxon style deregulation and inequality. First, not all protective measures impede employment creation or growth: it depends on the context. Thus, generous unemployment benefits are desirable for social cohesion, as long as they are accompanied by strict benefit durations and measures to help the jobless back into work. High levels of unionization and union coverage are also compatible with employment creation and growth, as long as they are offset by high levels of coordination in wage bargaining and unions do not become insider monopolies. Both such combinations of policies have been aspired to by new social pacts and their older corporatist counterparts. Selective deregulation, promoting part-time employment, has been achieved in the Netherlands within a broad social pact sustaining coordinated wage bargaining and minimizing the impact on real income disparities (Visser and Hemerijck 1997; van den Ploeg 1997). New forms of wage coordination and attempts to bolster the representative strength of union organizations have been undertaken in the Italian and Irish social pacts.

Crucially, the interaction of external pressures with domestic labour markets is also demanding centralization, as well as high levels of national (and European) employment protection. This has been one of the unexpected effects of the spread of new forms of 'human resource' management and work organization in highly unionized environments. Both imply the creation or maintenance of cooperative labour relations and a high-trust firm environment. As Negrelli (1997) shows in the Italian case (although the lesson also applies elsewhere) employers and workers become increasingly interdependent in such systems, and industrial relations systems make an important contribution. This is not to say that in weaker union environments (e.g. France) such developments do not compound existing labour movement problems. But the general point is that well-designed systems of labour market rules remain essential for the new world of work. As argued in a previous article (Rhodes 1998) (and following the prescriptions long made by Wolfgang Streeck 1992), the optimal world of internal flexibility is built not by unilateral management action but on teamwork and low levels of hierarchy within firms. High levels of skills and capacities for skills acquisition are critical. These depend, in turn, on national education and training systems which, again contrary to expectations, are proving to be flexible to new demands where they are institutionally strongly rooted. Too high a level of external flexibility—i.e. the absence of regulatory constraints on firms—destroys trust and undermines internal flexibility. This trade-off—producing a productive form of 'regulated cooperation'—is a critical one for sustaining both competitiveness and consensus in European labour markets.

Furthermore, both cost competitiveness and stability require a means of preventing wage drift and inflationary pressures. This has focused the attention of governments on revitalizing incomes policies. This has been true especially of the social pacts of Italy, Ireland, and Portugal, and now Spain is following with a similar set of institutional innovations as a means of moderating wage inflation (see Pérez 1999). As argued below, rather than disrupting these forms of concertation, and fragmenting governance in the European labour market, the completion of the single market and movement to full EMU is likely to lock the bargaining partners even more closely together.

Institutions and the Scope for Negotiated Adjustment

The argument to this point has stressed that pressures for change stemming from the international economic environment as well as from processes of economic change may well require concerted, coordinated national responses. This is not to say that there is one 'best way' or even convergence on a particular policy path or institutional model. The point to be stressed though is that neither neoliberalism nor institutional fragmentation follow logically from such pressures. Two other considerations confirm this view: the interlocking nature of national production, industrial relations, and welfare systems; and the institutional context of the 'new' European politics of welfare.

First, crude convergence arguments ignore three essential limits on radical deregulatory change in both policies and institutions in the organized market economies of Continental Europe: path dependence, the prevailing distribution of organizational power, and the 'efficiency' (or competitiveness) deriving from the complex links between systems of regulation and production firms (see Gourevitch 1996). This is also true for the liberal market economy of the United Kingdom where an absence of an 'organized' economic framework pushed governments in the 1980s towards deregulation as a means of improving efficiency (Soskice 1999). Path dependence and resistance to change derive from the fact that forms of labour market regulation are deeply embedded in national systems of law and collective bargaining. The fact that the existing distribution of power is located in the associational strength of both employers' and trade union organizations clearly limits the scope and content of reform. As for economic performance, Continental systems retain enormous economic strength and their large and successful export sectors and trade surpluses demonstrate that their regulatory systems—including their labour market rules—are far from dysfunctional.

This partly explains why flexible specialization has failed seriously to threaten corporatist arrangements or collaborative industrial relations. For, contrary to expectations, employers have typically not used it to weaken trade unions where flexibility of various kinds depends on their participation. The example of Italy has already been cited. German *Mitbestimmung* also retains its functional value in providing an effective framework for flexible and negotiated solutions to employment and innovation problems (Rhodes and van Apeldoorn 1998). As Thelen (1999) argues, most German employers are acutely aware of the costs of a decentralization strategy that seeks a radical shift in the balance of power with labour. It is this rather than union countervailing power that explains 'why German employers cannot bring themselves to dismantle the German model'. As discussed in Section 2 below, other countries which seek to follow a high-wage/high-productivity path of economic adjustment are seeking to develop similar coordinating capacities in their own economies.

Path dependence, power, and efficiency arguments also suggest that EMU will not lead to a radical restructuring of European national wage bargaining systems, as many have predicted. Because EMU places a greater burden of adjustment on labour costs, some argue that this may draw its member countries into a deflationary vicious circle of labor cost dumping, or competitive internal depreciations (see A. Martin 1998: 20). But neither an 'Americanization' of labour relations, nor a rapid shift to cross-border sectoral bargaining is likely, even if powerful unions like the German IG Metall are promoting such a project. Much more likely is what Martin (1998: 21) refers to as the 're-nationalization' of wage bargaining, a notion that fits with the resurgence of national wage coordination in the social pacts discussed below. We can also understand continuing attempts to shore up Scandinavian bargaining systems in this way. Just as German employers perceive the broader knock-on costs for themselves of decentralization in terms of competitive bidding for labour and wages among firms, so employers and governments elsewhere recognize the benefits—above all in EMU—of national coordination.

But in addition to the productive side of existing institutional trajectories, there is a downside when it comes to welfare reform. To use Esping-Andersen's (1996*a*) metaphor, despite some thawing at the edges, there is a 'frozen landscape' in European welfare. This is reflected in sustained levels of social transfer spending and limited institutional reform. Thus, according to a recent OECD study of fifteen countries (1996*h*), transfer spending fell in only seven cases, and generally by very modest amounts (Pierson 1997*d*). The most important institutional changes have been managerialism; attempts to make certain benefits (especially unemployment support) more 'incentive compatible'; a marginal degree of privatization (mainly in health, and mainly in Britain), some decentralization; and attempts to control budgetary expansion (see Therborn 1997 for a survey).

This is not necessarily cause for celebration. Indeed, the 'frozen landscape' indicates sclerosis rather than a stable and sustainable equilibrium. Pierson (1998) construes the crux of the problem in terms of 'irresistible forces' (post-industrial pressures, unmanageable increases in health and pensions budget) meeting 'immovable objects'. The latter stem from a mix of electoral incentives, 'institutional stickiness', and the veto points created by powerful vested interests devoted to defending transfer-heavy welfare states and their redistributive outcomes. Reforms to health care systems, pensions, and labour markets all require a careful process of adjustment if social cohesion is not to be sacrificed and if core constituencies and their representatives (welfare professions, the labour movement, citizens) are not to erect insuperable impediments to change. Complex policy packages are made inevitable by the imbrication of social security systems and employment regulation. The most difficult cases of reform can be found in those countries where labour market insiders are also social security insiders (in Italy, for instance, around half of the members of all three major union confederations are pensioners, creating major problems for left-wing reformists in the governing majority). This all suggests why, as Pierson (1998: 556) puts it, the 'new' politics of the welfare state in Europe 'involves a complex two-level game, incorporating both an electoral arena and a corporatist arena'. It is on the latter that we concentrate in the remainder of this article.

2. 'COMPETITIVE CORPORATISM' AND WELFARE REFORM

To recap the points made above, we have argued thus far that:

- globalization (and market integration in Europe) are interacting with domestic employment and welfare problems, making their resolution more difficult;
- but at the same time neither globalization nor socio-economic change are necessarily reducing the scope for a concerted process of social market reform. Indeed, in some respects, the necessity and capacity for such reform may both be enhanced.

Before examining a number of such 'pacted' transitions to reform in practice, we need to explore the logic and coalitional supports of 'competitive corporatism'.

The Logic of 'Competitive Corporatism'

In an earlier article (Rhodes 1998), I argued that the logic of the new social pacts is rather different from traditional forms of social corporatism. First, they are less routinized (although they may become so) because the very necessity of a pact signals the absence of a tradition of institutionalized political exchange. Second, and partly as a result, the partners will be institutionally weaker and the exit costs lower, although once again, this will change over time as 'emergency' or state-sponsored concertation consolidates and puts down stronger institutional roots. Third, unlike traditional Scandinavian corporatism, where the state was either a marginal or absent participant in the central incomes bargain, in the new pacts the presence of the state is much more strongly felt, either as a coercive force or provider of incentives.

In greater need of explanation, however, is how actors in weakly organized systems can strike bargains and then sustain them, given that only strong, centralized associations of capital and labour have been deemed capable of such exchange.

First there is the role of the state. Even in the Dutch case, we are talking about what Visser (1998) (after Fritz Scharpf) has called 'bargaining in the shadow of hierarchy'—in other words, a context in which the state legitimates and ratifies the bargain and sanctions or compensates potentially wayward, free-riding or 'free-booting' partners. This itself provides important cement for otherwise institutionally fragile bargains. Here, once again, European economic and monetary union has contributed to concertation over macro-economic policy issues via a process of what Della Sala (1997) has called 'hollowing out and hardening' the state. In countries where the boundaries of the state machine were always porous, making the state itself accessible to interest groups and therefore incapable of striking or enforcing clear-cut bargains, EMU has made state structures less permeable and displaced authority within them towards technocratic elites. Italy is the clearest case in point. One should acknowledge, however, that there is a danger in such an activist state role. For as Pekkarinen, Pohjola, and Rowthorn (1992) pointed out with regard to similar tendencies in traditional social corporatism, in the long run state action to shape or steer employers' and workers' organizations may inadvertently undermine their legitimacy and reduce their ability to mobilize support for government policies. This tension is already visible in a number of cases.

Second, there is a tendency, as Marino Regini (1999) has described it, for actors to be less conditioned by pre-existing institutions when 'an economy [is] close to a convergence between the opposing requirements of deregulation and concertation'. In this situation, it is therefore the set of constraints on, and incentives to change provided by each actor that largely determines the behaviour of the others: 'a co-operative game will last longer the more all actors have been able to develop a capacity for strategic learning'. All of the cases discussed below provide illustrations of such learning processes. One can also note in this regard that partisan politics becomes much less important as time goes on. Economic policy had already ceased to be a central valence issue after the mid-1970s, with both left and moderate rightist parties (Christian democrats, liberals) moving towards the pro-market right (Kitschelt 1997*b*). Under EMU, one can suggest that class-based differences regarding economic management have narrowed further, making it more likely that parties of all political stripes will seek pragmatic solutions to macroeconomic management and imperatives for micro-policy reform. Thus, contrary to the idea that 'turning vice into virtue' (Levy 1999) is a left progressive project, 'unfreezing' the Continental European welfare landscape has become a cross-party concern.

Third, not only does the interlocking nature of European social security and employment systems require simultaneous action on multiple fronts, but as Traxler (1997) has argued, broadening and deepening the bargain may also compensate for the absence of conventional organizational prerequisites. Thus, as has most explicitly occurred in the Irish and Portuguese cases, the best way to generalize the process of exchange is to synchronize industrial and structural with social and employment policy and/or extend concertation levels upwards or downwards by making associational strength itself a part of the bargain. This requires a complex and cautious process of coalition building. It is to this process that we now turn.

Social Pacts and Coalition Building

Not all of the new social pacts perform the same function, nor do they all rest on the same coalitional foundations. As Casey (1999) observes, social partnership and social dialogue can be involved at a number of different points. They can be involved at the level of planning, or involve simply consultation. They can be involved in policy formulation, monitoring, and the implementation of policy. In the pacts below, however, there has been a tendency for such functions to broaden over time from pay determination and macroeconomic policy, to issues of training, labour market policy, and social security. In the process the coalitional base may also shift correspondingly from a classic insider bargain on wage issues to what Casey (1999) calls a 'broad insider' bargain in which unions and employers bargain over issues affecting other groups. In its most expansive form, a social pact may include an 'augmented social dialogue' (of the Irish type) in which the 'outsiders' (in this case organizations of the unemployed) become parties to the bargain themselves.

If we take the objectives of these pacts, and consider their final goals, we can construe them analytically in terms of the constitution of two types of coalition—distributional coalitions and productivity coalitions—and the attempt to forge effective and enduring political and functional linkages between them. Although differing, sometimes markedly, from one country to another, these pacts derive precisely from their common attempts to link negotiations over both the formal and informal welfare states (i.e. formal welfare programmes and the labour market component of the social wage) with more general policies to bolster competitiveness. Some countries (the Netherlands, Denmark, and Portugal) are simultaneously building both types of coalition—although inevitably some are more successful than others in forging the complex links between them. Others have been relatively successful in creating a productivity coalition (Italy) but have been less successful—although much progress has been made—on the distributional side. Italy, for example, is struggling to find the distributional support for a further reform of the pensions system—something made rather difficult by the strength of pensioners in the labour movement. Ireland, by contrast, has put in place a broad distributive coalition, but the formal productivity bargain remains weak. We can hypothesize that the most enduring examples of competitive corporatism will be those that create the most complete coalitions of both types and forge the most functional links between them —functional, that is, for a politically acceptable and legitimate trade-off between equity and efficiency.

Prior to proceeding, it is important to note that the potential sources of tensions within these coalitions cannot be reduced to divisions between traded and non-traded capital and labour (Frieden 1991; Garrett and Lange 1995). Although such a division may make theoretical sense, in practice it is criss-crossed and may even be overridden by other, more conventional conflicts, some of which will be latent, others more explicit. This is partly because even a sophisticated analysis of the politics of traded/non-traded divisions such as that of Schwartz (1997) assumes that the main external influence is that of exposure to increased trade competition. Whereas in the European case there is in reality a much more complex mix of pressures, as illustrated in Section 1 above. The ways in which external pressures interact with and are filtered by domestic institutions and challenges to the welfare status quo rule out simple dichotomies in favour of more complex tensions between white collar and blue collar, service sector versus manufacturing, employed and unemployed, 'insider' and 'outsider' employees. Social pacts in the 1990s are highly vulnerable to such tensions, yet in unpredictable ways, since they rarely find organizational expression in terms of conventional capital/labour, traded/non-traded associational or party political terms. To one extent or another, the new social pacts attempt to bridge these divisions with complex strategic trade-offs, selective incentives, and solidarity deals, some ad hoc and transitional, others longer term and institutionally embedded. In certain cases (e.g. the Irish) even representatives of the socially excluded (the anti-poverty lobby) have also become part of the bargaining equation.

New Social Pacts in Practice

All of the social pacts that have emerged since the mid-1980s seek to combine wage moderation, the quest for lower social charges and greater flexibility of work conditions. The latter two objectives in particular imply (*a*) reform to social security systems (often with greater equity as a goal) and (*b*) a response to employers' demands for new productivity trade-offs. The latter will involve, for example, an exchange of shorter working hours or the maintenance of employment levels for greater freedom of labour use, in terms of hours and deployment of workers. To this extent all the pacts contain both distributive and productivity-linked innovations. But this does not necessarily mean that they will be based on stable or enduring distributional or productivity coalitions.

Creating or consolidating the first of these requires that the traditional social partners break with their defence of conventional insider privileges and entitlements, and accommodate the needs of other social groups, while building a productivity coalition demands a new deal between capital and labour based on a negotiated strategy of industrial adjustment.

Building a distributional coalition requires policies that are inclusive of former labour market 'outsiders', via, for example:

- a national incomes policy that has a degree of flexibility at lower levels so that less productive workers are not priced out of the labour market;
- the relaxation of high levels of security for full-time core workers, in return for greater protection for peripheral (although increasingly central) temporary and part-time workers, as in the Dutch 1996 central agreement on 'Flexibility and Security' (see below for details);
- a redesign of social security systems to prevent implicit or explicit disentitlement, in relation to two groups in particular: women workers (who are often discriminated against by male breadwinner-oriented social security systems); and those not in permanent, full-time employment who may also be discriminated against in terms of entitlements;
- and a parallel redesign of social security systems to allow a guarantee of access to skill acquisition and social services at any point during the life cycle, especially through education and training.

Constructing a parallel productivity coalition requires, at least in principle:

- a shift away from legislated or rule-governed labour market regulation to negotiated labour market regulation, e.g. in minimum wages, as has occurred, for example, in the Irish and Portuguese social pacts;
- the development of decentralized components within the national wage bargaining system that provides employers with the possibility of striking productivity-linked deals;
- the agreement on consultation through firm or company concertation that allows for a negotiated adjustment to new demands from markets or technologies;
- a shift away from adversarial industrial relations towards a more consensual model;
- and the joint implementation of training mechanisms and priorities.

It is important to note that key elements of both types of policy objectives can be found in all of the social pacts considered below. But in only certain cases are both types of coalition strongly present behind such deals.

The chart below summarizes roughly the strength or weakness of these coalitions in the countries examined here.

Country	Distributional coalition	Productivity coalition
Ireland	moderate	weak
Spain	moderate-strong	weak-moderate
Portugal	strong	moderate
Italy	moderate	moderate
Netherlands	strong	strong

The 'Dutch Miracle'

Perhaps the most interesting developments have been in the Netherlands where, as a result of monetary stability, budgetary discipline, and social security reform, something of a 'model' attracting policy emulation in other countries has begun to emerge (for the most extensive analysis, see Visser and Hemerijck 1997). In the Netherlands, the early and mid-1980s witnessed one of the most severe employment crises in Western Europe, with unemployment reaching 15.4 per cent in 1984. This was attributable in part to the immobilism in industrial relations between the early 1970s and early 1980s (which followed twenty years of centrally guided, corporatist governance before 1968), a period during which both trade unions and employers rejected a state-led system of incomes policy. In the 1970s, when the twin oil-price shocks fuelled inflation and rising unemployment across Western Europe, the negative consequences for the Netherlands were compounded by a breakdown in relations between the social partners that helped produce a vicious cycle in which real labour costs accelerated ahead of productivity gains, profits deteriorated, firms substituted capital for labour or relocated to low labour cost areas, and unemployment rose spectacularly (Hemerijck and van den Toren 1996).

Since 1982, however, the picture has been quite different. In the early 1980s, the Dutch social partners responded to the crisis the economy was then experiencing in similar ways to their Irish and Italian counterparts just over a decade later. Since the signature of a national social pact (the Wassenaar accord) between employers and trade unions in November 1982, there has been a return to corporatism, but a more flexible and responsive bipartite rather than tripartite version, one involving a considerable degree of decentralization in wage bargaining that is compatible with intensified competitive constraints. This has provided the basis for industrial relations peace, wage moderation, and an ongoing process of labour market reregulation that has helped to keep wage costs down, prevent increasing inequality, and boost employment (above all in part-time and temporary contracts) to the point where the present 4.5 per cent unemployed is one of the lowest in the OECD area. Between 1983 and 1993, job growth (at 1.8 per cent per annum) exceeded both the OECD and EU averages (Hemerijck and van den Toren 1996). The 1982 agreement was consolidated in 1993 at a time when a new rise in unemployment began to place the consensus under pressure. In the 1993 accord, there is provision for greater decentralization of bargaining to company level within the overall coordinated structure—described by Visser (1996*a*) as 'centralized decentralization'.

In addition to wage moderation, over this period, concertation has also produced agreements on social security contributions, work sharing and industrial policy, training, job enrichment, low-wage levels for low-skilled workers, the development of 'entry-level' wages and, most recently, the 1995 'flexicurity' accord in which rights for temporary workers have been strengthened in return for a loosening of dismissal protection for core workers. This consolidates the general trend in Dutch reforms to build a distributional coalition by breaking down the traditional barriers between labour market insiders and outsiders. In the 1980s, a relinking of the minimum wage and benefits to wage inflation was coupled with a decision to boost labour market participation by closing down easy exits from employment (early retirement, sickness, and disability schemes) and generally minimizing the incidence of moral hazard. Low-income workers have been compensated for low wages by targeted tax breaks. Trade unions rescinded their opposition to the creation of part-time and temporary jobs and became the champions of such workers, bridging the gap that usually divides the 'insider' from the 'outsider' workforce. Hourly wages for such workers have subsequently been bargained to the levels enjoyed by full-time workers: thus, employers can recruit such workers to bolster flexibility, but not as a means of following a low-price production strategy based on wage exploitation. The 1995–6 'flexicurity' accords mentioned above have guaranteed pension and social security benefits to all part-time and temporary employees.

There has also been a recent revival of tripartite corporatism, with the reorganization of Dutch employment services along tripartite lines in 1991 and calls by the tripartite Social and Economic Council (which has been marginalized by the shift to bipartism in recent years) for a renewal of national consensus creation, involving government, employers, and trade unions in the face of European integration and international competition.

The productivity elements in the Dutch pact would seem to derive mainly from the positive consequences for economic growth and labour market flexibility stemming from the distributional bargain. Most importantly, government intervention—an essential, albeit 'shadowing' influence, according to Visser (1998)—has been essential in helping break the blockage in negotiations on social security reform, an area where it has proven much more difficult to find agreement on changes to the amount and duration of benefits. The whole focus of social security, as a result, has been shifted away from providing protection through passive income support towards strengthening incentives for labour market participation.

Measures encouraging beneficiaries to actively seek work and reducing labour costs in general (and those of unskilled workers in particular) have been prioritized. Pay flexibility is being enhanced by an agreement on the part of employers and unions, encouraged by government, to close the gap between the legal minimum wage and minimum wages set in collective agreements. A new Social Insurance Organization Act (OSV), in force since March 1997, has shifted the governance of social security laws from bipartite Industrial Insurance Boards (run by the social partners) to a tripartite national public authority and their implementation to private organizations. This it is hoped will help minimize the flows of workers into social security schemes (OECD 1998*d*). This removal of the social partners from part of the social security system administration followed a unilateral privatization of the sick-leave scheme in 1994. It should be acknowledged that a weak spot in the Dutch system remains its dependence on disability benefits as a cushion for unemployment and the extension of subsidized employment programmes to compensate for the lack of jobs for the unskilled at prevailing wages. Despite the successes of the so-called 'Dutch miracle', broad unemployment (a measure which adds those on such schemes to the registered unemployed) is still a massive 25 per cent of the broad labour force (OECD 1998*d*: 6).

The Dutch case, then, as Visser describes it, is one of corporatism, but not one that is 'against the market'. Rather, it is a system of 'corporatism *and* the market' (Visser 1996*a*) in which monetary stability, budgetary discipline, and competitiveness have been achieved, while also reforming social security and boosting employment. It is important to note the absence of a master plan —which is also true of our other cases here. Rather, via a process of what Visser and Hemerijck (1997: 150) call 'learning and puzzling'—a 'cumbersome, uncertain and politically risky process of renegotiation over guaranteed social rights'—the Dutch social security system has been transformed. To its great credit, the increase in social inequality that has occurred in Britain, and the breakdown in consensus and large-scale social unrest suffered, for example, by France, have been avoided. *En bref*, it is perhaps the most advanced example of 'competitive corporatism' in Western Europe.

Ireland: Coalition Building and Incomes Policy in the Celtic Tiger

In the mid-1980s it was feared that Ireland was consigned to a vicious circle of weak economic performance, increasing public sector deficits and debt, and rising unemployment. The social partners hammered out their first tripartite response to the crisis in 1986, leading to the first neocorporatist deal in 1987 in the form of the Programme for National Recovery (1987–90). The PNR was negotiated amidst a crisis in public finances with government debt peaking at 117 per cent of GDP. The success of the PNR led to the 1990 PESP—Programme for Economic and Social Progress (1990). Subsequent pacts negotiated in 1990 (Programme for Competitiveness and Work), 1993, and most recently in 1996 (Partnership 2000), were linked to a centralization of wage bargaining and a growing willingness to address tax, education, health, and social welfare issues via central negotiation as well (O'Donnell 1998). The emphasis of all four agreements has been on macroeconomic stability, greater equity in the tax system, and enhanced social justice. Specific innovations include inflation-proof benefits, job creation (in manufacturing and international services sectors), and the reform of labour legislation in the areas of part-time work, employment equality, and unfair dismissal. Nevertheless, the labour market remains characterized by a high degree of rigidity, with unemployment and poverty still exacerbating the problem of long-term unemployment (Rhodes 1995).

Like several of the other case studies here (Spain, the Netherlands, Italy), Ireland has witnessed a remarkable transformation of its industrial relations system over the last ten years or so. It has made a transition from one bearing a strong resemblance to the British adversarial system, to one with strong corporatist elements, capable of delivering low inflation, a high rate of economic growth, and widespread innovation in social security, taxation, and labour market policy. There has been a gradual expansion of bargaining to include a wide range of social groups, creating, at least formally, one of the most inclusive distributional coalitions among the countries in this study. But problems of unemployment and social exclusion have still to be effectively tackled. Also, despite a growing convergence of opinion on the need for a 'high road' competitive strategy, and attempts to extend the neocorporatist consensus beyond distributive issues, little has been achieved so far in fostering industrial relations reform or in building a national productivity coalition. A fragmented industrial structure, with a large number of small firms alongside multinationals which dominate in particular sectors, has made reaching a consensus on a national strategy of industrial partnership (rather than firm-level, human-relations based strategies) difficult to achieve (Gunnigle 1997; Roche 1998).

Nevertheless, there do seem to be solid corporate foundations to Ireland's economic progress in recent years, based on an active diffusion of human resource management innovations across the country (McCartney and Teague 1997). For some commentators, this process has been facilitated enormously by the stability brought to the economy by the national incomes policy agreements. By introducing in the early 1990s a local bargaining clause (allowing management to tie negotiations to local labour market conditions) while maintaining wage moderation at the national level, this has encouraged employers to innovate in flexible work practices, employee status, and social organization (Taylor 1998). In this view, then, the distributive bargain has had important implications for productivity gains, even in the absence of an explicit productivity coalition (see Taylor 1996; cf. Durkan 1992). The most recent national bargain (Partnership 2000) explicitly addresses this issue by confronting issues of product development, training, and the introduction of new work and organizational patterns. A National Centre for Partnership has subsequently been established to develop partnership at the enterprise level by benchmarking and disseminating best practice (O'Donnell 1998).

There are dissenting voices though. Roche and Geary (1999) maintain that although collaborative production is undoubtedly significant in Ireland in the 1990s, exclusionary forms of decision making can be shown to dominate the postures of establishments towards handling change. O'Donnell (1998: 93) agrees that the challenge is now to build greater links between the distributive and productivity side of the bargain, using the atmosphere of solidarity to improve technology, products, marketing, and training in indigenous Irish firms. But the distributive side has also been criticized. A rather sceptical evaluation of these pacts has concluded that they have not delivered much when compared to Scandinavian 'social corporatism'. Main objectives such as employment creation have not been achieved, tax reforms have been only incompletely implemented and there has been little serious consideration of how training is linked to the wage-formation system or to how it should be developed as a collective good (Teague 1995). O'Donnell (1998) responds by pointing to trends in social and health spending and progress on employment legislation and in creating wage bargaining structures that work against greater income inequality. Meanwhile, social partnership agreements underpin the credibility of a non-accommodating exchange rate policy. As a result Ireland has escaped most of the negative effects of Britain's business cycle, while sustaining a higher level of social solidarity. Government commitments across a range of issues have been respected, including increasing resources in education, public housing, and health care, while also extending social protection to part-time workers and introducing legislation on unfair dismissal, employment agencies, and conditions of employment.

Until 1996, these agreements were largely tailored to the demands of the insider unionized sector and the main emphasis was on protecting the post-tax income of the employed 'insiders' (Kavanagh et al. 1997). The aim of the 1993 PCW sought to innovate in this respect and reduce taxes on low-income workers and raise the income threshold at which higher rates of taxation come into play. However little real progress was made in this respect. Single workers in 1996 were still liable for the top rate of tax at four-fifths of average male earnings while the married (spouse not working) become liable for the top rate of tax when earning just 1.5 times average male earnings (Taylor 1998). In a significant step forward 'Partnership 2000' (1996–7) was negotiated with a larger number of partners, including the Irish National Organisation of the Unemployed and other groups addressing the problems of social exclusion, includes a National Anti-Poverty Strategy, and was much more oriented to issues of poverty and industrial democracy than the previous PCW. It responded to union demands for a radical tax reform that would provide tax relief for public sector workers, a new flexible pay agreement to benefit the low paid, and initiatives to encourage profit-sharing in companies. With regard to welfare state reform, it introduced some major initiatives on public service provision, especially in the areas of health care, improving flexibility in the deployment of resources, and the use of performance measurements. In a separate deal, the growing problem of union derecognition was addressed and a landmark deal reached between employers and unions.

Although broadening the bargain has been a key element in sustaining the Irish pact, strengthening the associational base has also been important. Hardiman (1988) showed how attempts at national agreements in the 1970s failed because of an absence of a dominant social democratic party, cohesive employers' organizations, and a centralized trade union movement. But in the 1980s and 1990s there have been union mergers backed by state grants, helping to create a union movement capable of engaging in political exchange across a wide agenda, including pay, taxation, social policies, public finance management, and EMU convergence (O'Donnell 1998). As mentioned above in exploring the logic of the new social pacts, O'Donnell also argues that the absence of a strong social democratic party may no longer matter. A narrower ideological distance between the political parties than in the past tends to encourage stable and long-run agreements between economic interests, primarily by reducing the likelihood that a change of government will cause a sharp reversal of economic policy.

Italy: Steps towards a New National Bargain

In the Italian case, negotiations in the early 1990s that initially focused on reforming Italy's automatic wage-indexation system—the *scala mobile*—were extended to include the rationalization of bargaining structures and the reform of union representation in the workplace. In the significant agreement of July 1993, the *scala mobile* was abolished and a far-reaching reform of incomes policy and collective bargaining was achieved. Henceforth, biannual tripartite incomes policy and collective agreements were to set macroeconomic guidelines and establish a framework for incomes policy. Sectoral agreements were to be signed at the national level on wages (valid for two years) and conditions of employment (valid for four); and enterprise level agreements were to be concluded for four years and negotiated by workers' representatives. The latter innovation created a new form and level of representation within the firm—*Rappresentenza sindacale unitaria*—in which two-thirds of representatives were to be elected by the entire workforce (and not just union members as before) and one-third appointed by representative unions.

This emphasis on the associational basis of the agreement has played an important part in consolidating the Italian social pact, forging an important link between the workplace and higher levels of union organization (Regini and Regalia 1997). From late 1998, legislation has been developed on the basis of trade union proposals to consolidate the bargaining system and strengthen the role of the major unions in it. The main aim of the proposals, which employers strongly support, is to prevent the further fragmentation of wage bargaining and to marginalize breakaway and small unrepresentative organizations. By reregulating the relationship between representation, representativity, and the enforcement of collective agreements, unions hope to guarantee union democracy for workers but also consolidate their own positions. A major aim is a rule to ensure that only unions that represent an average of 51 per cent of workers (calculated through a combination of election results and union membership) should be able to sign national sectoral agreements. These will be enforced by law across the whole sector to which they apply (EIRR 1998). Centralization—and cross-sectoral coordination of bargaining—will henceforth be easier to achieve.

Apart from contributing to Italy's fulfillment of EMU entry conditions —which it has achieved by effectively taking inflation out of the labour market—the social pact signed in 1993 also covered a number of other areas. In broadening its areas of concern, the weak associational basis of the pact was strengthened. These included new measures to compensate those laid off in restructuring, improvements to the training system (boosting internal flexibility), the legalization of temporary work agencies (improving external flexibility), assistance for the unemployed to enter the labour market, and improving the general performance of Italian industry. The establishment of these principles of intent in 1993 led to the so-called 'Treu package' of reforms on labour market flexibility in 1997. Although not as extensive as employers wanted, these reforms simultaneously legalized temporary work agencies as well as the use of fixed-term and part-time work contracts, while also seeking to protect or improve the rights and entitlements of such workers. Important innovations were also made in the national training system to improve the quality of training, improve access to training, and promote the role of companies in shaping training courses.

One downside of the Italian deal is that the active labour market policy that accompanied the incomes policy of 23 July 1993 has not had much effect. This is due to the lack of effective mechanisms for policy implementation in Italy. This situation may begin to improve, however, with the decentralization of employment services introduced from 1997, which seeks to improve the operation of job placement and pro-active policies at the level of the regions and provinces. Although the evidence of success is so far limited, territorial pacts (*patti territoriali*) and area contracts (*contratti di area*) introduced between 1995 and 1997 should also assist in combatting unemployment, by linking private and public actors via concertation in pooling programmes, resources, and structures to promote economic growth and job creation (Ferrera and Gualmini 2000). Unemployment—at 12 per cent nationwide and rising to over 20 per cent in the south—remains Italy's number one problem. On the other hand, as noted by Negrelli (1997), the possibility of success-fully combining human resources management with industrial relations has already been realized in Italy. Negrelli maintains that an important degree of complementarity derives from the possibilities for mutual enrichment by these two different systems for organizing the workplace. The most beneficial effect has been a trade-off between job security and flexibility at work, beginning in public sector companies and spreading more recently to private ones. There, unions moved from a determined defence of rigid working practices at all costs to a policy of flexible working through collective bargaining, avoiding the dangers of deskilling. The emphasis in Italy has been on functional flexibility rather than numerical or wage flexibility.

Thus, from the industrial relations crisis in the 1970s, Italy has been edg-ing towards a new productivity coalition in which an uneasy truce between employers and unions has led to important labour market innovations. But it has also become the forum for bargaining the future of broader aspects of social regulation. To this extent, the distributive elements in the new Italian bargain are also being developed, although the future of this side of the bargain is now in doubt. The most significant step in this regard was the agreement signed between the unions and the government on pension reform in May 1995 (the employers abstained). The bargain was put to ref-erendum in the workplaces by the unions where it obtained a hard-won but significant majority backing. This consensus was achieved at the expense of a more radical reform (it retained the previous pension system for elderly workers and introduced, whether partially or in full, a more rigorous sys-tem for less senior workers). But it also, avoided protracted industrial dis-location, as occurred in the case of the Juppé reforms in France (Regini and Regalia 1997). Also prevented were any adverse knock-on effects on other aspects of the social pact, despite the fact the implementation of the incomes policy has favoured an increase in company profits at a time of reductions in purchasing power.

It remains to be seen whether the system can survive the current challenges. The Italian pact withstood the introduction in 1996 and 1997 of 'one last push for Maastricht' austerity budgets as well as discontent with constrained pay agreements in various powerful sections of the labour movement (notably the metal workers). And the fact that the October 1997 governmental crisis over the 35-hour week and pension changes provoked by the left-wing *Rifondazione comunista* only shook, rather than shattered, ongoing negotiations between the government, trade unions, and employers, provided grounds for optimism. So too did the distance taken by the trade unions from *Rifondazione* when it brought down the Prodi Government in 1998. Major reforms have been implemented which realize both efficiency and equity gains in the social security system. In pensions, despite the complicating—and delaying—concessions made to *Rifondazione comunista*, special privileges were eliminated for a whole range of public sector workers. The possibility of retiring with a full pension after 35 years of contributions, regardless of age, was terminated (although this innovation is being gradually phased in); the pensions of high-income groups were curbed; and self-employed workers henceforth have to shoulder a larger share of the costs of their pensions. With *Rifondazione* now outside the governing coalition, further reform in eliminating the many remaining inequities in the system should theoretically be possible. Nevertheless, the D'Alema Government encountered major resistance from the unions who wish to draw a line in the sand over pension reform. Their predicament—with pensioners forming around half of their membership—reveals the ongoing institutional fragility of the Italian case.

In sum, there have been major innovations in Italy, in terms both of institutional change and policy reform, and EMU entry has been guaranteed, as in the Irish and Portuguese cases, by the commitment of steadily more cohesive trade union organizations to an incomes policy pact. But as in Ireland—and unlike in Portugal—success on the employment front has not been great, and building a distributional coalition that can bring in the large number of unemployed younger people seems to be an insuperable challenge. High levels of unemployment—albeit among different categories of workers—in both countries remains the Achilles heel of their respective social pacts.

Portugal and Spain: Converging Southern Models?

Some observers suggest that, in the absence of adequate levels of human capital and physical infrastructure, these countries face a stark choice, neither of which is without high costs, between two 'models'. On the one hand is a so-called 'European model', entailing convergence in terms of entitlements, employment protection, and the expansion of an efficient, capital (or R & D) intensive high-wage sector. The disadvantage of such a strategy is that it may well hasten the demise of low productivity firms in Portugal and lead to high, long-term unemployment rates. This would bring that country into line with Spain where growth based on productivity has prevented the absorption of the unskilled workers coming from agriculture (Marimon 1997). The other alternative would be an 'American' or Anglo-Saxon model which would exacerbate unequal income distribution and entrench a dual labour market with very low-wage sectors in otherwise affluent economies (Barry, Bradley, and McCartan 1997).

In order to embrace the 'high-wage' alternative, while reducing its costs, a coordinated system of wage determination would seem essential to minimize the impact of high productivity growth coming from a relatively small section (in terms of employment share) of the economy. This is one more reason for pursuing the 'corporatist path' in these countries if the 'European model' is chosen. Portugal, like Ireland, has consciously sought to follow the 'high road' since the early 1990s, even though its industrial structure makes that difficult. Even if its productivity coalition is weak and that side of the national bargain underdeveloped, it has at least built a strong distributive coalition behind a national strategy of adjustment. Spain embarked on the same path much earlier but until recently has been unable to build either type of coalition.

In the Portuguese case, the period until the mid-1980s saw attempts at incomes policy and concertation, but an inadequate institutional framework undermined them. Particularly problematic—as in the Italian case—was the absence of strong authority on the part of the trade unions and the need for a strengthened role for the state, making it a more reliable and consistent bargaining partner (Rocha Pimentel 1983). In that period, the PSD–CDS (Social Democrat–Christian Democrat) coalition government was unable to control growing macroeconomic imbalances and the country experienced a severe balance of payments crisis. High inflation coincided with a commitment to full employment. In the mid-1980s, however, inflation was reduced even if public sector imbalances could not be tackled. Also as in Italy, it was the commitment to eventual EMU membership after 1990 (under an enlarged-majority PSD government) that led to an emphasis on an anti-inflation, lower public debt strategy. At the same time there developed a broad consensus on the need for a new distributional coalition linked to the country's aspiration for full EMU membership and the macroeconomic stability it was imagined this would bring.

There is thus a broad consensus linking the major parties and trade union and business groups on increased economic and social cohesion, including an active employment and social policy to help avoid the dependency of particular groups/geographic areas on social transfers (Torres 1994). Reflecting this consensus, and regardless of the continuing fragility of trade union structures (Stoleroff 1997), there have been five tripartite pacts since 1987 (the latest was signed in 1996) focusing on incomes and social policy and labour market measures. They have been presented from the outset as critical for improving the competitiveness of the Portuguese economy and for integration into EMU. The agreements have been very wide-ranging, covering pay-rise ceilings, levels of minimum wages, easing regulations on the organization of work (rest, overtime, and shift work)—i.e. internal flexibility—on the termination of employment contracts (external flexibility) and the regulation of working hours. Broadening the bargain has been Portugal's means of compensating for weak associational structures.

The critical difference with Spain was that while Portugal's reforms were slow and labour protective (building the basis for a distributional coalition —with productivity elements—that could be linked to broader economic goals), Spain's were faster and labour-compensating (Bermeo 1994: 198). This was partly for constitutional reasons: whereas the Spanish Socialists began liberalizing labour markets in 1984, Portugal's Constitutional Tribunal blocked the Portuguese Socialists when they tried to do the same in 1987. This meant that Portugal started restructuring its economy after having joined the EC (and when intra-European transfers were beginning to flow), while Spain began earlier in a different economic climate. This prevented the creation of either a distributional or a productivity coalition: indeed, during the late 1980s and 1990s, employment and social policy issues became the object of intense conflict at a time when they were increasingly the object of consensus in Portugal. Unemployment rose in Spain—accompanied by a massive increase in temporary contracts once these were liberalized in the 1980s—while insiders kept their protective privileges and wage levels (Rhodes 1997c; Toharia 1997). In Portugal, by contrast, insider barriers were reduced under a wages versus jobs trade-off. This helped reduce the persistence of unemployment in the face of various demand, productivity, and labour-supply shocks, while also providing foreign investors with lower labour costs and strike rates (Bermeo 1994: 198–206; Bover, Garcia-Perea, and Portugal 1997; Castillo, Dolado, and Jimeno 1998).

In Portugal, social pacts have played an important role in ensuring this result. Following the pacts of the late 1980s, the 1990s have seen a strengthening of both their distributive and productivity elements. The 1992 agreement, for example, was broadened to cover social security issues, including improvements in health insurance reimbursements and tax relief on housing. The 1996 short-term agreement (consolidated by a 'Strategic Social Pact' in 1997) also implements an incomes policy, linking wage rises to inflation and productivity forecasts (with scope for variation within margins at lower levels) (Campos Lima and Naumann 1997). Union agreement has been ensured by a commitment to training and employment placement services, to the enforcement of various rights for part-timers, and a broad programme of working time reduction, with the introduction of a 40-hour week in two stages. The new agreement also covers numerous social security issues, including the reduction of social security contributions for those employers belonging to employers' associations (a measure clearly conceived, as in the Irish case, to strengthen organizational cohesion) and the introduction of a minimum income on an experimental basis. In addition, income tax for those on low incomes will be reduced, a more favourable tax treatment will be made of a variety of health and education benefits, and old age pensions will also receive more favourable tax treatment. The government's commitment to improve the equity of the social security system has been honoured, with the latest (mid-1998) innovation taking the form of legislation to raise the level of state retirement and contributory pensions, requiring significant changes in the way the system is financed.

Recent developments in Spain reflect a general shift away from the pacts based on the protection of insider rights that emerged from the Franco period (Encarnación 1997), towards a more broadly based pact mirroring those struck in Portugal and Ireland. This reflects a commitment on the part of the state to reform in the labour market, demands from employers for greater flexibility, and the need of unions to strengthen their own organizational base. Given low membership and a correspondingly low level of financial resources, and their need for the legitimacy that bargaining with the state can confer on them, the incentives for union involvement are high. Innovations in wage bargaining have also been important. As in the Italian case, these reflect, as argued by Pérez (1999), a recognition by employers, unions, and government that a new wage bargaining structure—containing decentralized flexibility within a national framework—is essential for containing inflationary pressures under EMU.

The most important step so far has been the 1994 'Toledo Pact' signed by the government and the trade unions, which included a focus on the rationalization and consolidation of the public social security systems. The pact has facilitated subsequent deals on labour market flexibility and pensions, as well as—more recently—the first sectoral agreements on reduced working hours (in savings banks) and talks on incentives to encourage part-time working. Although more limited in content than many had hoped (and perhaps most important as a symbolic means of linking the unions to a centre-right government's policy ambitions) (Chuliá 1999), the pensions reform deal, struck between the government and the social partners in October 1996, made major innovations. These included the reduction in the number of special regimes (an equity increasing measure); an increase in the proportionality between contributions and benefits; the financing of health care and social services through taxes (so that contributions can only be used to finance contributory benefits); and the reduction of employers' contributions in order to foster job creation (Guillén 1998). The labour market reform of April 1997 was also extensive, and saw the first major concession by Spanish unions to labour market outsiders when they agreed to a decrease in high redundancy payments (a stricture on employers inherited from the Franco years) in exchange for a reduction of insecurity for those working on temporary contracts. Bolstered by such progress, Spain too appears to be working its way towards an institutionalized pact, although the coalitional supports in this case remain particularly weak.

3. CONCLUSIONS

Although more weakly embedded in social and institutional structures than in the traditional corporatist countries of Northern Europe, the new 'competitive' corporatisms cannot simply be dismissed as short-term tactical manoeuvres to improve EMU entry prospects or expedient combinations of nationalism and neoliberalism (cf. Streeck 1996). Nor, for reasons elaborated above, can they simply be seen as (mistaken) mechanisms for solving employment problems (cf. A. Martin 1997). It is certainly true that EMS membership and the movement towards monetary union have played a critical role in inducing and consolidating new consensual labour relations (cf. Teague and Grahl 1998: 5–6). However, while social pacts may not succeed in creating fully-fledged, corporatist-style, organized labour markets, they are frequently much more than short-term pay bargains, and combine traditional incomes policies with wider and more innovative forms of social security and labour market reform. This makes them critical for linking macroeconomic objectives with microeconomic adjustment. They may also prove to be a precondition for a European-wide expansionary policy, which as Martin (1997) argues will provide the real stimulus to employment creation that supply-side reform alone, cannot deliver. At the same time, while competitiveness may be a key concern, it is not the overriding concern. These pacts contain important trade-offs between equity and efficiency of the kind that have always characterized welfare states, even during their 'golden age', despite claims (e.g. Teague and Grahl 1998) that such trade-offs are no longer possible. In fact, the new trade-offs are often responses to the solidarity dilemmas and contradictions generated by those earlier bargains and may actually improve on them if older equity gaps are filled and new forms of disentitlement prevented.

We are witnessing a period of transition in which the market is clearly more important than in the past and in which international constraints and influences have increased. While domestically generated problems and solidarity dilemmas remain the key to understanding the contemporary politics of the welfare state, their interaction with globalization is complex but when linked with European market integration and EMU deserve serious consideration in understanding the genesis of these pacts. Despite much uncertainty about where current trends are leading, we can be clear, at least, about the following. If globalization is important, there is little evidence that states have lost their capacity for designing and redesigning social welfare systems. Nor does globalization appear to be irretrievably unravelling established national social compromises. Indeed, in many countries it seems to be one factor among many in sustaining them, while in others it has encouraged new social pacts to emerge. Welfare states are not in deep crisis; nor are they losing support from publics. Yet the creation of new distributional coalitions seems essential if the requisite reform is to proceed. No doubt, those coalitions are shifting, and their degree of support for traditional welfare arrangements is changing: and as a result, a process of adjustment and experimentation is occurring in the form, financing, and orientation of welfare provision. In addition, the nature of such coalitions is becoming more complex, partly because of the links being forged with parallel and overlapping productivity coalitions. But neither deadlock nor neoliberal convergence is the result of these developments. What we are witnessing instead is a concerted process of adaptation in which the core principles of the European social model are being sustained.

Thus, there may well be a European 'Third Way' (or at least a series of national 'third ways') at the dawn of the twenty-first century. In many countries, an elaborate social, economic, and institutional compromise is being found within pragmatic and productivity-oriented social pacts. Even in those countries that have failed thus far in their attempts to replace contested with concerted relations between public and private actors, a combination of strong external pressures and domestic demands for policy innovation may lead from experimentation with new organizational forms to their consolidation if the alternatives are deadlock and a blocked process of welfare reform. Capitalism is being liberalized but not unbound. Negotiated modes of adjustment are prevailing over unilateral implementation of welfare reform.

PART III

Adjustment Dynamics Parties, Elections, and Political Institutions

7

Political Institutions and Welfare State Restructuring
The Impact of Institutions on Social Policy Change in Developed Democracies

Duane Swank

SINCE the mid-1970s, governments of advanced capitalist democracies have in varying degrees attempted to retrench the welfare state. In many nations, policy makers have reduced the generosity of benefits and tightened programme eligibility; they have also imposed mechanisms for cost control in service delivery, privatized some social services, and increased targetting of benefits. As a result, social policy has tended to move in a 'market-conforming' (i.e. work and efficiency oriented) direction. Neoliberal policy changes have not been confined to right-of-centre governments in the Anglo democracies; even the most developed social democratic welfare states of Northern Europe have experienced some reductions in social protection (e.g. Stephens 1996; Swank 2000).

Numerous explanations for these changes exist. Synoptic overviews of new pressures on developed welfare states typically highlight the roles of post-1960s international and domestic structural changes characteristic of most advanced capitalist democracies (e.g. Esping-Andersen 1996*a*; George and Taylor-Gooby 1996; Pierson, in this volume; Rhodes 1997*b*; van Kersbergen 1997). Specifically, scholars highlight domestic pressures on social policy that arise from post-1973 economic stagnation and rising unemployment,

The original draft of this paper was presented at the 'Workshop on the New Politics of the Welfare State', Center for European Studies, Harvard University, Cambridge, Mass., 30 October–1 November 1998. I would like to thank the German Marshall Fund of the United States and the Marquette University Committee on Research for generous financial support; Marco Doudeijns and Willem Adema of the Social Policy Division, Organization for Economic Cooperation and Development, for unpublished data; Keith Banting, Francis Castles, Markus Crepaz, John Freeman, Geoffrey Garrett, Miriam Golden, Alex Hicks, Cathie Jo Martin, Paul Pierson, Jonas Pontusson, Dennis Quinn, Michael Shalev, and John Stephens for helpful comments on work incorporated in this paper; the other authors of this volume for comments on the original draft; and Dengming Chen, Craig Goodman, William Muck, and William Nichols for exceptional research assistance.

burgeoning public sector deficits and debt, demographic shifts (e.g. the 'crisis of ageing'), and changes in labour market structure (e.g. the rise in female labour force participation, structural unemployment). With respect to external factors, social policy analysts emphasize the downward pressures on welfare states that stem from the notable post-1970 rise in the international mobility of capital and the secular increase in trade openness and international competition for markets.

Yet, while neoliberal policy reform is widespread and programmatic restructuring is universal, the pace and depth of these changes (and their impacts on inequality and the quality of social protection) vary notably. In this paper, I outline and test the argument that democratic political institutions determine the depth and character of welfare state restructuring. This is so, I will argue, because national configurations of democratic institutions directly or indirectly shape the degree to which domestic and international pressures are translated into neoliberal policy reforms. Specifically, democratic institutions significantly influence the political strength and structure of opportunities of the interests ideologically opposed to neoliberal social policy reforms; institutions also shape the political strength and opportunities of the interests harmed or put at risk by domestic structural change and the heightened integration of world markets. Moreover, institutions influence levels of mass support for the welfare state and prevailing political culture (e.g. conflict and competition versus solidarity and cooperation) that impede or facilitate welfare state retrenchment. My argument is that, if anything, democratic institutions—interest representational systems, the formal structure of decision making within the polity, and welfare state structures themselves—are as important as ever in shaping the policy trajectories of welfare states.

In the following pages, I first provide an overview of two key domestic and international pressures on developed welfare states: domestic fiscal stress and international capital mobility. I then outline the theoretical argument that democratic institutions fundamentally determine government responses to domestic and international structural change. As suggested, I focus on formal and informal institutions and draw on and fuse insights from 'power resources' theory, the new institutionalism, and new cultural arguments about the determinants of social policy in advanced capitalist democracies. As such, this paper builds on and extends theory developed in my work on how domestic institutions mediate the domestic policy impacts of internationalization (Swank 1998*b*, forthcoming). Next, I utilize new data on social welfare effort, national political institutions, and internationalization to provide an econometric assessment of the social policy impacts of domestic fiscal stress and capital mobility during the period 1965 to 1995. First, I focus on the direct impacts of rises in public sector debt and in international capital mobility on social welfare provision. Then, I analyse the welfare state effects of fiscal stress and global capital flows across nationally and temporally divergent democratic institutional contexts. I initially focus on total social welfare effort and then shift analysis to changes in cash income maintenance and social services. In concluding, I assess the implications of my arguments and findings for the future course of social policy in the developed democracies. With this design, I extend the time frame and substantive focus of my complementary work (Swank 1998*b*, forthcoming) and potentially bolster the evidence for my central assertion that domestic institutions systematically determine the direction of welfare state restructuring.

1. INTERNATIONAL AND DOMESTIC PRESSURES ON CONTEMPORARY WELFARE STATES

As noted, scholars have typically identified a broad array of contemporary domestic and international pressures on the mature welfare states in developed capitalist democracies. Indeed, contributions by Iversen, Pierson, Schwartz, and others in this volume highlight the social policy consequences of several domestic and international structural shifts attendant to the post-industrial political economy. In the current paper, I would like to focus on two major features of domestic and international pressures on the welfare state—domestic fiscal stress and international capital mobility—and the ways in which political institutions shape the impact of these factors on welfare state restructuring.

Fiscal Stress and Welfare State Restructuring

Many observers of contemporary welfare state politics have highlighted the policy roles of rising needs, initially as sources of increases in welfare budgets and ultimately as imperatives for programmatic retrenchment. Two areas of rising needs stand out: ageing and unemployment.[1] As Table 7.1 makes clear, the relative proportion of the population over 65 as well as the share of population over 80 (i.e. the 'frail elderly') have increased substantially in recent years. The social policy consequences of these familiar demographic trends have been widely debated (see, among others, the OECD's 1994*b*, 1998*f* synoptic overviews). In fact, the direct budgetary implications are substantial. In the relatively encompassing models of 1965 to 1995 total

---

[1] One might also cite the (indexing based) expenditure impacts of inflation, rising wage inequality, and changes in family and labour market structure. However, in terms of the size of pools of claimants and potential impacts on the welfare state, the potential consequences of demographic and employment trends stand out.

TABLE 7.1. *Domestic fiscal pressures on developed welfare states*[a]

	1960–73	1979–82	1983–6	1987–91	1992–5
Ageing (% of population 65+)	11.7	13.1	13.5	14.3	14.7
Ageing II (% of population 80+)	1.8	2.6	3.0	3.3	3.5
Unemployment rate	3.2	5.9	7.7	6.7	9.0
Long-term unemployment	—	23.5	31.9	32.0	32.0
Real growth per capita	4.2	1.3	2.6	1.8	2.5
Aggregate public sector debt	—	45.0	56.9	58.8	71.4

Ageing	Percentage of population over 65 years of age (in last year in period).
Ageing II	Percentage of the population over 80 years of age (in last year in period).
Unemployment rate	Percentage of the civilian labour work force unable to find employment (period average).
Long-term unemployment rate	Percentage of unemployed population who are out of work for 12 months or more (period average).
Real growth per capita	Annual average (for period) of percentage change in real GDP per capita in international prices.

[a] Cell entries are 15 nation period averages of row variables. The nations are Australia, Austria, Belgium, Canada, Denmark, Finland, France, Germany (unified after 1990), Italy, Japan, the Netherlands, Norway, Sweden, United Kingdom, and the United States.

Sources: see Appendix Table 7.2.

social welfare effort presented below, an increase of 1 per cent of population over 65 is directly associated with an increase in aggregate social expenditure equal to 0.65 per cent of GDP (see Table 7.5 below). Over the long term, this estimate and Table 7.1 data suggest that the 1973 to 1995 absolute change in the size of aged population is alone responsible on average for an increase in social welfare outlays equivalent to roughly 2.6 per cent of GDP.

As to unemployment, A. Martin (1996) and Huber and Stephens (1998) have highlighted the role that low unemployment has played in sustaining the large social democratic welfare states of Northern Europe—the logic is generalizable. Increases in aggregate unemployment rates place substantial strains on social welfare budgets. Again, relying on estimates presented in Table 7.5, an increase of 1 per cent in the nominal unemployment rate is directly associated with an increase in total social spending equal to 0.33 per cent of GDP. In concrete terms, the growth of the average level of unemployment from roughly 3 to 9 per cent of the labour force between the 1960–73 and 1991–5 periods (row three in Table 7.1) generates increases in social outlays equivalent to 2 per cent of GDP. In addition, as Table 7.1 makes clear, the developed welfare states have also experienced relatively substantial increases in long-term unemployment. Rises in 'structural unemployment' place additional strains not only on unemployment assistance programmes but also on active labour market policies and a broad array of social supports and services (and, similar to rises in overall unemployment, reduce general and occupationally based taxes paid by employees). Thus, everything else being equal, most welfare states—and generous welfare states especially—face increasing pressure to reduce programme benefits, restrict eligibility, and otherwise reform policy to offset costs associated with long-term shifts in levels of unemployment.

These familiar trends in the size and composition of major clientele groups of mature welfare states—and the fiscal pressures they exert—tell one side of the story. The second part involves economic growth (and the productivity levels that underscore it); as is commonly understood, increases in the size of claimant pools have occurred in the context of a notable slowdown in economic growth rates, or what many observers describe as the 'end of the golden age' of strong macroeconomic performance in developed capitalist democracies (e.g. contributions to Crafts and Toniolo 1996). Utilizing data expressed in cross-nationally and temporally comparable international prices, Table 7.1 displays the average real growth rate of per capita GDP for the latter years of the 'golden age' (1960–73) and subsequent periods. The slowdown effectively amounts to a reduction by half or more of long-term real economic growth and, in turn, a substantial reduction in the amount of tax revenues that would have been collected at 'golden age' era economic growth rates.

The last row of Table 7.1 displays a general and consequential manifestation of the concomitant rises in the size of welfare constituencies and economic slowdown: a substantial increase in public sector debt. Moreover, it is arguably the case that the well-known political barriers to tax increases in the post-1970 era (e.g. Wilensky 1981) have made it very difficult to address fiscal imbalance through statutory increases in tax rates. Overall, these economic and political factors have contributed to the universal rise in public sector borrowing in the 1980s and 1990s and the notable average increase in public sector debt from 45 to 71 per cent of GDP between the late 1970s and mid-1990s. As to the course of contemporary social policy reform, accumulated debt and its budgetary and macroeconomic consequences (e.g. high interest rates, the prospect of future taxes) generate substantial pressure for neoliberal welfare state (and public sector) reforms. Indeed, the magnitude of public sector debt provides a parsimonious and encompassing index of the interaction of rising needs and economic slowdown and, in turn, the level of fiscal pressure on developed welfare states.

Global Capital and the Welfare State

Many observers have highlighted the role of internationalization—especially notable increases in the international mobility of capital—in contemporary efforts to retrench the welfare state. Indeed, international movements of

TABLE 7.2. *Internationalization of markets in developed democracies, 1960–95*[a]

	1960–73	1979–82	1983–6	1987–91	1992–5
Capital					
Total capital flows	6.7	18.6	26.1	32.3	46.3
Foreign direct investment	1.0	1.2	1.3	2.9	2.7
International capital markets	0.5	2.1	3.8	3.4	4.7
Trade					
Total exports + imports	46.9	61.7	62.7	59.3	60.6
Exports + imports developing	8.2	8.8	8.4	7.1	8.2

Total capital flows	Total inflows and outflows of foreign direct investment, portfolio investment, and bank lending as a percentage of GDP.
Foreign direct investment	Total inflows and outflows of foreign direct investment as a percentage of GDP.
International capital markets	Total borrowing on international capital markets as a percentage of GDP.
Total exports + imports	Total exports and imports of goods and services as a percentage of GDP.
Exports + imports developing	Merchandise exports and imports to and from developing nations as a percentage of GDP (where developing nation category excludes oil-exporting nations).

[a] Cell entries are 15 nation period averages of row variables. The nations are Australia, Austria, Belgium, Canada, Denmark, Finland, France, Germany (unified after 1990), Italy, Japan, the Netherlands, Norway, Sweden, United Kingdom, and the United States.

Sources: see Appendix Table 7.2.

capital, and the potential for such movements, have increased dramatic-ally since the early 1970s.[2] Table 7.2 illustrates these trends for the fifteen focal nations of this study.[3] Total transborder flows of capital increased on average from less than 10 to close to 50 per cent of GDP between the 1960s and mid-1990s. Foreign direct investment expanded nearly 300 per cent (from roughly 1 to 3 per cent of GDP in the typical country) while borrowing on international capital markets increased on average from 0.5 to nearly 5 per cent of GDP. In absolute terms, 1995 annual foreign direct investment flows

---

[2] The causes of the internationalization of finance have been analysed extensively. See Carnoy et al. 1993; McKenzie and Lee 1991; Williams 1993; and IMF 1991, for alternative perspectives on technical and economic determinants. In addition, several recent studies have highlighted the importance of the formal deregulation of international and national financial markets and, in turn, the role of political interests, actors, and institutions in shaping this process (e.g. Helleiner 1994; Sobel 1994; Quinn and Inclan 1997). For a synoptic survey of the contemporary literature on these issues, see Cohen 1996.

[3] The fifteen nations included here are: Australia, Austria, Belgium, Canada, Denmark, Finland, France, Germany, Italy, Japan, Netherlands, Norway, Sweden, the UK, and the USA. Ireland, New Zealand, and Switzerland as well as small developed democracies (e.g. Iceland, Luxembourg) are excluded in much of the subsequent analysis because of the unavailability of data on one or more key variables discussed below.

totalled $474 billion in the developed countries and $632 billion world-wide (United Nations Centre on Transnational Corporations 1996). Total borrowing on international capital markets (international and traditional foreign bonds, equity issues, intermediate and long-term bank lending) totalled $732 billion for the OECD and $832 billion worldwide in 1995. Reductions in some forms of interest rate differentials across countries and markets, as well as removal of legal restrictions on capital and overall financial movements have also proceeded rapidly. Today, few formal impediments to capital inflows and outflows exist in the large majority of advanced capitalist democracies. Similar patterns are observed for overall trade openness (exports and imports of goods and services in relation to GDP), although the rate of increase is not remotely close to the rate of growth of capital flows: trade flows in relation to economic product expanded on average from roughly 45 to 60 per cent of GDP between the 1960s and mid-1990s. The relative magnitude of trade with developing economies (excluding oil-exporting countries), a widely debated source of competitive pressures on the welfare state, has in fact not increased during the last thirty-five years. What are the consequences of the notable rise in international mobility of capital for the welfare state?

As noted, it is commonplace to link the dramatic increase in international capital mobility with reductions in social welfare effort. Classic political economists such as Adam Smith (1976 [1776]) as well as modern scholars such as Bates and Lien (1985) have argued that increasingly mobile capital poses substantial problems for governments that seek to raise revenues and pursue policies adverse to the economic interests and ideological orientations of (mobile) business. Contemporary neoliberal economists (e.g. McKenzie and Lee 1991), Marxian analysts (e.g. Gill and Law 1988; Ross and Trachte 1990), international relations theorists (e.g. Cerny 1996; Strange 1996), and popular analysts (e.g. Greider 1997) use nearly identical reasoning to argue that the globalization of capital markets has effectively increased the power of capital over governments that seek to expand or maintain relatively high levels of social protection and taxation.[4] This is purportedly the case because, in the presence of international capital mobility, governments must encourage internationally mobile firms to remain in the domestic economy, induce

---

[4] Moreover, Kurzer (1993), Moses (1994), and others have argued that capital's exit option weakens social democratic parties, unions, and neocorporatist institutions, important sources of the development and defence of the welfare state (e.g. Stephens 1979; Hicks and Swank 1992). With respect to revenues, Steinmo (1993: esp. ch. 6, 1994) has argued that redistributive taxation, always a difficult political and economic objective, is made nearly impossible by the ability of capital to move across national borders. Huber and Stephens (1998) have argued that international capital mobility has undercut the ability of governments in large social democratic welfare states to maintain low unemployment and hence the affordability of the welfare state.

foreign enterprises to invest, and satisfy international financial markets by reducing taxes, allaying fears of inflationary pressures, and eliminating a variety of distortions and inefficiencies associated with social welfare spending. It may also be the case because the 'exit option' enhances the conventional political resources of mobile businesses and the interest organizations that represent them and because greater capital mobility strengthens arguments embedded in neoliberal macroeconomic orthodoxy for market-oriented reforms in social policy.

As I have argued elsewhere (Swank 1998*b*, forthcoming), the globalization thesis rests on both an economic and political logic. As to economics, theory suggests governments of all ideological and programmatic complexions not only have to consider the domestic requisites of business confidence—of actual and anticipated profitability, but in a world of few impediments to international capital movements, they also have to consider international investment climates, the relevant policies of other nations, and policy assessments of internationally mobile asset holders and markets. The strategic interaction of governments and transnationally mobile business and finance becomes a prisoner's dilemma for national policy makers. That is, in the face of inherent impediments to international policy coordination, they each face incentives to engage in competition for investment. Such competition presumably leads to a bidding war where social welfare transfers, social services, and the tax burdens that support them are progressively lowered to a 'lowest common denominator', or what Jessop (1996) calls a 'Schumpetarian workfare state'. Such a welfare state tends to be residualist, increasingly organized along the lines of minimum means-tested benefits, reliance on private insurance, work and efficiency principles, and relatively low (and distributionally neutral) tax burdens.

Politically, the conscious political action of large enterprises with mobile assets as well as the interest associations that represent them may also produce substantial policy impacts. At a minimum, authoritative policy makers within the state have consistently given substantial weight to the explicit policy preferences of mobile capital in formulating substantive policies and in designing institutions (Bates and Lien 1985). At most, mobile asset holders and their interest associations are able to consistently and credibly use the 'exit option' as an implicit (or explicit) threat in legislative, centralized bargaining, and executive branch policy making forums, enhancing the conventional political resources that are commonly brought to bear in efforts to shape policy (e.g. Block 1987; Kurzer 1993; Schmidt 1995). Moreover, the impact of international capital mobility on domestic policies in recent decades may in part be channelled through the increasing acceptance of neoliberal macroeconomic orthodoxy. Specifically, the widespread ascendance of neoliberal macroeconomic ideas, which call for roll-backs in government intervention and highlight market distortions of social welfare programmes and redistributive taxation, provides a supportive theoretical framework for appeals for market-oriented reforms in social and tax policies to enhance trade competitiveness and business climate; arguments about the adverse impacts of moderate to high levels of social welfare provision and taxation on a nation's international economic performance lend further weight to neoliberal claims of general welfare state inefficiencies and calls for market-oriented reforms (see Evans 1997; Hay 1998; Mishra 1993; Singh 1997).

A Note on Trade Openness

It is important to point out that some of the work on globalization and the welfare state highlights trade openness and increasing competitiveness in international markets as sources of pressure for policy change (e.g. Pfaller, Gough, and Therborn 1991; for critical assessments, Pierson, in this volume; Schwartz, in this volume). In this familiar argument, policy makers in increasingly open economies may encounter pressures for reduced (social security and other) tax burdens on domestic producers in order to lower labour costs and promote price competitiveness of exports; increases in trade openness may also push governments to reduce social outlays in order to lessen a variety of market distortions (e.g. perceived work disincentives). However, despite these considerations, I exclude well-developed analysis of the question of trade impacts in the present paper. I do so for several reasons. First, a full analysis of trade impacts is a complex enterprise and would require a second paper. Second, as Huber and Stephens (1998) forcefully argue, the large welfare states of Northern Europe developed in the context of highly open markets for goods and services and played important roles in the process of structural adjustment to international competition; trade openness is not likely to be the central international mechanism generating pressure for welfare state retrenchment.[5]

I now turn to the explication of an alternative explanation of the dynamics of welfare state restructuring. My central proposition is that the welfare state pressures generated by the expanding national debt and the economic and political logics of globalization will be fundamentally conditioned and shaped by national configurations of democratic political institutions. Specifically, the general character of systems of interest representation, the organization of decision making within the polity, and the programmatic structure of welfare states should determine national policy responses to domestic and international pressures.

---

[5] Cameron (1978), Stephens (1979), Ruggie (1982), and Katzenstein (1985*b*) have argued that the income maintenance programmes of small open political economies, and complementary regulatory, labour market, and related policies, are central components of national strategies for adaptation to world markets (and see Garrett 1998*a*, 1998*b*; Pauly 1995; and Rodrik 1997 for contemporary extensions).

2. DEMOCRATIC INSTITUTIONS AND
THE WELFARE STATE

Democratic institutions are central to the determination of contemporary social welfare reform for three reasons.[6] First, national institutions provide (restrict) opportunities for resistance to unwanted policy change by those ideologically opposed to the common neoliberal responses to domestic and international pressures; institutions also provide (restrict) opportunities for seeking compensatory policies by those who are adversely affected by domestic structural shifts and internationalization. Second, national institutions also influence directly and indirectly the relative political strength (weakness) of affected groups (e.g. their votes, seats, organization, cohesion) and the relative strength of traditional welfare state constituencies and coalitions. Finally, political institutions promote or impede certain constellations of values important to social welfare policy change: some institutions foster cooperation and consensus as well as support for (and confidence in) the welfare state specifically, and the efficacy of state intervention generally; other institutions tend to promote competition and conflict and pro-market orientations. In sum, national political institutions shape the overall political capacity of relevant social aggregates to oppose neoliberal policy responses to domestic and international change. Who are these groups?

With regard to domestic socio-economic change, political institutions are an important determinant of the political capacity of increasingly large populations of elderly to defend their social policy interests. They are also crucial for those social aggregates who are disfavoured by post-industrial structural change (e.g. groups facing long-term unemployment). This change, in part, is associated with the expansion of the service sector and knowledge class; it is also associated with the decline of large-scale, geographically concentrated manufacturing of homogenized products and the ascent of specialized, flexible, small-scale, and spatially diffused production of high value-added products. Each of these changes—post-industrial occupational transition and post-Fordist production—contributes to a general climate of economic uncertainty for those in traditional occupations and industries. Marginalized groups consist of workers in low-skill positions within both the manufacturing and service sectors. Semi- and unskilled production and clerical personnel as well as less educated and less experienced workers are increasingly at risk in terms of stagnant and declining incomes and higher

---

[6] My theoretical argument draws on important work by Esping-Andersen (1990, 1996*a*), Crepaz and collaborators (Birchfield and Crepaz 1998; Crepaz and Birchfield, no date), Garrett and Lange (1991, 1995), Pierson (1994, 1996), and Rothstein (1998*b*). A more complete statement, esp. with regard to the institutional mediation of internationalization, appears in Swank (1998*b*, forthcoming).

probabilities of unemployment, particularly structural and long-term unemployment (see Esping-Andersen 1990; OECD 1995*d*). Moreover, focusing
on the overarching process of de-industrialization, the new economic uncertainties may extend to many skilled workers and middle-class strata as well
(see Iversen, in this volume).

With respect to globalization, the internationalization of markets also affects
economic and political interests in concrete ways. Specifically, as Rodrik's
(1997) review of the literature on the impacts of globalization on economic
interests suggests (1997: 4; cf. OECD 1994*c*):

reduced barriers to trade and investment accentuate the asymmetry between groups
that can cross international borders . . . and those that cannot. In the first category
are owners of capital, highly skilled workers, and many professionals, who are free
to take their resources where they are most in demand. Unskilled and semi-skilled
workers and most middle managers belong in the second category.

Moreover, in addition to diverse effects across class and occupational strata,
international financial integration produces differential short-run effects
on domestic economic sectors. As Jeffry Frieden has argued (1991: 426): 'in
the developed world, financial integration favors capitalists with mobile or
diversified assets and disfavors those with assets tied to specific locations and
activities such as manufacturing and farming.' The capacities of those actors
whose interests are threatened by globalization (in terms of both real and
perceived threats) to press for compensation of losses and insurance against
new risks is determined by the character of national political institutions.

Finally, national institutions shape the political capacity of those social
aggregates who may oppose neoliberal policy reforms on ideological grounds.
These groups, many of whom also have concrete material interests in preservation of extant levels of social protection, consist of trade union movements and labour-based political parties, communitarian Catholic parties and
groups, far-left and left-libertarian groups and parties as well as many social
aggregates that form the core constituencies for welfare state programmes.
The following dimensions of national political institutions are most relevant.

Institutions for Interest Representation

The basic character of democratic institutions for interest aggregation and
representation should matter quite a bit for conditioning the ways in which
domestic and international structural changes affect welfare state policy
trajectories. I focus on the system of interest group representation, or the
degree to which the interest group system is social corporatist as opposed
to pluralist, and the system of electoral-party interest representation, or
the degree to which the electoral rules and party structure fosters 'inclusive'
as opposed to 'exclusive' representation of societal interests.

Social Corporatist versus Pluralist Systems of Interest Representation

First, the character of the interest group system, especially the degree to which the system is social corporatist, should facilitate the extent to which affected actors can press their claims against adverse policy changes in the face of fiscal stress and internationalization. Corporatist institutions, particularly economy-wide bargaining in which broadly organized and centralized labour movements have regularly exchanged wage restraint for full employment commitments and improvements in social protection have been important in the development of welfare states in capitalist democracies (e.g. Hicks and Swank 1992; Katzenstein 1985; Lehmbruch 1984). Despite new pressures on such institutions (e.g. Kurzer 1993), we should expect that the continued existence of extensively organized and relatively highly centralized trade union movements as well as the surprising persistence of (political and economic) forms of corporatist bargaining in some nations (e.g. Hoefer 1996; Visser and Hemerijck 1997; Wallerstein and Golden 1997) will be important. Indeed, as Rhodes (in this volume) argues, national bargains or 'social pacts' on social policy reform have, if anything, become more common as nations have attempted to forge politically acceptable national policy strategies for equity and efficiency.[7] Generally, social corporatism provides an institutional mechanism whereby factions of labour affected adversely by different aspects of globalization and domestic change can articulate preferences and press claims on national policy makers to maintain (or in limited cases expand) social protection. Moreover, given the economic interests and ideological orientations of labour and labour's relatively powerful position in highly organized systems of interest representation, social corporatism should constitute a general political barrier to neoliberal policy change.

Indirectly, social corporatism has been an important element in the political success and policy strategies of social democratic parties. Indeed, in the post-World War II era, the relationships across time and space in the advanced democracies between the measure of social corporatism developed below and the percentage of votes and seats won by parties of the left is highly significant (Pearson correlations of 0.630 and 0.637, respectively ($N = 435$) for the years 1960–92 in the fifteen focal nations). In addition, as Katzenstein's seminal work has shown, social corporatism is dependent upon, and in operation reinforces, an 'ideology of social partnership' in which policy emerges from the cooperative and consensus-oriented routines of repeated interactions among peak associations of labour and business. Similarly, Visser and Hemerijck (1997) argue that corporatist exchanges are analogous to networks of engagement (see Putnam 1993) where norms

---

[7] Rhodes's analysis highlights the importance of negotiated social pacts not only in heretofore relatively corporatist polities (e.g. the Netherlands), but in nations where traditional corporatist institutions and practices have been less developed (e.g. Italy).

of reciprocity, trust, and a sense of duty to other social partners and the common interest are cultivated. Net of other forces, social policy change in such an environment will typically involve slow, marginal, negotiated changes in which all interests are accounted; relatively quick and non-trivial retrenchments of the welfare state in response to domestic pressures and internationalization are unlikely.

Inclusive versus Exclusive Systems of Electoral Institutions

In addition, different features of formal constitutional structures and associated institutions that facilitate inclusive forms of representation through the electoral and party systems should matter. Important in this regard is recent work by Crepaz and Birchfield (no date) who have argued that welfare state retrenchment should, at a minimum, proceed more slowly in consensus democracies. This is so because consensus democracies have institutional mechanisms which guarantee that potential 'losers' in the processes of domestic structural change and internationalization are represented and that policy change occurs with incorporation of their interests. In related work, Birchfield and Crepaz (1998) have highlighted particular institutional features associated with consensus democracy that are important to those who pursue maintenance of the welfare state and egalitarian ends. Specifically, Birchfield and Crepaz argue that it is the 'collective veto points' afforded by proportional representation and the number of effective legislative parties, in particular, that insures some protection of these interests and egalitarian policy goals. Indeed, PR and multi-party systems are more likely to afford workers and regional and sectoral economic interests relatively potent institutional mechanisms whereby to resist adverse policy changes and to pursue compensation; ideological interests opposed to market-conforming policy changes (e.g. communitarian Christian democratic parties, environmentalists) will also be relatively advantaged. Similar institutional opportunities are arguably weaker in polities with exclusive electoral systems (e.g. single-member plurality rules) and two-party dominant systems.

The existence of what might be labelled 'inclusive electoral institutions' has also historically advantaged those groups and parties that constitute the core ideological support for the welfare state. As to political parties, social democratic and Christian democratic parties have been important in welfare state development (e.g. Esping-Andersen 1990; Hicks and Swank 1992; Hicks 1999; Huber, Ragin, and Stephens 1993). Examining long-term relationships, the correlations between the index of electoral inclusiveness developed below and shares of votes and national legislative seats for left and Christian democratic parties are highly significant (Pearson correlations for 1960–92 data (N = 435) across the focal nations are 0.500, 0.477, 0.402, 0.407, respectively). In addition, inclusive electoral institutions tend to exist in broader constellations of consensus democratic institutions

(Lijphart 1984) and tend to involve repeated interactions between a multi-plicity of social interests within decision making institutions such as lower chambers of parliaments and coalition governments. As such, norms of co-operation, reciprocity, and consensus-building may be fostered and adopted policies may enjoy significant legitimacy (Crepaz and Birchfield, no date; Birchfield and Crepaz 1998). As in the case of social corporatism, relatively rapid and non-trivial roll-backs in social welfare provision are, on balance, unlikely in this context.

Organization of Authoritative Decision Making within the Polity

It is not only national institutional structures of collective interest repres-entation that matter; the organization of formal policy making authority in the political system should also influence the political capacity of focal groups and, in turn, shape the ways in which national policies respond to interna-tional and domestic change (see Bonoli, in this volume, for a complementary analysis). Indeed, work on the welfare state (e.g. Hicks and Swank 1992; Huber, Ragin, and Stephens 1993; M. Schmidt 1996*b*) has highlighted the way in which the 'dispersion of policy making authority' has shaped welfare state development. Federalism, bicameralism, and presidentialism constitute potentially important 'institutional' veto points that allow conservative interests the opportunity to oppose welfare policy development and slow policy change.[8] These institutional veto points may accord welfare state con-stituencies and coalitions similar opportunities to impede or otherwise shape neoliberal policy changes to their best advantage. However, not all 'veto players' are created equal. In the case of social corporatism and inclusive electoral systems, institutions create collective veto points (through encom-passing representation) that advantage pro-welfare state clienteles, groups, and coalitions. Both sets of institutional structures also promote directly and indirectly the political strength of these actors and foster values and policy making routines that enhance the ability of these interests to blunt radical neoliberal reforms. On the other hand, while dispersion of policy making authority creates potential institutional veto points, it also creates notably weak welfare state clienteles, groups, and coalitions as well as broad policy making orientations and climates that are conducive to retrenchment. These negative impacts on pro-welfare state actors and policy making orientations are particularly pronounced where dispersion of authority (e.g. federalism)

---

[8] The logic of institutional and partisan veto points, or what Birchfield and Crepaz (1998) label competitive and collective veto points, is fully explored by Tsebelis (1995). In that work, Tsebelis argues that the number of institutional or partisan veto players (the latter being, for instance, parties in lower parliamentary chambers) will be related to slower policy change, subject to the degree of divergence among veto players and the cohesion of the constituent units of veto players.

is historically embedded, as in Australia, Canada, Switzerland, and the United States. They are less pronounced where contemporary patterns of dispersion are relatively short-lived, as in post-World War II Germany.

Specifically, formal fragmentation of policy making authority has large effects on the political capacities of social interests that have traditionally supported the welfare state. Focusing on the decentralization of authority, Noble's (1997: esp. 28–34) survey of the literature suggests that decentralization of policy making authority has generally tended to mobilize socially heterogeneous forces, undercut progressive and egalitarian political forces at the national level (e.g. trade union movements, social democracy), and favour local economic and political elites (also see F. G. Castles 1998; Pierson 1995; Stephens 1979). Moreover, federalism accentuates differences between rich and poor regions and, in turn, generates conflicts over the content of policy, fiscal equalization, and the distribution of financial burdens of national expenditure (e.g. contributions to de Villiers 1994; Banting 1997). In addition, institutional structures that disperse policy making responsibility tend to undercut the formation of coherent national policy strategies by groups and parties; the organization of parties and groups tends to be concentrated at regional and local levels and politics tends to be focused on narrow distributional issues within regional and local jurisdictions (e.g. on Canada, see Bradford and Jenson 1992; on the United States, see Piven 1992 and Skopol 1995). In fact, the long-term relationships between institutional fragmentation, on the one hand, and the electoral strength of left parties and social corporatism, on the other, are strong. The correlations across time and space (1960–95 for the fifteen focal nations) between the index of 'decentralization of policy making authority' developed below (federalism and bicamerlism) and left parties' votes and seats are -0.468 and -0.522 ($N = 465$); for decentralization of authority and social corporatism the correlation is -0.513.

In addition, to the extent that dispersion of authority is associated with low levels of welfare state development, it will create weak welfare state programmatic constituencies. Indeed, I present evidence below that 'decentralization of policy making authority' is one of the largest factors—a substantial negative influence on social welfare provision—among those forces that directly shape welfare effort across time and space. Moreover,the climate for welfare state retrenchment may be enhanced by prevailing political culture in fragmented polities. That is, the dispersion of policy making power tends to complement and reinforce the competition and conflict of pluralist politics; norms of cooperation, reciprocity, and consensus-building, potentially conducive to defence of the welfare state against substantial and rapid cuts, will tend to be weaker in fragmented polities than in centralized polities. Overall, to the extent that dispersion of authority favours conservative forces and produces a small welfare state, pro-welfare coalitions, programme-specific alliances, and pools of social programme and service personnel will be relatively weak in systems of dispersed authority and relatively stronger in centralized polities. Indeed, one might argue that the institutional features of welfare states themselves (e.g. universalism), particularly those that cultivate strong constituencies and supportive public opinion and value orientations, should be considered as a separate set of institutional characteristics that condition the policy effects of external socio-economic and political pressures for retrenchment.

The Institutional Structures of the Welfare State

Pierson (1994, 1996) outlines the general logic of welfare state retrenchment by noting that, unlike the politics of welfare expansion, welfare retrenchment involves taking away concentrated, politically popular benefits from organized constituencies for the promise of future, diffuse benefits; institutional characteristics of programme structure constrain various retrenchment strategies. Esping-Andersen (1996a; 1996b) makes a similar point by arguing that institutional legacies of welfare states shape the impact of the variety of social, economic, and political changes on welfare state transformation. As Esping-Andersen's (1990) seminal work on 'worlds of welfare capitalism' argues, contemporary welfare states may be classified as social democratic, conservative-corporatist, and liberal (cf. F. G. Castles and Mitchell 1993). The core structural characteristics of these welfare states consist of universalism, occupationally based social insurance, and selectivity. As Rothstein (1998b) notes, universal welfare states consist of programmatic structures of extensive or full coverage of target populations, egalitarian benefits, and widely accessible social services; liberal welfare states are characterized by disproportionate reliance on means-tested and private benefits.

Opportunity Structures and Welfare State Retrenchment

These principal institutional features of existing programme structures can play significant roles in impeding or facilitating retrenchment of the welfare state in response to the economic and political pressures attendant internationalization and domestic fiscal stress. While universal and liberal programme structures centralize policy formation and implementation in the hands of governmental institutions and bureaucracies, conservative corporatist welfare states decentralize authority to networks of quasi-public administrative bodies comprised of constituency and professional groups, labour, business, and government.[9] As such, conservative-corporatist welfare

[9] An important exception is the union-administered (Ghent) system of unemployment insurance present in several universalistic welfare states.

states provide notable opportunities for constituency groups and their allies to resist adverse policy change (see Clasen and Freeman 1994 on Germany); such opportunities are, on balance, more restricted in universal and liberal welfare programme structures.

Political Support for the Welfare State

Institutional features of welfare states may also strengthen (weaken) constituency groups and their allies. Central to the politics of welfare retrenchment is the extent to which welfare state institutions promote large, unified constituencies and unify (fragment) the panoply of interests that may mobilize to resist roll-backs in social protection (Pierson 1994). Universal welfare states, most notably, tend to create large cohesive constituency groups organized around relatively generous, universal programmes of social welfare provision; conservative-corporatist and liberal welfare states tend to fragment programme constituencies (on the basis of occupational status in the case of the former and on the basis of social class in the case of the latter). However, the political division of constituencies in corporatist conservative welfare states may be mitigated by the relatively generous social insurance protections accorded both working- and middle-class groups and other features of contemporary occupationally based welfare programmes (see Swank, forthcoming).

Universalism may also generate high levels of mass political support and foster the development of broad political coalitions that support the welfare state. Specifically, Moene and Wallerstein (1996) have recently highlighted the importance of universal versus means-tested benefits in maintaining the support of median voters for national systems of social protection: the disproportionate use of universalism cultivates the political support of median voters for the welfare state, since median voters face relatively high probabilities of benefiting from universally structured social programmes; means-tested programmes do not generate such support, since median voters face low odds of benefiting from means-tested, targeted programmes. Supporting this rational calculus, historical analyses of welfare state development (e.g. Esping-Andersen 1990) suggests national programme structures providing high levels of universal coverage, basic security, and income replacement have effectively fused the interests of working- and middle-class strata in the development and maintenance of the universal welfare state (also see Rothstein 1998*b*). While some have suggested that the recent growth in tax preferences for upscale groups and private occupational schemes will contribute to growing fissures within this traditional welfare state coalitions (Ervik and Kuhnle 1996), the persistence of universalism should significantly blunt the policy impact of domestic and international retrenchment pressures when compared to liberal welfare systems.

Politics, Values, and Social Welfare Provision

Bo Rothstein's (1998*b*) important and insightful study of the universal
welfare state of Northern Europe extends the previous analyses of political
dynamics and offers an argument for the importance of the 'moral logic of
the welfare state' in retrenchment politics. According to Rothstein, support
for the welfare state hinges on the 'contingent consent' of strategically self-
interested and moral citizens. In turn, this consent is dependent on citizens'
appraisals of the substantive, procedural, and distributional fairness of the
welfare state. The principles of equal respect and concern embodied in
programme structure, broadly targeted universal benefits, carefully adapted
delivery organizations, and participatory administrative processes achieve
relatively high levels of citizen contingent consent. Solidarity, trust, and confidence in state intervention are promoted. In liberal welfare states, problems
related to substantive justice (e.g. conflicts over defining the 'deserving poor'),
procedural justice (perceptions of bureaucratic aggrandizement and waste),
and a fair distribution of burdens (e.g. constituency fraud) are endemic. In
sum, Rothstein's work suggests that net of other forces, we should observe
notably different magnitudes and paces of welfare policy reform across
universalistic and liberal welfare states.[10]

Overall, substantial theory suggests that roll-backs of social protection in
response to domestic fiscal stress and internationalization will be notably
more difficult in universal than in liberal welfare states: the relative political
strength of welfare state constituencies, and pro-welfare state coalitions as
well as high levels of mass political approval and supportive value orientations will constitute a significant barrier to social policy retrenchments. The
reverse may be true in liberal welfare states where institutional features may
facilitate neoliberal restructuring. In the case of conservative-corporatist
welfare states, the picture is mixed. While occupationally based systems
often provide institutional opportunities for resistance to retrenchment, the
fragmentation of constituency groups and of potential coalitions by programmatic structure may facilitate welfare state roll-backs (see Swank, no
date, for a discussion of features of occupationally based welfare states that
may blunt retrenchment).

I now turn to an empirical exploration of the paper's central questions.
Are there systematic, direct relationships between domestic fiscal stress
and internationalization of capital markets, on the one hand, and retrenchment of the welfare state, on the other? Or, alternatively, do institutional

---

[10] Svallfors (1995) presents detailed panel data on attitudes towards social welfare policies
in Sweden. Consistent with the theoretical and formal analyses of Moene and Wallerstein
and the arguments and evidence of Rothstein (1998*b*), Svallfors documents the continuation of high levels of support for much of the Swedish welfare state with one exception:
a clear erosion of support for means-tested programmes, most notably social assistance
(cf. Pierson 1994).

mechanisms for interest representation, the formal organization of policy making authority in the polity, and extant welfare state structures determine patterns of social welfare policy response to domestic and international pressures for retrenchment?

3. DEMOCRATIC INSTITUTIONS AND WELFARE STATE RESTRUCTURING: ECONOMETRIC ANALYSIS

Methodology

In the subsequent analysis, I examine the direct effects of the two features of domestic and international pressure on contemporary welfare states highlighted above—fiscal stress and international capital mobility. In 1965 to 1995 (and 1979/80 to 1995) empirical models of social welfare provision, I initially focus on an aggregate measure of welfare state size: total social welfare expenditures as a share of GDP.[11] To deepen the analysis and to provide a check on the robustness of findings for total social welfare effort, I also examine the effects of fiscal stress and capital mobility on cash income maintenance (for families and sick days, and for the elderly, disabled, unemployed) and on social services (for families, the elderly, and the disabled). (On precise operationalizations of all variables and on data sources, see the Appendix to this chapter.) I utilize three central indicators to measure focal dimensions of domestic and international pressures. For domestic fiscal stress, I use lagged gross public sector debt as a percentage of GDP; for capital mobility, I use two central aspects of cross-border capital flows: inflows and outflows of direct foreign investment and borrowing on international capital markets. These measures are standardized by

---

[11] Two points are in order. First, although aggregate welfare benefit spending has been criticized as a blunt measure of social policy (e.g. Esping-Andersen 1990), it is important to note that aggregate benefit spending is highly correlated with more theoretically and substantively important outcomes such as income redistribution (see Korpi and Palme 1998 for the most recent evidence). Indeed, with proper need, income, and business cycle controls, such measures provide useful (albeit very imprecise) summary indicators of benefit generosity and eligibility standards. Second, spending measures in part reflect concrete policy changes that have been made years before; this is particularly true in the case of pensions. (I thank John Myles for drawing this to my attention.) However, many concrete policy changes affect aggregate benefit outlays in the short term (e.g. changes in indexing, waiting days, some benefit and eligibility criteria, and so forth). Many of these reforms, and their determinants, are captured by models such as those used below. Generally, one should confirm results of benefit outlay analysis with models of more concrete policy change. I have done that in complementary work and results reported below are universally confirmed. (For instance, in Swank, forthcoming, an identical pattern of institutionally mediated effects of internationalization are reported for analysis of the 'social wage', or income replacement rates for the average unemployed production worker.)

a nation's GDP and, to smooth occasionally volatile annual movements, are operationalized as three-year moving averages (lags 1–3).[12]

To estimate the magnitude and significance of the direct policy effects of these facets of domestic and international change, I utilize empirical models of annual 1965 to 1995 (or 1979/80 to 1995) social welfare benefits (as a percentage of GDP) in the fifteen focal nations discussed in Note 3 above. I initially use 1965 to 1995 models to ascertain general welfare state effects of political institutions (and other factors), to test for differences in institutional effects across the contemporary era of welfare state retrenchment (i.e. 1979/80 to the present) and previous periods of welfare expansion, and to anchor contemporary models in a general model of social welfare provision. I then focus on 1979/80 to 1995 models of total and disaggregated social welfare effort.[13] These models incorporate core socio-economic determinants highlighted in theory and the extant literature. For all models, exogenous variables include (one-year) lagged annual economic growth, unemployment, inflation rates, and the relative size of the elderly population; the partisan character of the national executive; and the level of affluence defined as per capita GDP in international prices.[14] Finally, as noted above, I incorporate in empirical models a measure of trade openness, or total imports and exports as percentages of national GDP.

To ascertain direct welfare state effects of democratic institutions and to offer ready tests of the extent to which democratic institutions shape the impacts of domestic fiscal stress and international capital mobility, I include

[12] In complementary work on the effects of internationalization on tax policy and on the welfare state during the 1965 to 1993 era (Swank 1998a, 2000), I show that these categorical measures of actual capital flows are significantly associated with total capital flows and measures of capital and financial market liberalization. Results reported below for foreign direct investment and capital market borrowing do not change with alternative measures of international capital mobility.

[13] It is important to note that available data on total social welfare spending across the developed democracies for a long time span contain a number of breaks in the data series. To correctly test the paper's central propositions for the longer time-series, I control for eight significant series breaks through the use of dummy variables (i.e. 0 for country years before and outside of the country series break, 1.00 for country years following the break). For the 1980 to 1995 period, the OECD database utilized here provides a near universally consistent set of time-series cross-section data. I select the late 1970s as a threshold point for two sets of reasons. First, the late 1970s roughly demarcates the acceleration of capital mobility, domestic fiscal stress, the ascendance of neoliberal macroeconomic orthodoxy, and the weakening of Keynesian welfare state policies and political alliances (e.g. contributions to Crafts and Toniolo 1996; Scharpf 1991). Second, data for comprehensive measures of fiscal stress and for disaggregated social welfare effort are only available from the late 1970s on.

[14] For basic models reported in the paper, I used ten-year averages of the percentage of cabinet portfolios held by parties of the left and Christian democracy. In supplementary analyses, I explored various (re)specifications of these variables (e.g. short-term and long-term lags, cumulative years in office, and so forth). Generally, these alternative specifications are consistent with results discussed below for the focal measures. I provide an overview of partisan effects below.

in all empirical models indicators of institutional structures of interest representation—social corporatism and inclusive electoral institutions—as well as measures of the 'dispersion of national policy making authority' developed below (i.e. decentralization and presidentialism). In subsequent models, I test individually for the roles of welfare state structure in mediating the impacts of domestic and international change. Specifically, I use measures (circa 1980) of programmatic attributes of welfare states (Esping-Andersen 1990) in models of social welfare spending to test the proposition that impacts of domestic and international pressures vary across welfare institutions. (See below on precise measurement and related details.)

Measuring Democratic Political Institutions

To develop a measure of social corporatism, I utilize new cross-nationally and temporally varying data on the organization of trade unions and the labour and industrial relations systems in the advanced industrial democracies. Following the lead of Golden (1997), I employ correlation and principal components analysis of theoretically relevant dimensions of corporatism—union density, inter-confederal concentration, confederal power (e.g. control over strike funds, involvement in wage bargaining), and the level of wage bargaining—to develop a core empirical indicator. As presented in Table 7.3, three characteristics of unions and bargaining systems consistently cohere (i.e. factor loadings in access of 0.80): union density, confederal power, and the level of wage bargaining. A weighted standard-score index of these three factors—an index varying across time and space and weighted by each component's factor loading—is used as the principal indicator of social corporatism. Confirmatory analysis suggests that while the focal indicator inherently stresses economic features of social corporatism, it is highly correlated across time and space with measures of the incorporation of peak functional associations in the national policy process.[15]

In order to develop indicators of electoral institutions and the organization of policy making authority, I follow the precedent established by Lijphart's (1984) seminal work on dimensions of democratic political institutions and conduct analyses of the relationships between aspects of formal democratic institutions and their close correlates: the major institutional dimensions highlighted in the literature discussed above are the focus. Using operationalizations outlined in the notes to Table 7.3, I employ principal components analysis of cross-nationally and temporally varying measures of the degree of proportionality in the electoral system, the number of

---

[15] For instance, the correlation between the focal measure of social corporatism and Boreham and Compston's (1992) measure of the incorporation of labour in the national policy process is 0.759 (using 1970–1986 time-series data from thirteen nations). As to union concentration, I exclude for the present analysis exploration of independent effects of concentration, or the degree to which union members are concentrated in one or few national peak associations.

TABLE 7.3. *Principal components analysis for national political institutions*

Social corporatism	Factor 1	Factor 2	National political institutions	Factor 1	Factor 2	Factor 3
Union concentration	0.03	**-0.98**	Proportional representation	**0.82**	-0.04	0.47
Union density	**-0.86**	-0.18	Number of effective parties	**0.93**	0.13	-0.37
Confederal power	**-0.85**	0.05	Federalism	0.09	**-0.78**	-0.37
Level of bargaining	**-0.85**	0.28	Bicameralism	0.09	**-0.92**	-0.05
			Presidentialism—separation of powers	0.02	-0.14	**-0.54**

Union concentration	Herfindahl index of inter-confederal concentration, or the probability that any two union members are members of the same national confederation.
Union density	Percentage of employed labour force who are members of unions.
Confederal power	Index of largest confederation's involvement in wage-setting process, power of appointment, veto over wage agreements, veto over strikes, and maintenance of strike of funds.
Level of bargaining	Four-level scale for centralization of wage bargaining where 0 is plant level, 1 is industry level, 2 is sectoral level without sanctions, and 3 is sectoral level with sanctions.
Proportional representation	Three-level scale (0 = single member district with plurality rules, 1 = quasi-proportional, 2 = proportional) of degree of proportional representation.
Effective number of legislative parties	Laasko and Taagepera index as presented in Lijphart (1984: 120).
Federalism	Three-level scale where 0 = no, 1 = weak, and 2 = strong federalism.
Bicameralism	Three-level scale where 0 = no or symbolic second chamber, 1 = weak bicameralism, and 2 = strong bicameralism.
Presidentialism	Two-level scale where 0 = parliamentary and 1 = presidential government.

Sources: See Appendix Table 7.2.

effective legislative parties, presidentialism, bicameralism, and federalism.[16] As Table 7.3 reveals, and as prefigured in the literature, PR and the number of effective legislative parties strongly cohere. In addition, consistent with expectations about facets of the organization of decision making authority, federalism and bicameralism form a distinct institutional dimension. Presidentialism does not 'load' on this dimension. Thus, in subsequent analysis I focus on two dimensions of the 'dispersion of policy making power': the vertical separation of powers (i.e. presidentialism) and the horizontal dispersion of power (i.e. decentralization). For empirical indicators, weighted standard-score indices of PR and effective legislative parties and of federalism and bicameralism are used to measure 'inclusive electoral institutions' and 'decentralization of policy making authority', respectively.[17]

To measure attributes of welfare systems, I rely on Esping-Andersen's rankings of welfare states on the dimensions of 'socialism' or what might simply be called universalism (i.e. universal coverage with high benefit equality), 'conservatism' (i.e. occupationally stratified welfare programmes and special public employee plans), and 'liberalism' (i.e. means-testing and reliance on private pensions and health insurance). Clearly, 'universalism', 'conservatism', and 'liberalism' provide general indicators of the degree to which welfare states are characterized by those factors emphasized in the theoretical discussion above. The scores of the fifteen focal nations on these three dimensions of welfare state structure as well as the 1965–1994/5 average annual scores for social corporatism, inclusive electoral institutions, and dispersion of authority are listed in Table 7.4.

Statistical Estimation

Estimation of empirical models is conducted by Ordinary Least Squares regression with corrections for first-order autoregressive errors, panel correct standard errors (i.e. heteroskedastic-consistent variance-covariance matrices for panel data), and unit dummies (see Beck and Katz 1995). Given that inclusion of a full set of unit dummy variables produced R^2-deletes approaching 0.99 for institutional variables, a conventional fixed effects model is not used; country dummies to adjust for unit effects (and thus obviate potentially

---

[16] In companion work (e.g. Swank, 1998*b*, forthcoming), I have also included the use of referendums as an institutional dimension. However, because Switzerland is excluded in the present work on the basis of data unavailability, I exclude referendums here. Without Switzerland, there is very little variation in the use of referendums across the developed democracies as measured by Lijphart (1984) or Huber, Ragin, and Stephens (1993). Moreover, while the use of referendums 'loads' on the decentralization dimension with federalism and bicameralism, its inclusion or exclusion makes no difference to results reported below.

[17] I also examined different features of fiscal decentralization (i.e. the central government's share of total revenue) that have been highlighted in the literature (see Castles 1998). However, measures of fiscal centralization do not 'load' on any of the focal institutional dimensions nor do they have direct or indirect effects in empirical models discussed below.

TABLE 7.4. *Dimensions of national political institutions: country positions, 1965–95*

Country	Universalism	Conservatism	Liberalism	Social corporatism	Electoral inclusiveness	Decentralization	Presidentialism
Sweden	8	0	0	1.26	0.25	-0.58	0
Norway	8	4	0	1.02	0.30	-0.66	0
Denmark	8	2	6	0.74	0.76	-0.66	0
Finland	6	6	4	0.67	0.89	-0.66	1
Netherlands	6	4	8	0.08	0.73	-0.11	0
Austria	2	8	4	0.33	-0.10	-0.15	0
Belgium	4	8	4	0.08	1.28	-0.08	0
France	2	8	8	-0.72	-0.27	-0.66	1
Germany	4	8	6	-0.56	0.06	1.47	0
Italy	0	8	6	0.17	0.47	-0.11	0
United States	0	0	12	-1.02	-1.23	1.47	1
Canada	4	2	12	-0.78	-1.08	0.37	0
Japan	2	4	10	-0.55	-0.42	-0.11	0
Australia	4	0	10	0.26	-0.56	0.95	0
Britain	4	0	6	-0.42	-1.15	-0.66	0

Universalism	Esping Anderson's (1990) score for degree of universalism and benefit equality in social welfare programmes, circa 1980.
Conservatism	Esping-Andersen's (1990) score for degree welfare is occupationally stratified and public employees have special programmes, circa 1980.
Liberalism	Esping-Andersen's (1990) score for degree welfare state relies on means-testing and degree of private pensions and health care, circa 1980.
Social corporatism	Weighted standard score index of union density, union peak association power, and level of collective bargaining, annual average, 1965–94.
Electoral inclusiveness	Weighted standard score index of degree of proportional representation and number of effective legislative parties, annual average, 1965–95.
Decentralization	Weighted standard score index of degree of federalism and bicameralism, annual average, 1965–95.
Presidentialism	Dichotomous variable where presidential systems scored 1.00 and parliamentary systems scored 0.00.

Sources: see Appendix Tables 7.1 and 7.2 for descriptions of data and sources.

biased estimates of social policy effects of focal variables) are included when t-statistics for country dummies exceeded 1.00. Within the context of OLS models, I test for direct linear effects of political institutions, fiscal stress and international capital mobility, and the control variables of the general model. To assess core hypotheses about how welfare state effects of fiscal stress and international capital mobility vary by political institutional context, I employ interaction analysis in which multiplicative terms involving public sector debt, direct foreign investment, and borrowing on international capital markets, on the one hand, and political institutional variables, on the other, are added to the general empirical models of social welfare effort.[18]

4. FISCAL STRESS, INTERNATIONAL CAPITAL, AND POLITICAL INSTITUTIONS: RESULTS OF EMPIRICAL TESTS

Total Social Welfare Effort

The findings from the estimation of basic models of total social welfare provision are presented in Table 7.5. In the first two columns, I presents tests for direct linear effects of flows of direct foreign investment, four central facets of national democratic institutions, and exogenous factors composing the general model. As noted above, the models are estimated initially with 1965–95 data for the fifteen focal nations; I then shift the focus to the contemporary era (1979–95) and examine direct welfare state effects of fiscal stress, both measures of international capital mobility, political institutions, and the variety of socio-economic and political factors of the general model.

As the table reveals, three of the four dimensions of democratic political institutions have significant effects on total social welfare effort. In fact, social corporatism, inclusive electoral institutions, and decentralization of policy making authority all have substantively large effects. As theorized, the first two institutional factors have strong positive effects while decentralization has a large negative effect on total social welfare effort. For instance, net of other forces, the difference in social welfare provision between nations at −1.00 and 1.00 on the index of social corporatism (roughly the difference

---

[18] It may be helpful to discuss the interpretation of interactions. Briefly, the interaction of, let us say, X_1 and X_2, when the explanandum is Y, will tell us whether the effect of X_2 on Y varies with levels of X_1 (or vice versa). The significance test for the interaction simply tells us whether differences in the effect of X_2 at different levels of X_1 are significantly different from zero. The interaction term itself, when multiplied by a value of X_1 and added to the coefficient of X_2, becomes the slope for the effect of X_2 at that level of X_1. Moreover, standard errors necessary for testing the significance of the effects of X_2 at some level of X_1 are easily derived (see Friedrich 1982).

Duane Swank

TABLE 7.5. *The impact of political institutions on total social welfare effort*

	(1) 1965–95	(2) 1965–95	(3) 1979–95	(4) 1979–95
Democratic political institutions				
Social corporatism	0.8591*	0.9076*	2.2813*	2.2316*
	(0.3767)	(0.3588)	(0.4618)	(0.4408)
Inclusive electoral institutions	0.8549*	0.8678*	0.7130*	0.7018*
	(0.3027)	(0.3007)	(0.3413)	(0.3417)
Decentralization of policy making authority	−2.7485*	−3.0616*	−4.2301*	−4.1621*
	(0.7545)	(0.5760)	(0.7457)	(0.7378)
Presidentialism/separation of powers	−0.8524	—	—	—
	(0.9330)			
Domestic and international pressures				
Public sector debt	—	—	−0.0189*	−0.0209*
			(0.0114)	(0.0117)
Direct foreign investment flows	0.0770	0.0930	0.0079	—
	(0.1304)	(0.1265)	(0.1047)	
International capital market flows	—	—	—	0.0393
				(0.0672)
General model				
Left government	−0.0029	−0.0025	−0.0019	−0.0017
	(0.0078)	(0.0076)	(0.0067)	(0.0065)
Christian democratic government	−0.0044	−0.0041	−0.0061	−0.0065
	(0.0132)	(0.0132)	(0.0130)	(0.0130)
Elderly population	0.6536*	0.6145*	0.3896*	0.4005*
	(0.1744)	(0.1493)	(0.1705)	(0.1705)
Unemployment rate	0.3350*	0.3381*	0.3558*	0.3538*
	(0.0560)	(0.0551)	(0.0655)	(0.0642)
Inflation rate	0.0422*	0.0414*	−0.0201	−0.0201
	(0.0231)	(0.0234)	(0.0450)	(0.0455)
Level of affluence	0.8367*	0.8421*	0.8881*	0.8774*
	(0.1048)	(0.1038)	(0.1408)	(0.1385)
Economic growth rate	−0.1426*	−0.1429*	−0.2026*	−0.2034*
	(0.0232)	(0.0232)	(0.0490)	(0.0451)
Trade openness	0.0122	0.0127	−0.0203	−0.0204
	(0.0146)	(0.0146)	(0.0182)	(0.0185)
Intercept	−2.5996	−2.3596	3.3446	3.3032
Buse R^2	0.7973	0.7934	0.9157	0.9166

Note: Each model is estimated with 1965–95 (1979–95) data by Ordinary Least Squares; equations are first-order autoregressive. The table reports OLS unstandardized regression coefficients and panel correct standard errors. All models include nation-specific dichotomous variables (if $t > 1.00$) and dichotomous variables to control for series breaks in the dependent variable. * indicates significance at the 0.05 level or below.

between 1965–94 mean levels for the United States and Norway) is 1.7 per cent of GDP (0.8591 * 2). A similar difference of 2.00 on the index of electoral inclusiveness (e.g. the difference between mean levels of electoral inclusiveness in Canada and Finland) is associated with an equivalent difference in social protection of 1.7 per cent of GDP (0.8549 * 2). The social welfare impact of decentralization of policy making authority is even larger: the difference in social welfare effort between a nation at 1.00 on the index at a particular point in time (e.g. roughly the 1965–95 mean level for Australia) and a nation scoring −0.66 (e.g. the mean level for Denmark) is approximately 4.4 per cent of GDP (2.7485 * 1.61). On the other hand, presidentialism is not significantly associated with total social welfare outlays. Because of this initial finding and the absence of consistent direct or indirect effects in subsequent analysis, I drop this institutional dimension from the analysis. Column 2 of Table 7.5 displays the basic model after deletion of presidentialism; all other institutional effects retain or increase their substantive effects and significance.

These long-term general models of social welfare effort are also useful for testing for differences in social policy effects of political institutions in shaping welfare effort during the latter years of welfare expansion (i.e. mid-1960s to mid-1970s) and the post-1970s period of welfare state retrenchment. Using the basic model of column 2 and interaction terms for a post-1978 dummy variable and the three institutional variables, I estimated the effects of social corporatism, electoral inclusiveness, and decentralization of policy making authority during periods 1965–79 and 1979–95 (and tested for significance in the difference in magnitude of institutional effects across the periods). The effects of social corporatism are largely confined to the post-1979 period: its effect on total social welfare effort is a statistically insignificant 0.3763 in the pre-1979 era and a substantively large and significant 1.5185 in the post-1979 era. The effects of electoral inclusiveness are significant in both periods (regression coefficients of 0.6298 and 1.0919, respectively), although the post-1979 effect on social welfare effort is statistically and substantively larger. A similar pattern holds for decentralization: its effects on social welfare effort (−2.6376 in the pre-1979 era and −3.7532 in the post-1979 period) are significant in both eras but greater in the contemporary era of accelerating pressures on the welfare state. In addition, focusing on columns 3 and 4 of Table 7.5, estimations of institutional effects during the 1979–95 era confirm the conclusion that national political institutions continue to be very important (if not more important) in shaping social policy change in the contemporary era.

The second panel of Table 7.5 displays the direct social welfare effects of public sector debt and international capital mobility. With respect to capital mobility, neither rises in the level of flows of foreign direct investment nor borrowing on international capital markets is associated with declines in social welfare provision. However, the magnitude of public sector debt is related to social welfare effort (although the effect is moderate in substantive magnitude). Controlling for political institutions, economic openness, and the variety of socio-economic and political pressures on contemporary welfare states entailed in the general model, increases in government debt are negatively and significantly related to total social provision. Examining column 4 of Table 7.5, one can see that, net of other forces, an increase in debt equivalent to 10 per cent of GDP, would produce a decline in social welfare effort equivalent to 0.2 per cent of GDP; an increase in debt of 40 per cent of GDP (the mean change for our nations from 1978 to 1995) is associated with an absolute decline in social protection of 1 per cent of GDP. However, as I show below, where increases in debt are above the mean and where national institutional structures are conducive to welfare retrenchment, the impacts of debt are larger.

A Comment on the Combined Effect of Fiscal Stress and Global Markets

It is useful to note that in related work (Swank 1998*b*, forthcoming), I have examined the 1965–93 welfare effects of a variety of alternative measures of capital mobility (e.g. total capital flows, capital market liberalization, interest rate differentials, and various categories of capital flows standardized by gross domestic investment), plausible non-linear effects of capital mobility, and the interactions of each dimension of international capital mobility with trade openness. None of these alternative specifications produced findings of significant downward pressures of international capital on social welfare provision. Finally, in the present analysis, I explored the possibility that capital mobility would have significant negative effects on the welfare state at high levels of deficits and debt. Specifically, Garrett (1998*a*) has suggested the hypothesis that international capital markets impose a high interest rate premium on governments that run large deficits. That is, in the presence of high debt and deficits, capital markets anticipate higher inflation (and other adverse outcomes), engender currency depreciation, and hence necessitate higher interest rates in the fiscally imprudent nation. Ultimately, one might speculate that the interaction of high debt and deficits, on the one hand, and high capital mobility, on the other, will place serious downward pressures on the welfare state. I find (through a test of the interaction of public debt and the capital mobility variables) that, net of other forces, the social welfare impact of international capital mobility becomes significant and negative only when gross government debt exceeds 100 per cent of GDP (e.g. Belgium in the 1980s and Italy in the 1990s).[19]

[19] In complementary analysis of 1965–93 impacts of a variety of dimensions of international capital mobility, I find that capital mobility interacts with high short-term deficits. Specifically, when deficits exceed roughly 10% of GDP, international capital mobility begins to exert downward pressures on national welfare budgets. Coupled with results presented here, these findings suggest that policy makers in developed democracies enjoy some latitude in borrowing even in the context of open capital markets. It is only when debt and deficits exceed a relatively high threshold (or emerge in an institutional context conducive to retrenchment), that international capital market discipline creates significant downward pressure on the welfare state. In Swank (forthcoming), I present these quantitative findings and a variety of supportive case study evidence.

Turning to the bottom panel of the table, I present results for the general model of total social welfare effort. As to the other forces shaping social welfare provision, the size of the aged population, unemployment, inflation, and affluence are all positively and significantly associated with total social welfare outlays; the economic growth rate is negatively and significantly related to social welfare provision. Trade openness, inconsistent with the classic arguments of Cameron (1978) and Katzenstein (1985*b*) and the embedded liberalism thesis, is not significantly related to social provision in the models of Table 7.5.

A Note on Party Effects

Finally, in the presence of nation-specific dummy variables and controls for social corporatism, electoral institutions, and the decentralization of authority—all of which are related to partisan strength in direct and indirect ways (see above), the relatively short-term direct social welfare impacts of both left and Christian democratic government control are statistically insignificant in the basic models of Table 7.5 (and in the models of cash income maintenance and social services presented below). However, it is important to note that in the presence of unit dummies and institutional variables, levels of multicollinearity for partisan variables are high and thus it is difficult to draw conclusions about their exact relevance. In fact, if one deletes unit dummies in the column 3 equation, allowing institutional, partisan, and other variables to absorb cross-sectional variance, government control by Christian democratic governments is positively and significantly related to total social protection (e.g. the regression coefficient for Christian democratic government—per cent of cabinet portfolios held by these parties—is 0.0684 with a t-statistic of 4.803); left government is also marginally significant in this specification (regression coefficient of 0.0151; t = 1.472). In other formulations (e.g. cumulative years of left and Christian democractic government from 1950), left (and Christian democratic) government is clearly significant in Table 7.5 models in the absence of unit effects. (See Kitschelt, in this volume, for a systematic analysis of the strategic environment for partisan welfare state retrenchment/defence.)

Table 7.5A presents tests for the central argument of the paper: the social welfare impacts of domestic fiscal stress and international capital mobility should be notably shaped by configurations of national political institutions. As the table indicates, this indeed appears to be the case. Of the eighteen possible interactions between political institutions and domestic and international pressures, fourteen are correctly signed and moderately significant; a dozen are clearly statistically significant at conventional levels (0.05) and beyond. The strongest pattern pertains to the degree to which domestic political institutions shape international pressures. The character of the interest representational system, the inclusiveness of electoral institutions, and the

TABLE 7.5A. *The mediation of domestic and international pressures*
on welfare states by political institutions

	Public sector debt	Direct foreign investment	International capital markets
Political institutions			
Social corporatism*domestic or	0.0146[a]	0.4222*	0.2236*
international factor of column	(0.0108)	(0.1556)	(0.0823)
Electoral inclusiveness*domestic	−0.0089	0.1887*	0.3275*
or international factor	(0.0075)	(0.0765)	(0.0778)
Decentralization*domestic or	−0.0173[a]	−0.3666*	−0.3647*
international factor	(0.0116)	(0.1409)	(0.0903)
Welfare state programme structure			
Universalism*domestic or	0.0055*	0.2173*	0.0561*
international factor	(0.0027)	(0.0569)	(0.0278)
Conservatism*domestic or	−0.0026	0.0317	0.0689*
international factor	(0.0022)	(0.0270)	(0.0216)
Liberalism*domestic or	0.0024	−0.0964*	−0.0342*
international factor	(0.0024)	(0.0314)	(0.0133)

Note: Interactions are estimated in the focal equations of Table 7.5. Estimation is by OLS with AR1 autoregressive parameters and panel correct standard errors. Direct effects of Table 7.5 factors remain universally unchanged in terms of significance levels and substantive effects and, hence, full table results are not reported. Tables are available from the author.

* Significant at 0.05 level.
[a] Significant at the 0.10 level.
See Appendix Table 7.3 for full results of interaction analysis.

organization of policy-making authority, as well as universalism and liberalism in welfare programme structures, are all important in shaping the magnitude of impacts of international capital mobility. Computations of exact impacts of rises in international capital mobility at low, medium, and high levels of these five institutional dimensions suggest that direct investment and exposure to international capital markets exert systematic downward pressures on welfare states where decentralization and liberalism are high and where social corporatism, electoral inclusiveness, and universalism are low. At moderate to high levels of social corporatism, electoral inclusiveness, and universalism (and low levels of decentralization and liberalism), rises in international capital mobility are, net of other forces, either unrelated to social welfare protection or associated with small positive increases. (See Appendix Table 7.3 for estimates of the components of interactions. This information and procedures outlined above can be used to derive specific welfare state impacts of domestic and international pressures in particular institutional contexts.)

A similar but weaker pattern obtains for the case of domestic fiscal stress: three of the six interactions are correctly signed and modestly significant (although see below for evidence of stronger impacts of debt on cash income maintenance). The largest institutional effect—indicative of the broader pattern of findings for domestic and international pressures—occurs with regard to universalism: at high levels of universalism (Sweden, Norway, and Denmark), the effect of an increase of public sector debt equivalent to 1 per cent of GDP is 0.00. At moderate levels of universalism it is −0.023 and at low levels of universalism it is −0.045 (see information in Appendix Table 7.3). The welfare impact of an increase in government debt of 10 per cent of GDP in a nation where programmatic attributes of welfare states entail little universalism (e.g. the United States) is −0.45.

A Comment on Big Welfare States, Increasing Debt, and Global Markets

The above findings can be further illustrated with reference to the experience of Nordic countries. These welfare states possess highly universalistic programme structures, strong social corporatism and electoral inclusiveness, and are relatively centralized polities. Indeed, the experience of the Swedish welfare state in the early and mid-1990s, an experience grounded in rising public sector financial stress and international capital mobility, can serve to underscore and enrich the statistical findings reported above.[20]

In the early 1990s, Sweden experienced a dramatic fall in growth rates (for instance, real GDP per capita growth was only 0.5 per cent in 1990 and −1.7 and −2.1 per cent in 1991 and 1992, respectively). It also experienced a commensurate rise in unemployment, deficits, and public debt. For instance, total public sector debt increased from 44.3 per cent to 80.1 per cent of GDP between 1990 and 1995. The 1991–4 bourgeois government enacted two main 'crisis packages' in 1992 (largely with the cooperation of the opposition Social Democrats (SAP)). During 1992, the 'base amount' utilized to calculate social benefits was trimmed 3 per cent, sickness benefits (heretofore paid at 90 per cent with no waiting days) were reduced to 65 per cent for the second and third days, 80 per cent for the remainder of the first year of sickness, and 70 per cent of pay after that; one waiting day for sickness benefits was imposed and, to encourage better policing of the system, employers became responsible for the first two weeks of benefits. In addition, the system of work injury benefits was brought in line with sick pay, and unemployment and social assistance benefits were modestly reduced; a waiting period of five days (and new limits on duration) was introduced for unemployment benefits and new employee contributions for unemployment insurance were initiated. Perhaps the most important change was the initiation of major alterations in the earnings-related pension: in the future, the ATP would be based on lifetime contributions and not 30 years of contributions for full pension with the 'best 15 years' determining pension amounts; new social

---

[20] This section draws from my work on social democratic welfare states in global markets (see Swank 2000, forthcoming, esp. ch. 4).

insurance contributions were planned where the employee would ultimately contribute 9.25 per cent of pay to fund ATP. (A new 40-year residence rule, rather than citizenship, was enacted to determine eligibility for the basic, flat-rate pension.)[21] Finally, many new initiatives were taken in 1992 and 1993 to encourage the implementation of market mechanisms in social service delivery and to foster the establishment of private providers (e.g. doctors, child care businesses); additional user fees for a variety of social services were also implemented.

However, at the time of these entitlement cuts, the government increased outlays for Active Labour Market Policies (e.g. Stephens 1996). Indeed, expenditure on training, placement, and related services (as well as temporary public sector employment) increased from 1.63 per cent of GDP in 1989 to 3.11 per cent in 1994. Moreover, budgetary policy also emphasized (particularly from 1993–4 on) modest revenue increases; some of the early tax cuts (see note 21) were temporarily rescinded and moderate new revenue increases proposed (e.g. Gould 1996). The Social Democrats were re-elected in 1994 and preserved many of the roll-backs in social benefits and social services. However, some of the liberal provisions instigated by the bourgeois government concerning private providers were eliminated; social rights to services for the handicapped, elderly, and children were extended, and, again, the 1994 budget emphasized tax increases over further spending cuts.

Generally, while notable fiscal pressure engendered some retrenchment in social insurance benefits and eligibility, cuts in social entitlements were balanced with social support of the unemployed and with revenues. From the perspective of the mid- and late 1990s, most observers have noted that, while there have been cuts and modifications in the Swedish welfare state since the late 1970s, the basic elements of the social democratic model remain largely intact in Sweden (e.g. Sainsbury 1996; Clausen and Gould 1995; Gould 1996), albeit restructured in the direction of a more 'productivist' welfare state (Esping-Andersen, 1996a).

Income Maintenance and Social Services.

Table 7.6 reports the results of the supplementary analysis of the direct effects of political institutions, fiscal stress, and international capital mobility on 1980–95 cash income maintenance and social services. Overall, the findings reported above for the effects of these factors on total social welfare effort are reproduced in the case of these two important categories

---

[21] In addition to these changes in social welfare programmes, 1990 marked 'the tax reform of the century' in which marginal rates on individuals and capital were reduced substantially (along with the removal of a variety of exemptions, allowances, and deductions which benefited upper tier earners and corporations).

TABLE 7.6. *The impact of political institutions on cash income maintenance and social welfare services, 1980–95*

	(1) Cash benefits	(2) Cash benefits	(3) Social services	(4) Social services
Democratic political institutions				
Social corporatism	0.8256*	0.8188*	0.2994*	0.2869*
	(0.3338)	(0.3260)	(0.1165)	(0.1153)
Inclusive electoral institutions	0.6022*	0.5960*	0.0252	0.0291
	(0.2540)	(0.2507)	(0.0529)	(0.0510)
Decentralization of policy making authority	−4.1062*	−4.0547*	−0.5050*	−0.4948*
	(0.5238)	(0.5148)	(0.0814)	(0.0779)
Domestic and international pressures				
Public sector debt	−0.0055	−0.0052	−0.0074*	−0.0083*
	(0.0086)	(0.0088)	(0.0029)	(0.0027)
Direct foreign investment flows	−0.0226	—	0.0494*	—
	(0.1081)		(0.0231)	
International capital market flows	—	−0.0215	—	0.0170
		(0.0688)		(0.0181)
General model				
Left government	−0.0008	−0.0009	0.0005	0.0006
	(0.0028)	(0.0028)	(0.0009)	(0.0009)
Christian democratic government	−0.0068	−0.0065	−0.0012	−0.0009
	(0.0054)	(0.0053)	(0.0012)	(0.0012)
Elderly population	0.2154[a]	0.2125[a]	−0.0284	0.0008
	(0.1518)	(0.1511)	(0.0319)	(0.0319)
Unemployment rate	0.3330*	0.3326*	0.0571*	0.0504*
	(0.0541)	(0.0532)	(0.0108)	(0.0107)
Inflation rate	0.0518*	0.0492*	0.0030	0.0035
	(0.0314)	(0.0304)	(0.0062)	(0.0064)
Level of affluence	0.3995*	0.3912*	0.1396*	0.1437*
	(0.1135)	(0.1139)	(0.0278)	(0.0276)
Economic growth rate	−0.1078*	−0.1057*	−0.0144*	−0.0152*
	(0.0290)	(0.0287)	(0.0042)	(0.0042)
Trade openness	−0.0558*	−0.0520*	−0.0044*	−0.0034*
	(0.0138)	(0.0130)	(0.0010)	(0.0015)
Intercept	6.1500	6.2043	−0.5301	−0.8575
Buse R^2	0.8120	0.7960	0.8530	0.8439

Note: Each model is estimated with 1980–95 data by Ordinary Least Squares; equations are first-order autoregressive. The table reports OLS unstandardized regression coefficients and panel correct standard errors. All models include nation-specific dichotomous variables (if $t > 1.00$).

* Significant at 0.05.
[a] Significant at 0.10 level.

of social welfare provision. As to the direct roles of political institutions in shaping 1980 to 1995 changes in income maintenance and social service outlays, findings underscore the importance of all three dimensions of national institutions. This is particularly true for social corporatism and decentralization which have, net of the welfare effects of other forces, sub-stantively large and significant impacts in both areas of welfare. Electoral inclusiveness has significant direct effects on variations in cash income main-tenance but not on social services.

The second panel of the table reports the direct social welfare effects of public sector debt, direct foreign investment flows, and borrowing on inter-national capital markets; these results largely mirror those for total social welfare effort. The two dimensions of capital mobility are largely unrelated to social welfare provision; in the case of foreign direct investment, inter-national capital mobility is positively related to social services. With regard to this latter finding, the relationship between increases in social services (some of which are directly oriented to assisting families manage the combined demands of work and family life) and rises in international capital markets is consistent with the view that policy makers in (some) welfare states have increasingly emphasized human capital development and associated social policies in an era of internationalization of markets (e.g. Garrett 1998*a*, 1998*b*; Esping-Andersen 1996*a*). With respect to the direct effects of domestic fiscal stress, findings suggest that the impacts of fiscal imbalance on social welfare provision come primarily through downward pressures on social services. In fact, this finding is consistent with the conventional notion that more 'discretionary' social service budgets are relatively easier to cut than basic social insurance budgets whose relative importance to economic well-being, longer-lived status, and legal foundations pose relatively greater political difficulties for retrenchment-minded incumbent governments. However, as I show below, in institutional contexts that are conducive to welfare retrench-ment, rises in debt have negative effects on cash transfers.

Finally, the last panel of Table 7.6 reports evidence to suggest that the elderly population; unemployment, inflation, and economic growth rates; and the level of affluence play important roles in shaping contemporary income maintenance and social service spending. Trade openness (insignificant in general models of total social welfare effort) has small negative impacts on both income maintenance and social service outlays. Contrary to findings on the direct effects of international capital mobility, this finding is consistent with contemporary proponents of the internationalization explanation for welfare state retrenchment. However, in the absence of analysis of more detailed measures of trade flows, competitiveness indicators, and related dimensions of markets for goods and services, it is difficult to draw strong conclusions about the welfare policy roles of trade.

Further evidence on the effects of international capital mobility and fiscal stress, and findings about the paper's central proposition—that domestic and international pressures are mediated by national political institutions—are reported in Tables 7.6A and 7.6B. As the first table reveals, the findings reported above on the central role of political institutions in shaping social

TABLE 7.6A. *The mediation of domestic and international pressures on cash income maintenance by political institutions*

	Public sector debt	Direct foreign investment	International capital markets
Political institutions			
Social corporatism*domestic or international factor of column	0.0218* (0.0089)	0.3549* (0.1181)	0.2594* (0.0741)
Electoral inclusiveness*domestic or international factor	−0.0045 (0.0066)	0.0364 (0.0674)	0.2318* (0.0701)
Decentralization*domestic or international factor	−0.0144[a] (0.0109)	−0.0846 (0.1307)	−0.2814* (0.0798)
Welfare state programme structure			
Universalism*domestic or international factor	0.0079* (0.0024)	0.1173* (0.0334)	0.0420* (0.0241)
Conservatism*domestic or international factor	−0.0044[a] (0.0024)	0.0142 (0.0238)	0.0100 (0.0196)
Liberalism*domestic or international factor	−0.0038* (0.0021)	−0.0493* (0.0271)	−0.0406* (0.0117)

Note: Interactions are estimated in the focal equations of Tables 7.6. Estimation is by OLS with AR1 autoregressive parameters and panel correct standard errors. Direct effects of Table 7.6 factors remain universally unchanged in terms of significance levels and substantive effects and, hence, full table results are not reported. Tables are available from the author.

* Significant at 0.05 level.
[a] Significant at the 0.10 level.
See Appendix Table 7.3 for full results of interaction analysis.

TABLE 7.6B. *The mediation of domestic and international pressures on social welfare services by political institutions*

	Public sector debt	Direct foreign investment	International capital markets
Political institutions			
Social corporatism*domestic or international factor of column	0.0015 (0.0027)	0.1096* (0.0317)	0.0117 (0.0211)
Electoral inclusiveness*domestic or international factor	−0.0010 (0.0012)	−0.0013 (0.0400)	0.290* (0.0165)
Decentralization*domestic or international factor	−0.0037* (0.0020)	−0.0244 (0.0251)	−0.0213 (0.0220)
Welfare state programme structure			
Universalism*domestic or international factor	0.0009[a] (0.0006)	0.0332* (0.0123)	0.0105[a] (0.0070)
Conservatism*domestic or international factor	−0.0008 (0.0006)	−0.0052 (0.0056)	0.0058 (0.0060)
Liberalism*domestic or international factor	−0.0008* (0.0006)	−0.0252* (0.0084)	0.0058 (0.0060)

See note to Table 7.6A.

welfare responsiveness to domestic and international pressures are reproduced in the case of cash income maintenance programmes. Thirteen of the
eighteen interactions between domestic and international forces, on the
one hand, and political institutions, on the other, are moderately significant;
eleven are significant at conventional levels and beyond. In fact, the role of
institutions in mediating the impact of domestic fiscal stress is more pronounced in the case of income maintenance than in the instance of total
social protection. Fiscal stress is negatively related to income maintenance
at low levels of social corporatism and universalism and at high levels of
decentralization of policy making authority and liberalism (information for
derivations from interactions is reported in Appendix Table 7.3).

Turning to the findings on the role of political institutions in mediating
domestic and international pressures on social services, Table 7.6B suggests
that political institutions, while not irrelevant, are less systematically important to determining the magnitude of social welfare impacts of fiscal stress
and international capital mobility. Only eight of the possible eighteen relationships are statistically significant. However, in the case of direct foreign
investment for instance, the findings indicate that welfare states nested in
the context of social corporatist interest representational systems and universalistic programme structures will experience fewer cuts in social services than
liberal welfare states. Indeed, using the mathematics of interactions, one can
derive that an increase in the level of foreign direct investment of 1 per cent
of GDP is associated with a decline in social services equal to 0.23 per cent
of GDP in strongly liberal welfare states (i.e. those scoring 12 on the liberalism scale: Canada and the United States). Although limited in number,
additional institutionally mediated effects of domestic and international forces
exist for social services.

5. CONCLUSIONS

The preceding analysis has presented theory and evidence that highlight the
importance of national political institutions in shaping social policy responses
to domestic fiscal stress and internationalization. I have emphasized the ways
in which institutions provide (restrict) opportunities for collective action,
influence the political power of social groups and classes, and promote
(impede) the development and maintenance of value orientations that support social welfare states. To summarize the central findings about rising fiscal
imbalance, internationalization, and institutions, the welfare state effects
of notable domestic and international pressures vary systematically across
institutional contexts: where institutions of collective interest representation—
social corporatism and inclusive electoral institutions—are strong, where

policy making authority is centralized, and where the welfare state is based on the principle of universalism, the effects of fiscal stress and international capital mobility are absent, or they are positive in the sense that they suggest economic and political interests opposed to neoliberal reforms, or adversely affected by domestic and international structural changes, have been successful in defending the welfare state. Where corporatism and electoral inclusiveness are weak, where the dispersion of authority is substantial, and where liberal principles structure the welfare state, rises in public sector debt and international capital mobility are associated with downward pressures on social welfare provision. Indeed, countries such as Canada and the United States, and to a lessor extent Australia and the United Kingdom, seem particularly likely to have experienced a broad array of domestic neoliberal policy reforms and budget cuts with rises in debt and capital mobility.

On a more cautionary note, I should emphasize that the findings of the present study suggest a number of possibilities with regard to further welfare state retrenchment and the future impacts of demographic shifts, domestic economic stagnation, fiscal imbalances, and internationalization in domestic policy determination. First, my findings indicate that if social corporatism is further weakened (e.g. widespread declines in corporatist interest intermediation comparable to 1980s and 1990s changes in Sweden), a viable institutional mechanism for labour to resist domestic and international retrenchment pressures will be significantly diminished. Second, to the extent that authority for national policy formulation is further devolved to subnational jurisdictions (e.g. the contemporary USA and elsewhere) or to the extent power is ceded to supranational federations, most notably the European Union, the findings presented here suggest that the development of the resultant systems of decentralized authority may undercut the maintenance or expansion of systems of ample social protection (also see Huber and Stephens 1992). Finally, to the extent that governments continue to implement means-testing and related neoliberal principles (see Swank 2000, forthcoming, for a survey of this development in social democratic, Christian democratic, and liberal welfare states), the theory and results presented above suggest that the chances for further retrenchment in the face of domestic and international pressures increase in the long term. In each case, more significant cuts in the welfare state are likely as institutional mechanisms that support the welfare state are eroded. However, as noted in the introduction, the pace of these changes and their scope seem contingent on the conscious policy choices of elected governments and the institutional contexts in which they operate.

APPENDIX TABLE 7.1. *Principal variables*

TOTAL SOCIAL WELFARE	Total government expenditure for social welfare programmes as a percentage of GDP.
CASH INCOME MAINTENANCE	Total cash benefits for families and sick pay, the elderly, disabled, and unemployed as a percentage of GDP.
SOCIAL SERVICES	Total public social services to families, the elderly, and disabled as a percentage of GDP.
DIRECT INVESTMENT	Average (lags 1, 2, and 3 years) of inflows and outflows of direct investment as a percentage of GDP.
CAPITAL MARKETS	Average (lags 1, 2, and 3 years) of borrowing on international capital markets (e.g. bonds, equities, bank borrowing) as a percentage of GDP.
SOCIAL CORPORATISM	Weighted standard score index of union density, confederal power, and level of wage bargaining. Union density is measured as union membership (excluding retired, self-employed, and unemployed) as a percentage of wage and salary workers; confederal power is an unweighted standard score index of power of appointment, veto over wage agreements, veto over strikes, control of strike funds, and involvement in wage setting of largest union confederation; and level of wage bargaining is a 1–4 scale of centralization of wage bargaining in the economy.
INCLUSIVE ELECTORAL INSTITUTIONS	Weighted standard score index of degree of proportional representation (0, 1, 2 scale) and effective number of legislative parties (computed using the Laasko and Taagepera index as presented in Lijphart 1984: 120).
DECENTRALIZATION OF AUTHORITY	Weighted standard score index of federalism (0, 1, 2 scale) and bicameralism (0, 1, 2 scale).
PRESIDENTIALISM	Dichotomous variable for presidential (1) and parliamentary systems (0.00).
OLD	The percentage of the popoulation 65 years of age or older.
UNEMPLOYMENT	The percentage of the civilian labour force unemployed.
INFLATION	Year-to-year percentage changes in the Consumer Price Index.
GROWTH	Percentage change in real GDP.
AFFLUENCE	Per capita GDP in constant (1985) international prices (1000s of dollars)
LEFT	Annual percentage of left party cabinet portfolios.
CHRISTIAN DEMOCRAT	Annual percentage of Christian democratic party cabinet portfolios.
TRADE	Real imports plus real exports as a percentage of real GDP.

International variables

Total inflows and outflows of direct investment, portfolio investment, and bank lending in millions of current US dollars. *Source*: IMF, *Balance of Payments Statistics* (Washington, DC, selected years).

Total borrowing on international capital markets. *Source*: OECD, *International Capital Market Statistics* (Paris: OECD, 1996).

Exports and imports of goods and services in millions (billions for Italy and Japan) of national currency units. *Source*: OECD, *National Accounts of OECD Member Countries* (Paris: OECD, various years).

Data for computation of variables measuring the social welfare state

Total social welfare outlays. *Source*: for 1991–3, and for some countries for 1980–93, OECD, *Social Expenditure Statistics of OECD Member Countries*, Labour Market and Social Policy Occasional Papers, No. 17 (Paris: OECD, 1996). For 1961–91, OECD, *New Directions in Social Policy in OECD Countries* (Paris: OECD, 1994); for 1994–5, Work File, *OECD Social Expenditure Data Base, 1998*.

Cash income maintenance and social services. Work File of the *OECD Social Expenditure Data Base, 1998*.

Political data

Left party cabinet portfolios as a percentage of all cabinet portfolios. *Source* (for portfolios): Eric Browne and John Dreijmanis, *Government Coalitions in Western Democracies* (Longman, 1982); *Keesings Contemporary Archives* (selected years). *Sources* (for classification): (1) Francis Castles and Peter Mair, 'Left–Right Political Scales: Some "Expert" Judgments', *European Journal of Political Research*, 12 (1984), 73–88. (2) *Political Handbook of the World* (New York: Simon and Schuster, selected years). (3) Country specific sources.

Political institutions: Union membership. *Source*: Jelle Visser, 'Trade Union Membership Database', Typescript, Sociology of Organizations Research Unit, Department of Sociology, University of Amsterdam, Mar. 1992; 'Unionization Trends Revisited', Centre for Research of European Societies and Industrial Relations (CESAR), Research Paper 1996/2, Feb. 1996. Data on elements of confederal power, level of wage bargaining, and related union measures are from, Miriam Golden, Michael Wallerstein, and Peter Lange for access to the database, 'Union Centralization among Advanced Industrial Societies'. (Generally, the Visser data extend to 1993 and the Golden–Wallerstein–Lange data extend to 1992. To estimate 1993 and 1994, necessary for previous analyses, I used country-specific sources as well as linear extrapolation of data series); Union confederation power in the policy process. *Source*: Table A.1 in Boreham and Compston (1992); data on degree of proportional representation, federalism, bicameralism, and use of referendums are from Huber, Ragin, and Stephens (1993); data on legislative seats are from Mackie and Rose, *The International Almanac of Electoral History* and annual 'political data handbooks' in *European Journal of Political Research*.

Welfare State Institutions: Ranking of nations of socialism, conservatism, and liberalism, as defined above, are from Esping-Andersen (1990).

Socio-economic Data

Consumer price index. *Source*: IMF, *International Financial Statistics* (Washington, DC: IMF, various years).

Percentage of the civilian labour force unemployed, population 65 and older, population 15 and under; total population; and wage and salary workers. *Source*: OECD, *Labor Force Statistics* (Paris: OECD, various years).

GDP deflator, consumer price index, and Gross Domestic Product (national currency units and current US dollars). *Source*: OECD, *National Accounts* (Paris: OECD, various years).

Real Per Capital GDP in constant (1985) international prices. *Source*: The Penn World Table (Mark 5.6). National Bureau of Economic Research (http://www.nber.org).

Public Sector Gross Debt. OECD, *Economic Outlook: Data Appendix* (Paris: OECD, various numbers).

APPENDIX TABLE 7.3. *Estimates for components of interactions in Tables 7.5A, 7.6A, and 7.6B*

	Social corporatism	Electoral inclusiveness	Decentralization of authority	Universalism	Conservatism	Liberalism
Total social welfare						
Public debt	−0.0225*	−0.0145	−0.0225*	−0.0451*	−0.0086	−0.0260*
Institution (column)	1.4092*	1.3987*	−3.2774*	0.4824^	0.6813*	−1.1965*
Debt*institution	0.0146^	−0.0089	−0.0173^	0.0055*	−0.0026	0.0024
Direct investment	0.0687	0.0094	0.0281	−0.9299	−0.0064	0.6380*
Institution	0.1537	0.4698^	−2.3163*	0.3540^	0.2703	−0.1520
Direct investment* institution	0.4222*	0.1887*	−0.3666*	0.2173*	0.0317	−0.0964*
International borrowing	−0.1115^	−0.0302	−0.1030^	−0.3517*	−0.1273^	0.1682^
Institution	0.4033	0.3005	−3.1053*	0.5917*	0.1018	−0.1098
International borrowing* institution	0.2236*	0.3275*	−0.3647*	0.0561*	0.0689*	−0.0342*
Cash transfers						
Public debt	−0.0124^	−0.0027	−0.0101	−0.0421*	0.0147	0.0118
Institution (column)	−0.4215	0.9027*	−3.3222*	−0.6833*	0.4060*	0.3740*
Debt*institution	0.0218*	−0.0045	−0.0144^	0.0079*	−0.0044^	−0.0038*
Direct investment	−0.0520	−0.0530	−0.0403	−0.6120*	−0.0563	0.2137
Institution	0.0974	0.0542*	−3.9168*	−0.2624^	0.1165	0.2694*
Direct investment* institution	0.3449*	0.0364	−0.0846	0.1173*	0.0142	−0.0493*
International borrowing	−0.1844*	−0.0047	−0.1351*	−0.2773*	−0.0067	0.1545*
Institution	−0.0966	−0.0556	−3.7638*	−0.2225	0.1191^	0.4000*
International borrowing* institution	0.2594*	0.2318*	−0.2814*	0.0420*	0.0100	−0.0406*
Social services						
Public debt	−0.0078*	−0.0070*	−0.0085*	−0.0113*	−0.0048	−0.0045
Institution (column)	0.2088	0.0985	−0.2736*	0.0821	0.0069	−0.0006
Debt*institution	0.0015	−0.0010	−0.0037*	0.0009^	−0.0008	−0.0008
Direct investment	0.0387*	0.0503*	0.0440*	−0.1327*	0.0670	0.1226*
Institution	0.0810	0.0289	−0.4469*	0.1320*	−0.0226	−0.0212
Direct investment* institution	0.1096*	−0.0013	−0.0244	0.0332*	−0.0052	−0.0252*
International borrowing	0.0100	0.0113	0.0087	−0.0549^	0.0048	0.0244
Institution	0.2528*	−0.0478	−0.4674*	0.1726*	−0.0529*	−0.0692
International borrowing* institution	0.0117	0.0290*	−0.0217	0.0105^	0.0058	0.0058

APPENDIX TABLE 7.4. *The social welfare state, 1980–95*

	1980	1985	1990	1995
All countries				
Total social welfare	19.9	21.4	22.0	24.0
Cash transfers	13.1	14.4	14.4	16.0
Social services	6.8	7.0	7.5	8.0
Health care	5.5	5.8	6.0	6.3
Non-health services	1.2	1.2	1.5	1.7
Social wage	38.7	44.0	43.6	43.6
Public health share (% total)	76.8	76.8	76.9	75.8
Universal welfare states				
Total social welfare	24.1	24.9	27.3	29.3
Cash transfers	15.2	16.0	17.5	19.4
Social services	8.9	8.9	9.8	9.9
Social wage	54.2	65.3	66.1	65.4
Public health share	84.0	83.6	82.6	80.8
Conservative welfare states				
Total social welfare	22.6	24.4	23.7	26.1
Cash transfers	16.2	17.8	16.8	18.5
Social services	6.4	6.6	6.9	7.6
Social wage	32.4	35.4	35.9	35.7
Public health share	78.0	77.9	78.3	77.8
Liberal welfare states				
Total social welfare	13.1	13.6	14.9	16.8
Cash transfers	8.0	8.4	9.0	10.3
Social services	5.0	5.2	5.9	6.5
Social wage	29.5	29.9	28.7	29.6
Public health share	68.3	68.1	68.7	69.0

Universal, conservative, and liberal as defined in text	Countries: universal—Denmark, Finland, Netherlands, Norway, Sweden; conservative—Austria, Belgium, France, Germany, Italy; liberal—Australia, Canada, Japan, United Kingdom, United States.
Total social welfare	Total social welfare expenditures (see Appendix) as a percentage of GDP.
Cash transfers	Cash old-age and disability, unemployment assistance, sickness, family support, low-income, and miscellaneous benefits as percentage of GDP.
Social services	Government health care outlays and non-health services (elderly, disabled, families) as percentage of GDP.
Social wage	Gross income replacement rate for first-year of benefits for a worker at the average production worker's income.
Public health share	Government health care as percentage of total health care spending.

Sources: *The OECD Social Expenditure Data Base 1998*, Work File (Preliminary data); *OECD. Health Data 98*. CD ROM Version (Paris: OECD); OECD Database on Unemployment Benefit Entitlements and Replacement Rates (Paris: OECD, forthcoming).

8

Political Institutions, Veto Points, and the Process of Welfare State Adaptation

Giuliano Bonoli

THE capacity of governments to control policy outcomes varies substantially across countries. Depending on the rules which govern the law making process, political power can be more or less concentrated in the hands of the executive. These rules, which are enshrined in the constitutional order of a country, determine the extent of agreement needed to legislate, and thus establish the degree of influence that external groups, opposition parties, and lower tiers of governments can expect to have on national policy making. In a potentially controversial area such as welfare state adaptation, the impact of such rules on policy making can be highly relevant. Because welfare reforms generally involve changes in distributional equilibria, they are likely to be affected significantly by the degree of influence granted to actors other than the executive.

The impact on policy making of external groups is generally greater when constitutional structures provide veto points, i.e. instances in the policy making process at which a suitable coalition of actors can prevent the adoption of a given piece of legislation.[1] When, in contrast, veto points are few or non-existent, then governments can control policy making and outcomes to a much larger extent. In practice, veto points affect the level of threat-potential available to groups opposing government plans in a given area. If unsatisfied with government-sponsored legislation, these groups can threaten to make use of the available veto points with a view to preventing the adoption of unwanted measures. Under such circumstances, governments can more easily be persuaded to negotiate, to make concessions, and to grant quid pro quos to key actors.

The link between constitutional structures and social policy making has been largely explored in relation to the phase of expansion of modern welfare states (Immergut 1992; Huber, Ragin, and Stephens 1993). In general,

I would like to thank for comments, suggestions, and criticism of earlier drafts, Klaus Armingeon, Richard Balme, Bruno Palier, Paul Pierson, Nico Siegel, and Margaret Weir.

[1] For a discussion of the concept of veto point, see Immergut 1992 and Tsbelis 1995.

institutions which concentrate power with the executive have been found to be associated with big welfare states, whereas more fragmented political systems, which include veto points in their law making processes, have tended to produce smaller welfare states. The rationale behind this hypothesis is that fragmented systems have provided opportunities for anti-welfarist groups to prevent the adoption of given programmes, or to force governments to water down the content of their reforms. Empirically this thesis is successful in accounting for the comparatively low levels of state welfare found in Switzerland and in the USA: two countries characterized by high levels of power fragmentation and by the existence of various veto points in their law making processes.

The findings of these analyses, concerned primarily with the expansion phase of welfare state development, are only of limited use when applied to current change. The mechanisms observed during welfare state expansion, if present in the current phase of restructuring, can be expected to produce a range of different outcomes. On the one hand, one can expect to find retrenchment-minded governments enjoying strong power concentration to be more successful in cutting back social programmes. Since they have a substantial degree of control on policy making, they are more likely to reach their objectives. In contrast, governments operating in power-fragmented systems, will have to negotiate change with external interests, and thus be forced to make concessions to various actors. The result might come short of their initial policy goals, as the power of the pro-welfare coalition is magnified by institutional fragmentation (see Swank, in this volume). On the other hand, however, it can also be hypothesized that the degree of power concentration/fragmentation will be of little relevance, as pro-welfare coalitions, because they represent disadvantaged groups, are likely to be less capable to make effective use of veto points than their opponents were during the phase of welfare state expansion.

In addition, as some authors have pointed out, institutions which concentrate power, by the same token, tend to concentrate accountability. While power concentration enhances the capacity of governments to achieve their policy objectives, it also increases the risk of being held accountable by the general public for possibly unpopular decisions and of being electorally punished as a result (Weaver and Rockman 1993: 15; Pierson and Weaver 1993; Pierson 1994: 33). From this point of view, the overall effect of power concentration on welfare retrenchment remains uncertain, as a government might be more capable of steering policy if acting in an institutional context of power concentration, but it will also be more inclined to take into account the electoral consequences of its actions. In sum, the question of what kind of political institutions are more conducive to welfare restructuring, seems to be largely undetermined on the theoretical level.

This chapter explores the relationship between political institutions and patterns of welfare retrenchment, both on a theoretical level and on the basis of the observation of welfare reforms adopted in countries characterized by different levels of institutional power concentration. The main empirical focus will be on Britain, an exemplar of strong power concentration; on Switzerland, which has a political system characterized by high levels of power fragmentation, and on France, an intermediate case. For each of the three countries, I provide narrative accounts of how selected welfare reforms have been adopted. Their comparison suggests that the relationship between constitutional structures and welfare adaptation is not a linear one, whereby power concentration is directly linked to a higher or lower rate of success in achieving restructuring, nor to the amount of restructuring that can be obtained. Power concentration, however, appears to be related to the form that welfare state adaptation takes: in contexts of strong power concentration, reform tends to be unilateral and geared towards retrenchment. In contrast, in institutional contexts characterized by veto points, reform tends to combine measures of retrenchment with expansion and improvements of existing programmes.

1. POLITICAL INSTITUTIONS AND POWER CONCENTRATION[2]

Political institutions are powerful determinants of the level of power concentration granted to governments. In political systems with multiple veto points, power is fragmented, and external actors have the opportunity to exert a substantial influence on policy making. Power concentration, however, is not determined solely by institutional factors. There are at least two other features of a political system that are likely to have a considerable impact on the degree of control a government has on policy when dealing with welfare reforms: electoral results and the strength of the pro-welfare coalition. Electoral results affect the functioning of parliamentary politics. Minority governments and governments with small majorities, face more problems in controlling policy than governments which can count on substantial parliamentary majorities. Moreover, as will be shown below, different interactions of electoral result and political institutions can have opposite effects on power concentration.

Similarly, institutional power concentration can be contained by a strong pro-welfare coalition, which has an effective mobilizing capacity and ability

---

[2] This chapter covers only horizontal power concentration, i.e. at the national government level. A second dimension, vertical power concentration among the different tiers of government is not analysed.

to exert political influence. In English-speaking countries, pro-welfare coalitions generally consist of issue-based pressure groups, such as the AARP in the USA. In contrast, in Continental Europe, the pro-welfare coalition tends to coincide with the labour movement. Well organized and integrated trade unions, or more in general a labour movement which is capable of staging sustained and disruptive industrial action against welfare retrenchment, can provide a counterweight to a set of political institutions that concentrate power with the executive. In such contexts, the potential threat of the trade unions can de facto amount to an additional veto point.

In this respect, the impact of political institutions on policy making cannot be looked at in isolation from other factors. What we can expect to account for different approaches to welfare restructuring is not the shape of political institutions per se, but its interaction with electoral dynamics and with relative balance of power resources of the various actors which have a stake in the relevant welfare programmes. This section looks, on an abstract level, at the individual institutional features that can be expected to have an impact on power concentration, and as a result on patterns of welfare restructuring. Their interaction with non-institutional factors is discussed later, in the narrative accounts of welfare reform.

Parliamentary vs. Separation of Powers Systems

This is perhaps the most important feature determining the level of power concentration, as it establishes the degree of control that a government has over parliament, the principal locus of democratic decision making. Control is typically stronger in parliamentary systems, and this for three main reasons. First, since the executive is generally elected by a parliamentary majority, there is no risk of 'divided government', i.e. a situation in which the executive and the legislative are controlled by different parties. Second, in separation of power systems, the government cannot be brought down by a no confidence vote. This means that members of parliament can vote against their government without having to worry about its survival. Third, in parliamentary systems the government can resign or even dissolve parliament and call an early election. Often, the simple threat of doing that can constitute a powerful argument to convince parliamentarians to back the government on a controversial bill.

As a result, in separation of powers systems like the USA and Switzerland,[3] governments are less able to control the outcome of parliamentary votes, as they lack the instruments needed to ensure party discipline. This is particularly true in situations of divided government, but also when the same

---

[3] In the Swiss system the government is elected by parliament for a four-year period during which it cannot be brought down. As a result, divided government is unlikely but lack of parliamentary compliance to government guidelines is a rather frequent event.

party controls both levels of power. A case in point is President Clinton's failure to adopt compulsory health insurance in the early 1990s, when besides the Presidency, the Democrats controlled both houses of congress.

Structure of Parliament

The structure of parliament is also likely to affect the degree of control that a government can have on decision making. Unicameral parliaments (Sweden, New Zealand, Israel) and asymmetrical bicameral parliaments (United Kingdom, France), where approval of one chamber is sufficient to get legislation accepted, are generally associated with stronger governmental control over policy making. In contrast, countries with symmetrical bicameral parliaments have a second locus of decision making which increases the likelihood of amendment or even defeat of government-sponsored legislation.

The impact of bicameralism is particularly strong when the two chambers are elected on different bases, and can be dominated by different majorities, a system know as incongruent bicameralism. This is most notably the case of Germany, where the lower chamber (Bundestag) is directly elected but where the upper chamber (Bundesrat) is designated by the governments of the Länder. Until late 1998 the Bundestag was controlled by the right-of-centre coalition headed by Chancellor Kohl, while the Bundesrat, since 1991, was dominated by the SPD, then the opposition. The result was that in a large number of areas the government could not adopt legislation unless able to gain the approval of the opposition (M. Schmidt 1996*a*). This constituted an important limitation on the room for manoeuvre granted to the executive and a powerful incentive to seek consensual and negotiated solutions.

Electoral System

The electoral system of a country has a substantial impact on its politics. The number of parties, the type and stability of governments are related to how individual preferences expressed by voters are aggregated. In general, one-round single-member constituencies elections tend to enhance the representation of the largest party, to be associated with a lower number of parties (often only two), and to produce strong, single-party majorities (examples are the UK and the USA). In contrast, proportional representation with multiple-member constituencies tends to be associated with a large number of parties represented in parliament and with coalition government.[4] Examples are most Continental European countries, except France and Italy (since 1993).

---

[4] The link between electoral laws and party system has been qualified by Duverger as one of the few that in political science 'approximates a true sociological law' (Duverger 1963).

In relation to power concentration, the most important consequence of the electoral system is the type of government it produces. One-party governments are likely to be better able to control policy outcomes for two main reasons. First, governments made up of a single party are more likely to display a certain homogeneity of views. Cabinet members have similar ideological backgrounds and are likely to be used to working together. Such cohesion is likely to encourage power concentration (Weaver and Rockman 1993: 24). Second, coalition governments are made up of parties which will compete against each other at the next election. This might encourage coalition member parties (especially small ones) to adopt a distinctive policy approach in order to avoid being assimilated with their partners. In addition, in the case of unpopular measures such as welfare retrenchment, coalition members have a relatively strong incentive to defect, as this will promote them as the defenders of widely supported policies, and possibly be electorally rewarding. Defection from a coalition government at times of unpopularity is perhaps the biggest limitation on power concentration imposed by an electoral system (PR) which makes single-party government unlikely. In this respect, a single-member constituency system is likely to be associated with stronger power concentration than proportional representation.

Referendums

As noted by Lijphart, referendums do not have a clear-cut impact on power concentration. On the one hand, since they reflect the will of the majority, they can be used by governments to silence vociferous minorities and thus be an instrument through which to impose controversial policies. At the same time, however, referendums constitute an additional step in the policy making process at which legislation needs approval, or a veto point, and provide thus an opportunity for external groups to stop the adoption of an unwanted bill (Lijphart 1984: 31).

In fact, the impact of referendums on power concentration depends to a large extent on the procedure followed to call one. If these are called at the government's discretion (France), then they are likely to enhance power concentration. In contrast, when these can be organized by groups of voters (Switzerland, Italy, several states in the USA), they constitute a limitation on government's control over policy. This is particularly the case of the Swiss optional referendum, which can be called on any piece of legislation passed by parliament if 50,000 signatures of voters are produced. This constitutes an additional veto point in the policy making process, and introduces an element of uncertainty in it, which has traditionally been dealt with through the inclusion into decision making of groups likely to use the optional referendum (Neidhart 1970; Kriesi 1995).

Balanced dual executive

While most parliamentary systems have a dual executive, consisting of a head of state and a head of government, in most cases the former plays only a ceremonial role. In the case of France, however, the President, directly elected, has more substantial influence in the definition of policy (Duverger 1980). In addition, since presidential and parliamentary elections do not occur at the same time and have different frequencies, it is possible to have situations in which Parliament and the Presidency are controlled by different camps, which results in executive power-sharing between a President and a Prime Minister who have different political orientations. A situation that the French refer to as cohabitation and can, under certain circumstances, constitute a limitation on the government's control over policy making. As will be seen below, this is what happened in the 1993–5 period, when executive power was shared between a Socialist President and a Gaullist Prime Minister.

Power Concentration and Accountability

The various institutional features reviewed here affect the level of power concentration that governments can enjoy when restructuring their welfare states. Concentration of power, however, is not necessarily an element of strength for governments who wish to impose unpopular measures. The absence of veto points does concentrate power, but by the same token it also concentrates accountability, and thus makes electoral punishment for unpopular measures more likely. The two effects tend to counterbalance each other and the overall result is uncertain and highly contingent. (Pierson 1994; Weaver and Rockman 1993; Pierson and Weaver 1993). Besides power concentration, however, there are at least three other factors that can enhance the accountability effect.

First, the accountability effect is likely to be stronger in highly competitive political systems (Scharpf 1997c: 183). For the fear of electoral punishment to play a role in restricting the reforming ambitions of a government, there has to be an opposition party which can credibly put itself forward as an alternative for government. If there is no likelihood of a change of government in the near future, policy makers are less likely to be sensitive to the risk of electoral punishment. Second, the accountability effect is likely to play a relatively smaller role in proportional representation electoral systems than in single-member constituencies, as the losses due to electoral punishment are less likely to result in big losses of parliamentary seats. Single-member constituencies amplify the impact of swings in the public mood. Finally, the relative importance of the power and accountability concentration effects, is likely to vary according to the political cycle.

Typically, one would expect the power concentration effect to be stronger at the beginning of an electoral term, and accountability concentration to be stronger in the run up to an election, as politicians become more sensitive to the public's perception of their actions.

Overall, the importance of the accountability effect seems to be stronger in the United States than in most European countries. The United States combines the conditions that enhance the importance of the accountability effect: a bipartisan system in which both parties are equally capable of winning important elections, a single-member constituency electoral system, and, perhaps most crucially, an almost permanent state of electoral campaigning due to the two-year lag between presidential and congressional elections. In Europe, these conditions are combined in different ways, and one can expect the impact of the accountability effect to vary with time. In this respect, we can expect that most of the time in most European countries, the impact of power concentration on policy making will be felt more strongly than the accountability effect. The final assessment of the relative importance of divergent effects produced by power concentration, however, should be left to a case by case analysis of specific instances of policy change.

2. POWER CONCENTRATION AND POLICY STRATEGIES

The various institutional features reviewed in the previous section, contribute to determine the level of power concentration enjoyed by governments. When institutions provide veto points, they constitute a limitation on governments' ability to control the policy making process and to ensure the adoption of given policy outcomes. These features have an impact on government capabilities,[5] which from an institutional perspective, can be expected to be lower in political systems characterized by power fragmentation.

Governments operating in power fragmented systems, however, have been able to improve their capabilities by adopting policy making strategies based on the inclusion of external interests (Braun 1997; Lehmbruch 1993). Because political institutions create opportunities for external groups to block the adoption of legislation, governments have tried to control the impact of these groups by co-opting them among policy makers. This is most notably the case of Switzerland, where political elites have developed a system of constant and sustained concertation, which has been conceptualized in terms of

---

[5] Like Weaver and Rockman, I understand the concept of 'government capability' as 'a pattern of government influence on its environment that produces substantially similar outcomes across time and policy areas' (1993: 6).

consensus (or consociational) democracy (Lehmbruch 1979, 1993; Lehner 1984; and Lijphart 1984). Similarly, in Germany, the fragmentation of power brought about by the division between two branches of parliament controlled by different parties, has resulted in an increased tendency to negotiate legislative change with the opposition (M. Schmidt 1996*a*: 75).

The USA constitutes an exception in this respect, as its fragmented political system has not produced the sort of inclusive policy making strategies observed in some European countries. This has been explained by the fact that the US political system combines elements of power fragmentation with others that encourage majoritarian government, such as a single-member constituency electoral system and the concentration of executive power with the President (Lijphart 1984). This may help to account for the inability of the US political system to radically reform some areas of the welfare state, most notably old age pensions (Armingeon 1997).

The impact of political institutions on power concentration should not be considered as a fixed and constant feature. Depending on electoral dynamics (electoral results and the position in the electoral cycle) countries can move along the power concentration–fragmentation dimension and as a result display unexpected patterns of inclusive policy making. A weak government (like a minority government or a poorly integrated coalition government) may be more inclined to negotiate policy with external interests even if operating in an institutional context with few or without veto points. Changes in the partisan control of key institutions are also likely to affect the level of power concentration with governments. Among the examples mentioned above are the control of the different chambers of parliament (relevant in Germany) and of the two representatives of executive power (relevant in France). In this respect, the inclusive strategies observed in countries characterized by permanent power fragmentation, can emerge occasionally as a response to temporary reductions in power concentration in political systems which do not offer veto points. As will be seen below, this is arguably what happened in the French pension reform of 1993.

These considerations refer to general government policy making. In the area of welfare reforms, however, there is a further element that needs to be taken into account when considering the occurrence of patterns of inclusion–exclusion in policy making. As shown by opinion polls, by public reactions to proposed cuts and by the reluctance of politicians to radically cut back on welfare, current social policy arrangements are popular with large sections of electorates.[6] This constitutes an asset in the hands of political actors

---

[6] Comparative evidence on public opinion attachment to welfare arrangements is available in Ferrera 1993 and Taylor-Gooby 1995. France, Italy, Germany, and Switzerland have seen large-scale protest movements against planned cuts in social programmes. Even in the USA and in the UK, two countries which were ruled for a sustained period by openly anti-welfarist governments, cuts in welfare have come short of their leaders' ambitions (Pierson 1994).

willing to oppose retrenchment in social policy, as they find their mobilizing capacity increased. This is not just relevant in Switzerland, where through the referendum system such groups have the opportunity to prevent the adoption of unwanted legislation, but also in countries like France and Italy, where union-led mass protest movements have managed to force governments to back down on welfare reforms. More in general, the mobilizing capacity and threat potential of the pro-welfare coalition, which in most countries is mainly represented by the labour movement, can constitute an effective counterweight to institutionally based power concentration. A strong labour movement whose mobilizing capacity is enhanced by the popularity of the arrangements it sets out to defend, might constitute a powerful argument for governments to adopt a negotiated approach to welfare reform, even though political institutions allow them to operate without external support or acquiescence. This is particularly the case with pensions. As Myles and Pierson (in this volume) point out, there are substantial pressures for concertation and negotiated solutions in this area.

Welfare reforms, thus, because of their potentially controversial character, are under any circumstances likely candidates for inclusive policy making (Esping-Andersen 1996*b*; Pierson 1996: 156). However, on the basis of the above discussion, there are some conditions which make inclusive policy making more likely: institutional power fragmentation, lack of a stable and strong majority, and a labour movement with a strong mobilizing capacity. Without taking these factors into consideration, one cannot account for the occurrence of instances of negotiated welfare reforms in countries like Italy and France which lack a tradition of concertation with external interests.[7]

The next section looks at some specific instances of welfare retrenchment in Britain, Switzerland, and France.

3. WELFARE REFORMS IN BRITAIN, SWITZERLAND, AND FRANCE

The sample covered in this chapter was selected in order to include political systems characterized by different levels of institutionally-based power concentration. Two countries, the UK and Switzerland, represent two extremes of power concentration and power fragmentation, respectively. The third country, France, constitutes an intermediary case. In fact, depending on

---

[7] The Italian 1995 pension reform was the result of negotiations between a 'technical' government, i.e. without its own majority in parliament but supported by the left and the trade unions (see Ferrera 1997; Regini and Regalia 1997); on French reforms, see below.

TABLE 8.1. *Constitutional features affecting power concentration in Switzerland, France, and the UK*

	Separation of powers	Structure of parliament	Electoral system	Referendum system	Dual executive
Switzerland	Yes	Bicameral, symmetrical	Proportional representation	Yes	No
France	No	Bicameral, asymmetrical	Two-rounds single-member constituency	No	Yes
United Kingdom	No	Bicameral, asymmetrical	Single-member constituency	No	No

electoral results, France can move along the power concentration dimension. When President and Parliament are controlled by the same party, France is closer to the concentration end of the spectrum. When, in contrast, the two institutions are controlled by different parties, political power is more fragmented. Table 8.1 sums up the key constitutional features for the three countries.

A second selection criterion was the political orientation of ruling majorities in the three countries. At the time of adoption of the reforms, all three countries were ruled by right-of-centre majorities which were openly committed to achieving savings in the broad area of welfare.[8] Finally, all three countries were experiencing financial pressures on their welfare states. Although these were probably stronger in France than in Britain and Switzerland, the way they were translated into the government discourse was rather similar. The emphasis was on the non-sustainability of current arrangements.

The sample, thus, contains three countries facing welfare-related financial problems, in which governments are trying to do very similar things. The key variation between them lies in their very different political institutions and in the resulting patterns of power concentration fragmentation. The observation of welfare reforms adopted in different institutional contexts should highlight the impact of the latter on the content of welfare reform.

---

[8] The use of the term 'majorities' instead of 'governments' is not incidental. While in most parliamentary systems the two entities tend to overlap, in the case of Switzerland they do not. There is, in fact, a parliamentary right-wing majority, consisting of the Free Democrats, the Christian Democrats, and the former peasant party. Although these three parties represent slightly different constituencies, they share a common preference for limited state intervention in social policy. The government is composed of these three parties and the Social Democrats, which in economic and social policy take a more interventionist view.

Britain: The 1986 Pension Reform

The 1986 pension reform, which was part of the same year's Social Security Act,[9] had two main objectives: first it intended to deal with the expected rise in pension expenditure due to population ageing and to the maturation of the earnings-related component of the public pension system, known as the State Earnings-Related Pension Scheme (SERPS); second, it was meant to make life easier for employees who were members of employers' sponsored pension plans when changing jobs, as under previous legislation this entailed substantial losses in their pension entitlements.[10] While these were the declared objectives of the government, a number of commentators felt that the 1986 pension reform was part of a wider project for shifting to the market tasks that were traditionally fulfilled by the state. Rather than being the rational response to socio-demographic problems, the 1986 pension reform was seen as the practical implementation of the neoliberal ideas which were dominant within the British Conservative Party at that time (Walker 1991; Nesbitt 1995).

In the mid-1980s, in fact, the Conservative Party had particularly large room for manoeuvre in policy making. Besides the constitutional features reviewed above, which concentrate power with the executive, in that period the government could rely on a substantial majority in the House of Commons, which meant that it did not have to worry about getting legislation through in parliament.[11] In addition, the anti-Conservative camp was divided. This meant that, because of the single-member constituencies electoral system, electoral punishment resulting from unpopular policies would be to a large extent neutralized. These were obviously very favourable conditions for imposing policy in line with the government's ideological orientation.

Work on pension reform started towards the end of 1983, when the then Secretary of State for Social Services, Norman Fowler, decided to launch an 'Inquiry into provision for retirement' in order to 'study the future development, adequacy and costs of state, occupational and private provision for retirement in the United Kingdom' (DHSS 1983: 4). The format of the Inquiry was such that Fowler, and through him the government, had very strong

---

[9] Changes in pension legislation were undoubtedly the most significant part of the Social Security Act 1986. Other important elements included the introduction of an income support scheme, which replaced a number of means-tested benefits; the creation of a social fund which provides loans for particular circumstances (maternity, funerals); and a scheme of income supplement for the working poor (family credits).

[10] The British pension system consists of a basic pension, which grants flat-rate benefits, plus a second tier of earnings-related provision. For the latter, which is compulsory, employees can choose between the state scheme (SERPS); their employers' occupational pensions (if provided) or, since 1988, a personal pension.

[11] In the 1983 general election, the Conservatives achieved a majority of 187 over the Labour Party.

control over its outcomes. First, the Inquiry team was chaired by Norman Fowler himself. Second, its members were Conservative ministers, representatives of the insurance industry, and experts. Other groups with a stake in pension policy, like employees, pensioners, but also employers, were not included in the team. They were consulted through oral and written submissions of evidence, but the extent to which these were taken into account was entirely at the government's discretion.

The government's intentions in the area of pension policy were first spelt out in the Green Paper, *Reform of Social Security*, published in June 1985 (DHSS 1985*b*). Its main point was the gradual phasing out of SERPS which was to be replaced by privately run, individual, personal pensions. These, moreover, were to be available also to employees who were already covered by occupational pensions. The overall aim was the creation of a competitive market in supplementary provision for retirement (the basic pension scheme remained untouched) in which employees would shop around and buy the most convenient pension arrangement.

The Green Paper came quickly under attack from various directions. Besides the Labour Party, the Trades Union Congress and other left-leaning groups, which were obviously going to oppose a shift away from the state in pension provision, substantial criticism came also by some more unlikely opponents. For instance, British employers (CBI), were concerned with the phasing out of SERPS, because it meant a higher rate of contribution. Employers were to continue funding current SERPS expenditure, through National Insurance contributions, and the future pensions for current employees through contributions to their personal pensions.[12]

Moreover, there was not unanimity on the issue even within the government. In fact, even before the publication of the Green Paper, the Treasury had signalled its opposition to plans for abolishing SERPS. The episode was described by Norman Fowler as an 'all-out battle' with the Chancellor of the Exchequer Nigel Lawson (BBC 1996). The reason behind the Treasury opposition to the abolition of SERPS was the additional cost that this would have implied for the exchequer. In fact, while contribution rebates were to be granted immediately, the state would have remained liable to fund current pensions and those of people near retirement age. This was going to put additional pressure on the state budget and was seen as unacceptable by the Treasury.

Given the extent of criticism raised by proposals to abolish SERPS, and given the internal dissent, the government decided to opt for a less radical solution: a reduction in the value of future SERPS pensions. This change of direction was announced in a subsequent document, a White Paper. It was

---

[12] This problem is known as the 'double payment' issue, and occurs when pension financing is shifted from a pay-as-you-go to a funded system. See Pierson 1997*c* for a discussion.

justified with the argument that 'the aim of pension policy should be to seek as much agreement as possible' (DHSS 1985*a*: 3). In addition, it was argued that while not constituting an optimal solution, the reduction of SERPS was acceptable because it made it possible to achieve the government's two key objectives: 'to see the emerging cost of SERPS reduced' and 'to ensure that the conditions are created whereby individual pension provision can expand' (ibid. 4). The introduction of personal pensions as an alternative to state or occupational provision, however, was maintained.

The concessions made by the government did not manage to silence all of its critics. While the CBI came to accept the new proposal, the Labour Party, the Trades Union Congress, and the anti-poverty lobby maintained their opposition to the government plans. In 1986 Labour Party policy on pensions was to block the implementation of the Social Security Act 1986 if in government before April 1988, and to repeal it if elected after that date (Randall's Parliamentary Services 1986).

The new pension legislation, which came into force in 1988, resulted in a massive transfer from the state to the market in pension provision. In 1993 some 5 million employees had bought personal pensions. Of them, about 4 million were previously covered by SERPS (Waine 1995: 328). Despite the fact that the government was forced to compromise on the issue of SERPS abolition, the final outcome of the law making process was still in line with the government's initial intentions: to achieve long-term savings in pension expenditure and to transfer a substantial part of provision for retirement from the state to the market.

Moreover, it should be noted that on the abolition of SERPS, the government did not necessarily bow to external pressures. In fact, on that issue, there was a division within the cabinet. The fact that a senior minister, Nigel Lawson, opposed such plans, arguably reduced the government's ability to resist outside pressures and mitigated the effect of institutional power concentration over policy making. Finally, the concessions were made mainly to employers, a traditional ally of Conservative governments, but not to groups representing opposite interests. This suggests that resistance to external pressures remained strong even on that occasion.

Switzerland[13]

Until the early 1990s, the financing of social programmes was not seen as problematic in Switzerland. Thanks to a very low unemployment rate and to a buoyant economy, social policy debates were more about modernizing the welfare state, for example by introducing gender equality or a maternity insurance scheme. However, between 1990 and 1993 the unemployment rate

[13] This section draws on Bonoli 1997*b*.

soared from 0.6 to 4.6 per cent and has remained roughly constant since then. This, coupled with the biggest recession the country has known since World War II, has prompted concern over the financing of social expenditure. The 1990s, thus, signal a change of direction in social policy making. Since the 1990s, the main motive behind policy change is to contain or to reduce state expenditure on the relevant programmes (Bonoli 1997*b*).

The right-of-centre majority, though openly committed to achieving savings, has to operate in an institutional environment which offers external groups the opportunity to challenge legislation at various points, most notably through referendums. The result is limited scope for policy innovation (Cattacin 1996) but also strong pressure for negotiation. This appears to be having a significant impact on the policy strategy followed by those who favour retrenchment. Cuts in pensions and unemployment insurance have been successfully adopted, but at the price of substantial concessions targeted on key opponents.

The 1995 Pension Reform

Preliminary work on the 1995 reform started in 1979, but it was only in 1990 that a bill was presented in parliament. Its initial aim was to introduce gender equality in the basic pension scheme.[14] Under previous legislation, married people were granted couple pensions corresponding to 150 per cent of the husband's entitlement. In other words a married woman would lose her earned entitlement to a pension, this being replaced by a supplement on her husband's benefit (unless her pension entitlement was higher than his, in which case the benefit was calculated on the basis of the wife's contribution record). In addition, there were no contribution credits for raising children or taking care of relatives, which is common practice in most European countries.

The 1990 pension reform bill made provision for the removal of any reference to gender in the pension formula. In practice, married couples were to continue to receive couple pensions but these were to be based on the combined contribution records of both spouses. Upon request a couple pension could be split between two spouses and drawn separately. The bill did not include provision for the equalization of retirement age (then at 65/62), which had become incompatible with a constitutional article on gender equality adopted in 1981. The governments' interpretation of the Constitution was that since equality in the labour market (in terms of wages, career patterns, access to occupational pensions, etc.) was far from being

[14] The Swiss pension system consists of two tiers of compulsory provision. The basic level, referred to as the AVS, is a contributory scheme and works on a pay-as-you-go basis. While contributions are proportional to earnings, however, benefits vary between a minimum pension and its double, which is the maximum amount. The second tier consists of employer-sponsored funded pension plans.

achieved, positive discrimination favouring women in retirement age was justified. Equalization, thus, would have been dealt with in a subsequent reform.

Initially, the government decision not to increase women's retirement age did not attract much attention. Instead, the pension bill came under attack from women's organizations and progressive groups for failing to take a more far-reaching approach to gender equality. A few years earlier a number of organizations and political parties had published reports which had argued in favour of a system of individual pensions, granted regardless of gender and marital status and the subsequent abolition of couple pensions. Proposals were put forward by the Social Democrats, jointly with the Federation of Swiss trade unions (PSS/USS 1987); by a working group of the Liberal Democratic Party (PRD 1988); and by the Federal Commission for women's issues (CFQF 1988), a consultative body which includes MPs and representatives of other relevant interests.

The proposals were in fact remarkably similar. In general, they suggested the introduction of contribution sharing between married persons. Contributions paid by the members of a couple were to be added, divided by two, and counted separately for each of the two spouses. All the proposals argued also for the introduction of contribution credits for couples with children or for performing other caring tasks.

These proposals were going to be extremely influential. The bill, in fact, was substantially modified by parliament, precisely by adopting these measures. The pension bill, as amended by parliament, included the introduction of individual pensions regardless of gender and marital status and the abolition of couple pensions. As suggested in the various reports published in the late 1980s, contribution sharing and credits for couples with children were also included. Couples with children below the age of 16 were granted a contribution credit equal to the amount of contributions payable on a salary of approximately 56 per cent of average earnings. The credit is available regardless of whether one or both spouses give up work, and it is counted half each (entirely in case of a single parent).

The bill as modified by parliament, however, included also the controversial measure of raising the retirement age for women from 62 to 64. This measure was imposed by the right-of-centre parliamentary majority, allegedly in order to comply with the constitutional requirement of gender equality as well as to achieve some savings in view of the predicted worsening of the ratio between pension scheme contributors and beneficiaries over the next few decades. The measure was pushed through by a coalition of right-wing parties, against the will of the Social Democrats. Outside parliament, the trade unions and some women's organizations attacked the proposed increase in retirement age for women. In response, the Federation of Swiss Trade Unions organized the collection of the 50,000 signatures needed in order to call a referendum. The move was successful and the referendum on the pension bill was held in June 1995.

According to the constitution, referendums decide between the adoption and the rejection of a bill, but they cannot modify its content. Therefore the referendum called by the trade unions had to cover the age of retirement as well as the provision for gender equality, which had long been advocated by the trade unions and by the left in general. For the left, this situation constituted a powerful dilemma. The decision on whether or not to support the referendum against the pension bill depended on what was seen as more important between gender equality on the positive side and the increase in women's retirement age on the negative one. The result was that the Social Democrats declined to join the unions in supporting the referendum against the pension bill, therefore reducing their chances of defeating it at the polls. In fact, the bill survived the referendum obstacle, and it is now law. The division within the left obviously played an important role in making its adoption possible. To a large extent, the way in which the bill was designed encouraged the division, as it combined elements of retrenchment with measures that were among the key priorities of the left.

The 1995 Unemployment Insurance Reform

The sharp rise in jobless figures in the early 1990s caused a steep increase in the unemployment insurance scheme outlays. The result was that the scheme was unable to meet its liabilities and had to borrow funds from the general government budget. The perceived gravity of the problem convinced the federal government to act with an emergency decree, which unlike standard legislation cannot be delayed by a referendum, in 1993. On that occasion the replacement rate was reduced from 80 to 70 per cent of insured salary (unless the recipient had dependent children). A stricter definition of adequate work was also introduced, whereby unemployed persons could be required to accept jobs with salaries lower than their benefits with compensation paid out of the insurance scheme. These emergency measures lasted until December 1995 in order to allow policy makers some additional time to introduce a more substantial reform.

The 1995 unemployment insurance reform was drafted by a joint group of representatives of employers and trade unions, and passed by parliament without major changes. Like the 1995 pension reform, the new unemployment insurance law includes measures going in two diverging directions. On the one hand, the financing of the scheme has been strengthened and more funds have been made available for active labour market programmes, such as vocational training and job creation schemes. On the other hand, the entitlement period has been reduced to two years, whereas under the previous legislation benefits could be drawn virtually indefinitely if the recipient was prepared to participate in labour market programmes.

As far as financing is concerned, the joint contribution rate was raised from 1 to 3 per cent (1.5 per cent each for employers and employees), payable on earnings up to 160 per cent of average salary. An additional contribution of a joint rate of 1 per cent is charged on earnings between 160 and 400 per cent of average salary. This measure is temporary, in theory at least, until the debt accumulated by the scheme with the government is repaid. In addition, 5 per cent of current expenditure will be financed by a federal government subsidy. With these measures, it is hoped to repay the debt before 2000.

With regard to benefits, the changes introduced with the emergency decree (replacement rate of 70 or 80 per cent if with dependent children) are maintained. The duration of the entitlement period is set at two years, and during this period unemployed persons will be required to undertake retraining, to take part in a job creation scheme, or take up temporary work. Failure to do so will result in sanctions which can reach a 60 days' suspension of the benefit. Job creation programmes must be set up by the Cantons, but 85 per cent of the cost is met by the unemployment insurance scheme.

The 1995 unemployment insurance reform was adopted by parliament and, since it included measures able to attract approval from both the left and the right, was not challenged through a referendum. The left cared mainly about the introduction of the new labour market programmes, whereas the right was satisfied with the two-year limit imposed on benefits. Upon the expiry of this term, unemployed people have to rely on locally administered social assistance, which being means-tested, is less generous and more stigmatizing than unemployment insurance. In this respect, the 1995 unemployment insurance reform can be regarded as a legislative package which included a substantial element of retrenchment.

In September 1997 an attempt to introduce further cuts in unemployment benefits was defeated in a referendum by a small majority (50.8 per cent voted against). Unlike with the 1995 reform, on this occasion the planned legislation did not include measures of improvement in provision, or other concessions to the left and the unions. A year earlier a similar fate had occurred to a reform of the employment law which, if adopted, would have reduced regulation concerning extra working hours, working on Sundays, and women's work at night. Initially, the reform included some measures which responded to trade unions' demands, such as compulsory free time compensation of extra working hours. These measures, however, were eventually scrapped by the right-of-centre parliamentary majority. The result was a rejection in a referendum by a massive 67 per cent of voters. Unlike the reforms discussed above, these failed attempts constituted pure retrenchment. The fact that both of them were rejected, suggests that such unilateral reforms might be politically unfeasible in a fragmented political system like Switzerland's (see also Obinger 1998).

France[15]

The French case is a particularly interesting one. In the space of two years, different governments tried to introduce new pension legislation on two occasions. On the first one, in 1993, the Balladur Government managed to adopt some reductions in the pension formula of the country's largest pension scheme (*régime général*), covering private sector employees.[16] Two years later, a second attempt at cutting pensions, this time for public sector employees, resulted in a massive protest movement which eventually forced the government to withdraw its plans.

The two attempts at cutting pensions occurred under different political circumstances. In 1993 France was in a situation of cohabitation, i.e. with a Socialist President, Mitterrand, and a right-wing parliament and Prime Minister, Balladur. In contrast, the 1995 abortive attempt was made in a situation of united government, the right-wing candidate (Jacques Chirac) having won the 1995 presidential election. This change in the composition of the executive was accompanied by a shift in the government's policy strategy, from inclusion to confrontation, which helps to account for the different fortunes of the two reforms.

Cohabitation in fact had occurred a few years earlier, between 1986 and 1988. Then executive power was shared by President Mitterrand and Prime Minister Chirac. The main impact of executive power-sharing was a reduction in the influence of the President on policy (Duverger 1987; Bigaut 1995). On that occasion, the right-of-centre government tried to impose a number of neoliberal policies, some of which proved particularly unpopular. As a result, Prime Minister Chirac, who was also a candidate in the 1988 presidential election, experienced an important loss of popularity, which favoured the incumbent candidate, President Mitterrand, who won a second term in office.

As a similar situation occurred in 1993, the Prime Minister and presidential candidate Edouard Balladur was extremely wary not to repeat the mistakes made by his fellow party member Jacques Chirac a few years earlier. It was clear that confrontation with external interests had to be avoided if he wanted to secure widespread public support in the Presidential election (Bigaut 1995: 9). The second cohabitation, thus, saw a substantial reversal of the standard

---

[15] This section draws on Bonoli 1997*a*.

[16] The French pension system is characterized by a high degree of occupational fragmentation. The *régime général* provides basic pension coverage for private sector employees (65% of the working age population). In addition there are separate schemes for farmers (3%), public sector employees (29%), and self-employed people (12%). For the last two groups, moreover, pension coverage is further fragmented according to employer or profession. On top of that, complementary provision is also compulsory and follows roughly the same occupational divisions.

French approach to public policy. While traditionally the French state has been described as capable of imposing its own priorities without having to compromise with external interests (Badie and Birnbaum 1983; Merrien 1991), the Balladur Government proved to be rather sensitive to group pressure. Despite this particular political context, the government managed to push through a potentially controversial pension reform which previous governments all failed to adopt.

The 1993 Pension Reform

Soon after the 1993 general election, the newly elected right-wing government started working on the pension reform issue. Negotiations between officials at the Ministry of Social Affairs, employers, and employees took place throughout April and May. The trade unions, particularly the Communist CGT and the radical FO[17] were rather reluctant to accept cutbacks, as they had been before. Ministry officials were certainly aware of the fact that a fully consensual solution was not possible. Nevertheless, what could be achieved, was a situation in which at least the most radical sections of the labour movement would have refrained from staging an informal protest. According to a civil servant who took part to the negotiations:

It was important for us to gain the approval of the CFDT because we knew that FO and the CGT would be hostile anyway. . . . We needed at least the neutrality of the other confederations. It was also important to avoid that FO would adopt too a violent position. In fact they were against, but they did not react as they did in 1995 against the Juppé plan. They did not mobilize their members saying that the new legislation was shameful. (Interview, Ministry of Social Affairs, 20 Dec. 1996)

The government's position was to favour the adoption of the measures suggested in an earlier White Paper published by their Socialist predecessors in 1991. The number of contribution-years needed to be granted a full pension of 50 per cent of the reference salary was to be increased from 37.5 to 40. At the same time, the reference salary was to be calculated as the average re-valued salary of the best 25 years (instead of 10 years). Third, the indexation of benefits currently in payment was to be shifted from gross wages

---

[17] In France, the labour movement is divided along ideological lines. There are five major national federations of trade unions, which operate independently from each other. The divisions reflect the political spectrum. Starting from the left, the Confédération Générale du Travail (CGT) is of Communist inspiration. Force Ouvrière (FO) originated from a division within the CGT in 1947 and constitutes its non-Communist component (it is sometimes referred to as CGT–FO). The Confédération Française Démocratique des Travailleurs (CFDT) is a moderate union which in recent years has been much more cooperative with the government than its counterparts. Finally the Confédération Française des Travailleurs Chrétiens (CFTC) is a federation of Catholic unions. In addition, there is also a federation representing managers (CFE–CGC Confédération Française de l'Encadrement–Confédération Générale des Cadres).

to prices. The overall impact of this series of measures, which were eventually adopted, is a reduction of benefits and possibly also an increase in the age of retirement, since employees will qualify for a full pension 2.5 years later than under previous legislation.

These proposals, which were clearly unacceptable to the trade unions, were accompanied by plans to set up an 'Old Age Solidarity Fund' (*Fonds de Solidarité Vieillesse*), financed through general taxation (as opposed to contributions) with the task of paying for the non-contributory elements of the insurance-based pension schemes. The new fund takes financial responsibility for minimum pensions, which are granted on the basis of an income test and regardless of contribution record, and for contribution credits given to unemployed people, to those serving in the army, and to parents who give up work in order to raise their children. Before the 1993 reform these non-contributory benefits were to some extent financed by employment-related contributions. In fact, the shift in financing of non-contributory elements from contributions to taxation was a key demand of the labour movement.

The French trade unions view the social security system as not being part of the state apparatus, but as some sort of collective insurance plan covering all salaried employees. From their perspective, the inclusion of non-contributory elements constitutes an infringement of the insurance principle according to which there must be a strict link between payments and benefits. This understanding of the role of social security was the basis upon which the whole system was built in 1945. As a matter of fact, the management of social security was not given to civil servants but to joint committees composed of representatives of employers and employees. This perception, however, is not shared by state actors. For them, the social security system is primarily a social policy instrument, which must intervene where social needs are identified. As a result, throughout the post-war period governments of different political persuasion have adopted measures to extend adequate coverage on a non-contributory basis to those who had been unable to build up a sufficient contribution record.

This diversity of views is a constant source of conflict between governments and the trade unions on the definition of the objectives of social security (Bonoli and Palier 1996). The state has been trying to expand its control over the system, while the trade unions have resisted such moves. For the latter, in fact, the managerial role they play is of crucial importance. First, it gives them some sort of legitimacy in the eyes of public opinion, which somewhat compensates for their small membership. Second, it provides a substantial source of employment for union members (Rosanvallon 1995). For the trade unions, thus, it is extremely important that the social security system remains under their control and that its financing is guaranteed.

The creation of a new 'Old Age Solidarity Fund' must be understood as a move towards meeting some of the unions' demands. The acceptance by the government of the separation between insurance-based and non-contributory provision was de facto a recognition of the insurance character of the main scheme, and by the same token, of the managerial role played by the unions. Moreover, the fund brought additional finance to pensions and as a result a balance between cutbacks in provision and increases in financial means was achieved. The reform package, thus, included an element that was certainly going to be palatable to the trade unions, and that could be seen as a quid pro quo for their acceptance of retrenchment measures. This helps to explain why even the most radical sections of the labour movement refrained from attacking the new legislation through informal protest.

The 1995 Reform of Public Sector Pensions (Juppé Plan)

The 1993 reform affected only private sector employees. Because of France's fragmented pension system, civil servants and other public sector workers are covered by alternative arrangements, which are generally more generous. An attempt to deal with these schemes, which were also making substantial losses, was made in the context of the 1995 reform of social security (Juppé Plan). Among other things, the plan made clear the government's intention to extend to public sector employees the measures adopted in 1993 for the private sector. While the content of the two reforms was roughly the same, the political contexts in which these were discussed were radically different. In May 1995 Jacques Chirac was elected President for a seven-year term. Edouard Balladur, who had been a candidate in the presidential election, was replaced by Alain Juppé, the most senior figure in the Chirac camp. The result was a significant strengthening of the executive. President and Prime Minister now belonged to the same party and to the same area within the party. In addition, the next important national election was scheduled for 1998, and in parliament the right-of-centre coalition was still supported by a substantial majority. These conditions were probably viewed as particularly suitable to force the adoption of unpopular measures, which, according to the government, were badly needed.

The Juppé Plan was drafted between August and November 1995. The way in which this was done suggests that the government intended to adopt a confrontational approach to social security reform. While during this period Ministry officials had contacts with representatives of organized interests, the measures adopted were not negotiated with them. In fact, it appears that the content of the plan was to a large extent kept secret.

Beside the reform of public sector pensions, the plan included measures aimed at increasing the state's control over the social security system, and particularly over health insurance, which in France is part of social security.

Like the pension scheme, health insurance is managed jointly by representatives of employers and employees. In the case of health care, however, the absence of the state's participation in the management is widely regarded as an obstacle to effective cost containment. The social partners are seen as being unable to effectively contrast the power of the medical profession and of the pharmaceutical industry. As a result, the government has tried on various occasions to increase its control over the health care system, and particularly over health insurance. Moves in that direction, however, have generally been resisted by the labour movement, which fears to be excluded from the management of the system. Measures adopted in the Juppé Plan included a partial shift in health insurance financing from employment-related contributions to taxation, which means stronger government intervention. The plan also made provision for allowing parliament to vote on the social security budget, which previously was not the case. Finally, the composition of the administration boards of social insurance schemes was also affected, by the inclusion of civil servants.

The 1995 plan, thus, in addition to the extension of the retrenchment measures adopted in 1993 to public sector employees, included other elements which were likely to provoke a hostile reaction from the trade unions. Instead of sweetening pension retrenchment with concessions on the management side of the scheme, as had been the case in 1993, this time the government combined cuts with an attack on the trade unions' role in the system. In fact, contrary to what was reported by the international media, the fury of some of the most radical trade unions (particularly FO) was not directed so much against cuts in pension provision, but against increased government intervention in social security management. The general Secretary of FO described the fact that parliament would be allowed to vote the social security budget as the 'biggest theft in the history of the French Republic' (Blondel, in *Le Monde*, 17 Nov. 1995). The Juppé Plan was not merely a series of cuts in social provision, but constituted an attempt to change the fundamental structure of the French welfare state. One of its main consequences, was a reduction in the influence of the trade unions over the system.

The government was certainly aware of the potential for controversy embodied in the proposed measures. The conflict between state actors and the unions on the objectives of the social security system and, perhaps more crucially, on the issue of who controls it, has been going on for more than a decade now. Presumably, given its position of strength, the government decided to take an uncompromising stance. This confrontational approach, however, generated one of the biggest protest movements France has seen since 1968. Eventually, the government had to abandon its plans for public sector pensions reform, and to date the debate on that issue has not been reopened. The other measures included in the plan, however, were maintained and have been implemented gradually throughout 1996 and 1997.

4. POLITICAL INSTITUTIONS AND
WELFARE REFORMS

On the basis of the above account of welfare reforms in three countries, a number of considerations can be made with regard to the link between political institutions and welfare state adaptation. First, the link is two-tiered, in the sense that political institutions affect the level of executive power concentration which, in turn, has an impact on the kind of policy strategy governments are likely to follow when dealing with welfare reforms.

The first tier of the link refers to the level of power concentration generated by various elements of the constitutional order of a country, the most important of which have been reviewed at the beginning of this chapter. What is important to point out, however, is that power concentration is not entirely predetermined by constitutional rules. Other factors, like for example electoral results, can play an important role in determining the level of governmental power concentration. As seen above, in the case of France, power can be more or less concentrated with the government depending on which party controls key democratic institutions. When presidency and parliament are in the hands of the same party, then power concentration is strong. When, in contrast, the two are controlled by different camps, then there is an element of power fragmentation in the political system.

More in general, power concentrating institutions can be rather useless to governments, if their effect is offset by electoral results. In this respect, the focus on institutions should not result in neglect of the impact of social demands as expressed by vote. As argued by Immergut: 'to understand how these institutions work in practice, we must add the de facto rules that arise from electoral results and party systems' (Immergut 1992: 27). Hence, what best accounts for patterns of power concentration and fragmentation is the analysis of the interaction between institutions and electoral results. The logical consequence is that one should not consider power concentration as a fixed feature of a given constitutional setting, but as something that can change in time and needs to be reassessed in specific instances.

In addition, while institutional and electoral power concentration are powerful factors affecting governments' policy strategies to welfare reforms, they are not the only ones. What seems to be an important additional element is the structure of the labour movement, and in particular its mobilizing capacity and threat potential. In general, welfare reforms adopted in countries which have strong and well integrated trade unions movements have been characterized by negotiation and inclusion of external interests. Countries like Sweden or Germany have shown strong inclination for concertation in the adoption of cuts in social programmes (Pierson 1996). A negotiated approach is more likely to emerge in corporatist countries, partly because

corporatism is associated with strong and well integrated labour movements (Schmitter 1982), and partly because the existence of a corporatist
tradition of concertation in policy making provides a political climate which
can be more conducive to successful negotiation. The actors involved are
used to cooperating, and generally share a common inclination towards
problem solving.

While the existence of a corporatist tradition obviously favours a negotiated
approach to welfare reform, it does not seem to be an essential condition.
French and Italian pension reforms have shown that inclusive policy making is possible also in countries which lack a tradition of concertation between
governments and organized interests. On these two occasions, the adoption
of a negotiated approach seems to be related more to the weakness of the
government, due to contingent political factors, than to the strength of the
trade unions (on Italy, see Ferrera 1997; Regini and Regalia 1997).

The second tier of the institution–policy outcomes link, refers to the impact
of different levels of executive power concentration on patterns of reform.
This chapter looked at five instances of welfare reform. Three of these were
adopted in contexts of relatively strong power fragmentation. This was the
case of both Swiss reforms (pensions and unemployment insurance) and of
the French 1993 pension reform. What these three reforms have in common
is the combination of saving measures with quid pro quos aimed at gaining
the approval of key actors. In the case of Switzerland, gender equality in
pensions and increased expenditure on active labour market policies were
among the key demands of the Social Democratic Party and of the trade
unions. The inclusion of these measures in otherwise retrenchment-oriented
reforms, proved instrumental in guaranteeing their final adoption. Similarly,
in the French case, the combination of pension cuts with the creation of an
Old Age Solidarity Fund, a long-standing demand of the unions, made the
former more acceptable to the most radical sections of the labour movement.
Such quid pro *quos* were absent in the two reforms adopted in contexts of
strong power concentration: the British 1986 Social Security Act and the
French 1995 Juppé Plan.

These quid pro quos can be quite substantial. The active labour market
measures adopted in the 1995 Swiss unemployment insurance reform included
the creation of 150 Regional Placement Offices, employing more than 2,000
staff and providing 25,000 individual measures, for an unemployed population of around 200,000 (Pfitzman 1995; Nau 1998). These have to some
extent replaced previous Cantonal measures, which were generally less wide
ranging. In the case of France, the Old Age Solidarity Fund is financed
mainly by an increase of 1.3 percentage point of the *Contribution Sociale
Generalisee*, a flat-rate tax earmarked for social programmes. This amounts
to a fairly substantial increase in the level of finance available to state
pensions (Chadelat 1994).

On these three occasions, governments have managed to adopt reforms that could have been extremely controversial, as they included substantial cuts. One possible interpretation of this is to say that negotiation is a more effective road to welfare retrenchment than imposition (Esping-Andersen 1996*b*). The fact that the 1995 attempt at reforming public sector pensions in France failed, supports this view. What seems certain is the fact that negotiation is a more secure road to retrenchment, as it guarantees the adoption of a given level of savings. In contrast, imposition can potentially deliver bigger cuts, but at a more substantial risk of failure. In this respect, none of the two strategies is inherently more favourable to retrenchment.

The two strategies, however, are likely to lead to qualitatively different processes of welfare state adaptation. The fact that negotiated reforms need to include concessions and/or quid pro quos suggests that the overall direction of these reforms is unlikely to be pure retrenchment. Instead, changes can be introduced on other dimensions. This appeared strongly in the Swiss case, where cuts have been traded with modernization of the welfare state. The latter is being scaled back, but at the same time adapted to the new needs.

There are good reasons to believe that the combination of retrenchment and modernization is an effective strategy to neutralize the impact of veto points on welfare reforms. Welfare states are currently being exposed to various pressures. Financial constraints are the most pressing issue in welfare state adaptation, however, as the needs and aspirations of modern societies evolve, new requirements on the welfare state are likely to emerge. Examples of these are demands for gender equality, for a more active intervention in the labour market, or for meeting the social needs of increasing numbers of elderly people. In this respect, the institutional constraints which limit the scope for unilateral reforms in power-fragmented systems, might encourage an adaptation process which combines retrenchment with a modernization of the welfare state, or measures designed to take into account new social demands.

This does not seem to be a necessary outcome of welfare state adaptation in fragmented systems, as governments willing to contain social expenditure might also resort to other forms of quid pro quos, such as selective advantages targeted on key actors, as in the French 1993 reform. However, from the point of view of governments operating in power fragmented systems, the combination of retrenchment with welfare modernization seems a tempting option, as it allows them to overcome the institutional obstacles to retrenchment and, at the same time, it provides them with arguments that can be used for credit claiming. This seems to be the only viable road to welfare state adaptation available to Swiss policy makers. As seen above, attempts at imposing retrenchment-only policies have been rejected by voters.

It is important to point out the limits of this model. Political institutions do matter, but in interaction with other factors. As a result it is impossible to make predictions of individual instances of policy outcomes solely on their basis. As Immergut puts it: 'there is not an invariant correlation between a given set of political institutions and a specific set of . . . policies. Rather, by spelling out the effects of constitutional rules and electoral results at a high level of specificity, we can understand some recurring patterns of politics and policy making in individual polities' (1992: 231–2). The focus on political institutions as an independent variable, however, can still have some predictive validity, if looked at in the long term. The impact of political institutions is affected by its interaction with other factors, particularly electoral dynamics, which can either enhance or reduce executive power concentration and its effects on policy outcomes. In this respect, we can assume that over time, electoral dynamics will sometimes favour power concentration and sometimes not. In the long run, the likelihood is that the divergent impacts of electoral dynamics will offset each other, highlighting thus the influence of political institutions on policy. The work by Huber, Ragin, and Stephens (1993), which covering a thirty-year period found a significant correlation between institutional power concentration and a high degree of welfare state development, suggests that this might be the case.

In conclusion, what seems clear from this analysis is that particularly radical and unilateral reforms are more likely to be put forward in political and institutional contexts of strong power concentration. These reforms, however, entail a high level of risk for governments, both in terms of electoral consequences and of risk of informal protest. This option is generally not available in power fragmented systems. Governments there, in order to enhance their chances of getting controversial legislation accepted, are encouraged to adopt negotiated solutions to welfare problems characterized by the inclusion of quid pro quos targeted on key actors. The result is that the political risks are reduced, but at the same time their control over the content of reform is limited. While decisions concerning the choice of a policy strategy will depend on a number of factors, some of which are clearly of a contingent nature, political institutions are likely to play an important role in this process.

9

Partisan Competition and Welfare State Retrenchment
When Do Politicians Choose Unpopular Policies?

Herbert Kitschelt

WELFARE states protect citizens against the vagaries of the market place through compulsory insurance schemes (for health care, unemployment, occupational accidents, and old age), programmes to enhance citizens' human capital endowment (education, (re)training), social services (counselling, child care, old age assistance), and a variety of further policies to support income (housing, family allowances). The literature on the welfare state has amply documented the fact that since the 1980s it has become harder to assemble political coalitions supporting further expansions of the welfare state just about anywhere in the advanced industrial world and regardless of the level of social programmes reached at that time. Instead, efforts to reduce expenditure in existing programmes, or even to redesign and restructure the policies and institutions that govern such programmes, have intensified in most polities, although along diverging trajectories.

Policies to pair back and redistribute social programme benefits tend to be inherently unpopular in the precise sense that they do not capture the median voter in any advanced post-industrial democracy. Nevertheless, in some countries, rational vote- or office-seeking politicians and their parties have pursued such unpopular policies. What may be even more surprising, on a number of occasions, parties were elected into office that announced unpopular social policy changes ahead of elections, or successfully ran on a track record of social policy retrenchment engineered while being a government party in subsequent electoral campaigns. The main proposition of my paper is that the strategic configuration of party systems, net of public opinion on social policy reforms, is a critical force that shapes social policy reform programmes and their implementation. Thus, my paper lays out mechanisms that may induce politicians to pursue often unpopular reforms based on internal opportunities offered by the dynamic of competitive party democracy that have received only scant attention in the comparative political economy and social policy literature.

The central guiding proposition of my paper requires two important qualifications. First of all, the dynamic of party competition is only one of several mechanisms that affect social policy retrenchment. I do not claim exclusive causal efficacy for the electoral–partisan linkage between citizens and public policy. Many of the potential causes for welfare state retrenchment policies concern developments outside the political sphere, such as the demographics of ageing and infirmity, technology-induced changes in the relative demand for skilled and unskilled labour, and possibly the consequences of increased capital market openness for labour mobility. I sidestep controversies about the relative explanatory power of such factors external to the polity for social policy retrenchment and instead argue that once favourable external conditions for welfare state redesign and retrenchment exist, then the internal dynamics of competition in the electoral and policy making arena affect the adoption and implementation of social policy reform. The conditions of competition in party systems refract external shocks and trends that put pressure on social policy change (cf. Garrett and Lange 1995; Kitschelt et al. 1999*b*).

The second qualification concerns the empirical grounding of my argument. A comparative study of social policy change in the 1980s and 1990s would ideally rely on equivalent measures across a wide range of countries. Such measures would identify the extent of retrenchment in terms of the level of social policy programme expenditures per capita, criteria of eligibility for benefits, duration of benefits, and contributions necessary to qualify for entitlements. These programme indicators then could be summarized in an encompassing index of social protection and its change over time for each country. Given the lack of such cross-nationally comparable measures, scholars disagree at this time about the precise extent of welfare state change and retrenchment and therefore also about the causes that may account for these developments. Given my own research record and professional skills, I cannot remedy these deficiencies and I am therefore unable to compare rival explanations for social policy changes in an empirically rigorous fashion. While these data limitations currently make it impossible to determine the explanatory power of internal political conditions relative to external demographic and economic changes in accounts of social policy retrenchment, I employ case studies to illustrate how mechanisms of party competition impinge on social policy change. Beyond that, I attempt to generalize my argument based on a reading of much looser expert judgements about social policy retrenchment in a broader set of countries.

1. POLITICIANS' INCENTIVES TO PURSUE UNPOPULAR POLICIES

Citizens have little chance to fight against unfavourable policy changes if they are weakly organized and encompass a relatively small share of the electorate. The problem with the major social policy programmes, such as pension schemes, health insurance, and sickness benefits, is that they affect not only large groups, but often also well-organized groups with encompassing organizations or at least strategic resources to make their voices heard. We usually presume that the combination of large group size and strong organization tends to place insurmountable obstacles in the pathway of social retrenchment policies. Moreover, even where the constituencies for social policy programmes are large, but weakly organized, the electoral mechanism may give advocates of the status quo leverage in the party system they lack in the arena of organized interests and interest intermediation between governments and functional interest groups.[1] Nevertheless, in some countries, politicians dare to overcome the resistance of majorities to social policy reform, even if they are very large. This is a puzzle for the spatial theories of party competition and government coalition formation I outline first. I then argue that while public opinion is generally unfavourable to social policy retrenchment in virtually all advanced democracies, there are opportunities of 'framing' social policy issues that make it easier for politicians to overcome resistance to change. The focus of my theoretical analysis, however, is on the configuration of party competition that becomes decisive for politicians' calculations whether or not they will be persuasive to voters with new interpretive frames that justify social policy retrenchment.

Spatial Models of Party Competition and Unpopular Policy Reform

In a restrictive model of party competition voters cannot abstain from voting. They choose between two parties and prefer the alternative that announces a programmatic policy position closest to their own ideal point in a single policy dimension. At the same time, politicians cannot enter the electoral arena with new partisan alternatives, and they are purely motivated by the desire to win office. Under these conditions the median voter theorem implies that competing parties locate their political appeals slightly to the left and the right of the median voter at a minimal distance from each other that is just large enough to keep voters' interest in the alternatives (Downs 1957).

---

[1] The political economy literature (such as Olson 1982), puts a great deal of emphasis on group size and organization, but disregards the electoral connection as a countervailing force for weakly organized, large groups.

If the median voter theorem applies and social policy is the decisive issue, then parties can engage in social policy retrenchment only if the median voter withdraws support from social policy programmes.

The same result applies, with modifications, to a world with multi-party competition of four or more significant competitors in a single social policy/ economics dimension. On the one hand, in such systems some parties have strong incentives to advertise policy positions that substantially diverge from the median voter. Party positions thus tend to spread out over the entire issue space (Cox 1990; Shepsle 1991). But in multi-party systems, legislative and executive majority formation usually requires alliances among parties. If we assume that the ideological proximity and connectedness of the partners is a reasonable precondition for a working majority that can pass legislation, then the party that controls the median voter also tends to be the 'policy dictator' of the entire coalition (Laver and Schofield 1990), because no majority is viable that does not include that party. If the median voter opposes social policy reform, then the party representing that voter will do likewise and no government will be able to pass social reform.

A modification of multi-party coalition theory argues that the coalition government's policy position in the unidimensional competitive space will be equivalent to the 'centre of gravity' of the entire coalition. Multi-party competition thus creates the possibility of responsible partisan government with coalition policies distinctly to the left or the right of the median voter. The inclusion of the party controlling the median voter still constrains policy choice, but other coalition members have bargaining power that forces the alliance's centre of gravity away from the median voter. This will not damage the electoral prospects of each coalition partner, as long as no alternative majority coalition including parties currently in opposition permits the party that captures the median voter to bargain for a social policy package that is closer to the ideal position of the median voter it captures. Because coalitions with different centres of gravity to the left and right of the median voter may succeed each other, multi-party competition offers considerable possibilities for policy oscillation, while holding constant voters' preference distribution.

Centre of gravity theories of welfare state expansion have therefore argued that long-run government coalitions dominated by social democratic parties, 'centrist' Christian or secular parties appealing to cross-class voter alliances, or rightist market liberal parties yield different welfare states (cf. M. Schmidt 1982; Esping-Andersen 1990; Huber, Ragin, and Stephens 1993; and Huber and Stephens, in this volume). While empirically powerful, this theory has some analytical and empirical shortcomings that call for amendments and revisions of the central argument. First, the theory predicts policy formation based on the party positions supported by members of the governing coalition only, but does not take into account how coalition policy is strategically conditioned by the policy alternatives offered by the opposition parties. But government stances will also depend on the feasibility and likely policy appeal of alternative government coalitions.[2] The size of government majorities (Garrett 1993) and the durability of coalitions (Comiskey 1993) may affect government strategy. These, in turn, depend on the attractiveness and credibility of opposition party positions. Second, the centre of gravity theories of social policy making determine parties' policy positions and coalitional strategies based on their adherence to party families (social democratic, Christian democratic, conservative). If the overall configuration of party competition matters, however, parties belonging to the same party families may support different social policies, net of the government or opposition status. Third, the two analytical shortcomings of the centre of gravity theories may explain empirical problems of the theory accounting for the diversity in welfare state retrenchment programmes in advanced post-industrial democracies. As I theoretically elaborate and empirically illustrate below, in an environment of fiscal and economic crisis, it is not governments of the social democratic left that display the greatest propensity to defend existing welfare states and resist retrenchment, as the centre of gravity hypothesis might suggest. Instead, this resistance may be greatest in party systems configured around strong centre-right non-socialist parties. But before outlining the specific conditions of party competition that facilitate or impede unpopular social policy reform, let us first explore how unpopular social policy reform really is and what openings politicians might encounter to make arguments for such reform with some prospect of acceptance in the public sphere of democratic deliberation.

Public Opinion and the Framing of Social Policy Retrenchment

In the analysis of opinion surveys about social policy, responses vary based on three critical cues. First, does the question elicit an evaluation of current levels of welfare state protection or of change rates of social policy? Second, do respondents indicate their approval or disapproval of specific policy programmes (pensions, sickness compensation, education, etc.) or of the aggregate magnitude of the public economy and public social expenditure relative to the overall economy? Among programmes, those with universalistic coverage of all citizens command more support than those benefiting narrower groups. Favourable evaluations of the welfare state in opinion polls thus critically vary with the precise framing of the survey questions.

In general, Western publics in the 1980s and 1990s exhibit more support for current levels of welfare state expenditure and existing programme structures than for positive or negative change rates. It is always easier to defend the status quo because respondents perceive current benefit levels as less uncertain than those resulting from changes. Moreover, in the most affluent

---

[2] F. G. Castles (1978) made this point in his analysis of bourgeois party fragmentation as a condition of social democratic welfare state growth, but it has rarely been pursued by later contributions to the welfare state literature.

TABLE 9.1. *Public support of more state responsibility for citizens' social protection*[a]

Less developed countries		Post-Communist countries		Advanced post-industrial countries	
Chile	55	Latvia	55	Japan	55
Nigeria	54				
Turkey	50	Hungary	50		
		Lithuania, Slovenia	44	Spain	44
		Belarus	43		
Brazil	41				
South Africa	39			Italy	39
		Poland, Romania	37		
Mexico	35	Bulgaria, Estonia	35		
China, Argentina	33			Britain	33
		Russia	32		
				Ireland	30
				Portugal	28
				Iceland	26
South Korea	25				
		German Democratic Republic	23	Netherlands	23
				West Germany	22
				Norway	21
India	20			Finland	20
				France, Canada	19
				Denmark	16
				Austria, United States	14
				Sweden	11

[a] Approval (code 7–10 on 10-point scale) of the proposition: 'The state should take more responsibility to ensure that everyone is rovided for.' VAR 252, 1990 World Values Survey, reported in Ronald Inglehart, Miguel Basanez, and Alejandro Moreno, *Human Values and Beliefs: A Cross-Cultural Sourcebook* (Ann Arbor: University of Michigan Press, 1998).

countries, but not necessarily those with the largest welfare states, public opinion reflects ceiling effects. Large majorities realize they enjoy diversified packages of public and private social protection against the vagaries of the marketplace and infer that a further expansion of public social protection is either impossible or undesirable. It is thus not surprising that in a 1990 *World Values Survey* question that asks respondents in forty countries to evaluate the proposition 'The state should take on more responsibility to ensure that everyone is provided for' there is a moderately strong negative correlation between a country's economic affluence, measured in purchasing power parity terms, and the percentage of respondents advocating more responsibilities of the state for social protection ($r = -0.55$; see Table 9.1). Given that affluence, in general, also coincides with more public or private, but publically regulated social protection, it is clear that the demand for social protection increases levels off in the most advanced democracies.

Table 9.1 shows that the greatest support for stronger state responsibility for citizens' income provisions is in the post-communist countries that just started to undergo economic liberalization with a massive reduction of social protection in the early 1990s. Within the subset of advanced post-industrial democracies, the survey results reveal only a modest correlation between public opinion and affluence, but even less correlation between public opinion and the size of the welfare state. While it is true that Japanese respondents, facing a very small welfare state, are most insistent in their demand for its expansion, survey respondents not only in Sweden, with a very large welfare state, but also in the USA and Canada, with comparatively modest public social protection, are distinctly weary of expansionary social policies. What may influence political evaluations of social policy more than the sheer size of the welfare state is citizens' interpretation of a more encompassing quality of life package that influences social security and may be related more to personal affluence, including private hedging strategies against personal economic catastrophes.

Thus, in highly affluent democracies vote-seeking politicians may have an easier time in opposing welfare state expansions, although it is certainly not true that pluralities of respondents agree to a reduction in public social services and transfers. Here a second dimension of framing welfare state questions comes into play. Do respondents evaluate particular programmes —such as social security, sickness benefits, unemployment, etc.—or do they volunteer their opinions about the relative size of the public sector more generally without unpacking the aggregates and dividing them into programme expenditures? Data provided by the *International Social Science Surveys* in 1985 and 1990 show continued support for public health care systems and public pensions in European democracies included in the survey (Austria, Britain, Germany, Ireland, Italy, Norway, Sweden). If anything, in Britain, Germany, and Italy the demand for programme spending still increased in the 1980s (cf. Huseby 1995: 96–102; Confalonieri and Newton 1995: 139). At the same time, in a number of these countries, but not all of them, support for spending on programmes whose benefits accrue to more limited constituencies, such as unemployment insurance, declined (Huseby 1995: 96; Confalonieri and Newton 1995: 139). Thus, the evidence tends to bear out the expectation that small groups may become more vulnerable in an economic and political environment generally less favourable to large government expenditures, but support for large, encompassing programmes has held up well throughout the 1980s.[3]

---

[3] This statement is also empirically confirmed by the pattern of responses to questions concerning social policy areas in the European Union (Eurobarometer 37, 1992). In all EU countries, solid majorities of the respondents opposed the proposition that governments should pare back their social expenditure to the minimum level. In some isolated instances, certain aspects of operational social security prompted responses inconsistent with the general proposition that specific and universalistic programmes are untouchable. West European mass audiences, for example, argue that cutbacks in social security benefits are justified in the light of demographic developments. In a similar vein, many pro-welfare state respondents nevertheless are concerned about the all too frequent use of public health facilities and advocate more private solutions to public problems.

While specific universalist social policy programmes (health care, retirement) have continued to enjoy extremely strong public popularity, citizens'
approval of social policy activism more broadly conceived has often declined,
if questions do not mention key social programmes and focus on aggregate
expenditures. Above all, this applies more to change rates than levels of
aggregate spending, revealing a widespread aversion to further welfare state
expansion across a broad range of countries, no matter whether such countries have large or small welfare states (cf. Pettersen 1995: 210). Majorities
in most countries even favour outright government spending cuts in the 1980s,
although they wish to protect the large social programmes in health care
and pensions (Confalonieri and Newton 1995: 138–9). In the late 1980s,
in Britain, Denmark, the Netherlands, Norway, and Sweden usually thin
pluralities of respondents would like to see lower public spending levels
(Huseby 1995: 104). In a similar vein, support for income redistribution has
been waning in some, but not all advanced European democracies (Roller
1995*a*: 69). The same applies to public job creation programmes (Roller
1995*b*: 185). Therefore, if politicians successfully frame social policy reform
not as one of protecting or retrenching encompassing programmes, but as
an effort to reduce aggregate public expenditure and debt, or as reductions
in means-tested programmes benefiting small, well-defined groups, they enjoy
fair prospects to obtain median voter approval.

At the level of individual respondents, variables that correlate with a citizen's
probability to be or become a consumer or client of social policy programmes
at the time of the survey, such as lower education, lower income, higher age,
and working-class identification, but also gender (female) and public sector
employment shape evaluations of social policy (Pettersen 1995: 216–23). The
poorer and more vulnerable show greater support for the welfare state, and
this tendency cuts across class divides, but reflects skill levels and sectoral
affiliations within labour markets. Unfortunately, we lack the survey evidence
to test how political economic models of asset specificity and sectoral interests, as proposed by Alt et al. (1996), Baldwin (1990), or Swenson (1989),
affect emerging electoral coalitions about social policy.

For policy retrenchment in advanced post-industrial societies, the one
robust conclusion one can infer from this fragmentary evidence is that politicians may advance the cause of structural reform and retrenchment most
persuasively, if they focus on aggregate spending rather than individual
social programmes and talk about reductions in the rate of growth rather
than absolute cutbacks. Conversely, supporters of welfare state expansion best
frame their political appeals by highlighting the need to improve particular
universalistic programmes (health, pensions, education) and invoking the
defence of the status quo against market liberalizers who are portrayed as
trying to take away what generations of voters have fought for. In other words,
politicians may persuade the median voter more easily to support a party's

appeal to implement an across-the-board freeze of public expenditure than a cut of particular universalist programmes, such as pensions or health care. Given that the opponents of social policy retrenchment will strike back and highlight that such aggregate policy shifts necessitate painful adjustments at the programme level, the persuasiveness of retrenchment appeals does not depend entirely on the pitch of the message. It rather relates to the track record, reputation, and strategic situation in which each competing party is immersed in the democratic electoral and legislative competition and that endows its framing of the policy issue with greater or lesser credibility. An explanation for the varying tendency of contemporary democracies to engineer social policy retrenchment thus cannot be sought primarily in the realm of clever rhetoric and shifts in public opinion, but must start with an analysis of the strategic leverage politicians and parties have in different polities. The configurations of party competition determine which rhetoric enjoys more credibility in the interpretations of critical electoral constituencies.

Responsible Party Government and Social Policy Change in Democratic Party Competition

In this section, I try to show how a full consideration of competitive configurations can overcome the limits of centre-of-gravity theories of social policy formation and suggest when political rhetoric that facilitates or impedes social policy retrenchment is more effective in electoral and public policy terms. There is no single attribute of competitive party systems that accounts for different prospects of social policy retrenchment. Instead, I detail four mechanisms that may work in conjunction with each other to improve the prospects of social policy reform: the existence of a strong market-liberal party and the declining credibility of parties defending the welfare state; mild electoral trade-offs encountered by politicians when they diverge from the social policy preference of the party's electorate; a party organization that minimizes strategic inertia at the level of activists and party leaders; and a configuration of competition around economic rather than socio-cultural issues. It should be emphasized that I focus on structural relations among parties, not on run-of-the-mill party system properties, such as party fragmentation or polarization, that have often been invoked to account for different propensities of competitive party democracies to engage in economic policy liberalization (e.g. Haggard and Kaufman 1995: 166–9 and ch. 10).[4]

---

[4] The use of parameters such as system fragmentation and polarization tends to be purely inductive in the political economy literature. Hicks and Misra (1993) who employ a structural measure of fragmentation to tap the role of electoral competition to account for social policy cannot specify theoretical expectations of how fragmentation should affect the change in welfare state expenditures, but are happy to include this variable because it exhibits a statistically significant negative correlation with expenditures (as critique, see Amenta 1993).

I am most concerned with the actual capacity to engineer social policy reform, more so than the choice of appeal at the onset of the reform cycle. A party's track record in office speaks louder than words in subsequent campaigns. A party's decision whether to reveal or conceal reform intentions is relevant only as long as it is in opposition and has a prior record of opposing market-liberalizing social policy changes.

Market-Liberal Parties and the Defence of the Welfare State

The presence of parties with a track-record of liberal market advocacy is a facilitator of shifting the social policy debate towards containment and retrenchment of expenditures and institutional revisions. Without strong liberal parties in Western democracies that place the issue on the agenda and compel their competitors to take a position, decisive reform programmes have rarely gotten off the ground. At the same time, in the light of continuing broad popular support for the social policy status quo, such programmatic aspirations attract new supporters only if existing parties defending the welfare state have lost credibility in the eyes of many voters. Parties defending the existing welfare state may lose credibility as a result of a stint in government office that delivered bad economic performance. Examples are Britain under Labour (1974–9), the Netherlands under Labour and Christian Democrats (1972–82), New Zealand under Muldoon's National Party until 1984, or the United States under Carter (1976–80). Or an opposition party that advocates preservation of the welfare state sees its support erode because it supports anti-market social and economic policies that are much more radical than those endorsed by the median voter (British and Dutch Labour until the late 1980s). Socialist experiments may generate even more anxiety among status-quo oriented citizens than market liberal reform. Furthermore, an opposition party may have no credibility to defend the welfare state because it has never governed and voters hesitate to attribute the necessary competence to its bid to become the governing party.

Where the credibility of a major opposition party as defender of the welfare state is diminished, its competitors for government office, whether they run under social democratic or conservative ideological labels, have the opportunity to embrace unpopular social policy reforms with a reduced probability that they will earn the wrath of the voters. First of all, voters will have no reasonable alternative to turn to. From the perspective of status quo preservers, the retrenchment reforms offered by the government may be the best they can do, given the position and credibility of the opposition. And second, maybe the gamble works out and social policy retrenchment will, in fact, deliver economic recovery and growing affluence by the time new elections come around. The lack of reasonable alternatives and the outcome orientation of voters may entice politicians to embrace welfare state retrenchment because it makes it more plausible that voters will return to a party that did not deliver what they initially called for.[5] By contrast, where at least one major party, let alone all major competitors, has a strong track record and reputational credibility as defenders of the welfare state, social policy reform is much less likely to proceed, even under circumstances of high fiscal deficits.

When faced with a strong market-liberal competitor, social democratic parties may adopt social policy retrenchment in agreement with a modified 'Nixon in China' logic. An anti-communist Republican with a hawkish reputation in foreign policy could initiate reconciliation with Communist China more easily without raising suspicions of 'selling out' America than a liberal Democrat in the presidency. Applying this logic to social policy retrenchment, social democratic or labour parties engaging in social policy retrenchment that is unpopular with the median voter may be more acceptable to citizens because they represent the 'lesser evil' and enjoy more credibility in protecting the core of the system than right-wing market reformers.

The credibility of parties' defence of the welfare state, in conjunction with the outcome orientation of voters, plays a role in yet one other respect. In most circumstances, neither social democrats nor conservatives nor market liberals could win election by promising a harsh social policy retrenchment programme ex ante. Often parties that embrace market-liberal social policy reform after the election are elected on rather moderate or even social protectionist policy platforms they subsequently abandon contingent upon their competitors' ability to take on the mantle of social protection. After a term in office, however, during which retrenchment policies coincide with and, at least according to the interpretation of the governing parties, cause an economic recovery, market liberalizers as government incumbents in the second electoral bout may successfully run on their record and on promising more of the same, particularly if their opponents enjoy little credibility in delivering different and better results.[6] Thus, while there is a difference between implementing retrenchment policies and advertising them in electoral contests, the competitive configuration may allow governing parties sometimes to advertise unpopular policies without becoming concerned about voter defection. This applies to all parties with government incumbency after a round of policy retrenchments, but not to social democratic parties of the left that are confined to the opposition benches.

Electoral Trade-offs and Social Policy Reform

Even if a major party in government adopts unpopular social policies while simultaneously depriving its key rivals from rallying sufficient support to form an alternative majority after the subsequent election, social retrenchment

[5] On the role of outcome-oriented voter evaluations of parties in government incumbency, see Stokes and Baughman 1998.

[6] Most of the time, however, even then they will promise to sweeten reforms with selective measures of compensation for the losers.

policy may be costly in terms of electoral support for the governing party. For the sake of maximizing its bargaining power over government office, that party may be forced to sacrifice the votes of former supporters now disgruntled by the party's new social policies. These votes may accrue to new social protest parties or existing minor parties in the centre or on the left of the political spectrum. In other words, the office-seeking ambition of party strategists conflicts with the vote-seeking objective simultaneously supported by most activists and party leaders (Kitschelt 1994*b*: ch. 4 and Kitschelt 1999). Parties will be more inclined to embrace social policy retrenchment, if the trade-off between office- and vote-seeking strategies is likely to be mild at subsequent elections. For social democrats and labour parties, the existence of significant post-communist and left-libertarian parties, both of which are likely to become the recipients of disappointed social democratic voters sharpens the trade-off between office- and vote-seeking objectives and makes them more hesitant to embrace social policy retrenchment. For Christian democratic conservatives, the main threat may be small centrist or moderate social democratic parties supporting the welfare state in credible ways. Even market-liberal parties must carefully ponder how far to go in their pre-election appeals or their post-election policies as government parties in order to contain their electoral losses to parties more friendly to the welfare state. But market-liberals do not face a strategic trade-off. More radical reform initiatives are likely to reduce attainment of both their vote- and office-seeking objectives. But there is no linear relationship between cause and effect. Up to a certain point of reform commitment, market-liberals may still keep the opposition at bay because of its lack of credibility and/or its inability to form an alliance that could displace the market-liberal party.

Inertia of Intra-Party Strategic Capabilities

Political parties face difficulties in revising their political appeals and practical policies when they are tied down by a large apparatus of organized constituencies that participate in intra-party policy making. Either directly or indirectly, these constituents may derive an economic rent from maintaining a party strategy that endorses the welfare state status quo, prompting party leaders to oppose welfare state retrenchment if they are compelled to comply with internal organizational mechanisms of accountability. In social democratic mass parties, this strategic thrust characterizes labour union constituencies, particularly those in the public sector. In centrist and conservative mass parties, protected industrial sectors (agriculture, retail, etc.) and in all types of parties retirees and recipients of public health insurance schemes fight against social policy retrenchment.

What increases a party's strategic flexibility in revising its policy stances is a two-pronged organizational alternative to the classical mass membership party organization. On one side, party leaders in elected legislative or executive office gain more autonomy at the expense of the rank-and-file working through formal channels of intra-party deliberation and leadership accountability. On the other side, a numerical reduction of the membership yielding a transition from 'mass' to 'framework' party would make it more likely that relatively small groups of new entrants who push for a new strategy influence intra-party preference aggregation and overcome the status-quo lobbies (Kitschelt 1994*b*: ch. 5).[7] The problem of party strategy is thus not simply an ideological membership pitted against a pragmatic, office-seeking leadership (cf. Kitschelt 1989). The real problem is to increase the strategic responsiveness of parties to new competitive opportunities both from the bottom, via an entry of militants with fresh ideas, as well as from the top of the party, by enabling leaders to create some strategic degrees of freedom in their decision making process.

The problems of parties' strategic inertia are exacerbated, if citizen–party linkages are not based on programmatic party alternatives, as Downs (1957) and almost the entire literature on party competition in Western polities assumes, but on clientelist linkages. In the programmatic mode, parties engage in an indirect exchange with voters. Provided they obtain a favourable legislative and executive position, parties commit themselves to the realization of policies through legislation that will benefit voter constituencies, regardless of whether such individual beneficiaries have actually supported the party in the election. By contrast, in the clientelist mode, parties engage in a direct exchange with citizens where those who provide votes and financial resources to the party receive tangible, selective benefits in return, such as material gifts, public sector jobs, housing, favourable regulatory decisions, or public works contracts. Whether parties affiliate with voters based on direct clientelist or indirect programmatic exchanges hinges upon a host of conditions, such as the economic affluence of electoral constituencies, the professionalization of the state apparatus, the design of electoral systems and the relative magnitude of public sector employment. Electoral rules that personalize the relationship between voters and politicians promote direct clientelist exchanges.[8]

The impact of direct or indirect exchanges on welfare state retrenchment is complex. On the one hand, direct clientelist exchanges may facilitate social policy retrenchment. Since voters care more about the immediate direct tangible benefits they receive from politicians they support than the

---

[7] High leverage of small rank-and-file groups does not necessarily promote a strategic revision of social policy support in the direction of retrenchment. But it increases the volatility of a party's strategic stance and creates favourable organizational conditions for social policy retrenchment, when the political and economic climate leads to the entry of new activists supporting such positions.

[8] The institutional conditions of electoral personalization are detailed in Carey and Shugart (1995). A state-centred comparative-historical argument is advanced by Shefter (1978).

social policies that determine the disbursement of public benefits according to universalist criteria, politicians might buy their support for retrenchment programmes through clientelist side-payments. On the other side, where clientelist networks are crucial linkages between parties and citizens, the universalistic welfare state may already have a merely residual character and thus offer few opportunities for retrenchment. Instead, most social policy expenditure is funnelled through clientelist networks, such as unions and social welfare organizations subsidiary to the parties and directly benefits party constituencies. Such clientelist arrangements that penetrate, complement, or substitute for an encompassing welfare state tend to involve expensive public resource transfers into the hands of special interest constituencies with great leverage over party politicians. Policies of market liberalization would have to target such arrangements for cutbacks and institutional redesign rather than whatever universalistic social programmes exist. It is therefore primarily new outsider politicians and parties not entangled into such clientelist networks that are likely candidates to engage in social policy retrenchment activities. On balance, party systems that emphasize clientelist voter–party linkages may be more resistant to social policy retrenchment or market liberalization more generally than those relying on programmatic competition.

The Salience of Economic-Distributive Policy Conflict as a Dimension of Party Competition

The three variables mentioned so far presuppose that the main competitive divide in party systems is over economic distributive issues (arguments 1 and 2) and/or that clientelist networks trump whatever programmatic divides are detectable in party systems. But what if all or at least some influential parties in a democratic polity compete on other programmatic dimensions than economic distribution, such as socio-cultural divides over religion, environmental quality of life, multiculturalism, or moral conduct? A programmatic divide between parties constitutes a competitive dimension, if the elasticity of voters' electoral choices is highly contingent upon politicians' appeals. Politicians then have more reason to fight for voters by advertising the party's positions on this issue dimension than on dimensions of 'identification' where voters' opinions shape their party preferences, but modifications of party stances yield little elasticity in voters' party support (Sani and Sartori 1983).

Intuitively, one might expect that politicians enjoy greater freedom to engage in welfare state retrenchment the less economics constitutes a competitive dimension. Partisan supporters primarily observe signals parties send on non-economic issues and ignore whatever new initiatives they take on social policy retrenchment. More likely, however, the causality that links voter choices to politicians' appeals also has to be constructed in reverse order. Parties appeal to certain issue stances not just because voters find such issues salient for their choice, but voters' evaluations of salience is at least partially predicated on whether politicians advance alternative positions on an issue dimension. Thus, in Western democracies, the salience of socio-cultural, non-economic divides in the process of party competition is closely intertwined with and predicated on a broad 'centrist' agreement of all major parties on a mixed economy with a comprehensive welfare state. Social policy would become a competitive dimension, if some politicians find it advantageous to abandon this inter-party consensus. This option, however, is not all that attractive to politicians in all established parties for at least two reasons.

First, parties that question the underlying social policy consensus run a high risk of dividing their own electorates and disorganizing their support constituencies without reaping much electoral gain from other parties, provided the latter do not politicize social policy in parallel, internally divisive fashion, a process that would produce a general dealignment of voters from parties. Because of these transaction costs of policy innovation in established parties, the initiative to press for novel competitive dimensions usually comes from entirely new political parties.[9] At the same time, given the resources needed and transaction costs to be incurred in building new parties with a market-liberal appeal, the absence of established market-liberal parties (proposition 1) and of competition on the economic dimension makes it less likely that electorally strong parties advocating social policy retrenchment will appear.

Second, when pondering unpopular social policy retrenchment, the leading conventional parties find themselves in a prisoner's dilemma situation. Even if politicians in all major parties see social policy retrenchment not merely as a redistributive measure favouring affluent constituencies, but as a collective good that accrues to all citizens by boosting economic growth and a country's international competitiveness, no individual party may have the incentive of bringing about that good in a situation where all its competitors are credible 'centrist' supporters of the welfare state status quo.[10] These competitors would promptly exploit the governing parties' implementation of unpopular social policy measures to improve their own electoral standing

[9] Riker (1982) argues that parties permanently reduced to the status of an opposition minority party in an existing hegemonic competitive dimension will invent a new competitive dimension that tends to divide the ruling party internally. This strategy, however, is more difficult to engineer than Riker presumes because of the political transaction costs incurred by the challenging party in the process of building and maintaining a partisan coalition on the new dimension. Established parties therefore try to map new issues onto an existing unidimensional space of competition rather than risk their own integrity through cross-cutting divides or confusing voters with limited capabilities for cognitive processing. This argument can be developed from Hinich and Munger's (1994) instructive work on political ideology.

[10] In a different language, one can also characterize the dilemma of party politicians as one of choosing between the party's current popularity ('legitimation') and its probable future success based on choosing the appropriate economic and social policy ('accumulation'). Alber's (1996) work reminded me of this distinction originally found in Offe's (1972) seminal articles.

at the expense of the government party. Trapped in this prisoners' dilemma, party systems with only centrist parties in social policy terms that credibly defend the welfare state status quo and structure inter-party competition primarily around socio-political rather than socio-economic themes will deliver unpopular social reform only if all the major competitors can be incorporated in a 'grand coalition' for social retrenchment and thus engineer a 'blame diffusion' across the political spectrum.[11] Such over-sized grand coalitions, however, are rare occurrences confined to solving problems where no party can reap immediate benefits by abstaining or defecting from an agreement. This might apply to extraordinary crisis situations or to social policy problems that allow all participants to discount distributive effects at this time, such as very long-term changes of social security schemes, induced by inevitable demographic changes.

This is not the place to describe and explain why some party systems are more or less configured around economic or socio-cultural partisan divides.[12] Socio-cultural divides in the 1980s and 1990s are particularly salient in polities that earlier on had vibrant religious or other communitarian divides. Moreover, an encompassing welfare state, generating a large group of public or quasi-public employees in social services with often high educational skills contributes to the rise of salient left-libertarian socio-cultural views and tends to shift the competitive axes of party systems from economic to socio-cultural issues. The extent to which socio-cultural or economic conflicts inspire party competition cannot be gleaned directly from the opinion divides among citizens, but from the ways in which political parties combine economic and socio-cultural issue positions. In Anglo-Saxon countries, with residual welfare states and a history of economic policy conflict, parties divide primarily on economic issues whereas economic leftists are only marginally more libertarian than their economically rightist counterparts (Britain, New Zealand, Australia).[13] To a lesser extent these conditions also apply to the United States, where both distributive and communitarian socio-cultural conflicts have played a role over long periods of time. The socio-economic distributive conflict tends to be prevalent also among Scandinavian parties, although early communitarian-cultural conflicts and later the development of encompassing welfare states have given socio-cultural conflicts a higher profile that has been mapped onto their party systems.

By contrast to the Anglo-Saxon countries and Scandinavia, socio-cultural cleavages have always been more important for the party competition of Austria, Belgium, France, Germany, Italy, and the Netherlands. Whereas socio-cultural divides crystallized around religious themes in the past, they

[11] For the importance of dispersing blame, see Pierson 1994.

[12] For a discussion of this issue, see McGann and Kitschelt (1995) and McGann (1999).

[13] For empirical data pertaining to these comparative judgements in various European countries, compare Kitschelt (1994*b*: ch. 4) and Kitschelt, in collaboration with McGann (1995).

have now moved on to a host of new and overlapping controversies only a few of which are directly derivative of the old religious themes (gender and abortion, but not multiculturalism or ecology). In a somewhat different vein, the salience of socio-cultural issues also was high in Japan, where the ruling Liberal Democrats through economic growth and clientelist politics managed to depoliticize class and economic divides at least since the 1960s (Pempel 1998). Japan experienced, however, a rather sharp political-cultural division over the '1955 system', defined by Japan's American-designed constitution and its alliance with the United States (Sakano 1997). This divide collapsed with the end of the Cold War and the entry of the Social Democratic Party into government in 1994.

Public opinion data analysed by Wren and Iversen (1997) show that the cross-nationally different competitive dimensions that divide electoral constituencies also correlate with variance in the depth of economic-distributive disagreements among competing parties, as reflected by national political opinion. In Anglo-Saxon and Scandinavian countries where economic policy divides are clearly more salient than socio-cultural divides, the followers of different parties disagree not only about the size of the public sector, but also about standards of wage equality, with 'rightist' parties calling for small public sectors and merit-based wages, while 'leftist' parties advocate large public sectors and wage equality (Britain, Denmark, Norway, Sweden). At the other extreme, countries where party competition has emphasized socio-cultural themes to a greater extent, partisan divisions in the economic sphere primarily concern the size of the public sector, but not questions of wage equality. In some countries all parties support merit-based wage structures (Austria, Germany, Italy), while in others, such as Japan, all parties, including the Liberal Democrats, endorse egalitarian wages. Also in the United States, Belgium, France, and the Netherlands parties of the left are much more in favour of a large public sector, but only slightly more pro-wage equality than their conservative counterparts. Here we find an intermediate linkage that reflects party systems in which competition has always crystallized around both economic and socio-cultural themes.

The important and at first sight counter-intuitive proposition that follows from considering the impact of dimensions of party competition for social policy reform is that it is not the strength of social democratic or labour parties, per se, that impedes social policy retrenchment, as centre of gravity propositions of responsible partisan government would have it, but a partisan alignment of government and opposition parties in which competition is situated primarily on a socio-cultural dimension and all major established parties are credible defenders of the welfare state. In other words, social democrats in countries with consensual social policy appeal across the competitive spectrum may be less inclined to push for social policy retrenchment than their counterparts in countries with a clear economic-distributive divide, even if social democrats are electorally much more powerful in the latter! In such configurations, social democrats may find it to their advantage to take the wind out of their market-liberal competitors' sails by embarking on social policy retrenchment unpopular with social democratic core supporters, but perceived as necessary by social democratic politicians to preserve the country's economic performance and thus the future electability of social democratic governments. Here social democrats are not facing the prisoner's dilemma that the opposition can exploit the government party's provision of a collective good, because those 'bourgeois' opposition parties cannot credibly present themselves as defenders of the welfare state and hope to gain the support of disaffected social democrats at subsequent elections. Social democrats in countries without major social policy divide face a rather different strategic configuration involving the prisoner's dilemma as characterized above. Here embracing retrenchment policies would drive social democratic core supporters into the arms of other political parties who have contributed to the expansion of the welfare state and can credibly promise the defence of institutions against retrenchment in their efforts to undercut an unpopular social democratic government.

Alternative Configurations of Party Competition

Four variables influence the extent to which alternative configurations of party competition offer politicians opportunities to pursue unpopular social policy retrenchment with an office-seeking objective in mind: (1) the existence of liberal parties and of credible welfare state protectors; (2) the electoral trade-off faced by social policy retrenchers; (3) the strategic flexibility provided by existing party organizations to enable militants and party leaders to choose new policies; and (4) the alignment of party competition around economic or non-economic policy dimensions. Even if we simply dichotomize the values on each of these four variables, we obtain sixteen different configurations offering conditions more or less favourable to social policy retrenchment. Fortunately, there is some empirical association among the values on these variables so that for empirical comparative purposes it is sufficient to highlight four configurations, with the remainder relegated to the universe of counterfactual shadow cases. Let me underline again that my assessment of the conduciveness each of these configurations has for social policy retrenchment focuses on the net effect of political parties' strategic configuration within the system of democratic competition. In all cases, conditions external to the party system, such as an economic performance crisis (rising unemployment, net capital outflow, weakening balance of trade) or the past trajectory of welfare state expansion or contraction modify the chances that politicians embrace social policy retrenchment, but such forces are mediated by politicians' strategic calculations contingent on party system structure.

Configuration 1: United Market-Liberals versus United Social Democrats

In this configuration, the dimension of competition is centred on economics, with voter constituencies and their parties disagreeing both about the appropriate size of the public sector/welfare state and about wage equality. The dominant actors in this scenario are two major parties, one more redistributive and the other more market-liberal, and radical blackmail parties of the left and right are feeble. The market-liberal right is likely to blame economic problems on the size of the public economy and to create public uneasiness about state involvement in the economy (endogenous preference formation against the welfare state). These efforts are particularly successful in countries where economic crisis under governments of the left and a radicalization of left parties has undermined the credibility of leftist welfare state defence (empirical reference case: Britain in the 1970s and 1980s).[14] If the left still has social policy credibility, it may adopt a policy of wait and see when faced with a conservative government, hoping that market-liberal reforms prove reversible when such governments fall over unpopular social policy reforms. Alternatively, and particularly when in government office, the left may engage in a pre-emptory strike to embrace social policy retrenchment to steal the right-wing opposition's thunder at least to the extent that the left firmly controls the median voter (empirical reference cases: New Zealand and Australia in the 1980s).[15] Given the absence of credible left-libertarian parties, social democrats may expect only small losses among more radical voters due to abstentions or efforts to support new and ineffective leftist parties. If the left is initially in opposition to a conservative government that vigorously advances cutbacks on social policy because the left has lost credibility, it will sooner or later be compelled to buy into the conservative social policy reform agenda, if it ever wants to capture the median voter again and rule the country (empirical reference cases: Britain and the United States in the 1990s).

Configuration 2: Divided Market-Liberals and Centrists Versus United Social Democrats

Also in this configuration, the critical dimension of competition is still primarily centred on economics, even though libertarian-authoritarian socio-cultural themes matter a bit more (due to the size of the welfare state and communitarian discursive traditions). Here, the main centre-left social

---

[14] In my view, it is more important whether the left still has credibility as protector of the welfare state in order to explain the vigour with which market liberal governments pursue welfare state retrenchment than whether the right has a slim or large majority (Garrett 1993). Slim majorities may be durable, if the left is discredited by its intra-party politics and past record.

[15] I ignore here the rather substantial differences in the policy choices of Australian and New Zealand labour governments. See Castles, Gerritsen and Vowles (1996).

democratic and centre-right liberal and conservative parties are typically complemented by left-libertarian and right-authoritarian blackmail competitors. In this environment, market-liberal parties will make vigorous efforts to reform social policy in the direction of retrenchment, when in office and faced with a conducive economic policy climate. Social democrats, by contrast, face difficult trade-offs in this situation. In order to win or retain the median voter, a pre-emptive strike against the right (which cannot attract supporters of the welfare state) may be advantageous. But the electoral costs of such a strategy may entail a substantial loss of voters to radical leftist and libertarian parties. For social democrats, office- and vote-seeking strategies pose difficult trade-offs that can be managed only by flexible party organizations (see Kitschelt 1994*b*: chs. 4 and 5, 1996, 1999). Empirical reference cases for this dilemma are Denmark and Sweden. In both instances, social democrats may cultivate a 'new progressivist' discourse that recognizes how the creation of large public sectors and encompassing social policies has generated new privileged groups, particularly those of public sector employees, even social democrats should restrict in the name of public administrative efficiency and social equity considerations. This new progressivism in social reform affirms competition in the provision of social services and market incentives to improve the use of public resources. Political calculations permit social democrats to move to the right because disaffected voters can turn only to left-libertarian parties who are strategically captives of coalitions with more moderate social democrats. When these losses become heavy, however, social democratic parties may encounter internal disagreements as to whether vote maximizing strategies (catering to public opinion on social policy) or office-maximizing strategies (moving to the right on social policy issues and depriving non-socialist parties of a working majority) are the more beneficial objective to be pursued by the parties. A strong leadership and limited organizational entrenchment in a mass membership and labour union ties facilitate pursuit of the office-maximizing strategy.

Configuration 3: A Three-Way Divide between Liberals, Centre, and Social Democrats

Against the backdrop of long-standing communitarian socio-cultural conflict and a comprehensive welfare state, the dominant dimension of political competition is more strongly configured around the contrast between libertarians and authoritarians, dividing Christian democrats from social democrats and liberals. Nevertheless, economic issues, and particularly conflicts over the size of the welfare state, remain salient, particularly in an environment of economic crisis. Both Christian and social democratic parties have a reputation as protectors of the welfare state that is sometimes reinforced by patronage networks in the public sector and the partial delegation of responsibilities for policy implementation tasks to Christian and socialist organizational networks.

Nevertheless, such systems still contain electorally significant market-liberal parties that go back to powerful liberal movements in the nineteenth century (Luebbert 1991).

With the resurgence of economic problems and a waning enthusiasm for statist solutions, these parties have made a significant electoral comeback to about one-fifth of the vote. This success allows the liberals to reinvigorate political competition around issues of economic distribution and governance. It pits them against both Christian democrats and social democrats. Nevertheless, at least two reasons may tempt either party to make concessions to the market-liberal policy programme. First, they may care about the viability of the economy ('accumulation'), affecting their long-term electoral viability, just as much as their short-term electoral popularity ('legitimation'), particularly if they are rather autonomous cadre parties with a relatively flexible leadership. Second, they may seek to satisfy their office-seeking ambitions through alliances with the liberals.

If Christian democrats join a coalition with a liberal party, their willingness to embrace social policy retrenchment is still tempered by the existence of a credible and powerful alternative protector of the welfare state, the social democratic party in opposition. Alternatively, Christian democrats may contain the liberal parties' regained momentum to seek market-liberal retrenchment by joining coalitions with social democrats. Such alliances can promote social policy retrenchment also against public misgivings because liberal parties are no credible protectors of the welfare state. The greatest electoral risk for such coalition partners is the future loss of votes to left-libertarian parties or to new social policy protest parties (retirees, new leftist parties). Empirical reference cases for this configuration are Belgium, the Netherlands, and, with some qualifications due to its unique system of governance, Switzerland in the 1980s and 1990s. It is also conceivable that Austria and Italy since the erosion or outright collapse of the post-World War II party systems in the early 1990s begin to resemble the strategic configuration in the Low Countries, but not enough time has elapsed to yield social policy results that would converge on those of Belgium or the Netherlands.

Configuration 4: Weak Liberals, Strong Centre, and Strong Social Democrats

Here the communitarian discourse, the legacy of socio-cultural inter-party conflict and the nature of the welfare state have configured the competitive dimension primarily around the conflict between 'modern' libertarian politics and 'traditional' conservatism and authoritarianism, whether running under Christian democratic or other labels. Parties of the centre-right tend to be hegemonic organizations with distinctly conservative socio-cultural appeals, but a socio-economic compromise position that permits them to incorporate significant elements of the working class and of domestic protected economic sectors. These parties face social democratic counterparts with equally moderate positions on economic and social policy-making, but a more distinctly libertarian electorate and core activists. Both major parties have to cope with blackmail parties supporting more extreme authoritarian or libertarian socio-cultural positions. Liberal parties, by contrast, have remained weak and unable to gain momentum around a strictly antistatist position that would insist on a profound liberalization of capital and labour markets.

Because of the weakness of liberalism, only centrist parties can effectively push social policy retrenchment in this configuration. At the same time, as cross-class alliances that decisively contributed to the building of contemporary welfare states, such a strategic shift would make centrist parties run the risk of losing significant voter constituencies and a reputation for being a protector of the welfare state. Moreover, moderately leftist social democratic parties are waiting in the wings to assert their own social policy credibility, were centrist parties to adopt social policy retrenchment. Faced with these risks, Christian democrats have few incentives to push social policy retrenchment. At the same time, social democrats see no reason to engage in a pre-emptive strike and adopt social policy cutbacks, because Christian democrats would be the natural electoral beneficiaries of such policies, if the latter remain in the opposition where they can present themselves as credible protectors of the welfare state. In this configuration, only social democratic–Christian democratic coalitions that prevent either party from blaming the other for welfare cutbacks may be sufficiently daring to engage in painful social policy changes. Given the existence of radical left-libertarian and right-authoritarian parties and relatively modest thresholds for the entry of new competitors, such 'grand coalitions', however, may be electorally costly to both coalition partners and are thus quite unattractive.

Empirical reference cases for this configuration are all the countries with weak market-liberal parties, but either hegemonic centrist parties or a close competition between centre and moderate left, such as Austria, France, Germany, Italy, and Japan. All five countries experienced a disruption of democracy in the inter-war period and later gave rise to strong centrist hegemonic party blocs that welded together inter-class and urban–rural coalitions in the 1940s or 1950s (Pempel 1990). These coalitions are often based on patronage and clientelist networks just as much as a social class compromise built around a comprehensive welfare state or, in Japan's case, the functional equivalent of a system of labour relations and a financial governance structure that created very high employment security and private social policy safety nets. The hegemony of the centrist parties in these countries may have lasted so long because of the reputation they acquired based

TABLE 9.2. *The performance of incumbent parties from the 1960s to the latest election in the 1990s (% of cast votes)*

	1960–9 average performance	Latest performance	Change in performance
Configuration 1			
United Kingdom	88.7	73.9 (1997)	−13.8
New Zealand	99.1	62.4 (1997)	−36.7
Australia	97.8	85.6 (1996)	−12.2
United States	95.0	90.2 (1996)	−4.8
Configuration 2			
Sweden	93.2	69.1 (1998)	−24.3
Denmark	93.8	84.8 (1994)	−9.0
Configuration 3			
Belgium	91.7	83.6 (1995)	−8.1
Netherlands	85.4	77.2 (1994)	−8.2
Configuration 4			
Austria	96.4	66.4 (1995)	−30.2
France	92.7	67.6 (1997)	−25.1
Germany	95.1	82.4 (1998)	−12.7
Italy	95.0	45.4 (1996)	−49.6
Japan	90.9	52.2 (1996)	−38.7

on their success in the post-war decades.[16] In these five countries, I would expect the greatest obstacles to social policy reform, even in economic and demographic crisis situations.

The political inertia resulting from the strategic abstention of all major parties from daring policy reform initiatives may lead to a widespread sense of popular malaise and disaffection with the entire party system as a whole that manifests itself in the rapid decline of established parties in the late 1980s. Table 9.2 provides average electoral support for each country's major established parties in the 1960s compared to the levels of support for the same set of parties in the mid- to late 1990s. With the exception of Germany, the

---

[16] Voters engage in a Bayesian process of updating their expectations about party efficacy based on prior experience. Where this experience was positive, at least older voters hold on to hegemonic parties, even when their effectiveness manifestly declines. For a development of this argument in the case of Mexican party competition, see Magaloni (1997). A further argument for the maintenance of partisan hegemony can be derived from McGann's (1999) theory of party competition and empirical research on European democracies. If voter distributions on a competitive dimension are skewed to the left or the right and party activists make strategic appeals in the middle of a party's market, then parties that are located along the fat, long tail of the voters' preference distribution systematically will be pulled away from the densest areas of voter preference. This makes it difficult for them to coalesce among themselves and puts them at a disadvantage to hegemonic parties, situated in the most densely packed region of voter distribution.

losses of the major parties are greater in countries characterized by configuration 4 than in any other country except New Zealand which moved to a more proportional electoral system in 1995. In Italy and Japan, where a greater disproportionality of the new electoral system should have strengthened the largest existing parties, quite the reverse happened. In all instances, almost invariably the losses of the established parties translated into gains of entirely new parties, not the expansion of former fringe parties.

A comparison of configurations 1 through 4 reveals how the empirical puzzle for simple cabinet centre of gravity/responsible government models of policy choice can be resolved that leftist social democratic party governments might sometimes opt for more retrenchment-oriented social policies than governments dominated by centrist parties. It all depends on the existence of credible alternative protectors of the welfare state in the arena of party competition and their electoral threat potential that may prevent vote- or office-seeking politicians from embracing social programme cutbacks.

2. SOCIAL POLICY RETRENCHMENT AND PARTY COMPETITION: COMPARATIVE CASE STUDIES

In configuration 1, with bipolar competition between market-liberals and social democrats, responsible party government theories provide rather straightforward explanations of the dynamics of welfare state retrenchment, provided they relax the assumptions of the median voter theorem, as can be illustrated with the British case.[17] While the disastrous performance of the 1974–9 Labour government led to a decline of public support for social services (Pettersen 1995: 206), public opinion alone cannot explain Thatcher's victory on a radical retrenchment platform. Key was the loss of Labour Party credibility and its radicalization to the left before and after 1979. This process eventually prompted the exit of the social democratic moderates from Labour and the emergence of a centrist third party that split the opposition, making it easier for Thatcher's conservatives to maintain a majority of seats with a minority of votes in the British first-past-the-post single-member district electoral system. Nevertheless, in causal terms, the radicalization of Labour, not the resulting split of the opposition to Thatcher's Government, provides the key for understanding the policy leverage of the Tory government in the 1980s. The absence of credibility on the side of parties defending the welfare state (proposition 1), the absence of unattractive trade-offs between vote- and office-seeking objectives for the governing party

---

[17] For the theoretical reconstruction of intra- and inter-party dynamics in British politics, see Robertson (1976), Kitschelt (1989 and 1994b: 178–81, 249–52).

(proposition 2), intra-party politics in the Labour Party and in the Conservatives (proposition 3), and the general configuration of British politics around distributive-economic issues (proposition 4) were all favourable to profound social policy reversal promoted by the Conservatives.

Because configuration 1, exemplified by the British case, is intuitively obvious and widely analysed, I will now turn to the more complicated and sometimes counterintuitive trajectories in party system configurations 2 through 4 and discuss one country for each competitive alignment. For each case, let us empirically distinguish 'push factors', relating to the political-economic and mass demand for retrenchment of the state economy, including social expenditure, and 'pull factors' capturing politicians' opportunities to promote retrenchment with the prospect of 'electoral survival'. Since I am engaging in a heuristic and qualitative comparison of cases, I score countries in judgmental ways on a variety of indicators without a definitive set of quantitative variables. On the push side, judgmental indicators concern the intensity of economic crisis between the two oil shocks (the 1970s, actually from 1973 to 1983), the rest of the 1980s, and the 1990s during the long (American) boom and stock market asset inflation. A second indicator concerns the public mood about changes in social policy, as influenced by the solvency of the main social insurance systems, combined with the country's recent trajectory of social policy changes. Prospects for cutbacks are most promising where benefits and entitlements have recently been expanded, but now run into fiscal problems. They are least promising where the system is in fiscal balance after a round of unpopular retrenchments.

On the pull side, I score different aspects of the party systems' competitive configuration in order to capture propositions 1 and 2 above. How strong are market-liberal parties, centrist cross-class parties, and left-libertarian blackmail parties? These configurations change within countries over time, just as do the push conditions of economic-demographic retrenchment imperatives and (exogenous) public opinion moods about the welfare state. Two other factors are more or less fixed over the relevant time from the 1970s through the 1990s so that cross-national levels vary more than intra-national domestic conditions. One is the extent to which electoral competitiveness is configured around economic issues (proposition 4). The other is the extent to which mass-elite linkages (clientelist or policy?) and party organization (flexible 'cadre' or inert 'mass' parties) constrain politicians' strategic mobility (proposition 3).

Where both push and pull factors are strong, welfare state retrenchment is both necessary from the perspective of the imperative of economic 'accumulation' as well as possible from the viewpoint of political 'legitimation', i.e. the support of parties that venture into unpopular policy reforms. The reverse situation of little economic necessity nor political feasibility characterizes social policy throughout much of the expansion of social policy

from the 1950s to the early 1970s. Particularly interesting, of course, are
the asymmetric configurations, where social policy retrenchment appears
necessary, but politically difficult to engineer, or where it is economically
unnecessary, but politically feasible. In the latter configuration, reform is what
Huber and Stephens (in this volume) call purely 'ideological' reform. Over
the past twenty years, economic imperatives to engage in reform became
more intense in Germany, Japan, the Netherlands, and Sweden, but the political feasibility of such measures varies significantly across countries. Where
feasibility is limited, governments have either shied away from reform or,
where they eventually embarked on it, have suffered devastating electoral
defeats that brought to power rather different partisan configurations.

Sweden

Sweden experienced significant economic stress in the 1970s that waned
after a sharp currency devaluation in the early 1980s only to return again
in the late 1980s and intensify in the 1990s (Huber and Stephens 1998). Welfare
state expenditures and programmes kept expanding throughout the 1980s,
unimpeded by a six-year spell of non-socialist government dominated by
centrist forces between 1976 and 1982. In the course of that experience, and
particularly during the brief intensification of Sweden's economic crisis
during the second oil shock, the market-liberal Moderates gradually gained
ground at the expense of the Centre Party and the Swedish People's Party
within the non-socialist party spectrum. With the onset of the deep economic crisis of the early 1990s, characterized by falling investments, very large
public sector deficits, and rising unemployment, the Swedish party system
looked quite different than in the late 1970s. A weakened centre and a much
stronger market-liberal right were pitted against a social democracy facing
increasing competition from a libertarian left both on economic and socio-
cultural issues. In this situation, the Swedish social democrats in office began
to make rather sharp cutbacks in universalistic social programmes (sickness
insurance, pensions), continued to support this policy after a bourgeois minority government took office in 1992, and actually intensified the programme
retrenchment upon returning to office in 1995.[18] The reforms of Sweden's
superannuation pension scheme (ATP) in the mid-1990s, instituting tighter
rules on income qualifying for replacement by pensions and a changed
formula for calculating pension adjustments based on life expectancy that
is unfavourable to retirees, according to a probably pessimistic estimate sub-
mitted by labour union (LO) analysts might imply for someone employed for

---

[18] For a detailed empirical analysis of these programme cuts in comparison to social
policy retrenchment in Germany, see the diploma thesis by Schludi (1997) and the paper by
Anderson (1998).

40 years and contributing the maximum a fall from 65 per cent of her last wage to only 50 per cent of that wage.[19] Moreover, Sweden is a trailblazer by introducing a funded, contributions-defined component to its retirement plan consisting of 'investible' ATP contributions that constitute probably the most significant departure of a European social security scheme from pay-as-you-go financing outside Britain. Wage compensation for sickness was cut to 75 per cent of the wage, after one waiting day without compensation, and the collective bargaining parties have been legally prohibited from compensating such cuts by private wage agreements. It is true that some of these retrenchment measures have been partially repealed, as Sweden's economy recovered in the second half of the 1990s and the budget moved into surplus, but what is critical for my argument is that Swedish politicians, in contrast to their counterparts in other countries, in a challenging economic environment are able to take drastic politically unpopular action. In the light of these and other reforms, such as the insertion of competition into an increasingly decentralized public sector, Sweden appears to have undergone a probably more profound change of the welfare state than many other countries, when measured against the status quo ante of the mid- to late 1980s.[20] It must be kept in mind, of course, that these changes have taken place from a very high plateau of social expenditure and coverage and preserve basic distributive and organizational principles of the Swedish welfare state (Swank 1997). But for politicians, it is the change rate of programme benefits and institutional arrangements that matters more for their electoral prospects and abilities to govern than inherited programme levels and structures.

Social democrats paid for their leading role in social retrenchment policies in the 1989–92 and 1995–8 terms with very significant declines of electoral support. But in each case, the competitive configuration of the party system provided a rationale to embark on policies attending to the imperatives of 'accumulation' rather than those of 'legitimation'. Social democratic voters disaffected with social policy retrenchment certainly could not turn to the more market-liberal bourgeois opposition parties and thus found themselves with limited alternatives to voice their dissatisfaction. In 1992, many disaffected social democrats and new voters supported a maverick protest and flash party, the New Democrats, whereas in 1998 they opted for the post-communist Left Party. In both instances, the social democratic electoral losses did not empower a market-liberal right with a legislative majority and they thus did not substantially reduce the social democrats' bargaining power over policy (1992–5) or their capacity to hold executive office (after 1998).

---

[19] This LO paper is cited in Schludi (1997: 48).

[20] Scholarly opinion on the Swedish reforms varies from qualifying it as a major change (Schwartz 1994*c*; Clayton and Pontusson 1998) to a greater emphasis on the resilience of the existing system (Pierson 1996; Stephens, Huber, and Ray 1999).

Because the Swedish social democratic leadership has gained strategic manoeuvring space both vis-à-vis its large mass organization as well as the unions since the 1980s and thus could extend its time horizon over which to calculate political benefits and losses, the alternative to the retrenchment strategy was not very palatable. A populist policy supporting the party's core electorate would have maximized votes in the short run, but is likely to yield economic problems of accumulation in the longer run that then would set the stage for the ascent of market-liberal parties to electoral dominance with the consequence of much more dramatic departures from the Scandinavian model of the mixed economy.

Netherlands

This country belongs to configuration 3 with a significant liberal party, matched by stronger centrist-Christian and social democratic party formations and a growing left-libertarian sector. In the political climate of the 1970s and early 1980s, neither social democrats nor Christian democrats dared to engage in retrenchment. These strategies in an environment of declining economic performance and rising fiscal deficits contributed to a significant strengthening of the liberal pole in the Dutch political system. When the Dutch political economy slid into an intense crisis with close to one-sixth of those seeking jobs in unemployment, the Christian democrats finally entered a coalition with the liberals to bring about an economic policy reversal. But as a centrist force, they did not dare to touch major social spending pro-grammes, given that the social democrats were lurking in the opposition as the credible defenders of the welfare state. The liberal–Christian coalition did, however, manage to cut back public sector wages. The government's threatening demeanour towards the unions convinced the collective bargain-ing partners to resume corporatist bargaining resulting in a policy of low wage increases to improve the competitiveness of the Dutch economy.[21] It is no accident that the initial *Wassenaar* agreement in 1982 followed two days on the heels of a then shocking government programme presented by the incoming liberal-Christian democratic coalition to impose drastic budget cuts and a wage freeze, if business and labour were unable to agree on a low wage strategy (Visser and Hemerijck 1997).

The task of reining in on skyrocketing social expenditures, particularly on long-term disability payments, a convenient way to move almost one million of sometimes quite young unemployed citizens out of the labour market by the early 1990s, on sickness insurance costs, and on pensions, however,

---

[21] The authoritative account of Dutch economic and social policy change in the 1980s and 1990s is Visser and Hemerijk (1997). See also their earlier accounts in Hemerijk (1995) and Visser (1997).

could not be addressed in a Christian–liberal coalition government that left the Dutch Labour Party as the stalwart of welfare state protection in the opposition, ready to benefit from the disappointments the Christian democrats' inevitably had to inflict on their own electoral constituencies in pursuing such a policy. The all-out attack on the existing system of social protection thus began only in 1989, when the liberals were punished for their reformist zeal in the parliamentary election and the existing coalition lost its majority. The ensuing Christian democratic–social democratic alliance made drastic changes in the disability, sickness, and pension plans that affected benefit levels, eligibility, and governance structures, although both parties faced substantial internal opposition within their own camps from labour unions and pensioners' organizations. Both parties suffered severe defeats in the 1994 legislative election, but those losses primarily benefited social-protectionist peripheral parties and the social-liberal Democrats '66. In spite of losing one-quarter of their voters, the social democrats for the first time emerged as the relatively strongest party in the Dutch legislature and became decisive for coalition formation. Its skill in crafting a coalition with the social liberals and the conservative free-market liberals buttresses its now dominant role in the Dutch party system and has reinforced the social reform programme. When these efforts began to pay off in the Netherlands's economic performance, the governing parties reaped the benefits in the 1998 parliamentary election.

Germany

In Germany, the market-liberal challenge in the electoral arena has remained weak until the 1990s and the centrist Christian democrats, whether in opposition or government, did not dare to offend its labour union wing by dramatic cutbacks until 1995–6. It is quite telling that after the 1976 legislative election, when the governing social democrats changed the adjustment formula for the pension system to prevent pensions from rising from about 70 per cent of recipients' final wage to more than 90 per cent, it was the Christian democrats who attacked the changes as the 'pension lie' (*Rentenlüge*) of the incumbent government. While in opposition, Christian democrats repeatedly tried to stir up fears among pensioners that the governing social democratic–liberal coalition would reduce pension benefits. After Helmut Kohl's Christian democratic–liberal government came to office in 1982, it fell upon the new opposition party to play the same game. Nevertheless, the major government and opposition parties could agree on a reform of the pension system in 1989 that reduced expenditures in the longer run, but did not entail any imminent losses for current beneficiaries. The relevant baseline for the German party system is that direct social expenditure cutbacks in key programmes (sickness insurance, pensions) are politically difficult because the two major parties vie for the support of large beneficiary groups and, unlike the Netherlands, are not counterbalanced by a vigorous and growing market-liberal party. Within the social democrats, the German labour unions are a vocal constituency opposing social policy change. And the Christian democrats must heed the voices of both the Catholic minority current in the organized labour movement as well as those of the Protestant and Catholic churches which run much of Germany's means-tested welfare system with public funds, allocated to them according to the principle of subsidiarity (Alber 1996).

Nevertheless, Germany is one of the very few countries where social expenditure in the 1980s and early 1990s actually stagnated or even fell as a percentage of GDP (cf. Alber 1998*b*). The reason for this is Germany's demography of a temporarily declining share of pensioners in the population from the 1970s to the early 1990s, as weak age cohorts born during and after World War I and fighting in World War II retired. Furthermore, Germany's comparatively favourable economic performance throughout the 1980s kept unemployment relatively low, even though early retirement gradually began to increase the fiscal stress in Germany's social insurance systems. Thus, while Britain or Sweden have made deeper changes in individual benefit levels, eligibility, and entitlement schemes of their major social insurances than Germany, the German system shows less expenditure growth because the former countries experienced more need-based demand for social benefits (Alber 1998*b*).[22]

For Germany, the opportunity to test the ability of the party system to engineer welfare state retrenchment under conditions of high stress arrived only after 1993, when high unemployment in Eastern Germany, combined with sharply rising unemployment in Western Germany, and growing cohorts of pensioners have imposed high stress on the system. After much bickering, and under conditions of much business pressure and large net capital outflows from Germany, the Christian democratic–liberal government did legislate a reduction of the sickness income replacement rate from 100 to 80 per cent of the wage (compared to Sweden's reduction from 90 to 75 per cent, plus waiting days). But the social democrats in the opposition immediately attacked these measures and a strike wave in the strongest sector of German industry compelled employers to restore the full income replacement through collective bargaining agreements, a compensation outlawed in the Swedish sickness insurance reform (cf. Schludi 1997: 48–50). In order to contain the costs of pensions, reflected in rising employer and employee contributions to the pension funds, the Christian–liberal government also

---

[22] The evaluation of Germany as a case of only mild retrenchment, primarily in the late 1970s and early 1980s during the second oil crisis, is confirmed by Pierson and Smith (1993), Pierson (1996), Clayton and Pontusson (1997) and Stephens, Huber, and Ray (1999).

passed a pension reform law in 1997 that provides for a gradual fall in the wage replacement rate of pensions from 70 to 64 per cent of final income, in addition to tighter eligibility rules and a higher age qualifying employees for full insurance benefits. Also this reform was fought by the social democrats, Greens, and post-communist opposition parties and the candidate for the chancellor's office, Gerhard Schröder, promised to revoke these measures upon coming to office. While Christian democrats, after much hesitation, thus did engage in some social policy retrenchment, they paid a heavy price for it in the September 1998 election and lost control of the government.

In Germany the legislative term 1998–2002 constitutes a test case of whether a party system with centre-left bias can implement social policy retrenchment under conditions of a strong economic-demographic push. My theoretical argument predicts only limited efforts in this regard. It is true that the CDU has somewhat undercut its credibility as a welfare state stalwart due to its late retrenchment measures in 1996 and 1997, but new leadership might help the party to regain that image. If, however, the party moves to the market-liberal right, then the new red–green coalition enjoys more leeway to enact retrenchment without having to fear that dissatisfied voters will turn to the main opposition party.

Japan

In this final case, the situation of party competition is quite different than in Germany, although I subsume it under configuration 4 as well. The ruling hegemonic Liberal Democratic Party (LDP) is not a liberal party in anything but name and it has not encountered a credible market-liberal competitor since its inception. At the same time, for reasons of ideological origin, internal organization, and insertion in the single non-transferable vote electoral system, the major leftist party, the Japan Socialist Party (JSP), could never emerge as a strong contender for government office and did not give up its militant socialist appeals until the second half of the 1980s when it was too late to nourish a different reputation. While at first sight the JSP's intensely ideological discourse suggests a deep economic-distributive divide in Japanese politics, in reality the parties polarized more around approval or rejection of Japan's constitution and military alliance with the United States. The importance of the distributive-economic divide was further reduced by the importance of clientelist linkages between members of parliament and their local constituencies that are encouraged by the electoral system. When the end of the Cold War also undercut the JSP's militant socialism as well as the political-cultural divides over Japan's place in the world, there were no moorings available on which political entrepreneurs could build a new programmatic divide in the arena of party competition. In the mid- to late 1990s, the Japanese party system thus effectively lacked programmatic dimensions of competition. This situation has kept a credible alternative to the LDP from emerging, but it has also made the LDP hesitant to address the Japanese economic crisis with policies that would have the potential of creating a deep and lasting political divide ultimately endangering its hegemony.

In Japan, the role of competitive party configurations for social policy retrenchment is difficult to conceptualize also for a number of other reasons. First of all, Japan's demographic and cultural parameters made welfare state expansion a less visible issue than in Western advanced post-industrial countries since World War II. Japan's age distribution and comparatively high ratio of parents being cared for in the homes of their children has led to lesser demands imposed on the public purse until recently. Second, the spectacular performance of the Japanese economy with lifetime employment in core industrial and service sectors and rather safe employment in most other areas as well kept need-based demand for social policy programmes subdued. These developments lead to a third reason why it is difficult to bring the theory of competitive party configurations to bear on the Japanese case. It is inadequate to measure the Japanese welfare state in terms of formal-legal public programmes for income maintenance and social security. What is delivered in Western welfare state capitalism, is at least partially submerged in private sector social protectionist networks outside the reach of formal state authority (Pempel 1997). For this reason, in the assessment of social policy cutbacks it is not very meaningful to know that Japan expanded its public pension plan rather late and has been able to cut back on benefits since the end of the 1980s (Fushimi 1997; Pempel 1997). Increasing economic stress has led to industry-centred adjustment processes, primarily within the private sector. Private corporate strategy, sometimes in alliance with bureaucratic coordination, helped to distribute the costs of social policy changes across societal groups in the 1970s (Hiwatari 1998). This enabled Japanese parties to converge under conditions of economic stress, while Anglo-Saxon parties began to polarize ideologically.

The real test of the political system's adjustment potential has come only since the bursting of the real estate and stock market bubble in 1989/90 and the exhaustion of easy adjustment potentials within private firms that would not touch lifetime employment and private social benefits. In terms of public policy, the equivalent to social policy retrenchment in Western welfare states would be decisions by Japanese governments to let ailing firms go bankrupt (together with their in-house social protection plans), to expose private business to more domestic and international competition, and to set Japan's finance sector on a footing that requires Japanese banks and manufacturing companies to disclose realistic balance-sheets (with accurate debt/equity ratios) and to produce viable rates of return. Because such reforms would induce a sharp increase in business failures and prompt a need for social protection outside private sector companies, Japan's centrist parties, and above all the still hegemonic Liberal Democrats, have done everything to avoid policy changes that could force them to reveal painful choices to their electoral constituencies. Japan's foot dragging in the area of corporate and finance reform and in the realm of foreign trade is the functional equivalent of partisan resistance to welfare state retrenchment in Europe and North America.

Table 9.3 summarizes the judgements entailed in the analytical case studies I have just outlined, plus equivalent judgements I would apply to the main reference cases of Anglo-Saxon social policy retrenchment (cf. Alber 1996; Garrett 1993; Pierson and Smith 1993; Pierson 1994; Stephens, Huber, and Ray 1999). High values always indicate strong conduciveness to welfare state retrenchment targeting universalist, high visibility insurance programmes (sickness pay, pensions), either on the push side, reflecting the intensity of economic crisis and crisis perception, or on the pull side, specifying the opportunities for politicians to pursue social policy retrenchment, while remaining consistent with vote- or office-maximizing rationales. All variables are scored on a zero to two scale, except the left-libertarian blackmail party variable which is less important and is only on a zero–one scale. While at the margins there may be considerable disagreement about the scores for each country and each time point, the overall picture may be quite robust and is visually represented in Figure 9.1.

In the upper right-hand quadrant we find party system configurations involving both economic imperatives of reform ('accumulation') as well as opportunities for politicians to pursue retrenchment policies without giving up vote- and/or office-maximizing objectives ('legitimation'). In this quadrant, we encounter British and Anglo-Saxon politics in the 1970s and 1980s (marginally), Swedish politics in the 1980s and 1990s, and Dutch politics in the 1980s (marginally) and 1990s. The configurations underline that even social democrats in Britain, the Netherlands, and Sweden are willing to act on social policy retrenchment, while their colleagues in other countries may resist such efforts. In the 1990s, Britain and the United States are situated in a quadrant where parties' social policy strategies are not so much constrained by considerations of economic accumulation as by purely electoral concerns that induce politicians to pursue a retrenchment agenda even at a time when public opinion had become more favourable to social policy expenditures.

In many ways most interesting is the quadrant in which countries encounter rather intense economic pressures towards reform, but where politicians appear unwilling to deliver corresponding policies because the political configuration gives them incentives to pursue votes and/or office by avoiding unpopular social retrenchment programmes. My analysis leads to the

TABLE 9.3. *Forces pushing and pulling toward social policy retrenchment*

	Push factors: fiscal and economic crisis			Pull factors: opportunities for politicians to embrace social policy retrenchment					
	Economic growth crisis	Acceptance of social retrenchment*	Push index	Strong liberal parties?	Weak centrist parties?	Weak left-libertarians?	Strong economic divide?	Linkage through policy + cadre**	Pull index
Britain									
1970s	2	2	4	2	2	1	2	1.5	8.5
1980s	1	1	2	2	1	1	2	2	7.0
1990s	0	0	0	2	2	1	2	2	9.0
United States									
1970s	2	1	3	2	2	0.5	1.5	1.5	7.5
1980s	1	1	2	2	2	1	1.5	1.5	8.0
1990s	0	0	0	2	2	1	1.5	1.5	8.0
Sweden									
1970s	1	1	2	1	0	0.5	2.0	1.0	4.5
1980s	0	2	2	1.5	1	0	1.5	1.5	5.5
1990s	2	2	4	2	2	0	1.5	1.5	7.0
Netherlands									
1970s	1	2	3	1	0	0.5	0.5	1.5	3.5
1980s	2	2	4	2	0	0.5	1.0	1.5	5.0
1990s	2	1	3	2	1	0.0	1.5	2.0	6.5
Germany									
1970s	1	2	3	0	0	1	1.0	1.0	3.0
1980s	0	1	1	0	0	0.5	1.0	1.0	2.5
1990s	2	2	4	0	0	0.5	1.5	1.5	3.5
Japan									
1970s	0	0	0	0	0	1	0	0.5	1.5
1980s	0	1	1	0	0	1	0	0.5	1.5
1990s	2	2	4	0	0	1	0	1.0	2.0

* 0 = recent cutbacks of benefits, sound fiscal basis of social policy;
   1 = either recent cutbacks of benefits or sound fiscal basis of social policy;
   2 = both recent expansion of the system and fiscal crisis of social policy.

** mass parties = 0 / framework parties = 1; programmatic party competition = 1 / clientelism = 0.

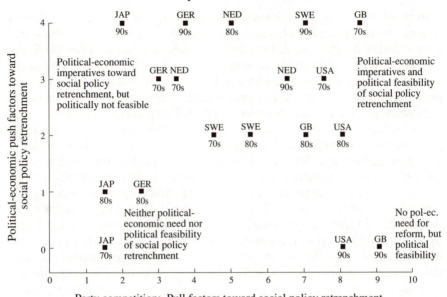

Party competition: Pull factors toward social policy retrenchment

FIG. 9.1. The trajectory of six countries through the opportunities
for political-economic reforms

contentious proposition that both leading cooperative market economies of
the world, Germany and Japan, are situated in this quadrant in the 1990s. If
they produce profound social policy retrenchment, it would count against the
validity of my theory, provided they do not first move out of this quadrant,
e.g. by improving political opportunities for retrenchment policies.

3. CONCLUSION AND GENERALIZATION
OF THE ARGUMENT

The absence of hard comparable data on social policy retrenchment
covering the big universalist social programmes and the small number of
countries whose social policies lend themselves to comparison constrain our
abilities to test rival theoretical arguments in a rigorous fashion. As Alber
(1996: 10–13) and Schludi (1997: 34–6) have correctly argued, the best way
to measure social policy retrenchment would be at the micro-level of individual entitlements, identifying changes in the average citizen's tangible
benefits from time t_1 before the policy change to time t_2 after the policy change,
plus changes in eligibility and governance structure of the programme. For
example, the efforts of the Swedish Moderates in 1995 to undercut the Ghent

system of unemployment insurance administration through the labour unions and to replace it with a state insurance board (Anderson 1998) would have entailed no changes in benefits disbursements, but a rather profound alteration of the long-run bargaining power of the labour unions due to the likely subsequent decline of union enrollment. Institutional design may have no immediate fiscal impact, but provides the tracks on which social policy change may move for decades thereafter (cf. Flora and Alber 1981).

As I suggested in outlining various reference cases for the four configurations of party competition I introduced above, the comparison of social policy change in the 1980s and 1990s can be expanded beyond the four illustrations of my theoretical argument. In addition to Britain and the United States, also New Zealand and Australia fit the first Anglo-Saxon configuration with political competition on the economic dimension between social democrats and free-market conservatives. In both cases, even the left seized upon incentives to pre-empt conservatives and move to freer markets which also entailed social policy retrenchment, yet tried to proceed more selectively than conservative parties and soften the blow of cuts with compensatory measures, for example by strengthening the national system of wage regulation in Australia (cf. F. G. Castles, Gerritsen and Vowles 1996; Stephens, Huber, and Ray 1999).

For the second configuration of party competition, aside from Sweden there is Denmark as a reference case for social policy change towards less generosity, more market incentives for welfare state clients as well as providers, and means-tested benefits (cf. Stephens, Huber, and Ray 1999; Schwartz 1994c). While most of the retrenchment took place under conservative governments, social democrats did not reverse the major reforms upon coming to office and at the margin increased the exposure of the labour force to market uncertainties.

In addition to the Netherlands, the third group of 'balanced' systems with market liberal, centrist, and social democratic parties includes Belgium and Switzerland. Moreover, changes in the Austrian and Italian party systems in the 1990s point in the direction of these countries joining the third configuration, although their limited actual retrenchment effort up to that point places them still in the fourth configuration. Hitherto that fourth configuration is represented not only by Germany and Japan, but also by France, Italy (pre-1994), and Austria (pre-1995) all of which have engaged in rather limited programme and institutional reforms. French governments have undertaken few benefits cutbacks or systemic reforms, although the growth of social expenditures has been slowed after 1983 through changing assessment and eligibility formula. The bottom line, however, is that neither socialist nor centre-right governments dared to touch the big social protectionist programmes in order to address their growing structural fiscal deficits (Stephens, Huber, and Ray 1999).

My emphasis on the configurations of party competition for the vigour of social policy retrenchment does not deny that a complete explanation of individual country trajectories must build on a multivariate explanatory model. Party competition is certainly not the only reason for social policy change. My theoretical model and the case studies have already taken into account one additional explanation, the intensity of economic crisis and the fiscal viability of social programme schemes, manifested by unemployment, government budget deficits, slow growth, and net capital outflows. This explanation has some plausibility in the light of party and government conduct in Britain (late 1970s) and New Zealand (mid-1980s) or policy reform in Sweden (early 1990s), but it is harder to sustain in many other cases. Economic and fiscal crisis most certainly play a role in governments' policy responsiveness, but these actions appear mediated by the political strategic feasibility of major retrenchment efforts, given the conditions of party competition. Thus, economic crises in France, Italy, or more recently Germany and Japan have prompted different response patterns in the social policy making arena than in the Anglo-Saxon countries under equivalent conditions.

Based on the same logic that external shocks or trends are refracted by party system configurations, demographic pressures and high rates of unemployment, taken by themselves, do not directly produce corresponding social policy reform. If demographic pressures, as measured by the net present value of future social security commitments and the ratio of contributors to beneficiaries of the social security system now and in the year 2020, or levels of unemployment mattered most, then countries such as France, Italy, and Germany should have long engaged in a vigorous policy effort to reshape their social policy programmes covering pensions, health care, and labour market policies. Conversely, Australia, Britain, and New Zealand with comparatively favourable demographic distributions and low social security commitments should have undertaken the least efforts to address these issues.

Other explanations run into similar difficulties that numerous cases will not fit the most plausible outcome pattern. The proposition that ceiling effects trigger social policy retrenchment is an example. The welfare state, in the widest sense of all state-mediated programmes of social protection, simply cannot be pushed above a certain upper threshold, say 40 per cent of GDP, beyond which the capitalist process of investment and accumulation begins to falter. But countries in our comparison set undertake welfare reform at very different levels of social policy effort. It must be strange from the perspective of the ceiling argument that the most vigorous reformers and retrenchers include precisely those countries that make the internationally weakest efforts to protect citizens through social programmes.

In a similar vein, the extra-political power of labour does not directly shape the degrees of freedom politicians enjoy in choosing social retrenchment policies. Also this explanation does not yield a promising pattern of predicted cases. Among countries with the least reform effort, we find corporatist polities (Austria), mixed corporatism (Germany), syndicalist systems with rather low labour and/or fragmented union collective mobilization and inclusion in systems of interest intermediation (France, to some extent Italy) and countries with a 'corporatism without labour' (Japan). Conversely, strong reform efforts happen under conditions of rather varied labour relations with either strong or very weak unions, more corporatist or more pluralist patterns of interest intermediation.

Finally, institutional veto points contribute relatively little to the explanation of differential pathways of social policy reform, although they may play some role at the margin (cf. Huber, Ragin, and Stephens 1993; M. Schmidt 1996*b*; Schludi 1997). The Anglo-Saxon countries with more or less majoritarian institutions fit the theoretical argument by opting for vigorous reform, yet the theory would expect a great deal more social policy retrenchment than actually took place in countries with relatively centralized political regimes such as France and Japan where powerful policy makers encounter quite feeble formal veto powers or veto players.

Nevertheless, given the limited opportunities for rigorous comparative analysis in the absence of better measures of the independent and dependent variables in the study of social policy change and the still small number of cases that lend themselves for inclusion in such studies, my paper represents nothing but an exercise to specify one possible set of strategic processes that may account for changes in the social policies of advanced post-industrial democracies. If nothing else, it provides a stimulus to model the role of party competition in social policy formation in a more sophisticated way than typically encountered in the simple partisan politics/government responsibility hypothesis.

PART IV

Comparing Policy Domains

10

The Comparative Political Economy
of Pension Reform

John Myles and Paul Pierson

THE remarkable expansion of old age security in the post-war period may represent the largest extension in the developed capitalist democracies of what Schwartz (in this volume) terms politically constructed property rights. Different countries initiated this process at different times and proceeded at different speeds, but in most countries it was more or less complete by the mid-1970s. Almost from the moment of maturation, however, discussions began over the looming 'pension crisis'. By the mid-1980s, the first serious efforts to reform national pension systems and resolve the 'crisis' were under-way. The pace of reform gained momentum in the late 1980s, accelerated in the 1990s, and there is still no end in sight. By 1998, almost all of the OECD countries had gone through at least one major reform. Old age pensions, long one of the most stable features of the post-war social contract, has become a sector marked by dramatic policy change.

The big question lurking behind any discussion of these reforms concerns the long-term future of the 'welfare states for the elderly' created in the post-war decades. Is the welfare state withering away or merely being redesigned and modernized? Does redesign mean convergence on some hypothetical neoliberal model as advocated for example by the World Bank (1994), one in which collective provision for income security in old age will be replaced by a privatized, market-based, model of retirement savings with the state retaining only the residual responsibility of meeting the income needs of the most impoverished? Will all these changes result in a return to the not so distant past when large numbers of the elderly found themselves in a state of relatively abject poverty?

Without claiming anything like a definitive answer to these 'big questions', our conclusions can be summarized as follows. With few exceptions, the size

For helpful comments and criticisms of earlier drafts we wish to thank Giuliano Bonoli, Gosta Esping-Andersen, Jay Ginn, Ana Guillén, Karl Hinrichs, Andrew Martin, Bruno Palier, Joachim Palme, Frances Fox Piven, John Stephens, Nick Ziegler, and the members of the New Politics Project.

of the welfare state for the elderly in the next century will be larger than it
is now if for no other reason than demand for benefits will rise more
quickly than the capacity of policy makers to cut entitlements. Reform
can slow down the rate of spending growth but with rare exceptions will
not reverse it. Nor will nations converge around a common level of spending or in the design of their pension systems for two reasons. First, the
options available to policy makers, whatever their politics, are constrained
by institutional and programmatic designs inherited from the past. In this
sense, we will argue, pension policy is a *locus classicus* for the study of
'path-dependent' change, processes in which choices made in the past systematically constrain the choices open in the future. Given quite different
systems of existing commitments and popular expectations, reformers
in different countries are choosing reform options from quite different
'menus'. The menu of options may include choices that represent novel, even
radical, departures from past practice (Myles and Pierson 1997). The point
is that particular departures are available only under particular conditions
inherited from the past.

The second reason for continued diversity in the 'new' welfare states is the
same as that which created diversity in 'old' welfare states. Cross-national
differences in the organization and political capacities of the key constituencies affected by welfare states—workers, employers, women, private insurers,
and public officials—continue to have an important impact on the character
of reform, just as they have in the past. Politics, including traditional partisan
politics between left and right, remains operative in the reconstruction of
the welfare states, albeit in new and sometimes unfamiliar ways.

A distinguishing feature of pension reform, one that appears with uncanny
empirical regularity, is that only rarely does reform come about through a
process of unilateral legislation by the government of the day. All-party agreements, referenda requiring the consent of the 'people', or corporatist 'social
pacts' (Rhodes, in this volume) involving organized labour and employers'
associations are the rule rather than the exception so that 'negotiated
settlements' (Bonoli, in this volume) are the usual political mechanism for
redesigning pension policies. During the 'golden age' of expansion, political parties were eager to claim credit for new programmes. Retrenchment,
in contrast, is generally an exercise in blame avoidance rather than credit
claiming (Weaver 1986). Blame is diffused, however, by bringing other key
institutional actors on board as co-signatories to the new 'social contract'.
Outcomes, then, hinge critically on precisely which social actors can be identified as legitimate co-signatories (the 'people', other political parties, labour)
to the new contract, and on the capacities of these actors to successfully
negotiate such reforms.

In Section 1, we argue that the problem driving pension reform is not
simply rising demand for pensions but also growing difficulties with a

particular method of financing and distributing benefits: pay-as-you-go (PAYG) defined benefit plans financed from payroll taxes. Payroll taxes constitute an increasingly problematic base for pension finance. In Section 2, we build on this analysis by showing how the method of financing and distributing benefits systems establishes the parameters of reform. Our principal claim is that the key variable shaping broad reform outcomes is the scope, maturity, and design of these PAYG pension schemes. Depending on this variable, reform has proceeded on one of two distinct tracks.

One cluster of countries is the 'latecomers'—those cases where significant pay-as-you-go, earnings-related programmes were not in place at the end of the golden age. Strikingly, among the latecomers, the dominant reform path has been an expansion of collectively organized retirement provision. In these countries, the last two decades have seen efforts to create viable systems of old age security, albeit of a very different sort from that provided by earlier models. Interestingly, the traditional explanation for welfare state growth —the power resources of organized labour and the political left—has remained salient for this set of countries. Where organized labour exerts greater influence, reforms were more likely and have taken a more 'collective' form —industry-based and generally with a strong organizational role for labour unions. Yet in the new environment of the 1980s and 1990s the form of expansion has been quite different from that of pension systems that matured earlier—funded and based on regulation rather than pay-as-you-go and based on public spending.

Most of the affluent democracies fall into a second group, where large earnings-related programmes were already mature by the mid-1970s. In these countries, the path of reform has been one of adaptation to austerity. Because of politically prohibitive transitional costs, radical shifts towards funding are precluded. And in view of the shared interest of key actors (labour, business, and government) in restraining the growth of payroll taxes, reform has meant retrenchment, albeit of a particular sort. The main avenue of change involves the reduction and rationalization (greater targeting) of interpersonal transfers so that future benefits will more closely reflect past contributions. Where pension systems result in a large volume of interpersonal transfers (horizontal or vertical) among beneficiaries the division between 'earned' and 'unearned' benefits is being made more transparent, so that financial responsibility for redistributive transfers can be shifted from payroll taxes to general revenue. Pension systems that provide an opportunity to reduce expenditures by means of 'rationalizing' or 'modernizing' redistribution provide policy makers with the opportunity to make cuts that are potentially self-legitimating. Where the volume of interpersonal transfers is low (where benefits have been closely linked to contributions), such a reform strategy is unavailable and change generally will be more difficult, since retrenchment requires universal—'across-the-board'—reductions in entitlements.

Our analysis contrasts sharply to both that of convergence analysts, who anticipate a move towards 'one best practice' but ignore the radically different starting points of different countries, and to naive versions of institutionalism that stress inertia and stability. In opposition to a naive institutionalism, we emphasize the big shifts that are taking place in systems of retirement provision. Against convergence theorists, we stress that there is no single 'destination'. Change is powerfully shaped by the constraints and opportunities presented in distinctively constituted pension systems, creating clusters of nations each with their own reform dynamic.

1. THE NATURE OF THE CRISIS

Explanations of the wave of pension reform currently sweeping the OECD countries typically invoke a familiar series of intertwined pressures (Weaver 1998) including demographic and budgetary pressures, concerns about competitiveness, and a resurgence of conservative ideology. Without disputing that all of these factors play a role, we think it is difficult to explain either the timing, extent, or type of reform as simple linear extrapolations of these pressures.

A striking feature of reform discussions is that the perception of crisis seems unrelated either to current or projected levels of expenditure on old age benefits (Table 10.1, cols. 4 and 5). The countries of Continental Europe face the highest levels of spending, now and in the future, in part because of generous pension schemes but also because of their very high rates of early retirement and labour force withdrawal by those under 65 (Table 10.1, col. 3). Nevertheless, one hears virtually the same rhetoric of 'crisis' whether one travels to high spending Italy or to low spending Australia.[1]

Population ageing is often invoked as a major motor of reform (see Pierson, in this volume). It is not population ageing alone that is the problem, however; rather, it is the design of the typical old age security system in interaction with population ageing and slow wage growth. The large pay-as-you-go defined benefit schemes that developed in Western Europe and North America in the post-war decades are financed with a tax on only part of national income, namely labour market earnings. Unlike programmes financed from general revenue, transfers financed exclusively from payroll taxes impose all of the cost of an ageing society on wage income. Since covered earnings are often limited to the bottom half or two-thirds of the earnings distribution, rising pension costs fall disproportionately on lower, and especially younger, wage earners.

---

[1] When one of the authors pointed out to a senior official in Australia's Department of Social Security that even the most dire projection for Australia's old age security budget left the country spending only about 4.5% of GDP, less than one-third of what Italy spends today, he was told: 'That won't cut any ice here.'

TABLE 10.1. *Ageing, work, and social expenditures, 16 OECD countries*

	(1) Population 65+ 1990	(2) Normal retirement age (Male/Female) 1992	(3) Employment/ population ratio men 55–64 1995	(4) Pension Expenditure as % of GDP 1995	(5) Projected Pension expenditure as % of GDP 2040	(6) Increase (5/4) 1995–2040	(7) Significant reform 1980–97
Nordic Countries							
Sweden	17.8	65/65	64.4	11.8	14.9	1.26	Yes
Norway	16.3	67/67	70.0	5.2	11.8	2.27	Yes
Denmark	15.4	67/67	63.2	6.8	11.6	1.71	Yes
Finland	13.3	65/65	34.9	10.1	18.0	1.78	Yes
MEAN	15.7	66/66	58.1	8.5	14.1	1.66	
Continental Europe							
Germany	14.9	65/65	47.2	11.1	18.4	1.66	Yes
Austria	15.1	65/60	40.8	8.8	14.9	1.69	Yes
Belgium	15.0	65/60	34.5	10.4	15.0	1.44	Yes
Netherlands	13.2	65/65	39.9	6.0	12.1	2.02	No
France	13.8	60/60	38.4	10.6	14.3	1.35	Yes
Italy	14.8	60/55	42.3	13.3	21.4	1.61	Yes
Spain	13.2	65/65	32.1	10.0	16.8	1.68	No
MEAN	14.3	63/62	39.0	10.0	16.0	1.60	
Anglo-Saxon							
Canada	11.3	65/65	54.0	5.2	9.1	1.75	Yes
Ireland	11.4	66/66	59.1	4.1	2.9	0.71	No
UK	15.7	65/60	56.1	4.5	5.0	1.11	Yes
USA	12.6	65/65	63.6	4.1	7.1	1.73	Yes
Australia	10.7	65/60	55.2	2.6	4.3	1.65	Yes
NZ	11.1	61/61	63.0	5.9	9.4	1.59	Yes
MEAN	12.1	65/63	58.5	4.4	6.3	1.43	

Sources: Population, Retirement Age, Pension Expenditures: Organization for Economic Cooperation and Development, *Ageing in OECD Countries* (Paris: OECD, 1997).
Employment/Population Ratio: Organization for Economic Cooperation and Development, *Employment Outlook* (Paris: OECD, 1997).

Thus, the pension dilemma facing policy makers has both a (widely recognized) demographic component and a (less well recognized) wage component. The demographic component is the declining ratio of wage earners to retirees, a result of reduced fertility exacerbated by a secular decline in the retirement age and increased longevity. The wage component is slow growth in real wages that most policy makers assume will continue into the future.

The problem is sometimes framed by comparing implicit 'rates of return' in a pay-as-you-go scheme to its major alternative, a fully capitalized scheme financed from returns on investments. The return in a funded model depends on long-term rates of return to capital. The implicit 'rate of return' in schemes financed by payroll taxes is the annual percentage growth in total real wages ('returns to labour'). Total wages are the product of the average wage multiplied by the number of wage earners. The latter term is a function of population growth and the rate of labour force participation. Quite simply, then, the financial soundness of old age pensions financed from payroll taxes depends on high wage growth, high fertility, and high rates of labour force participation.

Given the values of these parameters in the 1950s and 1960s—rising wages and a growing workforce—most 'sensible' treasury officials would have advised their ministers to opt for a PAYG design. Indeed, this is what most industrial democracies did, partly because PAYG offered additional advantages.[2] It pre-empted objections to state control over large capital pools and sidestepped widespread public distrust of capitalized pension schemes in countries where depression and war had devastated pension funds in the first half of the century. Furthermore, PAYG systems offered enormous 'front-end' political benefits during the initial phase-in period (Pierson 1997). Since there was no preceding generation of entitled pensioners, politicians could immediately offer a potent combination of modest payroll taxes, generous promises of future pensions, and 'unearned' benefits for those near retirement age.

Intense wage pressures in all advanced industrial societies reinforced the expansion of PAYG pensions during the 1960s and early 1970s. Current real wage increases could be traded off in exchange for promises of higher real pensions in the future. Pensions became a 'deferred wage' that could be used to purchase labour peace as well as political popularity (Myles 1988).

By the 1990s everything had changed. Figures produced by the Canadian Department of Finance illustrate the turnaround (see Table 10.2).[3] Clearly

---

[2] Canada and Sweden opted for high levels of capitalization in the initial years not for reasons of financial stability but to create large capital pools to achieve other political objectives.

[3] Similar figures for a broader range of countries can be found in Davis (1995: 37).

TABLE 10.2. *Real growth in total wages and salaries and real interest rates, Canada, 1960s–90s*

	1960–9	1970–9	1980–9	1990–4
Real growth in				
Total wages and salaries	5.1	4.8	2.1	0.0
Real interest rates	2.4	3.6	6.3	4.6

Source: Canada, *An Information Paper for Consultations on the Canada Pension Plan* (Ottawa: Department of Finance, 1996).

by the end of the 1980s a 'sensible' treasury official would be advising her minister that the model put in place in the 1960s was in difficulty. Irrespective of whether projected expenditures represent 5 or 25 per cent of GDP, the parameters that made pay-as-you-go the model of choice in the 1960s— rising wage rates, full employment, and comparatively high fertility—had changed dramatically. Real wages and the size of the labour force were now rising slowly if at all.

The threat of ever higher payroll taxes in the future generates several problems. In the light of the slowdown in real wage growth, trade union leaders as well as treasury officials face an intergenerational dilemma: how to reconcile the income needs of retired workers with the downward pressure on take-home pay of active workers while non-wage income is comparatively immunized from such pressures. At the same time, policy makers, employers, and unions have shared a growing concern about the employment effects of rising payroll taxes. As Scharpf (1997*b*) and many others have argued, payroll taxes raise the cost of labour, especially at the lower end of the labour market where the social safety net, minimum wages, or industrial relations systems make it difficult for employers to pass such costs on to employees. Whether or not high payroll taxes constitute a major 'killer of jobs' as often portrayed, rising unemployment levels in many economies in the 1990s created an unfavourable environment for calm acceptance of yet further increases.

In most countries the current wave of pension reform, then, is essentially a matter of adapting pension regimes designed for an 'old' political economy to one compatible with a new policy environment. If PAYG financing from payroll taxes is the problem, what is the solution? On the financing side, the choices include shifting the balance of financing towards capital investments, general revenue, or some mix of the two. Alternatively, benefits can be cut, but this raises the thorny question of 'for whom?' The choices are not endless but they are multiple. The analytical task is to account for which of the many possible strategies policy makers actually select in the reform process.

2. PENSION REFORM AS A PATH-DEPENDENT PROCESS: CAPITALIZING OLD AGE PENSIONS

Recent work in the 'new institutionalism' has drawn attention to the ways in which the 'rules of the game' help to structure political conflicts (North 1990; Skocpol 1992). While this discussion has often focused on formal institutions, extensive policy arrangements also become fundamental institutional frameworks, creating rules, constraints, and incentives for future political action. Where government activity is widespread, 'policy feedback' is likely to be a major contributor to the dynamics of reform (Skocpol 1992; Pierson 1994). The constraining effects of pre-existing pension systems render reform dynamics 'path dependent'. Because the term 'path dependence' is invoked with increasing frequency but little precision, some explication is necessary.[4]

In the standard world of neoclassical economics, nations are bound to converge on a single equilibrium as some choices prove their superiority over others (i.e. are more 'efficient' than others). The neoclassical model assumes a world of decreasing marginal returns which engender negative feedback leading to a (single) predictable equilibrium (Arthur 1994). Or more simply, if I choose a strategy that is inferior to the most efficient strategy, I will be 'punished' for my choice (negative feedback) and will soon change my behaviour or go out of business. Convergence is to be expected.

Many social processes are characterized by declining returns and negative feedback as the model assumes; but many other processes are not (Pierson 2000). Instead, they exhibit 'increasing returns' and self-reinforcement: each step along a path produces consequences which make that path more attractive in the next round and raises the costs of shifting to an alternative path. Timing, place, and sequence—in short, history—matter a lot in processes of the latter sort but not in the former.

Economists have made considerable headway in the study of such path-dependent processes in areas as diverse as technological change (why did the PC win out over the Mac?), economic geography (why Silicon Valley?), and international trade (should we subsidize Airbus?). One of the major factors Brian Arthur (1994) identifies as a source of path dependency, namely large set-up or fixed costs, is particularly relevant: when set-up or fixed costs are high, individuals and organizations have strong incentives to identify and stick with a single option. Once a low-density suburban infrastructure has been built up around roads and the automobile, for example, the shift to an urban design based on mass transport becomes prohibitively expensive.

---

[4] For an extensive discussion, see Pierson 2000.

The evolution of extensive pay-as-you-go pension systems represent an excellent example of this type of process. Once mature, any proposal to shift from a PAYG to a funded design, whether public or private, creates a huge 'double-payment' problem. A shift from PAYG to capitalization (or pre-funding) requires current workers to continue financing the previous generation's retirement while simultaneously saving for their own.[5] The 'double-payment' problem, coming on top of already heavy pressures to reduce benefits and increase taxes on the working population, is likely to present an insurmountable barrier to privatization or the capitalization of existing public schemes.[6]

Illustrating the Double-Payment Problem: Britain and the United States

Thus our central hypothesis is that how far one has gone down the path of PAYG provision is critical for delimiting reform options. We illustrate this point briefly here by contrasting the experiences of Britain and the United States and then pursue the same point more systematically in the next two sections, where we examine the less and more mature systems in turn. We focus on Britain and the United States because each is a 'liberal' welfare state where conservative politicians were interested in pension privatization. What differentiated the two cases was the degree to which pre-existing pension systems were institutionalized (Pierson 1994).

Because alternating Labour and Conservative governments had taken turns scrapping their predecessors' plans for two decades, the Thatcher Government inherited a relatively new PAYG earnings-related pension system, SERPS. Enabling legislation for SERPS was passed in 1975 and the first contributions made in 1978. Thus, in 1985, when the Conservatives began considering reforms, the new system had been in place for only seven years. The Tories were well aware that the immaturity of SERPS provided a brief window of opportunity for privatization. As then-junior-minister John Major noted in the House of Commons, 'the way in which SERPS works means that every year of delay leaves people clocking up expensive rights which must be honoured in the future' (House of Commons 1986: col. 105).

---

[5] The cost of financing existing obligations can of course be shifted to general revenue and financed out of current tax revenues or shifted into the future through debt financing (shifting the cost to future taxpayers). In this sense, the double funding problem is less an economic problem than a political problem of who pays and when. The 1997 Hungarian reform which introduced a partial privatization created a significant double funding problem. The formula chosen was to rely mainly on debt financing in the early years, shifting the balance towards tax financing in the following decade (Palacios and Rocha 1997). However, it will rarely be attractive to politicians to explicitly recognize such a massive debt burden.

[6] There are additional elements of path dependence associated with these systems. Where public PAYG schemes have crowded out funded private sector alternatives, financial markets for individual investors tend to be notoriously weak This may both make privatization more difficult to implement and diminish the scope of key political constituencies (Teles 1998).

Even for a system that had been in place for less than a decade, shifting to a funded regime created big problems. The Thatcher Government's initial gambit, to quickly shut SERPS down, was withdrawn following withering criticism from all directions. The opponents included not only the Labour Party and groups representing the elderly, but, revealingly, the highest reaches of the Treasury and powerful private sector allies of the government, including the major insurance companies and the Confederation of British Industry. The latter groups were concerned that the double-payment problem would lead to higher payroll taxes, lower benefits, or both. Forced to retreat, the Thatcher Government had to pursue a more gradual approach. The 1986 reforms incrementally but decisively shifted policy towards private pension alternatives to the state earnings-related scheme. Essentially, the government offered tax subsidies for personal pensions, along with significant cuts in the public sector scheme that left individuals 'free to choose' but made the decision to opt for private coverage attractive to almost anyone under the age of 40. By 1991, two-thirds of workers had 'contracted out' of SERPS. Further reforms under the Conservatives and new proposals from the Labour government have consolidated this fundamental reorientation of pensions policy.

Britain was a latecomer. It had not travelled very far down the path of PAYG earnings-related provision. Even so, and even under a committed and powerful conservative government, the transition was very difficult. Capitalization and, in this instance, privatization were possible only because of the system's immaturity, and only because the government agreed to shift a significant share of the 'double-payment' problem to 'itself' (i.e. to general revenue) through tax subsidies that will offset much of the budgetary saving anticipated.

In the United States, the 'double payment' problem was a much more formidable reality. When the Reagan administration arrived in 1981, Social Security had been in place for almost five decades. The window for full-scale privatization had long since closed. The financial resources needed to build a private-sector alternative were already committed, through payroll taxes, to the current generation of elderly. Those advocating steps equivalent to Britain's SERPS reform, like the CATO Institute's Peter Ferrara, remained marginal figures during the 1980s, and the reform of Social Security in 1983 quickly took the form of negotiated retrenchment, as we discuss further below.

By the 1990s, when Social Security reform again reached the agenda, a number of conjunctural factors had made privatization a more prominent political option. Republicans were in a far stronger position in Congress and had moved well to the right on welfare state issues. The previous decade's expansion of IRAs and 401(k)s, the mutual fund explosion, and the historically unprecedented performance of the stock market had heightened the allure of individualized accounts. The movement of baby-boomers into their peak earning years created a favourable demographic profile for the near term.

Finally, and perhaps most important of all, the movement of the government budget into surplus for the first time in twenty years opened the possibility that revenues might now be available to help fund a transition.

Despite this highly favourable convergence of contingent factors, the scale of the existing PAYG system put significant constraints on the scale and timing of any proposed transition. Even partial privatization proposals would require very substantial benefit cuts, sizeable increases in payroll taxes, or some combination of the two. As *The Economist* (11–17 Apr. 1998: 20) concludes, while privatization has moved from the margin to the mainstream, there is a long road ahead to persuade both ordinary Americans and the mutual fund industry (who fear greater regulation) that privatization is in their best interests (Teles 1998). A wholesale shift from a PAYG to a funded design would be radically more difficult in the United States than it was in the UK. At most, a very limited shift in the direction of funding seems likely. Examination of the conditions under which capitalization has emerged as the pre-eminent form of financing old age provisions does not augur well for proponents of privatization in the United States.

Path I: Latecomers and the Development of Funded Provision

By 1980, four advanced industrial countries had yet to establish universal 'second tier' PAYG earnings-related schemes (Australia, Ireland, the Netherlands, and New Zealand). Two others (Denmark, Switzerland) had very modest earnings-related schemes that did little to satisfy the income security needs of middle-income workers. A seventh (Britain) had enacted an extensive public earnings-related scheme but had only just begun to implement it.[7] It was among these 'latecomers' that capitalization was not only politically feasible but also the norm. By the early 1990s four of the seven countries (Australia, Denmark, the Netherlands, Switzerland) had created universal or quasi-universal capitalized pension schemes not as a replacement for, but as an addition to, their existing programmes. A fifth (Britain) had severely curtailed its new PAYG earnings-related public scheme (while cutting its basic flat-rate pension), and successfully shifted the balance in favour of capitalized private schemes.

Funded defined contribution plans were made mandatory in Switzerland in 1983 and in Australia in 1992. Dutch occupational pensions could be thought of as 'quasi-mandated'. While only 26 per cent of Dutch workers are union members, state regulation of the labour market (extension laws)

---

[7] Canada was also a potential candidate for supplementing the existing system with mandatory occupational pensions at the beginning of the 1980s. During the Great Pension Debate that ran from 1976 to 1984, the option was put on the agenda. The reformers and especially organized labour chose instead to push for an expansion of the PAYG CPP, a strategy that ended in failure.

TABLE 10.3. *Nations with capitalized earnings-related pension schemes, 1998*

	Defined contribution	Defined benefit
Fully capitalized	Australia	Netherlands*
	Denmark*	United Kingdom
	Switzerland	
Partially capitalized	Sweden	Canada

Notes: Does not include funds invested in government debt. Classification of DB and DC identifies the predominant pattern.

* = non-mandated but quasi-universal (see text).

requires that all benefits negotiated at the bargaining table be extended to non-union workers, while non-union firms inevitably follow the lead of the unionized sector to remain competitive. In 1980, only 60 per cent of Dutch workers were covered but by the 1990s coverage had risen to 90 per cent. In Denmark, where the vast majority of employees are unionized, labour went on a pension offensive in the late 1980s and coverage rose from about 35 per cent in 1986 to over 80 per cent of the labour force by 1997. Government officials concluded that mandating was unnecessary.[8]

With the exception of Switzerland, all of these countries also represent variants of what is often characterized as the 'Beveridge' path to old age security. Typically, these nations began with means-tested programmes for the elderly poor, then shifted to universal flat-rate benefit schemes with an additional tier of PAYG earnings-related benefits coming only much later. The 'latecomers' were Beveridge countries that did not make this last transition before 1980.[9] Switzerland is an ambiguous exception to this pattern, since, as Bonoli (1997a) notes, the Swiss scheme was a compromise between the Bismarckian tradition of earnings-related contributory pensions and the Beveridge flat-rate approach with the result that Switzerland is often counted among the 'flat-rate' countries in comparative research.

The political dynamics generating these changes were also broadly similar. In at least three of the four cases (we have been unable to uncover accounts of the Swiss case) the pressure for reform came from organized labour to spread entitlements traditionally available to civil servants, professionals, and workers in unionized sectors to all workers. In Denmark and the Netherlands, pension rights were won at the bargaining table. In Australia, pension mandating was the end product of a classical corporatist agreement between labour and government in which labour won new pension entitlements in exchange for wage moderation.

---

[8] For more detailed summaries, see Myles 1998.

[9] Denmark adopted a very limited second tier earnings-based scheme in 1964 but both contributions (about 1.2% of the average wage) and benefits were extremely modest.

The result of this development is a new 'family of nations' in pensions provision, one that will be characterized by a distinctive political dynamic in the twenty-first century. In none of these countries do governments bear direct responsibility for meeting future earnings-related pension obligations. In the defined contribution design prevalent in Australia, Denmark, Switzerland, and some UK plans, future benefits depend entirely on contributions and returns on investments. Beneficiaries bear all of the risk and future benefit changes can be 'blamed on' (or credited to) markets rather than governments. In the Netherlands and in some instances in the UK, where a defined benefit design prevails, responsibility for meeting future obligations lies with employers and plan sponsors, not government. Moreover, as these capitalized plans begin to mature in the next century, demand for means-tested benefits is expected to decline, reducing pressure on the tax revenues required for their financing.

This hardly means pension politics will disappear. Rather, they will revolve around the role of government as regulator to address problems of market failure and the uneven distribution of benefits among plans.[10] The way these issues are resolved will doubtlessly reflect the very different processes which brought these plans about. In the UK, capitalization was the result of conservative dismantling and replacement of a traditional PAYG defined benefit scheme. In Australia, Denmark, and the Netherlands, capitalization was the result of a struggle by labour to supplement existing plans. Rather than individualized personal retirement accounts, these plans are typically large industry-wide plans in which organized labour remains deeply embedded both in policy making and administration. How the presence or absence of these quasi-corporatist arrangements affects the resolution of the distributive problems that will inevitably emerge in the coming decades is an issue that invites close attention from future researchers.

What of the 'latecomers' that have yet to add a second tier of contributory pensions, notably Ireland and New Zealand? Ireland relies on a rather modest flat-rate benefit (27 per cent of the average industrial wage) and private occupational pensions that cover approximately half of the labour force.[11] The old age dependency ratio will actually decline through 2006 and not begin to rise until the middle of the next century. As a late industrializer with a weak Labour Party, pensions have not played a large role in Irish politics. Only recently have pensions become the topic of tripartite discussions. The 1998 report of the National Pensions Policy Initiative recommended

---

[10] These tensions have been very evident in the UK where governments have been 'blamed' for pension fund failures (the Maxwell affair) and misleading advice with respect to the advantages of alternatives to SERPS (Teles 1998).

[11] Pension politics have never occupied a prominent place in Ireland and rather little has been written on the topic. The discussion here relies on a personal communication from Julia O'Connor.

that employers provide mandatory access to a low-cost Personal Retirement Savings Account for all employees with consideration to be given to mandatory occupational pensions if 'insufficient progress' is made in increasing current coverage levels.

In New Zealand, the Labour Party implemented the New Zealand Superannuation Act in 1974, a fully funded state-run defined contribution pension. The plan was attacked by the National Party and wound down after only nine months of operation by the incoming National government in 1976 (Overbye 1997; St. John 1998). Instead, a tax-financed and comparatively generous flat-rate benefit scheme, New Zealand Superannuation (NZS), was implemented in 1977. The change was easily accomplished, since unlike the contributory plan which would only mature in the next century, NZS began to deliver full benefits immediately. Following the 1996 election, supplementary pensions returned briefly to the political agenda when the New Zealand First Party won an agreement with the ruling National Party to hold a referendum on the addition of a compulsory second tier 'savings scheme'. Instead, the National Party held the referendum on a proposal to replace, rather than supplement, the NZS with a compulsory savings plan. The result, which must be close to a record for a government-sponsored referendum proposal, was rejection by over 90 per cent of the voters.

Interestingly, the traditional explanation for welfare state growth in general —the power resources of organized labour and the political left (Korpi 1983; Esping-Andersen 1990)—and public pension development in particular (Myles 1989; Palme 1990) has remained salient for the 'latecomers'. Reforms generally have gone further and taken a more collective form where organized labour exerts greater influence. Perhaps the most striking contrast is between New Zealand, where the Labour Party initiated what was perhaps the most anti-labour agenda of any national government, and Australia, where organized labour remained a partner in the reform process over the same period (F. Castles and Shirley 1995; Grafton, Hazeldine, and Buchardt 1997). Yet in the new economic environment of the 1980s and 1990s the form of this labour-led expansion has been quite different from that of pension systems which matured earlier—funded and occupationally based rather than pay-as-you-go and public.

Path II: The Constrained Options of Mature Systems

None of the countries that developed mature pension systems by the mid-1970s are moving towards full funding. For these countries, the World Bank reform template is largely irrelevant to the practical problems facing policy makers. In a few cases, there have been modest moves towards partial funding or the promotion of private supplements, and we discuss these cases first. For most countries, however, reform activity has concentrated on the restructuring of pay-as-you-go schemes, and we devote the bulk of our discussion to the characterization of the issues at stake and the politics surrounding such initiatives.

Partial Funding in Mature PAYG Pension Systems

If whole-scale transformation is generally impossible, what of more modest, incremental shifts towards capitalization? Two rich democracies, Canada and Sweden, have taken steps in this direction, and the issue is on the table in a few other countries, notably the United States.[12] Strikingly, both the countries where these initiatives have occurred are exceptional by virtue of a post-war history of capitalization. During the start-up period of their national systems (the Canada and Quebec Pension Plans in Canada, the Swedish ATP) in the 1960s, both systems were more or less fully funded. The Swedish funds were used to finance housing; Canada Pension Plan funds were lent to the provinces to finance provincial debt while Quebec deployed its fund to finance both direct and portfolio investment in Quebec corporations.

In 1997 Canada passed legislation to accelerate the expected increase in contribution rates so that additional revenues could be invested in equities by an arm's length investment board. This was not a shift towards 'privatization' or to a defined contribution design, however. Rather, returns on investments will be used to finance the existing obligations of the plan.[13] The contribution rate will rise from 5.85 to 9.9 per cent by 2003. The intent is to stabilize the contribution rate at that level, well below the 14.6 per cent level otherwise projected for 2030.[14] This strategy is known as 'prefunding', raising the contribution rate sooner than required in order to spread the long-term costs over several generations.[15] The 1998 Swedish reform added a 2 per cent payroll contribution to finance government-administered, defined contribution, personal accounts with funds invested in a variety of market instruments. Both the prefunding and personal accounts strategy were

---

[12] Hungary, a country that lies outside the scope of this review, took a more dramatic step towards capitalization in 1997 by shifting 8% of payroll contributions (out of 30) into a mandatory DC scheme (Palacios and Rocha 1997).

[13] Reserve funds will increase from two to five years of benefits as a result.

[14] A similar proposal was part of the Advisory Council on Social Security's (1997) report in the United States. Often identified as the 'Ball proposal' because it is supported by Robert Ball, former Commissioner of Social Security, it is also identified as the 'left wing' solution because of support from labour representatives. In contrast, the Canadian proposal originated with a very conservative Finance Ministry and has received the support of business lobbies and the financial community.

[15] The 1983 US reform of Social Security introduced a modest dose of another variant of prefunding: contribution rates were raised and the surplus was invested in government debt rather than in market instruments.

presented as possible reform strategies for the USA in the 1997 report of the Advisory Committee on Social Security.[16]

In both Canada and Sweden, the choice of funding options reflected the imperative of reaching a negotiated settlement (see below) rather than unilateral enactment of new legislation. Traditional 'left–right' partisan politics also played a role. In Sweden, the Social Democrats had to concede to the 'personal account' model to reach an all-party agreement with the conservative opposition parties.[17] In Canada, the choice to increase funding to finance the current programme came to the top of the agenda when the nationalist and left-leaning Parti Québecois made clear Quebec would not support reform proposals that involved significant benefit cuts (Québec 1996). Together with the two provinces ruled by social democratic governments (British Columbia and Saskatchewan), Quebec had the potential to block any reform initiative under the legislation creating the plan.[18] With large benefit cuts off of the reform menu, the partial funding option emerged as one of the major instruments to bring down long-term increases in the contribution rate.

Though modest in scope, these reforms add a new element to the policy gene pool. One could speculate that the new gene will proliferate and become dominant in the future. To some observers, the addition of personal retirement accounts as in Sweden represents the thin edge of the wedge, opening the door to much larger individuation of benefits in the future. Alternatively, the Canadian strategy of investing public funds in the equity market to finance benefits could be seen as the beginning of 'creeping socialization'. The expectations of policy makers, however, are more modest—to stabilize or supplement the existing system rather than engage in the more radical 'paradigmatic reform' advocated by the World Bank. These two cases represent the most vigorous efforts to shift away from a PAYG system, and the transitional problems will become more acute as population ageing increases the scale of immediate pension outlays. Thus, rather than 'radical reform', the principal strategy in the large PAYG systems has been to contain expenditure growth through retrenchment strategies that combine across-the-board benefit reductions with programme rationalization and increased targeting of benefits.

The Moral Economy of Retrenchment

There is a profound difference between extending benefits to large numbers of people and taking those benefits away (Weaver 1986). For the past half

---

[16] Whether or not advance funding of either sort lowers the costs for future generations is a highly contested question. See, for example, Herbert Stein, 'Social Security and the Single Investor', *Wall Street Journal*, 5 Feb. 1997.

[17] Joakim Palme, personal communication.

[18] Bob Baldwin, personal communication.

century, expanding social benefits was generally a process of political credit claiming. Not surprisingly, the expansion of social programmes had until recently been a favoured political activity, contributing greatly to both state-building projects and the popularity of reform-minded politicians (Flora and Heidenheimer 1981). Retrenchment, in contrast, is generally an exercise in blame avoidance (Weaver 1986). The strategies available to policy makers to conceal and diffuse responsibility for cutting benefits by making the effects of policies difficult to detect or by making it hard for voters to trace responsibility for these effects back to particular policy makers are well known. (Arnold 1990; Pierson 1994). Successful efforts to trim public sector pension obligations often take the form of long-term revisions that phase in very gradually and primarily affect future retirees. When carefully crafted in ways that are not highly visible, these reforms have sometimes been introduced with relatively little opposition.

'Policy by stealth' (Battle 1990), however, is not always feasible or sufficient. As Stinchcombe (1997) recently reminded us, the 'old institutionalism' had a great deal to tell us about these matters. One of the main 'outputs' of the political system is its own legitimation. Justice, fairness, and the honouring of implicit contracts between policy makers and the electorate imposes an important constraint on the possibilities for radical reform (Rothstein 1998*a*). Pension systems are essentially a code of laws stipulating who may make claims on the state and under what conditions. Reneging on past contracts by unilaterally reducing benefits creates a profound problem of legitimacy for governments.

Employment-related, defined benefit schemes face a particularly acute problem, since the contract is highly individualized. Unlike generic schemes for those in 'need' or for 'citizens', each individual has his or her own contract with the government with specific benefits attached to their specific work record, years of contribution, and earnings history. Such programmes are not just another public service like roads or schools. Instead, they become invested with quasi-property rights in the same way as life insurance or equities.

National differences in the success and failure of efforts to cut expenditures through a strategy of 'means-testing' benefits for the 'rich' graphically illustrate the difficulties. As Myles and Quadagno (1997) show, selective targeting based on income has been widely used as a reform strategy in OECD countries. Since the early 1980s, Australia, Canada, Denmark, Finland, New Zealand, and Sweden have all adopted some form of selective targeting to reduce formerly universal flat-rate benefits for high-income seniors. However, no country has successfully income-tested earnings-related benefits to which quasi-property rights attach by virtue of past contributions.

Governments are pressed to identify reforms that will not generate electoral retribution. In parliamentary systems untroubled by elaborate checks and balances or government by coalition, it is technically feasible for governments to introduce large-scale reforms but no government wants to pass legislation that will lead to its early demise. The legitimation problem is overcome, however, if the new contract has (or appears to have) the consent of all parties concerned. Rather than reneging on an existing contract, the contract has simply been renegotiated. As a result, negotiated settlements and new social contracts are the rule rather than the exception when reforming public pension schemes.

The 1992 German reform was based on multi-party consensus and consultation with the social partners. Switzerland and New Zealand held referenda on major pension reforms in 1995 and 1997, respectively. Reform of the Canada Pension Plan was adopted after the federal government received the consent of two-thirds of the provinces containing two-thirds of the population (as required by law). The 1995 Italian reform succeeded after the Dini Government won the approval of organized labour (including a referendum of union members), whereas the Berlusconi Government failed in 1994 when it tried to introduce reforms over the heads of labour. In France, the Balladur Government succeeded in 1993 with labour's acquiescence while the Juppé Government was brought to its knees in 1995 when it introduced legislation in the face of union opposition. The 1996 'Toledo Pact' is an all-party 'framework agreement' ratified by the unions and employers' associations for the redesign of the Spanish old age security system. The 1997 Austrian reform was the product of prolonged bargaining between the government and the unions. The 1998 Swedish reform is the product of an all-party agreement. Even the 1983 Social Security Amendments in the United States had an unusually corporatist tone, as labour and business representatives were brought to the table and helped establish the parameters of a bipartisan consensus (Light 1985).

The rare exception may turn out to prove the rule. In a striking break with tradition, the 1997 German reform was imposed by the Kohl Government over the objections of the Social Democrats and the unions (Hinrichs 1998). The recently elected Social Democrats, however, promised during the campaign to reverse the legislation.

Reaching consensus depends critically on which actors can be considered legitimate signatories to the new contract—the 'people', organized labour, the other political parties, sub-national levels of government, or some mix of these. In Continental Europe and the Nordic countries, countries with the largest PAYG systems, the consent of organized labour has usually been a necessary if not sufficient condition for reform for several reasons. First, unlike Canada, the USA, or the UK, where labour is just one 'interest' group among many, in these nations organized labour is an 'encompassing institution' that represents virtually all employees.[19] Continental pension systems

---

[19] Although union membership rates are often much lower, coverage rates—the share of workers covered by collective agreements—are typically on the order of 80% (Traxler 1996).

are typically designed on corporatist principles, administered either by representatives of employers and the unions or by tripartite boards that include government. The origins of this pattern lie in the separate plans originally established for different occupational groups (civil servants, white-collar workers, blue-collar workers, miners, the self-employed, etc.). In this way, historical origins are reproduced institutionally in the design of the pension system and labour remains central to any reform process.[20]

How, then, does one get labour on side? Paradoxically, the reforms to which European labour has given consent appear to represent a profound shift from the model of old age security defended in the past. Two of the largest reforms since 1990—the Swedish and the Italian—provide especially dramatic illustrations. Palme (1994: 50) describes the 1994 Swedish proposals (which heavily influenced the Italian reform) as a 'shift from a system of defined benefits to a system of defined contributions'. Artoni and Zanardi (1997: 253) conclude that the 1995 Italian reform created a PAYG design that mimics a capitalized plan in which benefits are calculated on the basis of accumulated revenues plus investment returns ('virtually fully funded'). The Italian government describes the reform as a shift from a *sistema retributivo* to a *sistema contributivo* in its public documents.

To pension aficionados, the images associated with such change imply nothing less than a profound paradigm shift in the distributive logic of these welfare states. The defined contribution metaphor carries two implications: first, that financial risk is being shifted from the state to the individual worker/retiree; and, second, that the redistributive role of social insurance is being eliminated as benefits become strictly tied to past contributions.

The reality is decidedly more complex. The new design implemented in Sweden and Italy is on closer inspection a hybrid of the more familiar (PAYG) defined benefit (DB) and (funded) defined contribution (DC) models. To capture the distinctiveness of such plans a new language is required. Following Thompson (1997) and others, we shall refer to it as the notional accounts (NA) model.[21] To assess the implications of the change requires closer inspection

---

[20] The French case is a good example. In 1995, the strike by French railway workers against the reforms of the Juppé Government enjoyed broad public support despite the fact that the privileges they were defending (early retirement provisions) were specific to that industry. By failing to reach a mutual accord with the railway workers, the government threatened not the benefits but the principle of labour control over social security programmes. As Bonoli and Palier (1996) point out, French pensions are not considered 'part of the state'. Although the government sets benefit and contribution levels in the general scheme, pensions are considered part of the employment sector and the autonomy of the unions that direct the social security *Caisses* is jealously defended.

[21] The key elements of Thompson's definition of the notional account model include: a centrally managed, pay-as-you-go, notional contribution plan in which each worker has an account which is credited with the contributions made by or on behalf of the worker. Account balances are credited with the analogue of interest payments calculated either by the rate of increase in the average wage or the rate of increase in total wages.

of the actual mix of design features. As Thompson (1997: 6) observes, the promises made by NA models may not be that different from traditional DB designs. One has to examine the actual risks that each model insures.

A key difference between traditional DC and DB models is the protection they provide against economic risks that result from changes in the rate of wage growth and return on investments. As Thompson (1997) demonstrates, in the DC design the contribution rate required to finance a given retirement pension changes whenever wage rates and investment returns change and there is a very high risk of being wrong—of saving too little or too much. This is the risk faced by workers now covered by the Australian and Danish defined contribution plans described above. By contrast, notional accounts plans, like defined benefit plans, carry no such risk. The notional accounts designs implemented in Italy, Sweden, and, for the moment, Germany, do nonetheless transfer a significant element of the risk associated with demographic change to workers/retirees, a topic to which we return below.

The second referent of the 'defined contribution' metaphor in recent European reforms is more widespread, namely the tendency to tighten the link between benefits and total contributions. For pension experts, this application of the metaphor is misleading, since the reforms in question simply involve the shift from one defined benefit model to another: e.g. by making the Swedish design more like that of Germany where (defined) benefits have always been closely linked to contributions. As a way of communicating with publics, however, the metaphor is probably informative, since it correctly implies that, for many, future benefits will more closely reflect their earnings and contribution histories than in the past. Nevertheless, the metaphor remains misleading: interpersonal transfers are being changed but hardly eliminated.

Rationalizing Redistribution

Although defined benefit schemes have always ostensibly been 'earnings-related', all systems incorporate design features that produce significant interpersonal transfers. Eliminating transfers that can be identified as 'inequitable', 'perverse', or 'outdated', such as special privileges for civil servants and public employees can provide an effective solution to the blame avoidance problem, especially if backed by elite consensus. If the savings are sizeable, the policy maker is also in a position to use some fraction of the savings to make 'side-payments' to potential critics in the form of new transfers to risk groups now considered to have legitimate claims. The 'rationalization' of redistributive design features to achieve equity or to more clearly realize socially desirable distributive outcomes offers policy makers a potent tool for introducing cuts that are potentially self-legitimating (Levy 1999).

TABLE 10.4. *Change in assessed earnings period in final/highest earnings plans*

Country	1986	1996
Austria	10	15
Finland	4	10
France	10	25
Italy	5	Career
Norway	20	20
Spain	8	15
Sweden	15	Career

Source: OECD, *Reforming Public Pensions* (Paris, 1988) and Social Security Administration, *Social Security Around the World, 1997* (Washington: Office of Research and Evaluation, 1997).

A major feature of the Italian and Swedish reforms was the reduction of transfers that resulted from the use of final (or best) earnings formulas, a model that benefits workers with steep age-wage profiles or workers with fewer years of high earnings late in their career. Swedish pensions were calculated on the best fifteen years. In Italy, the earnings record was based on the last five years for private sector workers and the last year for public sector workers. Both nations modified their formulas so that, in the future, benefits will reflect average earnings over the entire working life. Other countries with final or best earnings models are also moving in this direction (Table 10.4).

Adjustment of the contribution period to compensate workers for irregular work histories is another method many countries use to calculate benefits, provisions that typically benefit women. Rather than basing benefits on a work history of say forty years, Swedish workers were eligible for maximum pensions after only thirty years of contributions. Italian workers were able to claim a pension based purely on years of service (thirty-five years for private sector workers and twenty years for public sector workers) allowing many to retire on a full pension in their early fifties (the so-called 'baby pensioners'). This created markedly different 'rates of return' (and implicit transfers) based on age of labour market entry and employment sector. In both countries, recent reforms reduced these transfers by basing benefits on total lifetime contributions.

The reforms, however, did not eliminate protection against irregular work histories; rather, social protection against irregular work careers was targeted on specific forms of labour market exit. In Sweden, pension credits will be granted for periods of parental leave, unemployment, and illness. As in the past, there is also a minimum guarantee pension. The Italian design imputes a contribution for years raising a child to the age of 6 and periods caring for disabled family members including parents. In the new design women (and men) will be compensated for shorter work histories due to child or elder care but not for providing housekeeping services to a spouse. Men (and women) will receive credit for periods of unemployment or disability (insurable risks) but not for periods of non-employment that are not insured.

Although few countries have design features that allow for the dramatic reforms of Italy and Sweden, most have elements that have produced an analogous logic of reform. Among the more significant is the harmonization of retirement ages and contribution years for men and women (e.g. Austria, Belgium, Germany, Italy, Switzerland). In EU countries, this shift was in part prompted by ECJ rulings on gender equality, but without exception reform has taken the direction of raising retirement ages for women (combining blame avoidance and considerable budgetary savings). Benefits formulas that privilege workers in some sectors (e.g. public servants) over others have also been reformed (Austria, Italy). A share of the savings, however, is typically used to compensate workers for time out of the labour force for child-rearing or care of other dependent family members.

The 1995 Swiss reform is especially striking, since the reform was about introducing gender equality and subject to a national referendum (Bonoli 1997a, in this volume). As in the USA, a married man with a dependent spouse was eligible for a 'couple pension' corresponding to 150 per cent of his own pension entitlement. Women's organizations successfully took the lead in demanding the end of the 'couple pension'. In the new design all contributions paid by the two spouses while married are added together, divided by two, and counted half each. Strikingly, however, couples with children below the age of 16 now receive additional credit equal to the amount of contributions payable on a salary three times the minimum pension (56 per cent of the average wage). By design, if not intent, childless couples now become penalized for being 'free-riders' on the old age security system.[22]

The trend towards reinforcing the link between contributions and benefits, on the one hand, and more systematic targeting of interpersonal transfers, on the other, is sometimes construed as representing a liberal dynamic in welfare state reform, a 're-commodification' of old age pensions (Palier 1997). How then to account for labour's consent (Bonoli 1996; Tuchszirer and Vincent 1997; Daniel and Concialdi 1997)? Labour's rationale is straightforward: to shift a larger share of the cost for rising pension expenditures from payroll taxes to general revenue. The upshot of reform, as Reynaud (1997 :11) points out, is to make the division between the contributory and 'solidaristic' (redistributive) elements of the welfare state increasingly transparent. The aim is to demarcate a clear separation between the two in order to shift financial responsibility for the latter from payroll taxes to general revenue, spreading the transition costs of an ageing society to a larger revenue base.

---

[22] Women's groups were not successful in blocking an increase in the retirement age for women from 62 to 65.

Bonoli's (1996) interviews with party officials and labour leaders in France and Germany provide striking evidence for the self-conscious character of the strategy. In the words of one French trade unionist: 'the financing of contributory benefits . . . must be done through contributions based on salaries. In contrast non-contributory benefits must be financed by the public purse.' German labour leaders and social democrats have been mainly concerned about winning general revenue funding to finance the huge transfers required for pensions in the former East Germany. Tuchszirer and Vincent (1997) point to the same logic as underlying labour support for the 1995 Toledo Pact, an all-party agreement on the framework for reforming the Spanish social security system.[23]

The limits of such a strategy are defined by the design of the existing system. The extent to which cuts can be made by rationalizing the distribution of interpersonal transfers depends critically on the volume of such transfers in the old design (Levy 1999). Hence, our hypothesis that where the old design generates benefits closely tied to contributions, benefit cuts are more likely to take the form of across-the-board reductions for everyone and generally will be more politically contentious as a result. The contrasting assessments by Palme and Wennemo (1997) and Schmael (1998) with respect to long-term impacts of recent reforms in Sweden and Germany, respectively, are consistent with this conclusion but the rigorous quantitative assessment required to support it lies well beyond the scope of this paper.[24]

Increased transparency is a two-edged sword, however. On the one hand, it provides policy makers with a potent tool for reducing expenditures. On the other, it sets the stage for new struggles that could lead to further rounds of benefit expansion, although in a context of austerity such expansions are likely to be modest, perhaps quid pro quos for cutbacks elsewhere. In the past, many of the redistributive features of the old age security system were hidden in complex technical provisions. In the age of expansion, this strategy was often deliberate, guided by the assumption that concealment made redistribution politically easier (Derthick 1978). In an age of retrenchment, increased transparency focuses attention on issues of how much redistribution and for whom. Assigning pension credits for periods of child-rearing, for example, opens up debate over the value of such credits. Women's groups were critical of the modest credits provided by the 1992 German reform,

---

[23] As both Palier (1997) and Guillén (1998) emphasize, in France and Spain where union membership is low, labour's eagerness to participate in these agreements is also motivated by institutional self-interest, a desire to preserve the corporatist design of, and hence labour's role in, national social security systems, a major source of union influence.

[24] Our suspicion, confirmed by researchers at the OECD (Peter Hicks, personal communication), is that quantification of the size and distributional effects of recent reforms is still technically impossible on a comparative basis. Any such quantification would have to make brave assumptions about future growth rates, wages, rates of labour force participation, and a host of behavioural responses to these reforms.

with the result that enhanced credits for child-rearing become part of the otherwise cost-cutting 1997 reform. The politics of redistribution has not been abolished but restructured. The outcomes to be explained by future generations of comparativists will doubtlessly include large cross-national variations in the quantity and quality of pension credits for child and dependent care, the unemployed, the sick, and other forms of economic risk.

The far-reaching, if still uncertain, implications of these reforms should not be underestimated. Especially important are attempts to reverse the secular decline in the retirement age by creating strong incentives to remain at work until the traditional age of 65 (or later). The 1995 Italian reform raises benefits by about 6 per cent for individuals retiring at age 65 and lowers them by 15 per cent for those retiring at 57 (Hamann 1997:16). In Sweden, a worker who contributes from age 22 will have a replacement rate of only 46 per cent if she retires at age 62, but this rises sharply to 60 per cent at age 65, and 82 per cent at age 68 (Palmer 1998: 8). Assuming such incentives have the intended effect and labour markets provide the required levels of employment, the result of reform may simply represent a return to the status quo of two or three decades ago. If not, the result will be a large benefit reduction for large numbers of future retirees.

A 'Hard' Budget Line for Old Age Pensions?

For policy makers, the Achilles heel of the defined benefit design is the quasi-contractual obligation to raise payroll taxes when expenditures exceed revenues. Raising taxes of any sort under conditions of slow real wage growth poses a problem for governments. But, as we have emphasized, raising payroll taxes poses a particular dilemma, since higher payroll taxes impose all of the costs on wage income. Several reforms address this problem by attempting to create a 'hard' budget line on future benefits so that post-reform payroll taxes stabilize at a fixed level. Prior to reform, Swedish contribution rates were projected to rise from 17–18 to 24–30 per cent in the next century. The reform aims to stabilize the contribution rate at 18.5 per cent (Palmer 1998: 30). In Germany contribution rates were projected to rise from 22 to 36 per cent between 2000 and 2030. The cumulative impact of reforms since 1992 stabilizes the rate at approximately 22 per cent (Schmael 1998).

One of the ways this is accomplished is especially fundamental, namely the introduction of provisions that automatically produce benefit reductions in response to population ageing. In essence, contributions will drive benefits, and in this respect the new system does resemble a defined contribution model (Thompson 1997: 6). In the German (1997) and Swedish (1998) reforms the benefit calculation at retirement incorporates a 'demographic component' to index future benefits to the life expectancy of the retiring cohort. A two-year increase in life expectancy among future cohorts, for example, will reduce the replacement rate for a hypothetical Swedish worker who begins work at age 22 and retires after 43 years of contributions from 60 to 53 per cent (Palmer 1998: 8). For the 'average' German worker who retires at 65 (after 45 years of contributions), the replacement rate falls from 70 to 64 per cent (Schmael 1998). The Swedish worker will have the option of maintaining a 60 per cent replacement rate by remaining in the labour force for an additional 18 months. If the recent reforms remain in place, German workers will not have this option.

The Italian reform introduces a similar strategy to ensure that benefits are reduced automatically as labour force growth declines. Under the new regulations, pension contributions will be indexed on the basis of GDP growth rather than real wage growth. The result is that benefits automatically reflect any decline in revenues that follow from slower employment growth. The Italian reform also provides for a review of benefit rates every ten years to take account of increasing longevity. Several countries have replaced the link between benefits and gross wages with a link between benefits and net wages, thus ensuring that any tax increases will automatically be passed on to pensioners in the form of lower benefits.

Such a strategy is a mirror image of the one introduced during the era of expansion when automatic indexing of benefits was adopted to raise benefits in line with price increases so that adjustment became a technocratic rather than a political exercise (Derthick 1978; Weaver 1988). Whether benefit reductions can be de-politicized in the same way as benefit increases were in the past remains to be seen. One suspects that technocratic retrenchment will produce a rather different response from the electorate than technocratic expansion did in an earlier era.

3. CONCLUSION: THE POLITICS OF CONSTRAINED REFORM

Pension reform has been an ongoing process in the OECD countries for well over a decade and will no doubt continue well into the next. Hazarding a guess about what the comparative pension landscape will look like fifteen or twenty years from now is a perilous exercise since that process is far from complete. Nonetheless, we believe it is possible to identify and make sense of some broad patterns.

In a fundamental sense, one needs to look to the past to make sense of the present. The particular combination of economic, demographic, and political conditions prevalent during the post-war 'Golden Age' created a unique opportunity to consolidate generous pay-as-you-go, earnings-related public pension systems. Lasting consequences stem from the success or failure of countries to move through that 'policy window' while it remained open. Our analysis has emphasized the strikingly different pathways of reform followed by two broad clusters of countries. What distinguishes the two clusters is the extent to which pay-as-you-go pension systems were already consolidated when the economic and demographic preconditions for the successful introduction of such schemes began to deteriorate rapidly in the mid-1970s.

The claim of path dependency advanced here is not an argument about institutional inertia—the simple claim that 'you get what you already have' or 'policy at time *t + 1* will resemble policy at time *t*'. Indeed, the emergent model among the 'latecomers' is a novel 'welfare state for the elderly' for which there is precious little historical precedent. The point, rather, is that this novel form is simply not available as a serious political option in many nations. A principle corollary of this general argument is that attempts to design an optimal system and then insist governments adopt it, as the World Bank has done, is unhelpful at best and a distracting form of utopianism at worst.

There is a considerable degree of compatibility between our projections and those implied by a power resource argument, since well-established PAYG systems tend to be highly correlated with a history of significant left power resources. However, a focus on the form of existing commitments allows one to account systematically for cases which are anomalies from other perspectives: Why does pension reform in social democratic Denmark look more like Australia, and the extremely 'liberal' United States look at least as much like Continental Europe as it does like the United Kingdom or New Zealand? Why are Italy and France, where most analysts consider labour's power resources to be modest, so constrained in their pension reform options? Moreover, identifying the scope of existing commitments also allows us to specify the key difficulties facing policy makers, and hence to provide a sharper analysis of viable reform options (and their difficulties) in different groups of countries. The embeddedness of current pension commitments (or lack thereof) tells us more about the trade-offs facing policy makers and the costs and benefits to different groups of possible reform initiatives than any other analytic frame.

The second task of this paper has been to go beyond the fundamental divide between these two paths and scrutinize the dynamics within each cluster of countries. The 'latecomers'—nations that never or only belatedly initiated significant PAYG defined benefit schemes—have been busy creating a novel form of 'welfare state for the elderly', that approximates in varying degrees the World Bank's model of choice. In this design governments provide a basic tier of protection against poverty but bear little or no direct responsibility for providing standard levels of wage replacement for middle-income workers. Indeed, as the funded contributory plans in these nations mature, the demand for government-financed income-tested benefits is expected to decline.

In the latecomer countries, future pension politics will focus on the regulatory role of government, a role, however, that will create no small measure of political conflict around issues of income security. Should capital markets continue to produce high rates of return, average living standards among the elderly may be as high or higher than those provided by traditional PAYG defined benefit designs but with much more 'heterogeneity' (i.e. inequality) of outcomes (Börsch-Stepan 1997). Should capital markets fail to meet expectations and the living standards of the elderly fall substantially, new pressures will emerge for yet another round of reform reminiscent of the 1950s and 1960s. The very different institutional environments of these systems, whether oriented towards the promotion of individual retirement accounts or more collective, industry-wide schemes, is demarcated by the institutional embeddedness of labour. The scope of labour power resources is likely to continue to play a key role in shaping policy outcomes—as can be seen in the contrasting developments of pension debates in Australia and Britain, for example.

The second, larger, cluster of nations, primarily those of Continental Europe and the Nordic countries (but excluding Denmark and including the United States and to a more limited degree Canada), already had extensive, mature, PAYG schemes in place at the beginning of the 1980s. Here, we have argued, the transition costs created by the double payment problem impede a shift to funding. Overcoming this hurdle is not technically impossible and the transition could be designed to spread the costs over several generations. Apart from modest changes in Canada and Sweden, however, none of the traditional OECD nations has thus far made serious efforts to tackle this hurdle.[25] History is not destiny of course. For almost two decades, conservative critics in the United States have invested large sums in creating a favourable ideological environment for the 'privatization' of Social Security and encouraged the spread of alternative private retirement savings instruments (IRAs, 401ks, and a large mutual fund industry) which, as Teles (1998) points out, provide a sort of 'parallel path' to the existing system. Whether a realignment of the political stars will create a sufficiently large 'window of opportunity' for this long-term project to succeed is yet to be seen. We remain sceptical.

The dominant track of reform in the mature PAYG nations has been a series of accommodations to austerity, typically modest in scale for current retirees or those near retirement but often substantial for future generations as reforms are phased in. We would like to close by considering briefly what we believe the evidence shows about the role of social actors in shaping these

[25] More radical reforms of traditional PAYG schemes have been implemented (Hungary) or planned (Poland) in the former Soviet block countries of Eastern Europe where financial crises unrelated to the pension problem made future payments under existing benefit formulae highly unlikely.

reforms. We certainly accept the general proposition that the power of employers has expanded in the past few decades, and that this shifting power balance helps to shape the general environment for reform, e.g. the policy alternatives that receive serious attention. But even here we see the impact of business as partial. For instance, while one could link business power to the growing critiques of the status quo and the increasing push for individualized, funded systems, we have argued that the 'logic' of funding (for those countries where it is feasible) is driven in large part by various economic and demographic trends. In other words, such initiatives 'make sense' to finance ministers even before someone starts to lobby for them.

At the same time, we have stressed that almost everywhere reform has been backed by either the active or passive consent of organized labour. Labour's consent (and/or the consent of political parties affiliated with labour) has often proven necessary to successful reform. In some cases, this reflects the role of labour as a 'signatory' with strong institutional power built into existing pension regimes. In others, it reflects the crucial mobilizing capacity of labour in many polities. Blame avoidance strategies of obfuscation and decremental cutbacks might fool untutored and atomized voters in fragmented, pluralist polities, but they are unlikely to fool trade union confederations or social democratic parties. To the extent that such groups can credibly threaten to galvanize voters (as has proven to be the case in France and Italy for instance), it becomes essential for policy makers to gain at least their tacit consent in advance.

We have constructed our analysis of the mature cases in large measure around the apparent paradox of labour consenting not only to cutbacks but also to reforms that seemingly undermine the distributive logic of systems that labour had been so active in constructing in the past. Our resolution of the paradox emphasizes that labour unions, as encompassing institutions that represent the majority of both active and retired workers, must internalize the trade-offs inherent in the prospect of financing ever rising pension demands from the wages of younger workers (Heclo 1988). While all of the consumption of the inactive population must ultimately come from wealth created by the working age population, financing population ageing primarily through payroll taxes places most of the burden on wage income. On this point unions and employers share incentives to seek solutions that contain future growth in payroll taxes through shifting the costs from payroll taxes to general revenue. This in turn, however, requires drawing a much sharper division than in the past between 'earned' and 'non-contributory' entitlements, as well as reaching new understandings of the meaning of these terms.[26]

---

[26] It has been difficult, for example, to persuade Italian workers who were eligible for full benefits after 35 years of work, and hence could retire in their early fifties, that a large share of their benefits are 'unearned'. Such an understanding is premised on an unfamiliar actuarial calculation that includes expected years of benefits as well as years of contribution.

Steps in this direction have been gradual, in part because government officials will often be more ambivalent about such a shift. While sharing a concern about payroll tax rates, governments see major advantages as well —as can be seen in the German government's heavy reliance on payroll taxes to finance unification (Manow and Seils 1999). At a time when governments struggle to meet their commitments, 'rationalizing redistribution' in pensions may require the imposition of taxes that are far less politically popular than payroll contributions. Increasing transparency of benefits may also politicize previously dormant issues of who gets (or loses) what. Yet despite this ambivalence of government actors there is a clear effort in many countries to move in the direction of constraining pressures on contribution-based finance. In the 'mature' countries, as in the latecomers, the politics of redistribution continues to animate the topic of pension reform, but it does so in ways fundamentally shaped by the particular configuration of pre-existing commitments.

11

Who Pays for Health Care Reform?

Susan Giaimo

THE extraordinary post-war boom came to an abrupt halt in the mid-1970s. The sluggish economic growth that followed ushered in a critical re-examination of the purposes and performance of the welfare state in all advanced industrialized societies. While social policy during the 'Golden Age' had aimed at expanding the scope and generosity of the welfare state and thereby redistributing the fruits of economic growth, by the 1980s and 1990s, 'retrenchment' had become the watchword. For many policy makers, business leaders, and research institutes, the welfare state had become synonymous with high costs and deteriorating economic performance. In their view, welfare state reform was critical to successful national or industry adjustment to tougher economic conditions (Pfaller, Gough, and Therborn 1991; OECD 1994*d*).

The 'new politics of the welfare state'[1] has also altered the relative position of various welfare state stakeholders. The views of those who finance the welfare state have steadily gained influence in policy debates, while those who provide and receive social benefits have increasingly found themselves on the defensive. Employers and government policy makers, and their interest in cost containment, have become the driving force behind welfare state reform.

Still, the project of containing welfare state outlays has been controversial. Such projects not only threaten the prerogatives of entrenched constituencies who benefit from social programmes (Pierson 1994), but also raise fundamental distributional concerns. Welfare states, after all, have sought to protect the vulnerable from the vagaries of the market (Polanyi 1944 [1957]: ch. 14). The critical questions surrounding the new politics of the welfare state, then, are whether payers' and policy makers' cost-containment projects have succeeded, and if so, whether the price of success has been the sacrifice of equity and solidarity. Have the burdens of welfare state reform and economic adjustment disproportionately fallen upon the shoulders of the weakest members of society, or have countries found ways to share this pain in a just fashion?

---

[1] The phrase is taken from Pierson (1996).

This chapter explores these questions through the lens of health care reform in Britain, Germany, and the United States since the late 1980s. Each country has a distinctive health care system. And each country undertook major reform initiatives designed to control health care outlays. Thus, Britain's National Health Service (NHS) is the model of a universal, state-administered health care system financed by general revenues; Germany has a statutory national insurance programme financed by employers and employees; while the USA relies primarily on voluntary, employment-based, fringe benefits to cover the majority of the workforce. Public programmes play a smaller role, covering only specified categories of the population. Looking at three different health care systems permits us to explore whether countries have converged on a common reform response in spite of their institutional variations, or whether institutional and political differences continued to shape reform paths in specific ways.

As this chapter will show, the three countries addressed the efficiency and equity goals in markedly different ways. Britain and Germany thus far have achieved good cost performance without surrendering the principle of universal access and without requiring the most vulnerable members of society to bear a disproportionate share of the burden of adjustment. Indeed, Britain's record on cost containment has been the best of the three cases. While the price has been explicit rationing of access to hospital care, Britain has done so in ways that address equity. Germany represents an intermediate case between Britain and the USA, spending more than the former but without resorting to the gaping inequities of the latter. The USA has only recently enjoyed markedly slower increases in health care outlays. But the cost-containment gains have come at the expense of worsening access to care for the sicker and poorer in society.

The reasons for these very different outcomes lie in the actions and preferences of payers and the state in each country. Specifically, payers' capacities to follow cost-containment strategies that were inimical to equity and solidarity depended on the health care system in which they found themselves, the political system and whether it provided them an avenue to influence health policies, and their own organizational capacity to pursue a unified, coherent line of action. In addition, because state actors had different roles in health care governance, they had varying expectations and capacities to ensure that cost-containment projects were compatible with equity. In brief, the universal health care systems of Britain and Germany blocked cost-containment strategies by payers or government actors that would have sacrificed equity, while the private, voluntary fringe benefits system of the United States, encouraged employers and insurers to take cost-cutting actions that worked in the direction of desolidarity.

The rest of the chapter proceeds along the following lines. Section 1 provides a broader background to situate the contemporary politics of health care reform. It explains how and why health care systems in Western countries have come under the stress of increasing cost pressures even as governments and employers have become more apprehensive about the possible effects of the welfare state on economic competitiveness. Section 2 develops the argument in greater depth. It explains how existing health care and political systems provide different opportunities or constraints for payers and the state to pursue unilateral cost-containment strategies, how health care institutions themselves shape policy preferences and strategies of payers, and how some systems require compromise solutions that reconcile equity with efficiency. Section 3 presents each country's case. The concluding section considers the broader lessons from health care reform for the contemporary politics of welfare state adjustment.

1. TO SPEND MORE OR TO SPEND LESS? COMPETING PRESSURES ON HEALTH CARE SYSTEMS

Payers' anxieties over rising health care costs are not unfounded. In general, health care has consumed a large and growing portion of social spending in all advanced industrialized societies, particularly in the past two decades. Beginning in the 1970s, health care systems experienced a 'cost explosion' that had the misfortune of coinciding with the global economic slowdown and concomitant worries about the fiscal viability of the welfare state.

However, our three countries did not fare identically. Britain has consistently been a low spender on the NHS when compared to its peers in the OECD. And having experienced a cost surge in the mid-1970s, Germany largely regained control over its health care outlays in the 1980s. The USA has had the greatest appetite for health care and remains at the top of the world league in health care spending (see Tables 11.1 and 11.2). The spending disparities are even more remarkable when one considers that both Britain and Germany have been able to extend access to care to the entire population while the USA has not.

Some of the reasons for escalating health care costs are, to varying degrees, common to all Western countries. First, the health sector is fertile ground for technological innovations that may prolong life but at considerable expense. In addition, once these discoveries are made, it is difficult—though not impossible—for insurers or governments to limit their diffusion, as patients demand access to such treatments (see Weisbrod 1985). Second, the populations of Western countries are graying, with direct consequences for health care. Older persons are likely to experience acute illnesses requiring high-tech interventions, or, more often, chronic conditions entailing long-term care. Both types of care do not come cheaply. At the same time, birth rates have

TABLE 11.1. *Health care spending as a percentage of GDP, 1960–97*

Year	Britain	Germany	United States
1960	3.9	4.8	5.2
1965	4.1	4.6	5.9
1970	4.5	6.3	7.3
1975	5.5	8.8	8.2
1980	5.6	8.8	9.1
1985	5.9	9.3	10.6
1990	6.0	8.7	12.6
1991	6.5	9.4	13.4
1992	6.9	9.9	13.9
1993	6.9	10.0	14.1
1994	6.9	10.0	14.1
1995	6.9	10.4	14.1
1996	6.9	10.5	14.0
1997	6.7	10.4	14.0

Source: OECD, *Health Data* (1998).

TABLE 11.2. *Health care spending per capita, 1960–97 ($/exchange rate)*

Year	Britain	Germany	United States
1960	54	48	149
1965	76	78	212
1970	99	149	357
1975	229	467	605
1980	537	913	1,086
1985	472	743	1,798
1990	1,024	1,650	2,799
1991	1,129	2,018	3,035
1992	1,252	2,433	3,276
1993	1,112	2,350	3,468
1994	1,213	2,533	3,628
1995	1,313	3,080	3,767
1996	1,358	3,017	3,898
1997	1,457	2,677	4,090

Source: OECD, *Health Data* (1998).

failed to keep pace with increasing longevity, so that there will be fewer working-age persons in the future to shoulder the financial obligations associated with caring for their elders. Third, the health sector is a huge generator of service sector employment. But jobs in this sector tend to be labour-intensive and have lower productivity than the manufacturing jobs they are replacing. If Iversen and Wren (1998) are correct, the smaller growth rates associated with the shift to a post-industrial economy will only make the question of adequate financing of health care that much worse.

Some of the causes for health care inflation, however, rest with the specific design of health care systems in individual countries. Fee-for-service arrangements for paying health care providers tend to be more inflationary than salary or capitation. The lack of a national budgeting mechanism to contain overall health care outlays is likely to produce cost-shifting rather than effective cost containment. Health care systems with multiple insurers tend to have higher administrative costs than single-payer systems. Some countries lack effective mechanisms to control the supply of specialists and hospitals and patients' access to them. Each of our countries has addressed (or failed to address) these issues in different ways. Section 3 addresses the particular problems they faced and their specific methods for dealing with them.

Regardless of their relative success or failure in ensuring cost discipline, governments or employers in the three countries believed that health care outlays posed immediate and long-term problems, and began to search for ways to address them. The reasons for such concerns are twofold. First, the developments exerting pressure to spend more on health care services have come at a time when economic growth has slowed from its historic post-war levels. This has raised concerns over how to finance current and future commitments in social spending, that is, whether mature welfare states can and will remain affordable. But the second concern has to do with the welfare state's impact on broader economic performance. While the exact date differed in each of our countries, from the 1980s and into the 1990s, the welfare state became inseparable from the question of national and firm-level adjustments to a more integrated and competitive world economy. In these debates, the welfare state was painted as a drag on or impediment to economic adjustment, and the solution seemed to be retrenchment measures of various sorts.[2]

Whether or how the welfare state has actually hurt economic performance may be open to question, but the change in the terms of political debate cannot be denied. The welfare state's impact on economic performance has become one of the most discussed topics among policy makers and academics, and has even spilled over into broader public discussions in Western

---

[2] However, different kinds of health care systems and welfare states appear to have different vulnerabilities in a more competitive and integrated economic environment. Where social provision is tied to employment, then the cost of fringe benefits or social insurance contributions has a direct impact on labour costs. Many analysts and employers recognize that high non-wage labour costs have adverse effects on employment, especially at the low end of the labour market (Scharpf 1997*b*). In voluntary fringe benefits systems, the problem of free-riding is rampant, and may place firms that provide benefits at a competitive disadvantage. Welfare states financed from general revenues can avoid saddling firms with higher labour costs. But they may present their own particular difficulties. Governments may have to raise taxes to levels that voters find intolerable, or choose to run expensive deficits and debts to cover spending commitments (see Genschel 1999; Pierson, Ch. 3 in this volume). If they opt for deficits, then governments run the risk of punishment by international financial markets, or exclusion from membership in regional economic clubs like Europe's single currency.

countries. Concomitantly, payers' concerns over cost containment have carried greater weight in social policy debates than in previous decades.

2. THE ARGUMENT: PAYERS AND THE POLITICS OF HEALTH CARE REFORM

By the end of the 1980s, the terms of debate, the goals, and the relative power of different actors had shifted. Cost containment had become a priority of health policy, and the question of economic competitiveness cast a long shadow over the calculations of policy makers and employers alike. Still, in some countries, the politics of health care reform required employers and state actors to forge negotiated settlements that accepted some cost control pain in exchange for equity gains (see also Bonoli, in this volume; Rhodes, in this volume). In other countries, however, such exchanges were absent, and the pursuit of cost control came at the expense of equity.

To explain these different outcomes, we must know who the payers were, what they wanted from health care reform, and what they were able to achieve in that regard. Whether payers were employers or the state, their policy preferences depended on whether they viewed the existing health care system as a help or a hindrance to their broader strategies of economic competitiveness. Furthermore, each country's health care system either granted or denied employers, insurers, or the state opportunities to take unilateral action to contain their own health care outlays at the expense of other stakeholders. In addition, the political arena provided different avenues for payers and other stakeholders to influence the course of health policy. Formal political institutions, contingent electoral outcomes, and the organizational characteristics of interest groups representing critical stakeholders worked to produce a particular brand of health care politics in each country.

The most critical variable, however, was whether the health care system was a universal, statutory system or not. If a country's health care system legally guaranteed a universal right to health services, then it placed serious constraints on unilateral cost-cutting strategies by either the state or employers. Such systems created broad constituencies or other countervailing actors to check employers' or governments' efforts at one-sided cost-shifting. The critical role of employees or taxpayers in financing or administering health care programmes granted them as much legitimacy as policy makers or employers in health care reform debates, while the political system provided them additional means of influence over the content of reform policies. In addition, because universal health care systems institutionalized equity and redistribution in their core design (see Stone 1993: 292), they made efforts to shift the burden of cost containment on to those least able to shoulder it politically difficult; such attempts were viewed as morally unjust. But while universal systems placed a heavy obligation on state actors to guarantee their solidarity, they also granted the latter the means to govern the behaviour of health care actors to ensure their compliance with both efficiency and equity. Voluntary fringe benefits systems, by contrast, contained none of these mechanisms or countervailing actors to constrain the behaviour of employers or insurers. If anything, it was government actors who found their freedom of manoeuvre and their authority over private actors in the health care system severely circumscribed. The three countries help elaborate the different parts of the argument.

First, each country's health care system designated different actors as payers and provided them with different capacities to realize their cost-containment goals. Thus, in Britain's National Health Service (NHS), the state is responsible for financing and providing health care. Its status as a single payer would seemingly grant the state unlimited freedom to decide health policy. But in fact there are limits: the state must answer to taxpayers who ultimately finance the health care budget. In Germany, employers and employees have equal responsibility for financing and administering national health insurance. Because both employers and unions are firmly embedded in these arrangements, it is difficult for one side to take unilateral action against the other. In addition, the statutory nature of health insurance closes off the option of 'exit' by employers, since they must provide insurance to their workers. In the USA, employers have been the pivotal players and payers in the politics of health care reform because most Americans obtain health insurance as a company-based fringe benefit. At the same time, employers are free to provide or withhold fringe benefits, since these are voluntary. And since employees and unions lack an institutionalized role in health insurance financing or administration, they have not been able to mount an effective opposition to employers' cost-cutting strategies. Lastly, many employers have viewed government efforts to intervene in the private fringe benefits system as an illegitimate intrusion in corporate governance.

Second, in addition to the health care system, the political arena has offered payers an alternative or complementary channel of influence over the course of health care reform. In Britain, taxpayers have two means of influence. One is the ballot box, which, admittedly, is a blunt instrument wielded infrequently. But the other is through members of parliament who regularly grill the government on the performance of the NHS. These accountability mechanisms partially offset the tendency towards a politics of imposition that the centralized political system encourages. In Germany, both employers and employees have found the various political parties to be willing advocates for their views. Coalition governments and parties associated with specific health care clients have made compromise and the balancing of the countervailing interests of employers and employees the norm in health politics. Federalism, too, has sometimes provided health care actors with an additional means of influence. In the USA, the fragmented political system—especially separation of powers—has provided employers ample opportunities or 'veto points' (Immergut 1992; Steinmo and Watts 1995) to influence the course of health care legislation. But while they may be good at wielding the veto, employers have been hampered in their ability to take positive, unified action by their organizational fragmentation in the political arena. In fact, the business 'community' is a misnomer that masks the reality of competing peak associations with few if any sanctions over wayward members. As David Vogel (1978) has pointed out, most business leaders tend to think of policy questions in terms of the interests of their own firm rather than of the business community as a whole. The weakness of American business as a collective actor in the political arena mirrors the autonomy of individual enterprises and the multiple cost-cutting options available to them in a private, voluntary fringe benefits system.

Third, statutory, universal programmes make the pursuit of cost containment at the expense of equity difficult, while voluntary fringe benefits systems do not. One reason for this is that universal systems create broad constituencies with a stake in preserving the quality and comprehensiveness of benefits. To put it bluntly, middle-class beneficiaries find themselves in the same risk community as the poor, but their reasons for fighting to protect these programmes from retrenchment may arise from simple self-interest rather than out of any sense of justice or altruism towards the less fortunate. Add to this the reality that the middle and upper classes tend to be more active in politics than the poor (though this is truer in the USA than in other countries), then the risk of electoral retribution for major retrenchment is high. Moreover, universal programmes carry legitimacy in the public eye because the majority of beneficiaries make some sort of contribution to them, either through payroll deductions to social insurance or through general revenues to finance a national health service. Benefits take on the status of entitlement based on contributions. Indeed, in some countries, courts have ruled that benefits are akin to property rights to be safeguarded by law (see Myles and Pierson, in this volume). Thus, the political risks are high for governments that launch retrenchment policies that appear to threaten the entitlements of a formidable range of stakeholders.

However, universal health care programmes go well beyond an appeal to self-interest or entitlement based on past contributions. In fact, they are the most redistributive of social insurance programmes, creating broad solidarities that encompass equity and that protect the more disadvantaged members of society. Unlike pensions and unemployment insurance programmes, in which benefits are calculated on the basis of past contributions and earnings, the universal health care programmes in Britain and Germany incorporate substantial redistribution through the pooling of risks. They involve cross-subsidies from richer to poorer, younger to older, healthier to sicker, men to women (Hinrichs 1995; Stone 1993: esp. 290–2). And despite differences in their institutional arrangements, the health care systems in both countries approach Marshall's (1963) ideal of social citizenship, whereby each person has a right to a decent social minimum as a necessary precondition for full participation and membership in the larger community.[3] In both Britain and Germany, definitions of social citizenship and a decent social minimum have been generously drawn to mean that every person has a right to the same level of high-quality care, based on one's medical need, not on one's ability to pay or past contributions. By contrast, two-tiered systems of provision based on ability to pay, which grant generous services for the wealthy and only residual benefits for the poor, violate the universality and comprehensiveness of social citizenship and their associated notions of equity.

In short, the universal health care systems of Britain and Germany equate equity with equality. Equity is defined as a broad solidarity, in which the poor and sick have the same status as the wealthy and healthy. This equation derives from the ideas of mutuality and reciprocity that underpin social insurance: people identify with each other in recognizing that they all share a risk of becoming ill or incapacitated, and respond by pooling their risks against this vulnerability (Baldwin 1990; Stone 1993). In doing so, universal programmes incorporate equity by extending their reach to include the disadvantaged with the better off and tying them together in a common fate. Put another way, these programmes achieve the goal of equity by 'targeting within universalism' (Skocpol 1991).[4] The institutionalization

---

[3] Baldwin (1990) points out that universalistic, tax-financed programmes are more solid-aristic because they consider the nation as the risk pool, while social insurance programmes segment risk pools along class, occupational, or regional lines. However, even in Germany's national insurance programme, the broader conception of solidarity has taken root. In the past two decades, the state has mandated that the sickness funds offer approximately similar benefits (on the basis that all are entitled to medically necessary care). And the 1993 reforms introduced a financial risk-pooling scheme among blue-collar and white-collar funds (see below and also Giaimo and Manow 1999).

[4] The debate between universal and targeted programmes as a more effective and efficient way to address the problems of the disadvantaged is not new. Skocpol echoes past advocates of universal programmes by arguing that such arrangements better address the needs of the poor because they have broader political support and higher levels of funding that residual programmes lack. Thus, she calls for universal rather than targeted programmes as the best way to meet the needs of the disadvantaged. Titmuss saw the dilemma between targeted and universal programmes as a key challenge of modern welfare states. However, he supported selective benefits targeted to needy groups in addition to universal programmes. In his eyes, a broader framework of universalism and a language of social rights were prerequisites to for targeted programmes to escape stigma. A universal framework was needed because it 'provides a general system of values and a sense of community; . . . sees welfare, not as a burden, but as complementary and as an instrument of change and, . . . allows positive dis-criminatory services to be provided as rights for categories of people and for classes of need in terms of priority social areas and other impersonal classifications' (Titmuss 1987*b*: 154).

of risk-sharing behaviour through social insurance thereby reinforces values of sharing and community among the population. Universal programmes thus rest on multiple bases of legitimacy that are broadly shared—from a notion of justice grounded on one's full inclusion in the community of social citizenship, through ideas of reciprocity and mutualism, to simple self-interest in preserving one's own entitlements—that together prove quite resistant to challenges of retrenchment.[5]

With social insurance, then, self-interest is compatible with reciprocity and pooling of risks. But self-interest can just as easily be conceived of in narrower terms, as 'one gets what one pays for'. This expresses the logic of actuarial fairness practised by private insurers. Actuarial fairness maintains that those who are healthier have no obligation to cross-subsidize those who are sick. Rather, insurance premiums should only reflect one's expected or actual use of health care. In practice, this kind of 'justice' encourages all sorts of inequities. Private commercial insurers, following the dictates of profit maximization and actuarial fairness, segment the market, 'cream skim' the healthier and wealthier patients, since they are the least costly to insure, and shun the unprofitable, expensive cases, namely, the sicker and poorer (Stone 1993). In sum, and in contrast to Britain and Germany, the private and voluntary nature of employee fringe benefits in the USA produces rampant inequities. Both employers and insurers are free to 'opt out' and refuse to cover the poorer and sicker on the grounds of competitiveness or profit.

Finally, statutory universal programmes and private fringe benefits systems affect state actors' freedom of manoeuvre as much as that of employers. In universal systems, the state has the legal obligation to guarantee that all citizens have access to comprehensive health care. This obligation holds not only in a nationalized health service like Britain's, where the state is the payer, but also in a social insurance system like Germany's, where the state is not. Such obligations have set political limits to how far governments could push retrenchment and whether they could do so in ways that burdened the most vulnerable. But at the same time, the statutory systems of Britain and Germany have provided governments with the legal authority and institutional means to set the parameters of the system and ensure that health care actors' quest for cost control did not destroy equity and solidarity. The government in London could use the hierarchical administrative apparatus

---

[5] Social insurance programmes might also incorporate (or least be compatible with) other motives or norms besides self-interest or mutual obligations and rights. Such programmes might also reflect a belief that in a civilized society, the stronger members have a responsibility to help the weaker, which would be expressions of paternalism or altruism. Nevertheless, Baldwin (1990) rightly points out that social insurance rooted in reciprocity removes the stigma and dependence of charity and instead accords benefits based on social rights or equal status in the risk community.

in the NHS to shape the pace and content of its reform programme in implementation, while the federal government in Germany could mandate new
implementation tasks and rules on public-law bodies of insurers, providers,
employers, and employees. But in the private employer-based health insurance system of the United States, government actors were denied the legal
authority and the institutional linkages to prevent employers and insurers
from following a range of go-it-alone cost-containment strategies that have
burdened the weaker members of society. Businesses and insurers have
viewed government efforts to regulate the health care system as an illegitimate intrusion in their private domain, while the peculiarities of regulatory
federalism have militated against coherent government action in this area.

The experiences of health care reform in Britain, Germany, and the
United States presented below bear out these conclusions.

3. THE CASES

Britain: The Limits of Neoliberal Reform in a Universal
Health Care System

In Britain's NHS, the state plays a predominant role in financing and
providing health care. Health care is financed from general revenues and
the central government determines the NHS budget. The state owns the
hospitals and governs the health service through successive tiers of heath
authorities emanating from the Department of Health (DOH) at the
centre. At the same time, state managers have shared authority in health
care governance with the medical profession, granting the British Medical
Association (BMA) an important role in policy making and administration (Giaimo 1994, 1995). British governments have also relied on hospital
doctors to ration scarce resources through waiting lists for non-emergency
hospital services. This amounted to an 'implicit concordat' with the medical
profession, whereby doctors took on the unpleasant task of rationing and
agreed to refrain from questioning governments' budgetary decisions; in
exchange, policy makers did not question their clinical freedom (Day and
Klein 1992: 471; Klein 1989: 235).

Britain's health care reform debates in the 1980s and 1990s were not couched
in terms of high labour costs because the NHS was financed from general
revenues rather than payroll taxes. And Britain had a very respectable record
of cost containment. Its fiscal discipline owed to global budgeting of health
care and limiting the number of hospital beds and specialist physicians. The
NHS also relied on general practitioners to act as gatekeepers to hospital

and specialist care, and rationed elective surgical and hospital procedures by means of waiting lists based on medical need.[6]

Still, the costs and effects of the welfare state on Britain's economic health remained an issue for Margaret Thatcher. Thatcher's disdain for the health service reflected her neoliberal distrust of 'big government' and collectivist politics generally, both of which she saw as responsible for Britain's economic decline.[7] And containing health care outlays was part of her broader agenda to bring public spending under control (Harrison 1988: ch. 5) and unleash private economic initiative to bring about Britain's economic regeneration.

Thatcher thus subjected the NHS to a severe austerity regimen throughout the 1980s.[8] But as Klein (1995) observed, the Prime Minister's success in holding down health care spending exacted a high political cost, provoking a bitter public quarrel with Parliament, health policy experts, and the medical profession. As waiting lists grew and hospitals closed wards and cancelled operations, critics charged that the government's 'underfunding' policy was starving the health service of needed funds, charges which only fuelled public fears that the NHS was not 'safe in the Conservatives' hands'.[9] Thatcher countered that inefficiencies in delivering health care, rooted in unaccountable doctors and managers eager to defer to them, were responsible for the burgeoning waiting lists. But with public criticism mounting, she initiated a full-scale review of the NHS in 1988.

The political system and the policy making process offered her the luxury to consider a range of radical proposals and to enact her reforms with relative ease. First, the review was a secretive affair involving Thatcher, a few trusted advisers, and outsiders whose political views mirrored her own. It was a break from the royal commissions of her predecessors, which had included all relevant interests. Second, party discipline and a huge parliamentary majority reassured Thatcher that her legislation would be enacted by Parliament.

But even with these political advantages, Thatcher discovered that there were limits to her reform ambitions, at least on the question of radically

[6] However, Aaron and Schwartz (1984) found that some procedures were rationed on social grounds rather than strictly clinical criteria.

[7] For the neoliberal critique of Britain's decline and accounts of the rise of the New Right in Britain, see Gamble 1994: ch. 2; Jenkins 1987; and D. Kavanagh 1990: esp. chs. 3 and 4. According to neoliberals, 'big government' and 'special interests' stifled individual initiative and economic growth. In Thatcher's eyes, the NHS epitomized these twin evils: it was a sprawling public bureaucracy full of rigidities, dominated by a medical profession unaccountable to elected officials, managers, and consumers.

[8] NHS spending increased 3% per year in the 1980s. But this rate was much lower than in previous decades and below what health care experts considered sufficient to keep up with technological advances, population ageing, and medical need (Ham, Robinson, and Benzeval 1990: 12–14; Klein 1995: 142).

[9] For an account of the health care debates in the 1980s, see Klein 1995 and Giaimo 1994.

transforming the financing arrangements for health care. The review team considered but rejected radical proposals for compulsory national insurance or mandatory private insurance on the grounds that the economic and political costs would have been prohibitive: both of these options would have done far worse in controlling health care costs than the centralized budgets and administrative simplicity of the single-payer NHS. And for all its shortcomings, the NHS was the most popular element of the British welfare state. Thatcher gauged that dismantling it would have only invited the retribution of voters (Timmins 1995: 392–4; 453–65).[10] In addition, national insurance would have shifted the cost of health care onto employers and almost certainly provoked their opposition. And it would have undercut her strategy to attract inward investment and aid industry competitiveness through low labour costs.

With privatization off the table, Thatcher decided that she would instead bring the market into the NHS itself. Hence, the 1989 White Paper called for an 'internal market' in the NHS, which split purchasers from providers. NHS hospitals were granted independence from district health authorities (DHAs). But hospitals now had to compete with each other and with the private sector for the patients of DHA purchasers or those of general practitioner fundholders. Fundholders were large, office-based, primary care physician practices that accepted a budget to purchase certain diagnostic and elective hospital procedures for their patients for which long waiting lists existed. In addition to the market reforms, the government also granted NHS managers a range of monitoring controls over doctors, from job descriptions to mandatory physician peer review, to ensure that doctors provided more cost-effective care (UK Department of Health 1989). The government hoped that competition would not only yield more efficient health care delivery but would also devolve responsibility for NHS performance failures down to local purchasers and providers.

In practice, however, the central state exerted tight control over the internal market. Thatcher's successor, John Major, streamlined the administrative tiers in the NHS, thereby increasing the capacity of ministers and managers at the centre to intervene in the day-to-day administrative

---

[10] A proposal for private health insurance that the Prime Minister's policy unit floated in 1982 met with fierce media criticism and public outcry, prompting Thatcher to disavow it (see Timmins 1995).

Thatcher's health care reforms thus differed from her policy towards state earnings-related pensions, which she gradually phased out (see Myles and Pierson, in this volume). But her caution in health policy was not only because the NHS was less expensive than other alternatives. Rather, the political risks of switching to a new health care system were considerable. The contrast with SERPS pensions is instructive. Unlike the NHS, which was more than 40 years old and upon which most Britons relied for health care, SERPS was an immature programme with relatively few pensioners dependent on it. Thus, the political and financial costs of phasing out SERPS were smaller in comparison to the NHS.

decisions of local units. And both he and Thatcher designed the market so as to limit the scope of competition among providers in order to ensure that they would not shy away from treating sicker, more expensive patients.[11] In some cases, this meant pre-empting market forces altogether, as with Major's decision to pursue a centrally directed rationalization policy for London hospitals rather than allow disruptive market forces to decide the winners and losers (see James 1995). For their part, health service purchasers and providers preferred co-operative, longer term contractual relationships than the one-off encounters characteristic of a spot market that the Thatcher Government had envisioned (Light 1997).

How can one explain the continued presence of the state in the market, and the very limited competition that was permitted? While the formidable technical difficulties of creating a market from scratch required detailed guidance and intervention from the NHS Executive, political considerations proved a more powerful brake on the market. First, the universalism of the NHS created a broad constituency with a stake in assuring access to quality care. Any cost-cutting programme that threatened a steep and visible decline in quality risked punishment at the polls from middle-class (and working-class) voters. Second, the universal citizenship rights in the NHS created a broad solidarity and commitment to equity that the public expected the government to guarantee. More than any other branch of the British welfare state, the NHS has epitomized—or has at least aspired to—a comprehensive notion of community based on Marshall's (1963) idea of social citizenship, and has expressed this solidarity as the right of all to a comprehensive level of care, (nearly) free of charge, on the basis of clinical need rather than on ability to pay (Klein 1995: ch. 1; Ministry of Health, no date; Speller 1948; Titmuss 1974, 1987*a*, *b*).[12] The deep attachment to the solidarity of the NHS not only ran strong within the Labour Party (which, after all, had created the health service), but also among the Tory wing of the Conservative Party that was sympathetic to state intervention in the economy and in social welfare. All of these political considerations compelled the Conservatives to carefully craft and constrain the workings of the internal market to avert the most egregious inequities and chaos that unbridled competition would have unleashed.

---

[11] Thus, the government limited GP fundholders' financial liability and the range of hospital services they could purchase, restricted the freedom of hospitals and fundholders to dispense with their 'profits', and mandated the development of a capitation system for purchasers that would adjust for inequities based on patients' health status (Maynard 1991; UK Department of Health 1989).

[12] Indeed, opinion polls have consistently shown that the public remains strongly committed to the principles of tax-financed, universalistic, and publicly provided health care and willing to pay higher taxes for health care (Klein 1995: 135–6, 240; Taylor-Gooby 1991: ch. 5).

Finally, the centralized structures of both the NHS and the political system made it hard for the government to 'let go' once the market was in place. Because the central government provided health care and determined the budget of the NHS, it had a direct stake in how that money was spent. Government ministers had to deal with the Treasury's perennial concerns over 'value for money', and Parliament's concern for the level of quality of services. Ministers had to face the regular grilling of members of Parliament (MPs) during parliamentary question time, and were held accountable for the performance failures even in the far-flung reaches of the NHS. Government ministers deemed it intolerable to cede control to lower level managers or to freewheeling market forces, while still being held responsible by voters and MPs.

And even as the NHS placed a heavy obligation on politicians to safeguard the equity of health care provision as they pursued cost containment, it also granted them the means to do so. The statutory guarantee of universal access gave government officials the authority to set rules on the behaviour of purchasers and providers in the health care market to ensure that their competitive behaviour did not come at the expense of the sickest and most costly patients. At the same time, the hierarchical tiers of health authorities served as the conduit through which the central government controlled the introduction and subsequent development of market forces in the NHS.

How well, then, did Conservative governments uphold their role as guarantor of equitable access for all while pursuing cost containment? On the question of equity, the record is mixed. On the one hand, the internal market reforms did not produce enough efficiency gains to make waiting lists noticeably diminish, much less disappear. In and of themselves, waiting lists do not offend equity, since one's place in the line is based on medical need. But since the inception of the NHS, those with private insurance have been able to jump ahead of the waiting lists for elective surgery. This inequality of access between those with private and public coverage has long been a point of contention in health politics, and only grudgingly tolerated by Labour politicians. Still, the extent of this inequity is often exaggerated. The segment of the population with private insurance has always been a small minority; in 1990, only 11 per cent of the population had private coverage (Klein 1995: 155; Timmins 1995: 507). Moreover, private coverage has served more as a 'safety valve' for unmet need, rather than providing the middle class a path of permanent exit from the public system. Those with private insurance still receive most of their care from the NHS as public patients, because private policies are restrictive in their scope of coverage, and tend to be confined to profitable elective procedures and amenities like private hospital room and choice of specialist (Klein 1995: 155–7; Timmins

1995: 507).[13] This means that the bulk of the population accepts (even if unenthusiastically) rationing of non-emergency hospital treatment through waiting lists whose criterion is medical need. The question for British policy makers is whether limiting access to non-emergency treatments still imposes suffering and reduced quality of life for those on the lists.

A greater criticism is that the internal market's fundholding scheme introduced a new kind of inequity of access among NHS patients themselves. Now, the wait for elective surgery was no longer solely a question of medical need but also of the ability of one's purchaser to pay. While the evidence was by no means definitive, it suggested that larger fundholding practices used their budgets and business savvy to achieve faster services for their patients than did non-fundholding practices.[14]

On balance, however, the NHS has weathered the changes of the internal market to retain much of its egalitarianism and universalism, and the Conservative reforms represented a quite limited challenge to solidarity. Universal access to medically necessary care remains a statutorily guaranteed, social right of citizenship. And as noted above, policy makers have taken great care to limit the play of market forces in the NHS to avoid flagrant inequities. Thus, fundholders and providers in the internal market operate under a number of constraints that discourage or prevent them from skimming the best patients. Moreover, the Blair Government's intention to abolish fundholding would presumably eliminate the threat that the scheme posed to equity.[15]

---

[13] Private insurance covered 6.4% of the population in 1980, rising to 11.5% in 1989. Twenty-three per cent of employers and managers had private insurance at the end of the 1980s, while 27% of professionals did (Klein 1995: 155). Private insurance was also a company fringe benefit highly dependent on the health of the economy; in the recession of the early 1990s, private insurance coverage stagnated. Among those with private insurance, more than half of their in-patient stays and 80% of their out-patient stays were covered as NHS patients (Timmins 1995: 507). Finally, while the number of private hospitals and providers increased, and the proportion of spending on institutional care rose from less than 10% in 1986 to 19% in 1993, most of this growth was in the area of nursing home care, which the NHS did not cover anyway (Klein 1995: 158–60; Timmins 1995: 507).

Waiting lists rose from 700,000 in 1992 to nearly 1.3 million by 1998 ('Bevan's Baby Hits Middle Age', *The Economist*, 4 July 1998, 56).

[14] Different contracts used by health authorities and fundholders accounted for some of the differences in access to hospital care (*British Medical Journal*, 12 Dec. 1992, 1451; 23 Jan. 1993, 227–9; Whitehead 1993). But some observers countered that fundholding had 'spillover' effects that benefited all patients, and pointed to health authorities that consulted non-fundholding GPs in their purchasing decisions or that devolved purchasing decisions to them (Klein 1995: 241–2).

[15] Fundholders will be replaced by larger primary care groups involving all GPs, who will purchase an array of services on behalf of DHAs for a population area of up to 100,000 patients. The Blair Government's proposals also indicate that it will continue with the centralizing tendencies of the Thatcher–Major reforms. The NHS Executive will have greater capacity to monitor doctors' practice patterns and intervene in the local decisions of managers and practitioners if deemed necessary (see Klein 1998; UK Department of Health 1997).

But did the market deliver the hoped-for cost discipline? The NHS has maintained its impressive record on containing costs relative to other OECD countries, but this is less a result of market competition than the effectiveness of other policy instruments. In areas with multiple providers, the NHS has become more responsive to patients or their fundholder agents. And as a whole, more patients have been treated (Klein 1995). But the internal market has been expensive to create and administer: it has generated substantial transaction costs in terms of administrative personnel, and required generous financial inducements for GPs to take up fundholding. In any case, such generosity proved fleeting, as the Major Government subsequently resorted to a policy of austerity.[16] Thus, the remarkable cost discipline of the NHS has been less an achievement of market efficiencies than of policy makers' willingness to deploy the weapon of tight global budgets and the public's tolerance of waiting lists in a government-created context of scarcity.

Germany: A 'Socially Bounded Market' within Corporatism[17]

Germany's compulsory national insurance system covers 90 per cent of the population through a network of approximately 500 quasi-public sickness funds (*Krankenkassen*) organized on class, occupational, and regional lines (Giamo and Monow 1999: 982). Despite their organizational differentiation, the sickness funds provide similar benefits packages as mandated by law. Employers and employees finance health insurance contributions in equal shares and have a role in health care administration through parity representation on the sickness funds' boards.[18] In granting employers and employees equal roles in financing and administration, the German health insurance system has institutionalized the idea of countervailing power in its very design.

Although the state does not finance health care, corporatist governance accords it a critical role in regulating the behaviour of sectoral actors and

---

[16] The number of managers soared from 700 in 1987 to over 13,000 in 1991. Between 1991 and 1992, there was an almost 25% increase in managerial personnel while only a 1% rise in hospital medical staff (Pike, 'NHS Managers' Wage Bill Soars', *Financial Times*, 5–6 Sept. 1992, 4; Pike, 'Rise of 25% in NHS Managers', *Financial Times*, 11 Dec. 1993, 6). The Blair Government calculated that managerial costs had risen from 9% to 12% (Klein 1998). GP fundholders initially received financial sweeteners to encourage their take-up in the scheme, though such payments were later discontinued (Sherman, '16,000 Pounds for Budget-Holding GPs', *The Times*, 14 Dec. 1989, 22). Critics charged that the amounts devoted to management merely siphoned off resources from direct patient care. Following its early generosity, the Major Government subsequently kept NHS spending increases well below the rate of inflation. Thus, NHS spending was projected to rise a mere 0.3% from 1996 to 1999 ('An Unhealthy Silence', *The Economist*, 15 Mar. 1997, 57).

[17] The title is borrowed from Henke (1997).

[18] The boards of the sickness funds set the level of contribution rates, though in practice that power is circumscribed by law: the sickness funds cannot run long-term deficits, so their contribution rates must cover their health care expenditures.

setting out the overall objectives for the system. Through the instrument of framework legislation, the government sets out broad policy goals and rules for the health care system but then delegates the job of implementation to quasi-public associations of sickness funds and physicians (*Kassenärztliche Vereinigungen*, or KVs) at the provincial level. Guided by the principles of subsidiarity and self-governance by sectoral actors, the state does not usually intervene directly in health care administration. But if sectoral actors refuse to implement the terms of the law, then the state may exercise its reserve powers of intervention until doctors and insurers prove able and willing to fulfil their public obligations. Once they do, the state pulls back and allows them to reclaim their collective rights of self-governance (Giaimo 1994, 1995; Giaimo and Manow 1999; Streeck and Schmitter 1985).

As part of its authority to set the parameters of the health care system, the state mandates that all employers offer insurance to their workers with incomes below a certain ceiling, finance contributions in equal shares with employees, and share with them in the administration of the sickness funds. In addition, the state also devises cost-containment policies that health care system actors are required to follow. For example, hospital doctors are salaried, while office-based practitioners must live within the confines of a regional or state-level budget cap for their services as negotiated by provincial-level associations of physicians and insurers.[19] In addition, providers and insurers are legally required to align their collective bargaining agreements with the principle of stable contribution rates (*Beitragssatzstabilität*). However, as we shall see, the state sometimes has difficulty getting doctors and payers to follow these provisions in their collective agreements.

Because health insurance is employment-based, rising health care costs have always had a direct effect on labour costs. But Germany's bleaker economic conditions in the past decade have placed serious strain on a welfare state financed from payroll contributions. The worldwide recession of the early 1990s, along with the costs of German unification, drove up the demand for unemployment insurance, while firms increased their use of early retirement and disability pensions to shed older and less productive workers (Manow 1997a).[20] Unemployment and labour force exit meant a smaller base of wages and salaries from which to finance growing demands for social insurance, so that by 1996, social insurance contributions had risen to nearly 41 per cent of wages (OECD 1996d: 76, and see Table 11.3). At the same time, German firms were coming under considerable competitive pressures from

---

[19] Ambulatory physicians receive fee-for-service reimbursement, but their level of payments may be adjusted downward over the course of the year in order to remain within the cap.

[20] The welfare state accounted for approximately 18% of the transfers to eastern Germany up through 1995, largely for unemployment benefits and early retirement pensions. Not surprisingly, these funds incurred enormous deficits as a result (see Heilemann and Rappen 1997: 13, 15).

TABLE 11.3. *Social insurance and health care contribution rates in Germany, 1960–96*
(as % of gross wages)

Year	Employer–employee joint contribution rate to social insurance	Average contribution rate to sickness funds
1960[a]	24.4	8.4
1970	26.5	8.2
1975	30.5	10.5
1980	32.4	11.4
1985	35.1	11.8
1990	35.6	12.6
1993[b]	37.4	13.4
1995	39.3	13.2
1996	41.0	13.6

[a] 1960: blue-collar workers' funds only; after 1960, all funds.
[b] Since 1991, western German states only.

Source: Manow 1997a: Federal Ministry of Labor.

globalization and the completion of Europe's single market. As a result, employers began to call upon government to stabilize social insurance outlays in order to help them bring their labour costs under control. In this they found support from scholars and policy makers who argued that high social insurance contributions were partly responsible for pricing labour out of the market, especially in lower productivity services (Esping-Andersen 1996c; OECD 1996d: ch. 3; Scharpf 1997b).

Even though pensions comprised the largest share of the social insurance bill and policy makers had reined in the medical inflation of the 1970s, health care costs remained a concern. Indeed, health care costs began to accelerate again from the late 1980s, and Germany had the dubious honour of ranking second in the OECD in health spending (OECD 1997b: 68–71; OECD 1998e). While some of the rise in expenditures lay in demographic developments and the costs of unification, inefficiencies within the health sector itself were also responsible. Chief among these was the per-diem reimbursement of hospitals, which encouraged unusually long in-patient stays. Another was the imbalance in the relationship between doctors and insurers. Corporatist self-governance was premissed on the KVs and sickness funds being in rough balance so that each could act as a counterweight to the other. But the reality was different. The KVs exploited their monopoly position in the face of a fragmented insurers side to negotiate generous fee settlements (Stone 1980). Thus, if record joblessness made it difficult to justify slashing unemployment insurance or early retirement pensions, the health sector seemed long overdue for efforts to seek out economies (Hinrichs 1995).

The Kohl Government's health care cost-containment strategy involved a mixed menu of delegating new policy tasks to corporatist actors, a careful experiment with market competition, and limited cost-sharing by patients. The 1988 Health Care Reform Law (GRG) relied on the usual method of corporatist delegation of policy tasks to doctors and insurers. Thus, the law required payers and providers to follow the goal of stable contribution rates in their collective agreements on remuneration, and mandated doctors' and insurers' associations to negotiate maximum prices for pharmaceuticals as well as practice guidelines with which to monitor physician prescribing and ensure that doctors practised cost-effective and clinically consistent medicine. The GRG also introduced minor co-payments on prescription drugs and hospital stays. But insurance contributions continued to rise, and the Kohl Government blamed the doctors for refusing to implement many aspects of the law.

Frustrated with the apparent failures of corporatist self-governance, the government passed the Health Care Structural Reform Law (GSG) in 1992. With this law, policy makers invoked their reserve powers to suspend doctors' and insurers' self-governance rights. Thus, the health ministry set budgets by decree for all areas of the health care system for three years, mandated a two-year price freeze for prescription drugs, and forced the medical associations to assume financial liability for cost overruns in physician prescribing. The law also promulgated slight increases in patient co-payments. Most important, the law introduced market competition among payers. Beginning in 1997, all patients were granted free choice of insurer. But a financial risk-adjustment scheme among sickness funds preceded choice of insurer in order to level the playing field among funds with very different health risks.

However, Kohl was not eager to have the state permanently enmeshed in the administrative domain of doctors and insurers. But neither could he afford a cost surge in the health sector once the budgets were lifted.[21] Kohl's answer to this dilemma was the two Health Care Restructuring Laws of 1997 (NOG 1 and 2). Under the NOGs, the state retreated from setting budgets for most subsectors of the health care system, returned to free collective bargaining between the KVs and insurers, and even extended the scope of their negotiations to the setting of practice guidelines for other subsectors of the health care system. But even as the government reiterated its commitment to corporatist self-governance, it compensated for the lifting of budgets on providers with a greater reliance on market competition among insurers and cost-sharing by patients. Hence, the NOG required that if a fund raised its contribution rate, it would have to increase its co-payments by the same

---

[21] As a short-term response to employers, the government enacted the Contribution Relief Act (*Beitragsentlastungsgesetz*) in 1996. That law required all funds to cut their contribution rates by 0.7% for 1997 (OECD 1997*b*: 85).

percentage. But patients facing a hike in contributions and co-payments would be free to switch insurers without the usual waiting period. In effect, the government's budgeting policy shifted from the sectoral level to that of the individual sickness fund.[22] The government reasoned that this would put sickness funds under severe pressure to not raise their rates and to instead take a tougher line in their negotiations with providers. Finally, the government also introduced provisions that required greater cost-sharing from patients: co-payments were now to be linked to the development of wages and salaries, while marginal benefits were struck from the statutory insurance catalogue and offered as 'extras' for patients to purchase from insurers.[23]

The NOGs signalled a shifting of the burden of cost containment onto patients and insurers. But they were far less drastic than some of the proposals considered during the reform debates between 1995 and 1997. The key goal was to relieve employers' of their share of non-wage labour costs. The most radical proposal would have called for employers' exit from financing health insurance altogether and substituting parity financing with compulsory, individual insurance borne solely by workers. However, a 'wage subsidy' would have compensated employees for this new expense.[24]

This proposal failed, however, not only because unions and the Social Democratic Party (SDP) predictably opposed it, but also because employers themselves had little interest in it. Employers argued that the Free Democratic Party (FDP) proposal would not have solved the problem of labour costs, but would have merely shifted the battle to the collective bargaining arena, where unions would have certainly demanded higher wages as compensation for the substantial new health insurance costs borne by their members ('Haarscharf' 1995). Furthermore, employers reasoned that relief from the responsibility of financing health care would also mean losing their representation on sickness funds' boards and their ability to influence health policy more generally ('Haarscharf' 1995). Finally, the coalition government itself was by no means of a common mind on the proposal. The CDU's trade union wing was adamantly opposed to it on the grounds that it violated the principles of parity financing and administration of health

---

[22] Manow has made this point in Giaimo and Manow (1999).

[23] The 1996 Contribution Relief Act removed the marginal benefits from the statutory catalogue. For details on the 1997 laws, see *Dienst für Gesellschaftspolitik* (20 Feb. 1997 and 27 Mar. 1997); Giaimo 1998; Giaimo and Manow 1999; and Manow 1997*b*.

[24] The strongest backer of this proposal was the Free Democratic Party in Kohl's coalition government. 'Union und FDP geben einander die Schuld am Abbruch der Gespräche über die Gesundheitsreform', *Frankfurter Allgemeine Zeitung (FAZ)*, 9 Oct. 1995, 1–2; 'Wettbewerb zwischen Krankenkassen soll verstärkt werden', *FAZ*, 15 Dec. 1995, 1; 'Haarscharf wieder so', *Der Spiegel*, 23 Oct. 1995, 30–1. The reform debate also considered more solidaristic proposals (such as taxing sources of income beyond wages and salaries, or bringing in segments of the population exempt from statutory insurance). For a discussion of the range of proposals considered between 1995 and 1997, see Giaimo 1998; Hinrichs 1995: 637–79; Advisory Council for the Concerted Action in Health Care 1995: 44–7, and 1997: 32–46). For a recent discussion of reform alternatives, see OECD 1997*b*.

care, while the health minister was fundamentally at odds with the FDP's neoliberal vision of individual responsibility and market provision for health care ('Die FDP unter Druck', *FAZ*, 9 Oct. 1995, 1; 'Haarscharf' 1995).

The interactions among actors in the German health care system, the broader political economy, and the political arena thus produced an overall reform pattern during the Kohl era that required a balancing of the goals of cost control with equity. All three arenas affected the strategic calculations of payers and policy makers and made it difficult for any one actor to pursue cost containment at the expense of other players. The health care system itself has limited the room for manoeuvre of employers, but so has its relationship to the larger political economy. Thus, the statutory nature of health insurance did not allow employers to reduce their labour costs by refusing to provide health insurance or by unilaterally curbing benefits. Moreover, even when given the option of exit, employers refused to take it because they recognized that they face a formidable counterweight in employees' presence in health insurance financing and administration, as well as in union strength in collective bargaining.[25] Business leaders knew that victory in one arena could just as easily translate into setbacks in another, and they saw their role in statutory social insurance as a valuable lever to control non-wage labour costs.

The German political system also granted key health care stakeholders a number of avenues to shape the content of reform legislation. The political parties and federalism were the chief avenues of influence for employees as well as employers. Both of the two main political parties—the Christian Democratic Union (CDU) and the SPD are heterogeneous *Volksparteien* or 'catch-all parties' (Kirchheimer 1966) representing the interests of employees and vulnerable groups in the population. The CDU institutionalizes both a business and Catholic trade union wing in separate internal party committees. The trade union wing of the CDU, with jurisdiction over the party's social policy matters, was the driving force behind the hardship exemptions on co-payments that featured in all of the health care reform laws. The GSG's measures reducing the disparities in choice of insurer and in contribution rates between blue- and white-collar workers were the product of a cross-party deal between the CDU's trade union wing and the opposition SPD in 1992. This 'de facto grand coalition' between the CDU and SPD was an expression of federalism and the Social Democrats' majority in the legislative upper house (Bundesrat), as well as of the ideological affinity between the CDU's labour wing and the SPD's moderate wing on the social market economy (*soziale Marktwirtschaft*) and a comprehensive welfare state.

---

[25] German unions only organize 35% of the labour force, but state extension of collective agreements grants them far more influence than membership numbers would suggest. Unions and employees are also firmly entrenched in the governance of the firm through co-determination arrangements.

But health politics and policies also were shaped by electoral outcomes and coalition politics. Encouraged by its improved showing in state elections in 1996, the FDP became a more pugnacious coalition partner eager to distinguish itself from the CDU and refusing to countenance further deals with the SPD. On top of this, Kohl's Government had only a razor-thin majority in the lower house (Bundestag) after 1994. To keep his fractious coalition together, Kohl had to yield to the FDP more than he had in the past. With the NOGs, then, the FDP played its familiar role as the patron of physicians and small business. Along with pressure from the CDU's business wing, whose influence had increased as the economic climate had deteriorated, Kohl chose the NOGs' provisions to stabilize employers' labour costs at the expense of patients and sickness funds.

Finally, the national insurance system both constrained and empowered state actors in the task of health care reform. Because national insurance guarantees all persons the same access to services based on medical need, and is modelled on contributory social insurance, it is very difficult for the state to pursue austerity at the expense of any one class or subgroup of the population. At the same time, however, the corporatist arrangements in the national insurance system provide the state with the legal authority and the institutional means—through its leverage over public-law bodies—to mandate cost-containment tasks on health care actors and to set the terms of market competition in ways that do not compromise the equity and solidarity of the system.

How, then, should we judge the Kohl Government's record on balancing costs and equity? Had they been fully implemented, it is clear that the NOGs would have shifted the burden of welfare state and economic adjustment from employers to patients. Dynamized co-payments and the linking of contribution to co-payment increases implied a gradual movement away from the principle of parity financing, since employees already paid half of the insurance contribution and patients would have also had to assume a growing portion of health care costs out of their own pocket (Manow 1997*b*).

But in important respects, the Kohl Government's policies largely preserved the equity of the health care system, and in some cases, even extended it. Health insurance has remained universal and the statutory catalogue of benefits generous; the services struck from the catalogue in 1996 were quite marginal. Hardship clauses have exempted low-income persons from the co-payment requirement or otherwise set a ceiling on the amount that those with chronic conditions would have to pay. And the government designed market forces in such a way as to advance both efficiency and equity concerns. Thus, insurers cannot compete on the basis of fewer benefits to woo healthier members but instead must accept all applicants and must offer, at a minimum, the same health services to all members contained in the catalogue of statutory benefits. Significantly, competition has granted wage earners nearly identical rights of choice of insurer as those long enjoyed by salaried employees. Likewise, the risk adjustment scheme has required substantial financial transfers from the company and white-collar funds, which had a history of healthier and wealthier members, to the local funds, which had had to levy higher contributions to cover the health care costs of their poorer and sicker blue-collar members. The risk-adjustment scheme has also narrowed contribution rates considerably among funds, to the benefit of blue-collar workers.[26] The risk-adjustment programme also reduces the temptation of sickness funds to compete by cream-skimming the healthier and wealthier persons, since they know they will have to make payments to funds with poorer health risk profiles. Finally, the most controversial provisions of the 1997 laws did not get very far in practice. Fearing punishment from voters in the 1998 elections, the Kohl Government refrained from implementing the provisions linking co-payments and contributions, while Kohl's Social Democratic successor, Gerhard Schröder, suspended the dynamization of co-payments and other market-like measures (Manow 1997*b*; Schneider 1998).[27]

Under Kohl's watch, the cost performance of the German health care system has also been respectable. To be sure, health insurance contribution rates have risen nearly every year, but the pace has been moderate: the average contribution rate, which stood at 12.6 per cent in 1990, was only 13.6 per cent in 1996 (Manow 1997*a*: table 3), despite the burdens of an ageing population, recession, and unification. This is not to say that Germany has found a way to permanently halt the upward trajectory of health care spending. But it has so far held the line and should be seen as an intermediate case between the tight-fistedness and unmet demand of Britain and the profligacy and cost-shifting of the United States.

The United States: The Triumph of 'Unmanaged Competition' and the Defeat of Equity

The most striking feature of the American health care system is the absence of a statutory universal health care programme and an employment-based fringe benefits system in its stead. Most Americans look to their employers to provide health insurance, while public programmes are confined

[26] One fund, for example, had to pay approximately half of its revenues to the risk adjustment fund (OECD 1997: 107). In 1993, approximately 32% of funds levied contribution rates 1% above or below the average. In 1996, less than 10% of the funds did so (Ministry of Health, cited in Giaimo and Manow 1999: 982).

[27] Kohl's successor, Gerhard Schröder, announced upon taking office that his SPD–Green government would not introduce the linkage provisions, and abolished the provision for dynamizing co-payments and some of the other market-like mechanisms, such as premium rebates for healthy patients, that the 1997 laws had introduced. The Schröder Government also reimposed legal budgets on all subsectors of the health care system as an interim cost control measure until it devised a comprehensive reform scheduled for the year 2000 (Schneider 1998).

to designated categories of the population, such as the elderly, disabled, the military, and the very poorest in society. Such arrangements make employers the pivotal players in the health care system and health care politics. They are free to decide whether or not to provide insurance as a fringe benefit, and when they do, most companies pay the bulk of the insurance premium (at least of the cheapest health plan). Unions offer little in the way of counter-vailing power because they have little or no presence in the workplace and no role in welfare state administration.[28] Likewise, government actors have few mechanisms to control the behaviour of employers and insurers in a voluntary, private fringe benefits system. State governments have limited regulatory authority over the employment-based insurance sector, while the federal government's reach is even more at arm's length.

Because of this patchwork system, the US health care system has always been plagued by costly gaps in access. The uninsured had access to emergency hospital care, and the safety-net providers who treated them recouped their losses by charging patients with private insurance higher fees. Insurers, in turn, passed on their cost increases to employers by charging them higher premiums (Reinhardt 1992). Thus, an elaborate but largely hidden cost-shifting game was being played, but with only some employers footing the bill. Rationing access by ability to pay was both inequitable and inefficient: it burdened vulnerable groups in society, encouraged free-riding by less efficient firms, and discouraged the uninsured from seeking out less expensive preventive care instead of costly hospital care.

But other reasons besides gaps in access and resultant cost-shifting were behind the high costs of the US health care system. Most physicians received fee-for-service payments for their services while hospitals were reimbursed for their costs, which gave them little incentive to seek out less expensive alternat-ives. Insurers largely paid what doctors billed without questioning treatment decisions, thereby deferring to physicians' economic and clinical freedom. The USA never had a mechanism like global budgeting to limit overall health care expenditures. Nor was there an effective system for controlling the diffusion of medical technology.[29] And until the advent of managed care, the USA had no gatekeeper system to limit access to specialists or to hospitals.

The cost-shifting game did not arouse too much complaint from em-ployers as long as the economy kept growing and American businesses were shielded from the effects of competition. But a number of factors converged to undermine firms' willingness to underwrite the care of the uninsured. First, medical inflation began to rise steeply in the 1980s (see Table 11.4).

---

[28] There are some exceptions, however. Some unions finance and administer insurance funds for their members. And employers who choose to self-finance their own health plans may directly administer these plans. But in many cases, employers contract with an insurance com-pany for administration.

[29] On state efforts to control high technology in hospitals, see Russell 1979.

TABLE 11.4. *Changes in medical care costs compared to Consumer Price Index, US (1967 = 100)*

Year	CPI	Total Medicine	Hospital	Physicians
1960	88.7	79.1	57.3	77.0
1965	94.5	89.5	75.9	88.3
1970	116.3	120.6	145.4	121.4
1975	161.2	168.6	236.1	169.4
1980	246.8	265.9	418.9	269.3
1985	326.6	413.0	722.5	407.9
1990	421.8	592.9	1096.1	533.1
1995	491.4	817.6	1577.1	692.5
1996	512.5	847.8	1638.6	717.0

Source: Peters 1999: 251: Bureau of the Census, Statistical Abstract of the United States.

Employers' health insurance premiums escalated at double-digit annual rates in the 1980s; between 1987 and 1993, employers' insurance premiums rose 90 per cent (Cooper and Schone 1997: 142).

More tellingly, the spike in health care inflation coincided with broader changes in the American economy since the 1970s. The shift to a post-industrial economy brought with it the disappearance of unionized jobs in manufacturing that had come with generous fringe benefits. In their place arose service sector jobs, temporary positions, and subcontracted labour in both manufacturing and services. Such contingent labour was one of the chief means for employers to hold down their labour costs, since these jobs often paid much lower wages than unionized jobs in manufacturing and did not come with health insurance and other fringe benefits (R. Freeman 1994).[30] Thus, the shifts in the American economy swelled the ranks of the uninsured, adding to the cross-subsidy burden of employers who did provide insurance. As their health insurance bills rose, these firms complained that they were at a competitive disadvantage relative to their domestic rivals who did not pro-vide insurance, or to those foreign competitors with lower labour costs.

As the 1980s wore on, employers who provided insurance became less will-ing to shoulder the access and cost deficiencies in the health care system. Many of them began to look to government to relieve them of their cross-subsidy burden through a national health insurance solution (C. J. Martin 1995a). Those advocating national insurance found a sympathetic ally in President Bill Clinton, who wanted to control the costs of public insurance

---

[30] The proportion of uninsured Americans had declined throughout the 1960s, 1970s, and the 1980s as a result of the expansion of Medicare, Medicaid, and employer-based insurance. However, the downward trend began to reverse itself in the late 1980s. Most of the uninsured were those in the labour market (Banks, Kunz, and Macdonald 1994: 19). In 1987, 14.8%, or 31.8 million non-elderly Americans had no insurance. By 1995, that figure had risen to 17.4% of the non-elderly population, or 40.3 million persons (EBRI 1997).

programmes, address employers' competitiveness concerns, and stem the rising tide of the uninsured.

With his plan for national health insurance and government-structured market competition, Clinton sought to solve both the cost and access problems simultaneously.[31] First, Clinton's Health Security plan would have required all firms to provide insurance, with the government subsidizing the costs to small firms or those individuals unable to obtain insurance through the workplace. Pooling all risks within a national insurance system would have achieved universal access and ended the cost-shifting and free-riding by firms that did not provide insurance. Second, Health Security mandated market competition among both providers and insurers to control health care costs, while largely pinning its hopes on health maintenance organizations (HMOs) to bring cost discipline to the market. By restricting patients' access to hospitals and specialists, HMOs tended to be much cheaper than other types of health plans. More expensive insurers would either have to reduce their costs to retain patients or else charge higher premiums and impose cost-sharing for additional benefits or greater choice of provider.[32]

Third, government actors would have played a leading role in structuring the market to ensure universal access and to prevent insurers and providers from engaging in competitive practices that harmed the sicker and poorer. States would have been key actors in this regard by establishing quasi-public 'health alliances' on a regional basis to ensure that small businesses and individuals had access to affordable coverage. In short, alliances would have organized the market and 'managed' the competition through extensive monitoring of insurers to prevent them from cream-skimming (Starr 1994: 53, 102). Large companies that self-insured could have chosen to opt out of the state alliances and instead constitute their own alliances (C. J. Martin 1995*b*).

Finally, the Clinton plan would have expanded the federal government's reach over employment-based insurance. The Health Security Act would have legislated a minimum but comprehensive benefits package that all plans had to offer. In addition, a National Health Board, with members appointed by the President, would have possessed wide-ranging powers to regulate alliances and health plans. And because the Clinton administration doubted that competition alone could control costs, the National Health Board would have had the authority to enforce a global budget cap over the entire health care system by limiting insurers' premium increases to the rate of inflation (Starr 1994).

---

[31] Unless otherwise noted, the description of the Clinton plan is drawn from the White House Domestic Policy Council (WHDPC 1993). Clinton's plan drew heavily on Stanford health economist Alain Enthoven's theory of managed competition (see Enthoven 1988, 1993).

[32] Employers would have shouldered 80% of the premium of the cheapest plan, with employees paying the 20% balance plus any additional premium costs if they chose more expensive plans.

Clinton's effort to introduce national health insurance came to an inglorious end, but this did not mean that health care reform was dead. Rather, transformation of the health care system continued apace at breathtaking scope and speed, with employers leading the charge in an uncoordinated, every firm-for-itself strategy. The centrepiece of this strategy was the deployment of competition against insurers and providers. Under pressure from employers to hold the line on premiums, managed care plans negotiated steep price discounts or capitation arrangements with doctors and hospitals.[33] Many employers also sought to control their health care costs by offering workers only one health plan, often an inexpensive HMO. Others rushed to self-insure in order to escape state risk-pools for the uninsured and other consumer regulations. In addition, employers engaged in a number of strategies that shifted their costs onto weaker market actors. For instance, companies required their workers to shoulder a greater share of insurance premiums or co-payments or curtailed the range of benefits that health insurance plans offered. Finally, some companies exercised their ultimate exit option by refusing to provide coverage at all (Giaimo 1996; Giaimo and Manow 1999).

Employers' strategies to contain their labour costs are best characterized as 'unmanaged competition' (Giaimo 1996), in which the application of market forces in health care has proceeded in the absence of an effective regulatory framework that would prohibit or compensate for market failures. Federal and state government controls over employers' and insurers' cost-cutting practices have been piecemeal, weak, or non-existent. Where government action has occurred, it has largely taken the form of incremental regulation of the insurance market to foster competition, as with federal and state oversight of mergers (Given 1997), or to make it conform to the dictates of the larger economy (Giaimo and Manow 1999).[34] The absence of a framework of rules over the market has permitted insurers to continue to segment the market and shun the worst health risks. And the absence of effective consumer protections in the world of managed care has also provoked a public backlash against the rationing decisions of HMOs (Blendon et al. 1998).

---

[33] By 1997, 85% of employees were in some type of managed care plan, up from slightly more than 28% in 1988 (Milt Freudenheim, 'To Economists, Managed Care is No Cure-All', *New York Times*, 6 Sept. 1994, A1, A10; Freudenheim, 'Health Insurers Seek Big Increases in their Premiums', *New York Times*, 24 Apr. 1998, A1, C4). For an excellent survey of recent managed care developments, see Wilkerson, Devers, and Given 1997: esp. ch. 1 and conclusion chapter. The editors point out that while managed care plans have a long history, the phenomenon of intensified price competition among these health plans is a recent development.

[34] The 1996 Kassebaum–Kennedy Act was an attempt to respond to employers' concerns with 'job-lock' by barring insurers from denying coverage to new employees with pre-existing medical conditions. But because the law made no provision that premiums would be affordable and allowed insurers to impose a waiting period before coverage began, it fell far short of its goal (Fuchs et al. 1997; GAO 1998; Robert Pear, 'Clinton to Punish Insurers Who Deny Health Coverage', *New York Times*, 7 July 1998, A1, A13).

How can we understand a reform path that started out as a solidaristic attempt at national insurance but ended up as atomistic cost-shifting at the expense of broader solidarity? The explanation lies in the critical role played by employers, their inability to forge a common line around a solidaristic solution to their labour costs problem, and the voluntarism of the fringe benefits system that instead encouraged their go-it-alone strategies of cost containment. Employers were critical to the fate of the Clinton plan because they financed health insurance and would have continued to do so under Health Security. As a result, the Clinton plan was held hostage to the veto of business. Firms' disarray in the political arena mirrored their actions in the health care system itself, with employers organizationally incapable of delivering support to the President. Moreover, the voluntarism of the American health insurance system encouraged employers to pursue multiple go-it-alone cost-containment strategies and blocked effective government action to limit their behaviour in ways that would protect solidarity. Let us consider each of these points in turn.

First, a firm's particular position in the health care system shaped its approach to controlling labour costs and the attitudes of its managers towards reform. For some employers, the voluntarism of the fringe benefits system aided them in their quest for low labour costs, but for others, it was a big part of the problem. As we have seen, many employers who already provided insurance blamed their high labour costs on the free-riding of their colleagues who did not offer coverage, and supported national insurance to level the competitive playing field among them. Most small businesses, by contrast, saw the voluntarism of employment-based insurance as vital to their economic survival; the freedom to not provide insurance was what allowed them to keep their labour costs at competitive levels. Not surprisingly, they vehemently opposed the Clinton plan on the grounds that it would saddle them with ruinously high labour costs. But even among firms that provided insurance, there were those who rejected the Clinton plan because they feared that it would have meant higher costs. Either they would have been forced into regional alliances and would have paid higher premiums in order to subsidize insurance for small businesses. Or, if they were large enough to constitute their own alliances, they ran the risk that the even larger regional alliances would have negotiated better rates from insurers and left them with higher premiums (Judis 1995; C. J. Martin 1995*a*, 1995*b*). For different reasons, then, these employers believed they could better control their own costs by 'going-it-alone'.

Second, the business community proved incapable of forging a common line on health care reform, in large part because the health care system granted its member firms multiple ways to control their labour costs, including not providing insurance at all. The freedom of action in the health care system, in turn, aggravated employers' collective action problems in the political arena.

Employers' peak associations—perennially weak, fragmented, and lacking sanctions over recalcitrant members—proved unable to overcome the centrifugal tendencies within their ranks to rally their members to support the Clinton plan at the critical legislative stage. Associations representing large and medium-sized firms remained on the sidelines and left the field open to small business, whose association waged a highly effective campaign of opposition.[35] Third, many businesses deemed Clinton's attempt to claim a greater government role in employment-based insurance as an illegitimate intrusion into their domain of corporate governance. Some employers—and not just small businesses—opposed Clinton's national insurance proposal because the employer mandate and statutory benefits package would have encroached upon their freedom to decide on insurance coverage for their employees. Others were even more alarmist, arguing that national insurance was an entering wedge for government intrusion into other areas of corporate governance (Judis 1995).

Subsequent government attempts to regulate the health care market after the Clinton plan's defeat have met with similar failure. Employers and insurers continue to regard government efforts to regulate employer-based health plans as illegitimate and as saddling them with unwanted costs. Moreover, the perversities of federalism have meant that state and federal officials work at cross-purposes, blocking one another's efforts to expand access or enact adequate consumer protections on employment-based insurance. The biggest obstacle is the Employee Retirement and Income Security Act (ERISA), which permits states to regulate private insurance but not employers' self-insured health plans. Not surprisingly, employers have seized upon self-insurance to avoid cooptation into state risk-pools for the uninsured and to evade state consumer protection regulations for private insurers. At the same time, however, federal regulation of self-insured plans and employer-based health insurance more generally is notoriously weak. The result is a dual system of government regulation that shields self-insured plans—whose numbers are increasing—from regulations that apply to other types of private insurers.[36]

---

[35] For accounts of business organizations' disarray towards the Clinton plan, see Adam Clymer, Robert Pear, and Robin Toner, 'For Health Care, Time Was a Killer', *New York Times*, 29 Aug. 1994, A1, A8–9; Judis 1995; Jurek Martin, 'Business Snubs Clinton Health Bill', *Financial Times,* 4 Feb. 1994, 5; Skocpol 1996; and Robin Toner, 'Autopsy on Health Care', *New York Times*, 27 Sept. 1994, A1 ff.

[36] For a discussion of ERISA, see Acs et al. 1996; Chirba-Martin and Brennan 1994; GAO 1995; Grogan 1995; O'Keefe 1995; and Polzer and Butler 1997. Seventy-eight per cent of companies with 1,000 or more employees and 89% with 20,000 or more employees were self-insured in 1993. Self-insurance has been growing: among firms with at least 100 employees, 46% of employees were enrolled in self-insured plans in 1993, compared to only 28% in 1986 (GAO 1995: 12–13). The Clinton administration had pushed for comprehensive consumer protection legislation at the federal level to regulate the rationing decisions by HMOs. But its efforts became bogged down in the impeachment scandal (see Giaimo and Manow 1999; R. Pear, 'Senators Reject Bill to Regulate Care by HMOs', *New York Times*, 10 Oct. 1998, A1, A8).

Health care reform through the market, led by private actors in the absence of public rules, has worrying implications for the achievement of both cost control and equitable access and financing. On the positive side, the USA experienced a noticeable slowing in health care outlays between 1993 and 1996. The spread of managed care plans in the private sector, with their restricted access to hospitals and specialists and their reliance on capitation or discounts to pay providers, has wrung out much of the excess capacity in the health care system and is responsible for much of the slowdown in health care outlays (Levit et al. 1998; S. Smith et al. 1998). However, it may be that the days of easy savings have come to an end, as mergers and acquisitions among plans and providers reach a saturation point (S. Smith et al. 1998). Indeed, after slowing considerably in the last few years, employers' health insurance premiums are set to rise substantially, as insurers seek to recover lost profits after years of belt-tightening.[37]

Moreover, cost savings for some have been realized at the expense of equity. While insurers have recently hiked their premiums, the biggest increases have fallen on small firms and individuals, not large companies.[38] In addition, firms' and insurers' cost-cutting strategies have segmented the market further and threaten what little solidarity there is in the health care system. The current trend shows the number of uninsured growing as employers—willingly or otherwise—exercise their exit option and refuse to offer coverage or as low-wage workers find insurance premiums beyond their reach (Cooper and Schone 1997). Those individuals with insurance coverage are also bearing a greater share of their health care costs. Finally, continued cost-shifting to weaker market players only aggravates the problem of the uninsured, as small firms and individuals find themselves priced out of the market by exorbitant premiums. The 'worst case' scenario predicts the disintegration of public hospital 'providers of last resort' and more restricted access for the most vulnerable members of society as employers' and insurers' cost-cutting actions, along with cuts in government programmes, destroy the cross-subsidy for the uninsured.[39] Thus, absent effective public intervention,

---

[37] Real per capita health spending averaged just below 5% per year between 1970 and 1993. Between 1993 and 1996, it averaged only 1.5% per year. But it is set to grow at 3.4% per year from 1997 to 2007, with the percentage of GDP predicted to rise to 16.6% in 2007 (S. Smith et al. 1998: 128–9).

[38] Milt Freudenheim, 'Health Care Costs Edging Up and a Bigger Surge is Feared', *New York Times*, 21 Jan. 1997, A1, D20; Freudenheim, 'Health Insurers Seek Big Increases in their Premiums', *New York Times*, 24 Apr. 1998, A1, C4. In addition to cost-shifting from stronger to weaker market players, the higher costs may be due to patients demanding greater choice of physician, and doctors organizing to counteract the growth of HMOs.

[39] For evidence of the 'worst case' scenario and the threat to the public hospital system, see the *Los Angeles Times* series in October 1995. Reinhardt (1995) paints a somewhat less pessimistic portrait, but one that still envisions safety-net providers bearing the brunt of the burden.

the ultimate logic of employer-led, go-it-alone strategies threatens both the cost-containment goals of many individual firms as well as the survival of the health care system itself.

4. CONCLUSION

The health care reform experiences suggest broader lessons for the politics of welfare state adjustment in the twenty-first century. The first lesson is that payers have become the driving force behind reform and they are likely to remain important actors in the politics of welfare state adjustment as long as economic difficulties associated with globalization or the post-industrial economy continue. But this should not lead to the conclusion that their views will always prevail. The terms of welfare state adjustment will depend on the presence of countervailing forces in the particular welfare state and political arena in each country.

Second, employers (and governments) are undeniably worried about the welfare state's effects on competitiveness. But their concerns need not translate into a policy stance that is anti-welfare state or anti-solidaristic. As the accounts of health care reform in the USA and Germany illustrate, many companies may favour a statutory, solidaristic solution because it pools risks and levels the competitive playing field among them. This suggests that employers' views towards the welfare state will depend on whether they see it as compatible with their competitiveness strategies. The strategies employers choose to contain their labour costs, in turn, will in part depend on the type of welfare state in which they find themselves and the freedom of action it grants or denies them to do so.

Thus, there is no one welfare state that best serves the cause of competitiveness, or even one particular welfare state type that automatically corresponds to a particular political economy. Instead, a number of different welfare state regimes may 'fit' together with the other components of a nation's political economy.[40] Thus, a voluntary fringe benefits system like that in the USA is an integral part of a broader liberal political economy, and is a critical part of a strategy of competition based on rock-bottom prices and low skills/low labour costs because it allows firms the freedom to not provide benefits. Of course, it also creates difficulties for other firms who must

---

[40] Put another way, there may be more 'varieties of capitalism' than the literature commonly assumes. The varieties of capitalism literature sketches only two models of capitalism: coordinated and liberal market economies. And it is only beginning to systematically integrate welfare states into its analysis. For examples of the varieties of capitalism literature, see Crouch and Streeck 1997; Hall 1998. For efforts to integrate the welfare state into varieties of capitalism models, see Ebbinghaus and Manow 1998; and Manow 1997*a*.

subsidize their compatriots' free-riding. The danger is that free-riding will gradually undermine this form of social provision, as more and more employers drop coverage to contain their labour costs.

But a tax-financed, state-administered system like the British NHS can be equally compatible with company strategies to compete on low prices and labour costs characteristic of a liberal political economy. Indeed, one reason that a social democratic oasis like the NHS could survive in Britain's neoliberal desert—aside from its track record of delivering low health care spending and its broad political popularity—was precisely because it did not threaten a competitiveness strategy premissed on low price and labour costs that Thatcher and employers advocated. A social insurance system like Germany's would seemingly pose the biggest disadvantage for firms seeking competitiveness through lower labour costs. Yet, as we have seen, employers have not been eager to part with their role in the social insurance system because it has provided them a lever over labour costs outside of collective bargaining.[41] This is a considerable advantage in a political economy that features a strong union presence in both industrial relations and in welfare state administration.

Third, some of the arguments advanced in welfare state reform debates argue for a roll-back of government and more privatization. But the health care reform experiences show that employment-based fringe benefits systems are a poor substitute for statutory social insurance programmes. As Esping-Andersen (1990) has noted, different welfare state regimes embody different kinds of social rights. In statutory universal systems, social rights are broadly defined and firmly anchored in the law. In fringe benefits systems, however, social rights rest on a precarious foundation. They depend on the economic power of unions to secure them through collective bargaining or on the discretion of employers to provide them, and generally do not have the legal backing of the state. This is not to imply that universal, statutory programmes are immutable or permanent, or that they should not or cannot adapt to new realities. But they may be harder to dislodge because they have a broader spectrum of the population interested in preserving them. And because they incorporate redistribution within their design, they may prove better able to adapt in ways that safeguard equity.

The task for all advanced industrialized societies is to adapt their welfare states to new economic and demographic challenges in ways that reconcile efficiency with equity. However, the outcome is likely to be quite different in welfare states with different kinds of social rights and social forces. Private

[41] Mares (1997*a*) and Swenson (1997) likewise found that firms have good economic reasons for wanting universal social programmes. Employers may also value their administrative role in social insurance if it provides them with a painless way to rationalize production and shed unneeded labour onto the broader risk community (see Manow 1997*a*; Visser and Hemerijck 1997).

fringe benefits systems appear to have a bleak future. Lacking countervailing forces to challenge or curb employers' freedom to pursue exit options, the anchoring of social rights in the law, or a broad notion of solidarity that ties people to a common fate, such systems will likely to continue down the path of desolidarity, unless those bearing the brunt of cost-shifting and economic adjustment can muster the political clout to seek a negotiated solution that advances equity alongside austerity.

The outcomes may be more hopeful in universal, statutory systems. If, as seems likely, economic and demographic pressures continue to strain the finances and generosity of such welfare states, then governments and employers will be hard-pressed to seek solutions that redefine solidarity and the content of social rights. But given the presence of powerful countervailing forces in such welfare states and reform politics, successful adjustment will hinge on forging a consensus with these stakeholders over a new conception of solidarity that continues to ensure broad provision, spreads the burden of adjustment fairly, and shelters the most vulnerable from harm.

There is no reason to expect countries to converge on a common path of welfare state adjustment. There are several possible options.[42] Each country's outcome will depend not only on past 'policy legacies' (Pierson 1993*b*; Weir and Skocpol 1985), but also on political choice and the particular settlements that stakeholders are able to forge among themselves.

[42] Future choices in health care reforms—and how they are viewed—will depend on the particular problems facing each type of health care system and the specific politics of reform in each country. For example, countries with universal health care provision might decide to adopt a defined benefits package that is mandatory, universal, and comprehensive, but that explicitly spells out the services that the national programme will cover. Individuals with the means to do so could then purchase extra benefits at an additional charge, but the most vulnerable would still have a right to fairly comprehensive coverage. Such a remedy, however, would officially sanction some differences in access based on ability to pay and may imply a stricter delineation of medical necessity. British and German citizens might view this solution either as a violation of solidarity, or as an attempt to redefine it to reconcile equity and cost containment goals. But if the USA adopted a defined benefits package as part of national health insurance, it would clearly signal a reversal of desolidarity. See Brown (1998) for a discussion of different health care reform options that European countries are contemplating or have recently adopted. See Advisory Council for Concerted Action in Health Care (1995, 1997) for a discussion of reform options for Germany. On redefining medical necessity to fit new policy goals, see Charles et al. (1997).

12

Labour Market Regimes under Threat? Sources of Continuity in Germany, Britain, and Sweden

Stewart Wood

IT seems impossible to study welfare states without studying the worlds of employment and unemployment to which they are attached. Yet the inclusion of labour market policy within the study and typologies of welfare states has been a recent development (Esping-Andersen 1990; Kolberg 1992; Stephens 1994). This is surprising in view of the multiple, though complex, interactions between labour markets and welfare states. First, many institutions and programmes (such as systems of unemployment insurance and schemes for early retirement) clearly belong to both domains. Second, the causal arrow from labour markets to welfare states goes both ways. On the one hand, variables such as the model of employment relations, the structure of bargaining systems, codes of employment protection, and types of non-standard employment fundamentally shape welfare state institutions and activities. On the other hand, welfare programmes construct incentives and constraints that impinge upon the terms and conditions of work, unemployment, and non-employment, as well as the transition between them. These linkages have long been exploited by policy makers—using the welfare state to shed labour, and labour market reform to reduce welfare dependency, for example. Finally, welfare states have in the past fifty years become sizeable employment systems in themselves (Kolberg and Esping-Andersen 1992).

The attempt to link models of welfare states systematically with patterns of labour market policy began with Esping-Andersen's paradigmatic analysis of welfare capitalism (Esping-Andersen 1990). In his view, each of the three worlds of welfare was accompanied by distinctive labour market regimes governing entry into, absence during, and exit from employment. Kolberg and Esping-Andersen (1992) used the term 'welfare regime' to denote the complex of institutions and policies that lies at the nexus of welfare states and

I would like to thank Peter Hall, Torben Iverson, Desmond King, Philip Manow, Iain McLean, Paul Pierson, David Stasavage, and Virpi Timonen for their comments on this paper, as well as those of other contributors to the volume.

labour markets. A wide range of research has since attempted to describe the distinctive patterns of work and unemployment associated with these regimes (Kolberg and Kolstad 1992; Pierson 1993*a*; Esping-Andersen 1996*c*). Despite a conspicuous lack of convergence on common terminology, this literature almost uniformly adopts the ideal-types developed by Esping-Andersen. Whether the specific subject is post-industrial employment trajectories, models of service sector growth, or the structure of unemployment, most accounts continue to divide national cases of welfare state–labour market interactions into 'the three worlds' (though see F. G. Castles and Mitchell 1993 for an influential amendment). Evidence strongly supports the claim for distinctive clusterings of welfare regimes (Huber and Stephens 1997).

A more pressing question, however, is whether or not these clusterings remain distinctive *over time*. Existing research was until relatively recently heavily biased towards characterizations of 'golden ages'. In the past five years, challenges to established welfare and labour market policies—both exogenous challenges and those deriving from 'Achilles heels' or 'hot spots' of existing regimes—have begun to receive more attention. But the predicted demise of distinctive welfare states has not resulted from the supposed onslaught of 'globalization' (Pierson 1997*d*; Garrett 1997; Krugman 1996). As many of the chapters in this volume show, variation between national welfare regimes remains pronounced, and market-induced convergence between them still seems a remote prospect. Furthermore, the effect of pressures such as de-industrialization, membership of the European Union, and high unemployment is not unidirectional. And rather than simply a casualty of these challenges, the welfare state should be viewed in part as offering resources for actors to manage them. The broader methodological point is that changing policy outcomes cannot be directly read off from social and economic pressures on the welfare state without reference to the preferences and strategies of the actors that respond to them.

Labour market policies in advanced industrial democracies provide interesting illustrations of these general points. On the one hand, the economic, political, and intellectual pressures on traditional forms of labour market policy have been particularly intense over the past fifteen years. Yet, as the evidence presented below testifies, labour market regimes in the late 1990s remain distinct in ways that demonstrate profound continuities with their 'golden age' incarnations. How can the resilience of these policy complexes be explained? What factors have propelled the policy choices of the relevant political actors? This chapter addresses these issues by focusing on recent labour market policy developments in three national cases—Germany, the United Kingdom, and Sweden—drawn from each of Esping-Andersen's three worlds. The central task is to assess the sources of policy continuity in each of these national cases, in an era of mounting economic, political, and ideological pressures for convergence and for fiscal retrenchment.

Comparisons of policy responses to common problems present a chance to assess competing arguments for distinctive policy trajectories over time. In this respect, this chapter picks up on some of the broader themes developed in Parts I and II of this volume. Its theoretical starting point is an examination of path dependence, perhaps the most popular contemporary approach to explaining the persistence of institutions and policies over time (Arthur 1994; Levi 1996; Pierson 1997*b*, Introduction, in this volume). Although path dependence in principle offers an enticing explanation of the resilience of national policy trajectories, the outcomes it explains have a tendency to be overdetermined. Not all mechanisms generating a bias towards the status quo are path-dependent ones. The theoretical work of this chapter, therefore, lies in deriving alternative (though not mutually exclusive) micro-level sources of policy continuity over time, and evaluating their relative contributions to the evolution of labour market policy in Germany, Britain, and Sweden. These alternative explanations thus offer a chance to revisit and evaluate the connections between the welfare state and political economy (Huber and Stephens), constitutional variables (Bonoli, Huber and Stephens), and partisan politics (Kitschelt) discussed earlier in the volume.

The chapter is divided into four substantive sections. In Section 1 the theory of path-dependent institutional and policy trajectories in politics is discussed. Section 2 presents three distinct sources of policy continuity —employer-centred, constitutional, and electoral—that are often bundled together as 'lock-in mechanisms' in path-dependent accounts. In Section 3 the changing context of labour market policy in the 1990s in Western Europe is sketched. An outline is provided of both 'golden age' policy regimes in the three country cases and of the new tasks confronted by governments in each labour market regime. The competing sources of status quo bias are then tested in Section 4 by examining national responses to unemployment, and related labour market problems, in Germany, Britain, and Sweden after 1980.

1. PATH DEPENDENCE IN POLITICS

Increasing Returns and Barriers to Exit

Political scientists have long wrestled with the problem of why national policy trajectories remain distinctive over time in the midst of pressures to change or even converge (Shonfield 1969; Hall 1986; Zysman 1983). In the 1980s a range of 'new institutionalist' accounts attempted to explain this continuity by linking stable institutional arrangements with stable policy outcomes (Thelen and Steinmo 1992). However, correlating institutions with policies raised the question of why these institutions were themselves so stable over long periods. At the same time the distinction and relationship between policies and institutions has come to seem less and less clear; policies give rise to institutions just as institutions give rise to policies, and policy stability may itself be a function of feedback from previous policies (Pierson 1993*b*). The explanatory imperative for political science has as a result become a much broader one of accounting for the 'change-resistant' properties of both policies *and* institutions.

The notion of path dependence offers a promising possibility for this more general explanation. At its weakest, path dependence is little more than the observation that history matters to current outcomes (Sewell 1996). Without understanding the sequences of events that precede an outcome of interest, we cannot understand that outcome fully. In this weak conception, there is no way of telling whether past events might result in continuity or change in the future. The claim is merely that influence is exerted. The stronger claim is that once a country or region has started down a certain path, it is likely to stay on it in the future. In other words, initial choices (or 'pushes') are not easily reversed, and paths cannot be left without large costs. This notion of path dependence 'refer(s) to those particular sequences which have self-reinforcing properties' (Pierson 1997*b*: 4–5).

If path dependence is to be useful as an explanatory framework, it must be able to specify the mechanisms that lock-in particular trajectories. In perhaps the most comprehensive and ambitious rendition of the theoretical framework, Pierson (1997*b*) presents a general typology of these mechanisms in the political world. Outcomes are path dependent for two central reasons. First, politics is characterized by various features that make it conducive to processes where 'each step along a particular path produces consequences which make that path more attractive for the next round' (Pierson 1997*b*: 6). Second, politics is characterized by various features that provide resistance to pressures that might otherwise force actors off a particular path. Each set of features merits discussion.

Increasing returns arguments, as Pierson's overview demonstrates, have found favour extensively within economics (David 1985; North 1990; Arthur 1994). Initial decisions and institutions can prejudice some future outcomes over others by providing strong incentives and constraints for actors to act in certain ways. Arthur distinguishes four such effects in the paradigmatic case of new technologies. First, high fixed or set-up costs may encourage individuals to persevere with certain investments in order to reduce unit costs. Second, repeated use improves operational knowledge of a given innovation and can generate efficiency savings and/or further innovations (learning effects). Third, the more a common technology is used by others, the greater the advantage for any individual in continued use (coordination effects). Fourth, in anticipation of the benefits to be gained from coordination on a common technology, expectations will adapt to select likely winners, and thus become self-fulfilling (adaptive expectations effects).

Pierson claims that there is considerable reason to suspect these 'positive feedbacks' to be as strong, if not stronger, in politics, because of three contextual features of the political world. The fact that institutions and policies (backed by the force of law and the power of the state) are authoritative constraints on activity induces high fixed costs, learning effects, coordination effects, and adaptive expectations. Second, the inescapably collective (or, perhaps more accurately, game-like) character of politics presents significant advantages from coordination on common institutions, policies, strategies, and outcomes. Lastly, the sheer complexity of political arrangements makes information gathering difficult and costly, particularly for the vast majority of individuals who seldom engage in political activity. Institutions and policies can be valuable in this opaque world by offering 'cues' for actors that can induce shared outlooks and expectations.

As a result of these increasing returns processes, inefficient institutions and policies may well persist over time. In the economic world, where market competition provides effective selection mechanisms, inefficiencies may be more easily corrected (Liebowitz and Margolis 1995). However, Pierson suggests, in the political world such corrections are especially difficult. Although policy makers and other actors are influenced by past successes and failures, there is no reason to believe that any process of learning acts to produce increasingly efficient outcomes over time. Inefficient political outcomes are not always selected out because of their inefficiency (in part because it is difficult to know what inefficient political outcomes *are*). Political actors tend to have short-term time horizons that reduce the incentive to tackle inefficiencies, particularly where the pay-off to doing so is diffuse or delayed. And finally, institutions and policies are notoriously 'sticky'. Sometimes this is the result of design, a means of binding one's successors (Moe 1990) or of binding oneself (North and Weingast 1989); often it is simply because reform processes are easy to stall and difficult to see through. In other cases, groups that benefit from programmes may be willing and well placed to mobilize in their defence once they become threatened.

A Critique and a Clarification

How persuasive is this picture of politics? Pierson's account of path dependence puts the strongest and most general case for the theory and is a powerful framework for understanding continuities in national policy trajectories. Before assessing its usefulness in explaining trends in labour market policy, however, two further clarifications are necessary. The first deals with the tendency of path-dependence explanations to exaggerate inertia and underestimate the possibility for change in politics. The second distinguishes the 'mechanism' of an increasing returns explanation from those of two rival explanations with which it can be confused and addresses the question of the sorts of evidence that would support one explanation rather than another.

Excessive Determinism.   Path-dependence accounts are often accused of implying too little variance in the dependent variables they seek to explain. If path-dependent mechanisms work in the way, and in the broad range of political contexts, that Pierson and others suggest, it is difficult to know why policies and institutions ever change at all. In part the problem of excessive determinism is a result of the misleading metaphor of 'the path'. If I am walking on a path, I can see the route it takes up ahead for metres or even miles. But only an ultra-deterministic social scientist would suggest that an initial policy decision fated a country into a unique and foreseeable series of policy moves in future periods. The central suggestion underlying path-dependence analyses is that certain moves are ruled out by past events in a sequence, *not* that there is only one possible route after a momentous initial 'turn'. The historical paths traversed by countries are ones which can be seen accurately only in retrospect. What is more important to path-dependence theory is the suggestion that sequences somehow make *certain* trajectories unlikely (or even preclude them) and others more likely. Viewed in this less deterministic way, path dependence becomes capable of accommodating change as well as continuity, by delineating the limits within which change can occur and identifying the factors that both mitigate against change and influence its direction.

A similar moderation of excessive determinism needs to be applied to the question of 'path inefficiencies'. It is clearly the case that selection mechanisms do not operate to privilege more over less efficient policies in the realm of politics. Inefficient outcomes have long lives. But inefficiencies do have welfare costs for actors, and the fact that these may persist or even accumulate as countries travel further down a particular policy path can serve to magnify their impact. At some point—a *tipping point*—the returns to be gained from network externalities of convergence on common practices may well become outweighed by the utility loss of living with 'bad' policies. Once this tipping point is reached, we should expect actors to seek policy change to correct the inefficiency. However, note that rectifying inefficiencies need not necessarily imply wholesale overthrow of a policy or complex of policies. If the benefits of long-standing coordination among actors are significant, and inefficiencies can be corrected through modifications to existing practice, we should expect to see strategies of adjustment that fall in between continuation of the status quo and complete policy reversals.

But what about the feasibility of such shifts? Pierson cites a variety of barriers to exit that militate against departures from policy trajectories. Although he acknowledges the possibility of governments orchestrating 'jumps' from one path to another, he contends that these are rare occurrences. But it is precisely the *authoritative* nature of politics which Pierson sees as central to positive feedback processes that offers opportunities for changes of direction. The concentration of authority in political contexts means that the interests of the few may dictate the fate of policies that apply to all. Where the relevant actors have access to law-making powers or significant political resources, significant shifts of policy are always possible. In particular, those in power have a strong *electoral* incentive to respond when policies go wrong or become unpopular. Failure to respond to dramatic turns of events, such as the appearance of persistently high levels of unemployment, can lead to dramatic shifts of support come election time. Furthermore, actors in the private sector can bring about important changes in policy. Governing parties may have their hands forced by key players such as core supporters, the preferences of swing voters, or coalition partners. And where policies delegate power to private sector groups such as employers' associations and trade unions (as in the case of insurance fund administration), policy shifts may be relatively easy for non-state actors *without* entering complex reform processes. For all these reasons, the existence of barriers to exit do not provide prima facie reasons for ruling out departures from policy paths.

Nor are these barriers to exit equally high across cases and across time. The complexity of reform processes varies considerably between one constitution and another. Even within the same constitutional arrangements policy changes may be easier at one time than another, depending on the distribution of support and opposition. Not all groups with preferences for the status quo will mobilize in its defence. And, as Pierson has discussed elsewhere, reformers may also be able to exploit the opacity of politics to hide, delay, or distribute the costs of change (Pierson 1994). Variance in factors such as these make the task of 'path deviating' easier in some contexts than others.

These observations suggest a more modest claim for the effect of path-dependence processes. Policies may generate increasing returns, but there is no necessary reason why these returns should compel policy continuity. If there are competing pressures on the direction of future policy—stemming from path inefficiencies, or the interests of other actors, for example—the outcome is a matter of contingency. Similarly, the fact that increasing returns exist does not mean that they will always be sufficient to preserve policies or institutions across different types of constitutional systems. In short, the mere presence of increasing returns processes is not sufficient to guarantee their dominance.

The Causal Mechanism of Increasing Returns Arguments. Pierson cites the prevalence of 'institutional stickiness' as a factor that 'intensifies' increasing returns processes. Not all sources of policy continuity are path-dependent ones, however. What distinguishes a path-dependent process is that the process is *self*-reinforcing: the probability of one outcome rather than another (or of one set of outcomes rather than another set) increases with each 'step down the path' after an initial event. The sources of policy continuity are endogenous to the policy and its 'interaction with certain qualities of related social activity' (Pierson 1994: 17). More specifically, increasing returns processes engender a status quo bias *indirectly* by influencing the interests and preferences of actors in ways that incline them to support a particular institution or policy, and to mobilize in its defence if necessary. Note that this implies a two-stage causal process: first, policies generating learning, coordination, and adaptive expectations effects shape the interests of key actors; second, these actors press for the maintenance of the conditions responsible for these effects.

The status quo bias induced by the effects of increasing returns on actors' preferences may be compounded by other factors, but the causal mechanism is a distinct one. Contrast the increasing returns argument with the claim that policy stability is the result of constitutional obstacles that make reform difficult. Whereas increasing returns arguments work through their effect on actors' interests and preferences, institutions shape policy outcomes through their effect on actors' strategies. Constitutions laden with multiple veto points and separated powers may make reform difficult, but they do so by frustrating reformers rather than by influencing their policy *preferences*.

A second and more subtle contrast is that between an increasing returns argument for policy stability and one which links policy outcomes to the interests of key actors. Many groups may have an interest in the continuation of a particular policy, and their activity may even be decisive in getting their desired outcome. But where these interests are *exogenous* to the policy itself—and its interaction with existing institutions and policies—it is not an increasing returns story. Trade unions, for example, will usually support the introduction of employment legislation and fight for its retention once in place. Their opposition to its reform or abolition is often crucial. Yet their interest in the policy is not engendered by any aspect of the policy itself and would exist whether statutory employment protection was high, low, or absent. Distinguishing an increasing returns dynamic from 'normal' interests-based politics therefore requires attention to the *source* of these interests.

Increasing returns accounts of policy continuity thus contend with rival institutional and interests-based explanations. All three explanations may point in the same direction, but the importance of each in any empirical case can only be determined by close examination of actual reform trajectories. The remainder of this paper assesses the relevance of these alternative sources of 'status quo bias' in the case of contemporary labour market policy. In the next section, variants of the three explanations are derived for the specific case of labour market policy in advanced industrial democracies. As argued below, although all three explanations are consistent with the policy stability we see in all three empirical cases (Sweden, Germany, and the UK), the lock-in mechanisms they emphasize are quite distinct, and the evidence required to lend them support differs correspondingly.

2. SOURCES OF CONTINUITY IN LABOUR MARKET POLICY

Increasing Returns: An Employer-Centred Approach

One of the key insights of path-dependence theory derives from the observation of the centrality of coordination to political life. This has also been a prominent theme in recent theoretical developments in political economy, notably in the 'varieties of capitalism' literature (Soskice 1999; Albert 1991; Berger and Dore 1996; Hall and Soskice 2000). Institutionalist arguments in the 1970s and 1980s explained policy continuity with reference to individual institutions. Distinct institutional regimes in banking or industrial relations, for example, were correlated with stable policy trajectories in corporate finance and collective bargaining, respectively. In the 1990s this literature progressed from matching policy areas with particular institutions to a more general argument about national institutional *complexes* and their tendency to be self-reinforcing over time.

The most sophisticated of these approaches has been that of David Soskice (Soskice 1994; Hall and Soskice 2000). Soskice's version of the varieties of capitalism model is strongly firm-centred (S. Wood 1997*a*). This continues a growing literature in political economic analysis of policy trajectories which has turned its attention away from labour towards capital (Fulcher 1991; Swenson 1991*a*; Thelen 1993). Underpinning this view is a conception of business as a privileged interest in capitalist democracies (Lindblom 1977), and a concern to provide proper microfoundations of preferences about public policy (Mares 1998). Yet the 'turn to capital' is also justified by a range of world-economic developments in the past two decades that have swung the balance of industrial power back to business, including the intellectual decline of Keynesianism, increased interdependence of trade, heightened capital mobility, and the return of high levels of unemployment. The centrality of employers to economic outcomes is therefore theoretically and empirically well grounded.

At the core of Soskice's theory is the distinction between two types of advanced industrial economy—coordinated market economies (CMEs) and liberal market economies (LMEs). CMEs, such as Germany and Sweden, are characterized by networks of formal and informal linkages between firms, and between firms and other economic actors (such as banks and trade unions), which facilitate the supply of collective goods involved in industrial production. Such goods include the supply of transferable skills, the provision of long-term finance, technological innovation, and industrial peace. LMEs such as the UK, on the other hand, involve no comparable level of capital coordination, and in consequence are unable to supply similar collective goods. Although the state can play a small role in redressing this balance, governments are not well placed to make the appropriate *firm-specific* investments that can only be provided by companies themselves.

The point of contact between Soskice's framework and the path-dependence approach comes when we examine the effect of these institutional complexes on employers' *strategies*. In CMEs, the availability of supply-side collective goods encourages companies to develop production strategies that exploit their use. In LMEs, however, companies are unable to sustain the institutional coordination required for key collective goods, and thus employ strategies that depend upon low costs, flexible production, and short-term returns. Companies in both forms of market economy thus adjust their strategies to exploit the *comparative institutional advantage* of the market economy in which they find themselves.

Over time, these institutional characteristics themselves get reinforced in various ways. Companies press for public policies that will complement the institutional arrangements that characterize production systems. Firms which attempt alternative strategies face strong countervailing incentives and constraints and are selected out. Where institutions and policies combine to keep labour costs high and employment protection strong, for example, firms are forced into investing in their employees' human capital. Coordination and adaptive expectations effects (not only for firms but also for governments, unions, and individual workers) thus produce positive feedbacks that make departures from the respective equilibria undesirable and difficult.

What makes exit from these trajectories particularly difficult is the fact that actors' preferences and strategies are configured by multiple interlocking institutions. This makes the process of movement away from equilibria through piecemeal reform difficult. Attempts to reform one institutional subsystem—such as the vocational training system—are likely to be ineffective if incentives and constraints in other subsystems continue to point actors the other way. Established institutional arrangements are self-reinforcing. In short, national market economies exhibit the processes of increasing returns at the heart of path-dependence theory.

How can this theory be applied to the case of labour market policy? As Pierson notes, there are functional similarities between institutions and public policies. Labour market policies, like institutions, structure actors' strategies. Policies as well as institutions interlock with one another to reinforce incentives and constraints. The sources of policy resilience thus lie in these institutional and policy complementarities, and the returns to actors to which they give rise. Where policies in combination with institutions perform functions that become established over time, and to which expectations adapt, actors will seek to preserve them. Furthermore, actors will resist reforms that bring about incongruent incentive structures. In the case of labour market policy, the key actors are employers, whose support or opposition for policies will prove central to their fate. Employers' preferences and strategies are therefore essential to an understanding of the embeddedness of national labour market policies.

These broad differences allow a more precise specification of how employers' preferences about public policy differ between CMEs and LMEs (S. Wood 1997*a*). One major area of difference concerns policy towards employment protection and the institutions supporting wage bargaining. In CMEs, for example, where firms are keen to cultivate implicit long-term contracts with skilled employees, employers will support strong statutory employment protection. On top of this, employers' associations, dominated traditionally by large and medium-sized firms, will seek to use strong employment protection and coordinated collective bargaining arrangements as a 'benign constraint' on companies that are potential defectors from the institutions of coordination (Streeck 1992; S. Wood 1997*a*). In LMEs, however, where competitive strategies are largely based upon low costs and high flexibility, firms and their representative associations will be strongly in favour of highly deregulated labour markets. Employers in LMEs will look to governments to engineer low levels of employment protection and non-wage labour costs.

Second, differences in the role of unions in CMEs and LMEs translate into differences in preferences about public policy. In CMEs, where the coordination of wages and other employment terms is negotiated, employers will want to protect the organizational strength of unions as bargaining partners. For coordination to be effective, employers must ensure that the parties to the bargain have high coverage across the domestic economy. They will therefore be hostile to government efforts to undermine organized labour's bargaining strength and representational coverage. In LMEs, where strong unions constitute impediments to flexible labour markets, employers will press government to weaken unions' statutory position.

A third difference concerns a more general preference about the role of the state in CMEs and LMEs. Coordination of supply-side outcomes in CMEs rests upon an informational and an institutional condition. The first condition is that firms be prepared to share sensitive information about needs, plans, and activities to facilitate coordination. The second is the need for authoritative monitoring institutions, such as employers' associations and banks, to ensure compliance, to apply pressure, and to impose sanctions. This framework of 'self-governance' in turn relies upon a certain restraint on the part of the state. Although governments play a key role in constructing *framework* legislation in CMEs, any attempts to undermine these private-sector governance structures will meet with strong resistance. Of course, companies everywhere are hostile to state intrusion into the business of management. But in LMEs, where coordinating institutions are absent, employers are more directly reliant upon statutory intervention to remove obstacles to market-clearing, especially in labour markets. Should the need arise, therefore, firms and their representative associations in LMEs will call on government to use its legislative arm (largely to overturn the legislation of previous governments!).

Employer preferences about labour market policy and structures therefore differ systematically between CMEs and LMEs. Furthermore, these preferences are grounded in the institutional and policy complementarities that characterize CMEs and LMEs. Labour market policies can serve a valuable role in reinforcing the incentive and constraint properties of these complementarities. As these policies become entrenched, they will interact with existing features of the institutional infrastructure to amplify coordination, adaptive expectations, and learning effects among employers. Employers should therefore be expected to defend such policies and institutions in virtue of these effects. The mechanism producing continuity exhibits the classic self-reinforcing properties identified with the path-dependence argument. In the first instance, institutions, practices, and policies emerge over time that encourage employers to structure their firms' production strategies and organization in ways that play to the institutional comparative advantage of their market economy; in subsequent periods, reliance upon this institutional and policy matrix engenders a strong interest in sustaining its core features. If this argument holds, an examination of the persistence of labour market policies and institutions during a period when they have come under severe economic and political pressures can offer a 'snapshot' of an increasing returns dynamic.

However, as argued above, path-dependent trajectories can bring inefficiencies to key actors. Often employers find that they are able to adjust their strategies to reduce some of the deleterious effects of policies. But some inefficiencies cannot be absorbed and may prompt employers into advocating change. Exogenous economic changes, for example, can render existing policies inadequate or inappropriate. In the case of labour market policy, the appearance of mass unemployment clearly over-burdened many traditional policy tools. Other unforeseen exogenous events—such as German reunification—can have an equally disrupting effect. Lastly, inefficiencies may result from activities of governments in other related policy areas that have an indirect impact on employers' preferences in labour market policy. Each national case discussed in this chapter provides examples of strategic changes by employers in the 1980s and 1990s prompted in part by the introduction of unwelcome policies. Yet each case also confirms the power of employers to obtain their most desired outcomes, often in the face of the opposition of governments.

Constitutional Constraints: A Veto Points Approach

An alternative explanation for policy stability points to the constraining effect of political institutions, the most fundamental of which are those that form the fabric of national *constitutions*.[1] Constitutional arrangements are harder to reform and have more pervasive effects, than other institutions set up by governments or private-sector actors. Recently the contribution of constitutions to reform processes has been reasserted (Huber, Ragin, and Stephens 1993; King and Wood 1999; Bonoli, in this volume), though also questioned (Pierson and Smith 1993; Pierson 1993*a*). In theory constitutions might influence the viability of reform in a number of ways (S. Wood 1997), but the dominant approach emphasizes the way in which constitutions preserve policy paths by erecting 'barriers to exit'. At least four dimensions of constitutions are of importance here.

First, constitutions disperse power (through separations of powers, federal arrangements, and vesting power in bodies outside government) to varying degrees and in different ways. As a result, the decisional autonomy of governments varies with the number of constitutionally protected veto points (Huber and Stephens, in this volume; Immergut 1992). The extent of this autonomy is central to governments' ability to navigate reform processes successfully. Where constitutions compel supermajorities to pass policy changes, or offer veto players ample opportunity to kill reforms, national policy paths will prove hard to exit. Second, constitutional rules shape the time horizons of political actors. Electoral rules and rules about parliamentary terms, notably, determine expectations about the length of office-holding. In systems where elections are more frequent, and/or where there is low continuity of elected personnel across elections, the ability to push through complex reforms with high adjustment costs will be low. Third, electoral systems affect the composition of governments by their propensity to generate one-party or coalition governments. As a rule, multi-party governments will find it harder to produce significant policy changes than single-party governments. Fourth, constitutions interact with the structure of particular programmes in ways that can make reform of these programmes more or less difficult. Where other constitutionally empowered bodies perform a key role in the administration of a particular policy, the ability of national governments to bring about policy change may be circumscribed.

---

[1] The term 'constitution' is meant to embrace the general class of fundamental institutional characteristics of a national polity. Whether or not the specifications for these institutional arrangements are encoded in a constitutional document is an open question. Thus, in Britain, which has no written constitution, constitutional features are a collection of conventions and long-standing practices; while in most countries, electoral systems, which are here regarded as constitutive of constitutional arrangements, are prescribed by statute.

The veto points approach argues that constitutions lock in policies by frustrating attempts at change. Where these variables are important, political struggles in the pursuit of reform agendas should be conspicuous. Yet the number and height of barriers to exit varies significantly between constitutions. The argument for constitutional barriers to reform is therefore actually a claim about variation in the capacity for policy change between alternative constitutional systems. The three countries examined here should demonstrate considerable variation in this regard. At one extreme, cabinets of single-party governments in the UK are faced with no significant formal barriers to radical policy changes. At the other extreme, German multi-party governments are situated within a constitutional framework that disperses powers, both horizontally and vertically, and both within and outside the formal boundaries of the state. A veto points approach would therefore predict that the project of policy change would be easiest to accomplish in the UK, hardest in the FRG, and somewhere in between in the Swedish case.

Electoral Constraints: An Organized Interests Approach

The third explanation for stable policy trajectories centres on the electoral constraints on governments provided by key supporters. If policy changes are proposed which are perceived to harm the welfare of core supporters, governments will face strong electoral incentives to back down. In some cases parties in power introduce policies in one period that create long-term electoral affinities with certain groups (the New Deal coalition of the American Democrats, for example). Electoral coalitions such as this offer leaders limited latitude to depart from traditional policies. Parties in power sometimes develop new policies to forge electoral alliances with new constituencies (Garrett 1993), but here too the electoral trade-offs between new and old supporters that come from policy movement can serve as a brake on radical change.

The way in which electoral constraints impinge on parties' capacity to initiate policy change varies. Sometimes the constraints are not party-specific, but affect any party whose reforming zeal is turned towards 'sacred cow' policies. Pierson's work on the limits to welfare retrenchment in Thatcher's Britain showed the constraining effect of hostile public opinion when privatization of the treasured National Health Service was contemplated. In contrast, Kitschelt notes the importance of party organization in reinforcing existing policy commitments, in particular the way in which 'internal party structures of interest aggregation as well as the composition of the party activists constrain parties in their strategic choices' (Kitschelt 1997: 3). One could also hypothesize that where key interest groups with close links to political parties enjoy stronger collective organization, their ability to block policy reversals will be correspondingly greater (Sheingate 2000). Internal constraints such as these are likely to vary significantly by country, as are the identities of the relevant veto players.

How might an electoral constraints argument apply to the case of contemporary labour market policy? One difference between labour market reform and welfare reform is that their impact affects different sorts of constituencies. Discrete cuts in transfer payments, for example, have clear political consequences in the sense that the distribution of costs and benefits is visible and can be calculated in monetary terms. Changes in collective bargaining arrangements, however, do not have such unambiguous or transparent economic consequences. Issues such as these are not conspicuous vote-winners or vote-losers. The impact of labour market policy is likely to be felt most by producer groups, in particular trade unions and employers' associations. This in turn suggests that there may be some asymmetry in the electoral sensitivity of different parties in power to the prospect of labour market retrenchment and deregulation. Where social democratic parties are in power, the electoral case for weakening unions, reducing employment protection, and lowering unemployment benefits will be less appealing. Conservative or bourgeois parties, on the other hand, whose support among the trade unions is relatively weak, may find such policies both more attractive and electorally more feasible.

However, the divide between parties of the left and right is not always so clear-cut. Social democratic parties vary in the degree and strength of linkages with trade union constituencies. The British Labour Party under Blair offers an illustration of a social democratic party that has loosened its ties with unions in order to engineer strategic flexibility over, among other things, labour market policy. Yet there is also variance within parties of the right. The CDU in Germany has strong organizational links to trade unions in a way that would be unimaginable in the cases of the British Conservative Party or the Swedish Moderate Party. An electoral constraints approach thus suggests variation across countries in the incidence and effectiveness of resistance to reforms offered by parties' constituencies.

These three explanations—concentrating on employers' preferences, constitutional obstacles, and electoral constraints—differ in the types of explanation they offer. Clearly each explanation sees a different veto player as central to the absence of radical change in the trajectory of labour market policy. The explanations also predict differences in the location of the relevant political battles involved in attempting reform. A constitutional veto-points approach would suggest that efforts at reform will suffer in the course of the legislative process, while an electoral constraints approach points to struggles inside governing parties between leaders and organized electoral constituencies. The employer-centred approach is more complex in this respect. Employer opposition to legislative proposals may be conspicuous during the reform process itself. But where employers are collectively organized, they may be able to implement collective abstention from implementation of the terms of reform once passed.

An evidential problem shared by all three explanations is that they rely on the appearance of conflict over reform proposals in order to assess who is responsible for the course of policy stability or change. Some constitutional processes may be so riddled with veto points, or some groups so influential within governing parties, that reforms to key policies do not even make it off the starting blocks. Where this is true, the explanations offered may be correct, but it will be difficult to know if they are or not. Fortunately, the case of labour market policy over the past two decades is unlikely to suffer from the absence of political confrontation and associated methodological problems. What makes the resilience of national labour market policies in the three worlds notable is the fact that they have come under enormous economic and political pressure since the 1970s—in particular from the appearance and stubborn persistence of mass unemployment.

3. NATIONAL RESPONSES TO UNEMPLOYMENT

The New Terrain of Labour Market Policy

The labour market policies of the 1960s and 1970s were designed for economies with low levels of unemployment. Contributions-based systems for financing unemployment insurance in Germany and Sweden relied in particular on unemployment remaining low in order to avoid the 'pro-cyclical' problem of increasing payments at a time of rapidly decreasing receipts. The viability of active labour market policy (ALMP) schemes aimed at reintegrating the unemployed into work (in Sweden and Britain, and to a lesser extent Germany) relied upon limited demand. Similarly the employment protection legislation of the 1970s that was introduced in Sweden, Germany, and the UK was justified as a constraint on company adjustment strategies during a period of moderate unemployment.

Between 1980 and the mid-1990s all three countries had experienced their highest rates of unemployment since the war (see Table 12.1). Equally frightening has been the persistence of high unemployment rates; these were not transitory peaks produced by sluggish demand (though in some cases this was a contributory factor), but the result of longer term and less reversible developments. The most important exogenous factors were, first, the enormous rise in world commodity prices from the 1970s to the 1980s and, second, a dramatic decline in the demand for low-skilled workers caused both by technological change and competition from NIEs (Nickell 1996).

TABLE 12.1. *Unemployment rates in Germany, Sweden, and the UK, 1975–97*

	Federal Republic of Germany*	Sweden	United Kingdom
1975	3.97	1.63	3.62
1976	3.93	1.60	4.84
1977	3.82	1.78	5.16
1978	3.66	2.23	5.01
1979	3.19	2.06	4.54
1980	3.19	1.97	6.10
1981	4.51	2.48	9.05
1982	6.44	3.14	10.43
1983	7.92	3.46	11.25
1984	7.93	3.11	11.40
1985	8.00	2.85	11.60
1986	7.66	2.49	11.76
1987	7.61	2.13	10.23
1988	7.60	1.74	7.83
1989	6.86	1.48	6.10
1990	6.2	1.65	5.86
1991	6.65	2.96	8.21
1992	7.61	5.27	10.21
1993	8.85	8.23	10.32
1994	9.56	7.95	9.36
1995	9.39	7.69	8.61
1996	10.32	8.05	7.99
1997	11.40	8.05	6.88

* Up to and including 1990, western Germany; subsequent data concern the whole of Germany.

Source: Database for Rob Franzese, 'The Political Economy of Public Debt: An Empirical Examination of the OECD Postwar Experience' <http://www.personal.umich.edu/~franzese/ PEofPubDebt.Public.TXT> (based on OECD, *Historical Statistics*, various years).

These factors impacted upon the three economies in different ways and at different times. In the UK and West Germany unemployment reached (then) historic highs at the beginning of the 1980s. Of these two, the UK was hit particularly hard; from 1983 to 1988 unemployment in West Germany remained between 7.5 and 8 per cent, while in the UK the 1981–7 *average* was just under 11 per cent. Sweden's impressive post-war employment performance continued throughout the 1980s, with unemployment rarely exceeding 3 per cent. In the first three years of the 1990s, however, unemployment soared to 8.2 per cent, and stayed at this level until 1997. Unemployment in Germany has remained high over the same period after dipping during the last half of the 1980s. Indeed after reunification the rate crept upwards continuously from 1990 to 1997, when it hit 11.4 per cent. Britain, however, has seen continuous though very gradual decline in its unemployment rate since 1993; by the end of 1999 it had fallen to its lowest level since the mid-1970s.

TABLE 12.2. *Allocation of labour market expenditures in Germany, Sweden, and the UK*

	Total expenditure (% of GDP)		Active expenditure (% of total expenditure)		Unemployment (% of labour force)	
	1985–9	1990–3	1985–9	1990–3	1985–9	1990–3
Britain	2.3	1.7	33.5	32.8	9.6	8.5
Germany	2.3	3.2	41.8	43.6	6.3	6.7
Sweden	2.6	4.0	70.6	55.6	2.1	4.2
Pre-95 EU	2.8	2.8	29.8	32.8	11.1	9.7

1985–90, figures are for West Germany; 1990–3 figure corresponds to 1991–3 for united Germany.

Source: Calmfors and Skedinger 1995.

The effects of the unemployment burden on labour market policies are mixed. On the one hand, fiscal pressures on insurance schemes, means-tested payments, and ALMPs have been intense. These expenditure constraints have been accompanied by an ideological shift, spearheaded by centre-right governments and the OECD, prescribing labour market flexibility and deregulation as the only remedy for European unemployment (OECD 1994*d*; Bradley 1998). Furthermore, the arrival of EMU and the pursuit of Maastricht convergence criteria since the early 1990s have resulted in a deflated west European economy, and strong political limits on domestic reflationary activity. Unemployment has also had the effect of weakening the position of trade unions, perhaps the strongest defenders of ALMPs and employment protection. The imperatives of economic liberalization, expenditure control, and European monetary integration thus all suggest a perilous future for a range of traditional labour market policies.

On the other hand, the strain on labour market policy imposed by unemployment is often exaggerated (Pierson 1997*d*). Between 1980 and 1993, average expenditures on labour market policies in Europe increased by only 3 per cent in response to a near-doubling of average unemployment from 6 to 11 per cent (OECD 1995*a*). With the exception of Germany, whose fiscal deficits have been largely the result of the reunification shock, countries have been able to adjust their patterns of spending to sustain high levels of unemployment in the 1990s without major dislocations. Partly this is because when unemployment is high automatic compensation payments increase, and it is harder to cut back policies that are aimed to boost employment. If anything, the political imperative to reduce the unemployment figures can make governments even more reliant upon labour market policies. As Table 12.2 demonstrates, both Sweden and Germany responded to rapidly accelerating unemployment in the early 1990s by increasing already high levels of labour market policy expenditures. In an era when governments are, for both political and economic reasons, loath to rely upon interventionist macroeconomic policies, supply-side reform and ALMPs can offer more appealing prospects for tackling unemployment. Finally, the task of policy makers in responding to high levels of unemployment also varies by the type or composition of unemployment. As argued below, the composition of unemployment varies strongly between regime types and is itself largely a function of prior labour market policies.

Three Worlds of Labour Market Policy in an Age of Mass Unemployment

Germany

Golden Age Labour Market Policies. The cardinal principle of German industrial relations is the autonomy of the collective bargaining partners (*Tarifautonomie*). Bargaining between the social partners—both at sectoral level and at firm level through the works council system—covers a wide range of employment terms. This bargaining model has delivered high but stable wages, and high employment security for company employees. Labour market policy has always played a supporting role to these negotiated outcomes, but it is one that has become increasingly important as the problem of unemployment has grown. Until the arrival of the SPD in power in 1969, interventionist labour market policy was almost non-existent. The unemployment insurance system, buttressed by two further layers of means-tested assistance, maintained high replacement rates and allowed workers to search for jobs that matched their skill levels. Indeed, perhaps the central pillar of labour market 'policy' until the 1970s was the apprenticeship system. Run autonomously by employers and their representative associations, the dual system of vocational training ensured a steady supply of skilled and highly productive labour in the post-war period, and helped to force down the proportion of low-skilled labour in the workforce to the lowest figure in the OECD. Its role in maintaining skill levels in the high value-added manufacturing sector in particular was pivotal to the coordinated capitalism of Modell Deutschland (Streeck 1992).

From the 1970s onwards, labour market policy was developed to assist the process of generational replacement, whereby older workers with fewer or outmoded skills were eased out of employment to make way for younger, newly trained workers. The legislative scheme introduced in the early 1980s allowed workers over the age of 59 to be phased out of work through receipt of unemployment benefit from 59–60, followed by premature qualification for pension benefits. Persistent unemployment in the 1980s and extension of the period of eligibility for unemployment pay increased the attraction

TABLE 12.3. *Long-term unemployment in Germany, Sweden, and Britain, average 1981–95*

	Total unemployment	Unemployed under one year	Unemployed over one year	% Long-term unemployment
Sweden	3.8	3.5	0.3	7.9
West Germany	5.8	3.2	2.6	44.8
United Kingdom	9.6	5.4	4.2	43.8

Source: OECD, *Employment Outlook*, various years.

of the early retirement scheme to employers. By 1988, labour force participation for men between the ages of 60–64 was 64.1 per cent in Sweden, 55.1 per cent in the UK, but only 31.5 per cent in West Germany (Pierson 1993*a*). Statutory reductions in the length of working lives was accompanied after 1984 by negotiated reductions in maximum working weeks (initially to 37.5 hours, later to 35 hours in some sectors). The main theme of SPD labour market policy in the 1970s was the introduction of extremely high levels of employment protection. Not only were individual employees equipped with a formidable array of employment rights, but employers were placed under additional constraints in the event of firm restructuring. Particularly onerous was the requirement on companies to negotiate, and pay for, a compensation package and retraining programme (*Sozialplan*) for all workers affected by changes in company strategy.

These policies reinforced companies' reliance upon, and incentive to invest in, the skills of their workers. From the workers' point of view, they constitute one of the most protective welfare regimes in the world. Rather than focusing on reintegrating the unemployed into work, German policy was oriented towards paying people to remain, or even to become, unemployed. Until 1989 subsidized employment and public training schemes were negligible elements of labour market policy, targeted only at 'disadvantaged groups'. Two aspects of this policy stand out. One is the stark difference in employment prospects between younger and older Germans that it entails. West German over 45s are significantly more likely to be unemployed, and more likely to be unemployed for long periods, than other age groups (see Table 12.3). In 1995, 60 per cent of the long-term unemployed in Germany were in this category (OECD 1996*d*). The second characteristic of these policies is their cost. Paying for rather than reducing unemployment meant an increasing burden on the productive sectors of the economy as the unemployment rate rose. By the end of the 1980s, therefore, labour market policy was acting as both a buttress to West Germany's coordinated capitalism and a growing fiscal burden upon the German economy.

Employer Preferences and Labour Market Policy.   With the formation of a
new centre-right coalition in 1982 under Helmut Kohl, West Germany seemed
to be entering an era of deregulation and retrenchment. Under pressure from
the CDU's own 'business wing' (*Wirtschaftsflügel*) and their coalition partners the neoliberal FDP, Kohl signalled an intent to reform Germany's highly
regulated labour markets in order to boost growth and employment. In spite
of the presence of separated powers, strong federalism, and entrenched
corporatism, the Kohl administration did produce significant pieces of legislation that empowered employers and weakened the formal position of
organized labour.

The 1985 Employment Promotion Act allowed for the introduction of short-
term contracts of between twelve and eighteen months. Its aim was to enable
companies to screen workers before committing to more standard forms of
employment contract, and thus to encourage employment as the economy
emerged from a period of low demand. Studies revealed, however, that after
controlling for cyclical factors firm take-up of these contracts was negligible before reunification (Büchtemann 1991). Similarly, legislation to weaken
the strike capacity of trade unions by denying benefits to workers indirectly
affected by industrial action has not been used to force unions into accepting
prejudicial collective bargains (S. Wood 1997*a*; Thelen 1999). In these and other
cases, government overtures to increase the strategic flexibility of employers
were rejected. Employers remained wedded to the institutional incentives of
'high-skill/ incremental innovation' production (Carlin and Soskice 1997) and
committed in particular to maintaining the collective strength of trade
unions and the long-term security of their workforce.

Labour market conditions were transformed by German reunification.
Contributions to the unemployment benefit system soared in order to cover
those made unemployed in the east by industrial restructuring. Increased
non-wage costs squeezed company profits in the east and generated a further
contractionary employment effect. At the same time, existing labour market
policies quickly became overburdened in the new economic environment. Early
retirement and short-time work benefits (*Kurzarbeitergeld*) were intended
as alternatives to lay-offs and were justified as methods of generational
replacement. In the new Germany, employers increasingly resorted to these
programmes simply to pay workers to stay at home at the state's expense.
The cost of these programmes rocketed, while their function as instruments
of employment policy disintegrated.

The explosive effect of reunification upon existing policies altered the incentives for employers in the West German economy to support them. The problem for employers was that they were now faced with two quite different
economies within the same legal and constitutional framework. The long-
standing coordinating institutions of the West German model were clearly
inappropriate and unworkable in the east. Increasing eastern employment

would require quite different labour market policies from those previously adopted for the west. But introducing 'flexible' labour market provisions risked undermining the regulatory constraints that supported the 'high-everything' model of west German production. Academics and journalists seemed to agree that Germany faced a choice between spiralling unemployment at an unsustainable social cost, and the dismantling of its characteristic economic institutions and policies.

Given these substantial pressures, the unravelling of the German model of labour market regulation has been widely anticipated. In some respects there have been departures from existing patterns, but their impact and significance should not be overstated. Most notable has been the emergence of an unfamiliarly interventionist role for the German state in the east. The CDU-led administration introduced a range of ALMPs in eastern Germany to absorb the newly unemployed, which were extended to western Germany in 1995. These have served as forms of emergency income transfer—in 1994, 40 per cent of the outflow from unemployment was to ALMPs—as well as a device to lower unemployment figures. Reliance upon public training programmes and subsidized employment represents a counter-cyclical policy stance that was never adopted for West Germany (Reissert 1994). Nevertheless, their use is a response to the employment shock induced by unification, rather than a concerted shift in government policy towards labour market regulation. There are no signs that Germany is moving from an employer-run to a state-run system for training workers; German employers have successfully resisted government attempts to increase control over training for decades (S. Wood 1997a). ALMPs, as in other countries, have come to serve the function of masking unemployment, rather than offering real prospects of reintegration into working life. There has also been moderate tightening of the terms of benefit receipt since 1997, and participation in ALMPs no longer suffices to re-establish eligibility for benefits. Cutbacks such as these (as well as the alterations to sickness payments discussed below) constitute fiscal rather than programmatic retrenchment (Pierson 1994), and in comparative terms benefit levels and conditions remain remarkably generous.

Despite the seismic shock of reunification and heavy non-wage labour costs, continuity of institutions and practice is striking. Underpinning this continuity is the resilience of the sectoral bargaining model. By 1995 over 72 per cent of western employees were still covered by industry-wide agreements; only 10 per cent were covered by company-level agreements. The story in the east has been different, where firms faced strong incentives to undercut western collective agreements. But even here the percentage of newly negotiated agreements that apply at the company level has declined by 23 per cent since 1990 (BMAS 1998). The primary effect of this resilience has been that adjustment within the labour market has been gradual and negotiated. Employers remain committed to the institutional framework for coordination and the method of bargained adjustment. Clearly they are seeking incremental changes in the structure of industrial relations—in particular the expansion of the role of works councils in agreeing supplementary company-level deals on pay and working conditions (Carlin and Soskice 1997)—yet this represents a quest for a more flexible form of collective bargaining rather than a more flexible *labour market*.

Employers' preference for the retention of the German bargaining model has had the effect of limiting the impact of the Kohl Government's moderate deregulation efforts of the 1990s. Legislation has repeatedly failed to have the desired effect in the face of employer reluctance to implement its key provisions. This dynamic is well illustrated by the government's attempts to limit firms' use of the unemployment path to early retirement as a means of engineering generational replacement in company workforces. In 1996 the Kohl administration announced its intention to re-raise the retirement age for both men and women to 65. Simultaneously, the early retirement legislation that was so pivotal to policy in the 1980s was reformed. Full-time retirement for 55 year olds and over was replaced by a provision for 'partial retirement', whereby employment costs for older workers on reduced hours are to be shared by the state and employers. Use of this instrument of labour market adjustment has become so widespread, however, that employers continue to rely on pre-retirement extensively. Partly as a result of employer pressure, extensive grandfathering clauses have been attached to the phasing out of pre-retirement which will delay its demise considerably.[2] Crucially the new law stipulated that the concrete conditions for implementation of partial retirement were a matter for collective agreements. Most sectoral agreements that have since been concluded have resulted in income floors for partly retired workers well above the minima prescribed by law. German employers thus remain reliant on various forms of early retirement practices and have shown their collective capacity to resist government efforts at reform.

The process bears a striking similarity to the story of reductions in sickness payment. After a protracted political battle, the CDU/FDP government managed to introduce a law in 1996 permitting companies to pay 80 per cent of wages rather than the previous 100 per cent. However, the Act merely succeeded in triggering collective and company-level agreements that maintained 100 per cent compensation. Even the decentralization of bargaining to firm-level in exceptional cases (through 'opening clauses') is regulated collectively by the social partners. Similarly, the effects of legislation aiming to deregulate hiring and firing have also been diluted by a widespread lack of enthusiasm among employers. Job creation measures, which (since 1997) require firms and Chambers to administer them, have suffered from lack of

---

[2] I would like to thank Philip Manow for clarifying this issue.

take-up. The introduction of a new, highly flexible work contract for the long-term unemployed which can be terminated at any time (*Eingliederungsvertrag*) has hardly been used. Even the looser form of employment protection introduced in 1996 only applies to one-third of the total German workforce (OECD 1998*c*).

Thus, although the content of labour market policy has changed somewhat since reunification, the relevance of these reforms to labour market outcomes is indirect and limited. Employers have continued to resist statutory intervention, even in the name of 'flexibility', preferring instead to negotiate adjustment privately while simultaneously reforming the organization of industrial relations gradually and consensually. This institutional resilience has meant that the main contribution of labour market policy has been to hide rather than reduce unemployment. In this respect its impact is little different from the policies of the 1980s.

Constitutional Factors and Labour Market Reform. The conservative coalition's foiled attempts at welfare retrenchment in the 1990s have given rise to a new German word—*Reformstau* ('reform-jam'). The second legislative Chamber (Bundesrat) proved to be the main obstacle to the governing coalition after 1991, when the opposition SPD became its majority party. As all bills with implications for the functions and fiscal position of the states require its consent, the Bundesrat effectively holds a veto power over the government's central economic and welfare policies. Crucial elements of the 1997 'Action Programme for Investment and Employment'—notably 'the tax reform of the century'—were rejected outright by the Bundesrat.

The prevalence of multiple veto points is widely seen as the reason for limited retrenchment in Germany (Katzenstein 1985*a*). Clearly the dispersal of authority horizontally and vertically in Germany does constrain the autonomy of governments. As in the USA, the judgements of the German Constitutional Court (BVG) have put a brake on some of the government's key reforms. For example the BVG curtailed the conservative government's efforts to reduce benefits by interpreting insurance contributions as equivalent to property rights. An equally important decision in 1992 was that the administration's attempt to tax individuals an amount equivalent to their annual entitlement of social assistance was unconstitutional, forcing allowances to rise to their previous level by 1996 (Clasen and Gould 1995). German governments are not exceptional in this respect, however; most Western European governments are forced to conform to judicial review, either at national or at EU level. What *is* distinctive about Germany is the way in which key tasks and programmes are delegated to institutions and actors outside the boundaries of the central state. Unemployment benefits are administered by the Federal Labour Office in consultation with the social partners. Their statutory responsibility for the system allows them to maintain the wage-replacement function of insurance benefits and to resist efforts by the government to raid funds to meet other expenditure needs. Whereas the responsibility of the municipalities for providing means-tested assistance to the unemployed (*Sozialhilfe*) gives them a direct interest in maintaining the health of the insurance system to prevent excessive demand on their own resources (Clasen 1994).

Nevertheless, the broader point is that despite the complexity of the legislative process in Germany, and despite the dispersal of power between a fragmented state and highly organized social actors, legislative reforms have been possible and have taken place. Some proposals have been shelved because of opposition in the Bundestag and Bundesrat; others have been watered down as a condition of their passage. But where the Kohl Government did succeed in passing reforms—to encourage more flexible forms of employment, for example—their effect has been small because of low employer interest. Examples such as this indicate that constitutional obstacles in Germany cannot provide a sufficient explanation for the absence of labour market reform. Although the inability of Kohl, and the likely inability of Schröder, to obtain parliamentary approval for a package of reform measures provides tangible evidence of political failure, a more satisfying account needs to address the question of why more radical reforms have not been attempted, and why those reforms that have been pushed through have not had their desired effect. In both cases the coordinated activities of employers—in the first case through pre-legislative pressure, in the second through collective non-compliance—offer a more compelling explanation for the resilience of the status quo.

Electoral Constraints and Labour Market Reform. The institutions of German welfare were established by the 'workerist' wing of the CDU–CSU. Benefits were made a function of contributions while in employment, and the trade unions given co-direction of their administration. Unlike conservative parties in Sweden and Britain, the CDU and CSU have always had close organizational ties to trade unions. These links have been crucial to the CDU's catch-all electoral strategy after 1949 (Pridham 1977). Within the CDU the workers' 'Social Committees' (CDA) have been an important influence on policy, upholding paternalism in welfare and labour market policy, and resisting the neoliberal intimations of the business wing of the party (*Wirtschaftsflügel*). The SPD, on the other hand, is in many ways a paradigmatic social democratic party. Relations between the main union confederation (DGB) and the SPD have always been extremely close, particularly during the 1970s when the SPD administration introduced a range of radical labour market and welfare policies. Both SPD- and CDU-led coalitions have in consequence been sensitive to the interests of trade union members, and have faced strong constraints in introducing policies that threaten them.

In the 1980s the CDA was the key veto player within the CDU–FDP coalition in the battle over weakening the DGB's control of works councils (S. Wood 1997*b*). After unification its influence has remained strong. One of its notable successes in recent years has been to force limitations on the use of 'short-time labour', exempt from additional labour costs, because of a fear that excessive use would undermine the liquidity of the social security system. Many of the most ferocious battles over labour market reform in the 1990s have in fact been *within the coalition*. While on one side the FDP and CDU business wing have campaigned for more extensive deregulation, on the other, the CDA and Bavarian CSU have defended the status quo. These internal tensions were compounded by the longevity of Kohl's Labour Minister, Norbert Blüm, a strongly pro-union Christian Democrat who remained in office throughout Kohl's tenure, and who used the significant autonomy of German ministerial posts to defend the position of workers and unions. The result was a government that found it almost impossible to introduce the 'flexibility' in labour markets that its leader repeatedly promised. Now that the SPD has returned to power the prospects for a concerted attack on labour market policies and institutions are clearly even dimmer than before.

As with the constitutional explanation for policy stability, however, it would be too simplistic to attribute too much leverage to trade unions as veto players within the governing coalition. On some issues—such as tightening eligibility for state-funded payments to workers affected by strikes—the unions lost despite vigorous protests. Even the moderate relaxing of employment protection under Kohl provoked the unions' wrath, but once again to little effect. Neither Kohl nor Schröder are the prisoners of their parties' constituencies. A second problem for the argument that the CDU was hamstrung by internal union vetoes is that it neglects the fact that the CDU is a highly polycentric party containing a wide spectrum of interests. Asserting the importance of electoral constraints to a party such as the CDU is therefore of little help in determining what its position will be on key issues where constituents' interests conflict. Increasingly the SPD under the 'neue Mitte' of Schröder is coming to emulate the CDU in this respect. Schröder is keen to cultivate employers as allies of the party, and clearly wishes to keep the demands of the DGB at arm's length. In neither case is there any reason to think that the demands of unions are more pressing than those of employers. If the Soskicean account of employer preferences is correct, the inability of parties to sustain a radical legislative attack on labour market structures is as likely to be the result of employer pressure as pressure from trade unions.

United Kingdom

Labour Market Policies up to 1979   Unlike the organized capitalism of Germany and Sweden, British employers have been unable to establish co-ordinated governance structures for domestic production. One main consequence of this has been a chronic undersupply of skilled labour (Hillman 1996). The secular decline in world demand for unskilled workers has thus hit Britain especially hard, giving Britain an 'early arrival' at mass unemployment in the early 1980s. But Britain's unemployed are also considerably more likely to remain out of work than in other countries. Long-term unemployment (unemployed for at least a year) grew with unemployment, rising from 25 per cent in the mid-1970s to over 40 per cent by 1989 (Clasen, Gould, and Vincent 1998). Unlike Germany, the group most vulnerable to long-term unemployment is school-leavers. Specific factors underlying these trends include the generosity of the unemployment benefit system until the mid-1970s (Nickell 1996), or more specifically the unlimited duration of benefits (Layard, Nickell, and Jackman 1994), and a sharp rise in trade union pressure on wages between 1964 and 1978.

Before the advent of mass unemployment in the 1980s there was little systematic labour market policy. In 1964 sectoral Training Boards were established on a tripartite basis with the aim of increasing the supply of marketable skills through a levy system, but to little effect. Its successor, the centralized Manpower Services Commission, introduced some public training programmes targeted at the young unemployed. However, there were no incentives or constraints to induce take-up of these programmes, and benefits were unconditional. Britain's failure to train coupled with the hysteresis effects of high and continued unemployment gave rise to a comparatively high incidence of *long-term* unemployment from the early 1980s onwards (see Table 12.3). In the labour market itself the strength of trade unions (or rather, of their plant-level shop stewards) rose gradually throughout the post-war period. As the labour market tightened, employers would concede wage deals that fuelled inflation at comparatively low levels of growth and employment. Meanwhile, attempts to construct organized collective bargaining by legislative fiat failed twice (in 1969 and 1971) because of combined employer and union opposition (Moran 1977). Equally fruitless were the attempts at national income policies in the context of poor employer coordination and a decentralized union movement.

Employers' Preferences and Labour Market Policies.   The welfare regime inherited by Margaret Thatcher in 1979 was thus fundamentally inconsistent with the interests of employers and the institutional characteristics of the British market economy. Employer strategies based upon low-cost, flexible production required drastic reform of the labour market. The new government acknowledged the affinity between its goals and those of British business, stating in 1985: 'The key contribution of Government in a free society is to do all it can to create a climate in which enterprise can flourish, above all by removing obstacles to the working of markets, especially the labour markets' (HMSO 1985).

The Conservatives' first target was the power of trade unions. Three Industrial Acts between 1980 and 1984 savaged an array of union rights and made unions liable in the event of industrial action that was not authorized using a stipulated procedure (Auerbach 1990). The balance of power in the workplace was deliberately swung towards employers. Perhaps more damaging for unions was the government's acquiescence in allowing unemployment to rise even further upon taking office. Employment in manufacturing fell by 36 per cent in the 1980s. The effect on unionization rates in Britain has been catastrophic—TUC membership fell from 12.2 million in 1979 to 6.9 million in 1995 (Bratt 1996). Second, the government set out to lower the price of labour. Labour market deregulation was accomplished through the abolition of Wages Councils, relaxation of unfair dismissal regulations, and privatization of state-owned industry and services (S. Wood 1997*a*).

Third, the terms of unemployment were tightened in three ways. First the link between benefits and earnings was broken, and benefit levels progressively eroded. By 1990 Britain had the lowest rate for insurance based unemployment benefit claimants in the EU, averaging 23 per cent of previous earnings compared to an EU average of 61 per cent (Murray 1994). Despite the enormous rise in unemployment, Britain is the only EU country in which expenditure on unemployment benefit has fallen since 1980 (European Commission 1994). Second, the burden of unemployment support was gradually shifted from the insurance basis to a means-tested programme (Income Support), whose generosity similarly declined. Third, entitlement to any unemployment-related benefit was made conditional upon claimants' ability to prove that they were available for employment and 'actively seeking work' (King 1995). In this spirit unemployment benefits were integrated in 1996 and renamed Jobseekers' Allowances.

Stricter benefit regimes were combined with a particular neoliberal brand of 'active' labour market policy. Individuals were offered assistance in job search through a twice-yearly interview with a 'claimant adviser'. The Conservatives also launched a succession of 'youth training' policies under different names throughout the 1980s and early 1990s. It was clear from early on that these programmes were designed to manage unemployment rather than offer genuine training. Only 4 per cent of participants in the main programme of this type (Restart) found a job. In fact they served not only a political, but also an economic function, by funnelling cheap, temporary labour to companies on a regular basis. Firms used programmes such as 'Youth Opportunities Scheme' and 'Youth Training' as 'revolving doors' for meeting their needs for low-skill, low-cost labour (King and Wood 1999). The government even handed control of this system to employers. In 1988 tripartite coordination of manpower policy was abandoned and a regional network of employer-run Training and Enterprise Councils (TECs) put in its place (S. Wood 1999).

It is important to note that employers were not simply the beneficiaries of this process, but worked with government in its preparation and execution (Auerbach 1990; S. Wood 1997a). Many of the more radical proposals introduced were taken directly from business think-tanks and employers' association publications, whose clear aim was to improve the flexibility of labour markets, and thus in turn to enhance company competitiveness by lowering labour costs. Non-standard forms of employment have flourished in Britain since the early 1980s, and inequality has risen. Britain after Thatcher is a country with one of the weakest trade union movements in Western Europe, very low levels of employment protection, a high level of contractual flexibility, and a thriving low-wage service economy. Employers' associations' enthusiasm for the radical neoliberal reforms that bequeathed this legacy derives from the absence of coordinated supply-side governance structures, and the consequent reliance on cost-based competitive strategies.

The Thatcherite revolution of the 1980s is therefore best seen as a restoration of employer dominance in British labour markets. The policy trajectory of the 1960s and 1970s was halted in its tracks and reversed. In retrospect it is the collectivist period from the late 1950s to the late 1970s that stands out as an aberration in recent British economic history. The governance structures required for the success of both Labour and Conservative governments' 'corporatist' experiments (such as the 'Neddy' apparatus after 1962, and the Industrial Relations Act of 1971) were never present in Britain. In an economy where transferable skills are in short supply, levels of investment in research and development historically low, companies depend upon short-term finance from equity markets, and collectivized industrial relations have never taken root, companies face few incentives to support regulation of labour markets (and large collective action problems should some wish to do so). Governments from MacMillan to Callaghan were in this sense always competing with the incentive properties of long-standing economic institutions and practices. Thatcherism was a *restoration* in the sense that the governance structures of labour markets were once more made congruent with those in other areas of the supply-side economy. The crucial juncture in British labour market policy is therefore a recent one—the May 1979 general election—but it is fair to speculate that it has given rise to a highly resilient policy path.

Constitutional Factors and Labour Market Reform. Concentration of power is the hallmark of the Westminster model. The unwritten British constitution allocates an exceptional degree of power to its central government. A combination of parliamentary sovereignty and a first-past-the-post electoral system, along with disciplined and hierarchical parties ensures that, with rare exceptions, Britain produces strong single-party governments. Once in power, governments are not constrained by constitutional veto points; the second Chamber, the House of Lords, has since 1911 been reduced to delaying rather than blocking powers; there is no constitutional court; and local government enjoys no constitutional protection. Even the newly created powers of the regional assemblies of Scotland and Wales exist by virtue of Westminster's consent alone.

In the 1980s this concentration of power was utilized to dramatic effect in the passage of neoliberal labour market reforms. The Conservative governments of the 1980s did not suffer a single legislative defeat or climbdown over these reforms. In part this was due to the fact that the Conservative Party in many ways mirrors the British political system—it has no written constitution and its leaders enjoy an immense concentration of power. After 1980 Thatcher used this pre-eminence to substitute 'dry' for 'wet' Tories inside the Cabinet. However, the most important facilitating condition was the first-past-the-post electoral system. As Huber and Stephens (in this volume) have argued, winner-take-all electoral systems allow single-party governments to emerge that do not cover median voters, and they are therefore likely to prove fruitful for radical politics. The Conservatives' room for manoeuvre was expanded further in 1981, when the centre-left Social Democratic Party broke away from a leftward drifting Labour Party. In the context of the electoral system this division was suicidal for the anti-Tory coalition. Britain's electoral system thus enabled Thatcher effectively to ignore her opponents and to develop a radical economic strategy that benefited a coalition of rising real wage earners in the south at the expense of Labour voters in northern urban constituencies.

Clearly these constitutional factors facilitated swift implementation of the Thatcher programme. It is far from clear, however, that the concentration of power in the Westminster model was a *necessary* condition for Thatcherism. Second, constitutional factors cannot explain why the Thatcherite agenda appeared in Britain and not in other countries, nor why it was so popular and successful. Third, the fact that central governments enjoy unparalleled autonomy in the British constitution cannot account for the durability of the Thatcherite settlement after the shift from Conservative hegemony to Labour hegemony under Blair, who has shown no inclination to reverse any of Thatcher's key labour market reforms. As the corporatist interlude of the 1960s and 1970s showed, governments can use concentrated power to implement policies that challenge the interests of employers, but in the long run they will not prove sustainable nor conducive to economic success if they conflict with national comparative institutional advantages (S. Wood

1997*a*). It was the political backlash against the corporatist consensualism of governments prior to 1979 that gave the Tories eighteen years of power. This backlash, however, is itself rooted in the incompatibility between the incentive properties of economic governance structures and public policies. A long-term perspective on the oscillating trajectory of labour market policy since 1945 thus finds the highly concentrated powers available to all British governments of little explanatory use.

Electoral Constraints and Labour Market Reform. Unlike the CDU in Germany or the SAP in Sweden, the Conservative Party has never developed strong organizational links with outside interest groups. Indeed the party has almost no organizational structure at all other than its parliamentary representation. Though the Conservatives supported paternalistic social policy from 1945 onwards, there was no electoral alliance which embraced organized labour in the manner of a Continental Christian democratic party. This organizational and electoral freedom was undoubtedly important in enabling the party to change its economic and welfare policies so radically between 1975 and 1979.

The case of the Thatcherite Conservatives during the 1980s exemplifies the absence of electoral barriers to exit from policy paths. The case of the British Labour Party illustrates quite the opposite. From its founding until the mid-1980s, the Labour Party was institutionally intertwined with the trade union movement. Labour leaders' room for policy manoeuvre was continually constrained by the party's financial dependence upon unions and by a constitution that vested so much power in union 'block votes'. After the electoral catastrophes of the 1980s (and 1992), Labour's political elites sought to move the party's policies sharply to the right. Tony Blair has since accomplished this strategic transition with remarkable speed. Integral to this transition, however, has been an organizational revolution from above within the party, designed to remove the connection with trade unions altogether. One motivation for this change is cosmetic, to project the image of a modernized party which has shed the skin of its former discredited self. But another, equally important, is to expand the leadership's strategic freedom to advocate many of the policies of the Thatcherite settlement in order to appeal to marginal voters in the ideological centre.

It is this startling transition of the Labour Party—from defenders of collectivism to proponents of neoliberal economic policies—that suggests most strongly the durability of Thatcher's labour market policy legacy, and that offers a strong counter-example to the claim that parties are the prisoners of their core constituents. Under Kinnock, Smith, and most notably under Blair, Labour has made a strategic gamble to uphold most of the Conservatives' labour market (and other) reforms, and to undertake internal structural change to detach itself from constituencies of support that would have held it back from doing so. There is no sign that any of the restrictive legislation regarding unions will be overturned. Labour has maintained deregulated labour markets and continued the Conservatives' neoliberal version of active labour market policy. In some respects it has even 'out-Thatchered' the Thatcherites. Its main employment programme, the 'New Deal', continues the theme of using training programmes to provide cheap labour to companies, but categories of the unemployed are now *required* to accept a training programme place or subsidized employment (or to join an 'environmental taskforce') rather than receiving unconditional unemployment assistance (Glyn and Wood 2000). In sum, rather than advocating traditional policies in order to appease client groups, Labour has engineered changes in its policy stance and its relations with key electoral constituencies at the same time.

Sweden

Labour Market Policy up to 1990 Sweden's employment performance in the 1970s and 1980s appeared to be nothing short of miraculous in international comparison (see Table 12.1). Between 1971 and 1989 unemployment oscillated around a 2 per cent trend figure, while the OECD average soared to over 10 per cent. The policy and institutional recipe responsible for this remarkable record revolved around a combination of distinctive political-economic institutions and government economic strategies (Martin 1992). In the arena of wage bargaining, the Rehn–Meidner model used wage equalization as a form of industrial policy. Minimizing wage differentials within skill categories served to penalize low productivity firms, and thus direct labour towards more efficient companies. Solidaristic wage deals thus promoted productivity growth and structural adjustment, as well as social-democratic egalitarian ambitions. The ability of the social partners to make such deals binding and with high coverage across sectors rested on one of the most highly centralized wage bargaining systems in the advanced industrial world (second only to Austria in Calmfors and Driffill's corporatist ranking of OECD countries— see Calmfors and Driffill 1988).

But the pursuit of wage equalization by the social partners through centralized bargaining was only one part of the Rehn–Meidner recipe. For its part, the state was expected to pursue a combination of tight fiscal policy (to control cost-push inflation) and active labour market policy (to enhance mobility between declining and expanding industries). Social democratic governments certainly delivered on the second of these two requirements. By 1987 Sweden was spending over 2.5 per cent of its GDP on labour market policy programmes. But more importantly, Sweden was distinctive in the proportion of this spending it devoted towards 'active' measures (70 per cent in 1987) rather than income maintenance (30 per cent). These measures came in three varieties—matching of the unemployed with vacancies by the Employment Service; funding of training for adults; and enrolling the un- employed on public relief programmes through the National Labour Mar- ket Board. Emphasizing reintegration into work rather than unconditional income support while unemployed was crucial for maintaining labour- market flexibility and for preventing hysteresis, i.e. the decline in the quality of human capital during absence from employment (Layard 1997). As a result, long-term unemployment in Sweden was virtually eliminated during the golden age (see Table 12.3).

This impressive record on employment coexisted with the maintenance of generous terms for the unemployed. Until the 1990s, replacement rates for the lower paid were high in international comparisons, while around aver- age for the higher paid. Coverage of unemployment compensation was also higher than in other Western European countries. Nevertheless, the max- imum duration of the compensation period was shorter than elsewhere, and tightly circumscribed according to age (up to 150 days for 16–55 year olds, for example). In addition the eligibility rules for drawing unemployment benefit were extremely strict. Long-term unemployment was thus minimized by a combination of activist labour market policy and strong incentives for indi- viduals to re-enter (skilled) work. The second part of the Rehn–Meidner policy recipe—maintaining a tight fiscal policy—was less strictly observed. Throughout the 1970s fiscal policy was consistently 'loose'. One of the chief causes of this was the expansion of public sector employment in the 1970s and 1980s, doubling between 1971 and 1986 to around 1.5 million employees (over one-third of the workforce). Most of this expansion occurred in local government welfare services, where female employment rose by 400 per cent between 1963 and 1992 (Rosen 1996).

Swedish labour market policy in the 'golden age' thus emphasized the importance of work to income stability and equality (in Pierson's (1993*a*) terms, 'hyper-commodification' rather than 'de-commodification'). Whereas policy in Germany and Britain was oriented towards subsidizing and man- aging unemployment, Swedish policy was genuinely employment-oriented. From one perspective this policy seemed extremely stable. Firms were sub- ject to 'benign constraints' that ensured a continuing demand for skilled labour, while the state assisted in eliminating frictional unemployment and preventing long-term unemployment. An expanding public sector under the direction of the hegemonic Social Democrats guaranteed near-full employment, and centralized collective bargaining delivered wage restraint. Until the early 1970s this was an institutional and policy matrix that was widely seen by most of the relevant state and societal actors as a virtuous circle.

Employer Preferences and Labour Market Reform.   The Swedish case is on the surface something of a hybrid between the German and British cases.

Swedish capitalism shares many of the institutional features of German capitalism; a high degree of business coordination, high exposure on export markets, encompassing trade unions, and institutionalized collective bargaining (Stephens 1996). Employers' interests and policy preferences are therefore structured in similar ways in the two countries. Where the two countries differ is in the role played by central government. The German state's economic role (at least before 1989) has been limited largely to framework legislation within which the social partners bargain. In Sweden, the social democratic state was crucial to the institutionalization of a *national* class bargain, and the public sector plays a far larger role in the economy (Pontusson 1997). Increasingly this difference has come to affect the interests of private sector companies. As with the British case, by the mid-1970s the size, role, and policies of the social democratic state had begun to generate clear costs for employers.

First, the growth of the public sector started to impede the operation of the collective bargaining system in the Rehn–Meidner model. The increasing weight of sheltered public sector unions within the trade union movement and thus in 'high coverage' centralized bargaining arrangements undermined the flexibility of real wages that had characterized Swedish wage politics in the 1960s and 1970s. Second, the Social Democrats' economic strategy, combining a loose fiscal policy with periodic devaluations, was becoming less and less effective in controlling inflation. Third, egalitarian economic and social policies had the effect of reducing incentives to work. Sweden's absenteeism rate produced the lowest average annual hours of work in the OECD for every year between 1960 and 1986 (OECD 1998*b*). A fourth and related problem was the weak incentive for workers to acquire skills in an economy where the marginal rewards were so low. As Pontusson and Swenson argue, technological change in Swedish manufacturing made the problem of recruitment of highly skilled labour a major concern for employers. Fifth, the effectiveness of ALMPs in reconnecting workers with genuine employment, rather than employment programmes, was increasingly questioned. Sixth, during the 1970s the Swedish Social Democrats (allied with the LO) radicalized their policy stance with the 'Democratization of Working Life' and wage-earner funds proposals. Employers' fierce opposition was ignored, and the tacit principle of consensual tripartite decision making on important economic and social policies seemed to have been repudiated.

In 1983 an organized employers' response to these developments began to take shape with unilateral withdrawal of the engineering employers' association (VF, now VI) from peak-level negotiations. By 1990, after a decade of struggle, the SAF dismantled its central bargaining unit altogether. Over the next few years Swedish employers also withdrew from the central boards of various manpower programmes that had hitherto been run on a tripartite basis (Thelen 1993). The SAF's chairman, Ulf Laurin, declared that there could be no return to centralized bargaining, and added: 'The course for our wage policy is totally clear. It is focused upon decentralization—with the intent of providing a dominant role for firm level bargaining' (quoted in Pestoff 1991). At the same time that employers were declaring the end of centralized bargaining, unemployment began to soar. Between 1989 and 1993 unemployment rose from 1.5 to 8.2 per cent, and stayed at around 8 per cent thereafter. The immediate effect was an automatic increase in public expenditure, triggering an enormous deficit, and provoking calls for retrenchment in ALMPs and deregulation of the labour market (Lundgren 1994).

Government policies in the 1990s responded to employer demands and fiscal crisis with moderate reforms. The conservative government under Bildt cut sick pay compensation and work injury pay by small amounts in 1991 and 1992. Between 1993 and 1995 the unemployment benefit replacement rate was reduced from 90 to 75 per cent, and a five-day period of uncompensated unemployment was introduced. Meanwhile absenteeism was attacked (quite effectively) by varying sickness benefit rates and making employers financially responsible for the first few weeks of an employee's absence from work. Incentives to take on the unemployed have been introduced in the form of exemptions from social insurance contributions for new hirings. Payment to those enrolled on ALMP programmes has also been restructured in important ways. Participants' compensation is now linked to unemployment benefit replacement rates, rather than to market wages as it had been since 1933 (Timonen 1997).

To many observers these trends appeared to mark the end of the Swedish model, and to herald the onset of British-style industrial relations and labour market structures. A closer look, however, reveals an overall picture of resilience rather than collapse and continuity rather than change. First, the changes introduced by Swedish governments have trimmed rather than transformed existing programmes. Traditional labour market policy remedies have survived the worst of Swedish unemployment, and in many respects have been reinvigorated by the Social Democrats in recent years. The 1996 Employment Programme is classic Swedish social democracy, calling for the reduction of unemployment by 4 per cent by 2000, in part through an expansion of the *public* sector of 40,000 jobs (Swedish Government 1996). In addition the raising of unemployment insurance benefit back to 80 per cent removed any suspicion that benefit rates were on an irreversible slide downwards.

Second, employers' disavowal of the Swedish industrial relations model is far more rhetorical than real. Employers remain committed to institutions of collective bargaining, although, as in Germany, the location of these institutions has moved from national to sectoral level. Indeed the repudiation of central bargaining itself is better seen as a move to weaken the political arm of the social democratic movement than as a rejection of the method of coordination between employers and encompassing unions. Pestoff characterizes the move as one intended to restore balance in the labour market by redirecting labour's attention away from the extraction of benefits through *political* exchange with the SAP, and back towards *economic* exchange with employers (Pestoff 1991). Despite the seemingly neoliberal rhetoric of Swedish employers' associations (e.g. Edgren 1995), coordinated bargaining at the sectoral level has been consolidated over the past eight years.

A landmark in this consolidation was the agreement in March 1997 between eight trade unions and twelve employers' organizations to establish common procedures for wage bargaining, and a forum for discussion of economic strategy. In many ways this agreement marks a return towards cross-sectoral wage bargaining. The first round of wage negotiations under the new system in 1999 was marked by low levels of threatened industrial action, moderate across-the-board pay increases, a significant breakthrough on the issue of more flexible working time, and agreements of an unusually long duration (three years). Although the SAF remains formally opposed to centralized bargaining, it played an influential role from the sidelines, particularly in getting export industries to set the standard-setting wage agreement (EIRO 1998). What has emerged in Sweden is an institutional set-up strikingly reminiscent of the German system of coordinated capitalism (Soskice 1994).

The similarity with German capitalism has increased in the case of ALMPs too. The overnight arrival of high unemployment in 1990 stretched Swedish ALMPs considerably. Labour market offices could no longer engage in intensive job placement for every individual, and employment and training programmes could no longer provide the bridge back to 'normal work'. When participation in ALMPs was ruled as acceptable for the reinstatement of eligibility for unemployment benefits, their employment function decreased even further. In the 1980s between 60 and 70 per cent of participants found work within six months, but by 1991 this figure had fallen below 30 per cent. There seems now to be a widespread concern that ALMPs may be ineffective in combating Sweden's new-found structural unemployment problem (though there is also disagreement over this; see the contrast between Calmfors and Skedinger 1995 and S. Agell 1995).

The response of the Social Democrats in recent years has been threefold. First, ALMPs have been restructured, and two new programmes (the 'Youth Practice Placement' and 'Working Life Development Projects') introduced on far less generous terms than their predecessors. Nevertheless, the proportion of the unemployed on ALMPs remains high, and approximately at the same level as during the early 1980s (Timonen 1999). Second, job search activity has been refocused towards constructing individual strategies for re-employment, rather than mass loading on to state training schemes. Third, the widening gap between rates of unemployment among workers of different skill levels has led the government to emphasize formal education more and ALMPs less. Although the payoffs to this change of policy emphasis are long term rather than short term, it does enable the government to keep unemployment down by delaying entry into the workforce. The result of these initiatives is that employment policy through public training schemes has declined in prominence. At the same time, raising the profile of formal education indicates a commitment to the view that increased investment in pre-career education (both academic and vocational) is the best way to ensure against labour market risks. In both respects—reducing the role of the state in vocational training for the unemployed, and increasing it in education for the pre-employed—Sweden seems to be moving towards a (west) German stance on labour market policy.

The Swedish labour market model has neither remained static nor collapsed. Neither centre-right nor social democratic governments have made serious inroads into long-standing institutions and policies. In spite of their hostile public declarations, employers have not striven to deregulate the labour market nor to weaken trade unions' bargaining position. Their strategy has been more subtle—to reconfigure the institutions of collective bargaining in order to eliminate accumulating inefficiencies whilst simultaneously retaining the benefits of labour market coordination. In other words, employers arrived at a tipping point, where the costs of centralized bargaining under an interventionist social democratic government began to threaten the returns to coordination between companies and between capital and labour. To the extent that change has occurred, however, it is the result of employers seeking to *adjust* rather than to *undermine* this coordination. In particular employers have succeeded in challenging the disruptive interventionism of the social democratic state by shifting the site of coordinated wage bargaining from national to sectoral level. As in Germany, the strong collective capacity enjoyed by employers has enabled them to take action autonomously of the state. But employers have now established new forms of wage coordination. The redrawing of the boundaries of state intervention may have been modest, but it has reinforced employer control without sacrificing the institutions and practices of labour market coordination that characterized the Golden Age.

Constitutional Factors and Labour Market Reform. The properties of the Swedish constitution, electoral system, and legislative process are rather indeterminate. Sweden was dominated by single-party social democratic governments until 1976, and the SAP has been in power again for all but three years since 1982. Swedish governments in a unicameral parliamentary system enjoy considerable external autonomy. The continuing electoral dominance of the Swedish SAP clearly underpins continuity of policy. However, the exercise of this power by the SAP in the 1960s and 1970s was one of the central reasons for the 'employer revolt' of the 1980s, in particular the proposals for co-determination and socialized investment in 1976. Another complaint of Swedish companies concerns the SAP's repeated statutory increases in employer contributions for workers' benefits, which increased from 1965 to 1998 by over 450 per cent (SAF 1998). This dynamic between the SAP's exercise of its legislative autonomy and the reaction of employers precipitated the demise of centralized bargaining.

In periods of social democratic ascendancy from the 1950s onwards the Swedish constitution seemed to offer considerable autonomy to governments. However Sweden's constitution can also be seen as an obstacle to policy change. Sweden's proportional electoral system is capable of producing internally constrained governments. Between 1991 and 1994 a four-party minority centre-right coalition came to power, but was paralysed by internal divisions. The government depended on the support of either the SAP or the protest party New Democracy, and rejected cooperation with the latter. In consequence the impact of the few reforms that the Bildt Government introduced was substantially reduced by the need for SAP support. All serious attempts at radical policy departures, such as Labour Minister Hörnlund's proposal to reduce wages for the young unemployed and Wibble's 1993 retrenchment programme, were vetoed either within the coalition or by the SAP (Timonen 1997).

Institutional obstacles to effective policy making were publicly aired by the Lindbeck Commission in 1993 (Lindbeck 1994). Lindbeck argued that Sweden's short three-year parliamentary terms made the passage of long-term and radical reforms especially difficult. (In direct response, four-year terms were introduced following the 1994 election.) Second, the report bemoaned the dominance of special interest pork-barrel politics in the Riksdag. Excessively high membership, the dominance of local interest groups in candidate nominations, and committees exercising vetoes on behalf of special interests meant that 'the main problem with the Riksdag today is that the public interest has difficulties asserting itself' (182). Of particular concern was the budgetary process, in which 'it is the parliament, often influenced by strong special interest groups, that struggles to raise expenditures against the restraining efforts of the executive' (185).

Given the ambiguous properties of formal constitutional features in Sweden, it is difficult to draw any firm conclusions about their effects on the long-term stability of public policy. Certainly the centre-right coalition of the early 1990s promised more reform than its fragile composition could deliver; yet two decades earlier, under the same constitutional arrangements, the social democrats had shown how autonomous and radical a single-party Swedish government could be. Constitutionally speaking, Sweden is a mixed bag, and it would be difficult to sustain the claim that the constitution's effects on the policy making process are either consistent over time or sufficient to lock-in policy trajectories.

Electoral Constraints and Labour Market Reform.   Traditionally the Swedish Social Democrats are seen as electorally constrained by the legacies of their own policies. If the creation of mass and cross-class support was not the goal of high levels of public employment and a commitment to a universalist welfare policy, it has been the consequence of it. Surveys suggest that support for established social democratic welfare and labour market policies remains strong and cross-class (Svallfors 1995). The deliberate expansion of the public sector since the 1950s has left the Social Democrats with a core electorate that depends upon an active state for its continued employment and welfare. This goes some way to explaining why the SAP's recent employment programmes have (much to the annoyance of the OECD) concentrated on reinvigorating public sector employment.

   The greatest strategic restriction on the SAP is the long-standing organizational and ideological affinity between it and the LO (A. Martin 1992). The influence of the 'organizationally entrenched' trade unions has been pervasive—in candidate selection, providing personnel, and particularly in reining in policy movement away from social democratic territory. Union pressure within the party prevented the leadership from developing a policy profile on 'left-libertarian' issues in the 1970s such as nuclear energy, greater citizens' choice over public services and feminism (Kitschelt 1994*b*). The LO also applied the brake on welfare retrenchment after the return of the SAP to power in 1994. Clearly the 'Halving Unemployment' programme and the return of unemployment benefit rates to 80 per cent of wages reflected an effort by Persson to mollify the LO after the cutback package of the previous year. Similarly, proposals in 1996 to lower employment protection were vetoed by the LO. After flirting with the idea of turning to the Centre Party to push through the reforms, the SAP eventually withdrew the bulk of them. Seen in this light the SAP is strategically bound by its previous policy successes and by the organizational solidity of its core constituency (Hine 1986).

   This view of the SAP as the pawn of Swedish unions is, however, excessively monolithic. Like the German SPD in the 1970s the SAP has been suffering from internal conflicts between old and new left groups, the latter comprising groups such as the youth and women's organizations (Stephens 1996). Perhaps more destabilizing has been the emergence of splits between trade unions, especially between public and private sector unions. As union demands have become more diversified, it has become harder for the party to represent a 'generalized working-class interest' (Kitschelt 1994*b*). A mark of increasing tensions between unions and the SAP is that by the mid-1980s the LO had recommended an end to the practice of collective affiliation of its members to the party. Furthermore it would be misleading to depict the SAP as internally decentralized. Its leaders enjoy relatively high levels of strategic control and autonomy, and have demonstrated a readiness to pass cutback measures that hurt union interests (e.g. retrenchment on public training programmes in the early 1990s).

4. CONCLUSION: EMPLOYER PREFERENCES AND PATH DEPENDENCE

Despite considerable pressures and apocalyptic predictions, labour market regimes remain distinct in the 1980s and 1990s. In two of the three cases, the characteristic institutions and policies of the golden age have been highly resilient. German labour market policy, despite the shock of unification and mass long-term unemployment, continues to focus on subsidizing non-employment and bargained adjustment at sectoral level. Over the same period Sweden has kept faith with its combination of ALMPs, public employment, and strong worker protection, against a backdrop of collective bargaining relocated from the national to industry level. In both cases changes have occurred—in Germany as a response to the economic shocks brought about by unification, in Sweden as a strategic response to the rigidities of excessive centralization in both the political and the industrial relations sphere. But in both cases these changes have been surprisingly limited and have failed to precipitate the extensive deregulation that many foresaw. The British case is slightly different. Unlike Sweden and Germany, Britain never enjoyed a 'golden age'. Labour market policy did not develop a characteristic pattern before the arrival of high unemployment and Margaret Thatcher. However, since 1979 a coherent liberal blueprint for labour markets has been legislated into existence and seems now to enjoy cross-party support.

The arguments centring on constitutional and electoral constraints on governments maintain that policy lock-in occurs as a result of 'barriers to exit'. The picture they paint is of governments frustrated in their efforts to initiate policy reforms. Certainly where these constraints have been at their weakest governments have been able to initiate radical changes, as the British case under Thatcher demonstrates. Conversely, the Kohl Government clearly experienced some setbacks at the hands of the Bundesrat and the Constitutional Court. Yet neither type of explanation offers an account of the source of preferences for labour market policy. One of the most interesting features of retrenchment politics in the sphere of labour market policy in Sweden and Germany is how little reform has been *initiated*. The assumption that policy responses to unemployment in all countries will prompt political elites into unravelling long-standing national labour market regimes is clearly naive.

A further problem with these arguments is that neither constitutional nor electoral constraints seem to be necessary nor sufficient conditions for preserving policy trajectories over time. One of the key reasons for this is that where employers are coordinated and collectively powerful, labour market institutions and practice can be altered *independently* of government. When employers in Sweden wanted to reconstitute the organization of collective bargaining they were able to do so autonomously, and irrespective of the institutional or electoral constraints that preyed upon their governments. Second, policy changes initiated by governments may not be sufficient to engineer changes in labour market structure where employers coordinate collective abstention from these policies. German employers since the early 1980s have repeatedly failed to bite when offered the carrot of deregulation by the CDU-led government. Here the formidable constitutional and electoral obstacles in the way of reform *were* overcome, but labour market structure, policy, and practice remain fundamentally continuous from the 1970s to the 1990s. In Britain, by contrast, where the constitutional obstacles to radical governments are low, New Labour shows no desire to overhaul Britain's highly deregulated labour markets. The argument that policy continuity is the product of electoral constraints on policy innovation within parties is also too simple. Even hegemonic parties such as the SAP in Sweden and the CDU in Germany contain competing constituencies struggling for influence over the party's policy commitments, and the relative weight of these groups within the party organization changes over time. It is therefore difficult to make determinate arguments about the policy stance of a party based upon the interests of any one of these groups. The arrival of new policy dilemmas, such as unemployment, pits the interests of different constituencies against each other, and forces elites to make difficult policy choices. Finally, these elites can also innovate to change the structure of their party and the constituencies on which they rely, as the emergence of 'New' Labour under Tony Blair has shown.

This chapter has sought to account for the trajectory of labour market policy by offering an employer-centred theory of preferences. Where employers are strongly coordinated (Sweden and Germany) they have sought to preserve the institutional and policy matrix that underpins this coordination. In these cases employers' collective interests in perpetuating certain sorts of labour market structure were based on the returns to coordination that accrued from them over long periods of time. Moreover coordination between employers in Sweden and Germany equipped them with the collective capacity to get what they wanted. The continuity of labour market institutions and policies in a period of political and economic stress therefore illustrates well the dynamics and effects of increasing returns.

However these cases also point to problems of applying increasing returns arguments to politics, and the limits of such arguments. The British case is one in which employers are weakly coordinated, and therefore enlist the state in the task of deregulating labour markets to support low-cost competitive strategies. Although the Soskicean framework explains this case well, what it explains is *not* policy lock-in, but policy *reversal* after 1979. As I have argued, the neoliberal revolution of Thatcherism is best seen as a restoration, both in a long-run historical sense and in the economic sense of restoring the incentive-compatibility of labour market structures with other supply-side governance structures in the UK. Nevertheless, prior to 1979 employers had for twenty years failed to obtain their desired labour market policy regime from both Conservative and Labour governments, and had actively and consistently undermined their policy initiatives. What this shows is that employers in weakly coordinated market economies sometimes do not have the required collective capacity to pursue their interests effectively. The moral for increasing returns arguments is that the extent to which institutions or policies are locked in is in part a function of the *power* of the actors who enjoy these returns. In political contexts the prevalence of returns to coordination may not be sufficient for lock-in over time.

A second contrast between the argument advanced here and the increasing returns argument is that the former avoids some of the latter's bias towards excessive determinism. Understanding employers' preferences enables us to explain variance in the *sorts* of change and continuity that we see in different national policy trajectories. As the Swedish case showed, the same institutions and policies that provide returns to coordination and adaptation over time may also have adverse distributional consequences. Whether or not the latter outweigh the former is a contingent question. Thus, even where increasing returns are produced by an institution or policy there will be other 'utility considerations' that influence actors' preferences about the desirability of change or continuity.

This suggests a final note of caution about transferring increasing returns arguments from economic to political contexts. In Paul David's classic discussion of the lock-in of the QWERTY technology he observes axiomatically that there are 'no inherent preferences about keyboards' (David 1985). Increasing returns stories in economics see lock-in as the product of convergent expectations *irrespective* of the content-specific preferences actors may have about the technology itself. The case of employer coordination shares many of the characteristics of technologies in this sense. But what distinguishes politics from economics is that institutions and policies are rarely (if ever) desired or despised *solely* in virtue of properties of their usage by other actors. Unlike technologies or traffic lights, the content and discriminating effects of political institutions and public policies are central to actors' preferences about them. Increasing returns processes may be widespread and crucial in politics, but they are unlikely ever to provide the whole story.

13

Coping with Permanent Austerity
Welfare State Restructuring in Affluent Democracies

Paul Pierson

THE welfare states of the affluent democracies now stand at the centre of political discussion and social conflict. Analysts frequently portray these conflicts as fundamental struggles between supporters and opponents of the basic principles of the post-war social contract. They often emphasize that the politics of social policy are played out against the backdrop of a transformed global economy that has undercut the social and economic foundations of the welfare state. While containing elements of truth, such portrayals distort crucial characteristics of the contemporary politics of the welfare state. Changes in the global economy are important, but it is primarily social and economic transformations occurring within affluent democracies that produce pressures on mature welfare states. At the same time, support for the welfare state remains widespread almost everywhere. In most countries, there is little sign that the basic commitments to a mixed economy of welfare face a fundamental political challenge. Nor is there much evidence of convergence towards some neoliberal orthodoxy.

Yet the chapters in this volume have also stressed that welfare states are undergoing quite significant changes. In this conclusion, I argue that the contemporary politics of the welfare state take shape against a backdrop of both intense pressures for austerity and enduring popularity. In this context, even strong supporters of the welfare state may come to acknowledge the need for adjustment, and even severe critics may need to accept the political realities of continuing popular enthusiasm for social provision. Thus, in most of the affluent democracies, the politics of social policy centre on the renegotiation, restructuring, and modernization of the terms of the post-war social contract rather than its dismantling. The crucial issue is whether particular national settings facilitate the emergence of such a centrist reform effort, and if so, on what terms.

Thanks to Andrew Karch and Effi Tomaras for research assistance. I have benefited from many conversations with participants in the *New Politics* project and the European Forum at the EUI. I owe special thanks to John Myles and Ann Orloff, although I suppose it would be unfair to hold them responsible for the end result.

The argument proceeds in three stages. In the first, I outline a basic framework for studying the politics of reform in a context of permanent austerity. In the second, I discuss two complications: the need to incorporate different dimensions of social policy reform and the need to recognize three quite distinct configurations of welfare state politics among the affluent democracies. In the third, I apply these arguments to analyse the politics of restructuring in the liberal, social democratic, and conservative 'worlds' of welfare capitalism.

1. AN INITIAL FRAMEWORK FOR STUDYING THE POLITICS OF PERMANENT AUSTERITY[1]

Despite some disagreement concerning the main sources of pressure on mature welfare states, the chapters in Part I all conclude that the welfare state now faces a context of essentially permanent austerity. Changes in the global economy, the sharp slowdown in economic growth, the maturation of governmental commitments, and population ageing all generate considerable fiscal stress. There is little reason to expect these pressures to diminish over the next few decades. If anything, they are likely to intensify.

Underlining the severe pressures confronting mature welfare states does not, however, imply that the expected result is a collapse or radical retrenchment of national welfare states. Major policy reform is a political process, dependent on the mobilization of political resources sufficient to overcome organized opponents and other barriers to change. The welfare state's opponents have found it very difficult to generate and sustain this kind of political mobilization.

I have developed this argument elsewhere (Pierson 1994, 1996) and present only a condensed version here. The sources of the welfare state's political strength are diverse, but are of two basic types: the electoral incentives associated with programmes which retain broad and deep popular support and the institutional 'stickiness' which further constrains the possibilities for policy reform. Together, these features have created tremendous resilience in the face of two decades of welfare state 'crisis' (Stephens, Huber, and Ray 1999).

Electoral Incentives

In market democracies, voters play a crucial role. Implementing and sustaining policy reforms over time generally requires electoral vindication. Voters, however, remain strongly attached to the welfare state. The broad public

---

[1] This section draws on material presented in Pierson 1998.

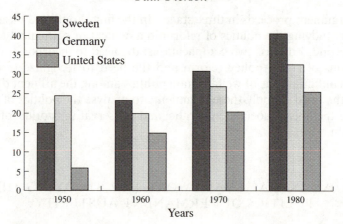

FIG. 13.1. Welfare state clienteles as a percentage of the electorate, 1950–80

Sources: Welfare state clienteles include public social welfare employment (excluding education)
as well as recipients of pensions, disability, social assistance, and unemployment benefits. All
welfare state clientele date comes from tables 4.5, 4.16, 6.3, 6.10, 7.4, and 7.14 in Richard Rose.
Public Employment in Western Nations (Cambridge: Cambridge University Press, 1985).
Electoral data comes from Thomas T. Mackie and Richard Rose, *The International Almanac of
Electoral History* (London: Macmillan, 1991), fully revised, third edition. All American welfare
state data covers 1952, 1962, 1972, and 1982. American electoral data covers 1952, 1964, 1972,
and 1984. German electoral data covers 1949, 1961, 1969, and 1980. Swedish electoral data
covers 1952, 1960, 1970, and 1979.

support consistently revealed in polls stems from several sources. As the welfare state has expanded, so has the size of its constituencies. As Peter Flora
has noted, 'including recipients of [pensions,] unemployment benefits and
social assistance and the persons employed in education, health and the social
services, in many countries today almost $\frac{1}{2}$ of the electorate receive transfer
or work income from the welfare state' (Flora 1989: 154). Figure 13.1 and
Table 13.1 offer a very rough indication of the political transformation associated with welfare state expansion. Figure 13.1 shows the dramatic impact
of welfare state growth from roughly 1950 to 1980. It tracks a conservative
measure of welfare state employment, plus a very conservative estimate of
transfer recipients, as a share of the total electorate for three representative
countries. From the beginning of the post-war expansion (1960) to the rough
end of the maturation period (1980) these ratios increase markedly in all
cases. Table 13.1 provides snapshots from the mid-1990s for the same countries. Again measured on a conservative basis, one can see both that the core
constituencies of the welfare state are very large, and that there are marked
variations across countries.

These crude indicators considerably underestimate the scale of the welfare state's reach into contemporary political life. Many voters who do not

TABLE 13.1. *Major welfare state clienteles in three countries, 1995*

	Sweden	Germany	United States
Pensions	1,584,304	21,630,000	43,388,000
Disability	408,576	1,180,000	5,857,656
Unemployment	37,734	1,990,000	7,900,000
Social assistance	474,159	2,080,000	4,869,000
Public welfare employment	1,245,800	1,590,000	2,540,000
TOTAL	3,750,573	28,470,000	64,554,656
Electorate	6,551,591	56,090,000	196,089,000
Percentage	57.25	50.76	32.92

Sources: Sweden—Statistiska Centralbyran, *Statistisk Arsbok '97* (1997). Germany—Statistiches Bundesamt, *Statistiches Jahrbuch für die Bundesrepublic Deutschland* (1998). United States—Committee on Ways and Means, *1996 Green Book* (1996). German welfare state clientele data and American electorate data cover 1996.

currently receive social benefits expect that they may at some point in their lives. Or they may be in the same household with someone who receives benefits from, or is employed by, the welfare state. In most countries, universal programmes, especially health care but also other social services, generate widespread support. Furthermore, the welfare state retains considerable legitimacy as a source of social stability and guarantor of basic rights of citizenship. Popular support generally appears to extend well beyond the confines of narrow economic self-interest.

Support for the welfare state is intense as well as broad. Intensity of preference matters because it is associated with higher rates of political mobilization and with voters' actual choices at election time. The intensity of support for the welfare state stems from two factors. First, while the benefits of retrenchment for welfare state opponents are generally diffuse and often uncertain, the large core constituencies for the welfare state have a concentrated interest in the maintenance of social provision. Huge segments of the electorates of advanced industrial societies rely on the welfare state for a large share of their income. It is one of the few basic axioms of political science that concentrated interests will generally be advantaged over diffuse ones.

The second source of intensity stems from the fact that welfare state supporters are in the position of fighting to sustain already existing benefits. Students of electoral behaviour and political psychology have found that voters exhibit a 'negativity bias'—they react more intensely to potential losses than to commensurate potential gains. Thus, the welfare state's electoral base is not only enormous, but primed to punish politicians for unpopular initiatives.

Institutional 'Stickiness'

Those seeking policy reform must confront not only the potential opposition of voters and programme beneficiaries but the stickiness of existing policy arrangements. By stickiness I have in mind two features of developed polities that reinforce the electoral obstacles to radical reform: formal and informal institutional 'veto points', and 'path dependent' processes, which in many cases tend to lock existing policy arrangements into place. Each of these characteristics pushes reform agendas in the direction of incremental adjustments to existing arrangements.

The basic point about veto points is straightforward and clearly spelled out in Bonoli's contribution to this volume (see more broadly Scharpf 1986; Tsebelis 1995). Most political systems make policy reform dependent on more than a simple 51 per cent majority, allowing minorities (including in some cases quite small ones) opportunities to block reforms. Examples of such institutional arrangements include federalism, a strong judiciary, bicameralism, use of referenda, requirements of super-majorities, and coalition-based governments.[2] Difficult as it is to create a majority coalition in favour of restructuring the welfare state, even that may not be enough. The multiplication of veto points can hamstring efforts at policy change, frustrating even an ambitious and aggressive reform coalition such as the Republican congressional majority in the United States after 1994, or an enduring conservative coalition such as the one governing Germany from 1982 to 1998.

A second major source of stickiness, path dependence, is more complex. Because path dependence is often invoked as an explanation without further explication, some elaboration is necessary.[3] Certain courses of political development, once initiated, are hard to reverse. It is not just that institutional veto points may make a reversal of course difficult. Individual and organizational adaptations to previous arrangements may also make reversal unattractive.

Recent work on path dependence has emphasized the ways in which initial social outcomes concerning institutional, organizational, or policy design—even suboptimal ones—can become self-reinforcing over time (Krasner 1989; North 1990). These initial choices encourage the emergence of elaborate social and economic networks, greatly increasing the cost of adopting once-possible alternatives and therefore inhibiting exit. Major social arrangements have major social consequences. Individuals make important commitments in response to government actions. These commitments, in turn, may vastly increase the disruption caused by institutional reforms, effectively 'locking-

---

[2] Veto points may also be policy-specific. The Canada Pension Plan (CPP), for example, cannot be reformed without a large super-majority among provincial governments.

[3] See also the discussions in the chapters by Myles and Pierson and Wood. A more detailed discussion can be found in Pierson (2000).

in' previous decisions. As a result, as Douglass North has emphasized, change in well-institutionalized polities is typically incremental.

Research on technological change has revealed some of the circumstances conducive to path dependence (David 1985; Arthur 1994). The crucial factor is the presence of increasing returns, which encourages actors to focus on a single alternative and to continue movement down a particular path once initial steps are taken. *Large set-up or fixed costs* are likely to create increasing returns to further investment in a given technology, providing individuals with a strong incentive to identify and stick with a single option. Substantial *learning effects* connected to the operation of complex systems provide an additional source of increasing returns. *Coordination effects* (or network externalities) occur when the individual receives increased benefits from a particular activity if others also adopt the same option. Finally, *adaptive expectations* occur when individuals feel a need to 'pick the right horse' because options that fail to win broad acceptance will have drawbacks later on. Under these conditions, individual expectations about usage patterns may become self-fulfilling.

As North has argued, all of these arguments can be extended from studies of technological change to other social processes, particularly to the development of institutions. In contexts of complex social interdependence, new institutions or policies often entail high fixed or start-up costs, may involve considerable learning effects, and generate coordination effects and adaptive expectations. Established institutions generate powerful inducements that reinforce their own stability and further development. 'In short', North concludes, 'the interdependent web of an institutional matrix produces massive increasing returns', making path dependence a common feature of institutional evolution (North 1990: 95).

Over time, as social actors make commitments based on existing institutions, the cost of 'exit' rises. Learning from past events may lead actors to act differently in launching new initiatives. Recapturing ground in previously institutionalized fields of activity, however, will often be quite difficult. Actors do not inherit a blank slate that they can remake at will when their preferences change or the balance of power shifts. Instead, they find that the dead weight of previous institutional choices seriously limits their room to manoeuvre.

Because this point is so often misconstrued, it should be stressed that the claim is not that path dependence 'freezes' existing arrangements in place. Change continues, but it is bounded change. North (1990: 98–9) summarizes the key point well: 'At every step along the way there [are] choices—political and economic—that provide . . . real alternatives. Path dependence is a way to narrow conceptually the choice set and link decision making through time. It is not a story of inevitability in which the past neatly predicts the future.'

One of the major themes of this volume is that contemporary welfare states, and the politics that surround them, strongly reflect these path-dependent effects. As Myles and Pierson argue, old-age pension systems provide a powerful example. Most countries operate pensions on a pay-as-you-go basis: current workers pay 'contributions' that finance the previous generation's retirement. Once they have been in place for a long time, pay-as-you-go systems may face incremental cutbacks and adjustments, but they are highly resistant to radical reform. Shifting to private, funded arrangements would place an untenable burden on current workers, requiring them to finance the previous generation's retirement while simultaneously saving for their own. Even partial privatization has generally proven possible only in the relatively few countries lacking extensive and mature pay-as-you-go systems.

Similar if less severe path-dependent effects are likely in areas of social policy where complex sets of institutions and organizations have 'co-evolved' over extended periods. The chapters by Giaimo, Manow, and Wood all emphasize this type of dynamic. In health care provision and many aspects of labour market systems, social actors need to coordinate their activities and they invest resources in line with the incentive structures of their existing environment (see also Giaimo and Manow 1999; Hacker 1998). This probably helps to explain why employers, for instance, have often been more half-hearted and internally divided over policy reform than many theories of political economy might have anticipated (Thelen 1999).

Both the popularity of the welfare state and the prevalence of 'stickiness' must be at the centre of an investigation of restructuring. The essential point is that welfare states face severe strains and they retain deep reservoirs of political support. For political analysts, the central question can thus be put as follows: What happens when the irresistible forces of post-industrialism meet the immovable object of the welfare state? Acknowledging the strength of both sides of this collision generates several implications for investigating the politics of reform.

There are strong grounds for scepticism about the prospect for any radical revision of the welfare state in most countries. Almost nowhere have politicians been able to assemble and sustain majority coalitions for a far-reaching contraction of social policy (Stephens, Huber, and Ray 1999). The reasons have already been outlined. The broad scale of public support, the intensity of preferences among programme recipients, the extent to which a variety of actors (including employers) have adapted to the existing contours of the social market economy, and the institutional arrangements which favour defenders of the status quo make a frontal assault on the welfare state politically suicidal in most countries.

Yet the chapters in Part I of this volume also suggest that pressures associated with post-industrialism, intensified in some respects by globalization, have rendered the maintenance of the status quo an increasingly unrealistic option. Continuing low growth coupled with the challenges of creating service sector employment, population ageing, and the overcommitments of existing policies are already generating intense pressures. Tax levels strain public tolerance. Payroll tax burdens and their possible adverse impact on employment and wages create tensions within the traditional support coalitions of the welfare state (Visser and Hemerijck 1997). Barring an extremely unlikely return to an era of high economic growth, fiscal pressures on welfare states are certain to intensify. While tax increases may contribute to closing the gap between commitments and resources, it is difficult to imagine that in many European countries changes in revenues alone could be sufficient to maintain fiscal equilibrium. Thus, even strong supporters of the welfare state increasingly acknowledge that sustaining basic arrangements will require significant reforms. It is a context of permanent austerity.

The prospect of permanent austerity transforms political conflicts over the restructuring of social policy. Welfare state conflict is often portrayed as a clash between those wedded to the status quo and those eager to dismantle basic social protections. In countries where aggressive advocates of neoliberalism have been in power, such as New Zealand and until recently the United Kingdom, this has not been too inaccurate a portrayal. Yet in a climate where social trends make pressures on budgets intense and unrelenting, political cleavages are likely to become more complex. Those advocating restructuring will include many who wish to preserve and modernize key elements of the social contract, but seek to do so in a manner which does not create unsustainable budgetary burdens, contributes to economic performance, and gives emerging social demands some chance of competing for public attention and resources with well-established ones. In the current climate, restructuring must be distinguished from retrenchment or dismantling.

My central contention so far is that neither the alternatives of standing pat or dismantling are likely to prove viable in most countries. Instead, as in many aspects of politics, we should expect strong pressures to move towards more centrist—and therefore more incrementalist—responses. Those seeking to generate significant cost reductions while modernizing particular aspects of social provision will generally hold the balance of political power. In Claus Offe's words, the objective for those wielding electoral power in most countries will be 'smooth consolidation' (Offe 1991).

A useful initial framework for fleshing out this claim is a simple version of the pivotal politics argument suggested in recent studies of American politics (Krehbiel 1998; Brady and Volden 1998). In any collective choice situation where policy preferences can be arrayed on a single continuum, there is a pivotal actor whose vote determines whether an initiative moves forward or is blocked. This pivotal voter is likely to wield disproportionate power, and policy outcomes should generally gravitate towards that location. Pivotal voters need not be median voters. A great deal turns on the institutional environment governing choice. Depending on the significance of multiple vetoes and super-majoritarian systems, the pivotal voter will generally be closer to the status quo than the median voter—often much closer. In the United States, for instance, if a President is prepared to veto legislation, the pivotal voter in the legislature is not the one generating a bare majority, but the one producing the two-thirds majority required for a veto override.[4]

In practice, the political vulnerability of those seeking to modify popular social welfare programmes is such that they will often seek relatively broad consensus on reform rather than a 'minimum winning coalition'. Broader consensus legitimates the claim that policy change is necessary and intended to sustain rather than gut the programme under review; it thus provides essential political cover (Weaver 1986). The desire to make reform durable generally points in the same direction. Especially with large, complex, and deeply institutionalized programmes like health care and pensions, social actors place a high value on predictability and continuity in policy. Reform is not enough; powerful interests seek reasonable assurance that the new policies can be sustained. This again encourages the assembly of grand coalitions. Such coalitions, often informal and issue-specific, extend the range of actors with a stake in the reform outcome, and increase confidence that the next election will not overturn the new initiatives.

In other words, the pivotal actor in practice will generally be closer to the status quo than the actor identified by a formal analysis of the institutional preconditions for minimum winning coalitions. In a wide range of countries, the coalitions engaged in the restructuring of welfare states have been far broader than minimum size, incorporating key interest organizations as well as political parties outside the current government. Such a broadening purchases the increased legitimacy and potential durability of enacted reforms. Most often, the price is a more incremental adjustment than would have been (theoretically) possible with a smaller coalition.

A final, related factor in pushing the 'pivot' towards the status quo is the possibility that the governments capable of enacting reform at a limited political cost will be those possessing the greatest credibility with voters on the issue (F. Ross 1998). Following a 'Nixon goes to China' logic, it will often be those governments with reputations of support for the welfare state that have the greatest room to manoeuvre. Yet the very factors that produce such credibility (past commitments, ideological orientations, and the nature of a party's core constituencies) make it unlikely that the favoured party will use its enhanced manoeuverability to dismantle established social policies. Again, political incentives point towards more moderate, modernizing reforms.

---

[4] More precisely, it is the voter producing a two-thirds majority in the chamber where that voter's preferences are closest to the status quo.

Q   C   V   M   R

FIG. 13.2. Identifying the viable space for policy reform.

Of course, students of comparative public policy have long recognized the role of positive-sum bargaining among crucial organized interests and political parties. In most advanced industrial democracies the new economic and fiscal environment has transformed, but not undermined the conditions for consensus-oriented policy making based on political exchange. What has changed is the 'currency' for such exchanges. Traditionally, labour's contribution to consensus was wage restraint. As Rhodes argues, even following the demise of Keynesianism this contribution remains important. Yet reformers of the welfare state also require credibility and legitimacy, particularly in the eyes of voters. Left and centre-left parties, and/or trade unions, generally need to be brought into reform coalitions to make the restructuring of welfare states politically sustainable.

The implications of the discussion so far can be seen in Figure 13.2. Depicting policy reforms on a continuum from the status quo (q) to a full-fledged neoliberal agenda of radical retrenchment (r), one would expect the median voter (m) to be a considerable distance from (r). The need to surmount institutional veto points pushes the government reform agenda back to (v), and the desire to gain legitimacy-enhancing and stability-inducing consensus promotes a further move to (*c*). My argument is thus that in most of the affluent democracies the viable reform space will be, at a maximum, in the region (c)–(v). Reform thus entails a substantial shift from (q), but it is a long way from (r).

2. TWO MAJOR COMPLICATIONS

This is of course an extremely stylized treatment of reform politics. A more satisfying account would need to complicate the analysis in two crucial respects. First, one needs to develop a more nuanced conceptualization of the reform agenda, or, in social science terms, the dependent variable. Second, one needs to consider the distinctive reform dynamics of different welfare state regimes. Each of these complications represents an important part of the current agenda for research on the politics of the welfare state.

Three Dimensions of Welfare State Restructuring

One of the striking features of current comparative research on the welfare state is the lack of consensus on outcomes. How much, and in what ways, have welfare states changed since the end of the post-war boom? The authors in this volume generally depict most reforms in most countries as incremental rather than radical, and focused on restructuring rather than straightforward dismantling. However, some have argued that the degree of cutbacks has been more severe (Clayton and Pontusson 1998). Even among those who see the overall degree of change as fairly limited, there may be little agreement about how to characterize the nature and scope of change cross-nationally.

It is difficult to exaggerate the obstacle this dissensus creates for comparative research. As Kitschelt notes in his chapter, it is impossible to seriously evaluate competing explanations when there is no agreement about the pattern of outcomes to be explained. Thus, it is important to ask why researchers have so much trouble with the dependent variable.

The problem lies partly in the concept of the welfare state itself, partly in data limitations, and partly in limitations of current theorizing about welfare state change. 'The welfare state' is generally taken to cover those aspects of government policy designed to protect against particular risks shared by broad segments of society. Standard features, not necessarily present in all countries, would include: protection against loss of earnings due to unemployment, sickness, disability, or old age; guaranteed access to health care; support for households with many children or an absent parent, and a variety of social services—child care, elder care, etc.—meant to assist households in balancing multiple activities which may overtax their own resources.

Needless to say, this list covers an extremely wide range of government activity. Furthermore, the trend in scholarship has been to broaden the already extensive domain of the subject matter. Recent analyses have advocated more attention to public/private interplay (e.g. Shalev 1996; Howard 1997) and to the interfaces between the public sector, the market, and the household (Orloff 1993; Esping-Andersen 1999; O'Connor, Orloff, and Shaver 1999). In this volume, Schwartz makes a similar appeal for extending attention to systems of social protection built into the regulatory arrangements governing particular economic sectors. There is little doubt that this broadening has had salutary effects, forcing attention to dimensions of social life that had previously received scant attention, and illuminating the extent to which welfare states are nested in a set of broader institutional arrangements.

Yet as the concept of the welfare state, or welfare regime, 'stretches', it becomes inevitable that quite distinct processes and outcomes will be joined together under the umbrella of a single master variable (Collier and Levitsky 1997). This in turn spreads confusion in two ways. First, it fuels a process where analysts discussing what has happened to 'the welfare state' find themselves talking past each other because each is concerned with distinct dimensions. Second, it makes efforts to develop summary measures of what has happened extraordinarily difficult. The complexity of this multifaceted concept cuts against our attempts to generate the relatively parsimonious measures of outcomes that make a serious enterprise of comparative explanation possible.

A second problem stems from data limitations. Even if we agree about the outcomes that we are interested in measuring, how do we carry out the measurements? This problem has become more acute as—again for quite good reasons—analysts have criticized simple efforts to characterize outcomes through indicators of public or social expenditure. Following Esping-Andersen's lead, there has been a broad recognition that many of the theoretically relevant outcomes of welfare state change will simply not be captured by expenditure data. Indeed, I have argued elsewhere (Pierson 1994) that this is especially true in the current environment. There is every reason to believe that policy makers will seek systematically to engineer changes that produce their major expenditure implications only at a later point in time. In short, there is probably no substitute for investigations that pay attention to fairly detailed dimensions of policy change, including attempts to map their (perhaps uncertain) long-term implications. Rigorously applying consistent criteria to even a small subset of the affluent democracies is a time-consuming and expertise-taxing enterprise.[5] Carrying out such research for the affluent democracies as a whole would require the efforts of a large and well-funded team. So far no one has carried it out.[6]

The final element of the 'dependent variable' problem stems from limitations of theory. It is this issue that I want to explore in more detail here. One of the hidden premises of much recent writing on the welfare state has been a return to the simple dichotomy of 'more' vs. 'less'. Implicitly, change is measured along a single continuum, stretching from the intact (or even expanding) welfare state on one end to the seriously eroded or dismantled on the other. Yet here again Esping-Andersen's core insights retain force. In a context where actors have complex motives, and the dependent variable is so heterogeneous, attempts to reduce change to a single dimension will be counterproductive.

Instead, starting from the perspectives of prominent actors in the reform process, we can think about change along three dimensions: re-commodification, cost containment, and recalibration.[7] Each constitutes a potentially important dimension of welfare state restructuring. Any effort to focus on only one will necessarily distort what the process of restructuring

---

[5] Two excellent examples are Alber 1998*b* and Lindbom 1999. Alber covers three countries, although he limits himself largely to transfer programmes. Lindbom covers one country.

[6] The voluminous Scharpf/Schmidt project probably comes closest, but it does not attempt to systematically measure policy outcomes at the level of programmes across the countries in their study.

[7] I am grateful to Jonathan Zeitlin for suggesting the term 'recalibration'.

is about. For any welfare state, or any particular welfare state programme, we can fruitfully think about the extent to which reform agendas and policy outcomes involve change along each of these dimensions.

Re-commodification

De-commodification, in Esping-Andersen's influential formulation, 'occurs when a service is rendered as a matter of right, and when a person can maintain a livelihood without reliance on the market' (1990: 21–2). For Esping-Andersen, the centrality of de-commodification stems from his earlier reflections on the construction of the social democratic welfare regime (Esping-Andersen 1985). He argued that this regime was fashioned through the efforts of a highly mobilized and well-organized working class, which sought to use political power to overcome its vulnerabilities in the labour market. Re-commodification essentially involves the effort to reverse that process—to restrict the alternatives to participation in the labour market, either by tightening eligibility or cutting benefits.

Particularly for those who see the current era as defined by the rise of business power, re-commodification stands as the key dimension for an investigation of welfare state restructuring. The transformation of social provision, from this perspective, is primarily about dismantling those aspects of the welfare state that shelter workers from market pressures, forcing them to accept jobs on employers' terms. This formulation has proven particularly central to analyses of welfare state reform produced by those who come to the topic from previous work on industrial relations. For these scholars, the shifting balance of power between employers and unions stands at the centre of political analysis (Clayton and Pontusson 1998; Swenson 1991*b*).

Re-commodification clearly represents an important dimension of welfare state change. Yet it is increasingly evident that the basic logic of de-commodification outlined in Esping-Andersen's *Three Worlds* was at least somewhat misleading even for the period of welfare state expansion during the post-war period.[8] It suggests an image of welfare states foisted on capitalists. The problem with this line of thinking is not that it takes capitalism too seriously, but that it fails to take capitalism seriously enough. These are, after all, economies where investment depends on the capacity of capitalists to earn profits, and where the need to induce investment therefore confers substantial political power (Lindblom 1977). The question thus arises: How would programmes seriously damaging to economic performance thrive so extensively for so long?

[8] As Ann Orloff has stressed to me, commodification's connotation of diminished autonomy or choice is also problematic when applied to women, for whom the shift from unpaid household work to participation in the paid labour market may enhance rather than diminish autonomy.

As Manow stresses in his chapter (see also the contributions of Rhodes, Swank, and Huber and Stephens) the attitude of private firms to the expansion of the welfare state cannot be reduced to one of recalcitrant opposition to de-commodification. To argue that employers have been enthusiastic builders of the welfare state would be revisionism run amok. Yet particular elements have been enormously appealing to particular employer interests, facilitating rather than impeding their core strategies (Mares 1998). Moreover, in many other respects employers have adjusted to welfare state arrangements—and policy makers have accommodated the welfare state to employers—over extended periods of time. As Soskice (1999) has argued, particular types of firms are likely to thrive in particular institutional settings. Thus, there is often a strong co-evolutionary aspect to the intersection between varieties of capitalism and systems of social provision.

This is not to suggest that commodification has not been a relevant dimension in recent struggles over the welfare state. For particular actors, in particular countries, with respect to particular programmes, this dimension has been highly salient. 'Work incentives' have been the focus of concern in many cases, ranging from the reform of Dutch disability pensions to the abolition of AFDC in the United States. Yet there remains considerable variation in the extent to which welfare state reform has focused on improving work incentives. All of the studies in Part IV emphasized that reform is often not primarily about re-commodification. As Wood argues, even actors who one might think would make this a high priority—e.g. German employers—have often had more pressing concerns. The task for analysts then becomes threefold: to identify the conditions under which a focus on re-commodification is significant, to establish the degree of change along that dimension, and to explain the observed patterns. At the same time, one must avoid the temptation to reduce the discussion of welfare state restructuring to this single aspect.

Cost Containment

In his powerful critique of expenditure-based analysis of welfare state variations, Esping-Andersen observed that spending levels were essentially derivative of, and often not a good proxy for, other outcomes (such as de-commodification, poverty relief, or status maintenance) which actors valued. During the period of welfare state expansion, he argued pointedly, 'it is difficult to imagine that anyone struggled for spending *per se*' (Esping-Andersen 1990: 21).

In the current climate, however, people do fight against spending per se. Indeed, this is a defining characteristic of the era of austerity. As I argued in Chapter 3, a range of pressures, including the shift from manufacturing to services, demographic and household change, and the maturation of governmental commitments are placing inexorable demands on government budgets. Deficit reduction is a high priority for many of the countries that have joined or seek to join the European Monetary Union. In many contexts, powerful actors are concerned first and foremost with the implications of reform for levels of government expenditure. Of course, the imposition of austerity may become a vehicle for the pursuit of other ambitions, but often the principal focus is cost containment itself.

With the exception of Wilensky's important work (Wilensky 1981), social scientists have generally treated social expenditure and taxation as two distinct realms of research. In reality, of course, they are two sides of the same coin, inextricably linked. The need to finance public spending in the current environment often becomes the most powerful constraint on existing social policy arrangements. Employers and financial interests worry about high tax levels because of their potential impact on profits—an impact that may be felt through a number of distinct channels. In many countries, for instance, a major preoccupation is the fear that high fixed labour costs, generated in part by payroll tax rates, are seriously impeding the ability of employers to hire low-skilled workers.

Of course, the other political channel for opposition to taxes runs through the electorate. As the welfare state has expanded, its financial underpinnings have shifted, necessarily, to heavy reliance on funds from middle-income households. Higher taxes, combined with slower growth of real incomes, have generated popular discontent. In most countries, politicians must also cope with the downside of pay-as-you-go financing. As Myles and Pierson argue, the current era marks the reversal of the favourable political dynamic that accompanied the phase-in of pay-as-you-go pension systems. During the 'golden age' politicians could make generous promises while deferring the cost (i.e. high payroll tax rates). Today's politicians, rather than being in a position to claim credit for new initiatives, act primarily as the bill-collectors for yesterday's promises. Although voters almost everywhere retain widespread allegiance to public social provision, these sentiments are now intermingled with stiff resistance to significant tax increases (Bonoli, George, and Taylor-Gooby, forthcoming).

Governments face the unenviable task of reconciling strong tendencies for higher outlays with the potential for voter backlashes and the possibility that new taxes will damage economic performance. At the same time, most countries face tighter constraints on their ability to run deficits (most obviously in countries subject to the convergence criteria of EMU). In this climate, cost containment itself emerges as a top priority. Again, the questions for analysts are to identify the circumstances where a focus on cost containment becomes prominent, to establish the degree to which that goal is achieved, and to explain the patterns identified.

Recalibration

Still, the agenda confronting contemporary welfare states cannot be reduced to cost containment plus commodification. By recalibration I mean reforms which seek to make contemporary welfare states more consistent with contemporary goals and demands for social provision. Two different types of recalibration should be distinguished. *Rationalization* involves the modification of programmes in line with new ideas about how to achieve established goals. *Updating* concerns efforts to adapt to changing societal demands and norms—e.g. changes in the household, the life course, the nature of the labour market, or the age composition of societies. Rationalization includes attempts to correct obviously 'incentive-incompatible programmes' or cases of overshoot which may become evident over time, especially if external circumstances change in a way which greatly changes the functioning of programmes. Examples might include disability programmes in the Netherlands, or public service pensions in France and Italy. This kind of modernization would also include reforms of service systems, including health care, designed to improve the efficiency of provision or the responsiveness of such systems to consumer needs and demands.

The reform of Sickness Pay in Sweden can serve as an example of rationalization. By the mid-1980s, absenteeism rates in Swedish workplaces began to reach extremely high levels. There was fairly broad agreement that sick pay programmes were being abused—that these programmes were helping to produce high rates of absence from work rather than, as intended, providing protection against an important social risk. Spending rose sharply, from under 2 per cent of GDP in the early 1980s to almost 3 per cent of GDP in 1988 (Benner, Vad, and Schludi 1999: graph 23). The result was a consensus—partial and not without conflict—on a set of reforms to correct these tendencies. Replacement rates were cut, and waiting days added. Revenue-neutral changes were introduced to increase the incentives of employers to monitor use of sick pay provisions. Both the pattern of reforms and their timing suggest that the dominant concern was to restore sick pay to its originally intended role rather than to worsen the terms on which genuinely sick workers could choose to be absent from work.

This is tricky territory analytically. Since in the current context these reforms will often be designed to save money, how do we distinguish the impact of new ideas about how to do things, or efforts to recalibrate errant programmes, from simple cutbacks in provision? Yet clearly we do not want to smuggle all modifications of programmes into a framework of 'assaults on the welfare state'. Over time actors will sometimes discover that particular programmes do not work as intended, or they will determine that there may be better ways of achieving their goals. In such a context, they will push for changes. Thus, recent reforms in Swedish health care provision have produced considerable reorganization and resulted in public employment reductions, particularly among the low-skilled. From one vantage point (Clayton and Pontusson 1998) this represents a fundamental assault on public sector workers. From another, however, it represents an attempt to increase productivity in the public sector in order to provide high-quality and flexible services to consumers at a politically sustainable cost. The equation of public sector reform with simple retrenchment or the roll-back of the state is highly questionable without evidence that cost-savings have reduced service quality.

Updating involves the modification of existing programmes, or the initiation of new ones, in response to newly recognized social needs. A defining characteristic of the current era is the coexistence of social conditions which are in many ways 'new' with welfare states which are in many respects decidedly 'old' (Esping-Andersen 1999). As has been discussed, mature welfare states will tend to be characterized by various forms of stickiness. In addition, many current policy outcomes are the lagged effects of decisions taken decades ago. There is thus often a considerable 'mismatch' between emerging social risks and shared understandings of appropriate targets for state intervention, on the one hand, and the existing array of government social policies, on the other. The various aspects of this mismatch constitute an important dimension of restructuring agendas in contemporary welfare states.

Problematic as the concept of recalibration might be, it is more problematic to reduce the nature of current welfare state restructuring to simple cost containment plus re-commodification. A variety of initiatives, dealing with issues such as gender equity and social exclusion, simply cannot be squeezed into these other categories. Consider some of the most striking initiatives of recent years: the introduction of 'private' but essentially mandatory superannuation in Australia (C. Pierson 1998); the establishment of long-term care insurance in Germany (Götting, Haug, and Hinrichs 1994); the enactment or expansion in many countries of a range of subsidies or 'contribution credits' for unpaid caring work (Daly 1997); and the marked expansion of various initiatives to 'make work pay' by subsidizing the terms on which workers enter the low-paid labour market (Myles and Pierson 1997). None of these initiatives can be incorporated into a simple vision of expanding markets (commodification) and contracting states (cost containment).

Introducing these three dimensions of welfare state restructuring confers several very considerable analytical advantages. First, breaking down the very broad category of 'change' into discrete dimensions sharpens our capacity to discern distinct patterns in outcomes. One can identify striking variations both across policy arenas and across countries. Particular sectors of the welfare state tend to be much more preoccupied with one or another dimension of welfare state restructuring. The differences are clearly highlighted in this volume's 'policy domain' chapters (Part IV). Wood shows that in the case of labour market reform the primary agendas are re-commodification and recalibration, in differing and quite interesting configurations. By contrast, cost containment is a much less significant motivation for policy reform. In the case of health care and pensions, on the other hand, cost containment is *the* issue in most countries, though flanked in some cases by efforts at modernization. Only rarely will re-commodification provide the primary lens for analysing the character of reform in these core welfare state sectors. To take a third example, in the case of family policies, the main pressure all welfare states face is the need to adapt social policy arrangements to the radically transformed interfaces between market, state, and households.

Distinct dimensions of welfare state restructuring will be of varied salience not only across programme areas, but across countries and over time. For instance, acute fiscal crises or the dash to meet EMU's convergence criteria obviously place a premium on cost-containment efforts. More generally, I will argue in the next section that the three different 'worlds' of contemporary welfare capitalism give rise to distinct policy agendas and, in part as a result, distinct competing political coalitions and reform dynamics. It has been in the liberal welfare states that a focus on re-commodification has been most pronounced. These already highly commodified welfare states have become more so—especially in Britain, New Zealand, and the United States. By contrast, recalibration and cost containment have been more central to the policy agenda in Continental welfare states, while cost containment has been the principal issue in the social democratic welfare states of Scandinavia. A focus on multiple reform dimensions thus allows the analyst to highlight the distinct problem loads of different welfare states.

Finally, disaggregating these reform dimensions increases our capacity to make sense of relevant political processes, facilitating more nuanced accounts of actor interests and political activity. Different actors may be concerned about distinct dimensions of reform; particular actors may have multiple but partly conflicting objectives. Furthermore, because of these multiple priorities there may be unsuspected opportunities for issue-linkage and negotiated change in which different actors trade off lesser concerns for greater ones. As noted in the chapters by Bonoli, Rhodes, and Myles and Pierson, one of the striking observed outcomes in some configurations is unexpected coalitions based on quid pro quos. One can place this in the framework outlined in the first part of this chapter. Recognizing the multi-dimensionality of reform is crucial in a context where many actors agree on the need for 'change' but have different interests and priorities. Analysts elsewhere (Levy 1999; Myles and Pierson 1997) have stressed the centrality of compromise and the search for positive-sum trade-offs under conditions where broad political coalitions are necessary and straightforward retrenchment is politically difficult to sell.

Three Distinct Welfare State Regimes

The second necessary complication of my initial framework stems from the need to recognize the existence of very distinct political and policy configurations—distinct regimes—within the ranks of the affluent democracies. Up until now I have spoken of essentially a single 'logic' of welfare state reform. Just as we have to distinguish different reform dimensions, however, we also need to recognize the existence of quite different settings for the emerging politics of restructuring.[9]

Esping-Andersen's typology of three worlds of welfare capitalism—liberal, conservative, and social democratic—has been enormously influential. At the same time, it has been subjected to frequent criticisms, mostly stressing that particular countries are poorly categorized, or arguing that other dimensions of variation are neglected. Any typology covering the complex realities of a large number of countries is vulnerable to this kind of challenge. Yet there are excellent theoretical and methodological reasons to organize the explanation of variance in outcomes around an analysis of distinct regimes rather than lumping all OECD countries into a single pool in which one scrutinizes variance along a single, continuous range of 'independent' variables.

'To talk of a regime', Esping-Andersen maintains, 'is to denote the fact that in the relation between state and economy a complex of legal and organizational features are systematically interwoven' (1990: 2). What was most compelling in Esping-Andersen's analysis of modern welfare states was his insistence that welfare states be seen as part of complex historical configurations.[10] The 'three worlds' did not result from 'more' or 'less' of a few discrete, independent master variables, but from the interactive and cumulative effects of a number of interdependent causal factors. 'Variables' may have a particular impact only when accompanied by a set of additional factors. This perspective has strong affinities with Ragin's concept of 'complex conjunctural causation' (Ragin 1987). As Shalev has put it, the argument is that welfare regimes should be seen as 'a limited number of

---

[9] In case it is not obvious, I should acknowledge that many of the arguments in Pierson 1994 and Pierson 1996, especially those which de-emphasize the contemporary role of organized labour, suffer from precisely this defect. This criticism is effectively advanced in Visser and Hemerijck 1997.

[10] In this respect, the analysis runs directly parallel to a very prominent theme in comparative political economy, emphasizing the varieties of contemporary capitalism (Kitschelt et al. 1999*b*; Hall 1999; Soskice 1999). In Soskice's influential account, 'there are strong *interlocking complementarities* between different parts of the institutional framework. Each system depends on the other systems to function effectively' (1999: 109). Spurred in part by Esping-Andersen's work, a number of researchers have begun to explore the connections between production systems and welfare state regimes (see Ebbinghaus and Manow 1998; Huber and Stephens, Manow, Rhodes, and Wood, in this volume).

qualitatively different configurations with distinctive historical roots'. Caus-ally, the claim is that '*countries cluster on policy because they cluster on politics*' (Shalev 1999: 13, emphasis in original). In this framework, it makes no sense to argue for a linear relationship between independent variables and dependent variables, e.g. that 'any discrete increment of Catholicism or absolutism ought to yield a discrete and uniform increment in pension "corporativism"' (ibid.).[11]

The arguments about path dependence discussed earlier in this chapter and elsewhere in this volume (Myles and Pierson, Wood), as well as the contributions which focus on linkages among regime features (Manow, Huber and Stephens) point in the same direction. Path-dependent processes are very likely to be prevalent in contexts where a set of organizations and institutions develop together over extended periods of time, reinforcing each other through processes of mutual adaptation and competitive selection. Institutions and organizational actors that constitute a poor fit are less likely to survive over time. Such processes foster the emergence of quite distinct configurations, containing many elements which 'make sense' in the context of the others. To take a prominent example (Huber and Stephens 1999) a number of factors operated together to create the 'Social Democratic service state'. In particular, the rapid entry of women into the workforce, in a con-text marked by social democratic party and union strength, fuelled demand for supportive social services. Efforts to meet that demand through public sector expansion both created additional opportunities for women's employ-ment and strengthened political forces pushing for further expansions.

Different welfare state configurations are the products of complex con-junctural causation, with multiple factors working together over extended periods of time to generate dramatically different outcomes. There is no theoretical justification for arguing that a 10 per cent shift in the value on one variable or another will have a simple, direct, linear effect on outcomes across all cases. To clarify, let me discuss one example: the impact of political institutions on the prospects for reform in the current period. Most discus-sion of this issue has addressed welfare states in general. Pierson and Weaver (1993) stressed that there was no clear theoretical basis for believing that increased institutional fragmentation necessarily made retrenchment more difficult. The concentration of authority also concentrated accountability,

---

[11] Esping-Andersen himself employed such regressions, but as Shalev argues persuasively, there is an 'obvious mismatch between Esping-Andersen's claims and his methods. . . . The regression approach . . . treats both policy and politics as continuous variables. . . . It is hard to exaggerate the fundamental incompatibility between [multiple regression] and Esping-Andersen's regime approach. . . . In his hands [multiple regression] was simply a blunt instrument for tapping gross differences between groups of countries that could have been conveyed by the use of tables and charts without the implication of constant linear effects across countries' (Shalev 1999: 13).

which might lead to difficulties in pursuing unpopular policies. This accountability/blame avoidance dynamic is important for understanding why even unified governments will often be cautious, for explaining the strategies that such governments employ, and for highlighting the possibility that aggressive action may lead to electoral backlash.

By now, however, the evidence would seem to show pretty clearly that on balance the concentration of political authority is an asset for those seeking reform.[12] As Huber and Stephens argue, the experiences of the two pure Westminster cases, New Zealand and the United Kingdom, are particularly striking. New Zealand's National government was able to move aggressively on multiple fronts. The British Conservatives gradually learned to shift from a strategy of frontal assaults to one of relentless, low-profile adjustments, which whittled away important elements of the welfare state over time. By contrast, veto points in other countries have generated significant, sometimes overwhelming, obstacles to radical change.

Yet it is no accident that both these examples of major retrenchment in the absence of formal institutional veto points concern liberal welfare states, where social actors are disorganized and popular support for the welfare state is (while still extensive) more limited than elsewhere. It seems highly unlikely that the same 'value' on this particular independent variable would have similar consequences in a configuration where popular support for the welfare state was broader and/or the power resources of labour were greater —a conclusion which Bonoli's discussion of the French reform experience supports. The 'freedom' to produce radical reform stems not just from a high concentration of political authority, but from that factor combined with a number of other features of a particular configuration.

In analysing the dynamics of social policy restructuring, one needs to attend to both the particular scale and shape of welfare states and particular political contexts. With respect to the latter, the scope of popular support for social provision, the connections between social provision and systems of economic production, and the relationship between the electoral/ partisan arena and systems of interest intermediation are especially critical. In short, we need to recognize the existence of distinct worlds of welfare capitalism.

---

[12] Again though, Swank's chapter suggests that while fragmented institutions might impede retrenchment efforts, they are also likely to slow welfare state expansion in the first place. This slowdown occurs both because of institutional fragmentation's direct role in blocking reform and because of its indirect negative effects on social solidarity through the promotion of interest heterogeneity. This is in keeping with a general presumption in much institutional research, namely, that the effects of institutions will generally be multiple and cross-cutting rather than simply direct and unidimensional. A different way to put this is that we need to distinguish between the short-term and long-term causal effects of institutional fragmentation. For a discussion of this point, see Shalev 1999.

Even if one accepts the basic case for treating cases holistically, as configurations rather than compilations of variables, one can nonetheless challenge Esping-Andersen's specification of regimes. A number of reasonable objections have appeared, and for particular purposes one might prefer a different typology. Yet I am struck by the extent to which other analysts, including those studying broader shifts in political economy, have gravitated towards similar demarcations (Iversen and Wren 1998; Kitschelt et al. 1999*a*; Scharpf 1997*b*). My view is that this reflects a reasonably tight fit between particular welfare state configurations and particular political configurations. This is indeed what one should expect if Esping-Andersen was correct in arguing that each regime type emerges from a particular political milieu.

As Walter Korpi has argued, in evaluating the heuristic merits of typologies, 'the analysis of causes and consequences of welfare states should be in the foreground' (Korpi 1999: 35). Ultimately, the crucial issue is whether the distinction among regimes provides leverage for explaining important variations across the relevant cases. In Section 3 of this essay, I argue that it does—although not always in the manner suggested by Esping-Andersen's own discussions. When combined with the disaggregation of reform dimensions outlined above, one can begin to make sense of variations both across regimes and among cases within each regime.

3. RESTRUCTURING THE THREE WORLDS OF WELFARE

What follows is a preliminary attempt to outline the distinct politics of welfare state reform in the three 'worlds', or regimes, of liberal, social democratic, and conservative welfare states.[13] I argue that the basic framework developed in Section 1 is helpful for making sense of what is happening in each of these three worlds. Each world, however, is composed not only of particular types of welfare states, but also of distinct political settings. Thus, the agendas for welfare state restructuring and the dominant political coalitions will vary. Furthermore, we can expect additional variation across cases within each world, and one of the major tasks for analysts should be to identify and explain that variation.

[13] A number of the cases sometimes considered in such comparisons are excluded from this analysis. Greece, Ireland, Portugal, and Spain are late developing welfare states, which were still very much in the process of welfare state construction at the end of the golden age. In my view this context raises quite different issues from those cases where affluence had been achieved and welfare states were already close to maturity by the mid-1970s. Switzerland and Japan represent distinct configurations that do not fit easily into any of the three regimes.

By distinguishing among regimes, and disaggregating different dimensions of restructuring, one can identify patterns that would not be evident in a more unified analysis which tried to explain a single outcome (e.g. 'retrenchment') over the whole set of cases. In these respects, I follow Esping-Andersen's regime typology (although utilizing different outcome dimensions). On the other hand, our accounts of the political dynamics in the three regimes are quite different.[14] The goal is to make the investigation complicated enough to capture and account for crucial elements of diversity, but not so complicated that it becomes impossible to identify general patterns.

The Liberal Regime

The liberal cases include Australia, Canada, Great Britain, New Zealand, and the United States.[15] The most politically salient features of the welfare state constellations in these countries include the following (data on most of these features can be found in the Huber and Stephens chapter in this volume). Taxes, and spending, have remained low by international standards. Public sector service employment is also low. Many transfer programmes are income-tested, although the range of coverage varies from very narrow (the United States) to quite broad (Australia). In part as a consequence of the failure of the welfare state to meet demands for social provision, private sector activity in pensions and social services such as child care (as well as health care in the United States and New Zealand) is extensive. In many cases, tax expenditures subsidize private provision for the upper middle class (e.g. Howard 1997). Finally, these welfare state arrangements operate in the context of liberal market economies. There is no overlap between the world of liberal welfare states and the world of 'organized market economies'. Thus, there are numerous linkages, explored below, between liberal welfare state arrangements and the liberal or 'disorganized' model of capitalism.

---

[14] This is not an issue that Esping-Andersen has pursued in detail. In *Three Worlds* he identified distinct political cleavages in each regime. In *Postindustrial Economies* he seems to maintain, although without much elaboration, that 'path dependence' and 'median voters' will prevent major policy change. The current analysis points to quite different political cleavages in the three worlds and argues that while path dependence and pivotal voters channel reform, they are unlikely to prevent it.

[15] F. G. Castles and Mitchell (1993) have persuasively argued that the two Antipode countries should be seen as a distinct 'wage-earner' model, in which protectionism combined with intensive labour market regulation to produce relatively egalitarian outcomes without extensive formal welfare states. However, the wage-earner model, grounded in protectionism, came under acute pressures from a changing international economy. For these countries globalization has clearly mattered enormously. This alternative model began to break down in the mid-1970s, forcing a gradual shift towards broadly liberal arrangements. Australia, in particular, remains somewhat distinct from other liberal cases in the continuing role of politically mediated wage bargaining. The differences are less pronounced than they were two decades ago, however, especially following the recent period of Liberal–National governance.

The political constellations of these cases also share a number of common features. First, and most crucial is the weakness of encompassing interest organizations. By comparative standards these are cases where organized labour has modest political capacities. Again, there is considerable variation among these countries, ranging from Australia at one end to the United States at the other. It is not only that labour is weak in these cases; the capacities of employers for collective action are also limited. In Soskice's words, 'companies have little capacity to coordinate their activities collectively. Their inability to act collectively means that they cannot combine to negotiate discretionary framework solutions with the state' (1999: 110). In short, with the partial exception of Australia, not only does labour lack the power to veto change, but the capacity of these systems to pursue negotiated reform through systems of organized interest intermediation is very low. Unlike the case in other welfare state regimes, policy changes must be executed almost exclusively through electoral and partisan politics.

Several crucial features of the electoral/partisan environments thus deserve special emphasis. First, until New Zealand's recent reform, none of these cases employed proportional representation. Instead, 'first-past-the-post' electoral systems have been the norm.[16] Thus, all of these countries have had strong tendencies towards two (or two-and-a-half) party systems. With the exception of the United States, where division between Congress and the President has become the norm, these systems tended to produce single-party governments. They varied, however, in the extent to which political institutions provided checks on these governments. New Zealand (pre-1996) and Great Britain constitute pure 'Westminster' models of 'elected dictatorship'. By contrast, the federal systems of Australia, Canada, and the United States create additional veto points, the severity and nature of which varies across countries, issue area, and electoral context.

Furthermore, there is little question that the scope of popular support for public social provision tends to be more conditional in these cases, although again with considerable variation (Svallfors 1997). One can see here how multiple features of a particular configuration point in the same direction. Because these welfare states are relatively small, the 'core' support group for social provision is also relatively small. Reliance on means-testing may divide those who benefit from many taxpayers. The political clout of labour unions, a traditional bastion of support, is also relatively modest. The institutionalization of (often state-subsidized) market alternatives weakens middle-class attachments to public provision. High levels of inequality are also associated, in many countries, with large class biases in electoral turnout. Low turnout among the economically vulnerable further diminishes their already limited political influence.

---

[16] Australia employs a 'preferential' voting system. Because voter's second choice matters, this will generally induce parties to moderate their policy stance.

To be absolutely clear, the claim is not that a majority of voters tend to oppose the welfare state in these countries; nowhere is this true. Compared to the social democratic and Continental countries, however, pivotal voters are likely to possess weaker attachments to social provision, and to be more susceptible to alternative political appeals (such as the demand for tax cuts). Liberal welfare states thus provide the greatest potential for parties to reconcile political success and a relatively aggressive, even openly hostile stance vis-à-vis significant components of the welfare state. Under particular conditions, pivotal voters may be within reach, and in some of these countries labour can be essentially excluded from playing a significant role. Thus, the political conflict between advocates of moderate restructuring and radical retrenchment is more equally matched than it is in the other two regimes.

This is reflected in the pattern of outcomes. By comparative standards, quite radical cutbacks have been achieved in New Zealand, and, to a lesser extent, in Great Britain (Stephens, Huber, and Ray 1999; Castles and Pierson 1996). Canada and Australia, on the other hand, have pursued a distinctive course, also marked by efforts at cost containment and commodification, but balanced by serious efforts to protect the most vulnerable. In the United States, change has been more limited, and contains elements of both tendencies.

Although the variations across countries both in policy outcomes and in inequality trends are quite striking, these outcomes are not sufficiently stable to allow firm conclusions about national trajectories. Australia's current National–Liberal government is seeking to erode many of the provisions that marked the accords reached between the Australian Labour governments and the trade unions between 1983 and 1995. Under the current British Labour government, important new policy initiatives emulate some of the Canadian and Australian strategies which combine a strengthening of work incentives with compensatory policies for those affected (Hills 1998). These recent developments suggest that partisan control of government may be most important in the liberal regime. This is indeed what we should expect given the relatively narrow base of welfare state support in these countries, and the dominance of the electoral/partisan arena for political action.

A defining characteristic of restructuring in all the liberal welfare states has been the priority placed on re-commodification. Indeed, both the emphasis placed on commodification and the degree of change has clearly been greater than in the other welfare state regimes. In all the liberal welfare states, programmes providing transfer payments to those of working age but out of the labour force—unemployment benefit and social assistance—have faced major cutbacks. Eligibility rules have been tightened, and benefit levels have been reduced significantly. Coverage rates (in Canada and the United States) and benefit levels (everywhere) for the unemployed have fallen sharply. Most dramatically, in Canada and the United States, national commitments to

social assistance have been severely weakened. Provincial and state authorities have often moved aggressively to push the poor off social assistance
rolls and into the workforce.

At first glance, this characteristic of liberal regime reform is puzzling.
Why would these systems, already the most 'commodified' in the OECD,
push so much more aggressively in this direction? Part of the answer lies in
the political weakness of those who might resist commodification. Equally
important, however, is the connection between income support and the
labour market in political economies where wage flexibility is treated as
the principal buffer against high unemployment. The deteriorating market
position of low-skilled workers has confronted policy makers everywhere with
difficult trade-offs (Iversen and Wren 1998; Scharpf 1997*b*). Consistent
with the basic workings of a liberal, 'disorganized' market economy, all of
these liberal countries have implicitly accepted that the new environment
requires larger wage differentials, and, in particular, deteriorating relative
wage conditions among the low-skilled. Yet this deterioration can only be
carried out if exit options ('reservation wages') are not attractive. That is, the
push for (downward) flexibility among the low-skilled implies a hardening
of conditions for income support to those out of work. Improving 'work
incentives' has thus been a common frame of reform, justifying stricter
eligibility, benefit cuts, or even outright abolition of programmes.

Many comparative analysts view the liberal welfare states primarily as
an analytical or normative foil for the 'real' welfare states of Continental
Europe and Scandinavia. For these analysts, the policy changes just described
are taken to define the essential outcomes for these cases. From this perspective, the United States is taken to typify the liberal world, and the
welfare 'reform' which abolished Aid to Families with Dependent Children
is taken as the paradigmatic policy change in the USA. Social policy dismantling and re-commodification are portrayed as the logical political
destination for liberal welfare states in the new era.

The actual patterns, however, are both more complex and more interesting. All the liberal welfare states have shared in the shift towards re-
commodification, albeit at different paces and to different degrees. Yet there
has been considerable variation in the extent to which this transition has
been subsidized or buffered. The main political debate in the liberal welfare
states has not focused on whether or not low-skilled workers should be in the
labour market, but on the terms under which their participation should take
place. The key issue is the extent to which commodification should be subsidized. Those advocating subsidization have accepted demands for reform
in social assistance and unemployment benefit, but have sought to 'make
work pay' by supplementing poverty-level wages available in an unregulated
market with various forms of targeted social provision. Arguments in favour
of such provisions emphasize both social equity concerns and the need to

foster the development of human capital. Many of these supplements are targeted on groups that are considered particularly vulnerable and/or particularly deserving of support, especially households with children.

The particular package of supplements varies, but may include some or all of the following: improved child allowances and access to affordable child care, reductions in social insurance contributions for the low-paid, an increased minimum wage,[17] expanded access to public health insurance (in the United States), and the expansion or introduction of tax-based wage supplements. The last provision has been particularly important. All the liberal countries have introduced significant wage subsidies, operated through systems of taxation, for at least some of the working poor—usually families with children. Most dramatic has been the major expansion of the Earned Income Tax Credit in the United States and of the Working Families Tax Credit (formerly Family Credit), in Great Britain. In Australia, the universal child benefit was means-tested (although 60 per cent of the population remain eligible), but an expanded Additional Family Payment provided significant additional cash on a per child basis to working families.

Some of these subsidization initiatives could be dismissed as cosmetic embellishments to harsh exercises in retrenchment. Yet the overall scale of these mediating efforts is difficult to ignore. In the United States, for instance, while there were considerable cutbacks in AFDC and Unemployment Insurance even before the 1996 welfare reform, overall federal spending on low-income groups rose significantly in the late 1980s and the first half of the 1990s (Weaver 1998). By the time AFDC was transformed and largely handed over to the states, the federal government was spending twice as much per year on the rapidly-expanding EITC as it spent on AFDC (Myles and Pierson 1997). Along with modest increases in the minimum wage, EITC expansions since 1989 have contributed to a large real increase in earnings for single employed mothers with two children.

Cost containment has also been a major political priority in all these countries. Deficit reduction has been a dominant theme, and it has been common for centre and centre-left parties (e.g. Blair, Clinton, and the Australian Labour government) to commit themselves to policies of not raising taxes. This outcome is striking, given the relatively low levels of public expenditure in these countries, and the absence of anything like the Maastricht criteria to generate an external constraint. Although in the cases of the three economies dependent on export of primary goods (Australia, Canada, and New Zealand) one could point to external pressures for budget balance, it is difficult to make this argument for Great Britain or, especially, the United States. Within the liberal regimes, the more right-leaning position of the pivotal voter

---

[17] In the UK the Labour government has introduced a minimum wage for the first time, and set its level significantly closer to the median wage than is the case in the United States.

appears to facilitate a focus on expenditure (and tax) restraint, along with deficit reduction, even in the absence of an institutional forcing mechanism such as EMU.[18]

Cost containment efforts, however, have not on the whole generated the kind of radical roll-backs popularly associated with neoliberalism. Indeed, it is hard to discern a distinct liberal response in the big spending areas of health and pensions. Unlike the case of income maintenance for the able-bodied, there is no clear policy imperative. In both health care and pensions, outcomes appear to be heavily constrained by the particular policy arrangements established before cost-containment demands became paramount. Where there were well-established, deeply embedded policy frameworks in these areas, continuity has been more evident than change. Thus, in health care, Australia, Britain, and Canada have all made modifications of their pre-existing systems in an attempt to cut costs, but without challenging basic rights to quality care and in contexts where overall expenditures were increasing. In the United States, the major policy initiative was a failed attempt to dramatically expand health care coverage, albeit as part of a cost-containment strategy. New Zealand again stands out as a divergent case. Only there was a major effort undertaken to roll back the contours of state provision for health care.

As Giaimo's chapter demonstrates, there is no logic of liberal market economies that generates a strong push for market expansion and state contraction in the area of health care. On the contrary, a good case can be made for the opposite proposition: a strong state role in health care will generally serve the interests of most employers. The Clinton administration's reform initiative was based on this presumption. Its failure arguably reflected the incapacity of a 'disorganized' polity to facilitate the negotiation of acceptable terms (Judis 1995) and the path-dependent accumulation of vested private interests in the policy status quo (Hacker 1998) rather than a more fundamental conflict of interest between employers and consumers.

It is also clear that there has been no convergence in pension systems. Canada and the United States have modified their mature systems, emphasizing cost containment, with Canada introducing a significant element of funding. Not locked-in by past commitments, the UK and Australia have embarked on new (but very distinct) paths of funded provision. New Zealand has been unable to proceed in any direction. As Myles and Pierson show, path-dependent effects in pensions are very strong. At the same time, however, these path-dependent qualities largely reflect the 'congealed liberalism' of an earlier period. It is no accident that liberal countries were less likely

---

[18] Again, the regime approach may help us to think about multiple paths to particular outcomes. Italy and the United States may both pursue vigorous deficit reduction, but this may reflect dramatically different political dynamics.

to have mature, earnings-related PAYG systems by the end of the post-war boom. Thus, the substantial expansion of funding in Canada and Australia, and private (but heavily tax-subsidized) funding in the United Kingdom reflected not only the unmet demand for earnings-related provision, but also the availability of fiscal space and the relative sophistication of private financial markets made possible by an earlier history of liberalism. Within a regime analysis, it is the American Social Security system (like Britain's NHS in the case of health care) that emerges as anomalous. What is revealing is the so far modest transformation of this essentially Bismarckian element of the American welfare state.

As in the case of re-commodification efforts, the Canadian and Australian experiences of cost containment demonstrate their distinct path of restructuring. While programmes have been cut, significant efforts have been made to protect the most vulnerable. In each country, 'means-testing from the top' has been a dominant strategy for generating savings, and some of the savings have been redistributed to low-income groups (F. G. Castles 1996; Myles 1996). This quid pro quo has facilitated the maintenance of a reasonably broad, centrist consensus on restructuring efforts. In a particularly dramatic example, a 'clawback' of pension benefits for high-income seniors in Canada has been accompanied by a major expansion of minimum pension benefits. This shift has been so successful that it has allowed low-spending Canada to sharply reduce poverty rates for the elderly, which now approximate Scandinavian levels (Myles 1999).

One can see the differences within the evolving liberal world most starkly in measures of income inequality and poverty. Poverty rates have risen massively in the United Kingdom and New Zealand—far more than in any other OECD country. They have risen much more moderately in the United States—but from a higher baseline. On the other hand, at least through the early 1990s there was little change in poverty rates in Canada and Australia. Although social welfare policy does not account for all of the differences across these cases, it has been quite important. Policy interventions that might have sheltered the poor from shouldering the costs of adjustment were actively dismantled in New Zealand and, until recently, Great Britain. In Australia and Canada (and much more tepidly in the United States) such protections were in many cases expanded to offset growing inequality in market incomes.

What explains this variation—straightforward and severe cost containment and re-commodification in New Zealand and the UK, compensated restructuring in Australia and Canada, with the United States as an intermediate case? New Zealand and the UK stand out as cases where there was little inclination or necessity for compromise in the pursuit of neoliberal goals. As has been discussed, the broad contours of the liberal regime type make such an agenda at least conceivable, while it is clearly beyond the reach of any likely political coalition elsewhere. In addition, however, two political conditions have appeared essential for such an aggressive coalition to achieve significant policy successes: first, a series of economic setbacks which discredited the policy status quo and its supporters; and second, a partisan-institutional configuration that translated an electoral plurality into a governing majority and allowed that majority to operate essentially unhindered (Huber and Stephens, in this volume; Schwartz and Rhodes 1999).

As Schwartz and Rhodes argue, the aggressive neoliberal agendas pursued in both Britain and New Zealand grew in part out of severe economic dislocations which underscored the need for major reforms. In both cases, the neoliberal projects were reactions to failed efforts to intensify policy strategies developed in the 1960s and early 1970s—Keynesianism, incomes policy, and expanded public spending in Britain, protectionism and state-subsidized production in New Zealand. The dramatic collapse of these projects lent credence to the neoliberal agenda, summarized in Thatcher's memorable phrase that 'there is no alternative'. At the same time, the loss of credibility and divisions generated by the failed projects demoralized and disorganized neoliberalism's political opponents.

A second, equally critical condition is a partisan-institutional setting that shifts the pivotal voter well to the right. I have argued that in general we can expect pivotal voters to be closer to the welfare state status quo than the median voter. Yet not only is that median voter likely to be comparatively far to the right in the liberal configuration, but the pivotal voter may actually be to the right of the median. As noted by Huber and Stephens, conservative parties in both Britain and New Zealand exploited Westminster, first-past-the-post electoral systems and a divided opposition to translate a plurality of votes into comfortable parliamentary majorities. During their eighteen consecutive years in office, for example, the British Conservatives never received more than 44 per cent of the vote. In New Zealand, parliamentary majorities in the four elections between 1984 and 1993 were based on electoral pluralities of 43, 48, 48, and 35 per cent.

Even under such circumstances governments face constraints or run the risk of backlash at the polls. The Thatcher Government was less aggressive in attacking the welfare state than other aspects of the post-war order, and particularly cautious with respect to popular middle-class programmes like the National Health Service (Pierson 1994). New Zealand's National Party attempted to 'crash through or crash'. Ultimately it crashed, as a popular referendum in 1993 scrapped the Westminster model, which had permitted the government to ignore the median voter. Nonetheless, compared with more typical settings, this partisan-institutional configuration provided governments with greatly increased latitude to pursue unpopular policies.

Unlike New Zealand and Great Britain, neither Australia nor Canada had institutional arrangements that gave national governments unfettered control over the reform process. And unlike the United States, these governments did have well-organized, relatively encompassing interlocutors with whom to negotiate and implement a more consensual process of restructuring. In Australia, the crucial mechanism was a series of accords between the unions and the Australian Labour Party, based on a relatively high (by liberal standards) capacity for concertation and a shared appreciation for the political risks associated with failure (Schwartz 2000). We lack a convincing and detailed account of the political dynamics in Canada, but part of the explanation must be the manner in which a decentralized federal structure encouraged negotiation on the contours of adjustment between a series of national governments and powerful (and politically diverse) provincial premiers.

The Social Democratic Regime

The Scandinavian or 'social democratic' cases include Denmark, Norway, Sweden, and (more marginally) Finland. The basic characteristics of this welfare state configuration are well known: generous transfer programmes covering a wide range of risks with high replacement rates; public social services which, by comparative standards, are extremely extensive; a set of supportive family and labour market policies which generate very high rates of labour force participation for both men and women. The wide scope of public provision has, of course, also filled spaces which elsewhere were occupied by market arrangements. The private provision of social services, as well as pensions, remains extremely limited.

The political constellation in these countries includes multiple features that create very strong pro-welfare state coalitions. Union density is high, and the unions have maintained strong links with electorally powerful social democratic parties. Public sector unions are also enormous by comparative standards. Women are highly mobilized and committed to the social service state (which is both the primary source of women's employment and provides crucial support for women's labour force participation). Not surprisingly given these elements of the political setting, public opinion remains strongly supportive of the key features of the social democratic welfare state (Svallfors 1995, 1997; Goul Andersen 1997; Rothstein 1998a). The formal political systems of these countries contain few checks on parliamentary majorities, but the frequency of coalition governments makes political authority less concentrated than in the Westminster setting. At the same time, governments in these systems operate in a context of well-established and encompassing employer and union organizations, which represent both possible partners in dialogue and potentially formidable political opponents in cases where dialogue is absent or fails.

The basic results of welfare state restructuring in the social democratic cases reflect this context of very broad support for public social provision.

In the words of Eitrheim and Kuhnle, 'politicians who blow the trumpet of neo-liberal economics too loudly, and those who blow the tune that the welfare state is an evil invention, have a hard time surviving in Nordic politics' (Kuhnle and Eitrheim 1999). As Huber and Stephens persuasively argue (see also Stephens 1996), the immediate challenge confronting this regime has been the adjustment to a context of increased unemployment. The social democratic welfare states were in fiscal equilibrium with 3 per cent unemployment, but given their generous transfer programmes they ran into trouble when unemployment rose sharply. Once the increase was recognized as permanent, which occurred at different times in different countries, a combination of benefit cuts, economizing reforms in social services (especially health care), and tax increases were introduced to restore equilibrium. Cross-national variation in the timing and degree of restructuring largely reflects the timing and severity of economic crisis, and the degree of adjustment required. Thus, the most painful reform process occurred in Finland, and changes have been most modest in Norway. A strong argument can be made that this shift has largely been accomplished in all these cases while leaving a modestly less generous version of the pre-existing welfare state structures intact (Stephens 1996; Goul Andersen 1997). The primary task is to understand this general adjustment path for the social democratic regime, rather than cross-national variation inside it.

Before directly outlining the basic reform dynamics, it is necessary to address the orthodox interpretation of contemporary social democratic welfare state politics, which focuses on cleavages between the 'exposed' and 'sheltered' (or traded and non-traded) sectors. Esping-Andersen (1990, 1996a) identifies this as the predominant line of cleavage in social democratic countries. This view has been elaborated in several analyses by scholars working from a perspective shaped by the investigation of collective bargaining systems (Swenson 1991b; Clayton and Pontusson 1998; Iversen 1998a). In this volume, Schwartz offers a nuanced version of this sectoral argument, stressing the fact that both workers and employers in the traded sector may continue to support significant aspects of social provision.

Yet the evidence that this potential cleavage drives the politics of welfare state reform is, to be generous, extremely limited. Even in the social democratic countries where large-scale public sectors might be expected to generate such effects, strong advocates like Clayton and Pontusson are forced to acknowledge that the empirical support is modest.[19] In his recent effort

---

[19] And even this modest evidence has been subjected to sharp criticism (Lindbom 1999). In Sweden, the case considered by Clayton and Pontusson, there is little sign that social service employment has been targeted at the expense of transfer programmes. In some cases, it appears that services have actually been expanded. In others, notably health care, there have been drops in employment, but these appear to be linked to efficiency gains rather than declining quality of service.

to determine if hypothesized cleavages over the welfare state are actually evident in public opinion Svallfors (1997: 292) concludes that 'public- versus private-sector employment does not seem to constitute a particularly important fault line. Differences are seldom statistically significant, and attitudinal differences point in different directions on different indices, sometimes showing public-sector employees to be more in favour of redistribution and small income differences than private-sector employees, sometimes the opposite.'[20] None of the 'issue area' chapters in this volume find evidence of such an alliance of 'tradeable' interests; nor do the chapters by Manow and Rhodes, which concentrate specifically on the contribution of economic actors to the formation of reform coalitions.

Why is there so little evidence for a claim that seems both credible and has received considerable scholarly support? The answers say a good deal about the current social democratic regime, and therefore help to provide a firmer basis for analysing its contemporary politics. First, the core assumption that 'productive' workers will rebel against 'unproductive' public sector ones is based on a doubtful interpretation of the role of public sector workers in the social democratic economies. Although often left implicit, explications of the tradeable/non-tradeable cleavage bear strong affinities to more extreme neoclassical treatments of the public sector which treat it as a domain dominated by 'rent-seeking'. From this perspective, a modestly paid public sector worker engaged in, say, the care of alcoholics or disabled children is essentially a parasite on the productive elements of society. Over time one would expect these productive elements to repudiate the extraction of rents and seek to roll back the public sector.

As Huber and Stephens (and, perhaps somewhat inconsistently, Esping-Andersen 1999) argue, there is a strong case to be made for the beneficial economic effects of large-scale public service provision in the context of the broader social democratic regime. Many of these services focus on the development of human capital. Active labour market policy, training, and education provide crucial support for skill development, which in turn has made a key contribution to the high standards of living in the social democratic countries. At least as significant, however, is the success of this regime in supporting the efforts of many women to combine caring responsibilities, including child-rearing, with active participation in economic life beyond the household. Both the direct expansion of economic activity related to these policies, and the contribution that they make to fertility, represent considerable social assets.

---

[20] He adds a modest qualifier for the social democratic cases: 'some support is found for the hypothesis about the sector cleavage being most important in the social democratic regime. It is only in Norway and Sweden that sector appears to have any importance at all when explaining (re)distributive attitudes, but even here differences are not very substantial.'

All of this is missed by standard analyses of the cleavage between exposed and sheltered workers. For accounting purposes, economists often treat the outputs of public services as equivalent to the inputs, but we need to clearly distinguish our inability or lack of interest in measuring productivity/output from the lack of productivity/output. The evidence in public opinion continues to show that most voters in the social democratic countries perceive public social services as important contributors to their quality of life.

There is a second problem with the exposed/sheltered cleavage argument. Ironically for an analysis based around classes or class fragments, the focus on cross-class alliances is strangely abstracted from social context.[21] Private sector workers, and their public sector counterparts, are treated as isolated monads. Yet we know that the labour markets in this regime are highly stratified by gender, with male workers overwhelmingly preponderant in the private sector and women concentrated in the public sector. In short, this hypothesized political cleavage is likely to run right down the middle of many households. If a private sector worker is married to a public sector worker, and they send their children to publicly financed child care, then what is the likely alliance pattern? Here is one clear advantage of bringing gender and household structure to bear on political economy approaches. It shows why some of the basic arguments about cross-class coalitions in welfare state restructuring may be far weaker than expected.

It is worth stressing that my arguments do not deny the relevance of the public/private divide with respect to wage bargaining processes. The division of the share of economic output going to labour has a zero-sum quality, and bargaining over this share is organized by unions structured along sectoral lines. Thus, the public/private cleavage is likely to be significant, and it is understandable that this cleavage occupies the attention of industrial relations scholars. What is in dispute is the extent to which this will carry over to the political determination of the 'social wage' in a context where the electoral realm constitutes an important domain of interest articulation. Here, evidence for the activation of a cross-class, private-sector-based coalition remains meager. Tendencies for wage-bargaining cleavages to spill over into welfare state politics are partially if not totally offset by the strong reliance of almost all Swedish households on public sector services. These services either directly provide employment or indirectly provide the means to juggle demands of work and family.

If the political agenda is not one of undercutting public sector workers, what, then, have been the pressing restructuring issues in the social democratic countries? Overwhelmingly, they focus on cost containment and the recalibration of programmes within an essentially fixed budget. By contrast,

---

[21] In this respect as well, the focus on cross-class alliances reflects the strange marriage of post-Marxism and neoclassical economics.

re-commodification has generally been a less important priority. This reflects the fact that while social democracy has traditionally been strongly 'de-commodifying', it has done so in a manner that produces very high rates of labour force participation and employment. 'Pushing (or pulling) people into the labour market' has always been part of the social democratic model. What have been distinctive are the quite favourable terms on which this occurred. Although what recent Swedish reformers have called the 'work-line' (everyone who can be working should be working) has been strengthened in all these countries, these changes have generally accentuated what had always been high expectations about work effort within the social democratic model. Much of the reform agenda has focused on rationalizing programmes which, either because of new labour market conditions or because of programme flaws, had gone astray from broadly accepted goals. As noted earlier, sickness pay in Sweden constitutes a clear example.

In most respects, however, the social democratic countries have had less need to focus on issues of recalibration—certainly when compared to the conservative regime which I will discuss in a moment. In particular, there has been relatively little need for what I have termed updating—the adjustment of old welfare states to new needs and demands. It should be emphasized that social democratic social policies already generate outcomes that the conservative Continental countries can only dream of achieving. The social democratic regime sustains very high rates of labour force participation for both men and women; it supports comparatively high fertility levels; it has extensive experience with active labour market policies designed to restrict exclusion and enhance skills; and it contains none of the clientelistic remnants that constitute such a costly problem on much of the European continent.

If the social democratic welfare states have succeeded in restoring their fiscal equilibrium over the medium term, their biggest long-term problem is reconciling the need for continuing cost containment with the maintenance of solidarity around the welfare state. As Rothstein (1998b) has forcefully argued, the political foundations of the social democratic welfare state have depended both on its compatibility with acceptable economic performance and on the ability to generate high-quality services for middle and upper middle income households. Sustaining the allegiance of these crucial voters, whose economic resources might provide an exit option, requires two difficult balancing acts. First, increasing heterogeneity in consumption tastes requires public sector services that provide meaningful choice, but without generating 'creaming' or 'tipping' effects which lead to class polarization in service consumption. Second, high-quality services must be sustained in a context where taxes are already high but 'Baumol effects' which accompany most social service provision generate continuing pressures for new spending. It is these dilemmas, rather than an effort to erode the position of public sector workers as part of a general liberalization, which have largely dictated public sector service reform in the social democratic countries.

The Conservative Regime

This third cluster of countries, variously termed conservative, Continental, Christian democratic, or Bismarckian, includes Austria, Belgium, France, Germany, Italy, and the Netherlands. The welfare state configurations of these countries generally include the following features: high levels of spending, strongly weighted towards transfers in general and pensions expenditure in particular; limited development of public sector employment; strong support for early labour market exit through early retirement schemes or unemployment and disability programmes (Ebbinghaus 1999); high levels of payroll tax financing; and explicit and implicit family policies (including tax structures, the absence of child care arrangements, and weak support for service sector job growth) which discourage women's labour force participation. These features are linked to a status-preserving 'Bismarckian' benefit structure, and, in many cases, to occupationally segregated (and often highly variable) pension and sickness funds. Unions and employers often play an important institutional role in the administration of these funds. In some cases (e.g. Italy), Conservative welfare states have also provided a strong basis for clientelistic welfare state politics (see Ferrera 1996).

The political constellations associated with these welfare state regimes are varied. Yet some generalizations are possible, and it should be stressed that in combination these generalizations suggest a political configuration quite different from those appearing in the other welfare regimes. Although not all these countries (e.g. France) could be defined as corporatist, systems of organized interest intermediation are generally important: 'across Europe, four out of five workers receive wages that reflect the outcome of a process of collective bargaining' (Golden, Wallerstein, and Lange 1999: 204). In many cases, such as France, organized labour's role in social insurance confers a degree of influence which it might not be able to achieve through wage bargaining systems (Bonoli and Palier 1996). These systems differ, however, in the extent to which the social partners are willing and able to negotiate over broad issues of relevance to the welfare state. At the same time, due to the modest role of public social services, public sector unions are smaller and politically weaker than in the social democratic countries.

The electoral systems of these countries tend to generate multiple veto points. The prevalence of proportional representation (although restricted in some countries) makes single-party governance rare. Federalism (Germany, and increasingly Belgium) and the institutionalized role of the social partners reinforce tendencies towards negotiated reform. A final feature of the political institutional setting deserving emphasis is that all of these countries are members of the European Monetary Union and subject to the Maastricht criteria. Given the fiscal circumstances discussed below, this membership may be of considerable importance.

As Kitschelt argues, party systems and public opinion in these countries have also helped to consolidate political support for the welfare state. Social democratic parties are far weaker than in Scandinavia but generally influential. The centre-right in many of these countries have been dominated by Christian democratic parties, which played leading roles in constructing these welfare state models (Van Kersbergen 1995). Despite including factions that are now more critical of extensive social provision, these parties contain significant elements committed to the basic contours of the social contract. Given the scale of these welfare states, it is not surprising that public opinion remains broadly supportive (Svallfors 1997). There is, however, probably less enthusiasm than in Scandinavia, and greater ambivalence where the inequities associated with clientilistic elements of social provision have been most in evidence (Ferrera 1997).

Although they might disagree on the root sources of pressure, there is a fairly wide consensus among commentators that these Continental countries face the greatest demands for adjustment in their core welfare state arrangements (Esping-Andersen 1996c, 1999; Scharpf 1997b). Esping-Andersen has provided an elegant diagnosis of the interlinked problems: high and rising costs associated with generous pensions and subsidized labour market exit; low women's labour force participation; disturbing rates of unemployment among the unskilled (linked to the high fixed labour costs associated with heavy payroll taxes); and low fertility rates.

As in the other regimes, there are powerful complementarities among these elements. In the current economic and social climate, however, these complementarities appear to work in a pernicious direction. High social insurance charges, especially to finance pensions, simultaneously block development of private service employment (by creating high wage floors) and public service employment (by generating fiscal overload). In turn, the unemployment and stagnation of labour force participation rates undercuts the revenue base for pension systems and creates political pressures to subsidize labour market exit through social insurance programmes, especially early retirement and disability schemes. All of these countries responded to initial employment problems by easing entry to various tax-financed paths out of the labour market (Kohli et al. 1991; Ebbinghaus 1999). Employment stagnation and increased reliance on transfers in turn precipitate further increases in payroll taxes. Compounding the difficulties, the blockage of public and private service development jeopardizes the capacity of women to combine labour force participation and child-rearing. This contributes to declining fertility rates, which further imperil the long-term fiscal equilibrium of these systems. Thus, the problem is not just that these countries face major pressures for adjustment, but that the possibilities for a 'bad' equilibrium of low employment and low fertility seem very real. In Esping-Andersen's gloomy synopsis, 'these systems find themselves locked into a self-reinforcing negative spiral' (1996c: 68).

The countries in the Continental regime face two quite distinct but potentially complementary reform agendas. First, there is a need to expand employment opportunities, which in the post-industrial world means service employment. This aspiration confronts a series of interconnected obstacles. Several impediments hinder women's efforts to combine paid-work and child-rearing (Gornick, Meyers, and Ross 1998). Already very high rates of taxation render the 'social democratic' path of social service employment expansion (which would also facilitate the movement of women into other forms of employment) implausible. High fixed social charges and reservation wages limit private service sector growth, especially for low productivity (and hence low pay) services (Scharpf 1997b).

The second agenda is to achieve cost containment in the main social insurance programmes—pensions, health care, and disability. The Continental systems are transfer-heavy, and in their most extreme form (e.g. Italy, but to a lesser extent France and Germany) approach the status of pensioner states. The combination of demographics and existing commitments generates projections of an even more severe shift in that direction. In most of these countries, health care has also been partly financed from social insurance contributions. These high levels of taxation strain public tolerance while crowding out fiscal space that might allow some social service expansion. As just noted, high social insurance contributions also raise fixed labour costs for firms, undercutting prospects for private sector job growth. Successful pursuit of cost containment would make an important contribution to the task of expanding service employment.

Thus, the Continental welfare states face an imposing list of reform demands, centring on cost containment and on a series of recalibrating adjustments to diminish reliance on payroll taxes, expand employment, and facilitate the efforts of women to combine paid employment with caring responsibilities. Needless to say, this reform agenda confronts formidable political challenges. The major social insurance programmes create powerful vested interests. Serious efforts to reduce expenditures by cutting benefits or tightening eligibility can threaten very broad voting blocs. It is these types of reforms that have prompted large public demonstrations in France, Italy, Germany, the Netherlands, and elsewhere mentioned at the outset of this chapter. Nor is it difficult to point to governments (Juppé in France, several coalitions in the Netherlands, Berlusconi in Italy) which subsequently paid large electoral costs for unpopular retrenchment initiatives. In addition, as shown in Wood's discussion of Germany, efforts to open the labour market for low-paid work may confront challenges from the social partners. It should be underscored that the resistance comes not just from unions, but often from employers as well. Having adapted to many aspects of the 'high wage-high skill' regime and benefited from the welfare state's subsidization of cost-shifting efforts, employers too may resist or only half-heartedly support labour market reforms.

Esping-Andersen (1990) has depicted the new cleavage in the conservative regime as one dividing insiders from outsiders. As in the investigation of the social democratic welfare regime, however, a simple political economy approach is likely to err by exaggerating the political significance of cleavages that run right through the middle of households. 'Outsiders' (e.g. unemployed women and young men) are often economically dependent on insiders, and this may in fact intensify resistance to anything threatening the existing social welfare and employment regime. Indeed, Esping-Andersen's recent acknowledgement (1999: 141) that political mobilization of outsiders was unlikely probably underlies his extremely pessimistic tone about these countries.

Yet a vigorous politics of restructuring is emerging in the Continental regime, captured by the concept (if not all the details) of Blair and Schröder's recent declaration of a 'new middle' ('neue Mitte'). The initial framework outlined in Section I presented the underpinnings for this political depiction. The basic claim made there—that welfare states both generate very strong support and face very severe pressures—applies especially clearly to the Continental regime. The dominant political struggle in the Continental countries is not between insiders and outsiders. Instead, it is between those who seek to create the foundations for a modernized, fiscally and politically viable system of social provision and their opponents, who generally advocate either the preservation of the status quo ('standing pat') or a more radical programme of liberalization ('crashing through').

Thus, the central political issue in Continental Europe during the past two decades has been whether or not particular countries could develop the capacity to initiate and sustain such a 'new middle' coalition of welfare state restructuring. I begin by characterizing the pattern of cross-national outcomes at the end of the 1990s, before turning to the issue of explanation. Regarding outcomes, the consensus view appears to be that the Netherlands represents a clear case of successful reform (the so-called 'Dutch miracle'), with Italy deserving the second prize. By contrast, Belgium, France, and Germany represent the 'frozen welfare state' outcome, showing so far very modest capacities for restructuring.[22] Particular emphasis is given to the contrast between Dutch success and German failure (Hemerijck and Manow

---

[22] See esp. the country chapters in the Scharpf/Schmidt project and, for an explicitly comparative assessment, Ebbinghaus and Hassel 1999. Levy's (1999) account of the French case has a more optimistic tone, but he acknowledges that his review of policy changes is highly selective, designed to illuminate a particular style of reform rather than to systematically assess the overall trajectory of policy change.

1998). Finally, Austria is often left to one side in these comparisons; its economic performance, and in particular its success in restraining unemployment, has so far generated only modest pressures for restructuring.

As I have argued earlier, establishing the pattern of reform outcomes across countries and over time is an extremely difficult task. Doing so systematically for these cases is well beyond the scope of this essay. Rather than attempting it, I wish to focus briefly on two revealing errors in the consensus judgement. On the one hand, it is overly generous in depicting the achievements of reform coalitions in the Netherlands and Italy; on the other, it exaggerates the extent to which the German welfare state has been locked into a politics of the status quo.

Derided as economic basket cases until recently, both Italy (Ferrera and Gualmini 1999; Baccaro and Locke 1996*b*) and the Netherlands (Visser and Hemerijck 1997) have since initiated quite substantial restructuring efforts. To deflate the depictions of 'miracles' is not to deny the significance of the reforms carried out in each case. Consider one telling statistic. Policies in place prior to the Italian reforms of 1992, 1996, and 1997 had been projected to generate public pension spending of over 23 per cent of GDP by 2035; current projections estimate that spending will peak at just under 16 per cent (from the current level of about 14 per cent) in 2030 before beginning to decline (Ferrara and Gualmini 1999: table 1). In the Netherlands, policies of labour market reform and negotiated wage restraint have generated a big increase in employment, especially part-time employment. There have been vigorous efforts, so far with uncertain results, to diminish reliance on disability and early retirement 'exit paths' from employment, including a restructuring of disability programmes that greatly enhanced the state's oversight role.

The comparative assessment of reform performance is heavily dependent upon the analyst's choice of time frame. Too often, it is also based on an implicit assumption that the countries being compared are starting from the same point. Yet if one takes the Dutch and Italian cases from 1973, the date usually adopted to demarcate the end of the Golden Age, then one's evaluation diverges from the consensus view. In both cases, conditions first dramatically deteriorated as policy makers resorted to a variety of short-term expedients, initially including further programmatic expansion, and later reliance on heavy borrowing and subsidized labour market exit. Arguably, the main achievement of the reform initiatives beginning in 1982 in the Netherlands and in the early 1990s in Italy has been to partially undo the policy damage done in prior years. Despite its jobs 'miracle', Dutch rates of labour force participation are still below the German level. Much of the heavily-touted expansion of women's participation appears to involve very part-time jobs. If one measures the number of hours worked in the paid labour market, rates for Dutch women remain at the very bottom end for

European Union countries (Daly 1998). Italy, despite notable reforms, continues to have the highest level of pension spending in the affluent world, a very heavy debt load, and alarmingly low rates of women's labour force participation and fertility. How one evaluates these reform efforts turns heavily on one's frame of reference. Their status as 'miracles' rests largely on the contrast with the economic disasters which preceded them.

Adopting a common baseline also suggests a kinder interpretation of the German case, which is widely regarded as an instance of failed adjustment (Manow and Seils 1999). As Wood argues, efforts to reform German labour markets roughly fit the conventional story. In a political system marked by veto points, efforts at reform have generally failed to overcome the resistance of organized interests committed to a deeply embedded labour market regime. Other aspects of the German welfare state, however, have seen rather considerable adjustments, particularly oriented around the goal of cost containment. Giaimo demonstrates that while health care reform came slowly and with difficulty it did come. By the early 1990s, an informal coalition involving the two major parties as well as unions and employers was able to impose significant new cost containment on providers, along with modest user fees. Two major quid pro quos, each an important instance of recalibration, made this painful restructuring acceptable. The reforms reduced inequities among sickness funds (a long-term goal of the unions) and allocated a considerable share of reform savings to a new programme of long-term care insurance.

In the case of pensions, there have been a series of major policy changes since the mid-1970s, all of which strived to control costs. Each successful reform involved extensive negotiations between the major parties and the social partners.[23] As Alber (1998*b*) shows, the upshot of all these efforts was not to reduce actual levels of pension spending or pensioner benefits from previous levels, but to essentially eliminate an extensive expansion of pension costs which had been built into previous pension policy. Pension benefits are roughly 30 per cent lower than they would have been if the policies in place in the mid-1970s had not been repeatedly modified.[24] Approximately half of the savings came from policies of the SPD–FDP government in place until 1982, and about half can be attributed to the Kohl governments which succeeded it. Efforts at cost containment have also taken place in other programmes, although Alber shows that the worst-off (e.g. families dependent on social assistance) have been treated relatively gently.

German restructuring has been discounted not only because in some areas it has been unimpressive (especially labour market reform), but because

---

[23] In at least one case, employers and unions made a joint submission of their position to the Commission charged with developing the reform.

[24] The German case thus illustrates the magnitude of loss imposition that is possible in pensions policy if policy makers pursue long-term goals, gain broad elite consensus, and do not markedly cut the real benefits of current recipients.

it has been undramatic. Furthermore, the magnitude of change has been partially obscured by the massive shock of German unification, which generated a severe fiscal disequilibrium. Under these exceptional adverse circumstances (which, unlike the case of the Netherlands and Italy were largely unavoidable), however, Germany has arguably done quite well. Germany has managed to keep social expenditure's share of GDP virtually level without sharply reducing benefits for the poor while at the same time introducing some important recalibration of core welfare state practices.

Thus, in my view, the Dutch, Italian, and German cases should all be classified as cases of moderately significant restructuring. Each combines a focus on cost containment with some efforts at recalibration. The reform paths differed, with the Netherlands and Italy first creating large problem loads, prompting economic crises, which then triggered the formation of political coalitions with a clear commitment to sweeping reforms. In Germany, reform has been more continuous and incremental. All these cases contrast with the French and Belgian experiences, where restructuring initiatives have generally been half-hearted.

In all three of the cases of substantial reform, the crucial political dynamic has been the construction of a 'new middle' coalition. The negative dynamic associated with these welfare state regimes prompts calls for fundamental reform. Yet the political configurations are such that serious reform generally requires careful negotiation among all, or at least most, major political actors—not only to surmount veto points, but in order to provide legitimacy for the imposition of losses and assure successful implementation. In the Netherlands and Italy this process has been apparent. In each case, broad centrist coalitions of varying shades have succeeded in convincing key actors, including voters, of the necessity of reform and have introduced major changes. Crucially, in each case vigorous efforts were made to provide reassurances that the ambition of reformers was to save, not destroy, the welfare state. In each case, reforms of social policy concentrated on costly elements (pensions in Italy, disability programmes in the Netherlands) that were both damaging to efficiency and normatively difficult to justify. Given the fiscal difficulties facing each country, opportunities for quid pro quos were limited, but in each country coveted enhancements of underdeveloped aspects of social provision rendered reforms more palatable. Finally, in each case efforts were made to support the most vulnerable; so far, considerable cost containment has not been accompanied by significant increases in poverty.

In Germany as well, successful reform reflects the employment of 'new middle' methods of elite negotiation and mutual legitimation. Both major parties, along with the social partners, have been active participants in sustained dialogue over major structural reforms. What was different in Germany was the informal, intermittent, and compartmentalized character of the process. In contrast with the Dutch and Italian cases, reform took place on a policy-by-policy basis rather than through a single, self-described, and well-publicized campaign of overarching reform.

Thus, the central issue for analysts of the conservative regime is to establish the factors determining the viability of such a new political middle.[25] At this stage, we can probably only begin the process of developing a reasonably convincing set of hypotheses. One can usefully distinguish between factors influencing the demand for a negotiated political response and those factors influencing the capacity of the system to generate that response. On the demand side are, especially, conditions that convince significant actors that 'standing pat' or 'crashing through' are not viable options. Marginalizing those who advocate 'crashing through' will often be easier. Given prominent features of the conservative regime, most important political elements are likely to be sceptical about the desirability of full-fledged liberalization in any event. Even for those who might consider such an outcome desirable in principle, the clear signals of public opinion, or the evident realities of veto points, may be sufficient to generate scepticism about crashing through. There may also be a need for political learning, however, through failed attempts at unilateral liberalization. Berlusconi's negative example appears to have played such a role in Italy, for instance.

Perhaps more critical is the determination by key political actors, especially in unions and left parties, that 'standing pat' is not a viable option. These actors may potentially (although not always) have relatively long time horizons, which allows them to pay attention to issues of policy sustainability (e.g. of old-age pension systems). Crucially, as Fiona Ross (1998) and Jonah Levy (1999) have emphasized, they are also politically positioned to sell reforms as both necessary and intended to revitalize the social contract rather than dismantle it.[26]

What convinces these actors of the need for reform? While a sense of policy imperative is always 'socially constructed', objective circumstances are likely to play a critical role. Well-established and highly valued policies, often the fruits of long political labour, are unlikely to be jettisoned easily. In the words of Maurizio Ferrera, actors must come to believe that 'there

---

[25] Aspects of the following analysis have some relevance for cases in the other regimes as well. Yet as discussed in the conclusion, those configurations vary because they generally face considerably more modest pressures for restructuring, and, in the case of the liberal countries (with the partial exception of Australia), because they have a much lower capacity for negotiated adjustment.

[26] Typical is the rhetoric accompanying German Chancellor Schröder's signing of the 'third way, *neue Mitte*' document with Tony Blair, which called for major welfare state restructuring including cost containment and labour market reform. In the words of a close aide, 'there is no other way . . . If we don't take steps to reform the welfare state, it will collapse.' Another adviser stressed that 'we must gradually convince people there is no alternative'. *Financial Times*, 9 June 1999, 1, 9.

is no status quo'[27]—that existing arrangements simply cannot be sustained. This is likely to involve both 'social learning' (about what the effects of particular policies will be) and 'political learning' (about the probabilities of achieving alternative policies). Social learning may be driven by focusing events (such as dreadful performance on key indicators) or financial crisis (such as a run on the currency). A more gradual process of learning, in which trial-and-error leads to the discrediting of alternative strategies, may also be crucial (Visser and Hemerijck 1997). Both these processes may be at work, with a period of cumulative learning punctuated by a focusing event that triggers the initiation of reform.

Political learning is likely to involve a similar trial-and-error process as actors explore the viability of alternative strategies. Here a plausible case can be made that political learning is most likely to lead to a 'new middle' outcome where left parties and unions are moderately strong. Moderately strong actors possess resources that are significant enough to place them at the bargaining table, but not so substantial that they can be confident that other actors (a right of centre government or employers) will not try to 'go it alone' if they attempt to exercise a veto.[28] This, for instance, was clearly the case in both the Netherlands (Visser and Hemerijck 1997) and Italy (Ferrera and Gualmini 1999), where decisions of 'left' and 'centre-left' actors to negotiate and on what terms occurred in the 'shadow' of possible exclusion (Scharpf 1997*b*). In the Netherlands and Germany centre-right parties have been integral participants in reform efforts. Thus, while Levy and Ross rightly argue that left participation in these restructuring processes is politically critical, they are wrong to portray these initiatives as essentially projects of the political left.

Yet if predispositions for reform among key actors are important, so are conditions which make the 'supply' of such restructuring initiatives possible. Success requires that the relevant social actors and political parties have both the desire and capacity to reach agreements and to make those agreements stick. A great deal of the traditional work on corporatism, which considered similar problems in the field of industrial relations, is relevant here. Two factors, however, appear crucial. The first factor is the quality of links between the social actors and the policy making process, which facilitate the effective implementation of agreements. The second is the ability of elites to maintain sufficient membership support for unpopular initiatives. As Kitschelt argues in this volume, this is an issue not just for unions but for political parties as well. Much is likely to turn on the extent to which potential negotiators find their organizations vulnerable to 'poaching' from competitive

---

[27] Personal communication.
[28] Of course, the Continental countries, except France, generally score in the middle range on most scales of left power resources.

organizations (or competing factions within their organization) who could exploit the opportunities created by efforts to impose losses.[29]

At first glance, this list of preconditions seems to imply that the prospects for negotiated reform would be bleak. After all, the conclusion of much of the traditional literature on corporatism was that breakdown was likely in the absence of relatively high levels of organizational concentration. Yet in fact, as Rhodes shows, there has been a rather striking sprouting of social pacts in recent years, even (or especially) in settings that might not have been considered fertile soil. In the current climate, those seeking a negotiated solution possess two significant advantages. First, in line with the analysis offered in Figure 13.1, they are likely to straddle the political space occupied by the pivotal voter. This position gives these elites considerable leverage, especially, as Kitschelt argues, if they are willing to trade off some erosion of membership support for sustained influence over policy.

The second advantage, as Jonah Levy has eloquently argued, is the possibility for turning 'vice into virtue'. In all these welfare states, Levy notes, there are opportunities to 'target inequities within the welfare system that are simultaneously a source of either economic inefficiency or substantial public spending. . . . [I]nherited welfare vices can be manipulated so as to soften or even obviate the supposedly ineluctable tradeoff between efficiency and equity' (Levy 1999: 240). In the terms employed in this essay, restructuring packages need not be limited to cost containment and re-commodification. They may also include substantial efforts at recalibration. As has been noted, the need for updating in many of these systems is evident, which may facilitate legitimation while generating crucial fiscal resources. When orchestrated through a broad, centrist coalition (formal or informal), which has credibility in claiming that the goal is restructuring rather than dismantling and that there are no viable alternatives, this can be a genuinely formidable political formula. In practice, the Dutch, German, and Italian cases all reveal a modest but very real possibility for the negotiated restructuring of conservative welfare states.

The argument presented in this section is summarized in Table 13.2. The three worlds of welfare capitalism differ in critical respects, which generate quite different political dynamics of welfare state restructuring. Most crucially, the different regimes vary in both the scope of support for the

---

[29] Both France and Belgium fall short in these respects. And unlike the case in the liberal regimes, the capacity of these two countries to concentrate political authority was not sufficient to generate major reforms. As Bonoli notes, French political authority is concentrated. In Belgium, governments ruling by decree were able for some time to exploit a similar concentration of formal authority (Scharpf 1999). In both cases, however, efforts to impose rather than negotiate reforms ultimately floundered in the face of widespread political opposition and the inability to implement key changes without consent. This underscores my earlier suggestion that the effects of concentrated political authority will be different within the conservative regime than they are in the liberal one.

TABLE 13.2. *Three worlds of welfare state reform*

	Liberal	Social democratic	Conservative
Political Support for Welfare State	Moderate	High	High
Adjustment Pressures	Moderate	Moderate	High
Reform Agenda	Re-commodification/ cost containment	Cost containment/ recalibration (rationalization)	Cost containment/ recalibration (updating)
Line of Conflict	Neoliberal retrenchment vs. compensated commodification	No dominant cleavage Negotiated, incremental adjustment	'Stand Pat' vs. Negotiated Reform
Distinct Key Variables	Concentration of political authority		Vulnerability of centrist reform organizations to 'poaching'

welfare state and in the scale and nature of adjustment pressures. In the liberal welfare states, adjustment pressures have been moderate, but so has been support for the existing welfare state. In the social democratic welfare states popular support is widespread and adjustment pressures have also been moderate. In the conservative welfare states, popular support of the existing regime is strong but so are pressures for adjustment.

These differences in the depth of popular support and the scale and nature of pressures in turn generates different political alignments, different plausible reform trajectories, and (somewhat more speculatively) different critical variables in the restructuring process. In short, *there is not a single 'new politics' of the welfare state, but different politics in different configurations.* In the liberal world reform focuses on cost containment and re-commodification, with the crucial divide between those advocating thoroughgoing neoliberal retrenchment and those seeking a more consensual and compensatory solution. In a context where support for social provision is relatively thin and the electoral/legislative arena plays a dominant role, partisan control of government and the degree to which institutions concentrate political authority become critical factors. In the social democratic world, the focus of reform is on cost containment and recalibrations, which aim at rationalizing programmes to enhance performance in achieving established goals. On the whole, reform has been negotiated, consensual, and incremental. In the conservative world, reform has centred on cost containment and recalibration, with a heavy emphasis on updating 'old' programmes to meet new demands. Neoliberal retrenchment is not a viable option, so politics centres on efforts to construct a viable reform coalition. The structure of interest intermediation and party systems—in particular, whether they allow reformers to overcome their fears of poaching—are crucial.

Two final observations about this summary statement underscore key features of the contemporary politics of social policy. The first, as indicated in Table 13.1, is that a critical factor in structuring reform in all three configurations is the severity of economic pressures. Intense disequilbria have a major impact on reform dynamics. These disequilbria may or may not stem primarily from 'globalization', but it is important to stress that it is not politics alone that determines how or when countries undertake significant reform initiatives. By implication, the future fate of mature welfare states is likely to be dependent upon the economic performance of the particular countries to which they are joined. This volume has offered grounds for scepticism about the deleterious economic effects of extensive social provision. However, if these negative effects are as severe and persistent as some critics allege, more wide-ranging reforms seem likely.

The second observation is that while reform agendas vary quite substantially across regime types, all of them place a priority on cost containment. This shared emphasis reflects the onset of permanent austerity. Welfare states are not being dismantled. Efforts to achieve recalibration can generate interesting innovations and even extensions of social provision. Yet everywhere, such adjustments occur in a context where the control of public expenditure is a central if not dominant consideration. The core structures of most welfare states are not in jeopardy. Nonetheless, the contemporary climate remains a harsh one for efforts to improve social provision for the vulnerable or to address newly recognized risks.

REFERENCES

AARON, HENRY, and SCHWARTZ, WILLIAM B. (1984). *The Painful Prescription: Rationing Hospital Care*. Washington, DC: Brookings.

ACS, GREGORY, LONG, STEPHEN H., MARQUIS, M. SUSAN, and SHORT, PAMELA FARLEY (1996). 'Self-Insured Employer Health Plans; Prevalence, Profile, Provisions, and Premiums'. *Health Affairs*, 15 (2): 266–78.

Advisory Council for the Concerted Action in Health Care (Sachverständigenrat für Konzertierte Aktion in Gesundheitswesen) (1995). *Health Care and Health Insurance 2000: A Closer Orientation towards Results, Higher Quality Services and Greater Economic Efficiency. Summary and Recommendations of the Special Expert Report, 1995*. Bonn.

—— (1997). *The Health Care System in Germany: Cost Factor and Branch of the Future*, ii. *Progress and Growth Markets, Finance and Remuneration. Special Report 1997, Summary*. Bonn.

Advisory Council on Social Security (1997). *Report of the 1994–1996 Advisory Council on Social Security*. Baltimore: Social Security Administration.

AGELL, JONAS (1996). 'Why Sweden's Welfare State Needed Reform'. *Economic Journal*, 106 (439) (Nov.): 1760–71.

AGELL, SUSANNE (1995). 'Swedish Labor Market Programs: Efficiency and Training'. *Swedish Economic Policy Review*, 2 (1).

ALBER, JENS (1996). 'Selectivity, Universalism, and the Politics of Welfare Retrenchment in Germany and the United States'. Paper prepared for delivery at the Annual Meeting of the American Political Science Association in San Francisco, 31 Aug.–3 Sept.

—— (1998a). 'Der deutsche Sozialstaat im Licht international vergleichender Daten', to appear in *Leviathan*, 26 (2): 199–227.

—— (1998b). 'Recent Developments in Continental Welfare States: Do Austria, Germany, and the Netherlands Prove to be Birds of a Feather?'. Paper presented to 14th World Congress of Sociology, Montreal, July 1998.

ALBERT, MICHEL (1991). *Capitalisme contre capitalisme*. Paris: Seuil.

ALDRICH, JOHN (1983). 'A Downsian Spatial Model with Party Activism'. *American Political Science Review*, 77 (Dec.): 974–90.

—— (1997). *Why Parties? The Origin and Transformation of Political Parties in America*. Chicago: University of Chicago Press.

ALT, JAMES, and GILLIGAN, MICHAEL (1994). 'Political Economy of Trading States'. *Journal of Political Philosophy*, 2 (2): 165–92.

—— FRIEDEN, JEFFRY, GILLIGAN, MICHAEL J., RODRIK, DANI, and ROGOWSKI, RONALD (1996). 'The Political Economy of International Trade: Enduring Puzzles and an Agenda for Inquiry'. *Comparative Political Studies*, 29 (6): 689–717.

AMENTA, EDWIN (1993). 'The State of the Art in Welfare State Research on Social Spending Effects in Capitalist Democracies Since 1960'. *American Journal of Sociology*, 99 (3): 750–63.

ANDERSON, KAREN M. (1998). 'Organized Labor, Policy Feedback, and Retrenchment in Swedish Pension and Unemployment Insurance'. Paper prepared for the 11th International Conference of Europeanists, Council of European Studies. Baltimore, 26–28 Feb.

ANDREWS, DAVID M. (1994). 'Capital Mobility and State Autonomy'. International Studies Quarterly, 38: 193–218.

APPELBAUM, EILEEN, and SCHETTKAT, RONALD (1994). 'The End of Full Employment? On Economic Development in Industrialized Countries'. *Intereconomics*, May/June: 122–30.

—— —— (1995). 'Employment and Productivity in Industrialized Countries'. *International Labour Review*, 134 (4–5): 605–23.

ARMINGEON, K. (1997). 'Globalisation as an Opportunity: Two Roads to Welfare State Reform'. Paper presented at the workshop 'Globalisation and the Advanced Capitalist State', ECPR Joint Sessions, Bern, 27 Feb.–4 Mar.

ARNOLD, DOUGLAS (1990). *The Logic of Congressional Action*. New Haven: Yale University Press.

ARTHUR, W., BRIAN (1989). 'Competing Technologies, Increasing Returns, and Lock-In by Historical Small Events'. *Economic Journal*, 99: 116–31.

ARTHUR, BRIAN (1994). *Path Dependence and Increasing Returns in Economics*. Ann Arbor: University of Michigan Press.

ARTONI, ROBERT, and ZANARDI, ALBERTO (1997). 'The Evolution of the Italian Pension System', in Bruno Palier (ed.), *Comparing Social Welfare Systems in Southern Europe*. Paris: MIRE, 243–66.

ATKINSON, ANTHONY B., and MOGENSEN, GUNNAR VIBY (1993). *Welfare and Work Incentives: A North European Perspective*. Oxford: Clarendon Press.

—— RAINWATER, LEE, and SMEEDING, TIMOTHY M. (1995). *Income Distribution in OECD Countries*. Paris: OECD.

AUERBACH, SIMON (1990). *Legislating for Conflict*. Oxford: Clarendon Press.

BACCARO, LUCIO, and LOCKE, RICHARD M. (1996a). 'The End of Solidarity? The Decline of Egalitarian Wage Policies in Italy and Sweden'. Unpublished manuscript, MIT, Apr.

—— —— (1996b). 'Public Sector Reform and Union Participation: The Case of the Italian Pension Reform'. *Sloan School of Management Working Paper*, No. 3922-96-BPS.

BADIE, B., and BIRNBAUM, P. (1983). *The Sociology of the State*. Chicago: University of Chicago Press.

BALDWIN, PETER (1990). *The Politics of Social Solidarity: Class Bases of the European Welfare State*. New York: Cambridge University Press.

BALL, ROBERT M. (1988). 'The Original Understanding on Social Security', in Theodore Marmor and Jerry Mashaw (eds.), *Social Security: Beyond the Rhetoric of Crisis*. Princeton: Princeton University Press, 17–39.

BANKS, DWAYNE, KUNZ, KIMBERLY, and MACDONALD, TRACY (1994). 'The Uninsured', in Banks, Kunz, and Macdonald (eds.), *Health Care Reform*. Berkeley: Institute of Governmental Studies, 17–26.

BANTING, KEITH (1997). 'The Social Policy Divide: The Welfare State in Canada and the US', in Keith Banting et al. (eds.), *Degrees of Freedom*. Montreal: McGill-Queen's University Press, 267–309.

BARRY, F., BRADLEY, J., and MCCARTAN, J. (1997). *Unemployment in the EU Periphery: Problems and Prospects.* Robert Schuman Centre, EUI Working Paper no. 97/47.

BATES, ROBERT, and LIEN, DA-HSIANG DONALD (1985). 'A Note on Taxation, Development and Representative Government'. *Politics and Society*, 14: 53–70.

BATTLE, KEN [published under the pseudonym, Gratton Gray] (1990). 'Social Policy by Stealth'. *Policy Options*, 11 (2): 17–29.

BAUMOL, WILLIAM J. (1967). 'The Macroeconomics of Unbalanced Growth'. *American Economic Review*, 52 (3) (June): 415–26.

—— BLACKMAN, SUE ANNE BATEY, and WOLFF, EDWARD N. (1991). *Productivity and American Leadership: The Long View.* Cambridge, Mass.: MIT Press.

BBC (1996). *Consequences: Personal Pensions*, broadcast on Radio 4, 27 Jan. 1996.

BEARDSLEY, SCOTT, and PATSALOS-FOX, MICHAEL (1995). 'Getting Telecoms Privatization Right'. *McKinsey Quarterly*, 1: 3–26.

BECK, NATHANIAL (1992). 'Comparing Dynamic Specifications: The Case of Presidential Approval', in James Stimson (ed.), *Political Analysis.* Ann Arbor: University of Michigan Press, 51–87.

—— and KATZ, JONATHAN (1995). 'What to Do (and Not To Do) with Time-Series—Cross-Section Data in Comparative Politics'. *American Political Science Review*, 89 (3): 634–47.

—— —— (1996). 'Nuisance versus Substance: Specifying and Estimating Time-Series-Cross-Section Models'. *Political Analysis*, 6: 1–36.

BENNER, MATS, VAD, TORBEN, and SCHLUDI, MARTIN (1999). 'Sweden and Denmark: Changing Places in Defense of the Welfare State'. Paper delivered at the conference on 'The Adjustment of National Employment and Social Policy to Economic Internationalization', Ringberg Castle, Germany, 17–20 Feb. 1999.

BERGER, SUZANNE, and DORE, RONALD (eds.) (1996). *National Diversity and Global Capitalism.* Ithaca, NY: Cornell University Press.

BERMEO, NANCY (1994). 'Comments on de la Dehosa and Torres', in John Williamson (ed.), *The Political Economy of Policy Reform.* Washington, DC: Institute for International Economics, 197–206.

BIGAUT, C. (1995). 'Les Cohabitations institutionnelles de 1986–1988 et 1993–1995'. *Regards sur l'actualité*, 211: 3–30.

BIRCHFIELD, VICKI, and CREPAZ, MARKUS (1998). 'The Impact of Constitutional Structures and Competitive and Collective Veto Points on Income Inequality in Industrialized Democracies'. *European Journal of Political Research*, 34: 175–200.

BLENDON, ROBERT J., BRODIE, MOLLYANN, BENSON, JOHN M., ALTMAN, DREW E., LEVITT, LARRY, HOFF, TINA, and HUGICK, LARRY (1998). 'Understanding the Managed Care Backlash'. *Health Affairs*, 17 (4): 80–94.

BLOCK, FRED (1977). 'The Ruling Class Does Not Rule: Notes on the Marxist Theory of the State'. *Socialist Revolution*, 33: 6–27.

—— (1987). 'Social Policy and Accumulation: A Critique of the New Consensus', in Martin Rein et al. (eds.), *Stagnation and Renewal in Social Policy.* Armonk, NY: M. E. Sharpe, 13–31.

BOIX, CARLES (1998). *Political Parties, Growth, and Inequality: Conservative and Social Democratic Party Strategies in the World Economy.* New York: Cambridge University Press.

BONOLI, GIULIANO (1996). 'Politics against Convergence? Current Trends in European Social Policy'. Paper presented at the conference on 'The Distributive Dimension of Political Economy', Centre for European Studies, Harvard University, 1–3 Mar.

—— (1997a). 'Pension Politics in France: Patterns of Co-operation and Conflict in Two Recent Reforms'. *West European Politics*, 20 (4): 160–81.

—— (1997b). 'Switzerland: Institutions, Reform, and the Politics of Consensual Retrenchment', in Jochen Clasen (ed.), *Social Insurance in Europe*. Bristol: Policy Press, 107–29.

—— and PALIER, BRUNO (1996). 'Reclaiming Welfare: The Politics of French Social Protection Reform'. *South European Society and Politics*, 1: 240–59.

—— VIC, GEORGE, and TAYLOR-GOOBY, PETER (forthcoming). *European Welfare Futures: Towards a Theory of Retrenchment*. Cambridge: Polity Press.

BOREHAM, PAUL, and COMPSTON, HUGH (1992). 'Labour Movement Organization and Political Intervention'. *European Journal of Political Research*, 22: 143–70.

BORRE, OLE (ed.) (1995). *The Scope of Government: Beliefs in Government III*. Oxford: Oxford University Press.

BÖRSCH-STEPAN, AXEL (1997). 'Retirement Income: Level Risk and Substitution among Income Components'. Paris: Organization for Economic Cooperation and Development.

BOUND, JOHN, and JOHNSON, GEORGE (1992). 'Changes in the Structure of Wages in the 1980s: An Evaluation of Alternative Explanations'. *American Economic Review*, 85 (May): 10–16.

BOVER, O., GARCIA-PEREA, P., and PORTUGAL, P. (1997). 'A Comparative Study of the Portuguese and Spanish Labor Markets'. Banca de España, Working Paper no. 9807.

BOYER, ROBERT, and DRACHE, DANIEL (eds.) (1996). *States Against Markets: The Limits of Globalization*. New York: Routledge.

BRADFORD, NEIL and JENSON, JANE (1992). 'Facing Economic Restructuring and Constitutional Renewal: Social Democracy Adrift in Canada', in Frances Fox Piven (ed.), *Labor Parties in Postindustrial Societies*. New York: Oxford, 190–211.

BRADLEY, DAVID (1998). 'The Comparative Political Economy of Employment Performance: Testing the Thesis'. Mimeo, University of North Carolina.

BRADY, DAVID W., and VOLDEN, CRAIG (1998). *Revolving Gridlock: Politics and Policy from Carter to Clinton*. Boulder, Colo.: Westview Press.

BRATT, CHRISTIAN (1996). *Labour Relations in Eighteen Countries*. Stockholm: Swedish Employers Confederation.

BRAUN, DIETMAR (1997). *Bringing State Structures Back In: The Significance of Political Arenas in Political Decision-Making*. Lausanne: IEPI, Travaux de science politique no. 12.

BROWN, LAWRENCE D. (1998). 'Exceptionalism as the Rule? U.S. Health Policy Innovation and Cross-National Learning. *Journal of Health Politics, Policy, and Law*, 23 (1) (Feb.): 35–51.

BRUNO, MICHAEL, and SACHS, JEFFREY D. (1985). *Economics of Worldwide Stagflation*. Cambridge, Mass.: Harvard University Press.

BÜCHTEMANN, CHRISTOPH (1991). 'Does (De-)Regulation Matter? Employment Protection in West Germany', in Egon Matzner and Wolfgang Streeck (eds.),

Beyond Keynesianism: The Socio-Economics of Production and Full Employment. Aldershot: Edward Elgar, pp. 111–36.

BMAS (Bundesministerium für Arbeit und Sozialordnung) (1998). *Bundesarbeitsblatt 1998.* Bonn: German Federal Government.

BURROWS, ROGER, and LOADER, BRIAN (eds.) (1994). *Towards a Post-Fordist Welfare State.* New York: Routledge.

CABLE, VINCENT (1995). 'The Diminished Nation State: A Study in the Loss of Economic Power'. *Daedalus,* 124 (2): 23–53.

CALMFORS, LARS, and DRIFFILL, JOHN (1988). 'Bargaining Structure, Corporatism, and Macroeconomic Performance'. *Economic Policy,* 3: 13–61.

—— and SKEDINGER, P. (1995). 'Does Active Labour Market Policy Increase Employment? Theoretical Considerations and Some Empirical Evidence from Sweden'. *Oxford Review of Economic Policy,* 11 (1): 91–109.

CAMERON, DAVID (1978). 'The Expansion of the Public Economy: A Comparative Analysis'. *American Political Science Review,* 72: 1243–61.

—— (1998). 'Economic and Monetary Union and Unemployment in Europe'. Paper presented at the Eleventh International Conference of Europeanists, Baltimore, Maryland, 26 Feb.–1 Mar.

CAMPOS LIMA, M., and NAUMANN, R. (1997). 'Social Dialogue and Social Pacts in Portugal', in G. Fajertag and Ph. Pochet (eds.), *Social Pacts in Europe.* Brussels: European Trade Union Institute/Observatoire social européen, 157–80.

CAREY, JOHN M., and SHUGART, MATTHEW SOBERG (1995). 'Incentives to Cultivate a Personal Vote: A Rank Ordering of Electoral Formulas'. *Electoral Studies,* 14 (4): 417–39.

CARLIN, WENDY, and SOSKICE, DAVID (1997). 'Shocks to the System: The German Political Economy under Stress'. *National Economic Institute Review,* 159: 57–76.

CARNOY, MARTIN, et al. (1993). *The New Global Economy in the Information Age: Reflections on our Changing World.* University Park: Pennsylvania State University Press.

CARROLL, EERO (1994). 'The Politics of Unemployment Insurance and Labor Market Policy'. Paper presented at the International Sociological Association Meetings, Bielefeld, Germany, July.

CASEY, B. (1999). 'Social Partnership and the Search for Solutions: European Experiences of the "80s" and "90s"'. Paper presented to the conference 'Globalisation, European Economic Integration and Social Protection', European Forum on 'Recasting the Welfare State', European University Institute, 11–12 Mar. 1999.

—— and GOLD, M. (1999). *The Impact of Social Partnership and Protection on Economic Performance.* Forthcoming.

CASTILLO, S., DOLADO, J., and JIMENO, J. (1998). 'A Tale of Two Neighbour Economies: Labor Market Dynamics in Spain and Portugal'. Centre for Economic Policy Research, Discussion Paper no. 1954.

CASTLES, FRANCIS G. (1978). *The Social Democratic Image of Society: A Study of the Achievements and Origins of Scandinavian Social Democracy in Comparative Perspective.* London: Routledge and Kegan Paul.

—— (1985). *The Working Class and Welfare.* Sydney: Allen and Unwin.

CASTLES, FRANCIS G. (1996). 'Needs-Based Strategies of Social Protection in Australia and New Zealand', in G. Esping-Andersen (ed.), *Welfare States in Transition: National Adaptations in Global Economies*. London: sage, 88–115.

—— (1998). *Comparative Public Policy: Patterns of Post-War Transformation.* Brookfield, Vt.: Edward Elgar.

—— and MAIR, PETER (1984). 'Left–Right Political Scales: Some "Expert" Judgments'. *European Journal of Political Research*, 12: 73–88.

—— and MITCHELL, DEBORAH (1993). 'Three Worlds of Welfare Capitalism or Four?', in Francis G. Castles (ed.), *Families of Nations: Public Policy in Western Democracies*. Brookfield, Vt.: Dartmouth.

—— and PIERSON, CHRISTOPHER (1996). 'A New Convergence? Recent Policy Developments in the United Kingdom, Australia, and New Zealand'. *Policy and Politics*, 24 (3): 233–45.

—— GERRITSEN, ROLF, VOWLES, JACK (eds.) (1996). *The Great Experiment: Labour Parties and Public Policy Transformation in Australia and New Zealand.* Sidney: Allen and Unwin.

CASTLES, FRANK, and SHIRLEY, IAN (1995). 'Labour and Social Policy: Gravediggers and Refurbishers of the Welfare State'. Presented at the meetings of the International Sociological Association, Research Committee 19, Pavia, Italy.

CATTACIN, S. (1996). 'Die Transformation des Schweizer Sozialstaates'. *Swiss Political Science Review*, 2 (1): 89–102.

CERNY, PHILIP (1996). 'International Finance and the Erosion of State Power', in Philip Gummett (ed.), *Globalization and Public Policy*. Brookfield, Vt.: Edward Elgar.

CFQF (Commission Fédérale pour les Questions Féminines) (1988). 'Propositions de la Commission fédérale pour les questions féminines en vue de la 10e révision de l'AVS'. *Questions au féminin*, 1 (88) (Berne).

CHADELAT, J.-F. (1994). 'Le Fonds de solidarite vieillesse'. *Droit Social*, 7/8 (July/Aug.): 727–33.

CHARLES, CATHY, LOMAS, JONATHAN, GIACOMINI, MITA, BHATIA, VANDNA, and VINCENT, VICTORIA A. (1997). 'Medical Necessity in Canadian Health Policy: Four Meanings and . . . a Funeral'. *Milbank Quarterly*, 75 (3): 365–94.

CHIRBA-MARTIN, MARY ANN, and BRENNAN, TROYEN A. (1994). 'The Critical Role of ERISA in State Health Reform'. *Health Affairs*, 13 (Spring II): 142–56.

CHULIÀ, E. (1999). 'The Future of the Spanish Pension System: Incremental Changes within the Limits of the Pact of Toledo'. Paper presented to the 2nd ECPR Summer School on 'The Welfare State: Challenges, Politics and Policy Responses in the 1990s', European University Institute, Florence, July.

CLASEN, JOCHEN (1994). *Paying the Jobless: A Comparison of Unemployment Benefit Policies in Great Britain and Germany*. Avebury: Aldershot.

—— and FREEMAN, RICHARD (eds.) (1994). *Social Policy in Germany*. New York: Harvester Wheatsheaf.

—— and GOULD, ARTHUR (1995). 'Stability and Change in Welfare States: Germany and Sweden in the 1990s'. *Policy and Politics*, 23 (3): 189–201.

—— GOULD, ARTHUR, and VINCENT, JILL (1998). *Voices Within and Without: Responses to Long-Term Unemployment in Germany, Britain and Sweden*. London: Policy Press.

CLAYTON, RICHARD, and PONTUSSON, JONAS (1998). 'Welfare-State Retrenchment Revisited: Entitlement Cuts, Public Sector Re-structuring, and Inegalitarian Trends in Advanced Capitalist Societies'. *World Politics*, 51 (1): 67–98.

CLINE, WILLIAM (1996). *Trade and Income Distribution*, Washington, DC: Institute for International Economics.

COHEN, BENJAMIN (1996). 'Phoenix Risen: The Resurrection of Global Finance'. *World Politics*, 48 (Jan.): 268–90.

COLLIER, DAVID, and LEVITSKY, STEVEN (1997). 'Democracy with Adjectives: Conceptual Innovation in Comparative Research'. *World Politics*, 49 (3): 430–51.

COMISKEY, MICHAEL (1993). 'Electoral Competition and the Growth of Public Spending in 13 Industrial Democracies, 1950 to 1983'. *Comparative Political Studies*, 26 (3): 350–74.

CONFALONIERI, MARIA A., and NEWTON, KENNETH (1995). 'Taxing and Spending: Tax Revolt or Tax Protest?', in Ole Borre (ed.), *The Scope of Government*. Oxford: Oxford University Press, 121–48.

Confederation of German Employers' Associations (CGEA) (1994). *Social Provision in Germany: The Welfare State at the Crossroads*. Cologne: CGEA.

COOPER, PHILIP F., and SCHONE, BARBARA STEINBERG (1997). 'More Offers, Fewer Takers for Employment-Based Health Insurance: 1987 and 1996'. *Health Affairs*, 16 (6) (Nov./Dec.): 142–9.

CORDES, JOSEPH J. (1996). 'How Yesterday's Decisions Affect Today's Budget and Fiscal Options', in C. Eugene Steuerle and Masahiro Kawai (eds.), *The New World Fiscal Order: Implications for Industrialized Nations*. Washington, DC: Urban Institute Press, 95–116.

CORNWALL, JOHN (1994). *Economic Breakdown and Recovery: Theory and Policy*. Armonk, NY: M. E. Sharpe.

COX, GARY W. (1990). 'Centripetal and Centrifugal Incentives in Electoral Systems'. *American Journal of Political Science*, 34 (4) (Nov.): 903–35.

CRAFTS, NICOLAS, and TONIOLO, GIANNI (1996). *Economic Growth in Europe since 1945*. New York: Cambridge University Press.

CREPAZ, MARKUS (1992). 'Corporatism in Decline? An Empirical Analysis of the Impact of Corporatism on Macroeconomic Performance and Industrial Disputes in 18 Industrialized Democracies'. *Comparative Political Studies*, 25 (2): 139–68.

—— and BIRCHFIELD, VICKI (no date). 'Global Economics, Local Politics: Globalization and Lijphart's Theory of Consensus Democracy and the Politics of Inclusion'. Typescript, University of Georgia.

CROUCH, COLIN (1986). 'Sharing Public Space: States and Organized Interests in Western Europe', in John A. Hall (ed.), *States in History*. Oxford: Blackwell, 177–210.

—— and STREECK, WOLFGANG (eds.) (1997). *Political Economy of Modern Capitalism: Mapping Convergence and Diversity*. London and Thousand Oaks: Sage.

CUSACK, THOMAS (1991). 'The Changing Contours of Government', WZB Discussion Paper.

—— (1997). 'Partisan Politics and Public Finance: Changes in Public Spending in the Industrialized Democracies, 1955–1989'. *Public Choice*, 91: 375–95.

CZADA, ROLAND (1998). 'Vereinigungskrise und Standortdebatte: Der Beitrag der Wiedervereinigung zur Krise des westdeutschen Modells'. *Leviathan*, 26 (1): 24–59.

DALY, MARY (1997). 'Welfare States under Pressure: Cash Benefits in European Welfare States over the Last Ten Years'. *Journal of European Social Policy*, 7 (2): 129–46.

—— (1998). 'Between Home and Work: Women and Labour Market Participation in International Comparison'. Unpublished manuscript.

DANIEL, CHRISTINE, and CONCIALDI, PIERRE (1997). 'La Réforme du système de retraite: Un difficile passage de la théorie à la pratique'. *Chronique Internationale de l'IRES*, 48: 73–9.

DAVID, PAUL (1985). 'CLIO and the Economics of QWERTY'. *American Economic Review*, 75 (2): 332–7.

DAVIS, E., PHILIP (1995). *Pension Funds, Retirement Income Security and Capital Markets*. Oxford: Oxford University Press.

DAY, PATRICIA, and KLEIN, RUDOLF (1992). 'Constitutional and Distributional Conflict in British Medical Politics: The Case of General Practice'. *Political Studies*, 40 (3): 462–78.

DE GREGORIO, JOSE, GIOVANNINI, ALBERTO, and WOLF, HOLGER C. (1994). 'International Evidence on Tradables and Nontradables Inflation'. *European Economic Review*, 38: 1225–44.

DE LA DEHESA, G. (1994). 'Spain', in John Williamson (ed.), *The Political Economy of Policy Reform*. Washington, DC: Institute for International Economics, 123–40.

DELLA SALA, V. (1997). 'Hollowing out and Hardening the State: European Integration and the Italian Economy'. *West European Politics*, 25 (1): 14–33 (special issue on 'Italy between Crisis and Transition', ed. M. Bull and M. Rhodes).

DERTHICK, MARTHA (1978). *Policy-making for Social Security*. Washington, DC: Brookings.

DHSS (Department of Health and Social Security) (1983). *Reply to the Third Report of the Social Services Committee*. London: HMSO, Cmnd. 9095.

—— (1985a). *A Programme for Action, White Paper*. London: HMSO, Cmnd. 9691.

—— (1985b). *Reform of Social Security, Green Paper*. 3 vols. London: HMSO, Cmnd. 9517–19.

Dienst für Gesellschaftspolitik (1997a). 20 (Feb.): 7–97.

—— (1997b). 27 (Mar.): 12–97.

DØLVIK, J. E., and MARTIN, A. (1997). 'A Spanner in the Works and Oil on Troubled Waters: The Divergent Fates of Social Pacts in Sweden and Norway', in G. Fajertag and Ph. Pochet (eds.), *Social Pacts in Europe*. Brussels: European Trade Union Institute/Observatoire social européen.

DOWNS, ANTHONY (1957). *An Economic Theory of Democracy*. New York: Harper and Row.

DOWRICK, STEVE (1996). 'Swedish Economic Performance and Swedish Economic Debate: A View from Outside'. *Economic Journal*, 106 (439) (Nov.): 1772–9.

DURKAN, J. (1992). 'Social Consensus and Incomes Policy'. *Economic and Social Review*, 23 (3): 347–63.

DUVERGER, M. (1963). *Political Parties: Their Organization and Activity in the Modern State*. New York: Wiley.

—— (1980). 'A New Political System Model: Semi-Presidential Government'. *European Journal of Political Research*, 8 (2): 165–87.

—— (1987). *La Cohabitation des français*. Paris: Presses Universitaires de France.

EASTON, BRIAN (1996). 'Income Distribution', in Brian Silverstone, Alan Bullard, and Ralph Lattimore (eds.), *A Study in Economic Reform: The Case of New Zealand.* Amsterdam: Elsevier, 101–38.

EBBINGHAUS, BERNHARD (1999). 'Any Way Out of "Exit from Work"? Reversing the Entrenched Pathways of Early Retirement in Europe, USA and Japan'. Contribution to the MPI Project on 'Adjustment to Economic Internationalization'.

—— and HASSEL, ANKE (1999). 'The Role of Tripartite Concertation in the Reform of the Welfare State'. *Transfer*, 5 (1–2): 64–81.

—— and MANOW, PHILIP (1998). 'Studying Welfare-State Regimes and the Varieties of Capitalism: An Introduction'. Paper presented at the 'Varieties of Welfare Capitalism in Europe, North America and Japan' Conference. Max Planck Institute for the Study of Societies, Cologne, Germany, 11–13 June.

—— —— (eds.) (forthcoming). *The Varieties of Welfare Capitalism: Social Policy and Political Economy in Europe, Japan and the USA*. London: Routledge.

EBRI (Employee Benefits Research Institute) (1997). 'Trends in Health Insurance Coverage'. *EBRI Issue Brief*, no. 185.

Economist (1995). 'Who's in the Driving Seat? A Survey of the World Economy'. 7 Oct.

EDGREN, JAN (1995). 'How Can We Reduce Youth Unemployment?'. UNICE Meeting Report, Swedish Employers Confederation.

EICHENGREEN, BARRY (1996). *Globalizing Capital: A History of the International Monetary System*. Princeton: Princeton University Press.

EIRR (1998). 'Proposals on Reform of Employee Representation'. *European Industrial Relations Review*, 295: 9.

ENCARNACIÓN, O. G. (1997). 'Social Concertation in Democratic and Market Transitions'. *Comparative Political Studies*, 30 (4): 387–419.

ENTHOVEN, ALAIN C. (1988). 'Managed Competition: An Agenda for Action'. *Health Affairs*, 7 (3): 25–47.

—— (1993). 'The History and Principles of Managed Competition'. *Health Affairs*, (Supplement 1993): 24–48.

ERTMAN, THOMAS (1997). *The Birth of the Leviathan: Building States and Regimes in Medieval and Early Modern Europe*. New York: Cambridge University Press.

ERVIK, RUNE, and KUHNLE, STEIN (1996). 'The Nordic Welfare Model and the European Union', in Brent Greve (ed.), *Comparative Welfare Systems: The Scandinavia Model in a Period of Change*. New York: St Martin's Press, 87–107.

ESPING-ANDERSEN, GØSTA (1985). *Politics Against Markets*. Princeton: Princeton University Press.

—— (1990). *The Three Worlds of Welfare Capitalism*. Princeton: Princeton University Press.

—— (1993). *Changing Classes: Stratification and Mobility in Postindustrial Societies*. London: Sage.

—— (1994). 'The Eclipse of the Democratic Class Struggle? European Class Structures at Fin de Siecle'. Paper presented to the study groups on 'Citizenship and Social Policies' and 'State and Capitalism', Center for European Studies, Harvard University.

Esping-Andersen, Gøsta (1996a). 'After the Golden Age? Welfare State Dilemmas in a Global Economy', in G. Esping-Andersen (ed.), *Welfare States in Transition: National Adaptations in Global Economies.* London: Sage, 1–31.

—— (1996b). 'Positive-Sum Solutions in a World of Trade-Offs?', in G. Esping-Andersen (ed.), *Welfare States in Transition: National Adaptations in Global Economies.* London: Sage, 256–67.

—— (1996c). 'Welfare States Without Work: The Impasse of Labour Shedding and Familialism in Continental Social Policy', in G. Esping-Andersen (ed.), *Welfare States in Transition: National Adaptations in Global Economies.* Thousand Oaks, Calif: Sage Publications, 66–87.

—— (1997). 'Welfare States at the End of the Century: The Impact of Labour Market, Family, and Demographic Change', in *Family, Market, and Community: Equity and Efficiency in Social Policy.* Paris: OECD, 63–80.

—— (1999). *Social Foundations of Postindustrial Economies.* Oxford: Oxford University Press.

—— and Kolberg, Jon Eivind (1992). 'Welfare States and Employment Regimes', in Jon Eivind Kolberg (ed.), *The Study of Welfare State Regimes.* Armonk, NY: M. E. Sharpe, 3–36.

Estevez-Abe, Margarita (1996). 'The Welfare-Growth Nexus in the Japanese Political Economy'. Paper presented at the American Political Science Association Meetings.

—— (forthcoming). 'Welfare Finance Nexus: A Forgotten Link?', in Ebbinghaus and Manow (eds.), *The Varieties of Welfare Capitalism: Social Policy and Political Economy in Europe, Japan and the USA.* London: Routledge.

European Commission (1994). *Employment in Europe 1992.* Luxembourg: Directorate General for Employment, Industrial Relations and Social Affairs.

Evans, Peter (1997). 'The Eclipse of the State? Reflections on Stateness in an Era of Globalization'. *World Politics,* 50 (1): 62–87.

Fearon, James (1991). 'Counterfactuals and Hypothesis-Testing in Political Science'. *World Politics,* 43 (2): 169–95.

Federal Reserve Bank of Cleveland (1999). *Economic Trends,* Jan.

Ferrera, Maurizio (1993). *EC Citizens and Social Protection.* Brussels: European Commission.

—— (1996). 'The Southern Model of Welfare in Social Europe'. *Journal of European Social Policy,* 6 (1): 17–37.

—— (1997). 'The Uncertain Future of the Italian Welfare State', in M. Bull and M. Rhodes (eds.), *Crisis and Transition in Italian Politics.* London: Frank Cass, 231–49.

—— and Gualmini, Elisabetta (1999). 'Italy: Rescue From Without?'. Paper presented to the MPI Project Meeting in Ringbergen.

—— —— (2000). 'Reforms Guided by Consensus: The Welfare State in the Italian Transition', in M. Ferrera and M. Rhodes (eds.), *Recasting the European Welfare State.* London: Frank Cass.

Flanagan, Robert J., Soskice, David, and Ulman, Lloyd (1983). *Unionism, Economic Stabilization, and Incomes Policies: European Experience.* Washington, DC: Brookings.

Fligstein, Neil (1998). 'Is Globalization the Cause of the Crises of Welfare States?'. *European University Institute Working Papers,* SPS No. 98/5.

FLORA, PETER (ed.) (1986). *Growth to Limits*. New York: De Gruyter.

—— (1989). 'From Industrial to Postindustrial Welfare State?'. *Annals of the Institute of Social Science*, special issue (Institute of Social Science, Tokyo).

—— and ALBER, JENS (1981). 'Modernization, Democratization, and the Development of Welfare States in Western Europe', in Peter Flora and Arnold Heidenheimer (eds.), *The Development of Welfare States in Europe and America*. New Brunswick, NJ: Transaction Books, 37–80.

—— and HEIDENHEIMER, ARNOLD J. (eds.) (1981). *The Development of Welfare States in Europe and America*. New Brunswick, NJ: Transaction Books.

FORSYTH, DOUGLAS, and NOTERMANS, TON (1997). *Regime Changes: Macroeconomic Policy and Financial Regulation from the 1930s to the 1990s*. Providence, RI: Berghahn Books.

FRANKEL, JEFFREY (1991). 'Quantifying International Capital Mobility in the 1980s', in B. Douglas Bernheim and John B. Shoven (eds.), *National Saving and Economic Performance*. Chicago: University of Chicago Press, 227–60.

FRANZESE, ROBERT (1998). 'Political Economy of Public Debt Database', located at <http://www.personal.umich.edu/~franzese/PEofPubDebt.Public.TXT>.

FREEMAN, JOHN R. (no date). 'Globalization, Welfare, and Democracy'. Unpublished manuscript. Department of Political Science, University of Minnesota.

FREEMAN, RICHARD B. (1994). 'How Labor Fares in Advanced Economies', in id., *Working under Different Rules*. New York: Russell Sage Foundation, 1–28.

—— (1995a). 'Are Your Wages Set in Beijing?'. *Journal of Economic Perspectives*, 9 (3): 15–32.

—— (1995b). 'The Limits of Wage Flexibility to Curing Unemployment'. *Oxford Review of Economic Policy*, 11 (1): 63–72.

FRIEDEN, JEFFRY A. (1991). 'Invested Interests: The Politics of National Economic Policies in a World of Global Finance'. *International Organization*, 45 (4): 425–51.

—— and ROGOWSKI, RONALD (1996). 'The Impact of the International Economy on National Policies', in Robert Keohane and Helen Milner (eds.), *Internationalization and Domestic Politics*. Cambridge: Cambridge University Press, 25–47.

FRIEDRICH, ROBERT (1982). 'In Defense of Interaction Terms in Multiple Regression Equations'. *American Journal of Political Science*, 26: 797–833.

FUCHS, BETH C., LYKE, BOB, PRICE, RICHARD, and SMITH, MADELEINE (1997). *The Health Insurance Portability and Accountability Act of 1996: Guidance on Frequently Asked Questions*. CRS Report for Congress. Washington, DC: Congressional Research Service, Library of Congress. Updated 10 Apr. 1997.

FULCHER, JAMES (1991). *Labour Movements, Employers, and the State: Conflict and Cooperation in Britain and Sweden*. Oxford: Clarendon Press.

FUSHIMI, YOSHIFUMI (1997). 'The Social Security System in Japan', in Peter Koslowski and Andreas Föllesdal (eds.), *Restructuring the Welfare State: Theory and Reform in Social Policy*. Berlin: Springer, 83–91.

GAMBLE, ANDREW (1994). *The Free Economy and the Strong State: The Politics of Thatcherism*. Durham, NC: Duke University Press.

GANGHOF, S., and GENSCHEL, P. (1999). 'National Tax Policy under International Constraints'. Paper prepared for the conference on 'Globalization, European Economic Integration and Social Protection'. European University Institute, Florence, Italy, 11–12 Mar.

GAO (General Accounting Office) (US) (1995). *Employer-Based Health Plans: Issues, Trends, and Challenges Posed by ERISA* (GAO/HEHS-95-167). Washington, DC.

GAO (Government Accounting Office) (1998). *Health Insurance Standards: New Federal Law Creates Challenges for Consumers, Insurers, Regulators.* GAO/HEHS-98-67. Washington, DC: GAO.

GARRETT, GEOFFREY (1993). 'The Politics of Structural Change: Swedish Social Democracy and Thatcherism in Comparative Politics'. *Comparative Political Studies*, 25 (4): 521–47.

—— (1995). 'Capital Mobility, Trade, and the Domestic Politics of Economic Policy'. *International Organization*, 49 (4): 657–87.

—— (1998*a*). 'Global Markets and National Politics: Collision Course or Virtuous Circle?'. *International Organization*, 52 (4): 787–824.

—— (1998*b*). *Partisan Politics in the Global Economy*. Cambridge: Cambridge University Press.

—— and LANGE, PETER (1991). 'Political Responses to Interdependence: What's "left" for the Left?'. *International Organization*, 45 (4): 539–64.

—— —— (1995). 'Internationalization, Institutions and Political Change'. *International Organization*, 49 (4): 627–55.

—— —— (1996). 'Internationalization, Institutions and Political Change', in Robert O. Keohane and Helen Milner (eds.), *Internationalization and Domestic Politics*. Cambridge: Cambridge University Press, 48–75.

—— and MITCHELL, DEBORAH (no date). 'Globalization and the Welfare State: Income Transfers in the Advanced Industrialized Democracies, 1965–1990'. Typescript, Department of Political Science, Yale University.

—— and WAY, CHRISTOPHER (1999). 'Public Sector Unions, Corporatism, and Macroeconomic Performance'. *Comparative Political Studies*, 32 (4): 411–34.

GENSCHEL, PHILIPP (1999). 'Tax Competition and the Welfare State'. Paper presented to the Study Group on Policy Reform in Advanced Industrial Societies, Center for European Studies, Harvard University, 23 Mar.

GEORGE, VIC, and TAYLOR-GOOBY, PETER (eds.) (1996). *European Welfare Policy: Squaring the Circle*. New York: St Martin's Press.

GERMAIN, RANDALL (1998). *The International Organization of Credit*. Cambridge: Cambridge University Press.

GIAIMO, SUSAN M. (1994). 'Health Care Reform in Britain and Germany: Recasting the Political Bargain between the State and the Medical Profession'. Ph.D. diss. Department of Political Science, University of Wisconsin–Madison.

—— (1995). 'Health Care Reform in Britain and Germany: Recasting the Political Bargain with the Medical Profession'. *Governance*, 8 (3) (July): 354–79.

—— (1996). 'Health Care Reform in Britain and Germany: Lessons for the United States'. Paper presented at the Robert Wood Johnson Foundation Scholars in Health Policy Research Program Meeting, Aspen, Colo., 29 May–2 June.

—— (1998). *Cost Containment vs. Solidarity in the Welfare State: The Case of German and American Health Care Reform*. AICGS Policy Papers No. 6. Washington, DC: American Institute for Contemporary German Studies.

—— and MANOW, PHILIP (1999). 'Welfare State Adaptation or Erosion? The Case of Health Care Reform in Britain, Germany, and the United States'. *Comparative Political Studies*, Dec.

GILL, STEPHEN (1990). *American Hegemony and the Trilateral Commission*, Cambridge: Cambridge University Press.

—— and LAW, DAVID (1988). *The Global Political Economy*. Baltimore: Johns Hopkins University Press.

GIVEN, RUTH S. (1997). 'Ensuring Competition in the Market for HMO Services', in John D. Wilkerson, Kelly J. Devers, and Ruth S. Given (eds.), *Competitive Managed Care*. San Francisco: Jossey-Bass, 167–97.

GLYN, ANDREW (1995a). 'The Assessment: Unemployment and Inequality'. *Oxford Review of Economic Policy*, 11 (1): 1–25.

—— (1995b). 'Social Democracy and Full Employment'. *New Left Review*, 211: 33–55.

—— (1997). 'Low Pay and the Volume of Work'. Typescript, Corpus Christi College, Oxford.

—— and WOOD, STEWART (2000). 'New Labour's Economic Policy', in Andrew Glyn (ed.), *Social Democracy and Economic Policy*. Oxford: Oxford University Press.

GOBEYN, M. J. (1993). 'Explaining the Decline of Macro-corporatist Political Bargaining Structures in Advanced Capitalist Societies'. *Governance: An International Journal of Policy and Administration*, 6 (1): 3–22.

GOLDEN, MIRIAM (1997). 'Economic Integration and Industrial Relations: Is Increasing Openness Bad for Labor?'. Paper prepared for the Workshop on the 'Political Economy of European Integration', Berkeley, Calif.

—— WALLERSTEIN, MICHAEL, and LANGE, PETER (1999). 'Postwar Trade-Union Organization and Industrial Restructuring in Twelve Countries', in Kitschelt, Lange, Marks, and Stephens, *Change and Continuity in Contemporary Capitalism*.

GOLDIN, CLAUDIA, and MARGO, ROBERT (1992). 'The Great Compression: The Wage Structure in the United States at Mid-century'. *Quarterly Journal of Economics*, 107 (Feb.): 1–34.

GOLDTHORPE, JOHN (ed.) (1984). *Order and Conflict in Contemporary Capitalism*. Oxford: Clarendon Press.

GOODMAN, J. B., and PAULY, L. W. (1993). 'The Obsolescence of Capital Controls: Economic Management in an Age of Global Markets'. *World Politics*, 46 (1): 50–82.

GORDON, ROBERT J. (1987). 'Productivity, Wages and Prices Inside and Outside of Manufacturing in the U.S., Japan, and Europe', *European Economic Review*, 31: 685–739.

GORNICK, JANET, MEYERS, MARCIA K., and ROSS, KATHERIN E. (1998). 'Public Policies and the Employment of Mothers: A Cross-National Study'. *Social Science Quarterly*, 79 (1) (Mar.): 35–54.

GÖTTING, ULRIKE, HAUG, KARIN, and HINRICHS, KARL (1994). 'The Long Road to Long-Term Care Insurance in Germany'. *Journal of Public Policy*, 14 (3): 285–309.

GOUGH, IAN, BRADSHAW, JONATHAN, DITCH, J., EARDLEY, TONY, and WHITEFORD, PETER (1997). 'Social Assistance in OECD Countries'. *Journal of European Social Policy*, 7 (1): 17–43.

GOUL ANDERSEN, JORGEN (1997). 'Beyond Retrenchment: Welfare Policies in Denmark in the 1990s'. ECPR Meeting, Bergen, Sept.

GOULD, ARTHUR (1993). *Capitalist Welfare States*. New York: Longman.

—— (1996). 'Sweden: The Last Bastion of Social Democracy', in Vic George and Peter Taylor-Gooby (eds.), *European Welfare Policy: Squaring the Circle*. New York: St Martin's Press, 72–94.

GOUREVITCH, PETER A. (1996). 'The Macropolitics of Microinstitutional Differences in the Analysis of Comparative Capitalism', in Suzanne Berger and Ronald Dore (eds.), *National Diversity and Global Capitalism*. Ithaca, NY: Cornell University Press, 239–59.

GRAFTON, R., QUENTIN, HAZELDINE, TIM, and BUCHARDT, BRUCE (1997). 'The New Zealand Economic Revolution: Lessons for Canada?'. *Canadian Business Economics*, 6: 3–19.

GRAHL, J., and TEAGUE, P. (1997). 'Is the European Social Model Fragmenting?'. *New Political Economy*, 2 (3): 405–26.

GRIEDER, WILLIAM (1997). *One World, Ready or Not*. New York: Simon and Schuster.

GROGAN, COLLEEN (1995). 'Hope in Federalism: What Can the States Do and What Are They Likely to Do?'. *Journal of Health Politics, Policy and Law*, 20 (2): 477–84.

GUILLÉN, ANNA (1998). 'Pension Reform in Spain (1975–1997): From Corporatism to Assistential Universalism'. Paper presented at the 14th World Congress of Sociology, Montréal, 26 July–1 Aug.

GUNNIGLE, P. (1997). 'More Rhetoric than Reality: Enterprise Level Industrial Relations Partnerships in Ireland'. *Economic and Social Review*, 28 (4): 179–200.

GUTIÉRREZ, R., and GUILLÉN, ANNA M. (1998). 'Protecting the Long-Term Unemployed: The Impact of Targeting Policies in Spain'. Working Paper 1998/116, Centro de Estudios Avazados en Ciecias Sociales, Instituto Juan March de Estudios e Investigaciones.

HACKER, JACOB (1998). 'The Historical Logic of National Health Insurance: Structure and Sequence in the Development of British, Canadian, and U.S. Medical Policy'. *Studies in American Political Development*, 12 (1): 57–130.

HAGGARD, STEFAN, and KAUFMAN, ROBERT (1995). *The Political Economy of Democratic Transitions*. Princeton: Princeton University Press.

HALL, PETER (1986). *Governing the Economy: The Politics of State Intervention in Britain and France*. New York: Oxford University Press.

—— (1993). 'Policy Paradigms, Social Learning, and the State: The Case of Economic Policy Making in Britain'. *Comparative Politics*, 25 (3): 275–96.

—— (1997). 'The Political Economy of Adjustment in Germany', in Frieder Naschold, David Soskice, Bob Hancké, Ulrich Jürgens (eds.), *Ökonomische Leistungsfähigkeit und institutionelle Innovation: Das deutsche Produktions- und Politikregime im globalen Wettbewerb*. WZB-Jahrbuch 1997. Berlin: Sigma, 293–317.

—— (1998). 'Organized Market Economies and Unemployment in Europe: Is it Finally Time to Accept Liberal Orthodoxy?'. Paper prepared for the 11th International Conference of Europeanists, Baltimore, 26–28 Feb.

—— (1999). 'The Political Economy of Europe in an Era of Interdependence', in Kitschelt et al., *Continuity and Change*.

—— and FRANZESE, ROBERT (forthcoming). 'Mixed Signals: Central Bank Independence, Coordinated Wage-Bargaining, and European Monetary Union', in

Torben Iversen, Jonas Pontusson, and David Soskice (eds.), *Unions, Employers and Central Banks: Wage Bargaining and Macroeconomic Regimes in an Integrating Europe*. Cambridge: Cambridge University Press.

—— and SOSKICE, DAVID (2000). 'An Introduction to Varieties of Capitalism', in Peter Hall and David Soskice (eds.), *Varieties of Capitalism: The Institutional Foundations of Comparative Advantage*. Cambridge: Cambridge University Press.

HAM, CHRIS, ROBINSON, RAY, and BENZEVAL, MICHAELA (1990). *Health Check: Health Care Reforms in an International Context*. London: King's Fund Institute.

HAMANN, A., JAVIER (1997). 'The Reform of the Pension System in Italy'. International Monetary Fund.

HAMEL, A. (1980). 'The Comparative Method in Anthropological Perspective'. *Comparative Studies in Society and History*, 22 (2) (Apr.): 145–55.

HANSEN, ERIK JØRGEN, et al. (1993). *Welfare Trends in the Scandinavian Countries*. Armonk, NY: M. E. Sharpe.

HARDIMAN, N. (1988). *Pay, Politics and Economic Performance in Ireland 1970–1987*. Oxford: Clarendon Press.

HARRISON, STEPHEN (1988). *Managing the National Health Service: Shifting the Frontier?* London: Chapman and Hall.

HAY, COLIN (1998). 'Globalization, Welfare Retrenchment, and "the Logic of No Alternative": Why Second-Best Won't Do'. *Journal of Social Policy*, 27 (4): 525–32.

HECLO, HUGH (1988). 'Generational Politics', in John Palmer, Timothy Smeeding, and Barabara Torrey (eds.), *The Vulnerable*. Washington, DC: Urban Institute, 381–411.

HEIKILLÄ, M., HVINDEN, B., KAUTTO, M., MARKLUND, S., and PLAUG, N. (1999). 'The Nordic Model Stands Stable but on Shaky Ground', in M. Kautto, M. Heikillä, B. Hvinden, S. Marklund, and N. Plaug (eds.), *Nordic Social Policy: Changing Welfare States*. London and New York: Routledge.

HEILEMANN, ULRICH, and RAPPEN, HERMANN (1997). *The Seven Year Itch? German Unity from a Fiscal Viewpoint*. AICGS Research Report No. 6, Economic Studies Program. Washington DC: American Institute for Contemporary German Studies.

HELLEINER, ERIC (1994). *States and the Reemergence of Global Finance*. Ithaca, NY: Cornell University Press.

HEMERIJCK, ANTON C. (1995). 'Corporatist Immobility in the Netherlands', in Colin Crouch and Franz Traxler (eds.), *Organized Industrial Relations in Europe: What Future?* Aldershot: Avesbury, 183–226.

—— and KLOOSTERMAN, ROBERT C. (1994). 'The Postindustrial Transition of Welfare Corporatism'. Paper delivered at the Conference of Europeanists, Chicago, 31 Mar.–2 Apr.

—— and MANOW, PHILIP (1998). 'The Experience of Negotiated Social Policy Reform in Germany and the Netherlands'. Max Planck Institute, Cologne, June.

—— and VAN DEN TOREN, J. P. (1996). 'The Resurgence of Corporatist Policy Co-ordination in an Age of Globalization'. Paper presented to the conference on 'Globalization and the New Inequality', Utrecht, 20–22 Nov.

HENKE, KLAUS-DIRK (1997). 'Sozial gebundener Wettbewerb als neuer Ordnungsrahmen im Gesundheitswesen', in Arbeitskreis Evangelischer Unternehmer in Deutschland e.V (eds.), *Die Soziale Marktwirtschaft als Wirtschafts- und Werteordnung*. Kölner Texte u. Thesen 36. Cologne: Deutscher Instituts-Verlag, 171–94.

HÉRITIER, ADRIENNE, and SCHMIDT, SUSANNE (2000). 'After Liberation: Public Interest Services and Employment in the Utilities', in Fritz Scharpf and Vivien Schmidt (eds.), *Welfare and Work in the Open Economy*, ii. *Diverse Responses to Common Challenges*. Oxford: Oxford University Press.

HERRING, RICHARD J., and LITAN, ROBERT E. (1995). *Financial Regulation in the Global Economy*. Washington, DC: Brookings.

HIBBS, DOUGLAS, JR. (1977). 'Political Parties and Macroeconomic Policy'. *American Political Science Review*, 71: 1467–87.

—— (1987a). *The American Political Economy: Macroeconomics and Electoral Politics in the United States*. Cambridge, Mass.: Harvard University Press.

—— (1987b). *The Political Economy of Industrial Democracies*. Cambridge, Mass.: Harvard University Press.

—— and LOCKING, HAKAN (1995). 'Wage Compression, Wage Drift and Wage Inflation in Sweden'. *Labour Economics*, 3: 109–41.

HICKS, ALEX (1988). 'Social Democratic Corporatism and Economic Growth'. *Journal of Politics*, 50: 677–704.

—— (1999). *Social Democracy and Welfare Capitalism*. Ithaca, NY: Cornell University Press.

—— and MISRA, JOYA (1993). 'Two Perspectives on the Welfare State: Political Resources and the Growth of Welfare Effort in Affluent Capitalist Democracies, 1960–1982'. *American Journal of Sociology*, 99 (3): 668–710.

—— and SWANK, DUANE (1992). 'Politics, Institutions, and Social Welfare Spending in the Industrialized Democracies, 1960–1982'. *American Political Science Review*, 86 (Sept.): 658–74.

HILLMAN, JOSH (1996). 'Education and Training', in David Halpern, Stewart Wood, Stuart White, and Gavin Cameron (eds.), *Options for Britain: A Strategic Policy Review*. Basingstoke: Dartmouth Press.

HILLS, JOHN (1998). 'Thatcherism, New Labour and the Welfare State'. *Center for the Analyses of Social Exclusion Paper*, No. 13, London School of Economics.

HINE, DAVID (1986). 'Leaders and Followers: Democracy and Manageability in the Social Democratic Parties of Western Europe', in William Paterson and Alistair Thomas (eds.), *The Future of Social Democracy*. Oxford: Clarendon Press.

HINICH, MELVIN J., and MUNGER, MICHAEL (1994). *Ideology and the Theory of Political Choice*. Ann Arbor: University of Michigan Press.

HINRICHS, KARL (1995). 'The Impact of German Health Insurance Reforms on Redistribution and the Culture of Solidarity'. *Journal of Health Politics, Policy and Law*, 20 (3): 653–88.

—— (1998). 'Reforming the Public Pension Scheme in Germany: The End of the Traditional Consensus'. Paper presented to the XIVth World Congress of Sociology, Montreal, July.

HIRST, PAUL, and THOMPSON, GRAHAME (1996). *Globalization in Question*. Cambridge, Mass.: Blackwell.

—— and ZEITLIN, J. (1991). 'Flexible Specialization versus Post-Fordism: Theory, Evidence and Policy Implications'. *Economy and Society*, 20 (2).

HIWATARI, NOBUHIRO (1998). 'Adjustment to Stagflation and Neoliberal Reforms in Japan, the United Kingdom, and the United States: The Implications of the Japanese Case for a Comparative Analysis of Party Competition'. *Comparative Political Studies*, 31: 602–32.

HMSO (1985). *Employment, the Challenge for the Nation*, White Paper, Cmnd. 9751 (Mar.). London: HMSO.

HOEFER, RICHARD (1996). 'Swedish Corporatism in Social Welfare Policy, 1986–1994: An Empirical Examination'. *Scandinavian Political Studies*, 19 (1): 67–81.

HOLLINGSWORTH, J., ROGERS, and BOYER, ROBERT (eds.) (1997). *Contemporary Capitalism: The Embeddedness of Institutions*. Cambridge: Cambridge University Press.

—— SCHMITTER, PHILIPPE, and STREECK, WOLFGANG (1993). *Governing Capitalist Economies: Performance and Control of Economic Sectors*. New York: Oxford University Press.

House of Commons (1986). Great Britain, House of Commons, *Hansard*, 19 May 1986, col. 105.

HOWARD, CHRISTOPHER (1997). *The Hidden Welfare State: Tax Expenditures and Social Policy in the United States*. Princeton: Princeton University Press.

HUBER, EVELYNE and STEPHENS, JOHN D. (1992). 'Economic Internationalization, the European Community, and the Social Democratic Welfare State'. Paper presented at the Annual Meetings of the American Political Science Association.

—— —— (1993). 'The Swedish Welfare State at the Crossroads'. *Current Sweden*, No. 394 (Jan.).

—— —— (1997). 'Welfare State and Production Regimes'. Paper delivered at conference on 'The New Politics of the Welfare State', Center for European Studies, Harvard University, Dec.

—— —— (1998). 'Internationalization and the Social Democratic Model'. *Comparative Political Studies*, 31 (3) (June): 353–97.

—— —— (2000). 'Partisan Governance, Women's Employment and the Social Democratic Service State'. *American Sociological Review*, 65 (3) (June): 323–42.

—— —— (forthcoming). *Development and Crisis of the Welfare State: Parties and Policies in Global Markets*. Chicago: University of Chicago Press.

——, RAGIN, CHARLES, and STEPHENS, JOHN (1993). 'Social Democracy, Christian Democracy, Constitutional Structure and the Welfare State'. *American Journal of Sociology*, 99 (3): 711–49.

—— —— —— (1997). Comparative Welfare States Data Set, Northwestern University and University of North Carolina (http://lissy.ceps.lu/compwsp.htm).

HUSEBY, BEATE (1995). 'Attitudes Towards the Size of Government', in Ole Borre (ed.), *The Scope of Government*. Oxford: Oxford University Press, 87–118.

HUSTED, THOMAS, A., and KENNY, LAWRENCE, W. (1997). 'The Effect of the Expansion of the Voting Franchise on the Size of Government'. *Journal of Political Economy*, 105 (1): 54–82.

IKENBERRY, JOHN (1994). 'History's Heavy Hand: Institutions and the Politics of the State'. Unpublished manuscript.

ILO (International Labour Office) (1990). *Yearbook of Labour Statistics.* Geneva: International Labour Office.

—— (1993). *Yearbook of Labour Statistics.* Geneva: International Labour Office.

—— (1997). *Yearbook of Labour Statistics.* Geneva: International Labour Office.

IMF (International Monetary Fund) (1991). *Determinants and Consequnces of International Capital Flows.* Washington, DC: IMF.

—— (1996). 'Fiscal Challenges Facing Industrial Countries'. *World Economic Outlook.* Washington, DC: IMF, 44–62.

IMMERGUT, ELLEN M. (1992). *Health Politics: Interests and Institutions in Western Europe.* Cambridge: Cambridge University Press.

INGLEHART, RONALD (1987). 'Value Change in Industrial Society'. *American Political Science Review*, 81: 1289–1303.

—— (1990). *Culture Shift in Advanced Industrial Society.* Princeton: Princeton University Press.

IVERSEN, TORBEN (1996). 'Power, Flexibility and the Breakdown of Centralized Wage Bargaining: The Cases of Denmark and Sweden in Comparative Perspective'. *Comparative Politics*, 28 (July): 399–436.

—— (1998a). 'The Choices for Scandinavian Social Democracy in Comparative Perspective'. *Oxford Review of Economic Policy*, 14 (1): 59–75.

—— (1998b). 'Wage Bargaining, Central Bank Independence and the Real Effects of Money'. *International Organization*, 52 (Summer): 469–504.

—— (1999a). *Contested Economic Institutions: The Politics of Macroeconomics and Wage Bargaining in Advanced Democracies.* New York: Cambridge University Press.

—— (1999b). 'Decentralization, Monetarism, and the Social-Democratic Welfare State in the1980s and 90s', in Torben Iversen, Jonas Pontusson, and David Soskice, *Unions, Employers and Central Banks: Macroeconomic Coordination and Institutional Change in Social Market Economies.* Cambridge: Cambridge University Press.

—— and CUSACK, THOMAS (1998). 'The Causes of Welfare State Expansion: Deindustrialization or Globalization?'. Prepared for presentation at 94th American Political Association Meeting at the Sheraton Boston, 3–6 Sept.

—— and WREN, ANNE (1998). 'Equality, Employment and Budgetary Restraint: The Trilemma of the Service Economy'. *World Politics*, 50 (4): 507–46.

—— PONTUSSON, JONAS, and SOSKICE, DAVID (eds.) (forthcoming). *Unions, Employers and Central Banks: Wage Bargaining and Macroeconomic Regimes in an Integrating Europe.* Cambridge: Cambridge University Press.

JAMES, JOHN H. (1995). 'Reforming the British National Health Service: Implementation Problems in London'. *Journal of Health Politics, Policy and Law*, 20 (1): 191–210.

JENKINS, PETER (1987). *Mrs. Thatcher's Revolution: The Ending of the Socialist Era.* London: Jonathan Cape.

JESSOP, BOB (1996). 'Post-Fordism and the State', in Brent Greve (ed.), *Comparative Welfare Systems: The Scandinavia Model in a Period of Change.* New York: St Martin's Press, 165–83.

JONES, CATHERINE (ed.) (1993). *New Perspectives on the Welfare State in Europe.* New York: Routledge.

JUDIS, JOHN B. (1995). 'Abandoned Surgery: Business and the Failure of Health Care Reform'. *American Prospect*, 2 (Spring): 65–73.

KAHNEMAN, D., and TVERSKY, A. (1979). 'Prospect Theory: An Analysis of Decision under Risk'. *Econometrica*, 47: 263–91.

KANGAS, OLLI (1991). *The Politics of Social Rights*. Stockholm: Swedish Institute for Social Research.

—— and PALME, JOACHIM (1993). 'Statism Eroded? Labor-Market Benefits and Challenges to the Scandinavian Welfare States', in Erik Jørgen Hansen et al. (eds.), *Welfare Trends in the Scandinavian Countries*. Armonk, NY: M. E. Sharpe, 3–24.

KAPSTEIN, ETHAN B. (1994). *Governing the Global Economy: International Finance and the State*. Cambridge, Mass.: Harvard University Press.

KATZENSTEIN, PETER J. (1984). *Corporatism and Change: Austria, Switzerland and the Politics of Industry*. Ithaca, NY: Cornell University Press.

—— (1985a). *Policy and Politics in West Germany: The Growth of a Semi-Sovereign State*. Philadelphia: Temple University Press.

—— (1985b). *Small States in World Markets*. Ithaca, NY: Cornell University Press.

KAVANAGH, DENIS (1990). *Thatcherism and British Politics: The End of Consensus?* (2nd edn.). Oxford: Oxford University Press.

KAVANAGH, E., CONSIDINE, J., DOYLE, E., GALLAGHER, L., KAVANAGH, C., and O'LEARY, E. (1997). 'The Political Economy of EMU in Ireland', in E. Jones, J. Frieden, and F. Torres (eds.), *EMU and the Smaller Countries: Joining Europe's Monetary Club*. New York: St Martin's Press, 123–48.

KENNY, LAWRENCE W. (1978). 'The Collective Allocation of Commodities in a Democratic Society: A Generalization'. *Public Choice*, 33 (2): 117–20.

KEOHANE, ROBERT O., and V. MILNER, HELEN (eds.) (1996a). *Internationalization and Domestic Politics*. Cambidge: Cambridge University Press.

—— —— (1996b). 'Internationalization and Domestic Politics: A Conclusion', in R. O. Keohane and H. V. Milner (eds.), *Internationalization and Domestic Politics*. Cambridge: Cambridge University Press, 243–58.

KIANDER, J. (1997). 'The 1995 Social Pact in Finland: Wage Restraint through Incomes Policy', in G. Fajertag and Ph. Pochet (eds.), *Social Pacts in Europe*. Brussels: European Trade Union Institute/Observatoire social européen, 135–44.

KING, DESMOND (1995). *Actively Seeking Work? The Politics of Unemployment and Welfare Policy in the United States and Great Britain*. Chicago: Chicago University Press.

—— and WOOD, STEWART (1999). 'The Political Economy of Neoliberalism: Britain and the United States in the 1980s', in Kitschelt et al. (eds.), *Continuity and Change*, 371–97.

KIRCHHEIMER, OTTO (1966). 'Germany: The Vanishing Opposition', in Robert A. Dahl (ed.), *Political Opposition in Western Democracies*. New Haven: Yale University Press, 237–59.

KITSCHELT, HERBERT (1989). 'The Internal Politics of Parties: The Law of Curvilinear Disparity Revisited'. *Political Studies*, 37 (3): 400–21.

KITSCHELT, HERBERT (1994*a*). 'Austrian and Swedish Social Democrats in Crisis: Party Strategy and Organization in Corporatist Regimes'. *Comparative Political Studies*, 27: 3–39.

—— (1994*b*). *The Transformation of European Social Democracy*. New York: Cambridge University Press.

—— in collaboration with ANTHONY J. McGANN (1995). *The Radical Right in Western Europe*. Ann Arbor: University of Michigan Press.

—— (1996). 'Defense of the Status Quo as Equilibrium Strategy? New Dilemmas for European Social Democracy'. Paper prepared for presentation at the 1996 Annual Meeting of the American Political Science Association, San Francisco, 28 Aug.–1 Sept.

—— (1997*a*). *The Radical Right in Western Europe: A Comparative Analysis*. Ann Arbor: University of Michigan Press.

—— (1997*b*). 'European Party Systems and Voting Behaviour', in Martin Rhodes, Paul Heywood and Vincent Wright (eds.), *Developments in West European Politics*. London: Macmillan, 114–30.

—— (1999). 'European Social Democracy between Political Economy and Electoral Competition', in Kitschelt et al. (eds.), *Continuity and Change*, 317–45.

—— LANGE, PETER, MARKS, GARY, and STEPHENS, JOHN D. (1999*a*). 'Conclusion. Convergence and Divergence in Advanced Capitalist Democracies', in Herbert Kitschelt, Peter Lange, Gary Marks, and John Stephens (eds.), *Continuity and Change in Contemporary Capitalism*. Cambridge: Cambridge University Press, 427–60.

—— —— —— —— (1999*b*). *Continuity and Change in Contemporary Capitalism*. New York: Cambridge University Press.

KLAUSEN, JYTTE (1995). 'Social Rights Advocacy and State Building'. *World Politics*, 47 (Jan.): 244–67.

KLEIN, RUDOLF (1989). *The Politics of the National Health Service*. London: Longman.

—— (1995). *The New Politics of the NHS* (3rd edn.). London: Longman.

—— (1998). 'Why Britain is Reforming its National Health Service—Yet Again'. *Health Affairs*, 17 (4): 111–25.

—— and O'HIGGINS, MICHAEL (1988). 'Defusing the Crisis of the Welfare State: A New Interpretation', in Theodore J. Marmor and Jerry Mashaw (eds.), *Social Security: Beyond the Rhetoric of Crisis*. Princeton: Princeton University Press, 203–25.

KLINGEMANN, HANS-DIETER, HOFFERBERT, RICHARD, and BUDGE, IAN (1994). *Parties, Policy, and Democracy*. Boulder, Colo.: Westview.

KOHLI, MARTIN, REIN, MARTIN, GUILLEMARD, ANNE-MARIE and VAN GUNSTEREN, HERMAN (1991). *Time for Retirement: Comparative Studies of Early Exit from the Labor Force*. Cambridge: Cambridge University Press.

KOLBERG, JON EIVIND (ed.) (1992). *Between Work and Social Citizenship*. Armonk, New York: M. E. Sharpe.

—— and ESPING-ANDERSEN, GØSTA (1992). 'Welfare States and Employment Regimes', in Jon Eivind Kolberg (ed.), *Between Work and Social Citizenship*.

—— and KOLSTAD, ARNE, (1992). 'Unemployment Regimes', in Jon Eivind Kolberg (ed.), *Between Work and Social Citizenship*.

KORPI, WALTER (1978). *The Working Class in Welfare Capitalism: Work, Unions and Politics in Sweden.* London: Routledge & Kegan Paul.

—— (1983). *The Democratic Class Struggle.* London: Routledge & Kegan Paul.

—— (1989). 'Power, Politics, and State Autonomy in the Development of Social Citizenship—Social Rights during Sickness in 18 OECD Countries since 1930'. *American Sociological Review,* 54 (3): 309–28.

—— (1996). 'Eurosclerosis and the Sclerosis of Objectivity: On the Role of Values among Economic Policy Experts'. *Economic Journal,* 106 (439): 1727–46.

—— (1999). 'Faces of Inequality: Gender, Class and Inequalities in Different Types of Welfare States'. Unpublished manuscript, Swedish Institute for Social Research.

—— and PALME, JOAKIM (1998). 'The Strategy of Equality and the Paradox of Redistribution'. *American Sociological Review,* 63 (5): 661–87.

KRASNER, STEPHEN D. (1989). 'Sovereignty: An Institutional Perspective', in James Caparaaso (ed.), *The Elusive State.* Thousand Oaks, CA: Sage Publications, 69–96.

KREHBIEL, KEITH (1998). *Pivotal Politics: A Theory of U.S. Lawmaking.* Chicago: University of Chicago Press.

KRIESI, H.-P. (1995). *Le Système politique suisse.* Paris: Economica.

KRUEGER, ALAN B. (1993). 'How Computers Have Changed the Wage Structure: Evidence from Microdata, 1984–89'. *Quarterly Journal of Economics,* 108 (Feb.): 33–60.

KRUGMAN, PAUL (1996). *Pop Internationalism.* Cambridge, Mass.: MIT Press.

—— and LAWRENCE, ROBERT (1994). 'Trade, Jobs, and Wages'. *Scientific American,* Apr.: 22–7.

KUHNLE, STEIN, and EITRHEIM, PAL (1999). 'The Scandinavian Model: Trends and Perspectives'. EUI European Forum Seminar Paper WS/23.

KUME, IKUO (1997). 'Cooptation or New Possibility? Japanese Labor Politics in the Era of Neo-Conservatism', in Michio Muramatsu and Frieder Naschold (eds.), *State and Administration in Japan and Germany: A Comparative Perspective on Continuity and Change.* Berlin and New York: de Gruyter: 221–45.

KURZER, PAULETTE (1993). *Business and Banking: Political Change and Economic Integration in Western Europe.* Ithaca, NY and London: Cornell University Press.

LANGE, PETER, and GARRETT, GEOFFREY (1985). 'The Politics of Growth: Strategic Interaction and Economic Performance in the Advanced Industrial Democracies'. *Journal of Politics,* 47: 792–828.

—— WALLERSTEIN, MICHAEL, and GOLDEN, MIRIAM (1995). 'The End of Corporatism? Wage Setting in the Nordic and Germanic Countries', in Sanford M. Jacoby (ed.), *The Workers of Nations: Industrial Relations in a Global Economy.* New York: Oxford University Press, 76–100.

LASH, S., and URRY, J. (1987). *The End of Organized Capitalism.* Oxford: Polity Press.

LAVER, MICHAEL, and SCHOFIELD, NORMAN (1990). *Multiparty Government: The Politics of Coalition in Europe.* Oxford: Oxford University Press.

—— and SHEPSLE, KENNETH (1996). *Making and Breaking Governments: Cabinets and Legislatures in Parliamentary Democracies.* Cambridge: Cambridge University Press.

LAYARD, RICHARD (1997). 'Sweden's Road Back to Full Employment'. *Economic and Industrial Democracy*, 18 (1).

—— NICKELL, STEPHEN, and JACKMAN, RICHARD (1994). *The Unemployment Crisis*. Oxford: Oxford University Press.

LAZONICK, WILLIAM (1990). *Comparative Advantage on the Shop Floor*. Cambridge, Mass.: Harvard University Press.

—— (1991). 'Organizations and Markets in Capitalist Development', in Bo Gustafsson (ed.), *Power and Economic Institutions: Reinterpretation of Economic History*. Aldershot: Elgar Publ., 253–301.

—— (1992). 'Business Organization and Competitive Advantage: Capitalist Transformation in the Twentieth Century', in Giovanni Dosi, Renato Gianetti, and Pier Angelo Toninelli (eds.), *Technology and Enterprise in a Historical Perspective*. Oxford: Clarendon Press, 119–63.

LEAMER, EDWARD E. (1984). *Sources of International Comparative Advantage: Theory and Evidence*. Cambridge: MIT Press.

—— (1996). 'A Trade Economist's View of U.S. Wages and "Globalization"'. Paper presented at the Political Economy of European Integration Study Group Meeting, University of California at Berkeley, Jan.

LEHMBRUCH, GERHARD (1979). 'Consociational Democracy, Class Conflict and the New Corporatism', in P. Schmitter and G. Lehmbruch (eds.), *Trends toward Corporatist Intermediation*. London: Sage, 53–61.

—— (1984). 'Concertation and the Structure of Corporatist Networks', in John H. Goldthorpe (ed.), *Order and Conflict in Contemporary Capitalism*. Oxford: Clarendon Press, 60–80.

—— (1993). 'Consociational Democracy and Corporatism in Switzerland'. *Publius: The Journal of Federalism*, 23: 43–60.

LEHNER, F. (1984). 'Consociational Democracy in Switzerland: Political-Economic Explanation and Some Empirical Evidence'. *European Journal of Political Research*, 12: 25–42.

LEIBFRIED, STEPHAN, and RIEGER, ELMAR (1998). 'Welfare State Limits to Globalization'. *Politics & Society*, 6 (24): 363–90.

LEVI, MARGARET (1996). 'Social and Unsocial Capital: A Review Essay of Robert Putnam's *Making Democracy Work*'. *Politics and Society*, 24 (1): 45–55.

LEVIT, KATHARINE R., LAZENBY, HELEN C., BRADEN, BRADLY R., and the National Health Accounts Team (1998). 'National Health Spending Trends in 1996'. *Health Affairs*, 17 (1): 35–51.

LEVY, JONAH (1999). 'Vice into Virtue? Progressive Politics and Welfare Reform in Continental Europe'. *Politics & Society*, 27 (2): 239–73.

LEWIS-BECK, MICHAEL (1988). *Economics and Elections: The Major Western Democracies*. Ann Arbor: University of Michigan Press.

LIEBOWITZ, STANLEY, and MARGOLIS, STEPHEN (1995). 'Path Dependence, Lock-In and History'. *Journal of Law, Economics and Organization*, 11 (1): 205–26.

LIGHT, DONALD (1997). 'Lessons for the United States: Britain's Experience with Managed Competition', in John D. Wilkerson, Kelly J. Devers, and Ruth S. Given (eds.), *Competitive Managed Care*. San Francisco: Jossey-Bass, 322–56.

LIGHT, PAUL (1985). *Artful Work: The Politics of Social Security Reform*. New York: Random House.

LIJPHART, AREND (1984). *Democracies: Pattern of Majoritarian and Consensus Government in Twenty-One Countries*. New Haven and London: Yale University Press.

—— (1997). 'Unequal Participation: Democracy's Unresolved Dilemma—Presidential Address'. *American Political Science Review*, 91: 1–14.

—— and CREPAZ, MARKUS (1991). 'Corporatism and Consensus Democracy in Eighteen Countries: Conceptual and Empirical Linkages'. *British Journal of Political Science*, 21: 235–56.

LIND, J. (1997). 'EMU and Collective Bargaining in Denmark', in G. Fajertag and Ph. Pochet (eds.), *Social Pacts in Europe*. Brussels: European Trade Union Institute/Observatoire social européen, 145–56.

LINDBECK, ASSAR (1994). *Turning Sweden Around*. Cambridge, Mass.: MIT Press.

LINDBLOM, CHARLES E. (1977). *Politics and Markets: The World's Political-Economic Systems*. New York: Basic Books.

—— (1982). 'The Market as Prison'. *Journal of Politics*, 44 (2): 324–36.

LINDBOM, ANDERS (1999). 'Dismantling the Social Democratic Welfare Model? Has the Swedish Welfare State Lost Its Defining Characteristics?'. Paper Presented to Workshop 26, European Consortium for Political Research, Mannheim, Mar.

LUEBBERT, GREGORY (1991). *Liberalism, Fascism, and Social Democracy*. New York: Oxford University.

LUNDGREN, HÅKAN (1994). *Sacred Cows and the Future—On the Change of System in the Labour Market*. Stockholm: SAF.

MCCARTNEY, J., and TEAGUE, P. (1997). 'Workplace Innovations in the Republic of Ireland'. *Economic and Social Review*, 28 (4): 381–99.

MACKIE, THOMAS T., and ROSE, RICHARD (1991). *The International Almanac of Electoral History* (3rd edn.). London: Macmillan.

MCGANN, ANTHONY J. (1999). 'The Modal Voter Result: Preference Distributions, Intra-Party Competition and Political Dominance'. Ph.D. thesis. Duke University, Department of Political Science.

—— and KITSCHELT, HERBERT (1995). 'Electoral Trade-offs and Strategic Choices of Social Democratic Parties in the 1990s'. Paper prepared for the 1995 Annual Meeting of the American Political Science Association, Chicago, 31 Aug.–3 Sept.

MCKENZIE, RICHARD, and LEE, DWIGHT (1991). *Quicksilver Capital: How the Rapid Movement of Wealth Has Changed the World*. New York: Free Press.

MCKINSEY GLOBAL INSTITUTE (1992). *Service Sector Productivity*. Washington, DC.

MACLEAN, DINAH (1996). 'Lagging Productivity Growth in the Service Sector: Mismeasurement, Mismanagement or Misinformation?'. Bank of Canada Working Paper, 97–6.

MAGALONI, BEATRIZ (1997). 'The Dynamics of Dominant Party Decline: The Mexican Transition to Multipartism'. Ph.D. thesis. Department of Political Science, Duke University.

MAIER, CHARLES (1985). 'Inflation and Stagnation as Politics and History', in Leon Lindberg and Charles Maier (eds.), *The Politics of Inflation and Economic Stagnation*. Washington, DC: Brookings, 3–24.

MANOW, PHILIP (1997a). 'Social Insurance and the German Political Economy'. Paper presented at the conference 'Germany and Japan: The Breaking Up of Nationally Organized Capitalism?'. University of Washington, Seattle, 10–12 April;

and to the Seminar on State and Capitalism since 1800, Center for European Studies, Harvard University, 16 April.

—— (1997*b*). 'Structural Characteristics and Potential Effects of Current Reforms in the German Health Care System'. July. Typescript.

—— and SEILS, ERIC (1999). 'Adjusting Badly: The German Welfare State, Structural Change and the Open Economy', forthcoming in Fritz W. Scharpf and Vivien A. Schmidt (eds.), *From Vulnerability to Competitiveness: Welfare and Work in the Open Economy*. New York: Oxford University Press.

MARES, ISABELA (1996). 'Firms and the Welfare State: The Emergence of New Forms of Unemployment'. WZB Discussion Paper FS I 96–308. Science Center, Berlin.

—— (1997*a*). 'Interwar Responses to the Problem of Unemployment: A Game-Theoretical Analysis'. Paper presented at the American Political Science Association Annual Meeting, Washington, DC, 28–31 Aug.

—— (1997*b*). 'Is Unemployment Insurable? Employers and the Introduction of Unemployment Insurance'. *Journal of Public Policy*, 17 (3): 299–327.

—— (1998). 'Negotiated Risks: Employers and Welfare State Development'. Ph.D. thesis. Harvard University.

MARIMON, R. (1997). *Reconsidering Spanish Unemployment*, Els Opuscules del Crei (Centre de Recerca en Economia Internacional), No. 1, Universitat Pompeu Fabra, Barcelona.

MARKLUND, STEFFAN (1988). *Paradise Lost? The Nordic Welfare States in the Recession 1975–1985*. Lund: Arkiv.

MARSHALL, T. H. (1963). 'Citizenship and Social Class', in *Sociology at the Crossroads, and Other Essays*. London: Heinemann, 67–127.

MARSTON, RICHARD C. (1995). *International Financial Integration: A Study of Interest Differentials between the Major Industrial Countries*. New York: Cambridge University Press.

MARTIN, ANDREW (1992). *Wage Bargaining and Swedish Politics: The Political Implications of the End of Central Negotiations*. Stockholm: FIEF (Trade Union Institute for Economic Research).

—— (1996). 'What Does Globalization Have to Do With the Erosion of Welfare States? Sorting Out the Issues'. *ARENA Working Paper*, No. 17, Oct.

—— (1997). 'Social Pacts: a Means for Distributing Unemployment or Achieving Full Employment?', in G. Fajertag and Ph. Pochet (eds.), *Social Pacts in Europe*. Brussels: European Trade Union Institute/Observatoire social européen, 37–44.

—— (1998). 'EMU and Wage Bargaining: The Americanization of the European Labor Market?'. Paper prepared for the 11th International Conference of Europeanists, Baltimore, 26–28 Feb.

MARTIN, CATHIE Jo (1995*a*). 'Nature or Nurture? Sources of Firm Preference for National Health Reform'. *American Political Science Review*, 89 (4): 898–913.

—— (1995*b*). 'Stuck in Neutral: Big Business and the Politics of National Health Reform'. *Journal of Health Politics, Policy and Law*, 20 (2): 431–6.

MAYNARD, ALAN (1991). 'Developing the Health Care Market'. *Economic Journal*, 101 (Sept.): 1277–86.

MELTZER, ALAN, and RICHARD, SCOTT (1981). 'A Rational Theory of the Size of the Government'. *Journal of Political Economy*, 8 (9): 914–27.

MERRIEN, F.-X. (1991). 'L'État par défaut', in J.-P. Durand and F.-X. Merrien (eds.), *Sortie de siècle: La France en mutation.* Paris: Vigot, 273–93.

MILNER, HELEN (1988). *Resisting Protectionism.* Cambridge: Cambridge University Press.

Ministry of Health and Central Office of Information (UK) (no date). *The National Health Service.* London: HMSO.

MISHRA, RAMESH (1993). 'Social Policy in the Post-Modern World', in Catherine Jones (ed.), *New Perspectives on the Welfare State in Europe.* New York: Routledge, 18–40.

MITCHELL, DEBORAH (1991). *Income Transfers in Ten Welfare States.* Brookfield: Avebury.

MJØSET, LARS (1987). 'Nordic Economic Policies in the 1970s and 1980s'. *International Organization*, 41 (3): 403–56.

—— (1996). 'Nordic Economic Policies in the 1980s and 1990s'. Paper presented at the Tenth International Conference of Europeanists, Chicago.

MOE, TERENCE (1990). 'Political Institutions—The Neglected Side of the Story'. *Journal of Law, Economics and Organization*, 6.

MOENE, KARL OVE, and WALLERSTEIN, MICHAEL (1996). 'Self-Interested Support for Welfare Spending'. Paper presented at the Annual Meeting of the American Political Science Association, San Francisco, 29 Aug.–1 Sept.

—— —— (1999). 'Social Democratic Labor Market Institutions: A Retrospective Analysis', in Herbert Kitschelt, Peter Lange, Gary Marks, and John D. Stephens (eds.), *Continuity and Change in Contemporary Capitalism.* New York: Cambridge University Press, 231–60.

MORAN, MICHAEL (1977). *The Politics of Industrial Relations: The Origins, Life, and Death of the 1971 Industrial Relations Act.* London: Macmillan.

MOSES, JONATHON (1994). 'Abdication from National Policy Autonomy: What's Left to Leave?'. *Politics and Society*, 22 (2): 125–48.

—— (1995). 'The Social Democratic Predicament in the Emerging European Union'. *Journal of European Public Policy*, 2 (3): 407–26.

MOSLEY, LAYNA (1998). 'Strong but Narrow: International Financial Market Pressures and Welfare State Policies'. Paper presented at the Eleventh Annual Conference of Europeanists, Baltimore, 26–28 Feb.

MUELLER, DENNIS C., and MURRELL, PETER (1986). 'Interest Groups and the Size of Government'. *Public Choice*, 48 (2): 125–45.

MUELLER, F. (1996). 'National Stakeholders in the Global Contest for Corporate Investment'. *European Journal of Industrial Relations*, 2 (3): 345–66.

MURRAY, I. (1994). 'Unemployment Benefits in Europe: UK Bottom of "Social Insurance" League'. Working Brief, Oct. London: Unemployment Unit.

MYLES, JOHN (1988). 'Postwar Capitalism and the Extension of Social Security into a Retirement Wage', in Margaret Weir, Ann Shola Orloff, and Theda Skocpol (eds.), *The Politics of Social Policy in the United States.* Princeton: Princeton University Press, 265–84.

—— (1989). *Old Age in the Welfare State: The Political Economy of Public Pensions.* Lawrence: University Press of Kansas.

—— 'When Markets Fail: Social Welfare in Canada and the United States', in G. Esping-Andersen (ed.), *Welfare States in Transition.* London: Sage, 116–40.

MYLES, JOHN (1997). 'How to Design a "Liberal" Welfare State: A Comparison of Canada and the United States'. Paper prepared for the Conference on 'Models of Capitalism and Latin American Development', Chapel Hill, University of North Carolina, May.

—— (1998). 'Discussion of Kent Weaver's "The Politics of Pensions: Lessons from Abroad"', in R. Douglas Arnold, Michael Graetz, and Alicia Munnell (eds.), *Framing the Social Security Debate: Values, Politics and Economics*. Washington, DC: National Academy of Social Insurance, 237–48.

—— (1999). 'The Maturation of Canada's Retirement Income System: Income Levels, Income Inequality and Low Income among the Elderly'. Unpublished manuscript.

—— and PIERSON, PAUL (1997). 'Friedman's Revenge: The Reform of "Liberal" Welfare States in Canada and the United States'. *Politics and Society*, 25: 443–72.

—— and QUADAGNO, JILL (1997). 'Recent Trends in Public Pension Reform: A Comparative View', in Keith Banting and Robin Boadway (eds.), *Reform of Retirement Income Policy: International and Canadian Perspectives*. Kingston: Queen's University School of Policy Studies, 247–71.

MYRDAL, GUNNAR (1957). 'Economic Nationalism and Internationalism'. *Australian Outlook*, 11 (4), December, 3–50.

NAU, G. (1998). 'Les Offices régionaux de placement passent à la consolidation'. *Sécurité Sociale*, 1: 40–1.

NEGRELLI, S. (1997). 'Social Pacts and Flexibility: Towards a New Balance between Macro and Micro Industrial Relations: The Italian Experience', in G. Fajertag and Ph. Pochet (eds.), *Social Pacts in Europe*. Brussels: European Trade Union Institute/Observatoire social européen, 45–62.

NEIDHART, L. (1970). *Plebiszit und pluralitäre Democratie: Eine Analyse der Funktionen des Schweizerischen Gesetzreferendums*. Berne: Francke.

NESBITT, S. (1995). *British Pension Policy Making in the 1980s: The Rise and Fall of A Policy Community*. Aldershot: Avebury.

NICHOLLS, ANTHONY (1994). *Freedom with Responsibility: The Social Market Economy in Germany 1918–1963*. Oxford: Oxford University Press.

NICKELL, STEPHEN (1996). 'Can Unemployment in the United Kingdom be Reduced?', in David Halpern, Stewart Wood, Stuart White, and Gavin Cameron (eds.), *Options for Britain: A Strategic Policy Review*, Basingstoke: Dartmouth.

—— (1997). 'Unemployment and Labor Market Rigidities: Europe versus North America'. *Journal of Economic Perspectives*, 11 (3): 55–74.

NOBLE, CHARLES (1997). *Welfare as We Knew It: A Political History of the American Welfare State*. New York: Oxford University Press.

NORTH, DOUGLASS C. (1990). *Institutions, Institutional Change, and Economic Performance*. Cambridge: Cambridge University Press.

—— and WEINGAST, BARRY (1989). 'Constitutions and Commitment: The Evolution of Institutions Governing Public Choice in Seventeenth Century England'. *Journal of Economic History*, 49 (4): 803–32.

NOTERMANS, TON (1993). 'The Abdication of National Policy Autonomy: Why the Macroeconomic Policy Regime Has Become So Unfavorable to Labor'. *Politics and Society*, 21 (2): 133–67.

—— (1999). *Money, Markets and the State*. Cambridge: Cambridge University Press.

OBINGER, H. (1998). *Politische Institutionen und Sozialpolitik in der Schweiz.* Frankfurt: Lang.

OBSTFELD, MAURICE (1995). 'International Capital Mobility in the 1990s', in Peter Kenen (ed.), *Understanding Interdependence: The Macroeconomics of the Open Economy.* Princeton: Princeton University Press, 201–61.

O'CONNOR, JULIA S. (1996). 'From Women in the Welfare State to Gendering Welfare State Regimes'. *Current Sociology,* 44 (2): 1–124.

—— ORLOFF, ANN SHOLA, and SHAVER, SHEILA (1999). *States, Markets, Families: Gender, Liberalism and Social Policy in Australia, Canada, Great Britain and the United States.* Cambridge: Cambridge University Press.

O'DONNELL, R. (1998). 'Social Partnership in Ireland: Principles and Interpretations', in R. O'Donnell and J. Larragy (eds.), *Negotiated Economic and Social Governance and European Integration.* Brussels: European Commission, Directorate-General, Science, Research and Development, 84–106.

OECD (1988). *Aging Populations: The Social Policy Implications.* Paris: OECD.

—— (1992). *International Direct Investment: Policies and Trends in the 1980s.* Paris: OECD.

—— (1994*a*). 'Collective Bargaining: Levels and Coverage', in *OECD Employment Outlook.* Paris: OECD, 167–91.

—— (1994*b*). *New Orientations for Social Policy.* Paris: OECD.

—— (1994*c*). *OECD Jobs Study: Evidence and Explanations.* Paris: OECD.

—— (1994*d*). *The OECD Jobs Study: Facts, Analysis, Strategies.* Paris: OECD.

—— (1995*a*). 'Effects of Ageing Populations on Government Budgets'. *OECD Economic Outlook,* 57 (June): 33–42.

—— (1995*b*). *Historical Statistics 1960–93.* Paris: OECD.

—— (1995*c*). *Income Distribution in OECD Countries.* Paris: OECD.

—— (1995*d*). *The Jobs Study: Taxation, Employment, and Unemployment.* Paris: OECD.

—— (1995*e*). *OECD Review of Foreign Direct Investment: Denmark.* OECD: Paris.

—— (1996*a*). *Aging Populations, Pension Systems and Government Budgets.* Paris: OECD.

—— (1996*b*). *Employment Outlook,* July (1996). Paris: OECD.

—— (1996*c*). *International Capital Market Statistics: 1950–1995.* Paris: OECD.

—— (1996*d*). *OECD Economic Surveys: Germany 1995–1996.* Paris: OECD.

—— (1996*e*). *OECD Economies at a Glance: Structural Indicators.* Paris: OECD.

—— (1996*f*). *Services.* Paris: OECD.

—— (1996*g*). 'Social Expenditure Statistics of OECD Members Countries'. *Labour Market and Social Policy,* Occasional Paper No. 17. Paris: OECD.

—— (1996*h*). 'The Experience of Fiscal Consolidation in OECD Countries'. *OECD Economic Outlook,* 59 (June) 33–41.

—— (1997*a*). *Employment Outlook.* Paris: OECD.

—— (1997*b*). 'Reforming the Health Sector: Efficiency through Incentives', in OECD Economic Surveys: Germany 1996–1997. Paris: OECD, 67–117.

—— (1998*a*). *Economic Survey: Australia 1998.* Paris: OECD.

—— (1998*b*). *Employment Outlook.* Paris: OECD.

—— (1998*c*). *OECD Economic Surveys: Germany.* Paris: OECD.

—— (1998*d*). *OECD Economic Surveys, 1997–1998: Netherlands.* Paris: OECD.

—— (1998*e*). *OECD Health Data 98: A Comparative Analysis of 29 Countries.* Paris: OECD, CD rom.

OECD (1998*f*). *Maintaining Prosperity in an Ageing Society*. Paris: OECD.
—— (various dates). *Financial Market Trends*. Paris: OECD.
OFFE, CLAUS (1972). *Struckturprobleme des kapitalistischen Staates*. Frankfurt. Main: Suhrkamp.
—— (1991). 'Smooth Consolidation in the West German Welfare States', in Frances Fox Piven (ed.), *Labor Parties in Postindustrial Societies*. New York: Polity Press, 124–46.
OHMAE, KENICHE (1991). *the Borderless World: Power and Strategy in the Interlinked Economy*. New York: Harper Perennial.
O'KEEFE, ANNE MARIE (1995). 'Will ERISA's Wall Come Tumbling Down?'. *Business and Health*, 35–40 Feb.
OLSON, MANCUR, JR (1982). *The Rise and Decline of Nations*. New Haven: Yale University Press.
ORLOFF, ANN SHOLA (1993). 'Gender and the Social Rights of Citizenship: The Comparative Analysis of Gender Relations and Welfare States'. *American Sociological Review*, 58: 303–28.
—— (1999). 'The Significance of Changing Gender Relations and Family Forms for Systems of Social Protection'. Study prepared for the World Labour Report 1999 of the International Labour Organization.
OVERBYE, EINAR (1997). 'Mainstream Pattern, Deviant Cases: The New Zealand and Danish Pension Systems in an International Context'. *Journal of European Social Policy*, 7: 101–17.
PALACIOS, ROBERT, and ROCHA, ROBERTO (1997). 'The Hungarian Pension System in Transition'. World Bank.
PALIER, BRUNO (1997). 'A "Liberal" Dynamic in the Transformation of the French Social Welfare System', in Jochen Clasen (ed.), *Social Insurance in Europe*. Bristol: Policy Press, 84–106.
PALME, JOAKIM (1990). *Pension Rights in Welfare Capitalism*. Stockholm: Swedish Institute for Social Research.
—— (1994). 'Recent Developments in Income Transfer Systems in Sweden', in Niels Ploug and Jon Kvist (eds.), *Recent Trends in Cash Benefits in Europe*. Copenhagen: Danish National Institute of Social Research, 39–59.
—— and WENNEMO, IRENE (1997). 'Swedish Social Security in the 1990s: Reform and Retrenchment'. Copenhagen: Centre for Welfare State Research, Working Paper 9.
PALMER, EDWARD (1998). 'The Swedish Pension Reform Model: Framework and Issues'. Stockholm: National Social Insurance Board.
PAULY, LOUIS (1988). *Opening Financial Markets: Banking Politics in the Pacific Rim*. Ithaca, NY: Cornell University Press.
—— (1995). 'Capital Mobility, State Autonomy, and Political Legitimacy'. *Journal of International Affairs*, 48 (2): 369–88.
—— and REICH, SIMON (1997). 'National Structures and Multinational Corporate Behaviour: Enduring Differences in the Age of Globalization', *International Organization*, 51 (1): 1–30.
PEKKARINEN, J., POHJOLA, M., and ROWTHORN, B. (1992). 'Social Corporatism and Economic Performance: Introduction and Conclusions', in J. Pekkarinen, M. Pohjola, and B. Rowthorn (eds.), *Social Corporatism: A Superior Economic Ststem?* Oxford: Clarendon Press.

PEMPEL, T. J. (1990). 'Exclusionary Democracies: The Postauthoritarian Experience', in Peter J. Katzenstein, Theodore Lowi, Sidney Tarrow (eds.), *Comparative Theory and Political Experience: Mario Einaudi and the Liberal Tradition*. Ithaca, NY: Cornell University Press, 97–118.

—— (1997). 'Labor Exclusion and Privatized Welfare: Two Keys to Asian Capitalist Development'. Paper prepared for the Conference on Comparative Capitalisms, University of North Carolina, Chapel Hill, 23–25 May.

—— (1998). *Regime Shift: Comparative Dynamics of the Japanese Political Economy.* Ithaca, NY: Cornell University Press.

PÉREZ, SOPHIA A. (1999). 'The Resurgence of National Bargaining in Europe: Expalining the Italian and Spanish Experiences'. Working Paper 1999/130, Centro de Estudios Avazados en Ciencias Sociales, Instituto Juan March de Estudios e Investigaciones.

PERRATON, J., GOLDBLATT, D., HELD, D., and McGREW, A. (1997). 'The Globalization of Economic Activity'. *New Political Economy*, 2 (2): 257–77.

PESTOFF, VICTOR A. (1991). 'The Demise of the Swedish Model and the Resurgence of organized Business as a Major Political Actor'. Working Paper PP1991: 2, Stockholm University, Department of Business Administration.

—— (1995). 'Towards a New Swedish Model of Collective Bargaining and Politics', in C. Crouch and F. Traxler (eds.), *Organized Industrial Relations in Europe: What Future?* Aldershot: Avebury.

PETERS, B. GUY (1998). *The Future of Governing*. Pittsburgh: University of Pittsburgh Press.

—— (1999). *American Public Policy: Promise and Performance* (5th edn.). New York and London: Chatham House.

PETTERSEN, PER ARNT (1995). 'The Welfare State: The Security Dimension', in Ole Borre (ed.), *The Scope of Government*. Oxford: Oxford University Press, 198–233.

PFALLER, ALFRED, GOUGH, IAN, and THERBORN, GORAN (1991). *Can the Welfare State Compete?* London: Macmillan.

PFITZMAN, H. (1995). 'La Nouvelle Législation sur l'assurance chômage', *Securité Sociale*, 5: 271–4.

PIERSON, CHRISTOPHER (1991). *Beyond the Welfare State?* Cambridge: Polity Press.

—— (1998). 'Globalisation and the Changing Governance of Welfare States: Superannuation Reform in Australia'. *Global Society*, 12 (1): 31–47.

PIERSON, PAUL (1993a). 'Welfare State Regimes in the New European Economy'. Paper presented at the Workshop on European Political Economy and Institutional Analysis, WZB Berlin, July.

—— (1993b). 'When Effect Becomes Cause: Policy Feedback and Political Change'. *World Politics*, 45: 595–628.

—— (1994). *Dismantling the Welfare State? Reagan, Thatcher and the Politics of Retrenchment*. Cambridge: Cambridge University Press.

—— (1995). 'The Scope and Nature of Business Power: Employers and the American Welfare State, 1900–1935'. Typescript, 6 July.

—— (1996). 'The New Politics of the Welfare State'. *World Politics*, 48 (2): 143–79.

—— (1997a). 'Path Dependence and the Study of Politics'. Florence: Robert Schuman Centre, European University Institute, Jan.

PIERSON, PAUL (1997*b*). 'Path Dependence. Increasing Returns, and the Study of Politics'. Center for European Studies, Harvard University, Working Paper No. 7.

—— (1997*c*). 'The Politics of Pension Reform', in Keith G. Banting and Robin Boadway (eds.), *Reform of Retirement Income Policy*. Kingston, Ontario: School of Policy Studies, Queen's University, 273–93.

—— (1997*d*). 'Skeptical Reflection on "Globalization" and the Welfare State'. Paper presented at the International Conference on Socio-Economics, Montreal, July.

—— (1998). 'Irresistible Forces, Immovable Objects: Post-Industrial Welfare States Confront Permanent Austerity'. *Journal of European Public Policy*, 5 (4): 539–60.

—— (2000). 'Increasing Returns, Path Dependence, and the Study of Politics! *American Political Science Review*, 94 (2), 251–67.

—— and Smith, Miriam (1993). 'Bourgeois Revolutions? The Policy Consequences of Resurgent Conservatism'. *Comparative Political Studies*, 25 (4): 487–520.

—— and WEAVER, KENT (1993). 'Imposing Losses in Pension Policy', in Kent Weaver and Bert Rockman (eds.), *Do Institutions Matter? Government Capabilities in the United States and Abroad*. Washington, DC: Brookings Institution.

PILAT, DIRK (1996). 'Competition, Productivity and Efficiency'. *OECD Economic Studies*, No. 27: 107–46.

PITRUZZELLO, SALVATORE (1997). 'Social Policy and the Implementation of the Maastricht Fiscal Convergence Criteria: The Italian and French Attempts at Welfare and Pension Reforms'. *Social Research*, 64 (4): 1589–1642.

PIVEN, FRANCES FOX (1991). *Labor Parties in Postindustrial Societies*. New York: Oxford University Press.

—— (1992). 'Structural Constraints and Political Development: The Case of the American Democratic Party', in Francis Fox Piven (ed.), *Labor Parties in Postindustrial Societies*. New York: Oxford University Press, 235–64.

PLOUG, NILS, and KVIST, JON (eds.) (1994). *Recent Trends in Cash Benefits in Europe* (Social Security in Europe 4). Copenhagen: Danish National Institute of Social Research.

—— —— (eds.) (1996). *Social Security in Europe: Development or Dismantlement* (Social Security in Europe 1). Copenhagen: Danish National Institute of Social Research.

POCHET, PHILIPPE, and FAJERTAG, GUISEPPE (eds.) (1997). *Social Pacts in Europe*. Brussels: ETUI.

POLANYI, KARL (1944 [1957]). *The Great Transformation: The Political and Economic Origins of Our Time*. Boston: Beacon Press.

POLZER, KARL, and BUTLER, PATRICIA A. (1997). 'Employee Health Plan Protection under ERISA'. *Health Affairs*, 16 (5): 93–102.

PONTUSSON, JONAS (1992). 'At the End of the Third Road: Swedish Social Democracy in Crisis'. *Politics and Society*, 20 (3) (Sept.): 305–32.

—— (1996). 'Wage Distribution and Labor Market Institutions in Sweden, Austria, and Other OECD Countries'. Institute for European Studies, Cornell University, Working Paper No. 96.4

—— (1997). 'Between Neo-Liberalism and the German Model: Swedish Capitalism in Transition', in Colin Crouch and Wolfgang Streeck (eds.), *Political Economy of Modern Capitalism: Mapping Convergence and Diversity*. London: Sage.

—— and SWENSON, PETER (1996). 'Labor Markets, Production Strategies, and Wage Bargaining Institutions: The Swedish Employer Offensive in Comparative Perspective'. *Comparative Political Studies*, 29 (Apr.): 223–50.

PRD (Parti Radical Démocratique) (1988). 'Avenir de l'AVS. Rapport final d'un groupe de travail du Parti radical-démocratique suisse'. *Revue Politique*, 67 (2): 34–45.

PRIDHAM, GEOFFREY (1977). *Christian Democracy in Western Germany: The CDU/CSU in Government and Opposition 1945–1976*. London: Croom Helm.

PRZEWORSKI, ADAM, and WALLERSTEIN, MICHAEL (1988). 'Structural Dependence of the State on Capital'. *American Political Science Review*, 82: 11–30.

PSS/USS (Parti Socialiste Suisse/ Union Syndicale Suisse) (1987). *Droits égaux dans l'AVS. Propositions du Parti socialiste suisse et de l'Union syndicale suisse pour la révision de l'AVS*. PSS/USS, Berne.

PUTNAM, ROBERT (1993). *Making Democracy Work: Civic Traditions in Modern Italy*. Princeton: Princeton University Press.

Québec, Government of (1996). *For You and Your Children: Guaranteeing the Future of the Québec Pension Plan*. Quebec City.

QUINN, DENNIS (1997). 'The Correlates of Change in International Financial Regulation'. *American Political Science Review*, 91 (3): 531–52.

—— and INCLAN, CARLA (1997). 'The Origin of Financial Openness: A Study of Current and Capital Account Internationalization'. *American Journal of Political Science*, 41 (3): 771–813.

RAGIN, CHARLES C. (1987). *The Comparative Method: Moving Beyond Qualitative and Quantitative Strategies*. Berkeley: University of California Press.

RANDALL'S PARLIAMENTARY SERVICES (1986). *Comparison of Party Policies: Pension Policies*.

REGINI, M. (1999). 'Between De-Regulation and Social Pacts: The Responses of European Economies to Globalization'. Working Paper 1999/113, Centro de Estudios Avazados en Ciencias Sociales, Instituto Juan March de Estudios e Investigaciones.

—— and REGALIA, I. (1997). 'Employers, Unions and the State: The Resurgence of Concertation in Italy?'. *West European Politics*, 25 (1): 210–30 (special issue on 'Italy between Crisis and Transition', ed. M. Bull and M. Rhodes).

REINHARDT, UWE (1992). 'The United States: Breakthroughs and Waste'. *Journal of Health Politics, Policy and Law*, Winter: 637–66.

—— (1995). 'Turning Our Gaze from Bread and Circus Games'. *Health Affairs*, 14 (1): 33–6.

REISSERT, BERND (1994). 'The Regional Impact of Unemployment Insurance and Active Labour Market Policy: An International Comparison', in Duncan Campbell and Werner Sengenberger (eds.), *Creating Economic Opportunities: The Role of Labour Standards in Industrial Restructuring*. Geneva: International Institute for Labour Studies.

REYNAUD, EMMANUEL (1995). 'Financing Retirement Pensions: Pay-As-You-Go and Funded Systems in the European Union'. *International Social Security Review*, 48: 41–58.

—— (1997). 'L'Avenir des retraites en debat'. *Chronique International de l'IRES*, 48: 5–16.

RHODES, MARTIN (1995). 'Regional Development and Employment in Europe's Southern and Western Peripheries', in Martin Rhodes (ed.), *The Regions and the New Europe*, Manchester: Manchester University Press, 273–328.

—— (1996a). 'Globalization and the Welfare State: A Critical Review of Recent Debates'. *European Journal of Social Policy*, 6 (4): 305–27.

—— (1996b). 'Subversive Liberalism'. *Journal of European Public Policy*, 2 (3) (Sept.): 384–406.

—— (1997a). 'Southern European Welfare States: Identity, Problems and Prospects for Reform', in Martin Rhodes (ed.), *Southern European Welfare States: Between Crisis and Reform*. London: Frank Cass, 1–22.

—— (1997b). 'The Welfare State: Internal Challenges, External Constraints', in Martin Rhodes, Paul Heywood, and Vincent Wright (eds.), *Developments in West European Politics*. London: Macmillan, 57–74.

—— (1997c). 'Spain', in Hugh Compston (ed.), *The New Politics of Unemployment*. London: Routledge, 103–22.

—— (1998). 'Globalisation, Labour Markets and Welfare States: A Future of Competitive Corporatism?', in Martin Rhodes and Yves Mény, *The Future of European Welfare: A New Social Contract?* London: Macmillan, 178–203.

—— and VAN APELDOORN, BASTIAN (1998). 'Capital Unbound? The Transformation of European Corporate Governance'. *Journal of European Public Policy*, 5 (3): 407–28.

RIEGER, ELMAR, and LEIBFRIED, STEPHAN (1998). 'Welfare State Limits to Globalization'. *Politics and Society*, 26 (3): 363–90.

RIKER, WILLIAM (1982). *Liberalism Against Populism*. San Francisco: Freeman.

ROBERTSON, JOHN (1976). *A Theory of Party Competition*. London: Wiley.

ROCHA PIMENTEL, J. M. (1993). 'Concertação social e política de rendimentos em Portugal: Experiência recente e perspectivas para a década de 80'. *Economia*, 17 (2): 357–94.

ROCHE, W. K. (1998). 'Between Regime Fragmentation and Realignment: Irish Industrial Relations in the 1990s'. *Industrial Relations Journal*, 29 (2): 113–25.

—— and GEARY, J. F. (1999). 'Collaborative Production and the Irish Boom: Work Organization, Partnership and Direct Involvement in Irish Workplaces'. Mimeo.

RODRIK, DANI (1996). 'Why Do More Open Economies Have Bigger Governments?'. NBER Working Paper No. 5537.

—— (1997). *Has Globalization Gone too Far?* Washington, DC: Institute for International Economics.

—— (1998). 'Why Do More Open Economies Have Larger Governments?'. *Journal of Political Economy*, 106 (Oct.): 997–1932.

ROGOFF, KENNETH (1996). 'The Purchasing Power Parity Puzzle'. *Journal of Economic Literature*, 34 (2): 647–68.

ROGOWSKI, RONALD (1987). 'Trade and the Variety of Democratic Institutions'. *International Organization*, 41 (Spring): 203–23.

ROLLER, EDELTRAUT (1995a). 'Political Agendas and Beliefs about the Scope of Government', in Ole Borre (ed.), *The Scope of Government*. Oxford: Oxford University Press, 55–86.

—— (1995b). 'The Welfare State: The Equality Dimension', in Ole Borre (ed.), *The Scope of Government*. Oxford: Oxford University Press, 165–97.

ROSANVALLON, P. (1995). *La Nouvelle Question sociale: Repenser l'État-Providence*. Paris: Seuil.

ROSEN, STEPHEN (1996). 'Public Employment and the Welfare State in Sweden'. *Journal of Economic Literature*, 34 (June): 729–40.

ROSS, FIONA (1998). 'A Framework for Studying Unpopular Policies: Partisan Possibilities, Institutional Liabilities and the Anti-State Agenda'. Unpublished manuscript.

ROSS, ROBERT J. S., and TRACHTE, KENT C. (1990). *Global Capitalism: The New Leviathan*. Albany: State University of New York Press.

ROTHENBACHER, FRANZ (1997). 'Public Sector Employment in Europe: Where Will the Decline End?'. *Eurodata Newsletter*, No. 6 (Autumn): 1–11.

ROTHSTEIN, BO (1991). 'Explaining Swedish Corporatism: The Formative Moment'. *Scandinavian Political Studies*, 15 (3): 173–92.

—— (1992). 'Labor Institutions and Working Class Strength', in Sven Steinmo, Kathleen Thelen, and Frank Longstrength (eds.), *Structuring Politics: Historical Institutionalism in Comparative Analysis*. Cambridge: Cambridge University Press, 33–56.

—— (1996). *The Social Democratic State*. Pittsburgh: University of Pittsburgh Press.

—— (1998a). 'The Future of the Universal Welfare State—An Institutional Approach'. Unpublished manuscript.

—— (1998b). *Just Institutions Matter: The Moral and Political Logic of the Universal Welfare State*. Cambridge: Cambridge University Press.

ROUBINI, NOURIEL, and SACHS, JEFFREY D. (1989). 'Political and Economic Determinants of Budget Deficits in the Industrial Democracies'. *European Economic Review*, 33 (May): 903–33.

ROWTHORN, ROBERT (1995). 'Capital Formation and Unemployment'. *Oxford Review of Economic Policy*, 11 (1): 29–39.

—— and RAMASWAMY, RAMANA (1997). 'Deindustrialization: Causes and Implications', in *IMF Working Papers*. Washington, DC: International Monetary Fund, WP/97/42, Apr.

RUGGIE, JOHN GERARD (1982). 'International Regimes, Transactions, and Change: Embedded Liberalism in the Postwar Economic Order'. *International Organization*, 36 (2): 379–415.

—— (1994). 'Trade, Protectionism, and the Future of Welfare Capitalism'. *Journal of International Affairs*, 48 (1): 1–11.

—— (1997). 'Globalization and the Embedded Liberalism Compromise: The End of an Era?'. MPIfG Working Paper 97/1. Cologne: Max-Planck Institute for the Study of Societies.

RUIGROK, W., and VAN TULDER, R. (1995). *The Logic of International Restructuring*. London: Routledge.

RUSSELL, LOUISE (1979). *Technology in Hospitals: Medical Advances and their Diffusion*. Washington, DC: Brookings.

SAEGER, STEPHEN S. (1997). 'Globalization and Deindustrialization: Myth and Reality in the OECD'. *Weltwirtschaftliches Archiv*, 133 (4): 579–608.

SAF (Svenska Arbetsgivareföreningen) (1998). *Facts about the Swedish Economy 1998*. Stockholm: SAF.

SAINSBURY, DIANE (ed.) (1994). *Gendering Welfare States*. London: Sage Publications.

—— (1996). *Gender, Equality, and Welfare States*. New York: Cambridge University Press.

ST JOHN, SUSAN (1998). 'Superannuation in the 1990s: Where Angels Fear to Tread'. University of Auckland.

SAKANO, TOMOKAZU (1997). 'Political Realignment in Japan: Resurgence of Predominant Party System in a New State?'. Paper prepared for presentation at the 1997 Annual Meeting of the American Political Science Association, Washington, DC, 28–31 Aug.

SANI, GIACOMO, and SARTORI, GIOVANNI (1983). 'Polarization, Fragmentation and Competition in Western Democracies', in Hans Daalder and Peter Mair (eds.), *Western European Party Systems*. Beverly Hills Calif.: Sage, 307–41.

SAUNDERS, PETER (1991). 'Noncash Income and Relative Poverty in Comparative Perspective: Evidence for the Luxembourg Income Study'. Paper delivered at the conference on 'Comparative Studies of Welfare State Development', Helsinki, Finland, 29 Aug.–1 Sept.

—— (1994). *Welfare and Inequality: National and International Perspectives on the Australian Welfare State*. Melbourne: Cambridge University Press.

SCHARPF, FRITZ W. (1987). *Sozialdemokratische Krisenpolitik in Europa*. Frankfurt: Campus.

—— (1988). 'The Joint-Decision Trap: Lessons from German Federalism and European Integration'. *Public Administration*, 61: 239–78.

—— (1991). *Crisis and Choice in European Social Democracy*. Ithaca, NY: Cornell University Press.

—— (1997a). 'Combating Unemployment in Continental Europe: Policy Options under Internationalization'. *RSC Policy Paper*, No. 3. Robert Schuman Centre, European University Institute, Florence.

—— (1997b). 'Employment and the Welfare State: A Continental Dilemma'. *Max Planck Institute Working Paper*, 7.

—— (1997c). *Games Real Actors Play: Actor Centered Institutionalism in Policy Research*. Oxford: Westview Press.

—— (1999). 'The Viability of Advanced Welfare States in the International Economy'. Mimeo.

SCHERER, PETER (1996). 'The Myth of the Demographic Imperative', in C. E. Steuerle and M. Kawai (eds.), *The New World Fiscal Order*. Washington, DC: Urban Institute Press, 61–83.

SCHLUDI, MARTIN (1997). *Kürzungspolitik im Wohlfahrtsstaat: Deutschland und Schweden im Vergleich*. Diploma thesis. University of Konstanz, Faculty for Public Administration.

SCHMAEL, WINFRIED (1998). 'Social Security Pension Reforms in Germany'. Paper presented at the annual meetings of the National Academy of Social Insurance, Washington, DC.

SCHMIDT, MANFRED (1982). *Wohlfahrtsstaatliche Politik unter bürgerlichen und sozialdemokratischen Regierungen*. Frankfurt, Main: Campus Verlag.

—— (1996a). 'Germany: The Grand Coalition State', in J. Colomer (ed.), *Political Institutions in Europe*. London: Routledge.

—— (1996b). 'When Parties Matter: A Review of the Possibilities and Limits of Partisan Influence on Public Policy'. *European Journal of Political Research*, 30 (2): 155–83.

SCHMIDT, VIVIEN A. (1995). 'The New World Order, Incorporated: The Rise of Business and the Decline of the Nation State'. *Daedalus*, 124 (Spring): 75–106.

SCHMITTER, PHILLIPE (1982). 'Reflections on Where the Theory of Neo-Corporatism has Gone and Where the Praxis of Neo-Corporatism may be Going', in G. Lembruch and P. Schmitter (eds.), *Patters of Corporatist Intermediation*. London: Sage, 259–79.

—— (1989). 'Corporatism is Dead! Long Live Corporatism!'. *Government and Opposition*, 24: 54–73.

—— and GROTE, JÜRGEN R. (1997). 'The Corporatist Sisyphus: Past, Present, and Future'. EUI Working Paper SPS No. 97/4. San Domenico (FI): European University Institute.

SCHNEIDER, ULRIKE (1998). 'What Goes Around Comes Around: Prospects for German Health Policy after the Change of Government'. Typescript. 11 Nov.

SCHULTEN, THORSTEN (1997). 'Collective Agreements on Partial Retirement'. *EIRO Online*, Aug. <http://www.eiro.eurofound.ie/servlet/ptconvert/de9708224f.sgm>.

SCHWARTZ, HERMAN (1994a). 'Public Choice Theory and Public Choices: Bureaucrats and State Reorganization in Australia, Denmark, New Zealand, Sweden in the 1980s'. *Adminstration and Society*, 26: 48–77.

—— (1994b). 'Small States in Big Trouble: State Reorganization in Australia, Denmark, New Zealand, and Sweden in the 1980s'. *World Politics*, 46: 527–55.

—— (1994c). *States versus Markets: History, Geography, and the Development of the International Political Economy*. New York: St Martins.

—— (1997). 'Bringing Coalitions Back In: Globalization and the Changing Face of Social Protection'. Paper Presented to the 'New Politics of the Welfare State' Conference, Center for European Studies, Harvard, 5–7 December.

—— (1998). 'Social Democracy Going Down vs. Social Democracy Down Under? Australian Labor's Strategies for Coping with International Capital'. *Comparative Politics*, 30 (3): 253–72.

—— (2000). 'Internationalization and Two Welfare States: Australia and New Zealand', in Fritz Scharpf and Vivien Schmidt (eds.), *Welfare and Work in the Open Economy*, ii. *Diverse Responses to Common Challenges*. Oxford: Oxford University Press.

—— and RHODES, MARTIN (1999). 'Internationalization and the Liberal Welfare States: The UK, Australia and New Zealand'. Contribution to MPI Project on Adjustment to Internationalization.

SEN, AMARTYA (1997). 'Inequality, Unemployment and Contemporary Europe'. *International Labour Review*, 136 (Summer): 155–72.

SEWELL, WILLIAM H. (1996). 'Historical Events as Transformations of Structures: Inventing Revolution at the Bastille'. *Theory and Society*, 25 (6): 641–81.

SHALEV, MICHAEL (ed.) (1996). *The Privatization of Social Policy? Occupational Welfare and the Welfare State in America, Scandinavia and Japan*. New York: St Martin's.

SHALEV, MICHAEL (ed.) (1998). 'Limits and Alternatives to Multiple Regression in Macro-Comparative Research'. Paper presented at the Second Conference on the Welfare State at the Crossroads, Stockholm, June.

—— (1999). 'Limits of and Alternatives to Multiple Regression in Macro-Comparative Research'. European University Institute, European Forum Paper WS/80, May.

SHEFTER, MARTIN (1978). 'Party and Patronage: Germany, England, and Italy'. *Politics and Society*, 7 (4): 403–51.

SHEINGATE, ADAM (2000). *The Rise of the Agricultural Welfare State: Institutions and Interest Group Power in the United States, France, and Japan*. Princeton: Princeton University Press.

SHEPARD, WILLIAM F. (1995). *International Financial Integration: History, Theory, and Applications in OECD Countries*. Brookfield, Vt.: Ashgate.

SHEPSLE, KENNETH A. (1991). *Models of Multiparty Electoral Competition*. Chur: Harwood Academic Publishers.

SHONFIELD, A. (1969). *Modern Capitalism: The Changing Balance of Public and Private Power*. London: Oxford University Press.

SIEBERT, H. (1997). 'Labor Market Rigidities: At the Root of Unemployment in Europe'. *Journal of Economic Perspectives*, 11 (3): 37–45.

SINGH, AJIT (1997). 'Liberalization and Globalization: An Unhealthy Euphoria', in Jonathan Michie and John Grieve Smith (eds.), *Employment and Economic Performance: Jobs, Inflation, and Growth*. New York: Oxford University Press, 11–35.

SKOCPOL, THEDA (1991). 'Targeting within Universalism: Politically Viable Policies to Combat Poverty in the United States', in Christopher Jencks and Paul E. Peterson (eds.), *The Urban Underclass*. Washington, DC: Brookings, 411–36.

—— (1992). *Protecting Soldiers and Mothers: The Political Origins of Social Policy in the United States*. Cambridge, Mass.: Harvard University Press.

—— (1995). *Social Policy in the United States*. Princeton: Princeton University Press.

—— (1996). *Boomerang: Clinton's Health Security Effort and the Turn Against Government in U.S. Politics*. New York: Norton.

SLAUGHTER, M. J., and SWAGEL, P. (1997). 'The Effect of Globalization on Wages in the Advanced Economies'. *Working Paper of the International Monetary Fund*, WP/97/43.

SMITH, ADAM (1976 [1776]). *An Inquiry into the Nature and Causes of the Wealth of Nations*. Oxford: Clarendon Press.

SMITH, SHEILA, FREELAND, MARK, HEFFLER, STEPHEN, MCKUSICK, DAVID, and the Health Expenditures Projection Team (1998). 'The Next Ten Years of Health Spending: What Does the Future Hold?'. *Health Affairs*, 17 (5): 128–40.

SMOLENSKY, EUGENE, DANZIGER, SHELDON, and GOTTSCHALK, PETER (1988.) 'The Declining Significance of Age in the United States', in John L. Palmer, Timothy Smeeding, and Barbara Boyle Torrey (eds.), *The Vulnerable*. Washington, DC: Urban Institute Press, 29–54.

SNOWER, D. J. (1997). 'Challenges to Social Cohesion and Approaches to Policy Reform', in OECD, *Societal Cohesion and the Globalising Economy: What Does the Future Hold?* Paris: OECD, 39–60.

SOBEL, ANDREW (1994). *Domestic Choices, International Markets: Dismantling Barriers and Liberalizing Securities Markets*. Ann Arbor: University of Michigan Press.

SORRENTINO, CONSTANCE (1990). 'The Changing Family in International Perspective'. *Monthly Labor Review*, Mar.: 41–58.

SOSKICE, DAVID (1990a). 'Reinterpreting Corporatism and Explaining Unemployment: Co-ordinated and Non-Co-ordinated Market Economies', in R. Brunetta and C. Dell'Aringa (eds.), *Labour Relations and Economic Performance: International Economic Association Conference*. London: Macmillan, 170–211.

—— (1990b). 'Wage Determination: The Changing Role of Institutions in Advanced Industrialized Countries'. *Oxford Review of Economic Policy*, 6 (4): 36–61.

—— (1994). 'Advanced Economies in Open World Markets and Comparative Institutional Advantages: Patterns of Business Coordination, National Institutional Frameworks and Company Product Market Innovation'. Mimeo, WZB Berlin.

—— (1999). 'Divergent Production Regimes: Coordinated and Uncoordinated Market Economies in the 1980s and 1990s', in Kitschelt et al. (eds.), *Continuity and Change*, 101–34.

—— (forthcoming). 'Macroeconomic Analysis and the Political Economy of Unemployment'. Ch. 2 in Torben Iversen, Jonas Pontusson, and David Soskice (eds.), *Unions, Employers and Central Banks: Wage Bargaining and Macroeconomic Regimes in an Integrating Europe*. Cambridge: Cambridge University Press.

—— and IVERSEN, TORBEN (1998). 'Multiple Wage Bargaining Systems in the Single European Currency Area'. *Oxford Review of Economic Policy*, 14 (3) (Autumn): 110–24.

—— HANCKÉ, BOB, TRUMBULL, GUNNAR, and WREN, ANN (1997). 'Wage Bargaining, Labour Markets and Macroeconomic Performance in Germany and the Netherlands', in L. D. E. d. Jong (ed.), *The German and Dutch Economies: Who Follows Whom?* Berlin and New York: Springer, 39–51.

SPELLER, S. R. (1948). *The National Health Service Act, 1946*. Annotated. London: H. K. Lewis.

STARR, PAUL (1994). *The Logic of Health Care Reform: Why and How the President's Plan Will Work*. New York: Penguin/Whittle Books.

STEINMO, SVEN (1993). *Democracy and Taxation*. New Haven: Yale University Press.

—— (1994). 'The End of Redistributive Taxation: Tax Reform in a Global World Economy'. *Challenge*, 37 (6): 9–17.

—— (no date). 'The New Political Economy of Taxation: International Pressures and Domestic Policy Choices'. Typescript, University of Colorado at Boulder.

—— and WATTS, JON (1995). 'It's the Institutions, Stupid! Why Comprehensive National Health Insurance Always Fails in America'. *Journal of Health Politics, Policy and Law*, 20 (2): 329–72.

STEPHENS, JOHN D. (1979). *The Transition from Capitalism to Socialism*. London: Macmillan Press Ltd.

—— (1994). 'Welfare States and Employment Regimes'. *Acta Sociologica*, 37 (2): 207–11.

—— (1995). 'Preserving the Social Democratic Welfare State'. *Nordic Journal of Political Economy*, 22: 143–62.

STEPHENS, JOHN D. (1996). 'The Scandinavian Welfare States: Achievements, Crisis and Prospects', in Esping-Andersen (ed.), *Welfare States in Transition*, 32–65.

—— HUBER, EVELYNE, and RAY, LEONARD (1999). 'The Welfare State in Hard Times', in Kitschelt et al. (eds.), *Continuity and Change*, 164–93.

STEUERLE, C. EUGENE (1996). 'Fiscal Policy and the Aging of the U.S. Population', in C. Eugene Steuerle and Masahiro Kawai (eds.), *The New World Fiscal Order: Implications for Industrialized Nations* (Washington, DC: Urban Institute Press), 19–41.

—— and KAWAI, MASAHIRO (1996). 'The New World Fiscal Order: Introduction', in C. Eugene Steuerle and Masahiro Kawai (eds.), *The New World Fiscal Order: Implications for Industrialized Nations*. Washington, DC: Urban Institute Press, 1–16.

STINCHCOMBE, ARTHUR (1997). 'On the Virtues of the Old Institutionalism'. *Annual Review of Sociology*, 23: 1–18.

STOKES, SUSAN, and BAUGHMAN, JOHN (1998). 'Is Neoliberalism a Mass Ideology in Latin America?'. Paper prepared for presentation at the Annual Meetings of the American Political Science Association, Boston, Massachusetts, 3–6 Sept.

STOLEROFF, A. (1997). 'Unemployment and Trade Union Strength in Portugal'. Paper presented at the conference 'Unemployment's Effects: The Southern European Experience in Comparative Perspective', Princeton University, 14–15 Nov.

STONE, DEBORAH A. (1980). *The Limits of Professional Power: National Health Care in the Federal Republic of Germany*. Chicago and London: University of Chicago Press.

—— (1993). 'The Struggle for the Soul of Health Insurance'. *Journal of Health Politics, Policy and Law*, 18 (2): 287–317.

STRANGE, SUSAN (1996). *The Retreat of the State: The Diffusion of Power in the World Economy*. New York: Cambridge University Press.

STREECK, WOLFGANG (1992). *Social Institutions and Economic Performance: Studies of Industrial Relations in Advanced Capitalist Economies*. London: Sage.

—— (1996). 'Public Power Beyond the Nation-State: The Case of the European Community', in R. Boyer and D. Drache (eds.), *States Against Markets: The Limits of Globalization*. London: Routledge, 299–315.

—— (1997a). 'Beneficial Constraints', in J. Rogers Hollingsworth and Robert Boyer (eds.), *Contemporary Capitalism: The Embeddedness of Institutions*. Cambridge: Cambridge University Press, 197–219.

—— (1997b). 'German Capitalism: Does It Exist? Can It Survive?', in Colin Crouch and Wolfgang Streeck (eds.), *Political Economy of Modern Capitalism: Mapping Convergence and Diversity*. London: Sage, 33–54.

—— and SCHMITTER, PHILIPPE C. (1985). 'Community, Market, State—and Associations? The Prospective Contribution of Interest Governance to Social Order'. *European Sociological Review,* 1 (2): 119–38.

—— —— (1991). 'From National Corporatism to Transnational Pluralism: Organized Interests in the Single European Market'. *Politics and Society*, 19: 133–64.

SVALLFORS, STEFAN (1995). 'The End of Class Politics: Structural Cleavages and Attitudes to Swedish Welfare Policies'. *Acta Sociologica*, 38: 53–74.

—— (1997). 'Worlds of Welfare and Attitudes to Redistribution: A Comparison of Eight Western Nations'. *European Sociological Review*, 13 (3): 283–304.

SWANK, DUANE (1992). 'Politics and the Structural Dependence of the State in Democratic Capitalist Nations'. *American Political Science Review*, 86: 38–54.

—— (1997). 'Global Markets, National Institutions, and the Public Economy in Advanced Industrial Societies'. Paper presented at the Conference on Economic Internationalization and Democracy, University of Vienna, 14–17 Dec.

—— (1998*a*). 'Funding the Welfare State: Globalization and the Taxation of Business in Advanced Market Economies'. *Political Studies*, 46 (4): 671–92.

—— (1998*b*). 'Global Capital, Democracy, and the Welfare State'. University of California Center for German and European Studies *Political Economy of European Integration Working Paper 1.66*.

—— (2000). 'Social Democratic Welfare States in a Global Economy: Scandinavia in Comparative Perspective', in Robert Geyer, Christine Ingebritsen, and Jonathan Moses (eds.), *Globalization, Europeanization, and the End of Scandinavian Social Democracy?* London: Macmillan.

—— (forthcoming). *Diminished Democracy? Gobal Capital, Political Institutions, and Policy Change in Developed Welfare States*. Cambridge: Cambridge University Press.

SWEDISH GOVERNMENT (1996). *A Programme for Halving Unemployment*. Stockholm: Prime Minister's Office.

SWENSON, PETER (1989). *Fair Shares: Unions, Politics, and Pay in Sweden and West Germany*. Ithaca, NY: Cornell University Press.

—— (1991*a*). 'Bringing Capital Back In, or Social Democracy Reconsidered'. *World Politics*, 43 (4): 513–44.

—— (1991*b*). 'Labor and the Limits of the Welfare State: The Politics of Intraclass Conflict and Cross-Class Alliances in Sweden and West Germany'. *Comparative Politics*, 23 (4) (July): 379–400.

—— (1992). 'Union Politics, the Welfare State, and Intraclass Conflict in Sweden and Germany', in Miriam Golden and Jonas Pontusson (eds.), *Bargaining for Change: Union Politics in North America and Europe*. Ithaca, NY: Cornell University Press.

—— (1997). 'Arranged Alliance: Business Interests in the New Deal'. *Politics and Society*, 25 (1): 66–116.

—— (1998). 'Efficiency Wages, Welfare Capitalists, and Welfare States: Employers and Welfare State Development in the United States and Sweden'. Paper presented at the Annual Meeting of the American Political Science Association, Boston, 3–6 Sept.

TANZI, VITO (1995). *Taxation in an Integrating World*. Washington, DC: Brookings.

—— and FANIZZA, DOMENICO (1996). 'Fiscal Deficit and Public Debt in Industrial Countries, 1970–1994', in Steuerle and Kawai (eds.), *The New World Fiscal Order*, 223–52.

TARROW, SIDNEY (1996). 'Making Social Science Work across Space and Time: A Critical Reflection on Robert Putnam's *Making Democracy Work*'. *American Political Science Review*, 90 (2): 389–97.

TAYLOR, G. (1996). 'Labour Market Rigidities, Institutional Impediments and Managerial Constraints: Some Reflections on the Recent Experience of Macro-Political Bargaining in Ireland'. *Economic and Social Review*, 27 (3): 253–77.

TAYLOR, G. (1998). 'Negotiated Governance and the Irish Polity'. Mimeo.

TAYLOR-GOOBY, PETER (1991). *Social Change, Social Welfare and Social Science.* Toronto and Buffalo: University of Toronto Press.

—— (1995). 'Who Wants the Welfare State? Support for State Welfare in European Countries', in S. Svallfors (ed.), *In the Eye of the Beholder: Opinions on Welfare and Justice in Comparative Perspective.* Umeå: Bank of Sweden Trecentenary Foundation.

TEAGUE, P. (1995). 'Pay Determination in the Republic of Ireland: Towards Social Corporatism?'. *British Journal of Industrial Relations*, 33 (2): 253–73.

—— and GRAHL, J. (1998). 'Institutions and Labor Market Performance in Western Europe'. *Political Studies*, 46: 1–18.

TELES, STEVEN (1998). 'The Dialectics of Trust: Ideas, Finance and Pensions Privatization in the U.S. and U.K.'. Paper presented to Max Planck Institute Conference on Varieties of Welfare Capitalism, Cologne, June.

THELEN, KATHLEEN (1993). 'West European Labor in Transition: Sweden and Germany Compared'. *World Politics*, 46 (Oct.): 23–49.

—— (1994). 'Beyond Corporatism: Toward a New Framework for the Study of Labor in Advanced Capitalism'. *Comparative Politics*, 27 (1): 107–24.

—— (1999). 'Why German Employers Cannot Bring Themselves to Dismantle the German Model', in T. Iversen, J. Pontusson, and D. Soskice (eds.), *Unions, Employers and Central Banks: Wage Bargaining and Macro-economic Regimes in an Integrating Europe.* New York: Cambridge University Press (forthcoming).

—— and STEINMO, SVEN (1992). 'Historical Institutionalism in Comparative Politics', in Sven Steinmo, Kathleen Thelen, and Frank Longstreth (eds.), *Structuring Politics: Historical Institutionalism in Comparative Perspective.* New York: Cambridge University Press, 1–32.

THERBORN, GÖREN (1997). 'The Western European Welfare State in its Hostile World.' Centro de Estudios Avazodos en Ciecias Sociales, Instituto Juan March, Working, Paper 1997/109.

THOMAS, KENNETH (1997). *Capital beyond Borders: States and Firms in the Auto Industry, 1960–94.* New York: St Martin's Press.

THOMPSON, LAWRENCE (1997). 'Predictability of Individual Pensions'. Paper presented to the Joint ILO–OECD Workshop: Development and Reform of Pension Schemes, Paris.

THYGESEN, N., KOSAI, Y., and LAWRENCE, R. Z. (1996). *Globalization and Trilateral Labour Markets: Evidence and Implications: A Report to the Trilateral Commission.* New York, Paris, and Tokyo: Trilateral Commission.

TILTON, MARK (1996). *Restrained Trade: Cartels in Japan's Basic Materials Industries.* Ithaca, NY: Cornell University Press.

TIMMINS, NICHOLAS (1995). *The Five Giants: A Biography of the Welfare State.* London: Harper Collins.

TIMONEN, VIRPI (1997). 'Welfare State Restructuring in the Face of Globalisation: Sweden and Finland Compared'. Mimeo, Oxford University.

—— (1999). 'Supporting the Unemployed in Sweden and Finland: Diversification of Benefits'. Mimeo, Oxford University.

TITMUSS, RICHARD M. (1974). *Social Policy: An Introduction.* Brian Abel-Smith and Kay Titmuss (eds.). New York: Pantheon Books (George Allen and Unwin).

—— (1987*a*). 'The Role of Redistribution in Social Policy', in *The Philosophy of Welfare*. London: George Allen and Unwin, 207–19.

—— (1987*b*). 'Welfare State and Welfare Society', in *The Philosophy of Welfare*. London: George Allen and Unwin, 141–56.

TOHARIA, L. (1997). 'El sistema español de protección por desempleo'. *Papeles de economiá española*, 72: 192–213.

TORRES, F. (1994). 'Portugal', in John Williamson (ed.), *The Political Economy of Policy Reform*. Washington, DC: Institute for International Economics, 141–52.

Trades Union Congress (1999). *Today's Trade Unionists*. London: TUC.

TRAXLER, FRANZ (1994). 'Collective Bargaining: Levels and Coverage'. *OECD Employment Outlook*, July: 167–94.

—— (1996). 'Collective Bargaining and Industrial Change: A Case of Disorganization?'. *European Sociological Review*, 12: 271–87.

—— (1997*a*). 'The Logic of Social Pacts', in G. Fajertag and Ph. Pochet (eds.), *Social Pacts in Europe*. Brussels: European Trade Union Institute/Observatoire social européen, 27–36.

—— (1997*b*). 'European Transformation and Institution Building in East and West: The Performance of and Preconditions for Corporatism'. In R. W. Kindley and D. F. Good (eds.), *The Challenge of Globalization and Institution Building: Lessons from Small European States*. Boulder, CO: Westview, 145–78.

TSAI, HUI-LIANG (1989). *Energy Shocks and the World Economy: Adjustment Policies and Problems*. New York: Praeger.

TSEBELIS, GEORGE (1990). *Nested Games: Rational Choice in Comparative Politics*. Berkeley: University of California Press.

—— (1995). 'Decision Making in Political Systems: Veto Players in Presidentialism, Parliamentarism, Multicamerialism and Multipartyism'. *British Journal of Political Science*, 25: 289–325.

TUCHSZIRER, CAROLE, and VINCENT, CATHERINE (1997). 'Un Consensus presque parfait autour de la reforme du systeme du retraite'. *Chronique Internationale de l'IRES*, 48: 26–30.

UK Department of Health (1997). *The New NHS: Modern—Dependable*. Cm 3807. London: HMSO.

UK Department of Health, Welsh Office, Northern Ireland Office, Scottish Office (1989). *Working for Patients*. CM 555. London: HMSO.

UN (1996). *World Populations Prospects: The 1996 Revision*. Population Division, Department of Economic and Social Affairs of the United Nations Secretariat.

UN Centre on Transnational Corporations (1996). *World Investment Directory 1995*. New York: United Nations.

UNCTAD (1993). *World Investment Directory 1992: Developed Countries*. New York: UNCTC.

UNGERSON, CLARE (1997). 'Social Politics and the Commodification of Care'. *Social Politics*, 4 (3): 362–81.

VAN DEN PLOEG, F. (1997). 'The Political Economy of a Consensus Society: Experience from Behind the Dykes'. *Economic and Social Review*, 28 (3): 307–32.

VAN KERSBERGEN, KEES (1995). *Social Capitalism*. London: Routledge.

VAN KERSBERGEN, KEES (1997). 'The Declining Resistence of National Welfare States to Change'. Typescript, Department of Political Science and Public Administration, Vrije Universiteit Amsterdam.

VERDIER, DANIEL (1998). 'Domestic Responses to Free Trade and Free Finance in OECD Economies'. Paper presented at the American Political Science Association annual meeting.

VILLIERS, BERTUS DE (ed.) (1994). *Evaluating Federal Systems*. Boston: Martinus Nijhoff.

VISSER, JELLE (1989). *European Trade Unions in Figures*. Deventer/Netherlands: Kluwer Law and Taxation Publishers.

—— (1996a). 'Two Cheers for Corporatism, One for the Market: Industrial Relations, Unions, Wages and Labor Markets in the Netherlands'. Max-Planck-Institut für Gesellschaftsforschung, Cologne, mimeo, Dec.

—— (1996b). *Unionization Trends: The OECD Countries Membership File.* Amsterdam: University of Amsterdam, Centre for Research of European Societies and Labor Relations (CESAR).

—— (1996c). 'Unionization Trends Revisited'. University of Amsterdam, mimeo.

—— (1998). 'La Concertation: Art de conclure des pactes sociaux'. Paper presented to the seminar 'Les Pactes nationaux pour l'emploi: bilan et perspectives', organized by the Groupement d'Études et de Recherches 'Notre Europe' and l'Institut Syndical Européen, Brussels, 10 June.

VISSER, JELLE and HEMERIJCK, ANTON (1998). *'A Dutch Miracle': Job Growth, Welfare Reform and Corporatism in the Netherlands.* Amsterdam: Amsterdam University Press.

VOGEL, DAVID (1978). 'Why Businessmen Distrust their State: The Political Consciousness of American Corporate Executives'. *British Journal of Political Science*, 8 (Jan.): 45–78.

VOGEL, STEVEN (1998). 'Can Japan Dis-engage? Winners and Losers in Japan's Political Economy, and the Ties that Bind them'. BRIE Working Paper 111. Berkeley: University of California.

WAINE, B. (1995). 'A Disaster Foretold? The Case of Personal Pensions'. *Social Policy and Administration*, 29 (4): 317–34.

WALKER, A. (1991). 'Thatcherism and the Politics of Old Age', in John Myles and Jill Quadagno (eds.), *States, Labour Markets, and the Future of Old Age Policy.* Philadelphia: Temple University Press.

WALLERSTEIN, MICHAEL (1990). 'Centralized Bargaining and Wage Restraint'. *American Journal of Political Science*, 34 (4): 982–1004.

—— (forthcoming). 'Wage Setting Institutions and Pay Inequality in Advanced Industrial Societies'. *American Journal of Political Science.*

—— and PRZEWORSKI, ADAM (1995). 'Capital Taxation with Open Borders'. *Review of International Political Economy*, 2 (Summer): 425–45.

—— and GOLDEN, MIRIAM (1997). 'The Fragmentation of the Bargaining Society: Wage Setting in the Nordic Countries, 1950 to 1992'. *Comparative Political Studies*, 30: 699–731.

—— —— and LANGE, PETER (1997). 'Unions, Employers' Associations and Wage-Setting Institutions in Northern and Central Europe, 1950–1992'. *Industrial and Labor Relations Review*, 50 (3): 379–401.

WATSON, SARAH (1996). 'Welfare State Regimes and Women's Autonomy'. Senior thesis. Department of Political Science, University of North Carolina, Chapel Hill.

WEAVER, R. KENT (1986). 'The Politics of Blame Avoidance'. *Journal of Public Policy*, 6: 371–98.

—— (1988). *Automatic Government*. Washington, DC: Brookings.

—— (1998). 'The Politics of Pensions: Lessons from Abroad', in R. Douglas Arnold, Michael Graetz, and Alicia Munnell (eds.), *Framing the Social Security Debate: Values, Politics and Economics*. Washington, DC: National Academy of Social Insurance, 183–228.

—— and ROCKMAN, BERT (1993). 'Assessing the Effect of Institutions', in K. Weaver and B. Rockman (eds.), *Do Institutions Matter? Government Capabilities in the United States and Abroad*. Washington, DC: Brookings Institution.

WEBB, M. C. (1991). 'International Economic Structures, Government Interests, and International Coordination of Macroeconomic Adjustment Policies'. *International Organization*, 45 (3): 309–38.

WEIR, MARGARET, and SKOCPOL, THEDA (1985). 'State Structures and the Possibilities for "Keynesian" Responses to the Great Depression in Sweden, Britain, and the United States', in Peter B. Evans, Dietrich Rueschemeyer, and Theda Skocpol (eds.), *Bringing the State Back In*. Cambridge: Cambridge University Press, 107–63.

WEISBROD, BURTON A. (1985). 'America's Health Care Dilemma'. *Challenge*, 28 (4): 30–4.

WEISS, L. (1997). 'The Myth of the Powerless State'. *New Left Review*.

WESTERN, BRUCE (1991). 'A Comparative Study of Corporatist Development'. *American Sociological Review*, 56: 283–94.

—— and BECKETT, KATHERINE (1999). 'How Unregulated is the U.S. Labor Market? The Penal System as a Labor Market Institution'. *American Sociological Review*, 1 (2): 157–84.

WHDPC (White House Domestic Policy Council) (1993). *The President's Health Security Plan: The Clinton Blueprint*. New York: Times Books.

WHITEHEAD, MARGARET (1993). 'Is it Fair? Evaluating the Equity Implications of the NHS Reforms', in Ray Robinson and Julian Le Grand (eds.), *Evaluating the NHS Reforms*. London: King's Fund Institute, 208–42.

WILENSKY, HAROLD (1981). 'Leftism, Catholicism, and Democratic Corporatism: The Role of Political Parties in Recent Welfare State Development', in Peter Flora and Arnold Heidenheimer (eds.), *The Development of Welfare States in Europe and America*. New Brunswick: Transaction, 345–82.

WILKERSON, JOHN D., DEVERS, KELLY J., and GIVEN, RUTH S. (eds.) (1997). *Competitive Managed Care: The Emerging Health Care System*. San Francisco: Jossey-Bass.

WILLIAMS, ROGER (1993). 'Technical Change: Political Options and Imperatives'. *Government and Opposition*, 28 (2): 152–73.

WILLIAMSON, JOHN B., and FLEMING, J. J. (1977). 'Convergence Theory and the Social Welfare Sector: A Cross-National Analysis'. *International Journal of Comparative Sociology*, 18: 242–53.

WILLIAMSON, OLIVER (1985). *Economic Institutions of Capitalism*. New York: Free Press.

WILSON, GRAHAM K. (1985). *Business and Politics: A Comparative Introduction.* Chatham, NJ: Chatham House Publishers.

WOLINETZ, STEVEN B. (1990). 'The Transformation of Western European Party Systems', in Peter Mair (ed.), *The West European Party System.* Oxford University Press, 218–31.

WOOD, ADRIAN (1994). *North–South Trade, Employment, and Inequality: Changing Fortunes in a Skill-Driven World.* Oxford: Clarendon Press.

—— (1995). 'How Trade Hurt Unskilled Workers'. *Journal of Economic Perspectives*, 9 (3): 57–80.

WOOD, STEWART (1997a). 'Capitalist Constitutions: Supply-Side Reform in Britain and West Germany 1960–1990'. Dissertation, Government Department, Harvard University.

—— (1997b). 'Weakening Codetermination? Work Council Reform in West Germany in the 1980s'. WZB Discussion Paper FS I 97–302. Science Center, Berlin.

—— (1999). 'Creating a Governance Structure for Training? The TECs Experiment in Britain', in Pepper Culpepper and David Finegold (eds.), *The German Skills Machine.* Oxford: Berghahn, pp. 363–402.

—— (2000). 'From Varieties of Capitalism to Public Policy: Employer Preferences and Labour Market Reform in Britain and West Germany in the 1980s', in Peter Hall and David Soskice (eds.), *Varieties of Capitalism: The Institutional Foundations of Comparative Advantage* (forthcoming).

World Bank (1994). *Averting The Old Age Crisis.* New York: Oxford University Press.

WREN, ANN and IVERSEN, TORBEN (1997). 'Choosing Paths: Explaining Distributional Outcomes in the Post-Industrial Economy'. Paper prepared for Delivery at the 1997 Annual Meeting of the American Political Science Association, Washington, DC, 28–31 Aug.

ZYSMAN, JOHN (1983). *Governments, Markets and Growth: Financial Systems and the Politics of Industrial Change.* Ithaca, NY: Cornell University Press.

—— (1996). 'The Myth of a "Global" Economy: Enduring National Foundations and Emerging Regional Realities'. *New Political Economy*, 1 (2): 157–84.

INDEX